A HISTORY
OF EDUCATION

An Essay Toward

A HISTORY
OF EDUCATION

CONSIDERED CHIEFLY
IN ITS DEVELOPMENT IN THE
WESTERN WORLD

BY

W. KANE, S. J.
LOYOLA UNIVERSITY, CHICAGO

OPTIMUS MAGISTER
BONUS LIBER

Chicago, Illinois
LOYOLA UNIVERSITY PRESS
1938

CUM PERMISSU

✦

T - NTT - R

To Edward A. Cudahy

PREFACE

The writer of this textbook is a Catholic priest. He is aware that in historical controversy there is a Catholic prejudice as well as an anti-Catholic prejudice. He has tried to keep that fact clearly in mind when writing this book. He has gone to sources as much as he could; when the sources were not accessible to him, or the field too large for him to cover directly, he has preferred the authority of non-Catholic scholars to that of Catholic scholars, in every instance where choice was reasonably possible.

Since the book is written as a textbook, he has tried to keep it brief, even though to do that meant to make the treatment deliberately inadequate. He believes that a textbook should be little more than a suggestive outline, not a complete treatise to take the place of the living teacher or to obviate the need of study and research on the part of the student. A textbook should be a stimulus and a guide to work, not a substitute for work. There is, apparently, no way open to mere human beings to educate a man, save by getting him to educate himself.

W. K.

CONTENTS

CHAPTER I

CHAPTER II

CHAPTER III

CHAPTER IV

CHAPTER V

CHAPTER VI

CHAPTER VII

CHAPTER VIII

CHAPTER IX

CHAPTER X

CHAPTER XIV

CHAPTER XV

CHAPTER XVI

CHAPTER XVII

CHAPTER XVIII

CHAPTER XIX

MODERN SCHOOL SYSTEMS 476

CHAPTER XX

SCHOOL EDUCATION IN THE AMERICAS 520

CHAPTER XXI

A HISTORY
OF EDUCATION

CHAPTER I

INTRODUCTORY

I

History a piecemeal record. History, in a general sense, is the record of human experience. As that experience is enormously complex, it is necessary that we break it up in various ways in order to make an intelligible record of it. Thus we limit our consideration of past experience, say to a definite period of time, or within certain geographical limits, or to a particular phase of human activity, such as the political, the artistic, the philosophical, and the like. And we do this, not merely for the sake of clearness, but because the extremely finite human mind cannot well grasp at one time more than a few details of the complicated and multitudinous acts that make up the life story of a single individual: to say nothing of the complexity of experience in the life of a nation or of the entire race. Such a splitting-up of human experience is not in itself desirable; it is an unfortunate necessity, resulting from the limitations of our intelligence. All too frequently, it leads to distortion of the historical record, to a lack of perspective in viewing the past. But with all its faults, it is the only practicable method at our command.

But not of political facts only. Thus the greater part of history has concerned itself with the broad political facts in the experience of large groups of people, of nations. The very word 'history' brings instantly to the minds of most persons such a record of the political organization and activity of a nation, of millions of people, through centuries of time: with the result, generally speaking, that this

meager record comes to stand for the complete story of the
life of those millions, and a man is considered well versed
in history who has a ready knowledge of the political facts
regarding, say, a dozen nations. Obviously, that sort of
knowledge may very well leave its possessor quite ignorant
of the most important truths concerning those nations.
Indeed, for lack of knowing something about the daily life
of the men and women who made up those nations, something of their manner of dress and housing, their food, their
amusements, their ideals, their religion, the student of
history generally does not understand even the bald political
facts he may have read.

Placing the history of education. All this has long
been realized by historians. Within the past few generations attempts have been made to record history more
intelligently and with better balance. As part of that purpose, much more attention has been paid to the study of
the principles and means by which each generation in the
past has tried to train and equip the succeeding generation
for the business of living. Histories of education, as well
as economic histories, social histories, and the like, have
been multiplied. In particular, the history of education
has been recognized as important, not merely for the technical student of education, to whom it is of immediate and
prime necessity, but for the general reader who aims at
being a cultured man. One cannot understand a people at
all without considerable knowledge of their aims and
methods in education. These tell us what they wished to
be and tried to be; whereas the best of general political
histories tell us, at most, only what they were.

Which is a difficult branch of history. Yet it would be
a mistake to think that the history of education is a simpler
matter than general history. The field of ideas and ideals
is even broader than the field of facts, and much more
tangled. There is great danger that the student of it may

be lost in details, not able, as the venerable tag has it, to see the wood for the trees. Any book dealing with the history of education, and more particularly a textbook, must interpret these infinite details, must stress certain of them as significant, and necessarily ignore thousands of them. This is obviously a delicate and difficult task. In carrying it out, the writer cannot but be guided by his own definite philosophy, his personal point of view. He must, of course, strive for objective truth. His aim, through all his selecting and summarizing, must be to give as exact and faithful a presentation of educational aim and procedure as the limits of his space and time will permit. But unless he be a singularly stupid man, he must realize the limitations, not merely of his ability, but of his prejudices (especially his unconscious prejudices), and of the pressure brought to bear upon his thinking by the traditions and even current opinions of his own civilization: and he must, with that intellectual humility which is the only honesty of mind, try to prevent these limitations from distorting his vision of the truth.

And a subject of controversy. It is because of the manifold limitations of the human mind that the history of education (of course, this holds for other histories, too) is a ground of controversy. All men, for instance, practically agree on the general meaning of education: that it is the development of a human being in all his capacities; yet they may disagree intensely, and to the point of quarreling, about the ultimate aim that should guide that development, about the relative value of man's diverse capacities, about ways and means of developing an individual, and so forth; and hence come to the widest divergence of judgment concerning any one scheme of education. Any man who ventures to write on education should at all times suspect and test his opinions, should guard himself against bias as earnestly as against falsehood; and, with all the watchfulness possible, he may still be morally certain of a margin of error in even his most considered judgments.

II

Education a larger affair than schooling. There are a few considerations which, from the outset, should be kept in mind by the student of the history of education. The first of these is the essential nature of education: that it is the complete development of the individual, in his body, in his mind, in his moral character. This is a most obvious truism; yet it is constantly being forgotten both in the educational process itself and in books about education. In the modern elaborate growth of schools, the training and equipment of the mind has been stressed almost exclusively; and in modern thought the *school* has all too often come to stand for the whole of the educational process. Most histories of education should more honestly and properly be called histories of the school. The influence of the home, the army, the daily toil and play of men, upon the shaping of individuals is generally ignored; though these exert a great force in forming even the habits and power of thought, to say nothing of their effect upon bodily development and the training of character.

Its value measured both by man's nature and by his conditions of life. The second consideration is that education, to be successful, must develop individuals to fit into the social, economic, political, and religious conditions of the actual society in which they live; and hence must be judged, in great measure, by the concrete circumstances of the particular time or period involved: though it is true that there are certain qualities and habits in men which education must at all times and under all conditions try to develop in the individual, because they are at all times and under all conditions proper to him as a human being.

Thus, education must always try to make men more reasonable, more self-controlled, more obedient to God and all lawful authority, more vigorous and well-balanced in bodily and mental activity: because these qualities are always essential to the ideal of man. But the particular forms of, say, self-control, or keenness of thought, called for by the conditions of life in Europe of the thirteenth or fourteenth century, may well be different from those needed for successful living in America of the twentieth century, or for life in central Africa today. It is a gross mistake to judge of an educational system of the past purely in the light of its usefulness for our own time: but it is not an uncommon mistake.

Each education a fresh beginning. The third consideration is the rather paradoxic one that, although education has a sort of cumulative character, in that we inherit the experiences of the past and should be able to profit by them, yet each new individual faces his problems as entirely new, comes into the world with the same limitations as hampered the child in ancient Athens or Carthage. The wealth of past experience is like wealth hidden in a mine, of service only to him who digs it out, and then only in so far as he knows or learns how to use it. We have, unquestionably, more educational tools today than, say, the Greeks had in 500 B. C. Does it at all necessarily follow that we know how to use them to better effect? Yet one of the unconscious prejudices that injure so many books on education is the assumption that an educational system, because it is later, must be better. It does not take much thinking to see that that is a dangerous and unwise assumption.

The goal of all human education includes more than the present. Finally, any study of education which excludes, as so many do exclude, all thought of the ulterior purposes of life, is a very faulty and unbalanced study. Human life has a value immeasurably beyond that of the daily details of living, and a purpose beyond its mere limited maintenance here on earth. It is a gift of God, who, in the very fact of giving it, implies a definite use and end for it. If it were only an accidental thing, to be held in insecure tenure for a few years, the whole business of training new generations for its use would be quite futile. All its significance comes from that at which it aims, and all its details are measured by the definitive test of their furthering an eternal achievement. Individuals forget that very often, nations profess to ignore it for long periods; but no individual of sound mind, nor any nation, can ever forget it entirely. Even the attempted negation of a destiny beyond the present violently colors the fabric of life in any man or group of men. Hence we must keep that purpose in mind, as a sort of background, for any intelligent study of the development of the individual, of education.

The aim of this book. This book, intended for use as a textbook, does not aim at covering the entire field of the history of education; and that for the simple reason that the field is too large. It will confine itself chiefly to an attempt to sketch, as clearly as its brief compass will allow, the aims and methods of education in our Western civilization. Even in that narrower field what it omits of historical detail must necessarily be enormously more than what it sets down. It has to be selective, to keep within reasonable bounds. Now, one must readily admit beforehand that in that process of selection the author will quite certainly make a great many errors: due both to limitations of knowledge and to defects of judgment. He has never yet read an entirely satisfactory textbook on the history of education, and he simply has not the conceit to imagine that this will be a satisfactory book. It will try to keep in mind, and to base itself upon, the four considerations just outlined. Each chapter will be followed by a short list of references and some suggestions for further investigation and discussion.

TOPICS FOR DISCUSSION

1. Some particular influences exerted by one's point of view (e. g., Catholic, Protestant, rationalistic, materialistic) upon one's concept of the history of education.

2. The meaning and limitations of impartiality in studying the history of education.

3. The place of supernatural aims and agencies in the history of education.

BIBLIOGRAPHIC NOTE

It may be appropriate to mention here some of the general works concerned with the history of education, such as encyclopedias, bibliographies, and periodical indexes. Of the encyclopedias, the following are the most important: K. A. Schmidt, *Encyklopaedie des gesammten Erziehungs- und Unterrichtswesens,* 11 vols., Gotha, 1859-76, revised ed., 10 vols., 1876-87; F. Buisson, *Dictionnaire de Pédagogie et d'Instruction Primaire,* Paris, 1882 sqq.; D. Raymond, *Dictionnaire d'Education Publique et Privée,* Paris, 1865 (good for accounts of some Catholic schools); R. Blanco y Sanchez, *Bibliografia Pedagógica,* 5 vols., Madrid, 1907-12 (valuable for Spain and Latin America; gives long excerpts from Spanish works or translations); P. Monroe, *Cyclopedia of Education,* 5 vols., New York, 1911-13; F. Watson, *Encyclopedia and Dictionary of Education,* 4 vols., London, 1921-22.

Most modern governments have issued serial publications which contain educational data: e. g., the *Bulletins* and *Reports* of the United States Bureau of Education; *Musée Pédagogique et Bibliothéque Centrale de l'Enseignement Primaire,* begun at Paris in 1884, and running to over 100 fascicules (contains such bibliographic aids as Bonet-Maury's *Catalogue des Ouvrages et Documents,* 1886-89, with supplements); *Special Reports on Educational Subjects,* begun by the Education Department of Great Britain in 1897 (valuable not merely for statistics, but for excellent monographs in a wide range of topics); *Preussische Statistik,* begun in 1890. W. T. Harris compiled *Publications of the United States Bureau of Education from 1867 to 1890, with Subject Index,* Washington, 1891.

Amongst the many bibliographies, the following should be particularly helpful: W. S. Monroe and O. Asher, *A Bibliography of Bibliographies,* University of Illinois, 1927; Monroe, Hamilton, and Smith, *Locating Educational Information in Published Sources,* University of Illinois, 1930; G. Stanley Hall and J. M. Mansfield, *Hints toward a Select and Descriptive Bibliography of Education,* Boston, 1886; Will S. Monroe, *Bibliography of Education,* New York, 1897.

J. I. Wyer and Isabel E. Lord began in 1899 an annual *Bibliography of Education,* taken over in 1907 by the United States Bureau of Education, and thereafter published every two years.   W. S. Monroe began in 1917 lists of *Graduate Theses in Education,* University of Illinois, continued to 1927, when taken over by the United States Office of Education, as annual *Bibliography of Research Studies in Education.*   All these publications include much on the history of education.

For periodical material, besides *Poole's Index* and *The Readers' Guide to Periodical Literature,* there are such aids as the following: W. J. Fletcher, *Analytical Index to Barnard's American Journal of Education,* published by the United States Bureau of Education, 1892; *Loyola Educational Index,* Loyola University, Chicago, 1928, supplanted after first year by *Education Index,* H. W. Wilson Co., New York.

CHAPTER II

PRIMITIVE EDUCATION

Its history based on assumptions. A desire for completeness, if no other reason, seems to demand of most histories of education some discussion of primitive education. If one kept only to known facts, that discussion might properly be as brief as the chapter on Snakes in Ireland. There is good evidence for the fact that men lived on this earth long before we have any intelligible record of *how* they lived. Nor have we any way of knowing accurately how long that unrecorded period of human life was. Conjectures run all the way from thousands to millions of years. The details of that life are almost absolutely unknown to us. But discussion of primitive education, in the present fashion, cheerfully ignores this paucity of facts, and tries to supply for them by a jauntily offered wealth of more or less gratuitous assumptions.

First assumption: Early men savages. Perhaps the most widely used of these assumptions is that men everywhere were first savages. We simply have no knowledge whatever of this as a fact. We have indications, it is true, of savage life in prehistoric times: such as is given by stone implements and the absence of the useful metals. From such indications we may conclude that *in some instances* there was development from a less civilized to a more civilized people. But we have no ground for asserting that these savage people were the *first* people, and that they did not degenerate from ancestors much more highly cultured than themselves.

Samuel Johnson is often quoted as saying, "One set of

savages is like another." Granting, even, the accuracy of
this as a broad generalization, what has it to do with the
assumption as an historical fact that men everywhere and
universally *were* savages before they became civilized? Yet,
with Johnson's saying as a text, authors of books on education, apparently serious, present sketches of the life and
customs of savage people of our own times as the reflected
history of races earlier than the dawn of history. The
procedure is more than unscientific: it is ridiculous. If it
could be based upon anything, it would be upon a very
nebulous theory of human evolution. Now, the theory of
human evolution, like all unproven theories, is very interesting, and may possibly one day prove very valuable; but
it is not history, nor the basis of history.[1] Until we actually
know something about the life of primitive peoples, discussion of their education is as futile as discussion of the contents of a sealed casket. Conjecture is not history.

Second assumption: Constantly ascending progress. Another assumption, closely akin to the preceding, perhaps
even part of it, is that civilization has developed in a continuously ascending scale, and that therefore we may infer
the history of earlier peoples by reasoning backward from
later known eras. It is a very tempting assumption. No
book of history, so far as I know, honestly offers this as
an assumption; but many act upon it. It is, of course, a
false assumption, refuted readily and abundantly by patent
historical facts. One need only compare the Egyptians
under Rameses II with the Egyptians, say of 1750 A. D.
(some 3,000 years later); or the Irish of 548 A. D. with the
Irish of 1848 A. D.; or, to take a briefer compass of time,
the Greeks of 479 B. C., after the Battle of Plataea, with the
Greeks at the time of the Macedonian domination, 338 B. C.;

---

[1] Cf. Goldenweiser, *Early Civilization,* pp. 20, 399, for a compact
and forceful criticism of the evolutionary theory as used in the study
of primitive history.

or the Romans of the Punic Wars with the Romans under Caracalla. Wars, famine, foreign invasions, endemic malaria, domestic tyrannies, the decay of public and private morality, economic disturbances, and a score of other causes, may partially destroy a civilization, may undo the development of centuries, and may so blunt the ideals of men that more centuries must pass before men even strive to regain the lost development. The history of education is always a history of new beginnings: a fact which finds plentiful illustration even in our own times. If the story of man's development, as known to us, were charted in the form of a graph, it would be represented, not by a straight line of continuous ascent, but by a very zigzag line of many ups and downs.

This assumption vigorously refuted by facts. Our researches into the hidden past of prehistory are more and more confirming the view that men in those remote times moved in much the same fashion as they have done in recent historical times, as often backward as forward. Take only a few instances. The excavations in Crete have revealed a superb culture thirty-five or forty centuries earlier than the Dorian invasion. Hogarth does not hesitate to say: "Man in Hellas was more highly civilized before history than when history begins to record his state."[1] At the annual meeting of British Scientists, 1925, Sir William Flinders Petrie reported the discovery, at Badar, some thirty miles south of Asyut in Egypt, of vases finer and thinner than any of later age, of glazed beads, of ivory statuettes of Asiatic type and pottery statuettes of Mediterranean type, all at a level covered by the water of the Nile since at least 10,000 B. C., and therefore five or six thousand years earlier than the first dynasty. Even Davidson, despite his emotional bias in favor of evolution, admits of the story

---

[1] *Authority and Archaeology,* p. 230.

of Egypt that "in some respects it is almost altogether a history of decay."[1]   Sir Robert Ball, the eminent astronomer, says:

The stars had been studied, and some great astronomical discoveries had been made, untold ages before those to which our earliest records extend. For example, the observation of the apparent movement of the sun, and the discrimination between the planets and the fixed stars, are both to be classed among the discoveries of prehistoric ages. Nor is it to be said that these achievements related to matters of an obvious character.[2]

And again:

I think we sometimes do not give the ancient astronomers as much credit as their shrewdness really entitles them to. We have all read— we have been taught—that the moon and the tides are connected together; but how many of us are in a position to say that we have actually noticed that connection by direct personal observation? The first man who studied this matter with sufficient attention to convince himself and to convince others of its reality must have been a great philosopher. We know not his name, we know not his nation, we know not the age in which he lived; but our admiration of his discovery must be increased by the reflection that he had not the theory of gravitation to guide him.[3]

The remarkable drawings and sculptures of the caves explored within the last fifty years in France and Spain have amazed the scientific world. In artistic perception and execution, these drawings, numbering thousands, often far surpass the much later work of the Egyptians and Babylonians. W. J. Sollas says of the group of bisons modeled in clay, found in the cave of the Tuc d'Audoubert, "It is probably 20,000 years old and yet quite modern."[4]

---

[1] *History of Education*, p. 38, footnote. But, in truth it is rather a succession of fine developments breaking down in decay. See Flinders Petrie, *The Revolutions of Civilization*, Harper, 1922.

[2] *The Story of the Heavens*, p. 2.

[3] *Ibid.*, p. 535.

[4] *Ancient Hunters*, p. 393. On the subject of prehistoric man, see C. Dawson, *The Age of the Gods*, London, 1933; the best and most comprehensive brief treatise so far appearing in English.

Any one of such instances (and they might be multiplied indefinitely) warns us to beware of the assumption that because any human process is later in time it is necessarily better, and vice versa. Facts deal roughly with such an assumption.

We have some real knowledge of early education. Leaving all such nugatory assumptions to one side, how shall we approach the history of education amongst primitive peoples? If by primitive peoples we mean those that are absolutely outside of history, they are equally outside of the scope of this book, or of any other book of history. If we mean merely *early historic* peoples, then we can in some way consider the processes by which they educated themselves. Our real knowledge of these early historic peoples is comparatively little, and generally speaking, less in quantity and accuracy as the peoples are more remote from us in time: a not unnatural thing.

Physical education. We know from the mere fact of their vigorous survival and growth through long centuries that their physical education must have been well looked after; that they knew how to get food and shelter, that they had a sufficient knowledge of hygiene, and that they passed that knowledge on from generation to generation. We know that they domesticated animals; and that, when their numbers crowded them, and wild fruits and plants were not sufficiently abundant, they tilled the soil.

Intellectual and moral education. Of their intellectual and moral education we have, if not detailed and accurate information, at least broad hints. The fact that Sargon I, about 3800 B. C., established a great library at Accad, in what was later the kingdom of Babylonia (and some 1,500 years before what we call the First Dynasty of that kingdom), does not, it is true, really tell us much about the intellectual education of his people, because we do not know what proportion of his people could or did make use of his library; quite exactly as the mere size of a modern university library tells us practically nothing of the intellectual processes of the undergraduates. We must go cautiously, therefore, when we single out particular instances of intellectual culture or moral comprehension as indicative of early education.

Facts drawn from the organization of early peoples. But the general organization of a people, the ideals shown in their social relations, their laws, their religion, these do tell us a great deal about their mental and moral status. We have enough knowledge of many early peoples to be able to grasp what that general organization was. We have got this knowledge from their memorial inscriptions, from their writings on clay and other substances, from their monuments, from their dwellings and household utensils, from their temples and burial places. The detail of it would be burdensome and out of proportion in such a book as this. But the broad outline is significant.

One of the most notable things in that organization is that it so closely resembled our own present society. It divided the people into great classes: upper, middle, and lower. The conditions which determined the particular class to which each person belonged were also, in general, the same as those which determine the present social status of the individual. They were chiefly his possession of wealth, prestige, and opportunity. The wealth may have been agricultural rather than industrial, the prestige may have been military rather than scientific or literary or purely political, the opportunity may have been won more by physical force than by cunning: but in their essence and their effects they were the same social determinants. There is a curious kinship between, say, an Assyrian usurer and an American bootlegger, or an Egyptian priest and a modern politician.

And there was the same restless seeking for material

advancement as now, the same 'divine discontent' with one's present state of affairs, the same succession of conflicts between individuals and between groups, the same shifting and uncertainty of ideals in all these conflicts, the same confusion of high and low purposes, worthy and unworthy. Men then as now puzzled over the ultimate meaning of life, and perceived by inevitable inference that it must have some purpose beyond the present, and were vague and discordant as now about the nature of that purpose and the means of attaining it. They worshiped God in various ways and measures. They appointed and accepted ministers of religion, specialists who should study these matters more profoundly and act as guides to those with lesser knowledge. They established civil governments, and quarreled about them. They changed both governments and forms of worship. They wrestled with the problem of compromise between the interests of time and of eternity, or at least of this life and a life other than the present. And all this involved purposive activity of mind and will, which is mental and moral education.

Early schools. Did they have schools as we know them now? The question is relatively unimportant; but we have made such a fetish of the school in education that it must be answered. There is evidence that they did have schools; though the school had not usurped the function of the family in education to the extent to which it now does.[1] But life itself was then, as it is now, as it must always be, the great school.[2] Each new generation of men and women faced the problems of living, as it always faces them, under

[1] Cf. Diodorus Siculus, *Bibliotheca Historica*, Bk. II, #29. Sayce, *Babylonians and Assyrians*, pp. 52-55.
[2] "No means can be found of exercising the higher faculties which can be compared with the actual relations of daily life." Quick, *Educational Reformers*, p. 313. Laurie also warns repeatedly "that we must not measure the education of a nation by its schools." *Pre-Christian Education*, p. 226.

the guidance of those who had a longer experience of living. And that longer experience sometimes was well interpreted and sometimes ill interpreted, sometimes condensed into formulas which were meant, as they always are meant, to be a short-cut to wisdom, but with very varying success in attaining their purpose. So arose literatures amongst these peoples, and with them schools of various sorts; but chiefly, as in all times, for those who had more wealth and the leisure that wealth brings.

Early relationships vague. Of the origins of these ideals, as of the detailed influences that carried them now to higher now to lower levels, we can say very little. There are curious parallels of thought between the Babylonians and the Egyptians and the Greeks, between the ancient Hebrews and all these peoples, which seem to point to some common origin; but that is not a sure ground of history. There is further a great, though vague, tradition, of some real historical value, which leads us back to a large mental culture as well as a great physical prowess and a high moral ideal. And there is a great deal of evidence, though not abundant enough nor well enough linked together, that generally the trend in these splendid possessions was downward:[1] with fitful periods of reform, and more or less sporadic attempts, under special influences and the leadership of exceptional individuals, to recover some of the former excellence.

[1] One might note, for instance, the evidence for a degeneration from monotheism to polytheism; or compare the tradition of the Flood as handed on by Abraham to the Hebrews and as recorded in the Gilgamesh Epic. For primitive monotheism, see W. E. Hocking, *The Meaning of God in Human Experience*, 5th ed., Yale University, 1912, pp. 322 sqq.; H. M. Gwatkin, *Knowledge of God and Its Historical Development*, 2 vols., Edinburgh, 1906, New York, 1907; and the excellent study of the nature and place of primitive religion in C. Dawson, *Progress and Religion*, London, 1929. J. R. Swanton, *History of Creek Indians*, United States Bureau of Ethnology, Bulletin 73, 1922, Annual Report, 1926-27, Washington, 1928, gives the argument from primitive stages of modern people.

Danger of underestimating early education. Looking back upon these fragmentary records of the most remote peoples known to us, we of the present Western civilization are in serious danger of despising their efforts. We glory in the manifest advance that humanity has made in the last three thousand years; even when we make allowance for the many halts and retrogressions in that advance. And the particular spirit of our present pride leads some of us to attribute that advance to the purely normal processes of unaided human nature. We toss aside, as a vague and insoluble puzzle, the fact that half of the human race, the Asiatic peoples, has stagnated for many centuries; and concentrate our admiring gaze upon our own Western world. And we forget (many of us even deny) the enormous influence upon our Western development exercised by the Incarnation. We forget that, in so far as we have really advanced, and have been able to educate each succeeding generation to more intelligent uses of life, that advance has been due to the fact that God became man, and brought to men not merely new ideals of life, but new supernatural aids to intellect and will. It is the very ungrateful fashion today, even amongst those who have profited most by the coming of Christ, to sneer at the influence of Christianity upon human education.

And what it owed to divine revelation. To such men— and with regret it must be admitted that they constitute a practical majority in our civilization—it would be hopeless to offer the tradition of a 'primitive revelation' as the starting point of all human education, and the Fall of Man, with its consequences, as the pitiful explanation of the later staggering record of ups and downs in education. A riotous and rebellious individualism prefers to put its submissive faith in a theory of natural evolution: to postulate men as initial savages, raising themselves by unaided natural processes to higher and higher levels of being and intelligence.

Yet one cannot, in mere reason, escape the evidence for a Creator; nor can one write human history intelligently and leave out of it the direct action of the Creator and Conserver of humanity. Add to this that the Christian teaching of a primitive revelation, made by God to the first human beings, is immeasurably better substantiated than the modern naturalistic assumption that man has 'evolved' in unbroken advance by his merely natural powers, and one cannot but admit that the idea of such a revelation is at least worth considering. To reject it *a priori* is unwarrantable and unscientific prejudice.

TOPICS FOR DISCUSSION

1. The hints offered toward an understanding of education in the Aurignacian and Solutrean periods by their drawings and sculptures.
2. The early domestication of animals as an indication of human education.
3. The common origin of certain scriptural and Babylonian narratives.
4. Babylonian libraries as educational indices.
5. The very early astronomical discoveries.

BIBLIOGRAPHIC NOTE

Besides the valuable *Age of the Gods,* mentioned in the notes to this chapter, Christopher Dawson offers enlightening suggestions in Chapter 3 of *Progress and Religion,* London, 1929. For the early cave drawings and carvings, the best reproductions are in H. Breuil, *Altamira, Font de Gawme, Cavernes Cantabriques, La Pasiega,* etc., in the Prince of Monaco Series, 1906-24. Two of the best discussions of the cave art are: H. Alcalde del Rio, *Las Pinturas y Grabados de las Cavernas Prehistóricas de la Provincia de Santander,* Santander, 1906; and H. Obermaier, *El Hombre Fósil,* 2d ed., Madrid, 1925. A fairly good account in English is G. Baldwin Brown, *The Art of the Cave Dweller,* Constable, 1928. A compact, readable, and well-illustrated introduction to prehistory is M. E. Boyle, *In Search of Our Ancestors,* London, 1927; and, for the Mesolithic to the Bronze Age, one of the best accounts is in V. G. Childe, *The Dawn of European Civilization,* New York, 1925. There is much of the current exaggerations of evolution in most books about early civilizations, but the following may be mentioned as reasonably free from such nonsense: R. H. Lowie, *Primitive Society,* New York, 1920; A. A.

Goldenweiser, *Early Civilization,* New York, 1922; H. O. Taylor, *Ancient Ideals,* New York, 1921; C. Seignobos, *History of Ancient Civilization,* New York, 1906.

Amongst the very large number of special studies in early civilizations, the following may serve as introductions to a few of the specific fields: for the Mayan culture, T. A. Joyce, *Central American Archaeology,* London, 1916, and *Maya and Mexican Art,* London, 1927; C. P. Bowditch, *The Numeration, Calendar Systems, and Astronomical Knowledge of the Mayas,* Cambridge, Mass., 1910; for the eastern cultures, the several monographs of S. H. Langdon in the University of Pennsylvania Museum Series, and his *Tablets from the Archives of Derhem, with a Complete Account of the Origin of the Sumerian Calendar,* Paris, 1911; A. H. Sayce, *Babylonians and Assyrians,* New York, 1889; J. H. Breasted, *Ancient Records of Egypt,* Chicago, 1907; A. T. Clay, *Light on the Old Testament from Babel,* Philadelphia, 1907; W. M. Flinders Petrie, *Social Life in Ancient Egypt,* Boston, 1923; C. H. and H. B. Hawes, *Crete, the Forerunner of Greece,* New York, 1909; H. Peake, *The Bronze Age and the Celtic World,* London, 1922. For the early discoveries in astronomy, see H. Shapley and H. E. Howarth, *Source Book in Astronomy,* New York, 1929.

CHAPTER III

Our debt to Hebrews, Greeks, and Romans. The three peoples to whom our civilization owes most are the Hebrews, the Greeks, and the Romans. All our Western world has been built upon these as a foundation. Some acquaintance with the character and history of these three peoples should be a common possession of all those amongst us who lay claim to any measure of culture. At least a brief study of their educational processes is a simple necessity for anyone who would understand the history of education since their times.

One of the first and most obvious things to be noted about these peoples is the curious fact that they so distinctively specialized in certain departments of living: the Hebrews in the religious and moral, the Greeks in the intellectual and aesthetic, the Romans in social organization and law. Each seems to have set before itself a definite and diverse purpose; or rather, in some mysterious way, to have had that purpose marked out for it, by special gifts of racial temperament as well as by external circumstances which it would be stupid to look upon as purely fortuitous. We have inherited from each in its own specialty.

Hebrew persistence. Of the three, the Hebrews have the longest known history, dating from some twenty centuries before Christ. Of Semitic origin, coming into our knowledge from somewhere in the vast vagueness of Asia, subjected through their long history to almost countless influences from other peoples, intermarrying with many other races, even dispersed throughout the world, they have still kept their racial continuity, their religious beliefs, and their distinguishing culture, with a persistence that sets them in strange contrast with all the other nations of the earth. No natural explanation seems to touch that fact, though men averse to a supernatural explanation have labored hard to find a natural one. Their written history, extant for many centuries before the Christian era, offers this explanation: that they were chosen by Divine Providence as the channel of a great tradition, of a divine revelation given to all men for their guidance in the most important business of life. If we reject this explanation, their history remains a puzzling mystery.

Explained by a divine purpose and guidance. In this view, God, many centuries after He had first made Himself known to men, singled out Abraham to be the head of a people who would keep alive that knowledge of Himself, already befogged and largely lost in the confusion of human transmission. The chronology of this early period is most uncertain. But this Hebrew people seem to have lived for some four hundred years a nomadic life, maintaining themselves by flocks and herds, in the region lying between the Arabian Desert and the Mediterranean. Driven by increasing numbers and lack of good pastures, they marched to the south, probably between the years 1700 and 1600 B. C. and came into a country called Gessen, or Goshen, east of the Delta of the Nile. They spent another 400 years, roughly, in that region, adding agriculture to their work as shepherds; at first tolerated by the Egyptian lords of the land, then for a time in favor, finally persecuted; always increasing in numbers, with the fertility that seems a mark of their race. Some time about 1250 B. C.,[1] under the leadership of Moses and Aaron, they departed from Egyptian lands, a great people, numbering in all, perhaps,

---

[1] Some authorities reckon it as much as two centuries earlier.

some 2,000,000.[1] After long wanderings and many battles
with neighboring tribes, they came back into their former
land of Canaan and took forcible possession of it. For the
sake of comparison, it may be noted that this took place
at about the same time as the Trojan War.

For nearly 150 years they lived as a more or less loose
confederation of twelve tribes, bound together chiefly by
their religion and their racial solidarity; with even these
bonds often weakened by lapses into idolatry and by inter-
tribal quarrels. They were ruled by tribal leaders, called
'judges': the last of whom, Samuel, seems almost to have
united all the tribes under his single government. About
1050 B. C. they chose Saul, of the tribe of Benjamin, as
king. After him succeeded David, about 1013 B. C., and
David's son, Solomon, about 973 B. C. About 965 B. C.,
Solomon built the first temple in Jerusalem. He died about
937 B. C.,[2] and almost immediately the kingdom was split
by dissensions, and divided into two kingdoms: that of
Israel, to the north, with the larger area (some 9,000 square
miles), and the greater number of the tribes, reckoning a
population of four or five millions; that of Judah, in the
smaller southern region (some 3,400 square miles), with
a population of somewhat less than two millions.

Both kingdoms rapidly declined in every way. In 722 B. C.
the Babylonian Sargon II captured Samaria, the capital of
Israel, and carried the people of the kingdom away into
captivity and dispersion.[3] In 608 B. C. Judah became a
vassal of Egypt under Necho II, and in 586 B. C. was conquered by Nebachadnezzar and its people carried captive
to Babylon. After forty-eight years some 50,000 Judeans

---

[1] The males alone, "from twenty years old and upward, that were
able to go to war, were 603,550 men." Num. 2:45-46.

[2] All these dates are disputed, but the margin of error regarding
them is comparatively small.

[3] These are the 'Lost Tribes' of Israel, whose later history is unknown to us.

returned, by permission of Cyrus, the new lord of Assyria. The temple was rebuilt in 516 B. C. Later more Jews returned, and the national life was reorganized, continuing with vigor until the Greek domination, begun under Alexander the Great in 332 B. C. and lasting for over 150 years. Then came the patriotic rebellion under the Machabees, from 168 B. C. to 63 B. C. After that the Romans ruled in Judea, until, in 70 A. D. when the Jews made their last effort for freedom, the temple and the city of Jerusalem were destroyed and the Jews driven for a final dispersion through the world. This was the end of their life as a nation, though their race has persisted through all the centuries since in a manner that is most amazing.

Their education chiefly religious and moral. This very long history may be roughly divided into three periods: from Abraham to the settlement in Palestine, perhaps nine or ten centuries; then the four centuries which include the rule of the judges, the kingdoms, and the Babylonian exile; and the final stage of national life, lasting some six centuries, so strongly marked by Greek and Roman influences. There are certain characteristics of Hebrew and Jewish[1] education which continue almost unchanged through all three, as well as distinctive educational traits for each period. Thus, in every stage, the chief content of their education was religious and moral training. This dominated in every way. Their great literature has no other purpose than the enshrining of religious and moral teachings; its charm and beauty exist only for that. To this end, too, they kept alive the study of the Hebrew language, when Aramaic or Greek had become the common speech of the Jews. If the young Jew was to be taught a trade, it was not merely to help him to make a living, but explicitly as a training in virtue and in that humble fellow-

[1] 'Hebrews' is the older and more general name of this people. The name 'Jews' is more properly limited to the inhabitants of Judea.

ship which is the only basis for a democracy. They were interested in astronomy, chiefly because that science was needed to fix their times of solemn worship. And so of all the other contents of education.

Resistance of Hebrews to external influences. Racially, the Hebrews have always been an intelligent and acquisitive people, quick to grasp the discoveries and advances of neighboring civilizations with which they came into contact, and eager enough to imitate these neighbors even in degrading and erroneous practices. But all such borrowing was always jealously suspected by the great leaders of the Hebrews, lest it should destroy their own high heritage of religious and moral truths. Thus it was that the influences of Babylonians, Assyrians, Egyptians, Phoenicians, and Greeks, as also of the lesser peoples immediately surrounding them, although at times very pronounced, never left a lasting impress upon their civilization nor shaped in any great measure their educational process. The arts and sciences of the gentiles were as suspect as their idolatries. For to the Hebrew mind it was profoundly true that every least detail of a civilization is colored by the religion of that civilization: a great truth which we have since learned to ignore.

The Hebrew educational ideal. The ideal of Hebrew education was to develop a human being who would be pleasing in the eyes of God, his Creator. It did not neglect such equipment as would help him to make his way in this material world; but it counted that as subordinate. It taught him language, and very early made use of reading and writing; it taught him the various industries needed for living; it made use of play and games[1] for the developing of his body, and music and dancing[2] for his amusement and delight. But it watched that none of these things

[1] Isa. 22:18; 1 Kings 20:20; Lam. 3:12; Ps. 19:5.
[2] Judg. 21:21; 11:40; 2 Kings 1:19-27; Judg. 5:11; 2 Kings 6:14.

should interfere with the first and most necessary education. Sculpture, for instance, was largely used round about them for idolatrous purposes; therefore it was forbidden them.

Hebrew education truly democratic. This education was open to all, with the only true democracy, that based upon our common origin and our common destiny. The Hebrews did not aim at social equality or equality of possessions, though their law did much to keep down gross inequalities; but they recognized an individual dignity underlying all inequalities. Each Hebrew was a child of God and a member of a race chosen by God for a divine purpose. That was the measure of his right to an education. A 'daughter of Israel' was as proud a title as that of a 'son of Israel.' No people of antiquity every treated women so justly. Of course, they recognized in simple common sense the physical limitations of women and their special adaptation for particular departments of the business of living. Thus, women were excused from the observance of laws which depended on a fixed time or season, and their labors were mainly in the home. But no advantage was taken of these limitations to degrade them, nor even to keep them from their proper place in the national life.[1] The education of orphans was a particular care of the community.

Education a family concern. The first and always the chief teacher was the family. Father and mother were charged with the education of their children as a religious obligation,[2] as well as a natural one. And the obligation was accepted and carried out rigorously. They taught the child its letters, and almost from infancy began its training in religious and moral truth. They too were to teach him

---

[1] Cf. Debbora, Judg. 4-5; Jael, Judg. 4:18-24; Judith; the 'Wise Woman of Thecua,' 2 Kings 14:1-23; of Abela, 2 Kings 20:16-22.
[2] Cf. Deut. 6:4-9.

his trade. Their authority was very great, and children respected it. They were urged often not to spare the rod— the Hebrews being sound psychologists. But the urging was needed because of the great love that Hebrews bore their children, and was meant only to keep that love from degenerating into harmful license. On the other hand, their authority was not absolute nor allowed to become tyrannical. Indeed, the family life of the Hebrews was thoroughly admirable.

The education of worship. In addition, the public worship was a great teacher. That worship was frequent in exercise and was interwoven with the whole life of the people. It kept before them their history as a theocratic nation. It impressed upon them with solemnity the ideals that should rule the details of their lives. It had dignity and beauty. It made use of a noble and divinely inspired literature.

The prophets as teachers. Formal schools were apparently unknown in the early history of the Hebrews. The training given in family life and through public worship was deemed sufficient. But after the national settlement in Canaan, during the period of the tribal rulers, and still more during the centuries of the kingdoms, there arose amongst them men of striking personality and great gifts, whom they called prophets, and who, claiming an inspiration from God, went about instructing the people. For the most part, they were not in a position of authority; their work was strictly educational, addressed to the mind and heart of their hearers. Many of them left their teachings in writing. They had a very great influence upon the Hebrew people, and more than once, by their teaching, brought about an impressive renascence of the national and religious life.

The scribes as teachers. After the Babylonian exile, in the sixth century before Christ, another body of teachers came into existence, the scribes. These were men learned in the law and in Jewish traditions, accepted by the people as authorities in an indefinite way, but not as divinely inspired. At the same time was begun the institution of the synagogues. These were not primarily places of worship, but of instruction in the law. The temple at Jerusalem remained the place of worship. Laurie calls the synagogues "the prototype of the Christian parochial system."[1] In the fourth century B. C. every town had its synagogue, and within 150 years they had spread even to the villages. There the people gathered on the Sabbath for instruction in the Torah, or Divine Law, and later for prayer and praise of God. Generally, the scribes presided over these meetings, but any competent person might be in charge of them and act as instructor.

The 'schools of the prophets.' The prophets and the scribes were real teachers, and the synagogue might be considered a school of some sort. But the Hebrews had more formal schools for many centuries. The earliest of these were the 'schools of the prophets,' which seem to have originated during the time of Samuel, in the eleventh century B. C. A number of young men gathered about each of the prophets, as his disciples, and shared in his frequent and intimate instruction. These groups would naturally be small, but membership in them was open to all classes, the only limitation being the essential limitation of all real education, that of intellectual and moral capacity. Although these schools of the Bene-nebi-im, the 'sons of the prophets,' were never numerous, they were, in effect, a sort of normal school, from which those who were trained in them went forth in their turn as instructors of the mass of the people.[2]

The schools of the scribes. Then, during the third great

---

[1] *Pre-Christian Education*, p. 87.
[2] St. Jerome notes in these 'schools' the germ of monasticism. Migne, *P. L.*, 22:583, 1076.

period of Hebrew history, the scribes, besides their general educational work as instructors in the synagogues, had definite schools for the training of other scribes. That training was chiefly in language and in knowledge of the Torah and of Jewish tradition. The sciences and other arts had practically no place in it. Even when the scribes came under Greek influences, the general type of their schools changed very little. Perhaps from the Greeks came that refinement and ultra-subtlety of reasoning notable in the later discussion of the schools. But the content of their education remained pretty much the same; they still studied chiefly the Jewish law. However, the attitude of many toward that law did change because of contact with the nimble, skeptical, and rather unmoral, mind of the Greeks; and out of the change arose the two noted parties amongst the Jews: the Pharisees, anti-Greek and zealous for the narrowest and most rigorous interpretation of the law, and the Sadducees, eclectic, politically and doctrinally in favor of the Greeks. The Pharisees were by far the dominant party.

Elementary schools: the shadow of the end. It was only with the shadow of destruction hovering over their nation that the Jews established what we would call elementary schools, and it was not until 64 A. D., six years before the final destruction, that attendance at them was made obligatory, under command of the High Priest Josue ben Gamala. It seems to have been a despairing effort to ward off calamity. It undoubtedly was a confession that the old family life and religious life of the Jews had lost vigor, and was no longer able to equip the new generation adequately for living. It is an interesting question to the student of history whether that decay of family life is always connected with a pronounced insistence upon schools, and whether the advent of compulsory schooling is a grim indication that the life of the nation that resorts to it is waning.

TOPICS FOR DISCUSSION

1. The Hebrew borrowings from Babylonian, Egyptian, and Greek cultures, and the influence of these upon their education.

2. Theocracy and democracy of Hebrews, as affecting their education.

3. The place of music and dancing in Hebrew education.

4. The form and order of worship in the synagogue.

5. The educational effect of the frequent struggles between monotheism and polytheism amongst the Hebrews.

6. The relative importance of schools in Hebrew education.

BIBLIOGRAPHIC NOTE

For the very early education of the Hebrews, the Old Testament must always remain our chief source of knowledge. Modern histories necessarily base themselves on the Old Testament, but often try to destroy its value as a source. Amongst general histories, H. H. Graetz, *Geschichte der Juden,* 11 vols., Leipzig, 1853-75, despite some faults, is the outstanding work for its scholarship. The best English translation is the abridged edition by B. Löwy, 6 vols., with index, Philadelphia, 1891-98. Of the many briefer, more popular accounts of the Hebrews, the following may be recommended: F. Gigot, *Outline of Jewish History,* New York, 1912; A. H. Sayce, *Early History of Hebrews,* London, 1897; G. A. Barton, *Sketch of Semitic Origins,* New York, 1902; and the chapters in C. Seignobos, *History of Ancient Civilization,* New York, 1906. Two other useful general works are: K. H. Cornill, *The Culture of Ancient Israel,* Chicago, 1914; and G. A. Barton, *The Religion of Israel,* New York, 1918. For a fairly thorough and scholarly study of the cultural relations between the Hebrews and other peoples, see G. C. C. Maspero, *The Passing of the Empires, 850 B. C. to 330 B. C.,* New York, 1900; and J. H. Breasted, *History of Egypt from the Earliest Times to the Persian Conquest,* 2d ed., New York, 1909. A compact and satisfactory discussion of the Babylonian borrowings is M. Jastrow, Jr., *Hebrew and Babylonian Tradition,* New York, 1914. With this may be consulted A. H. Sayce, *Light from Ancient Monuments,* London, 1909: a slightly antiquated, but essentially sound work.

Of books dealing more directly with Hebrew education, it may be sufficient to indicate these: J. Simon, *L'éducation et l'instruction des enfants chez les anciens Juifs d'après la Bible et le Talmud,* Leipzig, 1879; H. M. Leipziger, *Education amongst the Jews,* New York, 1890; B. Spiers, *School System of the Talmud,* London, 1898; F. H. Swift, *Education in Ancient Israel, to 70 A. D.,* Chicago, 1919; and the chapters in S. S. Laurie, *Pre-Christian Education,* New York, 1924.

CHAPTER IV

EDUCATION OF THE GREEKS

Early Greek history vague. Of the origins of the Greek people we know nothing. There are plenty of legends concerning their origins, but no sure history. Archaeologic evidence points to the existence of peoples of no small culture in Crete, in the islands of the Aegean, in the Peloponnesus, and farther up the mainland, from very ancient times: quite certainly fifteen centuries before Christ, perhaps much earlier. Later, the *Iliad* and the *Odyssey* give us some details of real historic value. Tradition even fixes the siege of Troy as closing in 1184 B. C., and speaks of migrations, considerable displacements of population within the mainland of Greece, as occurring within another lifetime before 1100 B. C. One of the most important of these migrations would be that which brought the Dorians into Sparta. But there is a certain mistiness about all this. The first sure date is only 776 B. C., the beginning of the Olympic games: from which the Greeks reckoned in cycles of four years.

Brief outline of later history. The later history of the Greeks is intricate. As a background to the study of their education, it must suffice to recall a few main features. The Greeks were a conglomeration of many little peoples; they lived in a small land, divided by mountain ranges and deep gulfs into many still smaller compartments; they were roughly grouped, according to some vague racial origins, as Achaeans, Dorians, Ionians, Aeolians, and these racial divisions still further subdivided. In definitely historic times the leading groups were the Dorians, settled chiefly

30

in Sparta and in Crete, and the Ionians in Attica and the colonies of Asia Minor. All seem to have been organized as monarchies in the earlier ages; the Spartans changing later to an oligarchy in which individual life was largely subordinated to the State; the Athenian Ionians to a modified democracy, after the tenth century B. C. Sparta was conservative, and for centuries changed little in government or in culture. The political life of Athens was more fluid, and was often unsettled and turbulent; successive reforms were attempted, most notably under the leadership of Solon in 594 B. C. and of Cleisthenes in 507 B. C. The latter, amongst other changes, extended citizenship to the people of Piraeus, who were not of Grecian stock, and thus brought in an infusion of Asiatic blood. The very numerous Greek colonies were settled chiefly between 750 and 550 B. C. The Persian Wars occurred between 502 and 479 B. C., and resulted in the temporary supremacy of Athens. From 460 to 430 B. C. may be set down as the Age of Pericles. The years 431 to 404 B. C. cover the Peloponnesian War, an internecine struggle chiefly between Athens and Sparta, at the close of which the leadership passed for a short time to Sparta. That was the beginning of the Grecian decline. After the brief hegemony of Thebes, Philip of Macedon began to master the Greeks by a sort of peaceful penetration. The Greek peoples were merged more and more into imperial policies imposed upon them from without. In 146 B. C. the Romans conquered Greece and made it part of their empire. But the real collapse took place almost within the space of a single lifetime.

Curious unity of the Greeks. There are two observations to be made preparatory to even a short study of education amongst the Greeks. First must be noted the curious fact that, although the peoples who called themselves Hellenes, and whom we call Greeks, cannot properly be said to be a nation, yet they were as distinctive a people as, say, the

Hebrews or Egyptians. They were made up of many races. They were not united politically; indeed they were almost constantly quarreling amongst themselves; nor did they have a common form of government.[1] The general type of organization, it is true, was the city-state; but there were more than a hundred of these in Hellas,[2] and more than a thousand in all, counting the Greek colonies. There were very considerable differences in their culture, and even some differences in their language. Yet, despite all these diversities, the Greeks have impressed themselves upon the world as a single people, and their differences resolve themselves into two broad types of culture, the Spartan and the Athenian. It is not necessary here to search into the reasons for this striking community of spirit amongst peoples in other ways so diverse. It is sufficient to observe that the educational history of Sparta and Athens really covers the education of all the Greeks.

Greek civilization based on slavery. The second, and more important, fact to be noted is that all Greek civilization was based upon slavery. Estimates of numbers are difficult; but perhaps it would be conservative to say that in general the proportion of slaves to free was at least four to one; in many cases it was undoubtedly much greater. Athenaeus,[3] with whom Dr. W. Richter[4] agrees, reckons for Athens, as of about the year 300 B.C.: 21,000 citizens; 10,000 *metics* (free men but not citizens, generally sons of

---

[1] The various *Amphictyonies* (Leagues of Neighbors) were loose and shifting federations, seldom counting more than a dozen city-states, originally religious in character, for the common worship of one of the gods, but often degenerating into predatory and vengeful associations for the prosecution of individual spite or greed. The oldest of them was the Delphic Amphictyony. They were never a true bond of political or social unity.

[2] A small country, less than half the size of the State of New York, with a population probably never exceeding three millions.

[3] *Deipnosophistae,* 6:20; written about 200 A.D.

[4] *Die Sklaverei in Griechischen Altertums,* 1886.

foreigners) ; and 400,000 slaves. But this estimate is revised by H. Wallon to: 27,000 citizens, 40,000 *metics,* and between 188,000 and 203,000 slaves.[1] The commoner figures for Sparta are: 9,000 Spartiate heads of families (Wallon reckons this as 32,000 souls in all), 120,000 *Perioikoi* (subject people but not slaves, scattered in about a hundred villages along the mountain sides), and 200,000 *Helots,* true slaves.[2] We know that the *Helots* were sometimes butchered to keep their numbers down. The lot of the slaves varied from that of the *Helots,* who were communal serfs of the land and might not be disposed of at will nor separated from the land, to that of slaves in Athens or Thebes, who were the absolute chattels of their masters. But in every case they are generally outside the scope of Greek education, which was concerned only with the small minority of free men. Incidentally, this fact must be kept in mind when speaking of Greek democracy; which was, to say the least, a very limited democracy.

I. SPARTAN EDUCATION

Its general character. The education of citizens in Sparta was determined by the character of the Spartan State. This was severely practical, hard, narrow. A people small in numbers, aristocratic, intensely exclusive, living upon the enforced labor of slaves, yet despising luxury whether of body or of mind, equally despising mere toil, hardy, militaristic, the Spartans organized their State as a compact unit, and looked upon each individual citizen as simply an integrating part of that unit. They were not religious (none of the Greeks were particularly religious) ; but they had a rigorous code of morality, in which the vir-

[1] *Histoire de l'Esclavage dans l'Antiquité,* 2d ed., 3 vols., Paris, 1879.

[2] Thucydides (5:14) gives slightly higher totals, but about the same proportions.

tues and vices were estimated chiefly by their effect upon the national life. They wanted their children to succeed them as strong, well-disciplined citizens. They planned their education to that end, and excluded from it anything that might interfere with that end.

The training of boys. Let us consider first the training of boys. All the male Spartans ate in common, at *pheiditia,* or clubs; each man being assessed a definite amount in kind and in money: monthly, about 75 quarts of barley meal, 60 or 70 pints of wine, 5 pounds of cheese, 2 or 3 pounds of figs, and 10 Aeginetan obols for extras. The dining clubs were exactly organized, even to the places of each at table and the order of precedence. But the food was the same for all. A member of the mess might bring game from his hunting or additional produce from his farm, and this was served as an *epaiklon,* after the regular meal. Until they were seven years of age, the boys went with their fathers to this dining club, where they sat on the floor, each near his father. This association was definitely part of their training.

Boarding school. At seven years, the boys were organized into *ilai* (packs of sixty-four); and these again organized into *agelai* and *bouai,* larger and less definite groups. This was their school, and it was a boarding school. They fed together, slept together upon bundles of reeds. They went barefoot, and winter and summer they had but a single garment. A citizen of rank and repute was put over them as *paidonomos,* 'master of boys,' and he had assistants who were called significantly 'floggers.' In each pack a boy was selected for his courage and good sense, as *ilarchos,* 'pack leader,' and had power to command and even punish the rest. Over each school was set a young man, over twenty in age, who was called the *eiren.*[1] The

---

[1] Plutarch, *Lukourgos,* 17.

boys were encouraged to fight amongst themselves; to make them hardy and enduring. The *eiren* watched over these fights.

Maintenance at school. Contrary to a common belief, the boys were not educated at the expense of the State. Each Spartan citizen had his allotment of land, tilled by his *Helots*. Out of this he paid his share for the maintenance of the dining clubs, and for the education of his boys. If he became, through mismanagement, too poor to pay, he lost his rights as a citizen. But some wealthier citizens often paid for the education of sons of foreigners or even of *Helots*. The payment was in kind, and was only for the maintenance of the boys, not for the services of those in charge of them. This payment was purposely fixed very low, so that the boys were on scant rations. They were to make up for the shortage of firewood and food by their own efforts. These efforts are often represented as stealing; but they were not really that. They meant filching wood and food by stealth, from the farms, from the larders of the dining clubs, from other *ilai*. But the boys were given a legal right to do this,[1] and if caught, were punished, not for theft, but for clumsiness. The purpose was not to teach them a disregard for property, but skill and craft in providing for themselves in time of need. The Spartans, though private owners, admitted a certain measure of communism; the use of one another's horses and dogs without permission, the use of another's food when out hunting—even if necessary to break open seals to get at the food. The boys' filching was simply a course in scouting and foraging. All was done under the orders of the *eiren*.

Physical education. Great part of their education was physical. They learned to ride horseback. They were forced to swim daily in the cold Eurotas. Under the close

---

[1] Xenophon, *Anabasis,* 4:6, 14.

inspection of their elders, they spent much time in gymnastics; and the Spartan gymnasia were not the soft lounging places of Athens. Plato says the rule was "Strip or withdraw." Every ten days the physical condition of the boys was inspected by the *ephors*. Yet these gymnastic exercises did not lead to one-sided specialism. Professional athletes were not allowed in Sparta. The training was for all, and its purpose was to give them healthy and serviceable bodies. And they had much training in endurance, from exposure to heat and cold, from constant fighting, and from not infrequent floggings.

Moral education. Their moral training was equally severe. They were taught prompt obedience. Not merely parents, *eiren, paidonomos* or assistants, but any elder might command them and even flog them. They were taught modesty and self-restraint; they walked the roads in silence, hands folded under their coat, with no looking about.[1] Loyalty to Sparta was made part of all their thought. Song and story exalted the hero for them; courage and devotedness to the State were the highest virtues. Even chastity had a value for them, beyond the esteem of the other Greeks, because it conserved manly vigor for the future citizen.

Intellectual education. As they were not a commercial people, the Spartans did not wish their boys to study arithmetic. Nor had they any enthusiasm for literature as such; though they knew Homer and admired him. Their songs and dances and poems were warlike, and were meant to stimulate courage rather than to satisfy a love of beauty. The boys' memories were trained by having to learn some of these poems. Most of them could not read.[2] But it would be a gross mistake to think the Spartans stupid, or

---

[1] Xenophon, *Constitution of Sparta*, 2:4.
[2] Isocrates, *Panathenaikos*, 276, 285.

without appreciation of intellectual training. This training was given chiefly by means of discussion; not the vague, wordy, though often charming, discussions of the Athesians; but sharp, keen talk, aiming at decisive and impressive brevity. Plato says: "If you talk with almost any Laconian, at first he seems a fool; then in a flash, at the right moment, he utters a pithy speech; and those about him seem like children beside him." The boys heard such discussion, reserved, penetrating, compact of wit and the grim Spartan humor; and in their turn, under the questioning of the *eiren* and their elders, exercised themselves in it. It was exercise in thinking before speaking.[1] Rhetoric was not merely despised; it was forbidden. A youth who studied it and came back to Sparta was punished by the *ephors*. Later, in the days of their decline, the Spartans enlarged somewhat this curriculum, and even permitted the teaching of the Sophists. But the training as indicated here was characteristic of the larger part of their history.

Social education. From eighteen to twenty, the Spartan youths were *epheboi,* and were given active training in hunting, in patrolling the country, in 'secret service,' in watching over the *Helots,* or even, under the orders of the *ephors,* in slaughtering those amongst the *Helots* who seemed likely to be rebellious.[2] But they were still under discipline, commanded by a regular officer. They organized deliberate, and often very bloody, fights amongst themselves, after a night spent in sacrifice to the gods. Every year, at the altar of Artemis Orthia, the *epheboi* voluntarily underwent terrible floggings, under which it often happened that some died.

Training of girls. The women ate at home. The girls took their meals with them. But the girls too were organ-

---

[1] Plutarch, *Lukourgos,* 19, 20.
[2] Thucydides, 4:80.

ized into packs, and like the boys, lived an outdoor life. They were trained in wrestling, running, swimming; in throwing the discus and the javelin. They went barefoot, and wore only a single garment, the woolen *chiton,* slit down the sides. Until their marriage, they mingled freely with boys and young men: in the gymnasia, in dances, in the religious processions; they learned the same songs as the boys, and were taught the same martial spirit. They were to have strong bodies and patriotic souls, to bear good citizens for Sparta. Because of their freedom, there was more chance for real love marriages for them than for girls at Athens or Thebes. After marriage, they wore veils in public, and for the most part stayed at home. They were famed for their beauty and strength of body, for heroic patriotism; and they had a good reputation for chastity.

Religion in education. There is some vague evidence that in very remote times the Greek peoples worshipped one God.[1] But in historic times they were polytheists. Their gods were very numerous, some of them quite local, some accepted by all the diverse and wrangling peoples. They were very human gods in every case, nor did they represent any very lofty ideals. Their influence upon conduct, never very strong, was bad rather than good. There was no lack of priests. Religious ceremonies and festivals were frequent. But the priests were in no sense teachers or preachers of religious doctrine. They were merely *hierophants,* 'exhibitors of sacred things,' guarding shrines, conserving rites. They did help to keep alive the vague religious instincts of the people, but they had practically nothing to do with either moral or intellectual education. The religion of the Spartans, as of all the Greeks, was a formal and emotional ritualism, almost completely empty of any doctrinal or ethical content.

[1] E. g., "the Pelasgian Zeus, dwelling afar," to whom Achilles prays.

Concluding estimate of Spartan education. This brief and incomplete sketch of Spartan education applies, with no substantial changes, to education in Crete and other Dorian centers. Opinions have always differed as to the value of such an education. Even in Athens there were some who esteemed it very highly, as Xenophon did.[1] Unquestionably it accomplished its purpose: to produce a vigorous and patriotic people. It had its points of nobility, in its development of courage, hardihood, loyalty, self-control, and a certain severe dignity. It had, it is true, an element of brutality; it lacked the humanly softening influences of the arts, of literature, and of the graces of life. Most of all, like all Greek education, it lacked the inspiration and the ennoblement of an outlook beyond this present life. Those who would advocate it as a model of 'efficiency' for imitation by other peoples, should remember, first, that it applied to a small nation: in Sparta, a population of about 350,000, kept down to that number in part by the exposure of weakly infants, in part by the deliberate butchery of *Helots:* and second, that its influence extended to less than one-tenth of that small population, the free and aristocratic Spartiates.

II. Athenian Education

The aim and ideal of Athenian education. When men praise the education of the Greeks, they have in mind chiefly Athenian education; both because it is representative of most Greek education outside of Sparta and Crete, and because at Athens this type of education reached its highest development. In the earlier days of Attica, education apparently had something of the Doric severity, and was not very unlike that of Sparta. But after the establishment of the Athenian democracy, both the spirit and the

[1] Cf. also Plato: in the *Laws, Republic,* and elsewhere.

method of education at Athens took on a new character, and became between the sixth and third centuries B. C. the model for most of Hellas. It was a training for elegant leisure. Unlike the Spartans and Cretans, the other Greeks had no lack of manufactures and commerce. But, except at Corinth, all forms of handicraft were looked upon as mean *(banausos)* and unworthy the dignity of a citizen.[1] The Athenians had abundant slaves, who maintained them in proper leisure; the business of the Athenian was to use that leisure for the development and enjoyment of his own powers, of body, of mind, of emotions, in as nice a harmony as he could accomplish. This is not merely a charming ideal of life, attractive in its graceful hedonism, but because of its impressive and intelligent stress upon comprehensive balance and harmony, it is a naturally worthy ideal. It is of interest to consider how closely the Athenians were able to approach it in practice; and it is only fair to confine that consideration chiefly to the great period of Greek history, before decay set in.

Limited to one twenty-fifth of the population. Athenian education was an attempt to equip each new generation for the task of attaining the Athenian ideal of life. But that attempt, to begin with, was severely limited. It not merely left out of account the enormous slave population; it just as rigorously excluded the wives and daughters of even Athenian citizens. It was concerned with certainly less than one in every twenty-five of the people at Athens. In the Athenian scheme of life, women were considered only for the purpose of procreation, and even grudgingly for that. Plato says that a man marries, not because he wants to, but 'because the law constrains him.' It was a civic duty to marry. Menander voices the mind of the Athenians, when he made a character in a comedy say: "Marriage, to

---

[1] Herodotus, 2:167.

tell the truth, is an evil, though a necessary evil." At Sparta weakly infants were exposed, to die; the same inhuman practice prevailed at Athens, but with this difference, that it was only girl babies who were so dealt with. If the girl child was allowed to live, she was kept in Oriental seclusion with the women until, at fifteen, she was married, often to a man she had never seen before. Her physical exercise was some work about the house, the supervision of the slaves; her mental and moral training no more than the company of other untutored women could give her. Even when she was wife and mother, she saw but little of her husband or son; for the male Greeks lived an outdoor life, and considered the house a place only for women and slaves.

Education prescribed, but not conducted, by State. The Athenian State did not control education, beyond making it a law that fathers must see to the education of their sons, and setting down certain moral regulations in the code of Solon. Davidson, with an eye upon the Spartan contrast, commends Athens for not establishing "a socialistic system of public schools, to relieve parents from the duty of educating their children, a duty which they had undertaken in bringing them into the world."[1] This is a very sound observation, and the principle expressed in it applies to all peoples and all times. Yet it is curious to note how Davidson, and other eulogists of Greek education, ignore the plain fact that Athenian *parents* had very little to do with the education of their children, although most Athenian citizens certainly had abundant leisure which they might have devoted to that purpose. Children were in the care of nurses during infancy, and boys handed over to the *paidogogos,* a guardian slave, and to the schools, at six or seven years of age, or even earlier.

---

[1] *Education of the Greek People,* New York, 1907, p. 72.

Paidogogoi and didaskaloi. The *paidogogos* (boy-leader) was not a tutor or teacher; he was always a slave, generally an old and decrepit or unfit slave,[1] whose office was to accompany the boy to and from school, carry his lyre or the like, guard him from bad companions. He had authority to whip the boy, it is true, but he had little real influence over him, and what little he had was by no means always good. The schools were private schools, and of course varied according to the wealth of the boys who attended them. Most of them were in some sort of building or enclosure, though the schools of the poor were often in the open. The *didaskaloi* (school teachers) were paid definite fees by the boys' fathers, niggardly fees for the most part, and for that reason, if for no other, were held in contempt by the Athenians. Demosthenes, in the speech "Peri Stephanou," can find no more bitter sneer against his great rival, Aeschines, than to say that he was the son of a schoolmaster.

Elementary schools. Primary education in the schools had three parts: instruction in letters, music, and gymnastics. The *grammatistes* taught reading and writing. The boys first learned the letters of the alphabet, then grouped these into syllables and words. They had the letters before them, painted on clay plaques. Writing was learned by following models, sometimes by tracing these model letters cut into wood. Their writing materials were, at first, wax tablets, on which they wrote with a stylus which had at its upper end a broad surface for erasing the writing. Papyrus and parchment were expensive, and were used only after the boys had acquired some skill. Paper, of course, was unknown to the Greeks, as it was first discovered by the Chinese only in 105 A. D. Though there is some uncertainty about it, arithmetic seems also to have

---

[1] There is a story that Pericles, seeing a slave fall out of a tree and break his leg, said: "There goes a new *paidogogos!*"

been taught by the *grammatistes*. The boys reckoned on their fingers; *pempazein* ('to five'), was a common word for counting. The Greeks had not our numerals, of course, but used a cumbersome system based on letters of the alphabet. For larger reckonings an abacus was employed. The *kitharistes* taught the boys, not merely to play the lyre and sing, but also how to use their voices in speaking; for the Greeks properly made great account of a good pronunciation and of a nicely cultured accent. The *paidotribes,* the 'boy-rubber,' was the master of gymnastics; his school was called the *palaistra*. He aimed at the development of beauty as well as health and strength in his pupils. He supervised exercises, prescribed diet, and was expected to train the boys to courage, endurance, and self-control. The boys exercised naked, and as the *palaistra* had no roof, they were well browned by the sun. The Greeks esteemed highly the hygienic value of sunlight. The *paidotribes,* or later, an assistant called *aleiptes,* rubbed the boys with oil before their exercises, and after the exercises bathed them with oil and water. Grown men were not allowed in the *palaistra* during the lessons, though they looked on from the dressing room.

Character of school life. The schools were not boarding-schools, as in Sparta, but the school day was long, beginning before breakfast and continuing until about sunset. Apparently the day began with some exercises in the *palaistra;* then, after breakfast, the boys studied their letters, and music, and memorized selections from the poems set them. The instruction was mostly individual, the *grammatistes* and *kitharistes* taking each boy in turn. The larger part of the afternoon seems to have been given to the *palaistra*. It will be noted that the boys were at home only for meals and sleep; after they had once begun to go to school they scarcely knew their mothers. Their moral training was largely in the care of the hired teachers and the rather irresponsible slaves who acted as *paidogogoi*. Such religious education as they got was derived in a concrete way from taking part in the public festivals, which were numerous and stately, and from the stories and songs of the gods and goddesses which formed a large part of their reading.

Extent of school education. This primary education occupied about eight or nine years, though of course the length of time depended upon the amount of money the father was able and willing to spend on his son's schooling. It was intelligently graded, advancing the boy from the rudiments of instruction in each of the three branches to more elaborate exercises. The boy, if his father were wealthy, might continue his study of the lyric poets and his training with other older boys in gymnastics until he reached the age of eighteen. If he were a poor boy, he might have only a few years of schooling, since only the elementary training in letters was compulsory, and he might even have to take to farm work or learn a trade under his father; but this was considered a great misfortune, and in general the Athenians were eager to send their boys to school as long as they could.

Training of epheboi. However, rich or poor, every Athenian boy at eighteen had to undergo a two-years' course of military training: the first year at Athens itself, the second in camp or in the frontier forts; and during those two years he was maintained by the State, in part out of the public funds, in part out of taxes levied specially upon the rich citizens of each tribe. His education then was, of course, chiefly physical and moral, a training for hardihood, endurance, loyalty to the State, sense of responsibility, and the like; but it was diversified by several solemn competitions each year, in athletics, in choral-dancing, and sometimes in reciting verses. The youth at this time was called *ephebos*. Ten officials, known as *sophronistai*, were appointed to watch over the morals of the young, particularly of the *epheboi.*

Moral influences. There was excellent reason for having such guardians of morality; though, as usual, they were futile guardians. The moral atmosphere of Athens was distinctly bad. The people were in general frivolous, conceited, and self-willed; notoriously lacking in truthfulness; though a gay people, they were not kindly; and they scarcely had any idea of chastity, beyond limiting sexual indulgence within the bounds of obvious and gross physical injury. Considering the very small esteem in which wives and mothers were held, it is not at all strange that the city should abound in purchasable women, or that unnatural sexual gratifications should have become of almost universal use. Aristophanes, in *The Clouds,* speaks of even the little boys at the *palaistrai* ogling their admirers.[1] All the schools in the world cannot combat such influences.

Aesthetic influences. On the other hand, the aesthetic influences were admirable. The climate itself was bright and joyous. Wit and intellectual keenness were enjoyed as thoroughly as bodily pleasures. The Greeks had developed a balanced and imposing architecture, and had produced sculptors never surpassed in the world. The public buildings at Athens were a delight to the eye and an inspiration to the mind. Their dramas are amongst the world's great literature. Their language itself was sonorous, rich, as graceful as it was vigorous. The city rang with vitality, a vitality tempered, even in its vicious manifestations, by a cultivated instinct for refinement, for that balance, that μηδὲν ἄγαν, which was as much at bottom of Greek levity as it was of Greek seriousness, and which had a charm about it even when it was detestable in its immorality.

---

[1] Cf. The Loeb Classical Library edition of *Aristophanes* (with English translation by B. B. Rogers), 3 vols., London, 1930, Vol. 1, pp. 350 sqq.

But neither drawing nor sculpture seems to have been taught in the schools until after 300 B. C. They were looked upon as parts of a technical education, and therefore beyond the scope of the general cultural equipment of an Athenian citizen. The boys who studied these arts did so as apprentices to painters and sculptors. The materials for practice drawings were white boxwood boards and charcoal or lead; and the drawings were erased by washing with a sponge. Before the time of Plato the Greeks had developed skill in the use of perspective and foreshortening.

Secondary schools. Of what we should call secondary or higher education, there is no evidence until after the Persian Wars, say about 460 B. C. Then it grew rapidly, in part as a result of the wider contacts of Athens with the outside world, in part as the natural outcome of the keen Greek intelligence and the spirit of critical inquiry to which it led.[1] A small number of men, exceptionally gifted, devoted themselves to the study of all the knowledge available to them, to the search for laws of thought and conduct, and to an understanding even of ultimate causes. Socrates, Plato, Aristotle, are, of course, amongst the world's greatest philosophers. And they were teachers, too, rather informally at first, through intimate conversations; later, in definite lectures quite like our modern university lectures. About the same time, another class of men, really learned, but perhaps less dignified than the philosophers, and certainly more practically concerned for the diffusion of knowledge, began to organize regular secondary schools, demanding payment from their pupils.[2] These were known

[1] "After the Persian wars, men, inspired by what they had achieved, ventured still farther; they sought all forms of knowledge, and set themselves to ever new inquiries." Aristotle, *Politics,* 1341.

[2] Much has been written about the place of the Sophists. Plato, in *Phaedo* and *Protagoras,* makes Socrates revile them for teaching for gain. For some source knowledge of them, see H. Diels, *Die Fragmente der Vorsokratiker,* 2 vols., Berlin, 1906-10; M. Schanz.

as Sophists; amongst whom were numbered such eminent men as Protagoras, Gorgias, Prodicus.

Philosophers and Sophists as teachers. There was bitter rivalry between the philosophers and Sophists. The philosophers, for one thing, scorned the Sophists for accepting payment for their wisdom; perhaps they also resented their greater popularity and influence; and they evidently knew that great truth, which the mass of mankind generally hates, that there is no democracy of intellect, that only a comparative few are equipped to do real thinking, and that intellectual poverty is more often a matter of lack of brains than of lack of opportunity. Their writings have succeeded in blackening the Sophist even to our own day, and in making us forget that the early Sophists were great men, great scholars, and great teachers. Later, it is true, the Sophists became mere crammers, offering to the well-to-do a superficial culture, which is, manifestly, always the enemy of real mental development. But of the two groups, whilst the philosophers are more important in the history of speculative thought, the Sophists are more important in the history of Greek education.[1] They taught skill in language, oratory, methods of logic, some higher mathematics and

Die Sophisten, Goettingen, 1867. J. Burnett has a brief account in *Greek Philosophy: Thales to Plato,* London, 1914, especially pp. 105-24. See also the still more summary account in *Cambridge Ancient History,* Cambridge, 1927, Vol. 5, pp. 377-82.

[1] The two greatest of the Greek philosophers are Plato and Aristotle. Plato has left us some scattered accounts of Athenian practice in education, chiefly in the *Protagoras* and, more at length, the *Laws.* But his true importance, not so much for Greek education as for the education of later ages, is based upon the *theories* of education which he elaborated in the *Republic.* Aristotle's writings on education appear to have come down to us only in fragmentary forms, and are mainly found in the *Ethics* and *Politics.* He follows much the same line of thought as Plato, but with the sharper definiteness characteristic of his own mental processes. A standard edition of Plato's works is that of I. Bekker, *Platonis Scripta Graece Omnia,* 9 vols., London, 1826, in which the ten books of the *Republic* occur in Vol. 6, 251-560, and Vol. 7, 1-230. There is an English translation of the *Republic* by H. Davis in Bohn's *Works of Plato,* London, 1899.

what was then considered physical science, and even some of the speculative truths discovered or formulated by the philosophers. It was inevitable that they should laugh at the silly cosmogony of the Greeks, and at their still more ridiculous gods. The witty Greeks eagerly followed them in this; though, for the most part, they were not interested to follow them in their positive attempts to search out a more reasonable explanation of the world; nor do they seem to have been willing to accept their intelligent suggestions leading to a higher morality. The Sophists added enormously to the accomplishments of the Greeks, but practically nothing to their character. And in their own day the philosophers influenced only a little handful of select disciples, though the influence of their writings upon much later ages of the world was, and still is, very great. Because of this later esteem of them, we are likely to forget that the philosophic 'schools' of Athens were little more than small and private coteries until they were practically merged into the system of the later Sophists, and the so-called University of Athens arose in the days of Greek decadence.[1]

The value of Greek education. There are violent differences of opinion about the worth of Greek education; the extremes of these opinions being, as usual, absurd. At present the more popular extreme is that of very indiscriminate praise. It is popular to forget the essential snobbery of an education based upon slavery; to 'point with pride'

Bekker has also excellently edited *Aristotelis Opera,* 11 vols., Oxford, 1837. The *Ethics* and *Politics* are translated into English in Vols. 9 and 10 of W. D. Ross' edition, *Works of Aristotle,* 11 vols., Oxford, 1910-31. Some extracts from Plato and Aristotle are translated into English in P. Monroe, *Source-Book of the History of Education: Greek and Roman Period,* New York, 1906. See also B. Bosanquet, *Education of the Young in Plato's Republic,* Cambridge, 1900; and J. Burnet, *Aristotle on Education,* Cambridge, 1903.

[1] The University of Athens developed after Greece had become a Roman dependency. See J. W. H. Walden, *The Universities of Ancient Greece,* New York, 1909; and W. W. Capes, *University Life in Ancient Athens,* London, 1877.

to the superb physical beauty of the Greeks, ignoring the obvious fact that the Greek statues, our main testimony to their perfection of body, represent the exceptional man, not the general type,[1] to instance Plato and Aristotle and Demosthenes as representative Greek intellects; and for the most part to pass over in silence the very low moral ideas and practices of the Greeks, their degradation of women, outside of Sparta, their almost utter lack of family life, and the terrible nemesis of a dwindling population that marked their later history. Greek freedom and independence are lauded, ignoring the huge slave population; and their aesthetic sense extolled, though it saw nothing ugly in the exposure of their own infants.

The plain fact is that Greek education did produce a vigorous and sprightly people, lithe of body and nimble of wit; but a people, at the same time, savagely cruel, hard, untruthful, unchaste; without any loyalty beyond a curious, though not very stable, civic pride; incapable of unified action, except in an emergency. It did create, at the great cost of slavery, leisure for its citizens, and gave those citizens a fine freedom of development which made possible the production of real, and even amazing, excellence in physical beauty, in artistic expression, and in profoundly penetrating thought. But it did not avail to save the race from physical and moral decay. "The glory that was Greece" was a doomed glory; it lives only in the romantic memory of a gay, clever minority of aristocrats, and in the artistic and philosophic works of a few geniuses. It is the greatest monument the world has known to the insufficiency of human nature when left to its own unaided resources.

---

[1] The combination of great vigor and fine harmony of body which is beauty is always as rare as the combination of great vigor and fine harmony of mind which is genius.

TOPICS FOR DISCUSSION

1. The relative position of schoolmasters at Sparta and at Athens.
2. The Greek notions concerning the moral value of music.
3. The proportion of Athenian youths who received a secondary education.
4. The influence of Socrates on the education of Greek youths.
5. The contrast between Plato's ideal of education and the Athenian reality.
6. The character and work of the so-called University of Athens.

BIBLIOGRAPHIC NOTE

There is a fair abundance of source material on Greek education; as, for instance, in the *Histories* of Herodotus (Rawlinson's translation, New York, 1897) and Thucydides (Jowett's translation, New York, 1883), and in the writings of Xenophon (Dakyn's edition, London, 1897), Plutarch's *Lives* (translated by Stewart & Long, London, 1880), and Athenaeus, *Deipnosophistae* (best edition, Meineke, 1859-67; translated by Yonge, in Bohn's Classical Library, 1854). Cassell, New York, publishes in pamphlet form, 10 cents each, partial translations of Plutarch, the *Crito* and *Phaedo* of Plato, Xenophon's *Memorable Thoughts of Socrates,* etc. A most useful selection of sources may be had in G. W. Botsford and E. G. Sihler, *Hellenic Civilization,* New York, 1915 (Vol. 2 of *Records of Civilization: Sources and Studies,* edited by Shotwell and Evans). A very interesting study is B. Bosanquet, *The Education of the Young in the Republic of Plato, Translated into English with Notes and Introduction,* Cambridge, England, 1900.

Some of the general works on Greek life in its various stages throw much light on Greek education: such as the excellent volume of D. Seymour, *Life in the Homeric Age,* New York, 1907; or, for the later period up to 323 B. C., J. C. Stobart, *The Glory that was Greece: A Survey of Hellenic Culture and Civilization,* 2d ed. rev., London, 1916, and H. B. Cotterill, *Ancient Greece, a Sketch of its Art, Literature and Philosophy,* etc., London, 1913; or, for the earlier and later periods, including the Graeco-Roman, F. Baumgarten, *Die antike Kultur,* Leipzig, 1922 (an abridgement of two larger, more detailed works by Baumgarten, Poland, and Wagner). G. Glotz, *Ancient Greece at Work,* New York, 1926, touches upon the economic background of education; W. H. S. Jones, *Malaria and Greek History,* London, 1909, indicates one of the causes of Greek decay; A. W. Gomme, *Population of Athens in the V and IV Centuries B. C.,* Oxford, 1933, discusses the slave problem; N. Fustel de Coulanges, *The Ancient City,* Boston, 1874, outlines the social structure of the Greeks.

Of the many books dealing directly with Greek schools and Greek education, the following may be suggested as fairly authoritative:

J. P. Mahaffy, *Old Greek Education,* New York, 1882; K. J. Freeman, *Schools of Hellas, an Essay on the Practice and Theory of Ancient Greek Education from 600 to 300 B.C.,* London, 1907; P. Girard, *L'Éducation Athènienne au Ve et au IVe siècle avant J. C.,* Paris, 1889; F. H. Lane, *Elementary Greek Education,* Syracuse, N. Y., 1895; A. S. Wilkins, *National Education in Greece,* New York, 1911; S. S. Laurie, *Pre-Christian Education,* New York, 1924; and the volumes of Capes and Walden on the University of Athens. For the last mentioned, see also the sketch in A. C. Allinson, *Roads from Rome,* New York, 1913.

CHAPTER V

Modern disparagement of Roman education. It is almost the universal fashion amongst our modern writers on education to disparage Roman education and to contrast it very unflatteringly with the Greek education which they admire and praise. The grounds for that disparagement are often concealed in a considerable fog of words, and a still thicker fog of ideas as to the meaning of education; but they seem to be in general that Roman education lacked the aesthetic ideals of the Greeks, that Roman life was ruled not so much by the concept of beauty, as by a rather stern consciousness of duty. The truth probably is that the Roman ideal and the Roman procedure in education were both farther removed from our present ideals and practices than were those of the Greeks: and we suffer from the tendency of all peoples to gauge another age by their own. But it is important to a proper understanding, not merely of Roman education, but of all education, that we view the education of the Romans as fairly as possible, and to that end divest ourselves of the prejudices engendered in us by momentary modern fashions of thought.

Roman character. The Romans come into history as a people small in numbers, of quite simply unknown origin, settled in and about what has been known for more than twenty-five centuries as the city of Rome. They were physically and mentally sturdy, energetic, practical: industrious, decidedly unimaginative, courageous, tenacious, and stern. They fought stubbornly with the other small peoples round about them, and dominated them. They had the

52

qualities that make for definite and strong social organization; they developed these qualities. They had, like the Hebrews, an intense appreciation of family life: differing in this very notably from the Greeks of the same period of history. Hence, though they perfected one of the greatest State organizations in the history of mankind, they built that State upon the family as an inviolable unit. The Roman State did not begin to decay until the Roman family had decayed.

Civil organization and growth. This State was ruled by kings from some time in their remote and vaguely known beginnings (tradition assigns 753 B. C. as the date of the founding of the city), until about 509 B. C. when it became a Republic, with the government in the hands of an aristocratic senate and a number of officials elected annually by the citizens. (It may be of interest to note that this change took place at the same time as the reform of Cleisthenes at Athens; though there is, of course, no connection between the two events). It was a small Republic, occupying a few hundreds of square miles in central Italy, and reckoning perhaps half a million people. It took some four hundred years for it to spread by conquest to the whole of Italy. After that, its power developed more rapidly, so that within another two hundred years it ruled practically the whole of the Mediterranean littoral; it became an empire in reality, and then changed to an imperial form of government. We may set the year 30 B. C. as the date of this last change. But this final change was so gradual as scarcely to be perceptible to the masses of the peoples concerned in it. It was a development rather than a revolution.

Class distinctions. Like all other peoples, the Romans were divided into classes. Even amongst its citizens there was a sharp division, existing from a time long before the Republic: the patricians, who held all the privileges of public office and religious ceremonial, and the plebeians, debarred from these, and even from intermarriage with patricians. The plebeians were, of course, by far the more numerous, and were often wealthy. If they became wealthy enough, they might be *equites,* knights; in the last century of the Republic the requisite fortune for a knight was 400,000 sesterces. From the very early years of the Republic the plebeians began a struggle for political recognition: a struggle which lasted for some two hundred years, and which gradually won for them the right of being under the same laws as the patricians (these laws were engraved on bronze tablets, about 450 B. C., and were known to the Romans as *The Laws of the Twelve Tables*), the right of intermarriage with patricians, and even the right to hold the highest offices in the Republic. But the social distinction between patrician and plebeian remained. Later, emancipated slaves, freedmen, were allowed to become citizens; but neither they nor their descendants ever lost the taint of slavery. They were not allowed to serve in the army; and in the assembly of the lower people, the *comitia tributa,* they voted last.

Slavery. Finally there were the slaves, who were never, of course, Roman citizens. Slavery was part of the Roman social system from the earliest times: an absolute slavery, in which not even the right to marriage was recognized. Most of the slaves originally came in as captives in the many Roman wars. Their numbers constantly increased, until at the end of the great period of conquest, say, about the time of the birth of Christ, they outnumbered the free men perhaps three to one. Exact figures are impossible. We know of authentic instances where a single Roman possessed more than four thousand slaves. Horace, who inherited seven slaves from his father, speaks of his 'modest patrimony'; and in the Rome of his time and later, to possess only three slaves was a mark of real poverty. Blair estimates, for the period about 50 A. D., the population of

Italy alone as consisting of 6,944,000 free men and 20,832,-000 slaves.[1]

Extent of education amongst Romans. It is customary to consider the education of the Romans in two or three great periods, determined by the varying amount of Greek influence upon Roman life. But few historians ever seem to consider the much more important division of that education according to the proportion of the people who profited by it. That proportion obviously was not at all times the same; it changed with the changing economic and social conditions of Roman life. Thus the number of those who received a characteristically Roman education was much greater during the earlier centuries, when a majority of the people of Rome were free and independent, and grew steadily less as the number of slaves increased and as the wealth of the nation tended to gather into the hands of a few and Rome developed a 'proletariat,' a people without land. It is evidently impossible to make anything like an exact estimate of such proportions. But perhaps we shall not be far from the truth if we say that in the first two centuries of the Republic more than three-fourths of the people were educated with care and in the manner which we have come to consider as Roman; in the next two centuries, half of the people were so educated; in the last century of the Republic and the first two or three centuries of the Empire, less than a tenth of the people, and these in a fashion differing largely from the older Roman and approaching more nearly to that prevalent in the decaying Greek civilization of the time. Some such perspective must be kept in mind for a just valuation of Roman education. The character of the Roman education remained fairly the

[1] T. Mommsen, *The History of Rome* (English translation by Dickson), New York, 1870, Vol. 3, p. 494, calculates on the basis of the census of 70 B. C. that the free population of Italy was not more than 6 or 7 millions, and the slave population was 13 or 14 millions.

same through the first four hundred years of the Republic, whilst the proportion of people who got a careful training in it lessened considerably; then a very small minority of the wealthy and privileged began to have a more elaborate sort of training, often called a Graeco-Roman education, whilst the enormous majority of the people received less and less education of any purposeful or intelligent sort. It should scarcely be necessary to add that not long after that came the end of the distinctively Roman civilization.

The Roman ideal in education. We are now in a position to consider what was the ideal and the practice of the education of the Romans. The ideal was the formation of a good citizen: which meant, both a vigorous and virtuous individual, and a competent and properly ordinated member of the State. It resembled not a little the ideal of Sparta, but with the very important difference that the individual did not exist for the State, but the State for the individual. It emphasized character. It intelligently recognized that character is made up of habits; and it wanted those habits to be good habits. It was, like the Hebrew ideal, fundamentally religious, even though the Romans quite early in their history had lost the clear notion of one Infinite Being. For the Roman, as for the Hebrew, duty to the State was recognized as duty to a Being above both State and individual; and although to the Hebrew that recognition was more definite and explicit, constituting the basis of a real theocracy, it was very genuine to the Roman too, and very strong. The enormous racial differences between the Hebrews and the Romans, and the very diverse material circumstances in which Providence placed each of these peoples to work out its destiny, greatly modified the development of that religious principle into national conduct; but they should not blind us to the common principle itself. The first of all virtues to the Roman was piety, obedience to the commands of the gods; and this was the foundation for obedience to parents and to the State.[1] Next, perhaps, came 'constantia,' the manly courage of fortitude, rather than mere bravery; then honesty and prudence in the management of one's affairs, 'gravitas' or sedateness, dignity, sobriety in manner and speech, and 'pudor' or modesty. These were not qualities to be speculated about, as amongst the Greeks, but to be acquired and practiced. It is not a graceful ideal, like that of the Athenians; it has in it little or no imagination, nor does it tend to develop any attractive artistry of expression; it is common sense, rather severe, and intensely practical. And it was powerful. Even in the later stages of Roman decay it did not entirely disappear.

Its realization depended little on schools. How did Roman education set about trying to realize this ideal? In the first place, as a negative yet important element of that education, must be pointed out the significant fact that it was not carried out by schools. That fact alone is quite puzzling to modern prejudices; it seems a paradox in education. It is true that Livy, in his account of the rape of Virginius' daughter by one of the decemvirs in 305 B. C., says that the girl was seized on her way to school: "Virgini venienti in forum—ibi namque in tabernis literarum ludi erant—minister decemviri libidinis manum injecit."[2] But scholars look upon the passage as an anachronism; Livy was reading into the story circumstances of his own time. There is no real evidence for schools until a much later period. The Roman family was the Roman school for all the Romans in the earlier centuries, and for most of the Romans even in the later. Horace, who was born in 65 B. C. and died in 8 B. C., at a time when schools had become fairly

---

[1] St. Ambrose might have made from his Roman tradition the statement he made as a Christian bishop: "Pietas omnium virtutum fundamentum est." (In Psalmum 118, Sermo 21.)

[2] Bk. III, 44.

common, tells us, in the First Book of his Satires, some details of his education. His father taught him in familiar speech, and by pointing out concrete examples for his guidance.

When he would exhort me to live a thrifty, frugal life, contented with what he had saved for me, he would say, "Do you not see how hard it is for the son of Albius to live, and how needy Barrus is: a signal warning to prevent any one from wasting his inheritance." If he would deter me from dishonourable love, he would say, "Do not be like Sectanus."

And he affectionately boasts of how his father, a poor man,

had the daring to carry me, when a boy, to Rome, there to learn the liberal arts which any *knight or senator would have his own sons taught.*

But he adds, almost immediately, that:

He himself was ever present, an incorruptible guardian, at all my studies. Why say more? My modesty, that first grain of virtue, he kept unsullied, not only by actual stain, but by the very rumour of it.

There was a school at Venusia, Horace's native town, kept, as he tells us, by Falvius,

to which the *leading youths of the town, the sons of centurions,* the great men there, used to go, with their bags and slates on their left arm, taking the teacher's fee on the Ides of eight months of the year.

But his father dared to look even higher for the education of the future poet.

The passage bears out clearly enough the conclusion that, even at the close of the Republic, schools were somewhat of a rarity, and were looked upon as the doubtful privilege of the rich. The true Roman still made the education of his children his personal care. The contrast to the education of the Greeks, which was almost entirely an affair of schools, is very marked; almost as marked as the contrast between the educational ideals of the two peoples.

But was primarily a concern of the family. The Roman family was very closely knit. The power of the father in it was supreme and all but absolute. In theory he might sell his children into slavery, might expose them to death as infants, or might for just cause put them to death when they were more mature. In practice his power over his children was shared with their mother, who had a large part in the education of the children. The Roman house was really a home; which the Greek house certainly was not. Father and mother lived in close contact with their children. Together they trained them to habits of virtue, and began from early years to instill in them the spirit of reverence and religious duty. Worship, domestic and simple in its exercises, was linked up with all the details of each day's life. Indeed, the religion of the Roman State was merely the religion of the family enlarged. Such an atmosphere of reverent obedience and devout care was in itself an important educative influence. Mommsen does not hesitate to say that "the Roman family from the first contained within it the conditions of a high culture in the mere moral adjustment of the mutual relations of its members."

Physical education. Most of the families were what we would call peasant families. Labor, though increasingly relegated to slaves, was not looked upon with contempt, as in Greece. Indeed, the moral value of a training to industry was clearly recognized, just as amongst the Hebrews. Hence a great deal of the education of the Romans was what the modern jargon calls industrial education. The Roman boy played games, of course; the most popular of which were various games of ball; but the Romans never took mere athletics with the seriousness with which the Greeks esteemed them. The boy's physical education was found to a large extent in plain work. And as the Roman peasantry was a fighting peasantry, ready to turn from the plow to the sword, fathers trained their sons from boy-

hood to the use of arms. But beauty and grace were not
the aims of physical education with the Romans, who looked
rather to the development of a man useful on his farm or,
at need, in the army. It might be mentioned in passing
that military service was considered a privilege as well as a
duty, and that for the best centuries of the Roman State it
was a service without pay. But when the Roman wanted
athletic display for his amusement, he paid the athlete. The
result of the physical education of the Romans was an exceptionally sturdy race, both active and enduring. The
story of the Roman citizen army testifies to that.

Intellectual education. It must be confessed, of course,
that the Romans never made any great contribution to the
world's store of speculative truth. They were doers rather
than searchers. But it would be a mistake to consider them
unintelligent, or that their education took no account of
the development of the intellect. Their intelligence was
displayed chiefly in the practical management of the means
of living, and very notably in the nicely balanced adjustment of the individual with the social group. To this end
they valued highly the arts which serve for communication.
Their language, whilst not as rich nor as subtle as that of
the Greeks, was clear, terse, and vigorous. Reading and
writing were, from early times, almost universal accomplishments, acquired by the child from his parents. The
method of instruction was essentially the same as that in
use amongst the Greeks, the alphabetical method. Arithmetic too was commonly studied by the child; and though
the Roman numerals were cumbrous enough, they were
more convenient than the Greek. In the matter of technical
equipment of the mind, these 'three R's' marked the ordinary maximum for the vast majority of the Roman people;
but it must be remarked that it was a maximum much
higher than, for instance, that found in England a scant
hundred and fifty years ago.

Mental development by practical application. Higher development of the mind was the privilege of only a small minority, as it always is, in every civilization. Amongst the Romans it was acquired by exercise in such practical arts and sciences as were involved in law-making, in governmental functions, in commerce, in the construction of buildings, roads, aqueducts, and in the organization and conduct of armies. Roman laws, for the most part, grew out of Roman practices; they were the formulation of customs. And it speaks very well for the mental as well as moral development of the whole people that the laws so based have won, as they have won, the admiration of the succeeding ages and peoples, and even have become models for most of the fundamental laws of all Western civilizations. In building, the Romans appear to have invented the round arch, that most important gift to architecture. Their great roads are still a wonder and an amazement to engineers. In their splendid aqueducts we scarcely know whether to admire more the daring of concept displayed in them or the skill with which the concept has been carried into execution. There is no need to dilate on these things; they are commonplaces of Roman achievement. And though they manifest a different sort of intelligence from that shown in the great Greek philosophies, sculptures, poems and dramas, it is a very high and keenly developed intelligence. If it lacks the charm of the Greek mind, may that not be because it moved under the restraint of duty, because it was always giving an account of its stewardship? Mankind has always hated restraints, even when it clearly sees and acknowledges the need of them. The Greek mind wandered delightfully like a child in a flowery meadow: the Roman marched with the heavy tread of a man on a bounden journey.

Religious education. A very competent and intelligent writer makes this amazing remark about the Romans: "Re-

ligion had little influence of an intellectual and aesthetic
character upon the life of the people and consequently upon
their education."[1] The implications of that statement go
far toward explaining some very curious things about modern education in general, about modern views on religion,
and about the consistent disparagement of Roman education in most modern histories. We must simply insist that
'intellectual and aesthetic' development is not the whole of
education, and that the primary purpose both of religion
and of religious education is not concerned with that sort
of development. Religion is the group of beliefs and practices which bind men in due subjection to God. It involves
an intellectual acceptance of truths, but not necessarily
philosophic speculations about such truths. In point of
fact, the Roman religion was much more intelligent than
the Greek, though it was much less speculative. It was
Roman intelligence which kept the Roman people to the
humility of high abstractions regarding the Deity, and kept
them away from the childishness of anthropomorphism.[2]
And it is not a sneer, but an encomium, to say that their
religion was eminently practical. It was because of its
practicality, and of its consequent influence upon character,
that the Roman religion was so important a part of Roman
education.

The Roman concept of God fell far short of the Hebrew;
but it was not a degrading concept. Back of all the confusion of polytheism, there persisted the clear idea of supreme dominion, and the correlative of human duty. It
had more of fear than of love in it, it is true; but it was a
noble fear, a calm recognition that no human being can
contend with the divine. The Romans prayed. There was

---

[1] Dr. Paul Monroe, *History of Education*, p. 179.
[2] In this connection it is worth noting that for nearly two centuries
the Romans had no idols. Cf. St. Augustine, *De Civitate Dei*, 4:11-
12, quoting Varro's *Antiquitates*. See also Plutarch, *Numa*, chap. 8,
and Pliny, *Historia Naturalis*, 34:4.

nothing strange to them in the practice of the great Scipio, who went daily to the temple of Jupiter to pray, and who attributed all his victories to prayer. There may be some superstition in that last, but there may be a great deal of real religion too; it was at least an acknowledgment of God's supremacy. Every day in the Roman home began with prayer: to Vesta, the goddess of the hearth, to the Penates, the guardian deities of the house, to the Lares, who stood either for what Christians think of as guardian angels or for those souls of the departed who are linked with us in the Communion of Saints. The father, as head of the family, led in these prayers; his wife and children joined with him. There was a formal ritual, which the child was taught; and there was a simple earnestness back of the ritual, which he was also taught. He was made to feel the ruling presence of the Deity through all his day. His instruction in the understanding and practice of the great Roman virtues was based upon that fundamental 'pietas.' To say that there was nothing highly educational in that constant training is to talk nonsense.

Social education. At the age, generally, of sixteen, the boy put off the 'toga praetexta' for the 'toga virilis,' and became a man. But his father still looked after his education, by making him his close companion, in his work, at ceremonial dinners, in the Forum, in military exercises, in public worship, and the like. The boy grew into full manhood in an atmosphere of self-control, simplicity, dignity, and patriotism, which breathed from the society in which he lived. For despite the inevitable distinctions of rank, and of wealth and poverty, there was in that earlier Roman society a remarkable homogeneity, the result of accumulated training to a common ideal and in a distinctive character. That society was, therefore, an educational force in itself.

The education of women. The training of girls seems to

have differed little from that of the boys. Certainly they were not in any way discriminated against. They seem to have been as well grounded as the boys in the 'three R's.' They were undoubtedly educated to the same standards of virtuous conduct. Of course their mothers taught them the necessary household arts, and naturally looked after details of their education more closely than their fathers did; but because of the close family life of the Romans, girls and boys were brought up together, shared the same social activities and the same general instruction, and each sex by its subtle and complex influence upon the other contributed not a little to the common education of both. The character of the Roman matron is eloquent of her early education. She takes her place as equal beside her husband—"ubi tu Caius, ego Caia"—respected and honored, protected by law in her property, socially free, and under no limitations save those which the functions of her sex impose upon her. Her position is like that of the Hebrew woman, and immeasurably higher than that of the Greek.

The effect of Roman conquests upon education. But a great change came over the Roman people and over their education. Like all really national changes, it was due to many causes; yet most of these derive from one source, the Roman conquests in Africa and in the East. We shall consider this change only in so far as it affects our study of the education of the Romans. That education now begins to split more sharply than ever before between the education of the very small minority of the rich and the education of the huge majority of the poor. For with the Roman conquests came appalling poverty, and almost equally appalling wealth. The three great wars between 264 B. C. and 146 B. C., which ended in the destruction of Carthage, gave Sicily, northern Africa, and Spain to Rome as provinces. Sicily and Africa, especially, became the granaries of Italy; they produced grain so abundantly and cheaply that the small farmers of Italy could not compete with them, and Italian farms began to lie idle. The richer men bought up these lands for little or nothing; the peasant ex-proprietors flocked into the cities, to waste in idleness. This meant two results: the creation of great, uncultivated estates (somewhat like the English parks), concerning which Pliny the Elder said, "Great domains are the ruin of Italy," and the creation of a proletariat. Both made for luxury and waste.

The rich import Greek culture. Consider first the rich. Their wealth had been increased enormously by the wars of conquest. At the same time they had been thrown into contact with the more elaborate civilization of other lands, and in particular had been much impressed by Greek culture; and, it must be remembered, by that culture when it had passed its best stage. During the lifetime of Cato (234-148 B. C.) Greek influence began to be very notable. Livius Andronicus, a freed slave, had already translated the *Odyssey* into Latin, about 250 B. C. Ennius, who died in 169 B. C., carried on the work begun by Andronicus. Rich men were too busily engaged in enjoying their wealth to have time for the education of their children. It became, at first a luxurious fad, later a prevailing fashion, to have a Greek slave as tutor for the children of the rich. The schools began to multiply, though they were still looked upon with suspicion, partly because of the unsavory repute of the Greeks, partly because the schools charged fees, a procedure contrary to Roman custom even in the law courts. There was a little nervous reaction; a decree of the Senate, in 161 B. C., even banishing 'philosophers and rhetoricians.' There was still more opposition to the introduction of Greek athletics, Greek music, and Greek dancing, which were all offensive to the modesty and dignity entrenched in the Roman tradition. With regard to the Greek custom of exercising naked in public, Ennius said: "Flagiti principium est nudare inter cives corpora." And indeed it was not until some 250 years later that Nero instituted the first imitation of the Greek athletic festivals at Rome. Dancing was even more despised by the Romans. It was a gross insult to call a man a 'saltator.' Even when the practice grew as a means of amusement, the Romans for the most part merely looked on, whilst hired Greeks did the dancing. Cicero says, "One would scarcely dance, unless drunk or crazy."[1] And in an often-quoted phrase Sallust said of Sempronia that "she played and danced more cleverly than a virtuous woman should."[2] But despite all opposition, Hellenism, at the death of Cato in 148, was triumphant. Two years later, the Romans completed the conquest of Greece, and more Greek slaves[3] poured into Rome. Cicero, born 106 B. C., tells us that the old education had been overthrown before his time. The last public protest, the edict of the Censors in 112 B. C., was a mere ineffectual gesture.

But Greek culture modified by Roman temper. Recall that all this affects only the wealthy and ruling class. Whilst still retaining a varying measure of the old basic Roman education, they began to build upon it a sort of Greek superstructure. The new education took in the Greek language and literature, Greek philosophy, Greek poetry and drama. But all these it passed through the alembic of the distinctive Roman character. It was frankly imitative, true enough, and made no attempt at concealing the fact; but it was selective in its imitation. It succeeded in modifying the Latin language considerably, and it produced a literature. But the literature was, for the most part, de-

---

[1] "Nemo enim fere saltat sobrius, nisi forte insanit." *Pro L. Murena,* 6:13 (Delphini ed., 12 vols., London, 1830, Vol. 4, p. 1395).

[2] "Psallere saltare elegantius quam necesse est probae." *Bellum Catilinarium,* chap. 25 (Delphini ed., 2 vols., London, 1820, Vol. 1, p. 74.)

[3] We must remember that many of these had been cultured free men.

cidedly snobbish; it circulated exclusively amongst the upper class; it was quite simply unknown to the mass of the people. This is a fact frequently overlooked by students of the 'Golden Age' of Latin literature.

Even of the small minority who went in for the new education, only a few seriously studied the Greek philosophies or the Greek drama. Most of them were attracted by the study of rhetoric, and the net aim of the Graeco-Roman education was the making of an orator. This was in keeping with the practical spirit of the Romans and with the character of their public life. The Romans had, even now, little or no interest in literature as such. They looked upon the new accomplishments almost solely as means to attaining social prestige or political power. If they eagerly mastered the Greek language, and sedulously studied Greek poets and philosophers, it was merely to equip themselves for the essentially Roman work of ruling. Cicero states that aim explicitly.[1] Even in the Augustan age, Horace complains that education is not tending to produce poets. The new education was professional rather than cultural. In detail it consisted largely in the analysis of Greek authors, with a view to understanding their logical and rhetorical processes, and in frequent efforts to imitate these in the students' own compositions. The method is obvious, and is in familiar use in our own day. It was narrowly intellectual, as professional study generally is. Its effect upon character was quite negligible.

The Roman proletariat. The great economic and social change in Roman life affected the poor just as powerfully, though of course in a different way. When the cheap grain of Sicily and Africa ruined Italian farming, the peasants sold their lands for a trifle to the rich and turned themselves to the cities. They were not lured to the cities by

---

[1] *De Republica,* 1:20, Mai's edition, in F. A. Nobbe (ed.), *Ciceronis Opera Omnia,* Leipzig, 1850, p. 1177.

manufactories, as was the case in England a few generations ago; they were driven by idleness. Naturally they
created a great economic problem. It was met by doles
from the State. Beginning in 123 B. C. grain was sold at
Rome to the citizens at half price, the Government shoulder-
ing the loss. Within the lifetime of a man, grain was being
distributed free; and in 58 B. C. this distribution was legalized by the Lex Clodia, and even a distribution of oil added.
Twelve years later, Julius Caesar found that at Rome alone
there were 320,000 citizens enrolled for these distributions.
Of course the same practice had spread widely through
other cities of Italy. Living quarters in the cities became
terribly crowded, the poor congested in great tenement
houses, called *insulae*. The idle mobs clamored for amusement, and got it in abundance. The chariot races in the
Circus Maximus, gladiatorial shows, a gross theatre pander-
ing to the vulgar taste, all were tossed out increasingly to
an urban proletariat which was rapidly losing all save the
name that had marked the old Roman people. *"Panem et
circenses!"* seemed to be the dominant thought of the mob.
The shows became more brutal and more frequent. From
the time of Julius Caesar as many as 320 pairs of gladiators
fought at a time. Nero enlarged the Circus Maximus at
Rome to accommodate 250,000 spectators. Vespasian built
the Colosseum to seat 87,000. The shows often lasted a
week or more, and they generally occupied the greater part
of each day when they occurred.

And its bad education. It is not in the purpose of this
book to consider the effect of these events upon the general
history of Rome. It is sufficient to note here that the chief
means of Roman education, the family life, was weakened
and in great measure destroyed. There is little family life
left to a people who live in huge tenement warrens, and
who spend their days abroad in vagabond idleness or in
gross and cruel amusements. Ideals of every sort soon die

out in such lives; the people may become more sophisticated, but they become less civilized. They have less and less of physical, mental, or moral equipment to pass on to their children; and they have increasingly less interest either in having any children at all or in preparing them with care for the business of living. During the later years of the Republic and the early centuries of the Empire, the life of poor people in Italy became more and more urban, idle, and debased; and education amongst them more and more disappeared. In the provinces, especially of the West, affairs were not in such bad case. The changes taking place in Italy were reflected in the provinces, it is true, but on a much smaller scale. There too one might find a certain Hellenizing of the rich, and a certain degrading paternalizing of the poor; but not to such an extent as in Italy; and there remained in both rich and poor a larger share of the ancient virility of the Roman spirit.

Concluding estimate. It is not easy to offer any summary conclusion as to the value of Roman education. In the field of mental and emotional activities which might lead to the development of a great philosophy or a keen perception of beauty, its limitations are evident; but equally evident is its intelligent balance in training the young Roman for a life of virtue and of practical usefulness. The measure of its success in forming a people sturdy in body and in soul may be gathered from the vigor with which Roman life withstood the influences that attacked it and lead to decay. The amazing thing is not that Rome died, but that she was so long in dying. The cycle of growth and decay is seen in everything human, and is painfully obvious in every national history. Greek civilization withered away like a cut rose; the Roman died like an old oak. It was impermanent, because it was merely human; but it was built upon the solidest things in humanity, the great natural virtues of fortitude, temperance, prudence, and justice.

TOPICS FOR DISCUSSION

1. Roman borrowings, in educational ideals, from the Etruscans.

2. Early educational contacts between the Romans and the Greeks.

3. Roman isolation from the educational influence of the colonies of Graecia Magna.

4. The influence of Eastern religious cults upon Roman education.

5. The development of Roman education in the provinces, particularly in Gaul and Spain.

6. Rome as a school of law; of architecture; of civic administration.

BIBLIOGRAPHIC NOTE

A convenient collection of Roman source material is to be found in the Oxford Library of Translations, begun in 1902, and in the Loeb Classical Library, Putnam's, New York, which gives the original texts and an English translation on opposite pages. In the latter series, see particularly the *Histories* of Polybius, Livy, Suetonius (*Vitae Caesarum*), Tacitus (*Annales*), for the general background; for more particular bearings on education, see the essays of Cicero, the *Dialogus* of Tacitus, the *Institutiones Oratoriae* of Quintilian, the Letters of Pliny the Younger, and the *Attic Nights* of Aulus Gellius. As a more compendious introduction to the sources, consult G. W. and L. S. Botsford, *Source-Book of Ancient History*, New York, 1912, with its good bibliography.

On Roman religions and their influence on education, a work rich in detail is J. F. Toutain, *Les Cults Paiens dans l'Empire Romain*, of which Vols. 1-3 deal with the Latin part of the Empire, Paris, 1907-20. For the local religious influences, there are two sound studies of the American Academy in Rome: R. M. Peterson, *Cults of Campania*, Rome, 1919; and L. R. Taylor, *Local Cults in Etruria*, Rome, 1925. For the Eastern cults, see F. Cumont, *Les Religions Orientales dans le Paganisme Romain*, Paris, 1909. A good study of the sources for the Etruscan period is in L. Homo, *Primitive Italy and the Beginnings of Roman Imperialism*, New York, 1926.

For the important period, 31 B. C. to 180 A. D., there is a wealth of information on Roman culture in general in L. Friedlander, *Darstellungen aus der Sittengeschichte Roms in der Zeit von August bis zum Ausgang der Antoninen*, 10th ed. rev., 4 vols., Leipzig, 1921-23; translated from the 7th ed. by Magnus, Freese, and Gough, as *Roman Life and Manners under the Early Empire*, 4 vols., London, 1908-13. Not so detailed, but wider in its range, is H. O. Taylor, *Ancient Ideals, a Study of Intellectual and Spiritual Growth from Early Times to the Establishment of Christianity*, 2d ed. rev., 2 vols., New York, 1913; this work includes Greece also. As further introduction to Roman life and culture, the following may be suggested: F. F. Abbott, *The*

Common People of Ancient Rome, Studies of Roman Life and Litera-ture, New York, 1911; J. E. Sandys, *Companion to Latin Studies,* 3d ed. rev., Cambridge, 1921; H. W. Johnston, *Private Life of the Ro-mans,* rev. ed. by Mary Johnston, Chicago, 1932; A. J. Church, *Roman Life in the Days of Cicero,* New York, 1883. On the history of slav-ery, besides the works referred to in the text, see W. Blair, *Inquiry into the State of Slavery among the Romans, from the earliest Period to the Establishment of the Lombards in Italy,* London, 1833; and J. K. Ingram, *History of Slavery,* New York, 1895. Valuable for social and cultural history is S. Dill, *Roman Society from Nero to Marcus Aurelius,* London, 1920, and *Roman Society in the Last Cen-tury of the Western Empire,* rev. ed., London, 1906. The latter deals largely with the provinces of the West.

The only extant early work on Roman architecture, written about 15 B.C. is Vitruvius Pollio, *De Architectura Libri X,* of which there is an English translation by M. H. Morgan, Cambridge, Mass., 1914. Of modern books, A. L. Frothingham, *Roman Cities of North Italy and Dalmatia,* New York, 1910, discusses the spread of Roman architec-ture; W. J. Anderson and R. P. Spiers, *Architecture of Greece and Rome,* 2d ed. rev., London, 1907, traces the development of Roman architecture (good bibliography); and H. B. Walters, *Art of the Ro-mans,* London, 1911, includes architecture in a wider survey. For Roman law, see R. Sohm, *Institutionen: Geschichte und System des romischen Privatsrechts,* 17th ed. rev., Munich, 1923 (English trans-lation, *The Institutes,* etc., 3d ed., Oxford, 1907); and E. Cuq, *Manuel des Institutions Juridiques des Romains,* Paris, 1917. On civic organ-ization, a work filled with interesting suggestions is N. D. Fustel de Coulanges, *La Cité Antique,* Paris, 1864, 19th ed., Paris, 1905, trans-lated as *The Ancient City, a Study on the Religion, Laws, and Insti-tutions of Greece and Rome,* 10th ed., Boston, 1901.

For education in the narrower sense of school education, the fol-lowing readings may be suggested: S. S. Laurie, *Historical Survey of Pre-Christian Education,* New York, 1924; A. Gwynn, *Roman Edu-cation from Cicero to Quintilian,* Oxford, 1926; G. H. Hulsebos, *De Educatione et Institutione apud Romanos,* Utrecht, 1875; G. Clarke, *Education of Children at Rome,* New York, 1896; A. S. Wilkins, *Ro-man Education,* Cambridge, 1905; W. Hobhouse, *The Theory and Practice of Ancient Education,* New York, 1910; E. Jullien, *Les Pro-fesseurs de Littérature dans l'Ancienne Rome,* Paris, 1886; P. R. Cole, *Later Roman Education,* New York, 1909.

CHAPTER VI

A New Ideal and New Forces in Education

I. The New Ideal

Christianity changes Western education. With the Incarnation of Jesus Christ, an enormous change began in the history of the world and this change very particularly affects the history of education. Christians and non-Christians will naturally estimate this change in different ways; but it is as patent and undeniable to the non-Christian as to the Christian. Christ came as "a sign to be contradicted," but whether accepted or rejected, He remains, obviously and historically, the greatest single influence upon our Western civilization. By far the larger part of humanity and of its various civilizations have, of course, not even known Him up to the present; a strange fact, for which we possess no adequate explanation. It is chiefly because of that fact that this book on the history of education confines itself almost exclusively to the story of the Western world; the education of the East, for all its engrossing interest, is out of the picture for the present.

By a new ideal and new educational forces. The effect upon education of the coming of Christ and the institution of Christianity is the introduction of a new ideal in education and of new forces for the shaping of humanity. We must understand this ideal and these forces, if we are to understand all education since their entry into the world. The new ideal is to equip all men for living in such a way as to assure them, not merely peace and growth and harmonious use of body and soul in this life (which was, in varying measures, the ideal of the Greeks and the Romans), but also an absolutely complete and perfect happiness, quite mysterious and inconceivable to us and entirely above our natural claims or capacity, which men are to enjoy forever in a life after this present life. This new ideal does not contradict or destroy such old and merely human ideals as the noble one of the Greeks; it includes them, but adds to them an element which dwarfs them in importance, both by its intrinsic superiority and by its eternity. Part of the resentment of the 'natural man' against Christianity has always been due to the fact that the Christian ideal thus surpasses and supersedes any merely human ideal. It is the petulant resentment of a child who prefers his shabby old toys to fine new ones; and it deserves, not scorn, but pity and patient understanding—with which, we may be sure, God meets it.

The new forces in education are manifold. First, and above all, comes a mysterious free gift of God, a supernatural quality or habit infused into the human soul, incapable of being acquired, which fundamentally changes the capabilities of that soul and confers upon it a real claim to that mysterious eternal happiness which God has made possible to men through Jesus Christ. It is more than merely educative, it is true, since it quite simply remakes the human soul and through that change will, after death, remake the human body. It is as much a mystery to us as perfect happiness itself is; but it is a fact. Catholics call it by the technical name of 'sanctifying grace.' Then there are other aids, or 'graces,' not permanent, as sanctifying grace is of its nature, but transient, or as they are called, 'actual.' These are both ideas and impulses, knowledge and moral motivations, exerted upon the mind and the will. They are given to men by God, not merely in and through the performance of certain rites instituted by Christ and called 'sacraments,' but through the apparently fortuitous incidents of human life, through contacts with others in speech or reading and the like, so that all life has become a sort of gigantic sacrament. Some of these ideas are contained in a direct revelation made to men by God, and transmitted either by certain inspired writings or in a divinely guarded tradition. In and through all these is the force of the concrete example of the life of Christ Himself, who, being God, became man and voluntarily endured the discomforts and difficulties of a very ordinary human life, in poverty, in toil, in obscurity, in pain, in human compensations of companionship and love, in acclamations and humiliations, in power and in weakness, in temptations, in loneliness, and in death.

Offered without distinction of sex, race, or rank. This new educational ideal and these new forces or agencies in education are offered to all human beings, without distinction of sex, race, age, rank, social or economic or political condition. They constitute a real and amazing equality. There is a mystery, impenetrable to us, in the manner in which this offer is made, and in the way in which its extension to individuals and races is brought about, so that some seem immeasurably more favored by God's providence than others. On a large scale, the contrast between the East and the West as regards Christianity is absolutely puzzling. It may be that that contrast is only temporary, and that time will solve the puzzle. It certainly is true that God is not limited in His providence by the institution of Christianity, and that He can aid in other ways those apparently beyond its range as an instrument of education. But, outside of that mysterious dispensation, there is no inherent distinction in the Christian ideal itself. It breaks down all barriers, it recognizes women on the same footing as men, slaves as well as free men, poor as rich.[1] It does not destroy these distinctions, it ignores them and transcends them.

[1] Gal. 3:26-28.

For free acceptance by the individual. Further, these
new elements in education are offered to all without compulsion.   The only Being who has absolute power to compel human beings is also the only Being who completely
respects their liberty.   Neither Christ nor the system He
originated *makes* men good or happy: they only offer men
the means to make themselves good and happy.[1] The education of each individual still remains primarily his own
concern.   Christianity holds out new helps, and points to
finer achievements; but it depends upon the individual to
make use of the helps and the guidance.   To forget or
ignore that fact is to confuse all Christian history.   Men
discuss the attitude of the Church toward education, when
they really mean the attitude of churchmen.   Men blame
Christianity for not stopping wars, when they should blame
Christians for not practicing Christianity and thereby ending wars.   And so of many other charges.   The Church is
the aggregate of all Christians as constituting the mystical
body of Christ: not each singly, in his opinions upon education or anything else, not even in the intelligence and
energy with which he tries to carry out Christ's purpose in
his life. The contribution of Christianity to education consists of the new version of truth, the new supernatural
aim, the new supernatural helps, given to mankind by Jesus
Christ.   The contributions of Christians to education are
varied, some good and some bad, and consist, quite simply,
of their more or less intelligent and purposeful efforts to
apply the Christian ideal to their lives.

Who must combine them with current needs of life.
Christianity did not simplify life; it complicated it.   It did
not replace old ideals; it built upon them.   It simplified the

---

[1] Cf. New Testament, Matt. 7:6; Mark 6:11. Even when Jesus
deals directly with His disciples, it is always by invitation, "Follow
Me."   Matt. 8:22; 16:24; 19:21; Mark 2:4; 10:21; Luke 5:27; John
12:26; 21:22.

values of life, it is true, by setting all the things of time against a background of eternity; but it left men still in need of the things of time, in order to carry on the affairs of this immediate, present life. It set new standards for all the uses of life; but it did not exempt the individual from the task of acquiring skill in those uses. It taught men, for instance, temperance; but it did not teach them how to improve the quality of their wine. It taught them chastity, but not eugenics; charity and justice, but not political economy; mercy and humility, but not medical science and social organization. It did not even teach men theology; it only gave them revelation. Christians, like pagans, must still have proper food and exercise to develop their bodies, must acquire and manage the means of physical and mental life, must train their powers of mind and emotion by study and play, must build up slow, laborious habits of virtue, must have sexual mating and the begetting of children and the organization of family life, must combine into social units for mutual help, must found institutions for passing all these things on to succeeding generations. The Christian ideal and the Christian helps will guide and assist them in every detail; but with a guidance external to the work, and concerned more with its ultimate purpose than with its immediate success; and with an assistance which is not direct, but indirect, affecting material achievement only through the medium of qualities of character. The education of a Christian is more comprehensive than that of a pagan. He must strive to develop himself physically, mentally, and morally; and, in addition, regulate all his efforts by an aim beyond that of the present life. He must master this world, though his home is beyond the world. He must combine toil for the present with purpose for the future; and under a conviction that the unseen and uncomprehended future is immeasurably more important than the visible and attractive present. His task is an endless balancing between two worlds; extremely difficult in any event, and simply impossible without the supernatural aids which are given him by the same Christ who sets this high ideal. He must use this world, because of the sheer necessity of living, yet as St. Paul says, "use it as if he used it not."[1] He must be in the world, yet not of it.[2] This thought runs throughout the teaching of Christ.

According to his own skill and energy. Obviously, that difficult combination is not achieved with equal success by all, nor with complete success by any. Christ Himself and His miraculously favored Mother were the only perfect Christians; all the rest fall short of perfection in differing degrees. There are other mysteries of providence in those differences, allotments of supernatural enlightenment and vigor into which we cannot examine. But from the human side, the differences will be differences in the intelligence and industry which each individual brings to the understanding, acceptance, and application of the Christian ideal. Laziness and stupidity are the foes of education in any system, under any ideal; they are the foes of Christian education: and every human being is more or less lazy and more or less stupid; neither pagans nor Christians, neither the orthodox nor the heretical, have any monopoly in these qualities. In fact, one might reasonably expect that, because of the high demands of the Christian educational ideal, the discrepancies between that ideal and Christian practice would be greater than the discrepancies between pagan ideals and practices, and that a Christian saint would be even a rarer phenomenon than a Greek Socrates or Aristotle. Yet the world in general is, and rightly, more critical of Christian achievement than of Greek achieve-

---

[1] 1 Cor. 7:31. Cf. also: Matt. 6:25-34; Heb. 13:14; 1 Tim. 6:7-11; 2 Cor. 6:8-10.

[2] "I pray not that thou shouldst take them out of the world, but that thou shouldst keep them from evil." John 17:15.

ment. We must only insist that the blame for any failure in that achievement be put where it belongs.

The Church in Christian education. The Christian Church has always claimed the superhuman prerogative of infallibility: a claim which is as irritating to the "natural man" as the superhuman Christian ideal itself. But it has also always been quite clear as to the limits of that infallibility. The infallibility of the Church, whether exercised in the unanimous functioning of the whole Christian body or by the authoritative leaders of the body, is limited to safeguarding what is called 'the deposit of faith,' the revealed beliefs and practices coming from Christ and His apostles. It does not extend to the 'disciplinary' regulations of the Church: which are mainly efforts, more or less wise, and often temporary in character, to co-ordinate the essential Christian ideal and Christian means of life with the purely human practices in education, in economics, in social and political organization, which Christians, like all other peoples, either inherit from the past or invent for their present needs. The Church claims and exercises authority over Christians by such disciplinary regulations; but it admits that the value of these regulations must depend upon the intelligence, prudence, and unselfishness with which they meet the situations they are meant to control. Churchmen exercising authority, because they are human and because they are in authority, may resent criticism of their efforts: but they are open to such criticism, precisely as are the men who exercise civil authority. Catholics, as well as non-Catholics, have often been guilty of great disservice to historical truth by a narrow and unintelligent claim for perfection in every effort of Churchmen toward solving the endless problems of adjustment which confront Christianity: as if the Church of Christ stood or fell by the mere skill and wisdom of its human leaders. As regards education in particular, the history of Christian education is the record of *how* individual Christians, acting either singly or in authoritative groups, have tried to combine the Christian ideal and Christian helps with the inevitable demands of human life as such. Like all other efforts at education, it is only a partial success. But it should be studied honestly as what it is, without prejudice for or against it, and without the absurd confusion between the Christian Church and Christian individuals which has distorted so much of history.

II. Early Strivings After the Ideal

The first Christian school. Jesus Christ conducted the first Christian school. It lasted for about three years. Its pupils were, for the most part, mature men and women: all Jews, as was the Master of the school: most of them from what we call the lower classes. They were divided into three sections: the large crowds, sometimes numbering several thousand, whom Jesus taught from time to time, in His wanderings through Palestine; a smaller group of a few hundred, whom He instructed more frequently; and a select dozen who were constantly in His company. Women were admitted, some of them on terms of intimacy with Jesus, but no woman was amongst the chosen twelve. His instruction was entirely oral, like that of Socrates, homely and familiar in style, much of it given in the form of short fictional narratives, or parables, so popular amongst His people. The school might be called peripatetic, since Jesus and His companions moved almost constantly from place to place. Its character was, of course, religious and moral. It aimed at introducing, bit by bit, in simple language, the knowledge of the high ideal and the superhuman aids which Christ brought to men. It both won adherents and made enemies, as might be expected. The teaching of Jesus stirred some to great enthusiasm, especially when He confirmed it by striking prodigies, healing the sick, feeding thousands with a few loaves, raising the dead to life; it stirred others to violent hatred, which was not content with less than His death. What it met with least was understanding. It did not succeed in ridding even the chosen twelve of laziness, vanity, selfishness, and stupidity. The closing exercises of the school were held on the night of Thursday, sixth of April, 29 A. D.,[1] in Jerusalem; when one of the Twelve sold Jesus to His enemies, another publicly denied Him, and, of the remaining ten, nine ran away. Jesus was crucified and died the next day. One man, a half dozen of the women, with His Mother, stood beside the cross.

The school of the apostles. On the third day after His death, Christ rose from the dead by His own power, the final proof of His divinity. For forty days He took up again the work of teaching His apostles. Then He left the earth. Ten days later, the Spirit of God filled the souls of the remaining apostles; and they, armed with amazing gifts, of command of many languages, of power to heal diseases, of knowledge of hidden thoughts, and the like, set out to carry on the teaching of Christ. Considerable numbers flocked to them; at first, quite naturally, of their own Jewish people, then of non-Jews; but the majority of the people were hostile to them. The new Christians formed themselves into close groups, rapidly developed throughout Asia Minor, Greece, Macedonia, Egypt, Italy, and even the far confines of the Empire in Spain and Gaul. For a time some of these groups were communist; all were small in numbers, isolated, fairly homogeneous in character; presided over by one of the apostles or by a man trained and authorized by the apostles.

---

[1] A disputed date. The custom of reckoning years from the birth of Christ was introduced only in 527, by Dionysius Exiguus, with an error in the reckoning of something between two and seven years. The correction ventured here is the most commonly accepted now.

They were, like the disciples of Christ's own school, most-ly adults, already trained and educated in some fashion. The new education was, therefore, almost exclusively con-cerned with Christianity itself. The method was still mostly oral teaching, though within a few years there were some small books for their use, summary accounts of the life and teachings of Jesus Christ, doctrinal and hortatory letters of the leaders of the Church; many of which were, in time, gathered into the collection known as the New Testament. Most of the members of these small, scattered schools were eager to learn and to practice, and made swift advance, in the measure of their intelligence, toward the carrying out of the Christian ideal. They worshiped God sincerely, they made diligent use of the sacraments and prayer, they prac-ticed a high and unselfish communism of wealth and a noble equality of brotherhood, they were chaste in the midst of an unchaste paganism, they were humble and unworldly in a proud world. But they were not all equally successful in their schools, as one may see from the letters of St. Paul and from the Acts of the Apostles. Human frailty was evident enough. Some of them defrauded in the communal ownership; some were ambitious and greedy of power and contentious; some sinned to fornication and even incest; some lapsed into idolatry.

The apostles, the masters of the schools, felt their way slowly in the difficult business of combining the Christian ideal with the immediate needs of life, and were willing to abandon schemes undertaken and to adapt themselves to changing conditions. Thus, for example, they gave up com-munism when mere growth in numbers made it imprac-ticable; they changed their policy with regard to admitting members, with regard to dietetic laws and the continuance of the Jewish practice of circumcision. They kept to the Christian ideal with absolute fidelity, but they realized that its application must vary with the inevitably varying circumstances of human life; and they had that prime quality of all great educational endeavor, infinite patience with the very imperfect material of human nature in which they had to work.

From the apostles to Constantine. The apostolic age closed with the death of John, about 100 A. D. During that time, and for two centuries after it, Christians were almost constantly subjected to persecutions of various sorts. They were a militant minority in an increasingly hostile world. Their continued growth in such circumstances is amazing, and humanly inexplicable; but they did grow enormously, and their members were found in every part of the Roman Empire and even in the farther East. Amongst a people so diversely situated, any uniform educational procedure was manifestly impossible. Each group, nay each individual, must make the practical application of Christianity to life according to his own best judgment dealing with the actual concrete condition. It was the most natural thing in the world that Christian education should differ in the East and in the West, in the cities and in the country, amongst poor slaves and amongst the cultured rich. It was inevitable that personal opinion, colored by the circumstances of individual temperament, talents, social position, and the like, should enter into those differences. It was inevitable that the fine balance of mind and character needed for the accurate adjustments of Christianity should not be universal possessions, and that ignorance and conceit and impetuosity should lead individuals into error in judging of those adjustments. There were extreme opinions, often uttered by men of talent and moral force, not infrequently leading to a wild distortion of the Christian ideal itself. Against that last, the Church was divinely armed; it promptly cast out such distortions as heresies. But though it could keep the plan of Christ from error, it could not make the individual Christian infallibly wise in his attempts to realize the plan. One of the astounding things in what is called history is to find the utterances of even heretical extremists, such as, say, Tertullian, quoted as the educational opinions of the Catholic Church.

The Christians were, during these first three centuries, a hunted people. To organize schools of their own was extremely difficult, and in many places quite impossible. They did set up religious classes for their adult new members, catechumenal schools, as they are called, in which these people were instructed in the teachings of Jesus Christ. There is plenty of evidence that infant baptism was in practice from the very early days of Christianity,[1] though the early growth of the Church was chiefly due to the conversion of adults. But during the centuries of persecution it became almost the universal custom to defer the baptism of even children of Christians to a mature age; in fact, the age of thirty came to be considered by many the most appropriate. Religious instruction was, therefore, continued for years previous to conferring baptism. In the latter half of the second century these catechumenal classes began to develop into something like theological schools, called catechetical, under the influence and leadership of men trained in the Greek schools. Pantaenus, who before his conversion to Christianity had been a Sophist of some note, became about 180 A. D., the first known teacher in the catechetical school of Alexandria, the most famous of its kind.[2] He was a Platonist, and seems to have introduced some attempt to express Christianity in terms of Platonic philosophy. He was succeeded, after six or seven years, by his pupil, Titus Flavius Clement, then about twenty-six years of age, and probably a native of Athens where he had received his preparatory training. Clement, driven out in the persecution of 202 A. D. under Septimius Severus, founded a like

[1] *E. g.,* Origen, in *Rom.,* v, 6; Cyprian, *Ep.* 59.
[2] Eusebius, *H. E.,* v. 10, 4.

school in Jerusalem. The famous Origen, a pupil of Ammonius Saccas the Neo-Platonist, was appointed successor to Clement by Bishop Demetrius in 203. He was only eighteen years old at the time. His learning was unquestionably very great; he enlarged the curriculum of the school to include some study of Greek grammar and rhetoric and some acquaintance, how much we cannot say, with Greek dialectic and philosophy in general. But he was not a man of great balance, as is instanced by the fact that in his dread of unchastity he went so far as to castrate himself. He was not ordained priest until twenty-five years after he had taken charge of the school at Alexandria. That same year, 228 A. D., he was excommunicated by Bishop Demetrius, and fled to Caesarea, where he opened a school like that at Alexandria, and where he had as pupils St. Gregory Thaumaturgus and his brother Athenodoros. There were other well-known catechetical schools, at Antioch, Edessa, Nisibis, Rhinocorura in Palestine, Carthage, and apparently even one at Rome, established as early as 160, under Justin the Martyr. But it must be remembered that these were schools of theology for the most part (though theology was still a science in its infancy), that they reached only a very small proportion of the Christians, and that in general any education outside of this theological training had to be sought for in the Greek or Graeco-Roman schools of the non-Christian world.

It must also be remembered that not merely the religious beliefs, but the moral principles and practices, of the pagan world were utterly opposed to Christian teachings, and that the decidedly decadent education of that Graeco-Roman world was intent upon practically nothing more than equipping youth for the enjoyment of this present life. There was war between the spirit of paganism and the spirit of Christianity; and the Christian educational ideal was not merely above the pagan ideal, but was even compelled to look upon many principles of the latter as actively hostile to itself. There was added to the innate and perpetual difficulty of combining worldliness and other-worldliness, an immediate and violent quarrel between Christian principles and the principles of the actual world in which Christians had to live. St. John Chrysostom, writing about 400 A. D. (long after the time we are considering; but this difficulty continued for centuries) puts the problem plainly:

The choice lies between two alternatives, a liberal education, which you may get by sending your children to the public schools, or the salvation of their souls, which you may secure by sending them to the monks. Which is to win, learning or salvation? If you can unite both, do so; but if not, choose the more precious.[1]

In these circumstances it is not astonishing nor unintelligible that the general leaning of Christians should be toward an excessive other-worldliness, that they should have shrunk from such secular education as they could get for their children, and that something of this fear should have persisted even after the days of persecution, when they were in position to have schools of their own, and should have left with them a vague mistrust of secular education in general. This is not to say that a certain measure of obscurantism to be found amongst the Christian body for centuries is justified. But it should win a tolerant understanding of their defective attitude, to see that the genesis of that obscurantism was not in mere ignorance or savagery, but in a very difficult and persistent conflict of interests and desires. Incidentally, it should go far to help us understand the origin of many of the heresies of the time, such as Montanism or chiliasm or even Manichaeism;

---

[1] Cf. John Evelyn's version of "The Golden Book of St. John Chrysostom, Concerning the Education of Children" (1659). Compare Quintilian's, "If it should appear that schools help studies, but harm character, I should prefer right living to even the greatest eloquence." Bk. I, c. 3.

all of which derived their attraction to Christians from the strong contrast between the Christian and the pagan ideals.

Conclusion. These early attempts at combining the diverse elements needed for a thorough Christian education were, obviously, very imperfectly successful. In the majority of instances they resulted in a comparative neglect of the arts and sciences which men had developed in the Greek and Roman civilizations. In some few cases they led to an opposite defect, an over-emphasis upon pagan culture to the distortion of the Christian ideal and the engendering of heresies. Only rarely, in the half dozen good catechetical schools of the East and of Carthage did they succeed, at least sporadically, under the guidance of exceptionally gifted men, in producing a small number of really learned Christians; and the numerical proportion of these to the entire body of Christians was almost infinitesimal. The task of educating both for this world and for the world to come was enormously difficult; and the circumstances of the debased civilizations of the time made it still harder. In spite of the manifest imperfections of Christians in carrying out that task, it is greatly to their credit that they made advance, even if slowly, in it, and above all, that they kept clear and undistorted the vision of their educational ideal, and bravely passed it on to succeeding generations, who might have better opportunities for realizing that ideal. It is very bad historical judgment to sneer at their efforts.

TOPICS FOR DISCUSSION

1. Details of the teaching of Jesus Christ.
2. The influence of Greek language and thought upon the early development of Christian theology.
3. The "disciplina arcani" as affecting the education of children in Christian families.
4. Educational effect of preponderant oral teaching amongst early Christians.
5. The growth and development of the catechetical schools; subjects studied in them; numbers of Christians educated in them.

6. The New Testament as an educational text in the second and third centuries.

BIBLIOGRAPHIC NOTE

For the teachings of Jesus Christ, the first and essential written source is the New Testament. Much of the important traditions concerning that teaching, not inscribed in the New Testament, may be found conveniently in the following group of translations: *Ante-Nicene Fathers,* translated and edited by A. Roberts and J. Donaldson, 24 vols., 1867-72; latest American edition, 10 vols., New York, 1911-19; *Select Library of the Nicene and Post-Nicene Fathers of the Christian Church,* translated and edited by P. Schaff, 14 vols., New York, 1886-90; Second Series, translated and edited by P. Schaff and H. Wace, 14 vols., New York, 1890-1900. Some of these early writings directly concern the process of education: such as *Stromata* of Clement of Alexandria in Vol. 2 of *Ante-Nicene Fathers;* others illustrate the general Christian aim and ideal in education. Two treatises embodying the Christian attitude toward education with interesting and significant fullness are: St. John Chrysostom, *Adversus Oppugnatores Vitae Monasticae Libri III,* in Migne, *Patres Graeci,* 47:319-86 especial Lib. III, addressed to Christian fathers, fol. 349-86; and St. Augustine, *De Doctrina Christiana,* in Migne, *Patres Latini,* 34:16-120 (English translation by J. F. Shaw in Vol. 9, pp. 1-171 of *Works of S. Augustine,* edited by M. Dods, Edinburgh, 1877), four books on preparation for the study of Scripture, the fourth book on rhetoric and style. A small selection of source material may be had in J. C. Ayer, Jr., *Source Book for Ancient Church History, from the Apostolic Age to the Close of the Conciliar Period,* New York, 1913.

Of the many excellent modern studies of the teachings of Jesus Christ, these two may be specially suggested: P. Battifol, *Enseignement de Jésus,* Paris, 1905; A. Goodier, *The Public Life of Our Lord Jesus Christ,* 2 vols., London and New York, 1931.

For the early conflict between the Christian and pagan ideals in education, the following may be consulted: A. de Broglie, *L'Église et l'Empire Romain au IV Siècle,* 6 vols., Paris, 1856-66; A. J. Thebaud, *The Church and the Gentile World at the First Promulgation of the Gospel,* 2 vols., New York, 1878; J. B. Lightfoot, *The Christian Ministry,* New York, 1878; T. J. Shahan, *The Beginnings of Christianity,* New York, 1903; P. Battifol, *Primitive Catholicism,* London, 1911; G. Boissier, *La Fin du Paganisme,* 2 vols., Paris, 1891; L. Duchesne, *Histoire Ancienne de l'Église,* 3 vols., Paris, 1906-10 (English translation, London, 1909-24); W. M. Ramsay, *The Church in the Roman Empire before A. D. 170,* 6th ed., London, 1900; A. von Harnack, *The Mission and Expansion of Christianity in the First Three Centuries,* 2d ed. rev., 2 vols., London, 1908; B. L. Kidd, *History of the Church to A. D. 461,* 3 vols., Oxford, 1922; J. J. I. Dollinger,

The History of the Church, 3 vols., London, 1840; F. X. Funk, *Manual of Church History,* 2 vols. (bibliography), London, 1914; M. C. D'Arcy (ed.), *The Life of the Church,* London, 1932.

Two books important for the understanding of the early Christian attitude toward life are: J. Lebreton, *La Vie Chrétienne au Premier Siècle de l'Église,* Paris, 1927; and M. Viller, *La Spiritualité des Premiers Siècles Chrétiens,* Paris, 1930. For the influence of Greek thought on Christian theology, see, in addition to works just mentioned, J. H. Newman, *An Essay on the Development of Christian Doctrine,* London, 1845. For the 'disciplina arcani,' see J. H. Newman, *The Arians of the Fourth Century,* London, 1833, Part 1; A. Weiss, *Die altkirchliche Paedagogik,* Freiburg im Br., 1869.

For the catechetical schools, see Brother Azarias (P. F. Mullany), *Essays Educational,* Chicago, 1896; E. Magevney, *Christian Education in the First Centuries,* New York, 1900; T. Drane, *Christian Schools and Scholars,* revised ed. by W. Gumbley, London, 1924, chap. 1; O. Willmann, *The Science of Education in its Sociological and Historical Aspects* (English translation of 5th ed. of *Didaktik*), 2d ed., 2 vols., Latrobe, Pa., 1930, Vol. 1, chap. 15-17. Of some value also for the early development of Christian education is P. de Labriolle, *History and Literature of Christianity from Tertullian to Boethius* (History of Civilization Series), New York, 1925. Touching more directly upon educational development are the two very good studies: H. J. Leblanc, *Essai Historique et Critique sur l'Étude et l'Enseignement des Lettres Profanes dans les Premiers Siècles de l'Église,* Paris, 1852; and G. Hodgson, *Primitive Christian Education,* Edinburgh, 1906.

CHAPTER VII

FROM CONSTANTINE TO CHARLEMAGNE

The general situation. From the supremacy of Constantine, in the first quarter of the fourth century, to the death of Charlemagne is about five hundred years. They were five centuries of enormous changes, political, social, economic, religious. During that time, the gigantic and really overgrown Roman Empire weakened internally, split into two empires, divided in the West into several independent kingdoms. More and more 'barbarians' came into the Roman confines, received various measures of the Roman civilization, built up political power for themselves, partly by violence, more largely, beyond doubt, by peaceful penetration, accepted Christianity in divers fashions; and mingled their own rude customs and ideas with all that they received. Civilization was in flux. This huge transition called, of course, for a new education; but the two supremely guiding influences in that new education were the established Graeco-Roman culture and Christianity. It was some fusion or combination between these two which was to reshape Europe.

Yet there was a certain hostility between Christianity and the Graeco-Roman culture. It was really that hostility, and not any mere political opposition, which had caused the persecutions. And when the sympathy and favor of Constantine brought an end to the persecutions, they brought, not peace, but only a sort of armed truce, between the old pagan culture and Christianity. The hostility has persisted to this day, and in all likelihood will persist to the end of the world. The reasons for this hostility have been touched upon in the preceding chapter. Nowhere is this hostility

89

shown more than in the field of education; and yet, as has been said, it is to some combination of these two hostile influences that the Western world has had to look for its policy and practice in education. The story of that fluctuating and uncertain combination is in reality the theme of the rest of this book.

The relations between the Church and the society of the Empire. It is a tangled story, complicated, of course, by many blunders on the part of all concerned; which is merely to say that it is human. When the Catholic Church was given its freedom in 313, it found that the schools were almost universally in the possession of the pagans: as were also the public offices and the positions of social leadership. The vast majority of the people, at any time and in any nation, are always poor in mental wealth as in material wealth; but the Christians of the fourth century were even poorer than their pagan neighbors; they had neither the money nor the developed intelligence to establish a great school system of their own. They did have schools of various sorts, as we have seen, for the teaching of religion. But their intellectual equipment in other matters had to be got from the existing public schools. All the 'Fathers of the Church' in those earlier times were educated in such schools.[1] And though Christians esteemed highly the knowledge and training furnished by the common schools, they were conscious of a hostile atmosphere in them, and feared both the secular schools and secular society in general. A certain spirit of aloofness, or at least of wariness, has always marked Christianity in its dealings with society. Its enemies scorn that spirit, its friends boast of it; though the

---

[1] Basil and Gregory Nazianzen studied at the University of Athens; John Chrysostom was taught by the pagan Sophist, Libanius. Jerome, after his schooling under the famous grammarian, Donatus, studied with Victorinus, still an eminent heathen philosopher. And so of the rest.

more sensible thing for both to do would be to accept it intelligently as an inevitable fact.

With their release from social and political disabilities, the Christians grew rapidly in numbers, more rapidly than in the years of persecution: but the growth was not so sturdy. Many men became Christians for less worthy motives than honest conviction, and apostatized from Christianity when to do so served some temporal purpose, and were conceited and restlessly ambitious and contentious within the Christian organization. The persecuted Christians had won a reluctant admiration from the pagans, but the free Christians often merited and got their contempt. The great Arian heresy had begun to divide Christians violently as early as 318; and in 366, only fifty-three years after the cessation of pagan persecution, the Christian adherents of the rival Popes, Damasus and Ursicinus, were murdering each other in internal political strife, on the pavements of Christian churches. The Roman emperors, who were baptized Christians, yet who still held the pagan office of Pontifex Maximus, issued edicts against paganism, forbidding the old sacrifice under pain of death. Julian, whom the Christians called 'the Apostate,' but who seems to have been entirely sincere in his devotion to the old culture and worship, turned the political scales against the Christians during his brief reign of twenty months, closing in 363. But, except for that momentary halt, the Christians gained an increasingly dominant position in the politics of the Empire; and the emperors thrust themselves ever more and more into religious affairs. The truce between the Church and the Roman State became an alliance, but an always dangerous and tottering alliance.

The Christians were mostly in the cities. Indeed, our name of 'pagan' comes simply from the Latin word for peasants or villagers. They were divided, with urban sharpness, into the many poor and the few rich. The Church made no distinction between rich and poor, but they, as always, made great distinction between themselves. The rich, who had leisure for culture, were on friendly terms generally with the cultured pagans. Mixed marriages were very common. St. Jerome's great friend, Paula, a most enthusiastic Christian, was married to the pagan Julius Toxotius.[1] Their son, Toxotius, married Laeta,[2] the devout Christian daughter of one of the great leaders of the pagan aristocracy, Publilius Caeonius Albinus,[3] who was a colleague in the pontifical college of that gallant defender of the old religion, the Senator Symmachus. Symmachus was intimate with St. Ambrose. St. Augustine writes in very friendly style to Longinianus, the pagan philosopher. There is no sharp social division between cultured pagans and cultured Christians.[4] Their religious interests apart, they shared the same training, the same tastes, and were linked together by the very strong bond of a culture much older than Christianity. But we must not extend this same solidarity to the great mass of the uncultured and rude Christians.[5]

The public schools. Although imperial and provincial laws regulated the schools in many ways, there was no state system of schools, such as we are familiar with in our times. The type of school was strikingly the same throughout the Roman Empire, it is true, but the uniformity grew out of social intercommunication, and was not imposed by authority. There was a uniform division into the *ludus,* or elementary school, the grammar school, and the rhetorical

[1] St. Jerome, Ep. 108, #4.
[2] To whom Jerome wrote a letter on the education of a Christian girl.
[3] St. Jerome, Ep. 107, #1.
[4] See the interesting study of Symmachus and Ausonius in Dill's *Roman Society in the Last Century of the Western Empire*, Bk. II. Boethius, who was executed in 525, and whose *De Consolatione Philosophiae* was one of the three great textbooks of the Middle Ages, leaves one in doubt whether he was a pagan or a Christian.
[5] Cf. Haarhoff's *Schools of Gaul,* pp. 124-32, for study of class distinctions in education.

school: corresponding, with loose approximation, to our modern divisions of elementary school, high school, and college. Of course, the schools differed in size, in equipment, in excellence, according to local conditions. This was particularly true of the higher schools, the character of which largely depended upon the personality of individual schoolmasters. The so-called University of Athens, for instance, (and this is true of most other higher schools of the period), was only a voluntary aggregation of professors and students, without any governing board, without examinations, without any fixed 'course of studies,' or any of the almost mechanical systematization of our modern schools, which carries along mediocre or even incompetent teachers by the momentum of the organization. A few good teachers made a great school; though obviously the character of the students had also much to do with the quality of the school. Thus, we find Augustine, who was a teacher of rhetoric before he became a Christian, leaving the school of Carthage for that of Rome because he believed that the Roman students were more docile and more studious than the Carthaginians.[1]

Elementary schools. Although the old Roman tradition of family education had not entirely died out, elementary schools became more and more numerous, and a larger proportion of children learned their three R's in them. Just what the proportion was, it is impossible to estimate. We may naturally expect it to vary in city and village, in the settled East and the migrating North and West. Density of population will affect it considerably. We may expect it to be much higher in Italy, with an old cultural tradition and a population of more than two hundred to the square mile, than in the still barbarian Germanies, with a popula-

---

[1] Also because the Roman schools paid better salaries. See *Confessions,* Bk. V, chap. 8 (in Loeb Classical Library, Text with English translation by W. Watts, 2 vols., London and New York, 1919, Vol. 1, pp. 232-35).

tion of only five or six to the square mile. Between these extremes comes populous Northern Africa, the malaria-ridden and dwindling peoples of Greece, the wealthy and socially ambitious men of southern Gaul, the developing peoples of Spain. There are indications that literacy was still a common possession even of the poor throughout the Graeco-Roman world up to the close of the fifth century. In the cities, where the Christians were steadily growing in numbers, the large majority of the teachers in elementary schools would be Christians; in the villages, they would be heathens.

Higher schools. In all the higher schools some sort of study of literature was the basic work; we may say it was the whole work of the grammar schools, and that it was carried into the rhetorical or philosophical schools to a greater or less extent. The higher schools of the East concerned themselves very much with philosophic and religious speculations. The schools of Italy, Northern Africa, and Gaul gave less thought to philosophy and more to rhetoric. The method in all was lecture and disputation; though the Western schools devoted much attention to written compositions, for the most part academic imitations of the poets and orators. In all there was a manifest decay of taste, a growing artificiality, an elaboration of rather empty theory, an increasing remoteness from the realities of life. They had practically no moral or religious influence upon the lives of their students. Their chief aim was to cultivate taste; and they failed in that aim more and more with each succeeding generation. In Gaul particularly, where there was a great enthusiasm for the higher schools during the fourth and fifth centuries,[1] rhetorical excesses and in-

---

[1] There were well-known higher schools at Lyons (founded by Caligula, about 40 A.D.), Autun, Vienne, Marseilles, Narbonne, Bordeaux, Arles, Toulouse, Poitiers, Besançon, Rheims (called 'The New Athens'), and Treves, which had a famous library. Ausonius (310-395) has left a group of poems on the Professors of Bordeaux.

sincerities grew like weeds; so that most of the writers of
the period are bombastic and magniloquent even to the
point of obscurity. Far from developing, the schools everywhere were degenerating. They had no new contributions
to offer to human thought, but only shallow and insincere combinations of old ideas, imperfectly grasped and
wretchedly expressed. The only real development in thought
throughout this period is in Christian theology. A few
great minds, trained in the public schools, it is true, but
surpassing the level of these schools, set themselves to
translate the teachings of Jesus Christ into the language
of Plato and Aristotle. St. Augustine, the Bishop of Hippo,
in Africa, stands pre-eminent in these beginnings of a science which was to be so fruitful of good and evil in the
centuries to come. St. Jerome, about the same time, made
use of the best linguistic studies available for the editing
and translating of the Bible; and his work was amazingly
good.

Women in education. It seems fairly certain that women
had as good opportunities for elementary education as men;
though it is likely that the training of girls was more confined to the home than the training of boys. But in general
women had no chance for any school education beyond the
most elementary. The occasional instance of a learned
woman merely stresses its unusualness. Hypatia of Alexandria is often cited as a type of learned women. She was
not a type, but almost a solitary exception. Her father,
Theon, was a teacher of mathematics in the Museum of
Alexandria; she was trained privately by him, and afterward went on to the study of philosophy which she taught
very successfully, until her tragic death at the hands of a
mob, in 416.[1] Similarly, the little group of learned women

---

[1] She seems to have been involved in a quarrel between Orestes,
the Prefect of Alexandria, and Cyril, the Bishop. Socrates (*Hist.
Eccl.*, 7:15; Migne, *P. G.*, 67:768) implies that it was the followers

around St. Jerome were exceptions, and were all taught in private.[1]　There is no indication up to the time of Charlemagne of higher schools for women, nor even of women sharing in the common schools with men.　The tradition seems to have lived on from the great days of Athens that it was abnormal for a woman to possess learning.　With all their admiration for the *hetairai,* the Ionian Greeks did not wish their wives and sisters to resemble them.　The Graeco-Roman world accepted and followed that opinion.

Christians in the higher schools.　Not merely did Christians study in the higher schools; they also taught in them. Scruples about that teaching cropped up, since it involved explaining the heathen gods and their often obscene worship.　But the Christian teachers somehow got around that difficulty.　In 362 an edict of the Emperor Julian forbade them to teach in the public schools.　St. Gregory Nazianzen and others wrote protests against the edict, and for the moment there appeared some likelihood of Christian rhetorical schools being set up.　But the very brief reign of Julian came to an end before anything could be done; and the Christian teachers returned to the public schools.　With the increasing favor of the succeeding emperors, and the constant numerical growth of the Christians, the grammar and rhetoric schools numbered more and more Christian teachers.　It is conceivable that in time the Graeco-Roman school system might have been Christianized, but in reality it was doomed, and the Christian schools, as we shall see, were to have another origin and history.

Decay of the public schools.　The decay of the schools was due to the same causes which brought about the decay

of Cyril who tore her from her litter and hacked her to death with shells and shards.　She was considered a pagan martyr.

[1] He had taught Eustochium, the daughter of Paula, and, after her mother, superior of the monastery at Bethlehem, to speak and write Hebrew.　He also praises lavishly Marcella, 'the glory of Roman ladies,' as a scriptural scholar.　(Ep. 127, Migne, *P. L.,* 22:1087.)

of the Graeco-Roman civilization in general. Those causes were many, and cannot be reduced to a simple formula; nor need we here try to venture upon the complicated explanation which has taxed, often futilely, the efforts of so many historians. This much may be said: that nations, like individuals, go through a cycle of growth, maturity, and senility; all history teaches that. Civilization, when it has grown complex, develops a curious fatigue, which lays it open to social diseases, just as fatigue lays a man open to organic disease; and it is restored, just as a man is, by the assimilation of new elements from without.[1]

Part of the efforts of government to check this process of decay was their interference in the schools. Back in the first century of the Empire, Vespasian began the practice of endowing rhetoricians in Rome. Antoninus Pius, about 160 A. D., extended the endowments to 'rhetoricians and philosophers in every province.' Hadrian and Alexander Severus continued the practice. Constantius Chlorus, about 305 A. D., ordered the municipality of Autun in Gaul to pay Eumenius, the master of the school of rhetoric, the almost incredible salary of 600,000 sesterces, equivalent to more than $30,000 today. His son, Constantine, in 321, exempted all teachers above the elementary schools from the burdens of municipal and military services. The Emperor Gratian, in 376, fixed a definite schedule of salaries for the prefecture of Gaul: twenty-four *annonae* to each master of a school of rhetoric, and twelve *annonae* to each master of a grammar school. An *annona* was the yearly pay of a common soldier or of a day laborer. Honorius and Theodosius, in

---

[1] Without venturing upon a discussion of the causes of the Roman decline, we may at least call attention to the often ignored fact that several frightful epidemics of plague had much to do with the break-up of Graeco-Roman civilization. Particularly virulent seem to have been the epidemics which, from the outbreak in Constantinople in 543, swept over Europe in almost continuous succession for fifty years. "Pestilentias sine cessatione patimur." (St. Gregory the Great, *Hom. I in Evangelia.*)

414, extended the privileges of schoolmasters to their families, and exempted their sons from military service. But all such encouragement of schools did not suffice to keep them alive and vigorous in the midst of the general social decline.

A persistent myth represents Christianity as opposed to education, and directly or indirectly responsible for the decay of the public schools. Of course, there is simply no evidence whatever for this. Christians, in general, were not entirely satisfied with the public schools; yet they attended them and taught in them: sufficient proof that at least they were not trying to destroy them. The one fact which is alleged as an indication of Christian hostility to the schools is the edict of Justinian I, in 529, by which he closed the pagan schools of Athens. Even granting that the edict was due to sectarian bigotry (which is debatable), how could the closing of two or three private schools have caused the general decay of all schools? Moreover, it is patent that the process of decay had begun long before Justinian's reign. Justinian may have been unwise in his edict, for with all his good will and ambitious enthusiasms he was not a very clear-headed man,[1] but why make his particular act the sign and symbol of a wholesale obscurantism on the part of Christians?

The cathedral schools. In the confusion and turmoil of every sort which ushered in what are called the 'Dark Ages,' the Catholic Church kept to her business of offering men Christ's means to attain supernatural happiness. She was, of course, only very imperfectly successful in getting men to accept and use these means: as she always was, and always will be. Part of that work of hers is essentially educational, carried on in the home, in the churches, as well

---

[1] His famous code is a very muddled performance. He himself toward the end of his life, became a heretic, adopting Aphthartodocetism: the doctrine that Christ had not a material body.

as in schools. Schools are, unquestionably, the least important of Christian educational instruments; still they are important; nor did the Church neglect them.

Her first care was for schools for her clergy. There was such a school at Rome from at least 190 A. D., when Victor, the Archdeacon, was put in charge of it by Pope St. Eleutherius.[1] Under Callistus I, about 220, it would appear to have grown into a large school. A decretal of Pope St. Siricius, in 385, addressed to Himerius, the Bishop of Tarragona, prescribes rules for the promotion of clerics to holy orders, and implies the existence of episcopal seminaries. St. John Chrysostom, St. Cyril of Alexandria, St. Athanasius, studied in the houses of bishops. After the conversion of Constantine, the Roman episcopal school was established in the Lateran palace. It had a great library, and the names of its librarians are recorded continuously from the fifth century. The evidence for the continued functioning of this school is abundant.

Eusebius, Bishop of Vercelli, in 354 established in his cathedral city a clerical school, which may be considered the first institution of regular clerks. In 394, St. Augustine organized at Hippo a similar group of students, which is looked upon as the model of all houses of canons regular. Many of the later cathedral schools were based upon such an organization, and in most of them the Roman practice was adopted, of placing the school under the care of the archdeacon. By the year 531, as is shown by canons of the second Council of Toledo, the bishop's seminary is taken for granted as a regular appendage to the cathedral.

St. Leander, Bishop of Seville, was one of the first who established a school of grammar and rhetoric as part of the cathedral school. His brother and successor in the see, St. Isidore, who had studied in that school, wrote for it his

[1] Cf. Bollandists, Acta Sti Feliciani, *A. S.,* Venice, 1734, Jan., Vol. 2, foll. 582, 583.

Origines, an encyclopedic textbook famous throughout the Middle Ages, and a valuable storehouse of ancient authors. It was the influence of St. Isidore which brought the fourth Council of Toledo, in 633, to command the founding of a school like that of Seville in every Spanish diocese. The apostle of England, St. Augustine, founded King's School in 598 as part of Christ Church Cathedral at Canterbury. It was a grammar school, and was endowed by King Ethelbert, and taught by Augustine himself and some of his clerks. A grammar school and a song school "are found side by side in connexion with all the great churches, that is in all the great centres of population, from the age of Augustine and Ethelbert to the age of Cranmer and Edward VI."[1]   St. Lubin, who was consecrated Bishop of Chartres in 544, had as pupil, and afterward as master of his school, Caletric, who succeeded him in the see. Bethaire came from Italy to study under Bishop Pappol at Chartres, and in 573 became head of the school there; he was made bishop in 594.   Pope Gregory the Great, in a letter written in 595, scolded Bishop Desiderius of Vienne because he took upon himself the office of teaching classic literature.[2]   In-

---

[1] A. F. Leach, *The Schools of Medieval England,* p. 6.   Theodore, a Greek monk, and Hadrian, together with the Northumbrian, Benedict Biscop, who founded the monastery of Jarrow, carry the schools to Aldhelm (born about 650) and Bede the Venerable (673-735).   Both Aldhelm and Bede owe much of their learning to Irish monks.   Much of Bede's work is a compilation, largely based upon Isidore of Seville; though it must be said his work is an improvement on that of Isidore. He was born thirty-seven years after the death of Isidore.   His voluminous works, all in Latin, are in Migne, *P. L.,* Vols. 90-95.   The best known is his *Historia Ecclesiastica.*   But within sixty years after his death the Danish invasions (in which his own monastery of Jarrow, together with many others, was destroyed) halted the work of the schools in England.

[2] A fact often ignorantly or maliciously distorted into an absolute condemnation of such teaching.   The letter is Ep. 54 in Bk. XI (Migne, *P. L.,* 77:1171-72).   Gregory had the common aversion to the pagan elements in classical writings, and considered it unbecoming that a bishop should teach them.   But he knew and appreciated the value of a training in classical literature, as may be seen in Bk. V, c. 3, n. 30 of *Comment. in Regum* (Migne, *P. L.,* 79:355-56).

stances might be multiplied, going to show that from the sixth century onward every cathedral had its organized school, and that these schools gave some sort of liberal education as a preparation for the special training in theology and scripture study.

The extent of their influence. It would, however, be an error to conclude from the existence of the widespread cathedral schools that school education was flourishing during the seventh and eighth centuries. The social conditions which worked against education at the time affected these schools also. Although the students were not limited to clerics, we may be sure that they were mostly clerics, and that the people at large were not in position to make much use of the schools. All indications point to their being small schools in general, perhaps averaging between a dozen and a score of students; and even the larger schools, during those centuries, would not reckon more than a hundred. But they were the little leaven in the mass, and they were destined, not to further decay, like the Graeco-Roman schools, but to a sturdy growth. The great mediaeval universities were to stem from them.

Parish schools. Elementary schools suffered too in the transition period, and in many parts of western Europe disappeared altogether. As it was the Catholic Church which chiefly civilized the new nations forming in the lands of the old Empire, it was that Church too which had to revive the schools. In the cities, the schools had made, of course, a better survival than in the villages. Indeed, the countryside was much neglected even in a strictly religious way during the first four centuries: Christianity grew almost exclusively in the cities. The first council to legislate for the establishment of rural parishes, and the appointment of priests to the villages, was the Council of Vaison, in 528. In the cities, some priests had, from very early times, established a sort of school for boys, with a view to

preparing them for the lectorship. No doubt, the custom
spread considerably, but not with any uniformity, nor did
it by any means become universal. The fourth and fifth
canons of the Ecumenical Council of Constantinople, in 682,
ordered all parish priests to teach children, or to establish
a school in which they might be taught. Some enthusiastic
writers thereupon conclude that the schools were universally established. But the conclusion shows a woeful lack
of understanding of how Church laws have been obeyed:
from the first legal pronouncement of St. Peter down to the
motu proprio of Pius X on Church music. We find the
command to found parish schools repeated in nearly every
century, by synods, local councils, general councils. Something undoubtedly came of the commands; but the constant
repetition of them is evidence that they did not meet with
complete obedience. In part, the difficulties of the time
are to blame for that; in part, the fine old inertia of human
nature. There were parish schools from the sixth to the
ninth century: how many we cannot say; but we are quite
sure there were not enough of them. There is no more
sense in canonizing every priest and Catholic school than
there is in damning them all in the statement, "The early
Church as a whole was opposed to education."[1]

Monastic schools. As has often been said, the entire
Church had something of a monastic character in the beginning: which, of course, it could not keep when it had
spread widely in the world. There were always, it is true,
some chosen souls who aimed at practicing the evangelical
counsels. But in the third century there was developed a
great, and at times unbalanced, enthusiasm for the ascetical
life. It produced thousands of monks, some of them saints,
many of them intolerable fanatics. They took no vows;
they were under no discipline save that of their own re-

[1] Leach, *Schools of Medieval England,* p. 10.

ligious impulses; they were turbulent,[1] ignorant, not infrequently heretical.   Eusebius of Vercelli, Cassian, and St. Martin of Tours, who died about 400, introduced the Eastern type of monasticism into the West; but it was never popular there, except in Ireland.   Some of the cultured Christians scoffed at it as much as the pagans.[2]   St. Jerome, although he constantly and strenuously praised the monastic life, recognized the disorders which had grown up in it.[3]   Yet the monastic idea could not die, in spite of the gross imperfections which hindered its development and propagation.   St. Basil, who died in 379, gave to Eastern monasticism a rule which did much to bring it into reason-

[1] It was the mob of Nitrian monks, not Cyril, who were responsible for the barbaric murder of the philosopher Hypatia.   Instances of their unruliness are abundant.   St. John Chrysostom, who had written a defense of the monks, recounts an attack made on him by a rabble (δροῦγγος) of monks at Caesarea in 404.   (Ep. 14 ad Diaconissam Olympiadem, in Migne, *P. G.*, 52:613-16.)   The Council of Chalcedon, in 451, legislated for monastic reforms in Canons 4, 6, 7, 8, and 23. (Mansi, *Concilia,* Vols. 6, 7.)   For the Eastern monks, the best collection of material is in L. S. de le Nain de Tillemont, *Mémoires pour servir à l'Histoire Ecclesiastique des Six Premiers Siècles,* 2d ed., 16 vols., Paris, 1701-02.

[2] Some reasons for that fact, in the persisting influence of pagan culture, may be found in the lives of such men as Synesius, Bishop of Ptolemais, in the East, and Ausonius in the West.   Cf. A. Gardner, *Synesius of Cyrene,* London, 1886; S. Dill, *Roman Society in the Last Century of the Western Empire,* 2d ed., London, 1906, chap. 1, pp. 181 sqq.

[3] Historians of anti-Catholic bias all too frequently exaggerate the extent of these disorders, seizing eagerly upon isolated faults, and trumpeting them as if they were the normal commonplace of all monastic life.   In particular, even eminent writers have grossly misrepresented the attitude of St. Jerome toward monks.   There is one misquotation (from Ep. 39, par. 5, in Migne, *P. L.*, 22:472) which has become a classic.   It reads: "Quousque genus destabile monachorum non urbe pellitur?   non lapidibus obruitur?   non praecipitatur in fluctus?"   Even such men as Professor Bury and Sir Samuel Dill present this as Jerome's own statement, whereas in reality it is a condemnation which Jerome dramatically puts into the mouth of critics hostile to the monks, and which he vigorously refutes.   In Ep. 125, par. 16 (Migne, *P. L.*, 22:1081) St. Jerome does portray and sharply condemn false monks, "monks only in garb and title, not in reality."

able order. But it was St. Benedict of Nursia, nearly a hundred and fifty years later, who introduced a form of monastic life destined to thrive amazingly and to influence very largely the whole course of Western civilization. He had had bitter experience of the degenerate character of existing monasticism,[1] before he founded his own great monastery of Monte Cassino, about 520, and wrote the rule which became the general model for cloistered life in the West.

We are concerned here with monasticism only as it affected education; which it did in two ways: first, by emphasizing to Christians and the world in general the important Christian idea of detachment; second, by establishing various sorts of schools. We shall not delay to stress the substantial value to men of the lesson taught by the living fact of monastic lives: that "we have not here a lasting city, but look for one that is to come." It is a hard lesson, and men never learn it well. The monastery schools played no small part in the educational history of Europe. We can only touch briefly upon them.

Catholic writers have often exaggerated the number and value of monastic schools. The early monks were very little concerned with learning; their educational work was strictly religious. When St. John Chrysostom speaks of sending children to the monks, he makes a definite contrast between their training and the acquisition of learning; it is a question of choice between virtue and scholarship. In the East, as in the West, monasteries later did establish schools, but they were almost exclusively for the merest elementary education of their own novices. Some of the Western monasteries developed better schools. Twenty years after the founding of Monte Cassino, Cassiodorus, a wealthy noble,

---

[1] At the request of the monks, he had assumed the direction of the monastery of Vicovaro. But the monks tried to poison him, harassed him in every way, and finally drove him out. (St. Gregory the Great, *Vita S. Benedicti,* c. 1, n. 3; in *A. S.,* 8:278.)

set up a monastery and school on his estate of Vivarium in Calabria, gathered books for a library, and himself wrote two treatises, *On the Teaching of Sacred Letters,* and a sort of encyclopedic work *On the Seven Liberal Arts.* Even earlier monasteries, like Marmoutier, the 'Great Monastery,' founded by St. Martin of Tours late in the fourth century, and Lerins, built by St. Honoratus on a rocky isle off the coast of Gaul, about 400, had schools; but though by the sixth century these monasteries reckoned a few scholarly men, such as St. Vincent and St. Caesarius of Arles, they confined themselves mostly to equipping their monks to read and chant the divine office and to copy manuscripts. It is true that after the sixth century they took in young boys, and had schools for them, but the boys were candidates for the noviceship, and the schools were both small and elementary. They had no effect upon the people at large.

In Ireland. During this disturbed period, Ireland was a sort of quiet backwater. Monasticism had been introduced there very early, and had flourished; and the monasteries had much better schools than those of the continent. This was due in part to the fact that the educational condition of the whole country was good; lay schools abounded, and were well organized. In 573, at the Convention of Drum-Ceata, St. Columba, who had himself been educated in a Bardic school, pleaded for harmony between the monastic schools and the lay schools; and thenceforth the two worked together to a considerable extent. Between 520 and 900 there were 168 monastic schools in Ireland. Their great period was from about 600 to the Danish invasion, about 800, when, in the general devastation, monastic schools and libraries were particularly singled out for destruction. The monastic schools were chiefly devoted to the study of theology and scripture; but they trained their students, as a preparation for these, in languages and the

classic literatures.   Students flocked thither from many
parts of Europe.   Aldhelm, Bishop of Sherborne, who died
in 709, bitterly resented that whole 'fleet loads' of English
went to Ireland for study.[1]   Scholars from Ireland went as
missionaries to other lands, or as teachers in continental
monasteries and schools.[2]   But only occasionally did laymen study in the Irish monastic schools.   Thus their influence upon general education was limited.

As schools of agriculture.   Men have always hated toil;
and the abominable institution of slavery made manual
labor particularly detested in the ancient world.   Jesus
Christ by His example gave a dignity to labor, and His
Church urged men to learn from that example.   St. Benedict had this very much in mind when he founded his great
order.   His monks were to be cultivators of the earth, and
to preach the gospel of work; that was the significance of
the sickle which they carried in their belts.   In the beginning the monks accomplished wonders; they chose the wild-

[1] *Monumenta Germ. Hist. Ep. Merovingi et Carolingi Aevi,* I, p.
231.   Migne, *P. L.,* 89:3.
[2] St. Columbanus was, perhaps, the most noted of these.   About the
year 590 he went into Gaul.   Guntram, a grandson of Clovis, gave
him a large Roman structure known as Luxovium or Luxueil, on the
boundary of the Austrasian and Burgundian kingdoms.   After the
death of Guntram, Columban was driven out by the queen-mother,
the famous Brunihildis, and went into Lombardy, where King Agilulf
gave him Bobbio, in a wild gorge of the Apennines, near Genoa.
There he established another monastery, which was one of the refuges
for learning during the later Middle Ages.   His letters and other
writings are found in Migne, *P. L.,* 80:209-96.   His *Life* by his disciple Jonas, is given in Migne, *P. L.,* 87:1009-46.   An English version,
by D. C. Munro, was published by the University of Pennsylvania,
1897.   Fearghal, or Virgilius, another Irish missionary, was Bishop
of Salzburg, 766-84.   Alcuin, in his letters, passim in Migne, *P. L.,*
Vols. 100, 101, speaks of various others.   Martin Haverty, in his
History of Ireland, Dublin, 1885, pp. 9-106, reckons 282 Irish missionaries to the Continent.   Of these the largest number, 150, went to the
Germanies, where nearly one-fourth of them were put to death.   The
Irish missionaries are credited with having founded 49 monasteries
in Gaul and Belgium, 13 in Scotland, 12 in England, 6 in Italy, 15 in
Switzerland, a dozen or more in the Germanies.   But the intellectual
and moral inertia against which they struggled was enormous.

est places, cleared, drained, tilled them, and turned them into splendid estates, as models to the semibarbarian peoples round about. But this work too dwindled and died. The monks became as lazy as the rest; they increased the number of illiterate lay brothers, and left the hard work to them; they entered into the feudal system, and held serfs to till their lands. They did not succeed in lifting the curse from toil; perhaps it was too much to expect of them.

The deepening darkness. There is a quarrel over the title of 'Dark Ages,' affixed to certain centuries of mediaeval history; extremist opinions representing those centuries as either the blackest night, or else as only a gentle twilight or, rather, a rosy dawn. There is further quarrel as to what centuries are included under the name. Obviously, the metaphor of darkness, applied to civilization, must be taken as a relative term, not as a scientifically accurate description. If we consider the plain facts of unrealized human ideals and unfulfilled capabilities, every age, including our own very boastful age, can be called dark. But there were some centuries, say from the sixth to the tenth inclusive, in which European civilization was lower than it had been just previously, and than it was to be shortly. The immediate cause of that failure, or at least partial failure, of civilization was the defect of education. In the great period of national transitions, the teachers had grown weary, and the pupils were unruly. The old society, which had of necessity to pass on man's accumulated tradition of culture, was heavy with fatigue, lacking in vigor of body, of mind, of will. Its essential function was to impress the new peoples, to help form in them the habits of intellectual endeavor, of eagerness to use wisely and resolutely all the means, natural and supernatural, for mastery in living; and through very feebleness it fumbled and blundered in that function. The marvel is, not that there were dark ages, but that light ever came again at all.

In the sixth, seventh, and eighth centuries, schools of any sort on the continent dwindled in numbers and in quality. In the monasteries, a part of the monks still kept up the copying of books, but few even of the copyists could understand the books they copied. The schools of England fared better; the Irish schools, during all that time the best in the West, compared favorably with the later Graeco-Roman schools. But throughout Europe as a whole, the influence of schools upon the people was small; illiteracy spread; and not one in a hundred of those who could read and write had opportunity for further school education. This meant in time, of course, ignorance in many of the civil and religious leaders. What Adalbero, Bishop of Laon, says of the early part of the eleventh century, was even more widely true of the eighth century: that "there was more than one bishop who was unable to tell the letters of the alphabet on his fingers."[1]

Moral and religious education was not quite so badly neglected as intellectual education. The essential vitality of the Catholic Church struggled against the mental and moral torpor of the age, but it was not a brilliantly successful struggle, and the results it produced in the souls of men were, in general, very meager. Anarchy ruled in Italy. Spain was torn by Arianism, and in 580 the dominant Arians began a persecution of the Catholics.[2] In Gaul, the cruel and corrupt Merovingian dynasty parcelled out bishoprics to despicable favorites. A competent and impartial historian writes: "The corruption of the Merovingian clergy is almost unbelievable. Yet never were there so

[1] Though we know on other grounds that Adalbero's testimony on this point is true, he is not in general a trustworthy witness. His own life was far from edifying, and his satiric and scurrilous poem is so poisoned by evident envy and malice as to discredit him pretty thoroughly. See Migne, *P. L.*, 141:773 sqq., *Adalpheronis Carmen*.

[2] It was in great part due to the jealousies and internal quarrels of the Christians that the Mohammedan Moors were able to conquer nearly the whole of Spain in four years, 711-715.

many 'saints' as in those stormy days. Rome was not consulted, and a halo seemed the birthright of every prominent bishop, even though he were embroiled in dark intrigues like Saint Pretextatus, or in constant civil war like Saint Leger."[1] Slavery, in the form of serfdom, spread everywhere. A capitulary of Charlemagne, in 789, urged that candidates for the priesthood should be sought for "not only from those of servile condition, but from amongst the sons of free men:"[2] a significant statement, which goes far to explain the very small influence which the clergy exercised over the lives of the people. The Church was worse off in these centuries than it had been during the great Roman persecutions.

A little light. Charles Martel, the bastard of Pepin of Heristal, broke the Arab wave that came up from Spain, in 732. His son, Pepin the Short, deposed Childeric, the last of the miserable Merovingians, and became King of the Franks. His grandson, Charlemagne, born ten years after the battle of Tours, succeeded Pepin in 768, established a really great kingdom and a vigorous government, and let in a little light on the Dark Ages.

Charlemagne was unquestionably a man of genius, but though he was twenty-six years old when he became king, he had not yet learned to write; nor, as his biographer Einhard says, did he ever succeed well in his later attempts to learn.[3] He had had some training in grammar under Peter of Pisa, could speak colloquial Latin as well as his native tongue, and had some slight use of spoken Greek. But

---

[1] A. L. Guerard, *French Civilization,* p. 111.
[2] *Capitulare Aquisgranense,* Baluze, *Cap. Reg. Franc.,* I, 209-42. Further light is thrown on the conditions in monasteries by a decree of the Council of Frankfort, in 794, which forbids the Abbot "to blind or mutilate the monks" (Baluze, I, 261). See also the letter of St. Boniface to Pope Zacharias (742) on the miserable state of the Frankish clergy and monks. Migne, *P. L.,* 89:776.
[3] *Caroli Vita,* c. 25; in Jaffe, *Bibliotheca Rerum Germanicarum,* 1867, p. 531.

he had the wit to appreciate learning, and was eager both
to acquire it and to help others to learn. In the midst of
almost constant military campaigns, his interest in the
schools never flagged. Many of his capitularies are concerned with the reformation of the clergy and the monks,
and great part of the reform was to be educational. More
than that, he wished that schools should be multiplied for
all his people, and that their intellectual and religious development should go hand in hand.

It may be remarked in passing, and it is worthy of remark, that the Charlemagne who strove for this educational
reform was an *educated* man. He lacked learning, it is
true; but that only emphasizes the distinction between
learning and education. The darkness of the 'Dark Ages'
does not mean that no one was educated during that time,
but only that fewer were educated. This is said, not as a
defense of the bad conditions then prevailing, but with a
view to keeping historical perspective.

Charlemagne's influence on education in the West would
have been impossible without the aid of teachers. And
there were teachers to be had. He personally selected a
good one, Alcuin, an Englishman trained in the cathedral
school of York, and set him at the head of a school established in his own palace at Aachen, in 782. In that school
the majority of the pupils were young nobles, destined to
be leaders in State and Church; but amongst them were
Charlemagne himself, then forty years of age, his wife
Liutgarda, his sister Gisela, Abbess of Chelles, his three
legitimate sons, his daughter Gisela, and many princes and
dignitaries.[1] After five years, in 787, Charlemagne issued
his famous capitulary on education, and at the same time
secured from Rome a number of teachers of singing, gram-

---

[1] The 'palace school' was not an innovation of Charlemagne's. It
had functioned under the Merovingians. Cf. S. Dill, *Roman Society
in Gaul in the Merovingian Age*, p. 138.

mar, and arithmetic, and sent them to the more important monasteries throughout the kingdom, to help in carrying out his reforms.   Two years later, the Council of Aachen commanded "that every monastery and every abbey have its school"; and with the king backing up the command, there was more likelihood of its being obeyed.   In 796, Alcuin became abbot of Tours, and Theodulfe, the Bishop of Orleans, who seems to have succeeded him as a sort of minister of education under Charlemagne, ordered the clergy of his diocese to open *free schools* for children in every town and village.   This order was issued in 797, ten years after Charlemagne's first great pronouncement.

The result of these and like efforts undoubtedly was a general stimulation of energy amongst the nobles, the clergy, the monks, a considerable improvement in morals throughout the country, and a very real impetus to schools. But a score of Charlemagnes could not civilize at a stroke the still half-savage peoples of his lands.   The disorder was too great to be remedied in one generation, or for that matter, in several generations.   The Archbishop of Toledo could reproach Alcuin, when he was abbot of Tours, that he was the master of 20,000 slaves.[1]   The court of Charlemagne himself gave no shining example of morality.   Lethargic bishops and abbots offered, not infrequently, only a half-hearted co-operation with the King's reforms.   Yet a beginning was made.   The slow and wearisome process of enlightenment was encouraged.   The little candlelight of Charlemagne and Alcuin could not brighten up the huge darkness: but it made men think of the dawn.

Conclusion.   A compact and adequate summary of educational conditions in these five hundred years is impossible. Europe was seething.   Waves of barbarism swept over it. The weary, old civilization, and the struggling Church,

[1] Monnier, *Alcuin et Charlemagne*, Pt. III, chap. 4.

fought against that barbarism, as men might fight against a vast forest fire, or succession of fires, that constantly broke out in new places. There is heroism in the age: in the pitiful, desperate struggle to save civilization and religion; and in the end there is at least the sure promise of victory (though of course the victory will never be complete on this earth).

TOPICS FOR DISCUSSION

1. Influence of the codes of Theodosius and Justinian on the Roman law schools.

2. Was the interference of the Roman government in education a cause, or only a sign, of the decay of the schools?

3. The contrast between the Irish and the Continental attitudes toward purely literary studies in the seventh and eighth centuries.

4. The character and history of the trivium and quadrivium.

5. The education offered to women by the convents during the seventh, eighth, and ninth centuries.

6. Curriculum and method in the palace school under Alcuin.

BIBLIOGRAPHIC NOTE

Source material for this period is fairly abundant; but only a small part of it can be indicated here. Besides Migne's collection of the Greek and Latin Fathers of the Church, there are the translations in the *Nicene and Post-Nicene Fathers,* 1st and 2d series: of which may be specially mentioned the *Histories* of Socrates and Sozomen, the writings of St. Augustine and St. Jerome, particularly the letters of St. Jerome in Vol. 6, 2d series. Orosius, *Historiarum adversus Paganos Libri VII,* is in Migne, *P. L.,* 21:663-1174, also in *Corpus Script, Ecclesiast. Lat.,* Vienna, 1882, Vol. 5. The *Chronicon Consulare* of Prosper of Aquitaine is edited by T. Mommsen, in *Monumenta Germaniae Historica,* Berlin, 1892, Vol. 9. The most important work of Gregory of Tours, *Historiae Francorum Libri X,* is in Migne, *P. L.,* Vol. 71: English translation, O. M. Dalton, *The History of the Franks by Gregory of Tours,* 2 vols., Oxford, 1927. The writings of St. Isidore, edited by Arevalo, take up Vols. 81-84 in Migne, *P. L.;* see especially *Etymologiae, Libri Duo Differentiarum,* and *De Natura Rerum.* W. D. Foulkes translated into English Paul the Deacon's *History of the Langobards,* London, 1907. C. Plummer edited Ven. Bede, *Historia Ecclesiae Gentis Anglorum,* 2 vols., Oxford, 1896. English translation by A. M. Sellar, rev. ed., London, 1912. There is an admirable collection of sources in M. Bouquet, *Recueil des Historiens des Gaules,* 23 vols., Paris, 1738-1876, edited by L. Delisle, 17 vols., Paris, 1869-79.   Translated extracts from some of the sources may be conveniently read in J. C. Ayer, Jr., *Source Book of Church History for the First Six Centuries,* New York, 1913; P. Monroe, *Source Book of the History of Education for the Greek and Roman Period* (pp. 445-509 for the *Institutes* of Quintilian), New York, 1901; B. J. Kidd, *Documents Illustrative of the History of the Church,* 2 vols., New York, 1920-23.   A full translation of *Quintilian's Works* has been made by H. E. Butler, 4 vols., London, 1921-22.   O. M. Dalton translated *The Letters of Sidonius,* Oxford, 1915; and H. P. Evelyn-White, *Ausonius,* 2 vols., London, 1920.   The *Works* of Julian the Apostate were translated by F. Wright, in Loeb Classical Library, 3 vols., London and New York, 1923.

For the later development of Roman law schools, see J. B. Bury, *History of the Later Roman Empire from the Death of Theodosius I to the Death of Justinian, A. D. 395-565,* 2 vols., London, 1923; and T. Mommsen and P. Meyer (eds.), *Theodosii Libri XVI,* Berlin, 1904-05, revised by E. Kiegel, 1926-28.   R. W. and A. J. Carlyle, *History of Medieval Political Theory in the West,* 5 vols. (bibliography), Edinburgh, 1903-28, admirably covers the entire development from the time of Cicero to the thirteenth century.   Another valuable work is N. D. Fustel de Coulanges, *Histoire des Institutions Politiques de l'Ancienne France,* 6 vols., Paris, 1888-92.

On the general culture of the West during this period, the following works may be particularly recommended: S. Dill, *Roman Society in the Last Century of the Western Empire,* London, 1921, and *Roman Society in Gaul in the Merovingian Age,* London, 1926; H. Belloc, *Europe and the Faith,* New York, 1920; E. K. Rand, *The Founders of the Middle Ages,* Harvard University Press, 1928; C. Dawson, *The Making of Europe* (bibliography), London, 1932; C. E. Stevens, *Sidonius Apollinaris and His Age,* Oxford, 1933.

For the Celtic influences in education, see J. F. Kenney, *The Sources for the Early History of Ireland,* Vol. 1, *Ecclesiastical,* New York, 1929 (Series: *Records of Civilization: Sources and Studies,* J. T. Shotwell and A. P. Evans (eds.), 1915 sqq.); L. Gougaud, *Les Chretientés Celtiques,* 2d ed., Paris, 1911 (English translation by M. Joynt, *Christianity in Celtic Lands,* London, 1932); H. Zimmer, *Ueber die Bedeutung des irischen Elements fur die mittelalterliche Kultur* (Preussische Jahrbucher, 59, 1887), translated by J. L. Edmands, *The Irish Element in Mediaeval Culture,* New York, 1891.

For school education, perhaps the best single work so far published is M. Roger, *L'Enseignement des Lettres Classiques d'Ausone à Alcuin,* Paris, 1905.   A. T. Drane, *Christian Schools and Scholars,* London, 1881, 1909, 1924, contains much valuable data, but is often uncritical.   For the trivium and quadrivium, see A. F. West, *Alcuin and the Rise of the Christian Schools,* New York, 1892; and P. Abelson, *The Seven Liberal Arts,* New York, 1906.   The following are good studies of the particular fields indicated in their titles: J. B. Mullinger, *The Schools of Charles the Great,* London, 1877, new ed., New York, 1911; P. Lahargou, *De Scholis Lerinensibus Aetate Merovingiaca,* Paris, 1892; T. Haarhoff, *The Schools of Gaul,* Oxford, 1920; A. F. Leach, *The Schools of Medieval England,* London, 1915; J. Healy, *Insula Sanctorum et Doctorum: or Ireland's Ancient Schools and Scholars,* Dublin, 1850, 5th ed., 1908. For the convent education of women, see the earlier chapters of L. Eckenstein, *Women under Monasticism,* Cambridge, 1896; and H. Wilms, *Aus mittelalterlichen Frauenklostern,* 3d ed., Freiburg, 1918. Alcuin's school is competently treated in C. J. B. Gaskoin, *Alcuin: His Life and His Work,* London, 1904; and G. F. Browne, *Alcuin of York,* London, 1908.

For the sixth century, an interesting source is the work of Aurelius Cassiodorus; see especially, in Migne, *P. L.,* Vol. 70, *De Institutione Divinarum Litterarum,* foll. 1105-50, and *De Artibus et Disciplinis Liberalium Litterarum,* foll. 1149-1220. There is much information about education in H. von Schubert, *Geschichte der christlichen Kirche im Fruehmittelalter,* Tubingen, 1917, 2d ed., 1921; and in Dom H. Quentin's edition of the uncompleted work of L. Duchesne, *L'Eglise au VIe Siècle,* Paris, 1926.

CHAPTER VIII

FROM CHARLEMAGNE TO THE RISE OF THE UNIVERSITIES
NINTH TO TWELFTH CENTURIES

Scope of chapter: How light came to the 'Dark Ages.' To be obsessed with the idea that education and schools are synonymous is a handicap in studying any period of the history of education; but it makes simply impossible an intelligent evaluation of education in the 'Dark Ages.' It is that obsession which has misled many historians to exaggerate the value of Charlemagne's influence upon the education of the period, and even to trace a connection between his efforts on behalf of schools and the marked intellectual revival which took place in Europe in the twelfth and thirteenth centuries, three or four hundred years after the death of Charlemagne. There is a manifest huge gap to be bridged between these two ages; and it is not bridged by schools.[1] This chapter will try to show how the barbarian Europe of the ninth century came to be the civilized Europe of the thirteenth century; the process is essentially one of education.

The 'Dark Ages' continue after Charlemagne. It is no injustice to Charlemagne's fine efforts to say that they had little to do with bringing light to the 'Dark Ages.' *If* the vigorous government of Charlemagne had been maintained with equal vigor by his successors, and *if* these successors had shown the same wise interest in education which was one of the chief glories of Charlemagne, a scant hundred years might have put an end to the 'Dark Ages.' But the statement is painfully like the old saying in the army, "If

[1] Cf. Laurie, *Rise and Constitution of Universities*, Lect. III. See especially S. R. Maitland, *The Dark Ages*, Rivington, London, 1844.

we had some ham, we could have ham and eggs, if we only had some eggs." Charlemagne's efforts on behalf of schools practically died with him. His successors were, for the most part, incompetent to further them. More than that, important as those efforts were, they were limited even in his own time. They had not a wide enough influence to affect the general state of education in Europe. The Germanies were scarcely touched by them. Spain was almost wholly in the power of the Saracens. The Christian East, struggling desperately against the Moslems, was in disorder; it was only in 860, half a century after the death of Charlemagne, that Michael III was able to refound the University of Constantinople; and the restoration was not very vigorous even then.[1] In Charlemagne's own domain, the schools he set up would have needed generations to make an impression upon the feudal anarchy of the times.

Early feudalism anarchic. We must not let the military successes and glory of Charlemagne blind us to the fact that Europe was still seething in barbarian ferment. The civilization of the Middle Ages was still in its feeble infancy. The most important organization of society was in *local efforts* to climb out of anarchy. Small freeholders banded together for mutual aid, their immediate aim being merely *security* of life and property. It was an organization primarily for war, not for the development of civilization. It was a most necessary organization; but its very necessity is a terrible revelation of the bad conditions which prevailed. Out of it some fine things were to grow; but they were not envisaged in the early organization itself. It affected but very little the wretched slavery which the various peoples of Europe had inherited from the Romans or had brought from their own vague antiquity. Feudalism of itself did nothing to improve the lot of the slaves and

[1] Cf. Finlay, *Byzantine Empire,* Bk. I, p. 265.

serfs; it merely included them in the compacts which their masters made. Later, as we shall see, it tended indirectly to give to the serf a slightly better status, by attaching him to the land. He was no longer to be a mere chattel; he had some roots in the soil. But the whole of society, despite its elaborate organization in detail, was so loosely knit together as scarcely to merit the name of a society. This exaggerated local independence was a great hindrance to the spread of any general scheme of education, such as Charlemagne had hoped and striven for. Even in 885, seventy years after the death of Charlemagne, a like attempt of Alfred in England came to practically nothing, and for precisely the same reasons.[1]

The Church involved in feudalism. It is to be noted that all of Charlemagne's zeal for schools found its practical expression through the clergy and the monks. Not even the most hostile writer disputes the fact that these churchmen were in almost exclusive possession of what educational tools the age could look to.[2] Charlemagne had no choice but to use the clergy and the monks. And it must be frankly admitted that most of them were poor instru-

[1] The educational influence of Alfred has been as much exaggerated by some writers as has been that of Charlemagne. Historical perspective would seem to be rare. It is almost amusing to note that, whilst Charlemagne sent to England for Alcuin to direct his 'palace school,' Alfred, when he in turn wished to establish a 'palace school,' had to send to the Continent for masters: Grimbald, of St. Omer, and John, a monk of Corbie. Learning had no real foothold anywhere in that age, which needed first to be civilized before it could be interested in such things as books and schools. Alfred's 'revival' failed even more signally than Charlemagne's.

[2] In the matter of schools, this was true until after the year 1000. Indeed, the fact is constantly made the basis of a malevolent charge that the Catholic Church in the Middle Ages held a monopoly in education. Of any monopoly by design, there is simply no evidence: beyond the essential monopoly conferred on it by its Founder, when He commissioned it to 'teach all nations,' and gave His revelation into its keeping. The monopoly in fact (i. e., that there were no other schools) is patently explained by the equally evident fact that no other organization made any attempt to establish schools.

ments.   One Alcuin does not make a learned and pious
clergy, any more than one swallow makes a summer.   The
bishops and abbots had become feudal lords; no doubt, by
sheer necessity.   But the fact involved them, and through
them the priests and monks, in the turbulent anarchy of
the time, in the riot of individualism, which, sifting all elements, we find at the bottom of barbarism.   For all practical purposes, each bishopric, each abbey, stood by itself;
concerned chiefly, if not only, with its relations to its feudal
suzerains and feudal subjects.   Bishops and abbots were
more interested in caring for their feudal rights than in
raising the tone of civilization, either morally or intellectually.

Conditions made worse by further barbarian raids. Bar-
onius is perhaps the first to give to the ninth and tenth
centuries the name of the 'Iron Age.' It was an age marked
not merely by constant feudal quarrels, but by savage and
destructive inroads from the still less civilized outer world.
There are three of these invasions to be specially noted.
The first is the Norman raids, which occupied the greater
part of the ninth century, and ended only in the shameless
bribe by which Charles the Simple, in 911, turned over to
the pirate Rollo the splendid Duchy of Normandy.   Then,
beginning in 831, the Saracens ravaged northern Italy and
southern France, pushing up the valley of the Rhone.   More
terrible still, huge armies of Huns devastated central Europe during most of the tenth century.   In 926 their savage
waves had come up to the very frontiers of Lorraine; and
they continued in a succession of invasions until the death
of their leader Tatsong in 972.

With particularly disastrous results to clergy and monks.
Such events alone would demoralize even a well-established
civilization; they were incredibly injurious to the difficult
beginnings of mediaeval civilization.   All the elements of
society suffered through the confusion and insecurity

brought about by these invasions, but perhaps the clergy and the monks suffered most of all. Their material losses were great. The Norman pirate, Hastings, in 851, burned the monasteries of Fontanelles, St. Ouen, and Jumieges. Within a few years, Marmoutier was pillaged, St. Martin of Tours was burned, Malmedy, Corbie, Liége, and scores of others, were destroyed. In the course of the ninth century, the abbey of Nonantula in Italy was plundered seven times, ending with the last savage onslaught of the Huns, who in 899 killed all the monks together with their abbot, Gregory. It has been said that by the beginning of the tenth century scarcely one of the great French abbeys was left standing. Many of these monasteries had possessed considerable libraries. Fontanelles had a famous one. The chronicles of Novalesa in Italy record that when the Saracen invaders came, in 906, the fleeing monks carried away with them to Turin more than six thousand volumes. Most of these were later burned by the Saracens in the sack of Turin. Beyond a doubt the monastery libraries suffered great losses in all these raids and invasions. But more grievous to mediaeval society was the demoralization of the monks and clergy, caused by their dispersion and the inevitable breakdown of what religious discipline the rude times had been able to boast. Wars always tend to breed license.[1]

The darkest part of the 'Dark Ages.' Shepherds and sailors and other watchers of the night have made us believe that the darkest hours come before the dawn. Certainly, the latter part of the 'Dark Ages' grows steadily more gloomy. Rulers were incompetent; and what energies they had were almost entirely devoted to war. There

---

[1] Cf. *Acta Conc. Metz, 909,* Mansi, Vol. 18, pp. 270 sqq. Odo, the second abbot of Cluny (927-42), expressly attributes the corruption of the monks to the dispersion caused by the invasions. Cf. *Vita Odonis a Joanne,* 3:2, Migne, *P. L.,* 133:96.

was no cohesion in the social order, little or no intercommunication of ideas.   Roads had pretty nearly ceased to
exist.[1] All life was narrowed to the small circle of feudal
domains; and even that life was made sullen and savage by
its insecurity. The Catholic Church, the one great hope of
civilization in these turbulent times, found only pitifully
feeble instruments to its hand, in a dispersed and demoral-
ized huddle of monks, in its swaggering, incontinent, and
ignorant bishops and priests.[2] Perhaps in no part of
Europe were conditions worse than in Rome itself, during
most of this time torn by factions which made the papacy
the sport of their ambitions.

Optimistic writers try to see an area of light amidst all
this darkness, in the Germany of the Ottos. But the exception there is more apparent than real. In the tenth century,
the descendants of Henry the Fowler, and notably Otto the
Great, who ruled as king from 936 to 973, and was crowned
emperor of the West by the Pope at Rome in 962, established a strongly autocratic government in Germany, and
made a vigorous stand against the Hun invaders. But far
from curbing the turbulence of the age, they added to it by
engaging in the factional wars of Italy. Otto the Great
appointed his brother, St. Bruno, and his cousins, Poppo
and Henry, to episcopal sees. These were three good men,
who tried earnestly to stir up some enthusiasm for learning
and piety amongst their clergy. But the little good they
did was more than offset by the vicious policy which gave
them their appointment as bishops, and which led to such
grave abuses in the Church. And they no more succeeded
in making a home for learning in Germany, or in effecting
any widespread reform in the German clergy or people,
than had Charlemagne in France or Alfred in England.

The needed revival. What the age needed was, not a

[1] Cf. H. Belloc, *The Road,* New York, 1925, pp. 147 sqq.
[2] Cf. *Collationes Odonis,* Migne, *P. L.,* 133:518 sqq.

scattering of learned men, not an occasional pious bishop here and there, not even a wise sovereign who would encourage schools. If the education of men was to develop in any way befitting human beings, society needed two things. The first was a definite stabilizing, on some sound and healthy basis, suited in a practical way to what the men of the time were capable of appreciating. And the second was a moral reform, some return to Christian principles of conduct. These two processes would constitute the real education of Europe, and upon them alone could be built any further development of civilization. The instruments of these two processes were at hand; in the tradition of Roman law and the civil organization, which, though obscured, had never been wholly lost to Europe; and in the Catholic Faith, which smouldered with a divine vitality under all the ashes of violence, simony, ignorance, superstition, and immorality. But that Europe of the ninth and tenth centuries should be so revivified would seem to be a greater moral miracle than even the survival of the Church during the first three centuries of persecution.

Brought about through Cluny. It is no exaggeration to say that the foundation of Cluny marks the turning point in the history of education in the Middle Ages. Cluny was a Benedictine abbey, about four miles from Macon, founded in 910 by Berno, on a grant of land from William, the Duke of Aquitaine. There had been Benedictine monasteries continuously for nearly four hundred years. In their early history, as we have seen, the Benedictine monks were a most important factor in the civilizing of the barbarians. But although all the monasteries had a common 'rule,' or way of life, each monastery was an isolated unit. That fact involved them in the feudal organization which grew up round about them. Further, it exposed them to the great weakness of being unable to resist or oppose the bad conditions which might prevail in their particular locality; they had no common fund of spiritual vigor upon which to draw in their need. Hence they inevitably suffered decay in the social anarchy of the ninth century. Berno saw the need of closer organization, for the mutual support of the monasteries. During the seventeen years of his government of the new abbey of Cluny, he succeeded in getting five other monasteries to revive the spirit of the old Benedictine rule,[1] and to place themselves under the central jurisdiction of Cluny. His successor, St. Odo, abbot from 927 to 942, added seventeen more abbeys to the organization. Both Odo and Maieul, who was abbot from 948 to 975, carried the new spirit into Italy, which had perhaps suffered more grievously from the distress of the times than any other country. Bishop Gennadius of Astorga, in Spain, restored a number of abbeys destroyed by the Saracens, and placed them under the rule of Cluny.[2] And so the organization grew, until, in the twelfth century, three hundred and fourteen Benedictine houses were included in the Cluny system.[3] It was this growing system which changed the character of feudalism, and therefore of all mediaeval society. *The change was an amazing work of education.* We shall have to consider it a little in detail, though as briefly as possible.

Which brought back the Roman concept of organization. As has been said, early feudal society needed stabilizing.

---

[1] Benedict of Aniane, who died in 821, had, with the aid and encouragement of Louis the Mild, reformed the monks of a number of Benedictine abbeys; but his work died with him. The changes he introduced into the Benedictine 'rule' were adopted by Berno, and made the base of his new reform. They may be read in Migne, *P. L.*, 103:701-1380.

[2] A. K. Porter, *Romanesque Sculpture on the Pilgrimage Roads*, 10 vols., Boston, 1923, recounts in detail how the influence of Cluny spread first to Burgundy, then to England, northern Spain, the Germanies, southern Italy; and most strikingly how it passed along the great highway which led to the shrine of St. James at Compostella.

[3] Under Hugh, abbot from 1049 to 1109, the total number of Cluniac monks was reckoned at some ten thousand. At the general chapter of 1132, summoned by the abbot, Peter the Venerable, more than two hundred priors attended.

All its elements were in flux. A great man like Charlemagne could hold them together momentarily with his
strong hand; but when his grasp was relaxed, they scattered
again. Yet the memory of the great Roman organization
was never wholly lost, even during the wildest times of
anarchy in Europe. Indeed, from the time of Charlemagne
on, there were repeated efforts to revive the Roman Empire itself. For the most part the revivals were in name
only. When they approached any reality, it was always by
a mere forced imposition of physical power: a necessarily
unstable condition. Now the reform of Cluny was modeled
on the Roman idea of a central organization; but it did not
impose that central government; *it got men to accept it
voluntarily*.[1] It is true, Cluny was concerned with organizing a comparatively small number of men, in the distinctive (and what some would stupidly call 'unsocial') monastic life. But those monks were an influential part of
mediaeval society, and their monasteries were intricately
involved in the feudal system. The drawing together of
the monks could not but affect the complicated feudal world
in which they lived. A new idea of union was actively at
work in that world, and its value appealed to many, who
had no notion whatever that it was a very old idea brought
again into practice.[2] It would be out of proportion, and

[1] It is significant that, although Odo definitely aimed at a general
reform of monasticism, and was empowered by Pope John XI in 931
(Migne, *P. L.*, 132:1057) to receive "any monk from any monastery
who should wish to pass over to your manner of living," he reformed
twice as many monasteries as those which he added to the Cluny
system; and although he had the backing of civil lords, he used no
force, but relied upon persuasion. (See the reform of Fleury: Migne,
P. L., 133:81. *Vita Odonis a Joanne*, 3:8.)

[2] The Cluniac monasteries were placed directly under papal jurisdiction. This fact and its political consequences, in establishing an
influential organization within the various feudal states which was
free of control by those states, are of enormous importance in the
social and political history of Europe. Whether men managed that
new central political power well or ill in the succeeding centuries,
there is no denying that in the eleventh and twelfth centuries the

beyond our purpose, to follow the development of that idea in the feudal system. Every honest history of the Middle Ages shows it. But we should not forget that it takes its beginning at Cluny.

And revived the Christian spirit. More important even than the civil reform of feudalism, was the revival of Christian principles of living; without which, indeed, the civil reform itself would have been impossible. It must not be forgotten that by the tenth century most of western Europe had accepted Christianity in theory at least; but it is always a harder task to get people to reduce a theory to practice than to get them to accept the theory. Even those who may not admit that moral and religious education is more important than intellectual education,[1] must confess that it is more difficult. Cluny set about the moral education of Europe both by example and by precept. Within fifty years of its foundation, the holy lives of its own monks had made the name of Cluny famous throughout the Western world, had impressed the imagination of peasants and nobles alike, and had begun to leaven the mass of Europe.

Immediately by its influence on the clergy and monks. The Popes John XI and Leo VII welcomed and furthered this revival. By their charters they exempted Cluny from all jurisdiction save their own. They made of the Cluniacs a rock in the swirling waters of feudalism. Bishops turned to Cluny for aid in reforming various monasteries; often to find the peaceful Cluniacs ending by reforming the bishop himself. It is impossible to reckon accurately the number of restorations and new foundations of monasteries in the tenth century, but in the lifetime of Odo alone we

papal power was the great source of social unity in Europe and a most potent influence in bringing Europe out of barbarism.

[1] It is stupid, furthermore, to ignore the obvious fact that moral and religious education involves a very energetic use of the intellect in grasping and applying great truths.

have record of more than fifty in France, Italy, and the
Germanies. The Christian fervor of the monks was con-
tagious. Often, as in Upper Lorraine, laymen and the
lower clergy besieged the bishops with clamors for reform;
this was very notable in Toul, Verdun, and Metz. *Corruptio
optimi pessima:* a bad bishop is harder to Christianize than
a prostitute; but at times even a bad bishop gave way to
popular demand, as Adalbero did at Metz in 933.[1] It is not
implied that suddenly all the clergy and monks became
saints; but unquestionably the moral and religious tone of
the clergy and monks was raised, the scandal of dissolute
clerical lives was lessened, the teachings of Christ were
more earnestly preached to the people at large. There are
three particular effects of this educational movement to be
noted.

By introducing the truce of God. First, and perhaps
most important, was the repression of feudal violence. In
989, at the Council of Charroux,[2] was decreed the *Pax Dei;*
by which the sentence of excommunication was uttered
against all who should attack unarmed travelers, steal from
a church, or steal from the poor. It was declared again at
Narbonne and at Le Puy, in 990; more solemnly at Poitiers,
in 999.[3] *Twenty* like councils repeated the decree between
1000 and 1038. This was a significant stand against the
anarchic violence of feudalism; and it is to be observed
that it is distinctly based on religious belief and backed by
religious sanction. But it was to go further. At the Council of Elne, in 1027, the 'truce of God' was first proposed:
an agreement by which the knights bound themselves not
to fight "from the ninth hour on Saturday to the first hour

---

[1] Bollandists, *Acta SS.,* 27 Febr., p. 697.
[2] Mansi, *Concilia,* Vol. 19, 89-90. It is worth remark that at this
council, as also at the councils of Hery (1024) and Elne (1027)
women took part. Cf. Mansi, Vol. 19, 483.
[3] Mansi, Vol. 19, 267.

of Monday."[1] Within fifteen years the movement had grown so that Odilo, the fifth abbot of Cluny, backed by Reginald, the Archbishop of Arles, Benedict, the Bishop of Avignon, and Nithard, the Bishop of Nice, could appeal to the clergy of Italy to receive and keep the *Treva Dei*, "which we have accepted and firmly hold."[2] This developed truce of God was to extend from sunset on Wednesday to sunrise on Monday. The days of peace between Wednesday and Monday were to be kept sacred to the memory of the Christian mysteries; the motive of peace was the Christian religion. For a homicide committed on a day of the Truce, the penalty was exile from the province and pilgrimage to Jerusalem; for other offenses against the peace, reparation under the civil law, and a *double* canonical penance. It is astounding to know that the truce of God was accepted; even though it was not perfectly kept, its acceptance marked a great educational advance; and it *was* kept in sufficient measure to lift Europe out of anarchy.[3]

By Christianizing the institution of chivalry. Chivalry at first meant only cavalry, soldiers on horseback. Later it meant the order of feudal nobility, based upon the military and social distinction of knighthood. In theory, knighthood was not hereditary. It was to be conferred as a recognition of valor and worthiness. It was to be a democratic institution, open to every one who could earn entry into it. In reality, of course, it was practically hereditary; with rare exceptions, only the sons of knights became

[1] Mansi, Vol. 19, 483.
[2] Mansi, Vol. 19, 593.
[3] It may help us to realize the educational significance of the truce of God, if we compare the effort which brought it into existence with the efforts expended, since the World War of 1914-18, upon a covenant of peace: (1) in the conditions under which the two have been made (a semibarbaric feudalism, and a supposedly high civilization); (2) in the means employed (the universal Catholic religion, and congresses of diplomats); and (3) in the relative success of the two attempts.

knights. For centuries the distinction of knighthood was nothing more than a distinction of physical prowess; and if to our modern minds the very name is filled with the fine moral flavor of loyalty, devoted courage, courtesy, if today chivalrous means considerate, unselfish, and morally noble, we must recall that the change in meaning came from that Cluny which introduced the truce of God. The *Chansons de Geste* read back into the earlier chivalry a spirit which it did not have until the influence of the Cluniac monks made Christian principles an essential part of chivalry. Without ceasing to be military, chivalry became religious.[1] Its ceremonies of initiation were acts of worship of God. The oath of knighthood was an oath to defend religion, to practice justice and charity and mercy.[2] The penalties for violation of the oath were religious penances. The knight was a man *dedicated*. It was this fusion of the martial and the religious which prepared the way for the Crusades, the epic adventures of the Middle Ages. When Pope Urban II, once a Cluniac monk, proclaimed the First Crusade at Clermont, in 1095, the chief inducement he offered to the Christian knights for taking part in the Crusade was an indulgence.[3]

And by improving the lot of the serfs. It is not within the purpose of this chapter to go into the history of serfdom. But a reform which opened the way for serfs to

---

[1] Cf. L. Reynaud, *Les origines de l'influence française en Allemagne*, Paris, 1913, pp. 43, 339. Kenelm Digby, *The Broadstone of Honour.*

[2] The distinctive education of a knight is well known. In its later development, it included an elementary training in letters and in moral conduct, then a training in the use of arms and the military art, and finally training in elaborate courtesy and such graces of life as the age knew: the whole strongly pervaded by the spirit of religion. Although it was concerned with only a small percentage of the population, its influence was considerable, because that small part of society constituted the social leaders.

[3] Can. 2: Quicunque pro sola devotione, non pro honoris vel pecuniae adeptione, ad liberandam ecclesiam Dei Jerusalem profectus fuerit, iter illud pro omni penitentia reputetur. Mansi, *Concilia,* Vol. 20, 816.

develop themselves is a very important event in the history of education, and its importance is stressed by the fact that in the tenth and eleventh centuries the serfs constituted by far the largest part of the population of Europe. Old Roman laws[1] had forbidden rural slaves to be removed from the land of their origin. The barbarians, besides adding greatly to the number of slaves, suppressed these laws. The Church revived them for her own serfs, and gradually, both by the influence of her example and by the persuasions of Cluniac monks in the various regional councils, got the feudal lords to accept them.[2] Seebohm points out that serf-

[1] Constantine in 332, Valentinian I in 377. Cf. *Cod. Justin.*, XI, xlvii, 2.

[2] St. Ives of Chartres in his *Decretum,* collects many of the ancient canons which imposed upon churches the duty of defending the liberty of freed slaves. See particularly pars xvi, cap. 46-54 (Migne, *P. L.,* 161:915 sqq.). There is an interesting letter of Pope Gelasius I (492-496) to Bishop Bonifacius, which implies that churches had even gone much further than this, and given sanctuary to runaway slaves (Migne, *P. L.,* 59:152). In the laws of St. Stephen, King of Hungary (who died in 1038) there is clear evidence that the manumission of slaves was a frequent act, done out of the motive of Christian charity (Ch. xvii; Migne, *P. L.,* 151:1248). The 66th chapter of the laws of William the Conqueror, granting liberty to any serf who dwelt for a year and a day in one of the King's cities or camps, or in a walled town, is an outgrowth of the Christian practice of monasteries and churches (Cf. Migne, *P. L.,* 149:1320). The freeing of the serfs was necessarily, and wisely, a slow and gradual affair; but it would never have had its beginning except in the spirit of Christian charity. The influence of the great St. Hugh, Abbot of Cluny from 1049 to 1109, in furthering the growth of this spirit both by precept and by example, may be gathered from various details in his life, as recounted in the *Bibliotheca Cluniacensis,* pp. 413-38; 447-62; 557-60. Stubbs, in *Select Charters,* says that serfs might not become clerics or monks, and quotes the Assize of Clarendon, under Henry II, of 1166. But that decision merely repeats the law of cap. xvi, Constitution of Clarendon, 1164, which does not forbid the ordination of serfs, but only cautions that before a serf be accepted as monk or cleric due inquiry be made to safeguard the rights of his feudal lord. The text is: "Prohibet dominus rex ne monachi vel canonici vel aliqua domus religionum recipiat aliquem de populo minuto in monachum vel canonicum vel fratrem, donec sciatur de quali testimonio ipse fuerit, nisi ipse fuerit infirmus ad mortem"—in which latter case, of course, the rights of the serf's lord were on the verge of eternal cancellation.

dom was a transitional stage between slavery and freedom.[1]
And it was the application of Christian principles to feudal
society by and through Cluny which furthered that transition. Peter the Venerable, Abbot of Cluny, replying to the
Apologia of St. Bernard in 1125, says: "We look upon our
serfs, not as slaves and handmaids, but as brothers and
sisters."[2] The way to freedom opened through Christian
charity and the Christian sense of spiritual equality. In
the twelfth century Walter Mapes could say that the villeins
were educating their ignoble offspring in the liberal arts.[3]
In France and Italy serfs increasingly gained their freedom
during the eleventh and twelfth centuries, and serfdom had
practically disappeared by the end of the fourteenth century. There were, obviously, many causes at work in this
change;[4] but a notable impetus comes from Cluny.[5]

---

[1] *The English Village Community*, London, 1833, Vol. 8, pp. 252-
316. He is in agreement with Fustel de Coulanges, *Histoire des Institutions Politiques de l'Ancienne France*, Paris, 1901.

[2] Epist., 28; Migne, *P. L.*, 189:146.

[3] Nicholas Breakspear, who, as Adrian IV, was the only English
pope, had been a serf. He was pope from 1154 to 1159. See his *Life*,
by Cardinal Boso, in Migne, *P. L.*, 188:1351-60.

[4] Many writers have exaggerated the influence exerted through all
the developments of the tenth century by the superstitious fear that
the year 1000 was to see the end of the world. Contemporary records
make clear that, though this fear was widespread amongst the
peasants and the more ignorant of the nobility and clergy, it had
little hold or influence upon the men who were shaping the course of
events, and its influence upon the common people was neither profound nor lasting. See, for instance, the quarrel between Arnulph
and Gerbert (five years later to be the first French pope, under the
title of Sylvester II) over the see of Rheims, and the decision against
Gerbert by Pope Gregory V in 996 (Mansi, *Concilia*, Vol. 19, 103 sqq.
and 173 sqq.). See also the Life and Letters of Sylvester II, pope
from 999 to 1003, in Mansi, Vol. 19, 240 sqq.; especially Sylvester's
letter of 999, proposing to arm Christendom in a crusade to deliver
the holy sepulchre from the hands of the Moslems, in Muratori,
Script., Vol. 3, p. 400, and *Recueil des historiens des Gaules*, etc.,
Palme, Paris, 1874, Vol. 10, p. 426. In the same way, the English monastic and educational reforms of Sts. Dunstan, Ethelwold,
and Oswald, and the famous Abbot of Fleury, during the last quarter of the tenth century, are the work of forward-looking men, not
of men paralyzed by fear of an impending end of the world. In

A restored society ready for intellectual development. It is unwise to forget that all educational development is not merely slow (and not always in a forward direction), but that it is continuous, linking a constant succession of causes and effects. A mere handful of intelligent and energetic men may speed up the process, but only when the mass of men are ready to follow their leadership. It is this fact which at times tempts the historian of education to despair; he can never catch and put upon paper adequately that most elusive yet most important element of development, the temper and spirit of the people. Now it was that temper of the age which Cluny had changed, in every part of society, from the highest nobles to the lowest of the peasants. It is perhaps significant that schools begin to multiply in the eleventh century; but it is more significant that there is a growth of *interest* in things of the mind. Yet it appalls one to find modern historians sneering at the fact that great part of that interest should concern itself with revealed truths. The Christian ideal was finding a home again in the family, that basis of all society. The home life of

the eighteen years he was Archbishop of Canterbury (he died in 978), St. Dunstan founded or restored more than forty abbeys, reformed large numbers of the clergy, and to some extent revived the system of parish elementary schools which had been destroyed in the Danish invasions. See also the *Annales* of Thietmar of Merseburg, for the Germanies, referring to the year 1000; in Pertz, *Mon. Germ. Hist.,* Vol. 5; and the life of Bernward, Bishop of Hildesheim from 992 to 1021, by his teacher Thangmar, in Migne, *P. L.,* Vol. 140. The *Chronicon Venetum* of John the Deacon, in Migne, *P. L.,* 139:871, covers the period to 1008. The only man of note who seems to have been affected by the popular fear was the boy-Emperor, Otho III, crowned in 996, poisoned in 1002 by his mistress, Stephania, whose husband he had ordered beheaded in 997 for a conspiracy against Pope Gregory V. But Otho's age (he was only sixteen when he became emperor) may help to account for the exception.

  5 There is pitiful irony in the fact that later on Cluny too fell into decay, through wealth and the inertia of overgrown numbers and power. Its place was taken by the new reform of Citeaux, under the great St. Bernard. But the incomparable work of Cluny in the education of western Europe was well done before Cluny itself went the way of all human institutions.

Guibert de Nogent, appealingly described in his autobiography,[1] was typical of an increasingly large number of homes. Family life began to take precedence over the business of war. It is a sort of symbol of the age that within little more than a long lifetime, the pirate Normans became builders, founding between 1050 and 1125 a new and admirable style of architecture. Christendom was beginning again to indulge in the luxury of thinking.

Material for intellectual revival supplied in part by Saracens. Left to itself, Europe would have revived the arts and sciences. The peoples who created Gothic architecture and sculpture, who made the glass of the marvelous windows of Saint-Denis and Chartres, who determined the diatonic scale in music, who invented the mariner's compass, and who wove the tapestry of Bayeux, were not intellectually or aesthetically helpless, to say the least. Gerbert, born about 950, who became a monk in the Benedictine abbey of St. Geraldus at Aurillac in Auvergne, might seem to sum up in his one person the learning of the time; and a study of his extant writings, and the life by his disciple Richer, make clear that that learning was not inconsiderable.[2] The ferment of thought in Europe was vigorous.[3] But it moved more swiftly for the help it got from a strange source, the once threatening Saracens or Moors of Spain.

[1] *De Vita Sua sive Monodiarum;* Migne, *P. L.,* Vol. 156. It has been rather clumsily translated into English by C. C. Swinton Bland, Dutton and Co., New York, 1926. See also B. Monod, *Le Moine Guibert et Son Temps,* Paris, Hachette, 1905. Guibert was born at Clermont-en-Beauvaisis in 1053, died Abbot of Notre Dame de Nogent in 1124.

[2] Richerus, *Historiarum Libri IV,* Migne, *P. L.,* 138:17 sqq. See especially lib. iii. Cf. also Picavet, *Gerbert, un Pape Philosophe,* Leroux, Paris, 1897.

[3] Evidences of the intellectual awakening of Europe in the eleventh century are found also in the growth of scholarship outside the monastic and cathedral schools. For the first time in centuries lay teachers begin to appear, and soon become rather numerous. Possibly the elevation to the papacy of Gerbert, the brilliant school teacher of Rheims, stimulated the ambition of men, and pointed to the fact that books might be as useful as the sword in achieving success.

The contribution of the Saracens should not be undervalued. It consisted chiefly in reintroducing to Europe the learning of the Greeks, particularly their writings in philosophy and medicine, and in bringing to Western civilization the great gift of the Hindu numerals and some of their mathematics.[1] But two facts should be remembered, in this connection. The first is that the new acquaintance with foreign learning would have been useless unless the peoples of Europe were actively ready to profit by it. Mere exposure to learning is not education (though many schools are conducted on the supposition that it is). It was what Europeans of the eleventh and twelfth centuries *brought to the new learning* that determined its value to them.[2] The second fact is that, at the very time that Europe was entering upon the astonishing intellectual development of the thirteenth century, the Saracens were slipping back into stagnation and decay.

Cf. Rodulfus Glaber, *Historiarum Libri,* Migne, *P. L.,* 142:611-98. Berengar, of unhappy fame, was one of these teachers. He was born about the year 1000. Cf. *Ep. Adelman.,* Migne, *P. L.,* 143:1264 sqq.

[1] Von Humboldt (*Cosmos,* II, p. 226, note to p. 358) considers it "more than probable . . . that the Christians in the west were familiar with Indian numerals even earlier than the Arabs," and bases his acceptance of the statement on the work of the mathematician Charles, *Aperçu historique des Méthodes en Géometrie,* 1837, pp. 464-72. The question is discussed in the *Comptes rendus de l'Académie des Sciences,* Vol. 8 (1839), p. 78; Vol. 9 (1839), p. 449; Vol. 16 (1843), pp. 156-73, 218-46; and Vol. 17 (1843), pp. 143-54.

[2] Even in the latter half of the tenth century there are evidences of intellectual enthusiasm in the reformed monastic and cathedral schools. See, for instance, Richer's Life of Gerbert, in Pertz, *Monumenta Germaniae Historica,* Vol. 3, and Richeri, *Hist.,* Lib. iii, 47-53, in Migne, 138:102-05, where Gerbert is said to have taught rhetoric from the classic Latin poets, dramatists and satirists, and astronomy with the aid of globes, showing a knowledge of the sphericity of the earth, the elliptical planes, and the movements of the stars. Gerbert's pupil, Fulbert, Bishop of Chartres from 1006 to 1028, and a friend of Odilo of Cluny, founded a great school, or rather re-established an old school, at Chartres, which was deservedly famous. Cf. *Les Écoles de Chartres au Moyen Âge,* by the Abbe Clerval (Memoires de la Societe archeologique d'Eure-et-Loir, Vol. 11, 1895).

The strange history of learning amongst the Saracens.
Lack of space forbids going into any study of the *education*
of the Saracens; but it is important to our history to consider their *learning*. Mohammed, an illiterate man, founded
his religion about 621 A. D. It was not an intellectual movement, but one of militant fanaticism; the Koran, committed
to writing only after the death of Mohammed, is a jumble
of disconnected sentences. The new religion spread rapidly.
Before the close of the seventh century it came into contact
with the cultured peoples of Syria. Some Nestorian monks
had made a Syriac version of the writings of Aristotle and
the neo-Platonists and some of the Greek authorities on
medicine; these they again translated into Arabic. When,
about 750, the Khalifate was moved to Baghdad, some of
the influential Moslems favored the new learning. Harun-al-
Raschid, Khalif from 786 to 809, urged the establishment
of schools. His son, Al-Mamum, who ruled from 813 to
833, founded a great school, with a library and observatory,
at Baghdad.[1] A small number of Moslems developed enthusiasm for study. They borrowed a good deal in mathematics from the Hindus, including, of course, their convenient system of numerals; which we today commonly call
Arabic. But the enthusiasm never spread widely. The
mass of the people looked upon it with suspicion and aversion. Nevertheless it persisted for centuries, based chiefly
upon two noble interests: an interest in medicine, and a
desire to rationalize the fanatic vagaries of Mohammedan-
ism. Both these pursuits reached their best development,
in the East, in Avicenna (Ibn Sina) a Persian physician,
who was born in 980 and died in 1037. However, the popu-

---

[1] By way of comparison, it may be pointed out that Al-Mamum's
astronomers never attained to an accuracy in determining the solar
year equal to the work of the Etruscans (Cf. Niebuhr, *Hist. of Rome*,
Vol. 1, 274) or the even better work of the Mayas in America (Cf.
Humboldt, *Vues des Cordillires et Monuments des Peuples indigènes
de L'Amerique*, p. 125).

lar opposition to learning had been growing, and was driving the scholars out of the East into the new Khalifate of Spain. In the East the movement dwindled into the writing of silly chronicles and lascivious romances. In its new home in Spain it thrived mightily. It became the fashion for men of wealth to collect manuscripts[1] and to act as patrons to scholars. Most of the learning was centered in the study of medicine, based upon the writings of Galen and later of Hippocrates and Aristotle. But the medical studies involved chemistry and even astrology: in the search for the elixir of life and the philosopher's stone and a control of the influence of the stars. These researches often carried keen minds into real philosophy and real discoveries in the sciences. Geber discovered nitric acid, and Rhazes sulphuric acid. Back in the time of Al-Mamum, Ptolemy's geography and astronomy had been translated into Arabic as the *Almagest;* and in 1196 Geber had built an observatory in Seville and made real developments in astronomy. Very many of the so-called 'Arabian physicians' were not Arabs, but Jews; and it was a group of Jewish scholars who founded the famous school of medicine at Montpellier, about 1090. The Moors of Spain were proud of their scholars as physicians, but began to look askance at them when they went into the study of philosophy. The greatest of their philosophers, Averroes (Ibn Roshd), was driven into exile before his death in 1198. The Jews received him and befriended him. After his death, the orthodox opposition to philosophical study triumphed; and in fact all zeal for learning began to die out amongst the Moors of Spain, as it had already died in the East.

How the Saracen learning came into Europe. From the tenth to the close of the twelfth centuries, the peoples of

[1] The Khalif Al-Hakem II (961-76) is said to have gathered together in his library at Cordova 600,000 books and manuscripts. Though this is a manifest exaggeration, the legend testifies to the prestige attaching to the possession of a great library.

western Europe had many contacts with the Saracenic learning developed in Spain. Perhaps the first to be noted is that which came through the Moorish physicians, who were welcomed throughout Europe. Although their primary concern was with medicine, many of them had picked up no small smattering of other sciences. They impressed the awakening intellects of Europe, and were able to give them, both in speech and in writing, a great deal of information. Next, there are indications, in part historical, in part legendary, that Europeans went into Moorish Spain to study. Such a seeker after knowledge was the Englishman, Aethelhard of Bath, often called the greatest English scientist before Roger Bacon. He lived in the time of William Rufus, and probably went into Spain about 1090. Such were the English Robert de Tetines and the Dalmatian Herman, whom Peter of Cluny found studying astrology at Evora when he went there himself to enquire more exactly into Moslem doctrines. Peter persuaded the two to translate the Koran into Latin, in 1143. But the most important of all the media of communication between Europe and the Saracen learning were the Christian Spaniards themselves, who, in the course of the heroic reconquest of their country from the Moors, took over also the intellectual importations which the Moors had made from the Greeks and the Hindus.

The story of the *reconquista* has no place here. Unfortunately, though it is one of the great epic stories of the world, it has very little place in any modern writing of history. From the Battle of Covadonga, in 718, in which King Pelayo defeated the invading and conquering Saracens, and saved the little foothold of the Asturias, to the Battle of Las Navas de Toledo in 1212, covers the most inspiring part of the great struggle, which in its entirety lasted nearly eight hundred years. During the reign of Alfonso VI (1065-1109), Rodrigo Diaz, Count of Vivar, the hero whom the Spaniards call El Cid Campeador, stirred the soul of a whole people. With the capture of Toledo in 1085, the way began to open for a mastering of the Saracen learning. Christian Spain partook of the intellectual revival of all Europe, and she found at hand a considerable store of the ancient lore of the East as material to work with. Most of the men who came from various parts of Europe to profit by the Saracen learning did not actually go to Moorish teachers, but studied in Christian schools attached to monastery or cathedral. So Gerbert had studied, at the Abbey of Cusan in Catalonia, before the close of the tenth century. At the end of the eleventh and beginning of the twelfth centuries, the monastic and cathedral schools of Spain were flourishing; and by 1150, Raymond, the Archbishop of Toledo, had gathered a group of fifty scholars, from nearly all the countries of Europe, to make a huge translation into Latin of all the learning that the Moors had compiled.[1]

Conclusion. This whole chapter is a summary. But to compact it still more, we may say that for a hundred years after the death of Charlemagne Europe was thrust farther back into barbarism by internal conflicts and foreign invasions; that it was raised from this bad state by the renewal of the Christian spirit and the revival of Roman principles of social organization, brought about largely

---

[1] It must not be forgotten that, during the twelfth century, the Crusades brought western Europe into direct touch with the Greeks and other peoples of the East, and were the occasion of at least some slight infiltration of learning into the West. But that, at best, was a thin stream. More came by way of Northern Africa and Sicily. But Spain was the chief channel. Roger Bacon (*Opus Majus*, pars I, cap. xiii) credits the introduction of Aristotle to the version by Michael Scot which appeared in 1230. However, the greatest of the translators was Gerard of Cremona, who was born in 1114 and died at Toledo in 1187, and who turned into Latin more than eighty Arabic works: three on logic, a half dozen on mathematics, a score or more on astronomy and other sciences, and a long list of medical treatises.

through the Cluniac reform; that, with the restoration of some social and moral stability, the intellectual life of Europe began to function once more; and that it providentially found a rich mental provender awaiting it in the antique learning which the Saracens had so strangely carried out of the East. The twelfth century marks the definite passing of the Dark Ages, and the coming of a new civilization, as sharply characterized as has been that of the Greeks and the Romans.

TOPICS FOR DISCUSSION

1. The training of a knight.
2. The place of women in the education of chivalry.
3. The educational function of the Jongleurs.
4. Schools in the Cluniac monasteries.
5. Gerbert and his disciples.
6. The schools of Rheims and Chartres.
7. The libraries of this period.

BIBLIOGRAPHIC NOTE

Source material for the period dealt with in the present chapter may be found in such large collections as Migne, *Patres Latini,* the earlier volumes of *Monumenta Germaniae Paedagogica,* Berlin, 1886 sqq., and *Histoire Litteraire de la France,* begun by the Benedictines of St. Maur, Paris, 1733, and extending to 36 volumes by 1927. The significant *Continuationes Isidorianae* have been edited by Mommsen in Vol. 2 of *Monumenta Germaniae Historica.* A valuable source is Guibert de Nogent's *De Vita Sua, sive Monodiarum Libri Tres,* in Migne, *P. L.,* 156:838-1018, with the notes of Dom L. D'Achery in foll. 1047-1202; it has been rather clumsily translated into English by C. C. Swinton Bland, *The Autobiography of Guibert,* London, 1926. John of Salisbury, *Opera Omnia,* are in Migne, *P. L.,* Vol. 199, and have been translated into English by J. A. Giles, *The Works of John of Salisbury,* Oxford, 1848. There is a great deal of source material on the education of chivalry, although awkwardly presented, in Kenelm Digby, *The Broad Stone of Honour,* 5 vols., London, 1877 sqq. (Vol. 1 first published 1822), and *Mores Catholici, or Ages of Faith,* 11 vols., 1831-40 (reprinted, 3 vols., London, 1845-57, 4 vols., New York, 1888-94). F. J. Furnival has edited *The Babees Book,* London, 1868. For the early history of Cluny, there is *Bibliotheca Cluniensis,* Paris, 1614; republished, Macon, 1915.

On the education of chivalry, see J. Batty, *The Spirit and Influence of Chivalry,* London, 1890; L. Gautier (translated by H. Firth), *Chivalry,* London, 1891; and the popular account in W. S. Davis, *Life on a Medieval Barony,* New York, 1923. The Prolegomena of B. Guerard to his edition of the *Polyptique de l'Abbé Irminon,* 2 vols., Paris, 1844 (new ed. by A. Longnon, 2 vols., Paris, 1886-95) illustrates the feudal relations of an abbey from those of St. Germain de Prés in the time of Charlemagne. There are interesting and valuable data on the education of chivalry in La Curne de Sainte-Palaye, *Memoires sur l'Ancienne Chevalrie,* 3 vols., Paris, 1781; new edition, *Avec une Introduction et des Notes Historiques,* by C. Nodier, Paris, 1826. For the education of women, see A. A. Hentsch, *De la Litterature Didactique du Moyen Age s'Addressant Spécialement aux Femmes,* Cahors, 1903; C. Jourdain, *Memoires sur l'Education des Femmes au Moyen Age,* Paris, 1890. For the troubadours, see J. H. Smith, *The Troubadours at Home,* 2 vols., London, 1899; G. Doutrepont, *Les Types Populaires dans la Litterature Française,* Brussels, 1927, Vol. 1; and J. Bedier, *Les Legendes Epiques,* 3d ed., 4 vols., Paris, 1926-29.

For Cluny, the standard work is E. Sackur, *Die Cluniacenser in ihrer kirchlichen und allgemeingeschichtlichen Wirksamkeit bis zur Mitte des elften Jahrhunderts,* 2 vols., Halle, 1892-94; a brief account is in L. M. Smith, *Early History of the Monastery of Cluny,* Oxford, 1920. The best account of Gerbert is in F. J. Picavet, *Gerbert, un Pape Philosophe,* Paris, 1897. The best single work on the schools of the period is L. A. Maitre, *Les Écoles Episcopales et Monastiques en Occident (768-1180),* Paris, 1866; rev. ed., Paris, 1924. (See pp. 187-202 for libraries.)

On the Saracen contribution to European education, see Ali Amir, *History of the Saracens,* London, 1899; R. Dozy, *Recherches sur l'Histoire et la Litterature de l'Espagne pendant le Moyen Age,* Paris, 1881; H. Middeldorpf, *Commentatio de Institutis Litterariis in Hispania quae Arabes Auctores Habuerunt,* Goettingen, 1810; F. Codera, *Estudios Criticos de Historia Arabe-Española,* Zaragoza, 1903; J. Ribera, *La Ensañanza entre los Musulmanes Españoles,* Zaragoza, 1893; G. Le Bon, *La Civilisation des Arabes,* Paris, 1884; and H. Suter, *Die Araber als Vermittler der Wissenschaften in ihrem Uebergang vom Orient in den Occident,* 2d ed., Aarau, 1897.

For the general situation in education, see S. R. Maitland, *The Dark Ages,* London, 1844 (many reprints); F. A. Gasquet, *English Monastic Life,* London, 1910; L. Reynaud, *Les Origines de l'Influence Française en Allemagne,* Paris, 1913; N. D. Fustel de Coulanges, *Recherches sur Quelques Problèmes d'Histoire,* Paris, 1885, and *Histoire des Institutions Politiques de l'Ancienne France,* Paris, 1901. Some educational details may be found in B. Monod, *Le Moine Guibert et son Temps,* Paris, 1905, and in such biographical studies as these: A. Du Bourg, *Saint Odon (879-942),* Paris, 1905; P. Jardet, *Saint Odilon, Abbé de Cluny: sa Vie, son Temps, ses Oeuvres (962-1049),*

Lyons, 1898. Although St. Gall is earlier than this period, the introduction to Maud Joynt's *Life of St. Gall,* London, 1927, offers valuable
data. For Italy, see G. Salvioli, *L'Istruzione Pubblica in Italia nei
Secoli VIII, IX, X,* Florence, 1898. Concerning the year 1000, besides
the reference mentioned in the text, see J. Roy, *L'An Mille: Formation de la Legende de l'An Mille, Etat de la France de l'An 950 a l'An
1050* (bibliography), Paris, 1885.

CHAPTER IX

SCHOLASTICISM AND THE RISE OF THE UNIVERSITIES

The return of school education to Europe. The work of
education, as has been seen, was carried on for several
centuries without much assistance from schools; and that
lack was, as we know, a great handicap in the work. It
must be insisted upon once more that schools are by no
means essential instruments of education; but they are, or
can be, very useful. Schools are *short-cuts to experience,*
systematized attempts to convey to a new generation, in
condensed formulas, the experiences and acquisitions of
preceding generations. They are limited in their effectiveness (a) by the skill or want of skill of those who formulate these past experiences; (b) by the immaturity of the
students; (c) by the essentially imperfect process implied
in attempts to reduce living knowledge to a theoretical
formula. Within these limits they can be of real and great
value in education: as *supplementary* to the students' actual experience of living, and to the more vital influences
of their homes and surroundings. Now, once again, the
peoples of Europe had reached a stage and condition of
social life which made schools in any number possible; and
the schools began to appear and multiply.

The cycles of school education. It may be of service here
to take a broad preliminary survey of this school education
which, from the twelfth century to our own time, is to play
so large a part in the history of education. A very interesting fact to note is that school education moves in curious
cycles; of which there have been three, clearly marked, in
the past eight hundred years; and a fourth is, apparently,
now well begun. The beginning of these cycles is often

called a 'renaissance,' or rebirth; which is rather an absurd name, springing from the perennial vanity which leads each generation of men to see in its efforts a splendid improvement upon the efforts of preceding generations.[1] Each of these 'renaissances' has been characterized by a strikingly similar cycle of progress: (1) an intense, and fairly widespread, enthusiasm for some particular line of studies is the first stage; (2) then comes a period of more careful organization in the studies; (3) then a fixed method, a formula of procedure, tending to become more and more rigid and dwarfing in importance the actual subjects studied; (4) then boredom, discontent, reaction, ending in (5) a final turning away from the now discredited line of study, and the eager acceptance of a new line. Thus the cycle begins over, and repeats itself with exquisite precision. In a large view, the process is both amusing and pathetic. To add to the humor, we may note that the close of each cycle sees the recurrent use of a wildly exaggerated appeal to the theory of 'formal discipline' for a justification of the waning system. We shall have to consider that theory in its place.

Dominant subjects in each cycle. The subjects that

[1] The only 'renaissance' that in some way really deserves such a name is the one that took place in the eleventh and twelfth centuries. So far as schools are concerned, that was a genuine 're-birth,' inasmuch as schools had so nearly ceased to exist in the preceding centuries. But it must be noted that the term 'renaissance' has a wider range than this application to schools. In that wider meaning, in which it embraces the whole culture of a people or of a world, it is much more tragic than conceited; since it is an implicit confession that the culture of the time is decaying. Indeed, there is even much humility of mind in each of the great 'renaissances,' in so far as the men who bring them about turn to an earlier generation for light on the problems of living. So, when Roman culture failed, there was a 'revival' of a dead Greek culture. When that earlier Greek civilization failed, there was in Greece a 'revival' of a dead Eastern culture. There are manifest strong agencies at work today toward a 'revival' of mediaeval culture. We can never entirely get away from our roots in the past; that past which repeatedly revenges itself on our scorn of it by becoming again a present.

claimed enthusiastic attention in the schools of the first 'renaissance,' from the twelfth to the middle of the fifteenth centuries, were predominantly logic and metaphysics; during the second 'renaissance,' from the middle of the fifteenth to the end of the eighteenth centuries, Latin and Greek 'classic' literature; during the third 'renaissance,' from the eighteenth to the latter part of the nineteenth centuries, the positive sciences. At present we are developing in our schools an enthusiasm for the application of these positive sciences to industry, communication, and comfort of living.

These cycles closely bound up with social changes. In order to keep our view clear upon education in general, it must be recalled that these cycles in school education have been associated with great social, religious, and political changes, which are, in many ways, much more important in education than the changes in the school, and which have even conditioned the school changes, since the schools by their very nature must follow the social environment. Thus, for example, the school change from metaphysics to a borrowed antique literature came upon the heels of an increase in wealth and material comfort of living, and was accompanied by a change from the principles of Christianity to an outworn, but ever appealing, pagan delight in the world of the senses. The change from 'classic' literature to positive science was influenced, not merely by the striking scientific discoveries of a handful of geniuses in the seventeenth century, but also, and profoundly, by the breaking away of a large part of Christendom from Catholic unity and the consequent growing skepticism in the separated fragments.[1] With it came an increase of individualism in

---

[1] "History shows that the inevitable tendency of non-Catholic opinion is to sporadic division and individualism." Sir Samuel Dill, *Merovingians,* p. 93. The late Sir Samuel Dill was not a Catholic.

society, and of so-called democratic forms of government.[1]

And each still affected by its predecessors. The whole process is enormously complicated, as all living activities are. For one thing, each cycle is not so sharply set apart as might be indicated in this brief summary; but instead, carries over a confused heritage, from one generation to another, from one cycle to another, of educational methods largely discredited yet still curiously persisting. Schools, like men in general, drag a lengthening chain of memories. One may be tempted to sympathize, at least momentarily, with Rousseau in his desire to sever the chain and leave it behind him. But of course the thing cannot be done. Then too the swirling cross currents of social changes strongly affect life in the family as well as procedure in the schools; sometimes with consequences which set the home and the school in conflict. It is easy for the historian to ignore that great fact, and to look upon schools as isolated instruments of education. To make matters still worse, these eight hundred years are a period of quarrel between upholders of diverse educational procedures: a fact which adds to the difficulty of being even honest and unbiased in trying to outline their history. A great many histories of education blow up about the year 1100.

It will be a natural division of the later history of Western education to consider each of the cycles of school education; attempting, at the same time, to keep in mind the very important forces, other than the schools, which shape the development of each new generation of men.

The first cycle: logic and metaphysics. Interest in sharp, hard, clear thinking was no new thing to men; but it offered considerable novelty to the tumultuous peoples coming out

---

[1] Perhaps it is scarcely necessary to note that changes in school curriculum lag a long way behind those in general interests. For instance, a marked general interest in the positive sciences existed for fully a century before it affected the schools.

of the semibarbarism of the 'Dark Ages.' Metaphysical speculation, that last fine luxury of the mind, had fascinated ages long since dead. It began again to fascinate the peoples settling down, after their centuries of turmoil, into a shaped and coherent mediaeval civilization. The Catholic Church, with her divine mission of spreading certain exact, definite, though often incomprehensible, truths, had done most of the shaping of that civilization. Its truths offered a field for organized, systematic thought. Its mysteries provoked speculation. When leisure came to Europe, the challenge was accepted. It was often riotously, exuberantly accepted; and led to heresy, to an implicit or explicit rejection of the truths themselves. Then, and only then, did the raw metaphysician find himself in opposition to the supernaturally endowed guardian of the truth. For the rest, churchmen encouraged the new intellectual interest, indeed took a foremost part in it; and it thrived mightily.[1]

[1] The twelfth and thirteenth centuries were rich in heresies; and these are often hailed today as evidences of superior rational development amongst men. Yet it is a plain fact, and one not astonishing to the thoughtful mind, that these heresies are singularly lacking in originality. Nothing in the history of man seems so painfully stereotyped as his intellectual and emotional revolts. The Bogomili, apparently the first of the significant mediaeval heretics, came out of the East, from the borderland between Christianity and Islam. Intellectually, they date back to the Persian Manes, and the fourth century Manichaeans. The many European sects of the 'Cathari' (the Pure) derive from the Bogomili. Some modern Protestants like to think that they derive from the Cathari. Many of them still raise a cry against the Catholic Church, because it strove to protect its truths against these revolts; and accuse it of obscurantism, because it refused to admit novelties in its doctrines. But whether one likes the Catholic Church or not, it is intelligent to recognize that, granted its concept (which alone marked it as a Church), it was bound to reject opposing doctrines, and to guard against the corruption of what it held to be truth. Thus, even the new enthusiasm for Aristotle underwent an ecclesiastical scrutiny during the first half of the thirteenth century. In 1215, the Papal Legate at Paris forbade teachers to lecture on Aristotle. In 1231, Pope Gregory IX appointed a commission to expurgate his works before they might be used in the schools. Yet thirty years later, we find Aristotle accepted freely everywhere, with all ecclesiastical suspicion quite allayed. There is

The genesis of Scholasticism. There had been great minds exercised in this same organization of thought and in metaphysical speculation, long before intellectual darkness had crept out of the forests of Europe with the barbarians. Their writings were at hand, voluminous, weighty: Tertullian, Cyprian, Jerome, Ambrose, and greatest of all, Augustine. Cassiodorus at the Vivarium in Italy, Isidore in Seville, had made redactions of these: clumsy enough, without the personality and charm of the original writers; but reduced to the tabloid form perhaps best suited to a people beginning to take the first tottering steps out of their intellectual infancy.[1] Aristotle supplied the method, the cold, hard method of formal logic. Formal logic is not a glory of the human mind, but a sign of its weakness. The syllogism is a mental crutch. A finer intelligence than ours would not move upon truth by slow and laborious inference; it would apprehend. But for halting human beings the syllogism is a pitiful necessity. Armed with it, the mediaeval peoples set out in the footsteps of the great thinkers of the fourth and fifth centuries. That was the real genesis of Scholasticism.[2]

Scholasticism not a conscious, planned development. Few, if any, of the great movements in society are consciously and definitely planned.[3] Like Topsy, they 'just grow.' A

---

an excellent brief discussion of intellectual liberty in the Middle Ages in Haskins' *The Renaissance of the Twelfth Century*, pp. 360-65.

[1] And whilst our historians are sneering at the compends of Isidore, they might also think for a moment of the almost incredible popularity today of "Outlines of History," "Outlines of Science," "Outlines of Philosophy," and the like. There is food for thought in the comparison.

[2] The name is derived from the title of "Scholasticus," the head of a cathedral school.

[3] Some maintain that the revolutionary movement, evident in Western history since the early 18th century, and still functioning very vigorously, is a planned social movement; and that the three "Internationales" are connected in a direct and purposive line of descent. Cf. *World Revolution* by Nesta Webster, Boston, 1921.

countless multitude of minor changes in agriculture, commerce, manufacturing, housing, social relations, religious practices, ideas of civic government, accumulate through several generations, give to society a certain momentum in a more or less well-defined direction. The men and women who are both the causes and the subjects of these changes scarcely notice them, so gradual are they. But in time they acquire a cumulative power; each one small, the mass of them is great; and they produce a great change, a real revolution in society. As a rule, only the long perspective of history makes clear how great the final change is. It was in this gradual way that Scholasticism developed: from a multitude of causes, operating through a long period of time.

Its character traceable through three preceding centuries. Interest in the logical systemization of knowledge and thought had shown itself for a generation or two in the Carolingian times. Rabanus Maurus had insisted on the value of logical training,[1] had applied an exact logical procedure in his theological dispute with Gottschalk over the knotty problem of predestination, and had made a systematic redaction of patristic commentaries on Scripture.[2] His contemporary, the neo-Platonist John Scotus Erigena, had ventured, on the crutch of logic, into the trackless lands of divine mystery. His exploration not unnaturally led him into heresy; for which, of course, the moderns praise him.[3] Walafrid Strabo, a disciple of Rabanus, polished up his master's *Commentaries* and brought them into more exact systemic form; so that his *Glossa Ordinaria*[4] became a sort

---

[1] *De Cleric. Inst.*, iii, 20; in Migne, *P. L.*, 107:397.

[2] Migne, *P. L.*, Vol. 108. He wrote also, somewhat after the model of Isidore of Seville, an encyclopedia, *De Universo Libri XXII*, Migne, *P. L.*, 111:9-614.

[3] Some of his writings are given in Migne, *P. L.*, Vol. 122.

[4] It takes up two volumes in Migne's collection: *P. L.*, Vols. 113, 114.

of standard and model of system for centuries to follow. The dialectic method of Paschasius Radbertus,[1] Abbot of Corbie, and of Ratramnus,[2] a monk of Corbie, in their controversial works on the Eucharist, are not remote in manner from the theological treatises of three and four centuries later. Thus, although the troublous tenth century, following upon these efforts, made intellectual expansion practically impossible, the lines of future development were already well indicated. When the schools revived, they had a subject matter and a method ready to hand.[3]

Its cradle at Bec. In the very nature of this new enthusiasm for schools, it is rash to assign to any one particular place the honor of having given the first impetus to the movement. Yet this may be ventured: that, as Cluny was the starting point of the important moral and social education of the tenth and eleventh centuries, so the monastery of Bec in Normandy may be looked upon as the radiating center of the interest in intellectual education which was growing into Scholasticism. Bec was founded in 1039 by Herluin, a Norman knight, who became its first abbot; its monks were few in number, poor, and illiterate. But three years after its foundation, there came to it an Italian noble, Lanfranc of Pavia, learned in letters and the law. He was then thirty-seven years old, and had already been engaged in teaching, at Avranches and other places. He had gained a certain notoriety by his disputations with the heretic Berengarius. When he opened his school at Bec, men, lay and clerical, noble and baseborn, came in numbers to hear him. He taught there for some twenty years, and

---

[1] *De Corpore et Sanguine Domini* in Migne, *P. L.,* 120:1267-1350.
[2] Migne, *P. L.,* 121:125-70.
[3] It is interesting to note that the revival took place so rapidly that Guibert de Nogent (died 1124) can complain of a distressing scarcity of teachers in his boyhood, although within his lifetime good teachers had become abundant. (*Monodiarum,* Bk. I, c. IV; Migne, *P. L.,* 156:844.)

reckoned amongst his pupils Ives of Chartres, Anselm of Bagio (who later became Pope Alexander II), and the more renowned Anselm of Aosta,[1] who was to succeed Lanfranc, both at Bec and in the archbishopric of Canterbury. From a time shortly after its beginning, Lanfranc's school never numbered less than a hundred students; and a hundred students made a large school in those days. Many of those students went forth, in their turn, to found other schools, and to carry through Europe the new enthusiasm for studies.

The trivium and quadrivium. The basis of these studies was the long-established system of the seven liberal arts, divided into the trivium and the quadrivium, and formulated as long before as the time of Cassiodorus. The trivium consisted of grammar, rhetoric, and dialectic or logic; the quadrivium, of arithmetic, geometry, astronomy, and music. Medicine was a later supplement to the quadrivium; and all the liberal arts were looked upon as the handmaids to theology, the 'queen of sciences.'[2] In spite of the work of Gerbert, Hermann Contractus,[3] Adelard of Bath,

[1] Born in 1033, died in 1109. His life is excellently written by his companion Eadmer (Migne, *P. L.,* 158:50 sqq.). His works are in Migne, *P. L.,* Vols. 158, 159. His famous argument, proving the existence of God from the very concept of God, is in the *Proslogion,* cap. 2 (Migne, *P. L.,* 158:227).

[2] The theological side of Scholasticism was unquestionably its most important work. Although it was much concerned with purely philosophical and metaphysical speculation, its great accomplishment was that it *dogmatized* Christian truths, set them in molds of rigorous definition, in a *scientific* system. It is much derided for having done that. But is not that a human tendency with all knowledge? Why should we exclude it when there is question of knowledge given us through divine revelation? When Bateson says, "No one can survey the work of recent years without perceiving that evolutionary orthodoxy developed too fast, and that a great deal has yet to come down . . . " (*Darwin and Modern Science,* Cambridge Press, 1909, p. 101) he admits that evolutionists too are *dogmatizing,* gathering fragments of fact, opinion, theory, into a system. All he asks is that they go slowly. The Scholastics had *eleven centuries of Christian teaching* back of them before they began a scientific synthesis.

[3] Writings in Migne, *P. L.,* Vol. 143.

and of the many Jewish and Moorish scholars who influenced European thought, the mediaeval schools in general paid little attention to the physical sciences. The simple fact is, of course, that many of these sciences did not even exist in the Middle Ages. It is scarcely fair, therefore, to carp at the mediaeval schools for neglecting them.

Particular branches of the trivium and quadrivium were emphasized in various schools. Grammar, in the broad sense of a study of the Latin language, was everywhere a fundamental school subject; but the earlier emphasis on rhetoric more and more gave way to the new enthusiasm for dialectic, and this enthusiasm tended even to swamp the quadrivium altogether. The trend of study became more severely and narrowly logical, hard, sharp-edged. However, the ancient scheme of the seven liberal arts, with something in it still reminiscent of Greek balance and grace, was never entirely abandoned throughout the Middle Ages, even when the chief studies had become logic, metaphysics, and scholastic theology.[1] Logic was studied largely in Boethius' translation of the *Categories* and *de Interpretatione* of Aristotle, with Porphyry's *Introduction*. There is evidence of acquaintance with the *Timaeus* of Plato, in a Latin version.[2] Of course, in grammar Donatus continued to be the textbook for beginners: Priscian, and the *Etymologiae* of Isidore, for those more advanced.

The studia generalia. The twelfth-century enthusiasm

---

[1] Hugo of St. Victor has an interesting discussion of the subject matter of studies in *Didascalion,* iii, 4 (Migne, *P. L.,* 176:768-69). See also Henri d'Andeli, *Bataille des septs arts,* in *Histoire littéraire de la France,* t. xxiii, p. 225, in which allegorically, Logic, at Paris, vanquishes Grammar, in its stronghold at Orleans. This was written at Rouen, about 1259.

[2] Even this translation, done by Chalcidius in the fourth century, is incomplete, comprising only the first fifty-three chapters. Aristippus of Catania furnished Latin versions of the *Meno* and *Phaedo* about 1156, but they seem to have made little impression on the students at the time.

for school education was bound to bring about great changes in the character and organization of the schools themselves. For over five centuries, it will be recalled, the types of schools throughout Europe were almost exclusively the monastic and cathedral schools: uniformly small in the number of their students, and closely allied to religious purposes. These were to give place to new types: foremost amongst them those which we now call 'universities,' but which in their earlier stages were known as *studia generalia*.[1] There were also, as we shall see, lesser schools, burgher, guild, chantry.

The rise of the *studia generalia* is closely bound up with another very interesting fact, the growth of towns and cities. The Dark Ages had seen the decay of city life, especially outside of Italy. For centuries, the monastery and the feudal castle were the chief centers of civilization. The great mass of the people lived rather isolated lives, travelled little, had few occasions for wide social relations. But the Crusades, beginning in 1095, stirred men out of their isolation, set them in motion in huge masses, gave them new contacts, not only with their fellows of the West, but with the men of the old Eastern civilization. The result was new ideas, new tastes, new standards of living. Industries began to develop on a larger scale, men banded together for manufacture and commerce, villages grew into towns.[2]

As might be expected, the seething ferment of intellectual life was more marked in the towns than in the sparsely

[1] "Universitas" was originally a legal term, signifying any corporation or group of persons organized for commerce, industry, or like purpose. It was not applied to the great schools until long after their origin.

[2] By the year 1200 there were over two hundred city-republics in Italy alone. In passing, we may refer to one detail of mediaeval life, which has been much misrepresented: cleanliness. For a good account of bathing in mediaeval times, see T. E. Bridgett, *Blunders and Forgeries*, 2d ed., London, 1891, pp. 20-51.

settled countryside. The monastery was no longer the most important center of ideas. Bec gave way to Chartres and Paris. The monastery school had seen the beginning of the twelfth-century renaissance, but it was the cathedral school which carried it on: in a city.

Their origins obscure. Various circumstances, not always clear to us now, determined which of the growing cities should become seats of the new and great schools. Some medicinal springs near Salerno brought the ailing to the place; and therefore brought physicians. A school of medicine was almost inevitable. Great teachers, like Irnerius (who codified civil law) and Gratian (who redacted Church law) drew students to Bologna, or, in the case of William of Champeaux, Hugo of St. Victor, and Abaelard, gathered them to be the making of a university at Paris.

Owing to the gradual character of the change from a cathedral school to a *studium generale,* it is rash to set any very definite dates for the beginnings of the various universities, more especially the earlier ones. Bologna came into recognizable existence some time between 1100 and 1150. The organization of the university was largely in the hands of the students themselves, who elected the rectors of the various *nationes,* paid the professors their salaries, determined the time and manner of lectures. The University of Paris, a more direct growth from the cathedral school of Notre Dame, which William of Champeaux had made famous, became a *studium generale* about 1150, and a recognized university about 1210. In it the corporation of masters, originally licensed to conduct schools by the Chancellor of Notre Dame, was the governing body. Bologna furnished the type of organization for many, if not most, of the universities of the South, and Paris the type for the North. Occasionally, a migration of students from one university led to the founding of another: such as that of the law students from Bologna to Arezzo in 1215 and to Padua in 1222; or that of the Paris students who, according to Rashdall, flocked from Paris in 1167 to swell a small school at Oxford into a university. In one way or another, between 1100 and 1250 some fourteen or fifteen universities came into existence, in France, Italy, Spain, and England.[1] The Germanies developed universities considerably later. At the time of the Reformation the number of universities in Europe is variously estimated at from seventy-seven to eighty-one.

General structure of universities. It is to be noted that, primarily, a *studium generale* or university was a corporation of students with their masters, rather than an impersonal institution, and that it had for its purpose the training of students to be masters in their turn: pretty much like an apprenticeship in one of the craft guilds. It began quite simply in that essential relation of pupil to teacher, though in time it developed a complex social code too elaborate for discussion here. The term of years of study seems to have been generally seven, but with an increasing tendency to shorten that period. Students might enter as young as twelve or thirteen years of age; twenty or twenty-one was the common age for reaching the mastership. After some four years the student became *baccalaureus,* rather equivalent to a journeyman in the craft guild. The ceremony of his admission into this stage was called 'determination.' After three years more came his 'inception' or 'commencement' as a master. Rashdall notes that at least one half of the students did not go on even so far as the *baccalaureatus.*

Student life. The students were by no means drawn entirely from the locality of the school. As a cosmopolitan body, they grouped themselves according to the regions of their origins into *nationes,* which to a greater or less ex-

[1] There is dispute over Salerno. Rashdall denies that there was ever a university there.

tent they determined and regulated by a sort of home rule.
Some of them banded together and lived in a rented hall,
under the management of one of their own number whom
they elected as principal.[1]   Some lodged with the towns-
folk.   They had, from very early times, their own legal
privileges, and were exempt from much of the ordinary
civic control.   They were frequently turbulent.   The often-
quoted account of their disorderly lives, by Cardinal
Jacques de Vitry,[2] who was a student at Paris shortly after
the rise of the *studium generale,* may be representative of
the rude beginnings; but it is too drastic to be true of
university life in general.[3]   After the coming of the friars
(the Dominicans settled at Paris in 1217, at Oxford in
1221; the Franciscans at Paris in 1230, and at Oxford in
1224), colleges were founded for the poorer students, and
discipline was much improved.[4]   But youth, then as now,

[1] Brother Azarias, *Essays Educational,* pp. 111, 113, 123-24.

[2] *Historia Occidentalis,* lib. ii, c. vii.   He was born 1160, died 1240.
In the edition of *Historia Occidentalis,* Douai, 1597, the passage oc-
curs on p. 278.   Rashdall quotes it, *Universities of Europe in the
Middle Ages,* Vol. 2, p. 690.   It is commented on and interpreted by
Denifle, *Universitaten des Mittelalters,* Vol. 1, p. 672.

[3] Possibly the strictures on student conduct are to some extent
based on a comparison with the discipline students were subjected to
in monasteries.   Chapter 21 of the *Decreta pro Ordine S. Benedicti*
of Lanfranc, when he was archbishop, lays down disciplinary regulations for the monastery students which are appallingly stringent: the
strictest surveillance, an attitude of suspicion and mistrust worthy of
a prison.   (Migne, *P. L.,* 150:506-07.)   On the other hand, the daily
order of students, as outlined by Marbodus (1035-1128) in *Carmina
XXX, XXXI* (Migne, *P. L.,* 171:1724) indicates great industry on the
part of the students, a routine of hard work as the normal thing:
four hours of study before dinner; a short period for rest or play
after dinner; then meditation, writing, study until supper; after
which, another brief period for play; and then to bed.   For an excellent short study, see "Life of Medieval Students," by C. H. Haskins,
in Vol. 3, *Amer. Hist. Review,* pp. 203 sqq.   Rashdall, *Universities,*
Vol. 1, p. 218, has a good account of a day's work at Bologna in the
thirteenth century.

[4] The first college was founded at Paris, in 1248, by Pope Innocent
IV for the study of oriental languages, and was followed in 1257, by
the Theological College of Robert de Sorbonne.   These furnished the
model for most of the succeeding colleges.   The first English uni-

was ebullient and rough. Quarrels between 'town and gown' were frequent and violent. The boisterous manners of the age possibly accentuated all this. But we must not let it make us forget that these students worked hard. Their hours of lecture and disputation were long. Poverty forced many of them to wearisome copying out of textbooks. From that poverty also came the custom, distasteful, of course, but not at all looked upon as dishonorable, of spending their vacations in begging tours to gather funds for their maintenance at the schools.

Methods. The mediaeval universities aimed chiefly at intellectual education.[1] The method centered about *books,* and consisted of lectures on the texts by the masters, and disputations carried on by the students under the supervision of the masters. The plan of lecture was analytic: explanation and definition of terms used in the statement of a truth to be discussed; a detailed division and subdivision of the subject matter under consideration, followed by a summary recapitulation; the presentation of problems suggested by the text; and the solving of objections to the doctrine taught. At certain of the lectures, the students were encouraged to ask questions, or to express their doubts, or their opinions on the meaning of the texts. The disputations were of two kinds: the ordinary, which took place every week, and lasted from early morning to noon, or often to evening; and the extraordinary, or *disputatio*

versity college was founded at Salisbury, in 1262, by Bishop Giles of Bridport, "for two chaplains, and twenty poor, honest, and teachable scholars" (A. F. Leach, *Schools of Medieval England,* p. 165). Walter de Merton's college at Oxford, founded the same year, was for future secular priests (Maxwell-Lyte, *History of Oxford University,* pp. 73 sqq.). Colleges were at first looked upon with suspicion, as nurseries for friars. It was not until 1550 that they became dominant in the universities (Maxwell-Lyte, *op. cit.,* p. 69; Brother Azarias, *Essays Educational,* p. 122).

[1] See the treatise *De Magistro* of St. Thomas Aquinas; English translation, pp. 39-86 of M. H. Mayer, *The Philosophy of Teaching of St. Thomas Aquinas,* Milwaukee, 1929.

de quodlibet, which was held only once a year, covered a wide range of subjects, and lasted from two or three days to even a fortnight. Discussion was carried on in strict syllogistic 'form.' Objections were cast in a syllogism or series of syllogisms, and were answered in the rigorously analytic method of dialectic. The method makes for clearness, of a narrow analytic sort, but is cold, rather inhuman, and utterly lacking in persuasion. Out of these lectures and disputations the written works of the doctors were developed. The whole method, with all its good and bad points, survives to this day; and in many Catholic universities, and particularly in ecclesiastical seminaries, survives quite unchanged.

Numbers and influence. Estimates of the number of students in the various universities differ to an almost grotesque extent. Richard Fitz Ralph, who died in 1360, says that Oxford at one time had 30,000 students, and 6,000 in his own time. Wycliffe, who died in 1384, set down 60,000 as the ancient attendance at Oxford, but claimed only 3,000 for his own day. Paris has been credited with as high as 40,000 students at one time. Odofredus gives Bologna 10,000 in the year 1200. All these numbers are exaggerated. Modern estimates allow Paris a maximum of 6,000 or 7,000, Bologna rather less, Oxford between 1,500 and 3,000. The later German universities were still smaller in number of students, ranging from the one hundred or so at Freiburg in 1460 to about one thousand at Prague in 1380.

The total number of students at any time in the Middle Ages was small in proportion to the entire population: though possibly by the fourteenth century it was relatively larger than it is now. But their influence upon the culture of the time was pronounced. They were not numerically strong enough to raise the whole intellectual quality of mediaeval civilization to such a level, say, as that of Greece in the time of Pericles. But they did form a core of accurate and clear-cut thinking which made definite intellectual principles a common possession, in fact a rather amazingly common possession, throughout all Europe; and for one great century they tended to stabilize the civilization of Europe upon a plane of thought more lofty than it had ever before known as a whole. The complete and perfect stability of civilization upon that plane was, of course, not reached; one may reasonably doubt that it ever will be.

The great weakness of the mediaeval universities was that they were almost exclusively intellectual in their character and their influence: an inhuman and dangerous thing. And though something of that danger was lessened by the atmosphere of living faith, of supernatural religion, which clothed the great age of the universities, the blight of intellectualism was to spread more and more over the schools as time went on, and ultimately to render them dry and sterile. The Middle Ages learned the lesson which we today are learning over again; that to unbalance education is to destroy it. The mediaeval universities were concerned with Christian truths, but rather as subject matter for analysis and discussion than as a guide to living.[1] And if the thirteenth century can lay claim to have approached more nearly than any earlier century to a successful combination of training for this life and training for the next, the basis of the claim is not to be found exclusively, or even chiefly, in the work of the universities. There was education of another sort shaping the people. We shall consider it in the next chapter.

TOPICS FOR DISCUSSION

1. The development of scholastic method, from the *Sic et Non* of Abaelard to the *Sentences* of Peter Lombard and the *Summae* of St. Thomas Aquinas.

2. The mystical and rational schools in Scholasticism.

[1] H. Rashdall, *Universities of Europe in Middle Ages,* Vol. 2, pt. 2, p. 687.

3. The function of colleges in the mediaeval universities.

4. Peter of Blois on the relation between metaphysics and the liberal arts.

5. The subjects studied in mediaeval universities.

6. The method of Bernard of Chartres in teaching.

7. Guibert de Nogent on the discipline of students.

8. Mediaeval libraries.

9. The Friars at the universities.

BIBLIOGRAPHIC NOTE

There is a great deal of source material for early scholastic writers and teachers and the beginnings of universities in such collections as Martene and Durand, *Veterum Scriptorum et Monumentorum Amplissima Collectio,* 2d ed., 9 vols., Paris, 1724-33; L. A. Muratori, *Rerum Italicarum Scriptores ab Anno Aerae Christianae 500 ad 1500,* 28 vols., Milan, 1723-51 (new ed., G. Carducci and V. Fiorini, Citta di Castello, 1900 sqq.); Migne, *Patres Latini,* 221 vols., Paris, 1844-64. More narrowly concerned with the early universities are such collections as *Chartularium Studii Bononiensis,* edited by L. Nordi and E. Orioli, 8 vols., Bologna, 1909-27; *Chartularium Universitatis Parisiensis,* edited by H. Denifle and E. Chatelain, 4 vols., Paris, 1889-97; *Munimenta Academica: Documents Illustrative of Academical Life and Studies at Oxford,* edited by H. Anstey, 2 vols., London, 1868 (Rolls Series). The writings of St. Anselm are in Migne, *P. L.,* Vols. 158, 159; John of Salisbury, *Metalogicus,* is in Migne, Vol. 199 (see foll. 866 sqq. for subjects studied, and foll. 854 sqq. for Bernard of Chartres); St. Anselm, *Proslogium,* is translated into English by S. N. Deane, Chicago, 1903 (see also L. F. H. Bouchitté, *Le Rationalisme Chrétien à la Fin du Xie siècle,* Paris, 1842, for French translation of *Proslogium* and *Monologium*); Hugo of St. Victor, *Eruditionis Didascalicae Libri VII,* is in Migne, Vol. 176; the *Opus Majus* of Roger Bacon has been translated into English by R. B. Burke, Pennsylvania University Press, 1928, who also translated Robert Goulet, *Compendium Universitatis Parisiensis, 1517,* Pennsylvania University Press, 1929; L. J. Paetow edited and translated Henri D'Andeli, *The Battle of the Seven Arts,* Berkeley, Calif., 1914, and *The Morale Scholarium of Joannes de Garlandia,* Berkeley, 1927; Pseudo-Boethius, *De Disciplina Scolarium,* is in Migne, *P. L.,* 64:1223-38. Extracts from the sources may be had in R. L. Poole, *Illustrations of History of Mediaeval Thought,* 2d ed. rev., London, 1920; and A. O. Norton, *Readings in the History of Education: Mediaeval Universities,* Cambridge, Mass., 1909. T. F. Crane has translated *The Exempla of Jacques de Vitry,* London, 1890, useful as illustrating student life.

The best brief introduction to mediaeval universities is C. H. Haskins, *The Rise of the Universities,* New York, 1923, and *The Renaissance of the Twelfth Century,* Harvard University Press, 1927 (see *Rise of Universities,* pp. 58 sqq. for libraries; see also his *Studies in Mediaeval Culture,* Oxford, 1929, pp. 1-91 for life of students). The two standard works on mediaeval universities are: H. Denifle, *Die Entstehung der Universitäten des Mittelalters bis 1400,* Berlin, 1885 (he did not live to complete it); and H. Rashdall, *The Universities of Europe in the Middle Ages,* 2 vols. in 3, Oxford, 1895 (new edition shortly expected). On scholastic method, the best book is M. Grabmann, *Die Geschichte der scholastichen Methode,* 2 vols., Freiburg im Br., 1909-11; see also E. Vacandard, *Pierre Abelard et sa Lutte avec Saint Bernard, sa Doctrine, sa Methode,* Paris, 1881; and M. de Wulf, *Histoire de la Philosophie Medievale,* 5th ed., 2 vols., Louvain, 1924-25 (English translation by E. C. Messenger, 2 vols., London, 1925-26).

There are valuable data on the early developments in these: A. Porée, *L'Abbaye du Bec et ses Écoles, 1045-1790,* Paris, 1892; E. C. E. Domet de Vorges, *Saint Anselme,* Paris, 1901; A. J. MacDonald, *Lanfranc, a Study of His Life, Work, and Writing,* Oxford, 1926. For the subjects studied, see Peter of Blois, Ep. 101, in Migne, *P. L.,* 207:311 sqq.; L. J. Paetow, *The Arts Course at Mediaeval Universities,* Urbana, Ill., 1910; and the two very valuable works: C. Douais, *Essai sur l'Organisation des Études dans l'Ordre des Frères Prêcheurs au XIIIe et au XIVe Siècles,* Paris, 1884; and C. Thurot, *De L'Organisation de l'Enseignement dans l'Université de Paris au Moyen Âge,* Paris, 1850. For theology, see G. Robert, *Les Écoles et l'Enseignement de la Théologie pendant la Première Moitié du XIIe Siècle,* Paris, 1909.

For student life, see Guibert de Nogent, *De Vita Sua,* Bk. I, c. 1, n. 5 (in Migne, *P. L.,* 156:837, 962); R. S. Rait, *Life in a Mediaeval University,* Cambridge, 1912; D. C. Munro, *The Mediaeval Student,* Philadelphia, 1895; G. Zaccagnini, *La Vita dei Maestri e degli Scolari nello Studio di Bologna nei Secoli XIII e XIV,* Geneva, 1926; the excellent account of class work in F. Cavazza, *Le Scuole dell' Antico Studio Bolognese,* Milan, 1896; and such histories as J. B. Mullinger, *History of the University of Cambridge,* Cambridge, 1873 (an abridged edition, London, 1888); H. C. Maxwell-Lyte, *A History of the University of Oxford to 1530,* London, 1886; V. de la Fuente, *Historia de las Universidades, Colegios, y demas Establecimientos de Enseñanza en España,* 4 vols., Madrid, 1884-89.

G. H. Putnam, *Books and Their Makers during the Middle Ages,* 2 vols., New York, 1896-97, is a good general introduction to the subject of mediaeval libraries. The *Philobiblion* of Richard de Bury, Bishop of Durham from 1333 to 1345, was edited and translated by E. C. Thomas, London, 1888 (translation published separately, London, 1902 and again 1903). A more thorough work is J. W. Clark,

The Care of Books, an Essay on the Development of Libraries from the Earliest Times, Cambridge, 1901, 3d ed., 1909.   There are excellent brief sketches of mediaeval libraries in F. A. Gasquet, *The Old English Bible and Other Essays,* 2d ed., London, 1908.

For the place of the Friars in the early universities, see H. Felder, *Geschichte der wissenschaftlichen Studien im Franziskanerorden,* Freiburg, 1904; F. A. Gasquet, *Monastic Life in the Middle Ages,* London, 1922; A. Jessopp, *The Coming of the Friars,* 6th ed., London, 1928; W. D. G. Fletcher, *The Black Friars of Oxford,* Oxford, 1882; A. G. Little, *The Grey Friars in Oxford,* Oxford, 1892; and for an excellent summary account of both Friars and colleges, C. B. Dawson, *The Mirror of Oxford,* London, 1912.

CHAPTER X

THE LARGER EDUCATION OF THE MIDDLE AGES

Its agencies complicated. For more than three hundred years historians had represented the Middle Ages as almost completely benighted. Then came a reaction to this gross untruth which was often equally violent and tended to exaggerated praise. For a time the Middle Ages were a battlefield of biased writers. Latterly, under the lead of such accurate and scientific historians as Fustel de Coulanges, Denifle, Maitland, Poole, Langlois, Sandys, Paetow, Rand, and Haskins, a genuine history of the Middle Ages is being written. Cool and dispassionate consideration of the evidence at hand shows us the Middle Ages, from the eleventh century onward, as a period of great achievement in education, which deserves to stand out in history, both for its absolute excellences and by comparison with the educational development of mankind in other ages. The educational agents shaping the minds and characters of Europeans during those centuries which are the real Middle Ages were numerous and complicated. This chapter can try to give only a general survey of them.

The Crusades. First in time, and possibly in importance, are the Crusades. It cannot be too much stressed that these were more than mere military ventures; they were great social and religious movements. They affected, directly or indirectly, every man, woman, and child in Europe. They profoundly influenced thought, feeling, and conduct. They were more significant, in their social effects, than the westward movement of peoples some seven or eight centuries before, which played a considerable part in what we think of as the 'fall of the Roman Empire.' There were four of

160

these Crusades between 1096 and 1204. They began in an amazing enthusiasm, made up, in part of religious zeal, in part of sentimental and chivalrous romance, which gathered the isolated units of Western society into a united activity and a common purpose: the recapture for Christendom of the Holy Land. Although they failed in that purpose, they achieved something much greater for Europe.

Important, though not lasting, in their moral influence. The educational effect of such a gigantic unifying of thought and emotion can scarcely be exaggerated. Its moral results were, as is always the case, only temporary; but whilst they lasted, they were very great: in the sudden sweep of high purpose lifting a crude lot of men, for the moment at least, above the humdrum plodding selfishness of their individual lives. The enthusiasm flickered and very nearly died entirely; and when it was revived, it was revived by motives much more secular in character, by greed for wealth, by mere vagabond love of adventure. The First Crusade was what the modern commercial mind considers a sublime insanity; but even that type of mind concedes that it was sublime. The Fourth Crusade culminated in the brutal sack of Constantinople: it fell to the level of a modern war. In 1095, the cry, "God wills it!" electrified Europe. In 1254, even so chivalrous a man as de Joinville is delicately balancing the call of the Crusade against his castle life in Champagne. In 1270, Rutebeuf's *Descroizié* bluntly argues for staying at home.

Even more important as means of social education. Yet, however much the moral influence of the Crusades diminished, their social effect was maintained and grew. They bound men together with new bonds, they stimulated communal effort, they brought about new industries, new intellectual efforts in organizing human relations, new activities of commerce. The growth of towns and cities is a direct result of the Crusades; the mediaeval guilds are at least an indirect result; and one would be very lacking indeed in historical sense who could not see how powerfully the momentum of closely organized town life influenced the education of Europe. Its effect upon the development of law has been studied. But much more important is its general social effect, upon manners, speech, customs, amusements, worships, industries, and arts.

The guilds. The most significant feature of that town life in the Middle Ages was the guild. There were four sorts of guilds: the strictly religious confraternity of layfolk; the frith (peace) guild, closely allied to the religious; the merchant guild; and the craft guild. Some of the religious and frith guilds date as far back as the early eleventh century, the oldest guild charter extant being that of Abbotsbury in Dorset, in the time of Canute. But the great period of the guilds is in the twelfth and thirteenth centuries. During the reign of Edward I, ninety-two of the one hundred and sixty towns represented in the English parliament had merchant guilds. It was the merchant guilds that formed the basis of the Hanseatic League, which was begun in the thirteenth century, reached the height of its influence in the fifteenth century, and held its last meeting in 1669. The craft guilds were still more important as part of the larger educational influences of the Middle Ages. They were the last type of guild to come into existence, and began to appear in the twelfth century. The merchant guilds promptly had come to be the real executive power in most of the municipalities; but gradually the craft guilds supplanted them. By 1340 there were forty-eight craft guilds in London alone.

Informed with Catholic principles. All of these types of guild were permeated with Catholic principles. Each had its chaplain, its religious services, its masses for deceased members of the guild; each recognized and accepted the moral obligations of charity, care of orphans, justice amongst its members. Each was a relatively small company, a sort of overgrowth of the family, its members so closely bound together that a common spirit animated them. To compare them to modern labor unions is as absurd as to hope to revive them; for one thing, we should first have to revive the Catholic atmosphere of the Middle Ages. Particularly in the craft guilds was this spirit manifest. The members were divided into apprentices, journeymen (from *journée,* the day: as they were paid a daily wage), and masters. The guild demanded a proof of skill in its craft, the 'masterpiece,' as a condition of admission to the grade of master; but it further demanded high moral qualifications before it allowed a master to take any youth as apprentice. The apprentice was bound to a fixed term of training, varying from two to ten years, according to the difficulties of each craft; he lived as a member of the master's household; and the master was bound to give him the best training within his power. Wage disputes were settled within the guild. There were no class distinctions, no falsely opposed interests of employer and employed. Every master was simply an educated apprentice, and every apprentice a future master. Thus the whole industrial life of the towns was essentially a process of education, with carefully planned aims and methods, and with a balance of physical, intellectual, and moral elements which commands our admiration.

Mediaeval architecture and art. Detailed studies of the guilds are matters for the historical experts. But the guilds have left eloquent monuments throughout Europe which must impress even the dullest minds. These monuments are the cathedrals, town halls, and guild halls of the Middle Ages. The architecture and art of a people may always be taken as one of the soundest displays of its culture. They represent, not merely the technical skill of artists and artisans, but the mental and moral qualities of the whole society back of them.   The Parthenon throws light upon the entire fabric of Attic civilization: so too does Chartres illumine the Middle Ages.

A spontaneous growth. Mediaeval architecture and art, which we now rather stupidly call 'Gothic,'[1] is most amazingly the lively and self-originated expression of the Middle Ages. Ralph Adams Cram says very significantly: "Normandy in the eleventh century was simply Cluny in action."[2] From Normandy the new art sprang, and when political turmoil checked its further development there, it leaped up like a flame in the Champagne and the Île de France. The twelfth century saw the growth of architectural structure that still remains one of the great triumphs of human intelligence; the thirteenth century made beauty grow about that structure in exquisite sculpture, glass, and mural decoration. A very passion of church building swept over western Europe. "It was," says Rudolph of Cluny, in the midst of it, "as if the world, shaking itself, and casting aside old things, were putting on a white robe of churches."

And an unmatched educational movement. When a man of today looks at what remains of that 'white robe of churches,' not great cathedrals alone, but parish churches in the smaller cities and towns and villages, he may not realize at first that whole peoples built them. They are not the work of an isolated genius, here and there, but the enthusiastic product of tens of thousands of craftsmen who

[1] The name 'Gothic' is an honored one today, but it was first applied to mediaeval architecture and art as a term of derision. The fifteenth-century 'renaissance' in Italy, enamored of all things Greek and Roman, affected to despise mediaeval art; and because that art had come to Italy through some German craftsmen, it was called 'Gothic' as a synonym for 'barbaric.' Cram insists that its proper name is 'Catholic architecture and art.' But of course such a name would damn it today as thoroughly as 'Gothic' damned it in the mouth of Giorgio Vasari.

[2] *Catholic Encyclopedia,* Vol. 6, p. 667.

seem to our modern minds almost incredibly inspired. There is abundant evidence to show that *each locality* furnished the skilled and devoted craftsmen who built the local church or town hall or guild hall. When we consider, as Thorndike points out, that in our own time skilled workmen are too few even to build a *copy* of a mediaeval church,[1] we may get some concept of the nature and extent of mediaeval guild education.

Mediaeval drama. Another large factor in the education of a people is its drama, which mirrors as well as forms popular taste and ideals. It is most significant of the chaos of the 'Dark Ages' that they had no drama. The old Roman theatre had disappeared entirely, and nothing took its place until Europe was ready to produce a new drama of its own, expressing its own new spirit and its own new concept of art. The mediaeval drama owes nothing directly to antique Greek or Roman models; it is as fresh and vitally new as mediaeval architecture, and like that architecture it centers supremely in Catholic faith and worship.

Its development. Mediaeval drama took its origins from liturgical sources. It may be said to begin as far back as Carolingian times, in the dramatization of sequences in the Mass. Catholic churches were its first habitat, and continued exclusively to shelter it until the twelfth century, when it moved out, first into churchyards, then into town squares and marketplaces. Its structure grew from a brief scene, with a few figures, into complete plays which would not appear at all strange to a Shakespeare. Its language was Latin in the beginning, but Latin was gradually supplanted by the developing vernaculars. Thus in the 'mystery' of *The Wise Virgins,* about 1130, the chorus chants in Latin, Christ and the virgins speak a mixture of French and Latin, the angels speak French only. The *Adam* mys-

---

[1] *History of Medieval Europe,* p. 418.

tery is in French, but all the directions to the actors are in Latin.[1] The subject matter too changes. In the earlier plays the subject is strictly liturgical or scriptural; by the twelfth century, the 'miracles' of saints become more prominent; and in the fourteenth-century 'renaissance' in France and England, the greater number of plays are 'moralities,' concerned with a personification of vices and virtues.[2] The institution of the feast of Corpus Christi in 1264 gave a great impetus to mediaeval drama.

Its influence. Mediaeval drama was much more intimately a part of common life than is modern drama. It was produced, not by a small group of professional actors, but by the people themselves. The plays quite simply grew up in the parishes and the guilds. They had the same local influence that mediaeval architecture had, since they drew their performers from the same town or village group which furnished the audience. There is a manifest educational character in this close conjunction of the drama with the people. It may not make for the highest dramatic art, but it does stimulate very widely the impulse to dramatic expression. After many generations, our 'little theatres' are trying to get back to it today. Further, as an important work of education, the mediaeval drama admirably Christianized one of the chief recreations of the people.

Mediaeval poetry. It is not too much to say that the huge masses of the mediaeval people had a finer apprecia-

---

[1] The oldest extant English play, *The Harrowing of Hell,* dates from the thirteenth century. There are one hundred and eight of the earlier mystery and miracle plays still in existence. *The Towneley Mysteries,* published by the Surtees Society, 1836, contains thirty-three plays, which cover almost the complete historical outline of the Old and New Testaments. The 1912 edition of *Everyman* (Everyman's Library, London and New York) contains eight miracle plays, in modernized English, including *The Harrowing of Hell;* and has a useful introduction.

[2] The 'miracle' plays of the fourteenth century are almost all about our Lady. Forty-two of them survive.

tion of poetry than many even of our 'educated' people have today. It is hard to imagine an average college graduate of the present getting as much enjoyment out of poetry as did the simple common folk of the Middle Ages. Their poetry, like their drama, grew out of the Church. The mediaeval hymns led the way into new forms of Latin verse,[1] into the development of vernacular verse. To the modern mind the mingling of sacred and profane subjects in mediaeval poetry is often shocking; but it was not shocking to a people for whom the most sacred elements of religion were part of their daily life. It is not without significance that the composition and popular spread of the *chansons de gestes* are bound up with religious pilgrimages, or that the wildest burlesques of the *carmina burana* are linked with Catholic worship. The road to Compostela or to Rome was, in the Middle Ages, also the road to Parnassus. The technical excellence of that poetry, both religious and secular, is very high.[2] For all its simplicity, it is vivid, intensely imaginative, melodious. And it went everywhere, was chanted in hovels as well as in castles. From mouth to mouth it travelled across western Europe, for books were scarce, and the people depended more upon hearing than upon reading. There was not a tavern in Europe that had not often rung to the splendor of epic song. The wandering minstrel of the Middle Ages was a great educator.

[1] Mediaeval *rhymed* verse appears here and there even in the four thick volumes of *Poetae Latini aevi Carolini*. It reached its finest development in the twelfth century. Abaelard wrote great poetry. The *De Contemptu Mundi* of Bernard of Morlaix, a Cluniac monk, is an astonishing work of versification in intricate triple rhyme. It contains nearly three thousand hexameter lines, and was written about 1140 and dedicated to Peter the Venerable, Abbot of Cluny. It has been edited by Thomas Wright, Master of the Rolls Series, Vol. 59 (ii), 1872.

[2] See the interesting technical discussion of mediaeval poetry in G. Kar, *Thoughts on the Mediaeval Lyrics,* Oxford, 1933; and for a handy collection of original texts (with English translation by H. Waddell), *Mediaeval Latin Lyrics,* London, 1929.

The lesser schools. All these social, industrial, commercial, religious, and aesthetic activities are most vital agencies of popular education. The fact that they are not formally and consciously educational increases, rather than lessens, their influence upon the people. But to our modern minds, rooted in the mob conviction that formal schools are the most important means of education, it may be of comfort to know that the Middle Ages were also well supplied with schools. These were of several sorts: grammar schools attached to cathedral or collegiate churches, chantry schools,[1] parish schools, burgh or town schools, guild schools, 'venture' schools conducted privately.

The work of the Church. As is to be expected, the earlier elementary and grammar schools were always bound up with some church or monastery or hospital. Even in the twelfth century, most of these schools were actually conducted in a church or monastery;[2] and when they multiplied so as to need space beyond the church, they were still taught by priests and clerics. There was some jealousy of the growing schools. Bishops and abbots were loath to see them pass in any way from under their immediate control. The Third Lateran Council, in 1179, had to forbid local authorities to exact money from schoolmasters for license to teach,[3] and the Fourth Lateran, in 1215, had to renew the decree. But this only shows that the Church as

[1] Endowed schools connected with some chapel or church, in which the priest was bound by terms of the endowment to chant Mass for the repose of the souls of the founders, and to teach a certain number of children free of charge. It is estimated that there were over three thousand such chantries in England at the time of their suppression in the 'Reformation'; and though there is much uncertainty as to how many of them had schools attached, the most hostile reckoning concedes that there were some three hundred chantry schools.

[2] See the story of Reginald of Durham, in Grant, *History of the Burgh and Parish Schools of Scotland,* p. 5.

[3] Mansi, *Conc. Ampl. Collectio,* tom. xxi, col. 523, canon xviii. Pope Alexander III made notable efforts to increase schools, and to make them readily accessible to the poor. Cf. Leach, *Schools of Medieval England,* pp. 132, 133.

opposed to some churchmen, was doing all it could to facilitate the spread of schools. When the first new enthusiasm
for schools for the people at large began to affect Europe,
there were no religious orders dedicated to teaching; these
were first instituted only in the fourteenth century, one of
the earliest and most noted being the Brothers of the
Common Life, founded at Deventer by Gerard Groot, about
1380. But in the meantime the Church fostered schools by
every means which it found to hand.[1]

Increased steadily. It was naturally the demand for
schools which caused the supply of them to grow. In the
tax rolls of Philip the Fair, for the year 1292, Paris is
shown to have, outside of the many church schools, eleven
schoolmasters and one schoolmistress. Within sixty years
the number had grown to forty-one masters and twenty-two
mistresses. Grant says that by the fifteenth century
"schools were planted in every considerable town in Scotland."[2] Babeau asserts that schools were relatively more
numerous in mediaeval France than in modern times.[3]
Leach, from a careful compilation of figures taken from
contemporary records, estimates that in England, in the
fourteenth century, there was one grammar school to every
5,625 people, as contrasted with one to every 23,750 people
in 1864.[4] This means a supply of schools in the fourteenth

---

[1] "There can be no manner of doubt that all the cathedral and
collegiate churches kept schools, and that the schoolmaster was one
of the most important of their officers, and school teaching one of
the most important of their functions." Leach, *Schools of Medieval
England*, p. 115. "It may be stated with some confidence that, at
least in the later middle age, the smallest towns and even the larger
villages possessed schools where a boy might learn to read and to
acquire the first rudiments of ecclesiastical Latin, while, except in
very remote and thinly populated regions, he would never have to
go far to find a regular grammar school." H. Rashdall, *Universities
of Europe in the Middle Ages*, Vol. 2, p. 602.

[2] *History of the Burgh and Parish Schools of Scotland*, p. 25.

[3] *L'Instruction Primaire dans les Campagnes avant 1789*, p. 41.

[4] *The Schools of Medieval England*, p. 331.

century about four times more abundant than in the nineteenth.

The character of the schools. In spite of natural diversities, the mediaeval elementary and grammar schools are of a distinct and common type. They were mostly small schools,[1] and most frequently under a single teacher. Although there was, of course, progression in studies, there was no distinction of grades, no grouping into classes, but each pupil was taught individually, just as had been done in Athenian schools of fifteen centuries earlier.[2] The discipline was rigorous; the bundle of rods was the schoolmaster's insignia.[3] Until the close of the Middle Ages, the first instruction was in Latin, the vernacular coming later.[4] The Catholic religion and Catholic practices, as is obvious, were interwoven with other instruction, since the whole Western world was still Catholic. After his ABC book (and even that contained Latin prayers), the child's first book was the collection of psalms and prayers for the

[1] The number of pupils might be as small as twenty or thirty, and very rarely was more than a hundred and fifty. Leach, *ibid.,* gives some definite figures, p. 330.

[2] John of Salisbury (1110-1180) in *Metalogicus,* lib. ii, cap. x, gives a sketch of school occupations which impress us by their variety, and which might come with a shock of surprise to modern opponents of the simultaneous method.

[3] Though St. Anselm of Bec had shrewdly argued against the rod (Cf. Drane, *Christian Schools and Scholars,* 2d ed., 1881, p. 314) yet Guibert de Nogent, born a generation after him (c. 1053), tells us of getting such a severe beating in school that his mother in tears wished to forbid him to continue his studies. *Monodiarum,* lib. i, cap. 6 (Migne, *P. L.,* 156:894).

[4] The change to primary instruction in the vernacular was not completed in England until the sixteenth century. (Cf. Mulcaster, *Positions,* p. 31.) St. Jean Baptiste de la Salle had a hard struggle to introduce the change in France in the seventeenth century. "In the twelfth century the common language of western Europe was Latin. . . . Men prayed in Latin, sang in Latin, preached in Latin. . . . It was the language of learning and education everywhere. . . . Latin remained a living language until it was killed by the revival of antique standards in the fifteenth century." C. H. Haskins, *The Renaissance of the Twelfth Century,* pp. 127-29.

Sunday 'office.'[1] Reading was more stressed than writing. Indeed, up to the fifteenth century, the general run of people were but little able to write. One reason for that is that writing was looked upon as a professional work, and since the schoolmaster was also frequently the village scribe, he jealously guarded his privilege, and was not eager to teach his art to others.[2] Arithmetic was mostly limited to little more than simple enumeration. Even though Leonardo Febonacci, a Pisan merchant, published a book on arithmetic in 1202, in which he used what we now call the Arabic notation, and decimals, the primary schools did not study arithmetic during the Middle Ages. There is no mention of it in the schools up to 1541.[3]

Management of schools. In the management of such small schools, with so limited a curriculum, and with the comparatively simple methods of individual instruction, the chief problem of management was the supply of competent teachers.[4] It may seem curious to many persons that the procedure for the control of teachers should have changed so little from the Middle Ages to the present time. It consisted in the grant of a license to teach, issued by various corporate bodies: such as a cathedral chapter, or its official, a chancellor of a university or a diocese. In some

[1] "Beyond a doubt we must attribute to the study of the psalms made in school the universal taste preserved by all classes of mediaeval society for the almost daily recital of the psalter." De Charmasse, *Etat de l'Instruction Primaire dans l'Ancien Diocese d'Autun,* Paris, 1878, p. 22. See also P. J. McCormick, *Education of the Laity in the Early Middle Ages,* Washington, 1915.

[2] Cf. E. Rendu, *De l'Education populaire dans l'Allemagne du Nord,* p. 8.

[3] Even in 1719, an arithmetic published at Lille, and called "Instruction nouvelle pour enseigner aux enfants le chiffre et a sommer," was looked upon as a novelty. Resbecq analyzes it in his *Histoire de l'Instruction Primaire dans le Departement du Nord,* Paris, 1878, pp. 84, 85.

[4] With all our complications of schools, that may be said to be still the chief problem of management. It is an open question whether or not we have made any nearer approach to a solution of it.

cases, the license was granted "only to those who had already shown their capacity by actual teaching under supervision."[1] But so much care was not always taken. There were plenty of wandering schoolmasters, 'vagantes,' 'grammarians,' such as Erasmus so bitterly describes in the *Encomium Moriae*.[2] In time, each town of any considerable size took over the control of licenses and of schools; and guild schools and venture schools merged into burgh schools. It was naturally a gradual process, and although the resultant organization varied somewhat in different towns, its general similarity throughout Europe was striking. The Middle Ages had a genius for uniformity, because of the spiritual and traditional bonds which linked one country with another. Such uniformity, however, could not, and did not, extend to the age at which children began to go to school; that age, and the number of years spent at school, obviously varied with varying conditions and circumstances. But roughly we may estimate three or four years of school as the average for the great mass of children. The school day was long, beginning at half-past seven in the summer and an hour later in winter.

Games. As in all ages, mediaeval children played various games of ball, the most popular being football and a form somewhat resembling hockey. In another game, two contestants, standing each on one leg, and putting the soles of their free feet one against the other, strove by pushing to topple each other over. They tilted at rings, in imitation of the jousts. They flew hawks. But the prime school-boy

[1] In the "Ancient Ordinances for Masters in Grammar" of the thirteenth century. Cf. Leach, *Schools of Medieval England,* pp. 174, 175. The method of our normal schools is nearly as ancient as all else in school education; but their distinct organization dates only from St. Jean Baptiste de la Salle.

[2] Pp. 34, 35 of ed. Florentiae, 1518. In translation by White Kennett of 1683, edited by H. Bridges, Chicago, 1925, pp. 108-12. See also H. Waddell, *The Wandering Scholars,* London, 1927.

sport was cockfighting, or, where the boys were too poor to own fighting birds, the still more savage sport of chasing and killing a cock with sticks.[1]

Financial support of schools. Most of the earlier primary schools were endowed by pious founders, and made no charge for tuition. The guilds also maintained free schools in some places. When the towns took over existing schools or established new schools, they usually made some provision for their support from communal funds. But as the number of pupils grew, these ancient foundations frequently became inadequate, and had to be supplemented by fees. In general, throughout the Middle Ages, the schoolmaster was both more respected and better paid than in classic antiquity; in many of the English schools, for instance, his salary amounted to three or four times the wages of a skilled craftsman.[2]

Town and country. Schools were by no means limited to the towns, yet in general town children fared better than country children in opportunities for school education, just as they do today. The children of burghers, merchants, craftsmen, had no legal disabilities in the way of their schooling, but the children of farm laborers had. It must be remembered that the common people of the countryside were still in thrall under the feudal system, and were only gradually being freed from serfdom. In England, it was only as late as 1406, in the 'Statute of Apprentices,' that all restrictions regarding school were lifted from the farm-laborers. Up to that time, the villein had to get leave of his feudal lord to send his child to school, and failure to

[1] Leach, *Schools of Medieval England*, p. 174. In many instances, the schoolmaster himself was bound to furnish the cocks. Delisle cites a schoolmaster of Dieppe, in 1282, who was under obligation for four. *Études sur la Classe Agricole en Normandie au Moyen Âge*, p. 185.

[2] Leach gives some detailed statistics concerning fees and salaries, *op. cit.*, pp. 171-75, 184, 196, 210, 211.

get such leave was punishable by fine. It must be said, however, that in the thirteenth and fourteenth centuries such leave was generally granted. But the mere fact of having to ask for it militated to a great extent against school education for children outside the towns.

Conclusion. It would be absurd to claim that these various agencies of education achieved anything approaching perfection in the development of the people of mediaeval Europe. But it would be unfair to deny that they did accomplish a great deal. They did develop in the people a broad grasp of great truths, a sound moral judgment, an appreciation of beauty, many social virtues, and a considerable capacity for organization. They did not appreciably raise the level of material living, in comfort of housing, sanitation, hygiene, and means of communication; and for that reason, we of today, who so highly esteem our progress in these matters, are likely to undervalue the great educational work of the Middle Ages, which was decidedly more in the spiritual than in the material order. It was very imperfect in that order too; but it lifted Europe to a balance between the temporal and eternal which it had never known before and seems never to have gained again since that time. That balance is the chief aim of Christian education.

TOPICS FOR DISCUSSION

1. The educational effect of the Children's Crusades.
2. The influence of the Crusades on hospitals and medical education.
3. The guild schools.
4. Comparison between mediaeval parish players and the modern "Little Theatre."
5. The relations between education and material progress in the Middle Ages.
6. The intimacy of mediaeval religion as shown in the miracle plays.

BIBLIOGRAPHIC NOTE

A good collection of sources for the Crusades is *Recueil de Historiens des Croisades,* 16 vols., Paris, 1841-1906. Some source illustrations for the guilds may be found in *Documents Relatifs a l'Histoire de l'Industrie et du Commerce en France,* edited by G. Fagniez, 2 vols., Paris, 1898-1900. For architecture, see *De Consecratione Ecclesiae Sti. Dionysii,* and *De Rebus in Administratione sua Gestis,* in *Oeuvres Completes de Suger* (Abbot of St. Denis, 1121-51), edited by Lecoy de la Marche, Paris, 1867; also in Migne, *Patres Latini,* 186:1211-1468. For mediaeval hospitals, see L. Le Grand, *Statuts d'Hotels-Dieu et de Leproseries: Recueil de Textes du XIIe Siècle,* Paris, 1901; E. Nicaise (ed.), *La Grande Chirurgie de Guy de Chauliac,* Paris, 1890. For mediaeval poetry, besides the sources mentioned in the text, see M. Edelstand du Meril (ed.), *Poesies Populaires Latines du Moyen Age,* Paris, 1847, and *Poesies Inédites du Moyen Age,* Paris, 1854.

An excellent general discussion of this period in education is H. O. Taylor, *The Mediaeval Mind,* 4th ed., 2 vols., London, 1927. There are some interesting details in C. G. Crump and E. F. Jacobs, *The Legacy of the Middle Ages,* Oxford, 1926; C. V. Langlois, *La Vie en France au Moyen Age de la Fin du XIIe au Milieu du XIVe Siècles,* 4 vols., Paris, 1924-28; L. Delisle, *Etudes sur la Condition de la Classe Agricole en Normandie au Moyen Age,* Evreux, 1851, new ed., Paris, 1906; F. J. Furnivall, *Manners and Meals in Olden Time,* London, 1868; P. Boissonade (translated by E. Power), *Life and Work in Mediaeval Europe,* New York, 1927; J. J. Jusserand, *English Wayfaring Life in the Middle Ages,* 3d ed., London, 1925; B. Jarrett, *Social Theories of the Middle Ages,* Boston, 1926; E. M. Hulme, *The Middle Ages,* New York, 1929.

On the Crusades in general, see L. Brehier, *L'Église et l'Orient au Moyen Age: les Croisades,* 5th ed., Paris, 1928; E. Barker, *The Crusades,* London, 1923. For their cultural results, see O. Henne am Rhyn, *Kulturgeschichte der Kreuzzuge,* Leipzig, 1894. For the Children's Crusades, see G. de Jannsens, *Etienne de Cloyes et les Croisades d'Enfants au XIIIe Siècle,* Paris, 1890. For the effects on medical education, see H. Haeser, *Lehrbuch der Geschichte der Medicin und der Volkskrankheiten,* 3d ed., Leipzig, 1872-82; and J. J. Walsh, *Education: How Old the New,* New York, 1910, and *Old Time Makers of Medicine,* New York, 1911.

For the miracle plays, see K. A. von Hase (translated by A. W. Jackson), *Miracle Plays and Sacred Drama,* London, 1880; K. Young, *The Drama of the Medieval Church,* 2 vols., Oxford, 1933; E. K. Chambers, *The Mediaeval Stage,* Oxford, 1903; F. G. Bates, *English Religious Drama,* New York, 1902; M. Sepet, *Les Origines Catholiques du Theatre Moderne,* Paris, 1901. For mediaeval poetry, see J. Bedier, *Les Legendes Epiques,* 2d ed., Paris, 1921; E. Faral, *Les*

Jongleurs en France au Moyen Age, Paris, 1910; J. A. Schmeller, *Carmina Burana,* 3d ed., Breslau, 1894.

Something of the part the arts played in mediaeval education may be gathered from C. Norton, *Church Building in the Middle Ages,* New York, 1902; J. Addison, *Arts and Crafts in the Middle Ages,* Boston, 1908; L. Pillion, *Les Sculpteurs Français du XIIIe Siècle,* Paris, 1912; G. Baldwin Brown, *The Arts in Early England,* 5 vols., London, 1903-21; F. H. Kendon, *Mural Painting in English Churches during the Middle Ages,* London, 1923; W. Lethaby, *Mediaeval Art,* London, 1904, rev. ed., 1912, *Westminster Abbey and Craftsmen,* London, 1906; and E. S. Prior, *The Cathedral Builders in England,* London, 1905.

There are some data about the early common schools in E. Allain, *L'Instruction Primaire en France avant la Revolution,* Paris, 1881; J. Resbecq, *Histoire de l'Instruction Primaire dans le Departement du Nord,* Paris, 1878; E. Rendu, *L'Education Populaire dans l'Allemagne du Nord,* Paris, 1852; A. E. Leach, *The Schools of Medieval England,* London, 1915; J. Grant, *History of the Burgh and Parish Schools of Scotland,* London, 1876; F. A. Gasquet, *Parish Life in Mediaeval England,* London, 1909.

On the part played by the guilds, see G. Renard (translated by G. H. D. Cole), *Guilds in the Middle Ages,* London, 1919; L. Olivieri, *Le Forme Medievale d'Associazione,* Ancona, 1890; Toulmin Smith, *English Gilds,* London, 1870. For the development of town life, see F. G. Bates, *The Emancipation of Mediaeval Towns,* New York, 1908; H. Pirenne, *Les Villes du Moyen Age,* Brussels, 1927; F. Schevill, *Siena: The Story of a Mediaeval Commune,* New York, 1909.

CHAPTER XI

The Break-up of Mediaeval Education

The nature of the catastrophe. Moral equilibrium is always an unstable equilibrium; unfortunately, it even takes very little to upset it. Europe had reached, in the thirteenth century, a momentary moral equilibrium. In the fourteenth century, it toppled and crashed. That, in briefest outline, is the story of what many persons gloat over as the beginning of the Renaissance. The only possible justification for that gloating would be in the excellence of the education which, after some hundred years of confused struggle, took the place of the destroyed mediaeval education. We shall consider that new education in the chapter succeeding this. In the present chapter we shall try to get some clear view of what happened in the break-up of mediaeval education.

In the eleventh, twelfth, and thirteenth centuries, there did occur in Europe a true renaissance, a true revival of civilization. It was moral, social, intellectual, artistic. It was, in the most complete sense, educational. That education was informed by the spirit of the Catholic religion. Its leaders were religious leaders: priests, monks, bishops, popes. For all its limitations and imperfections (and they were many) it was, in the judgment of competent and impartial historians, singularly successful. Its great monuments are scholastic philosophy and theology, the universities, the cathedrals, the developed social organization of Europe.

In the fourteenth century, the forward movement spent itself: in part, because of the strange inertia in all human activity; in part, through the gradual failure of its leaders;

in part, because of the inevitable tendency to stasis and
inflexibility in human institutions, a sort of social hardening of the arteries; in part, because of a terrible physical
disaster, the Black Death, which destroyed within a few
years nearly one half of the total population of Europe.
The result was an approach to moral anarchy, beginning
in the decay of the religious spirit of the various European
peoples.

Churchmen largely to blame for it. Jesus Christ had
promised that His Church would not fail; He had not promised that churchmen would not fail. Their failure in the
fourteenth and fifteenth centuries was fraught with disaster to Europe. They had become increasingly immersed
in secular politics, neglecting the care of their spiritual
charges. They had become wealthy, and greedy for wealth;
and their wealth had led them to pompous pride and luxury. It seems to be a law of human endeavor that difficulties call forth finer efforts, and that ease atrophies our
powers. Certainly it is an evident historical fact that the
vitality of the Catholic Church in its members thrives under
persecution and hardships, and decays in what the world
looks upon as success. Catholic churchmen, being human,
did not well endure the accumulated prosperity of the thirteenth century. The popes were too much taken up with
their temporal power, embroiled in endless and often immoral squabbles with the petty principalities of Italy, and
through these with the developing nations of the rest of
Europe. As one result of this, the papal residence was
transferred to Avignon from 1305 to 1377, and the papacy
became almost an appanage of the French crown. When
Pope Gregory XI died, at Rome, in 1378, a struggle broke
out between the French, Italian, and Spanish powers for
the control of the papacy, which led to the Great Western
Schism, a chaotic condition of rival popes and partisan contentions, lasting forty years, and incredibly scandalizing

the masses of Catholic people.   The bad example of the popes affected bishops and priests throughout Europe.   An atmosphere of gross worldliness prevailed in the upper ranks of the Church.   The people largely lost confidence in their religious leaders.

Sporadic and misguided attempts at reform.   St. Bridget of Sweden and St. Catherine of Siena tried, but with feeble success, to influence the popes spiritually; the former persuaded Urban V, in 1367, to return from Avignon to Rome, where, however, he stayed less than three years; the latter had much to do with the final return of Gregory XI, ten years later, just before the Great Schism.   John Wycliffe, an English secular priest, out of mixed motives of pique and zeal, set himself up as a reformer, during the papacy of Urban V.   Lingard says of him: "Wycliffe, exemplary in his morals, declaimed against vice with the freedom and severity of an apostle . . . but chiefly against the clergy."   He organized bands of 'poor priests,' barefoot, coarsely clad, who went about England, teaching the people the welcome doctrine that the laity might rightfully despoil sinful priests and monks.   Anarchy was in the air. John Ball, another priest, was the associate of Wat Tyler in leading the peasant rebellion of 1381 in England.   John Huss of Prague, influenced by the writings of Wycliffe, preached another politico-religious 'reform,' was condemned by the Council of Constance in 1415, and was burned to death.   The attempts at reform were violent, impassioned, and therefore often unbalanced.   They made the mistake, which Protestantism, a century later, was to make: of throwing out the baby with the bath, of condemning right uses as well as abuses, of rejecting Christian truths as well as the distorted misapplications of those truths.   There was no remedy in such 'reforms'; but the people acclaimed them because they knew there was terrible need of some reform.

The Black Death. Such a gross and widespread failure of Church leadership might alone have disrupted the civilization of Europe, which was built upon the Catholic Faith. But there was added to it an appalling physical calamity, one of the most dreadful in the history of the human race, the Black Death. It seems to have been a particularly virulent form of bubonic plague, which, after raging in the East for three or four years, was carried to Europe by Italian trading ships in the autumn of 1347. During 1348 it swept through France, Spain, Switzerland, Bavaria, and by August 15th of that year had reached England, from which country it crossed to Flanders, Norway, Sweden, Poland, Hungary, the lower Rhine valley, in 1349. Within three years, from a third to a half of the population of Europe died of it. The mortality was all the more terrible because of the swiftness with which death struck, and the fact that it attacked chiefly the young and vigorous. There was a rather bad recurrence of the plague ten years later, in 1361, and other minor outbreaks occurred during the rest of the century and well into the next century.

Effects on survivors. One might possibly expect this enormous disaster to sober those who survived, to call forth a moral revival, to turn men's minds from this life-in-death to the hopes and aspirations of Christianity. As a painful matter of fact, it did just the opposite. Matteo Villani, a contemporary historian, paints a picture of idleness, dissolute morals, frantic revelling.[1] "Priests and doctors fled in fear from those ill."[2] The laboring classes were intent chiefly on extorting higher wages.[3] The clergy too were engaged in profiteering, and the evil of plural benefices

---

[1] Muratori, *Scriptores,* tom. xiv, coll. 11-15, Palatine ed., Milan.

[2] *Idem,* tom. xvi, col. 286. Marcha di Marco Battagli da Rimini, C. xxix, p. 54.

[3] *Chronicle* of William Dene, a monk of Rochester, in MS. Brit. Mus. Faust. B, v, fol. 99.

multiplied.[1] Li Muisis has a shocking account of the churches of Tournay tolling the bells continuously for the sake of the fees, and of the town officials having to enact moral ordinances to meet the situation.[2] All contemporary accounts represent the moral apathy of the people as something more distressing to contemplate than the mortality itself.

And upon education. Schools and universities were obviously badly affected by this huge disaster, in the loss of both students and teachers. There is a manifest break in the development of architecture, and of stained glass: a change of style so marked as to help in dating many structures.[3] The arts in general begin to decay. Society becomes grosser in every way, more materialist, lacking in inspiration. Its educational leaders, already weakened in fiber of character and in equipment, suffer an enormous loss in both after the plague. Gasquet estimates that, for England, the loss in numbers of the clergy was about 25,-000;[4] but their loss in quality was even more important. In the urgent need of the times, illiterate and untrained men were ordained priests; and these were, of course, the chief guides and educators of the people, in the churches, in the schools, in the homes. It is small wonder that mediaeval education went to pieces in the fourteenth and fifteenth centuries.

War. One human activity which the Black Death itself could not halt was the lust of fighting. The Hundred Years'

[1] Wharton, *Anglia Sacra,* i, pp. 375, 376. Cf. also Wilkins, *Concilia,* ii, pp. 735, 736.

[2] De Smet, *Recueil,* Bruxelles, 1841, ii, pp. 279-81, 361-82.

[3] Gasquet, *The Black Death,* 2d ed., London, 1908, p. 235.

[4] *Idem,* pp. 237-39. He reckons that, prior to the plague, one in every fifty men in England belonged to the clergy. This goes far to explain why the common schools of England could be so well supplied with teachers, and why there were so many chantry priests and "Morrow Mass" priests to devote most of their time to the care of schools.

War, between France and England, began in 1346. Within seven years after the great plague, Edward of England and his son, the Black Prince, again invaded France, and at Poitiers defeated King John of France and captured him and his son Philip. It was in the midst of the Black Death that the populace of Rome drove out of the city Rienzi, whom seven months before they had acclaimed as their reforming leader. Whilst the plague was raging in the Germanies, the new emperor, Charles IV, was fighting with Gunther of Schwartzburg and other princes. The *condottieri* in Italy fought each other amidst rotting corpses; and in Naples Louis of Hungary waged his war against Queen Joanna I, even whilst half of his army died of the disease. The Black Death brought peace only to its victims.

Scholasticism decadent. The great philosophical and theological system which was the intellectual core of the thirteenth century fell into feeble hands in the fourteenth. The number of students of philosophy multiplied, but they lacked thoroughness as well as originality. They lined up as partisan adherents of one of the three great schools, Ockhamists, Scotists, Thomists; and made up in contentiousness what they lacked in knowledge. Dialectic, which in the thirteenth century was only a preparatory discipline to real philosophical studies, became in the fourteenth the main subject of study, or rather of quarrel. Clearness and vigor of thought were lost in a fog of distinctions and subdistinctions. Even the language of the schools suffered: the terse, precise Latin of the thirteenth century giving way to a hodge-podge of barbarisms. Conceit took the place of intelligence; and skepticism, as always, was ready upon the heels of conceit. The English Franciscan, William of Ockham, who was born about 1300 and died in the Black Death at Munich, 1349, shook the foundations of Scholasticism and prepared the way for agnosticism. With him, Scholasticism lost its place and force in the scheme of

European education, and was ready for the gibes of the coming humanists.[1]

These changes reflected in the universities. It must be repeated that schools do not lead social changes, but follow them. The school of life always dominates the school of formula. As the vitality of the twelfth and thirteenth centuries built the universities, so the decadence of the fourteenth century enfeebled them. Even in the earlier, vigorous ages, the universities suffered from the educational weakness of being too exclusively intellectual in their training; but it was, at any rate, a fine, clear, and noble intellectuality. Now it becomes petty, contentious, querulous, lost in insignificant details.[2] The faculty of theology is a hotbed of intrigue. True zeal for study disappears before the trivial ambitions of vanity or greedy campaigning for ecclesiastical preferment. Political jockeying, and even bribery by money, make easy the approach to the 'doctorate.' In the faculty of arts the years of study are shortened, and "beardless boys fill with infantile stammerings" the chairs of the masters.[3] The students are sputtering dialectic; and the 'form' of a syllogism has become more important than the truth it may contain. There are more and more monks and friars in the schools, but they are neither good students nor edifying religious.[4] Moreover, one of the glories of the mediaeval university, its cosmopolitanism, now vanishes, owing to the increasingly

[1] Maurice de Wulf, *History of Mediaeval Philosophy,* London, 1926, Vol. 2, pp. 159-69.

[2] University work also began to be more a task of training than of educating, due to the fact that the doctorate was a necessary step on the way to teaching. The universities became trade schools of a sort, when even the logic-chopping was done chiefly as a preparation for teaching others to chop logic.

[3] Richard de Bury, *Philobiblion,* c. lx, p. 87 (published 1344; reference to edition of 1888, London, by Ernest C. Thomas).

[4] Denifle and Chatelain, *Chartularium Universitatis Parisiensis,* Paris, 1891, Vol. 2, p. 11. The entire introduction to Vol. 2 is concerned with the early fourteenth-century conditions.

sharp demarcation between the developing nations of Europe. The fine solidarity of the Middle Ages is passing; culture is becoming insular, provincial. New universities spring up, particularly in the German-speaking countries; and they are all national, or even local, in character. Europe is splitting up; and European education is turning into French, English, Italian, Spanish, German education.[1]

And in the lower schools. Throughout the Middle Ages, the lot of the peasant was a hard one. The Black Death, by making labor scarce, helped much to improve the material position of the laboring man; but it seems also to have stirred up in him an increased bitterness and resentment toward the higher classes, including, by all means, the clergy. The social atmosphere was filled with conflict. The country schools became more and more lay schools; in which, of course, fees were demanded for tuition. M. Simeon Luce indicates that the schoolmaster had considerable difficulty in collecting these fees.[2] Moreover, competent schoolmasters were increasingly scarce.[3] The towns fared better. Commerce and industries were only temporarily halted by the plague. There was an actual increase in individual wealth, since there were suddenly fewer people to share possession of the total wealth. The burgher class solidified its social standing. One notable change in the lower schools was brought about by the growing spirit of nationalism; that was the increased use of the vernaculars in school instruction.[4] We shall have to note a curious re-

[1] Cf. H. S. Denifle, *Die Universitäten des Mittelalters bis 1400.*

[2] *Histoire de Bertrand du Guesclin et son Epoque (1320-1364),* p. 15. The incidents narrated are of the year 1377.

[3] A. F. Leach, *The Schools of Medieval England,* London, 1915, pp. 210 sqq.

[4] Up to the year of the Black Death, children in the schools of England construed their lessons in French. Shortly after 1350 a schoolmaster named Cornwall introduced the use of English into the instruction of his pupils. His example was eagerly followed; within a single generation, the custom became nearly universal. About the

sult of this when we consider the growth of humanism. And it must not be forgotten that the quality and intensiveness of religious instruction in these most important lower schools greatly fell off during the fourteenth and fifteenth centuries. The children trained in these schools had no little ground for discontent with their clerical teachers; the good-humored anti-clericalism of the thirteenth century becomes rather bitter in the fourteenth. Yet the Catholic religion had a more tenacious hold in these lower schools than in the higher; and throughout the troublous fourteenth century, the mass of the people everywhere retained the Faith, although it was gradually enfeebled through lack of adequate instruction. During this century and the next, diocesan and provincial synods repeatedly urged upon parish priests the duty of religious instruction of their people: a fact which testifies to the need of such urging.[1]

Conclusion. Even so cursory a sketch as this of educational conditions in the fourteenth century may make clear that Europe had pitifully gone back from the crest of mediaeval accomplishment. Nor can one hesitate a moment as to where to place the chief blame for that great failure. Just as the reform of Cluny had been the principal agency in bringing about the amazing improvement in education which ushered in the twelfth-century renaissance, so too the moral and religious decay of the bishops and clergy was now the greatest single factor in destroying the educational achievements of the Middle Ages. There were other destructive forces at work, just as there had been other upbuilding forces besides Cluny; but the failure of the Catholic leaders was the most powerful disintegrating agent, pre-

same time, Chaucer was writing the Canterbury Tales. Cf. F. A. Gasquet, *The Black Death*, 2d ed., London, 1908, p. 234.

[1] See monograph by F. A. Gasquet on "Religious Instruction in England during the Fourteenth and Fifteenth Centuries," *Historical Papers*, Vol. 3, Catholic Truth Society, London, 1908.

cisely as Cluny had been the most powerful constructive agent. The fourteenth and fifteenth centuries were the secular Spy Wednesday: the mystical body of Christ betrayed by some of His leading disciples, as His actual body had been betrayed by Judas.

One immediate result of this spiritual decay is to be found in the intellectual conceit of theologians. By the fourteenth century they had begun to take themselves very seriously as THE guardians of Catholic truth; assuming an authority which was not from God; making the human science of theology the final test of the Faith. Theirs is a position singularly like that of the scribes at the time of Christ. Its effect upon the people was bad; it stirred a vague rebelliousness, which is never capable of distinguishing between assumed authority and true authority. It set up the conciliar idea, the subversive notion that a general council was superior to the spiritual authority of the pope; and so prepared the way for future division of Christendom.

The Black Death was merely a hastening and intensifying incident in the general process of decay. It gave a violent thrust to a stumbling age; but the age would have fallen without it. It sprinkled corpses about what was already becoming the ruin of the Middle Ages; and mingled the effluvia of the dead with the stench of spiritual decadence. It made impressive in human bodies the greater horror that was happening in human souls. The fifteenth-century Renaissance was to spring up in a physical and moral charnel house.

TOPICS FOR DISCUSSION

1. The decay of the education of chivalry: how far affected by loss of religion? by growth of burgher class? by introduction of firearms?

2. Comparison between the German universities, sprung up in the fourteenth and fifteenth centuries, and the universities of France, England, Italy.

3. The educational influences, good and bad, of the mendicant religious orders during the fourteenth and fifteenth centuries.

4. The Brothers of the Common Life and elementary schools.

5. The effect upon education of the widening concept of geography during the fourteenth and fifteenth centuries.

6. The influence of Wycliffe and Huss upon the religious education of this period.

BIBLIOGRAPHIC NOTE

Many of the sources indicated for the early universities are of value also for this later period. See also such collections as *Recueil des Chroniques de Flandres,* 56 vols., Bruges, 1839-64 (the *Chronicon Majus* of Aegidius Li Muisis is in Vol. 2, foll. 378 sqq.); Muratori, *Rerum Italicarum Scriptores,* Milan, 1723-51 (the *Historia* of Matteo Villani is in Vol. 14, foll. 1-770); L. Wadding, *Annales Minorum,* 2d ed., Rome, 1734-35 (see especially Vol. 8); Thomas de Walden, *Doctrinale Antiquitatum,* 3 vols., Venice, 1571. There is much of interest and value in the *Opera Omnia* of St. Bernardino of Siena, edited by de la Haye, Paris, 1536 (reprinted Paris, 1650; Venice, 1745); extracts from the *Sermons* were edited by N. Orlandi, Siena, 1920. E. Baluze, *Vitae Paparum Avenoniensium,* 2 vols., Paris, 1693 (new ed. by G. Mollatt, Vols. 1-4, Paris, 1914-22), contains some source material. For England, see Thomas Walsingham, *Chronicon Angliae,* edited by Sir E. M. Thompson (Rolls Series), London, 1874. W. W. Shirley has edited *Fasciculi Zizaniorum Magistri Joannis Wyclif cum Tritico* (Rolls Series), London, 1858; and D. S. Schaff has edited and translated, *Jan Hus de Ecclesia,* New York, 1915. Brief selections of sources may be found in O. J. Thatcher and E. H. McNeal, *A Source Book of Mediaeval History* (some Papal Bulls and other material), New York, 1905; F. A. Ogg, *A Source Book of Mediaeval History,* New York, 1908; F. M. Fling, *European History Studies,* 10 numbers, Chicago, 1900; *Translations and Reprints from Original Sources in European History,* University of Pennsylvania, 1894-99 (see especially Vols. 2 and 3). V. Scudder, *S. Catherine of Siena as Seen in Her Letters,* New York, 1926, translates some letters that illustrate problems of the period.

A valuable summary of university conditions is the Introduction to Vol. 2 of Denifle and Chatelain, *Chartularium Universitatis Parisiensis,* Paris, 1891. For the entire period, see E. G. Gardner, *St. Catherine of Siena: a Study in the Religion, Literature, and History of the Fourteenth Century,* London, 1907; L. Pastor, *Geschichte der Papste seit dem Ausgang des Mittelalters,* Leipzig, 1884 sqq. (English translation by F. I. Antrobus and R. F. Kerr, *The History of the Popes from the Close of the Middle Ages,* London, 1898 sqq.) (especially Vols. 1 and 2, 1305-1458); H. Bruce, *The Age of Schism (1304-1503),* London, 1907; L. Thorndike, *Science and Thought in the Fif-*

teenth Century, Columbia University, 1929; M. De Wulf, *History of Mediaeval Philosophy,* Vol. 2, London, 1926; W. Cunningham, *Growth of English Industry and Commerce,* 5th ed., 3 vols., Cambridge, 1910-12.

For the Black Death and its effects on education, see A. Philippe, *Histoire de la Peste Noire,* Paris, 1853; F. A. Gasquet, *The Black Death of 1348 and 1349,* London, 1908; J. Nohl (English translation by C. H. Clarke), *The Black Death,* London, 1926; A. M. Campbell, *The Black Death and Men of Learning,* Columbia University, 1932. For the effect of firearms on the education of chivalry, see C. H. Ashdown, *Armour and Weapons in the Middle Ages,* London, 1925; H. Belloc, *Warfare in England,* London, 1912; H. W. L. Hine, *The Origin of Artillery,* New York, 1915. The *Fabliaux* satirize the break-down of chivalry; for a selection of them, see C. Oulmont (ed.), *La Poesie Française du Moyen Age (XIe-XVe Siecle): Recueil de Textes etc.,* Paris, 1913.

For Wycliffe and Huss, see J. Loserth, *Hus und Wyclif,* Prag, 1884; R. L. Poole, *Wycliffe and Movements for Reform,* London, 1889; J. Herbern, *Huss and His Followers,* London, 1926; B. Manning, *The People's Faith in the Time of Wyclif,* Cambridge, 1919; J. Gairdner, *Lollardy and the Reformation,* 4 vols., London, 1908, Vol. 1; W. W. Capes, *The English Church in the Fourteenth and Fifteenth Centuries,* London, 1900; J. P. Whitney, "Religious Movements in the Fourteenth Century," *Cambridge History of English Literature,* Cambridge, 1908, Vol. 2.

A. Hyma, *The Christian Renaissance,* Grand Rapids, 1924, besides discussing the reform movement in the north of Europe, has a good account of the Brothers of the Common Life.

CHAPTER XII

THE EDUCATION OF THE CLASSIC RENAISSANCE

Some preliminary considerations. Before attempting a sketch of education in the Classic Renaissance, it seems advisable to consider briefly a few important facts about that Renaissance itself. First to be noted is that the vast, slow, tortuous upheaval of European civilization which is generally known as the Renaissance stretched over a period of about two hundred years: considerably longer than from the American War of Independence to our present day. Its limits may be roughly set as between 1350 and 1550: between the enthusiasms of Petrarch and the cold formalism of Sturm and the Jesuits. The second great fact is that the character of that social upheaval varied in different lands, in different stages of its progress, under the varying local conditions of life. It is a fatal mistake to think of the Renaissance as a compact, coherent, and unified movement of Europe as a whole. Indeed, diversity, division, even separatism essentially marked the movement. Europe was not merely changing; it was breaking up. A third, and very important, fact to be kept in mind is that the period of the Renaissance was largely a period of negations. This may the more readily be seen when one compares it with the twelfth-century renaissance, which built up European institutions. The Classic Renaissance found much of its enthusiasm in hatred and destruction of the immediate past; and all warmth tended to leave it when that function was fulfilled. Except in the one great art of painting, it had no creative force; even its panegyrists make that clear.[1]

[1] The invention of printing occurred in a Germany scarcely touched as yet by the Renaissance. The importance of printing is obvious;

189

In none of its efforts did it have any of the joyousness and ease of the twelfth century. It was restless, turbulent; the whole period was one of turmoil and bitterness.[1] These facts have much to do with the difficulty of estimating the Classic Renaissance aright; and they complicate any study of its educational efforts. In attempting that study, we must first draw a distinction between Renaissance education outside the schools and within the schools; and of these the former is by all means the more important.

I. EDUCATION OUTSIDE THE SCHOOLS

Its general character. This new education affected the minds and characters of grown men and women; it sprang from the social and intellectual tendencies of the age, and

though it would be interesting to compare its importance with that of the mediaeval discoveries, such as chimney flues, clocks, plumbing, stained glass, spectacles, gunpowder, the rudder, and the mariner's compass. Further, it is instructive to consider the fact that the Chinese had already invented printing some six hundred years or more before Johann Gutenberg printed his bible at Mainz from cast metal types. (See *The Invention of Printing in China,* by T. F. Carter, Columbia University Press, 1925.) If we contrast the use of printing in China and in Europe, we must note how greatly the value of an invention depends upon the circumstances which surround it. The Renaissance profited enormously from the use of printing, in so far as printing gave it a cheap and abundant means of spreading its ideas. The educational significance of that fact must, of course, be measured by the worth to mankind of the ideas it had to spread.

[1] It must not be forgotten that the dreaded bubonic plague, which was an important element in the break-up of mediaeval civilization, continued to harass Europe all through the Renaissance, although never with the widespread virulence of the 'Black Death.' In Italy especially, with its crowded cities, its frequent sieges of towns, its lack of sanitary regulations, foci of infection lurked everywhere, ready at any time to burst forth into sweeping disaster. Cf. A. von Reumont, *Kleine historische Schriften,* Gotha, 1882, pp. 67 sqq.; and the large work of Corradi, *Annali delle epidemie occorse in Italia,* 8 vols., Bologna, 1865-94. Even in the sixteenth century, Erasmus, whilst travelling in Italy, was nearly mobbed, because his garb resembled that of a plague doctor. These frequent outbreaks of pestilence added to the confusion of the period, and were in part responsible for the mingled superstition and moral apathy which marked Italy during the Renaissance.

in turn strongly shaped those tendencies; it was intensely vital. It began in Italy, which had always been the closest Western link with the long-dead past; but in a chaotic Italy, torn by dissensions, insecure in principles, groping amidst ruins. It began in a revolt with the immediate past, which men were inclined to blame for their present social ill-ease: in a revolt against an intellectual system which undeniably had become hard, dry, sterile; against a moral system which had become insincere through the almost complete divorce of practice from precept. It turned men's minds in a great hope to a culture, a philosophy of life, which had been brought to its highest development more than a thousand years before. It saw in the revival of that ancient culture the cure for the moral and intellectual dry-rot which was everywhere manifest in the decadent mediaeval civilization. There was not lacking nobility of purpose in the leaders of the movement; there was fine enthusiasm, which spread with amazing rapidity amongst the leisured classes; and there was tremendous industry. Every trace of the old Graeco-Roman culture was eagerly ferreted out, and acclaimed as a treasure.[1] The first new welcome to the antique was not at all pedantic; it thrilled with life, it was looking for a solution of living problems; and it thought to find that solution in the many-sided interests of a civilization more elaborate than the mediaeval civilization.

Shaped by individuals. Such a turning-back of the clock is in itself remarkable; but more remarkable still is the

---

[1] The manuscripts so eagerly hunted for by Petrarch and the succeeding humanists are all mediaeval copies, not a single one of them dating back to 'classic' times. (Cf. Thorndike, *History of Mediaeval Europe*, p. 589.) The greatest single find, a complete Quintilian, was made by Broccolini Poggio, about 1417, in the monastery of St. Gall. Burckhardt points out that the work of these fifteenth-century copyists was very inferior, compared with "the conscientious precision of the old monks." (*Civilization of the Renaissance in Italy*, p. 192; translation by S. G. C. Middlemore, 1898.)

way in which it was done. It was done, not by the slow evolution of a whole people, but by the energetic action of a few gifted individuals. Even when we recall that, in the very midst of the Italian Renaissance, the invention of printing came to increase the power of the individual over the masses, this power is amazing. From that time onward, *names* begin to count more and more in European history; single individuals more and more shape the principles and conduct of multitudes of men.[1] It is significant that, in the past, great men came most often at the tail of an educational movement, not at the head. Socrates, Plato, Aristotle appear just before Greece decays; St. Augustine stands at the edge of the Dark Ages; St. Thomas Aquinas is only a long lifetime away from the break-up of mediaeval education; and Dante died in 1321, just twenty-six years before the Black Death. The great man more naturally marks the completion of a stage in the up-and-down progress of humanity. He is debtor to the lesser dead for what made him capable of high development. He follows, even more than he leads. And if he comes when the wheel of human achievement is on the down-swing, he is powerless to swing it upward, or even to keep it level. But with the Classic Renaissance the procedure seemed to change. Men who disclaimed all allegiance to the immediate past, who scorned its offered helps, who broke with it in complete condemnation, took the lead in a new movement; and the people followed them.

Toward an appealing objective. One explanation of this new power of the individual is that the old, established leadership had lost its hold upon men, and that a leaderless people welcomed new guides. But a more important

[1] In the matter of school education, this prominence of individuals becomes very marked in the eighteenth and nineteenth centuries, as we shall see later. Rousseau, Pestalozzi, Herbert, Froebel, Horace Mann, exert an influence which is nothing short of astounding.

explanation lies in the fact that the goal of the new leaders was so obvious, so immediately appealing. They pointed to no remote, supernatural standard of excellence; they imposed no rigorous discipline, called for no difficult faith. There, on the near horizon, was a rich culture, purely human, easily attainable, outwardly alluring. It promised nobility without restraint, excellence without more than moderate effort. By contrast with the otherworldly ideals of mediaeval civilization, it appeared joyous, warm, glowingly colored; it appealed to the senses, to the emotions; it was rich in promises of immediate delight, with no grim portals of death standing in the way. No wonder that men who had so largely lost the vision of the Faith, turned at the first shout of the new leaders, to follow this new ideal of achievement! Petrarch and Boccaccio, for all that they were still Catholics, set back the ill-disciplined peoples of Italy at a point where Augustine had stood as a young man; and equivalently told them to take up the path that Augustine was abandoning. The modern world has ever since been divided in its opinion as to whether or not the choice urged by the Renaissance leaders was a disastrous choice; and that division of opinion is, beyond question, the most important division separating men today.

But at once divides into two. As a matter of fact, not all of Italy (nor later, all of Europe) accepted the lead of the Renaissance into a break with Christianity. For the moment, the Italians of influence were in three very unequal groups: the first group frankly pagan, positively hostile to Christianity; the second, largely made up of monks, friars, clergy, and theological faculties of universities, violently Catholic (at least in speech), fanatically opposed to the revival of the ancient civilization in any form; the third, composed of laymen and ecclesiastics alike, eager to seek a compromise, some blending of Graeco-Roman culture with Christian beliefs and practices, such as had been sought a thousand years earlier by Christians of the age of Ambrose and Jerome and Augustine. In the course of time, the second group was absorbed into the first and third, and there remained but two: the pagan humanists, and the Catholic humanists. As representatives of the former, may be mentioned Giovanni Boccaccio (1313-1375), Braccolini Poggio (1380-1459), Francesco Filelfo (1398-1481), Nicolo Machiavelli (1469-1527); as representatives of the latter, Francesco Petrarca (1304-1374), Pier Paolo Vergerio (1349-1420), Gasparino Barzizza (1370-1431), Lionardo Bruni, Aretino (1369-1444), Battista Guarino (1434-1513). There is no denying that, owing in great measure to the wretched condition of the Church at the time, the paganizing group was by far the more influential, and that the temper of the Renaissance in Italy was predominantly pagan. Nicolo Machiavelli, writing when the Italian Renaissance was at its highest point of development, says bluntly: "We Italians are irreligious and corrupt beyond all others."[1]

Aims of the pagan education: fame and pleasure. The first principle of the paganizing education of the Italian Renaissance was insistence upon education for this world. Its leaders, by speech and writing, emphasized the worldly ideal of 'success,' an ideal which we should have no difficulty in understanding today, and which, on their lips as on ours, meant chiefly two things, fame and pleasure:[2] the gratification of our human craving for personal glory, and the satisfaction of appetite and emotional desire. The only immortality worth while for them was the immortality conferred by poets and biographers: to live in the memory of succeeding generations.[3] In many cases, mere notoriety

[1] *Discorsi,* lib. I, c. 12 (translated by N. H. Thompson, London, 1883).
[2] Money, except by the mentally unbalanced miser, is always valued only for its power to procure fame and pleasure.
[3] Burckhardt, *Civilization of the Renaissance,* 3d ed., Vol. 1, pp. 173 sqq.

was considered a sufficient goal of endeavor; even some of the most detestable crimes of the period are frankly attributed to the ambition to attract attention, to be remembered, if only as a moral monster.[1] Lorenzo Valla, about 1430, wrote a book on pleasure, which represents the views of many leaders of the Renaissance. He takes the outspoken position that enjoyment alone is the aim of life, and praises the ancients who raised voluptuousness to a cult.[2] Naturally, such an ideal implies very active hostility toward Christian aspirations; nor did the pagan Renaissance writers leave any doubt about their attitude toward Christianity. They attacked it constantly, with open scorn, with ridicule and parody: in poems such as Luigi Pulci's "Morgante Maggiore," Boccaccio's "Three Rings"; in plays such as Machiavelli's comedies, *Mandragola* and *Clizia*.[3]

Exaggerated individualism. In line with this emphasis upon fame as one of the great goals of living, the pagan Renaissance developed an exaggerated individualism. It was an era of boastfulness, of vigorous assertion of one's personality, of resentment toward authority. Everyone insisted upon his right to criticize, and, if he had the power to do so, to repress all criticism on the part of others. A touchy sort of pride prevailed everywhere, yet without any high principles of conduct or very keen sense of responsibility. A decidedly empty 'honor' took the place of re-

[1] Pastor, *History of the Popes* (English translation), Vol. 2, pp. 215 sqq., cites instances of this curiously disordered craving, leading to assassinations.

[2] Pastor, *History of the Popes* (English translation), Vol. 1, pp. 13 sqq. Valla was about twenty-three years old when he wrote this book. The year following, 1431, he was ordained priest. He became a great scholar, denounced the Donation of Constantine in 1440, was an important secretary under Pope Nicholas V, and died at the age of fifty, a Canon of the Lateran.

[3] J. Owen, *The Sceptics of the Renaissance*, London, 1893, pp. 147 sqq., 153 sqq. Cf. also W. B. Skaife, *Florentine Life during the Renaissance*, Baltimore, 1893, pp. 131 sqq.

ligion as the basis of moral conduct.[1]   The effective result
of all this was a pretentious sophistication, which seems
curiously modern, a cynicism at once arrogant and childish.
"An easy-going contempt of everything and everybody was
probably the prevailing tone of society."[2]   The pagan Renaissance, in casting away divine faith, seemed also to have
lost human faith; and for all the current prating about
honor, few ages have ever been so horribly and so persistently stained by treachery as this was.

Yet it is a strange fact that, with rare exceptions, these
Italian Renaissance pagans, when death gave them any
warning of its approach, turned to the religion they had
travestied and scorned, and tried to die as Catholics.   Even
Machiavelli, and Sigismond Malatesta who seemed to revel
in crime for its own sake, called for a priest at the end,
made confession of their sins, and received the Viaticum
with devotion.[3]

The Christian education.   These deathbed repentances,
for one thing, testify to the latent vitality of the Christian
spirit.   It never died out in Italy, even in the worst stages
of the Renaissance.   In spite of adverse conditions, of failure of spiritual leaders, of multiplied temptations, thousands of the people continued sincerely and steadily in their
Catholic belief and Catholic lives.   For them, the changing
enthusiasms of the time, the new flair for the long-dead
antique culture, were simply a new circumstance which
they must adapt to the unchanging Faith.   Petrarch himself made some efforts toward this adaptation; but it was
not until the Classic Renaissance was well under way, in
the succeeding generation, that Catholic efforts became
vigorous and well organized.

---

[1] See Rabelais, *Gargantua,* lib. I, cap. 57, for satiric discussion of
this.

[2] J. Burckhardt, *Civilization of the Renaissance in Italy* (Middlemore's translation, 1898), p. 161.

[3] L. Pastor, *History of the Popes* (English translation), Vol. 1, p. 28.

Pier Paolo Vergerio (1349-1420) wrote an admirable treatise, *De ingenuis Moribus et Studiis Liberalibus,* in 1392. His educational aims are the recognized Catholic aims, with which he combines the new feeling for style, for classic excellence, for a larger and more rounded culture.[1] Gasparino Barzizza (1370-1431), who taught rhetoric and Latin literature at the University of Padua, and who was prominent in classic scholarship, was completely Catholic in his character and influence. One of his pupils was Vittorino da Feltre, a man recognized as worthy of a place amongst the little handful of the world's great teachers. Contemporary with Barzizza was Lionardo Bruni (1369-1444), often called Aretino from his birthplace, Arezzo. He too wrote an excellent, and thoroughly Catholic, treatise, *De Studiis et Literis.* Two pupils of the paganizing Filelfo became popes: Tommaso Parentucelli, as Nicholas V, who founded the Vatican Library about 1450; and Aeneas Silvius Piccolomini, as Pius II; and, what is more, they were good popes. The period draws to a close in Italy with the really remarkable treatise of the younger Guarino (Battista, 1434-1513), *De Ordine Docendi et Studendi.*

Extent of its influence. These men represent large numbers back of them. But it is hard to make any exact estimate of the relative influence of the Catholic spirit in Renaissance education. It certainly failed in its efforts to keep the drama Christian, in spite of the impressively large number of religious plays produced,[2] and the momentary success of such dramatic organizations as that of the Dominicans at Pistoja.[3]

---

[1] See C. Bischoff, *Studien zu P. P. Vergerio dem Älteren,* Berlin and Leipzig, 1909.

[2] D'Ancona, *Sacre Rappresentazione de' secoli XIV, XV, e XVI;* 3 vols., Firenze, 1872. This work contains also excellent introductions.

[3] P. Vigo, *Una Compagnia di Giovinetti Pistoiesi a principio del secolo XVI,* Bologna, 1887.

On the other hand, in the one new art of the Renaissance, painting,[1] the Christian spirit is strikingly manifest. Muntz, in a careful listing, estimates that the Italian *Quattrocento* pictures present twenty religious subjects for one classical subject.[2] The guilds kept alive the Catholic spirit that had always animated them.[3] Pious confraternities flourished, most of them dedicated to works of charity; some of them an inheritance from mediaeval times; some of them new, such as the famous *Misericordia* of Florence,[4] founded in 1488, or the many confraternities established at Rome under Alexander VI and Leo X.[5] At the time, no other country had such splendid hospitals and charitable foundations as Italy.[6] Nor was there lacking abundant influence from the greatest sources of Christian education, religious instruction, prayer, and the Sacraments. The effect of this is shown in the admirable family life to be found so widely existing amongst the middle classes, in the earnest, even if sporadic, attempts at social reform, above all in the large number of men and women whose lives displayed heroic virtue.[7] But there was a certain unsteadiness about this essential religious education amongst the people at large; it had a tendency to extreme fluctuations, to flare up violently at one time, and die down to a faint spark at another. It must further be admitted that, although there

[1] Renaissance architecture was imitative; its sculpture had only the originality of being dissociated from architecture.

[2] Eugene Muntz, *Histoire de l'Art pendant la Renaissance,* 3 vols., Paris, 1889-95, Vol. 1, pp. 232-73.

[3] E. Rodocanachi, *Les Corporations ouvrières a Rome depuis la chute de l'Empire Romain,* 2 vols., Paris, 1894, Vol. 1, pp. 75, 99 sqq.

[4] C. Bianchi, *La Compagnia della Misericordia,* Firenze, 1855. In Florence alone there were, about 1500, seventy-three religious associations.

[5] Carlo Piazza, *Opere Pie di Roma,* Roma, 1679, pp. 391 sqq., 429 sqq., 462 sqq., 546, 549.

[6] W. B. Skaife, *Florentine Life during the Renaissance,* pp. 180 sqq.

[7] Ulysse Chevalier, *Repertoire des sources historiques du moyen-âge,* Paris, 1877-83. For the fifteenth century alone, he gives references for over eighty Italian saints and blessed.

were many zealous preachers and priests of exemplary lives, especially amongst the new Benedictine congregations,[1] too many of the clergy were swamped in greed and licentiousness, too many of the preachers were conceited and bombastic, parading their smattering of heathen mythology in the pulpit, indulging in exaggerated accounts of the abuses of the day, aiming more at fame, or at least notoriety, for themselves than at real religious influence over their hearers; so that the direct power of religious education was much impaired by the gross lack of Christianity in the educators.[2] The general impression produced by a careful study of the period is that Christian education was less effective upon Renaissance society than was the pagan education. Unfortunately, this is most true as regards the clergy, high and low.[3]

Effects of the Renaissance on language. One of the aims of the Classic Renaissance was to replace the mediaeval forms of the Latin language by the literary forms of Latin in the stage of its highest academic development. The leaders of the movement either did not know, or else simply ignored, the important fact that such literary Latin was never the popular speech of the Roman people, that classic Latin, at the very time it was produced, was remote from the popular forms. All literature, it is true, is remote from common speech; but Latin classic literature peculiarly so. It was an exotic. It could not grow in the wide fields of

[1] F. Fabri, *Evagatorium,* edited by Hassler, Stuttgardiae, 1849, Vol. 3, pp. 393 sqq.

[2] Cf. also Burckhardt, *Civilization of the Renaissance,* Vol. 1, p. 243, for instances of humanists in the pulpit, political announcements, etc. Often the pulpit was used least of all for religious instruction. It might be interesting to compare the Renaissance pulpit with the American Protestant pulpit of today.

[3] C. Cantu, *Italiani illustri. Ritratti,* 3 vols., Milano, 1873-74, Vol. 1, pp. 201 sqq., gives a general description of the low state of the clergy. It is notable that much of the best work done in Christian education during the Renaissance was done by laymen.

Europe. The net result of the forcing process attempted
by the humanists of the Renaissance was, as Haskins has
clearly pointed out,[1] to destroy the living Latin language,
and thus indirectly to open the way for further growth of
the vernaculars, which were so despised by the fifteenth-
and sixteenth-century humanists. One of the stock ironies
of history is the error of Petrarch in contemning his Italian
poems and putting his hope of fame in his Latin verses;
whereas in fact his Latin work is forgotten, and his name
established solely by his Italian writings. But the humanists were, for the most part, so out of touch with actual
life that they never learned the power of the growing vernaculars. Even in the sixteenth century, Erasmus not only
wrote his books in Latin, but would not speak any other
language; and still dreamed of a universal republic of Latin
letters, when Cervantes, Shakespeare, Lope de Vega, and
Corneille were already in the gate. St. Thomas More, a
master of vigorous English, turned to Latin for the writing
of his great work, Utopia. The simple, yet amazing, truth
is that the Classic Renaissance made Latin a dead language,
and succeeded chiefly in cluttering our school rooms for
four hundred years with the whitened bones of Latin
grammar. It is a curious instance of how limited is the
educational power of even gifted leaders, who fail to observe and follow the trend of forces which no human leader
can turn, the huge, spontaneous developments of the people
at large.

The Classic Renaissance beyond Italy. The Classic Renaissance had almost run its course in Italy before it began
to affect very seriously the education of the rest of Europe.
In that widening out of its influence, several important
facts are to be noted. First, there was a striking similarity

[1] C. H. Haskins, *The Renaissance of the Twelfth Century*, pp.
127-29.

in the manner of its propagation: that is, in the other countries of Europe, just as in Italy, the new enthusiasm for antique culture did not spring from the people, or even from the schools, but was introduced and urged by a small number of influential men, for the most part attached to courts and under the patronage of rulers. Second, in contrast with the Italian development, Renaissance education in the rest of Europe seldom took on an anti-Christian character. Indeed, northern Europe was largely shocked by this quality of the Italian Renaissance, and tended to draw from a consideration of it an increase of national dislike and distrust of Italian culture in general, and an aversion from and contempt for the corrupt papal court in particular. From this last circumstance many historians erroneously infer a close causal connection between the Renaissance in northern lands and the politico-religious revolution commonly known as the Reformation. As a matter of fact, the two are more nearly linked in mere coincidence of time than in any other way. The anti-Christian influence of the Renaissance was powerfully felt in the north only *after* the Protestant Revolution had succeeded in devitalizing Christianity amongst the northern peoples: a slow process, scarcely completed in our day, when so large a majority of, say, the population of the United States is now quite pagan in principle and in conduct. A third fact is that the Renaissance in the north made much more account of Greek than did the Italian Renaissance. Interest in Greek writings had never had a really strong hold in Italy. By the time the Renaissance was passing out into other lands, even that feeble interest was dying, and the leadership in bringing Greek to the Western world definitely came to France.

In England. England, although geographically so remote from Italy, seems to have been the first country to be notably influenced by the Classic Renaissance in Italy.

Early in the fifteenth century, English ecclesiastics, coming into contact with the humanist secretaries of the Papal Curia, brought back to England vivid impressions of the new learning. Poggio himself visited England in 1419. William Gray, of Balliol College, Oxford, studied under Guarino at Ferrara, and returned to Oxford in 1449 with a valuable collection of Latin manuscripts, which are still treasured in Balliol library. At the close of the Wars of the Roses, in 1485, Italian teachers came to Oxford, seeking pupils. In the same year, Linacre went to study in Italy. Grocyn, after a like period of study in Italy, taught Greek in Oxford, in 1491; and Colet, with the same background of Italian training, began to lecture in theology at Oxford from the Greek text of St. Paul's letters, in 1496. But the true center of humanism in England was the house of St. Thomas More in Chelsea. It was from his association there, from 1505 onward, with More, Erasmus, Linacre, Warham, Colet, Fisher, and Grocyn, that Sir Thomas Elyot gathered the ideas which he embodied in his famous *The Boke named the Governour,* published in 1531, the first book written in English to present the humanist ideal in education. A few years later, out of fear of Henry VIII, Elyot repudiated his religion, as well as his friendship for More and Fisher. It is to be noted that, with this one exception, the leaders of the Classic Renaissance in England were Catholics, and most of them priests or bishops.

In the Germanies. The two earliest importers of the Classic Renaissance into the Germanies (in which are included here the Low Countries) were Rudolph Agricola (1443-1485) and Alexander Hegius (1420-1495). Agricola, a Hollander, after getting his master's degree at Louvain in 1461, finished his education at Paris, Pavia, and at Ferrara under Guarino. On his return, in 1479, he strongly influenced Hegius, who had his school of St. Lebuin at

Deventer. The teachers in this school were chiefly members of the Brothers of the Common Life, although Hegius himself was not a member. Agricola passed on to Heidelberg in 1484, at the invitation of Dalberg, the Bishop of Worms. Although he died only a year later, at the early age of forty-two, and had done but little writing, his vigorous personality and genuine scholarship did much to turn German thought toward the new learning, especially to the study of Greek. He was intensely Catholic in his ideals of education.

A still more important person than either of these in the Classic Renaissance in Germany was the distinguished priest, Jacob Wimpfeling (1450-1528) of Schlettstadt in Alsace. He studied and taught at Heidelberg, and was rector there in 1482. Whilst he was at Speyer, in 1497, he published his first treatise on education, *Isidoneus Germanicus*, in which he drew largely upon the excellent Catholic manuals of Barzizza. Four years later, he urged the city authorities of Strassburg to found a school in which education would be conducted on the new lines; the school over which Sturm was to preside, a generation later. But the Teutonic mind responded very grudgingly to these new ideas. The progress of the Classic Renaissance in the Germanies was slow.

Johann Reuchlin (1455-1522) was the foremost of the German laymen who took an interest in classic studies. He taught Greek at Heidelberg under Bishop Dalberg, in 1496. His chief distinction is that of having introduced into Germany the study of Hebrew as one of the learned languages. He was always a sincere Catholic, and tried, though unsuccessfully, to win over his grand-nephew Melanchthon (Philip Schwarzerd, 1497-1560) from adherence to Luther. The University of Heidelberg, after the death of Bishop Dalberg, was unable to maintain its early leadership in classic influence. It was to Tübingen, Erfurt (under the scholarly Eobanus Hessus), Wittenberg, and Leipzig, that German humanism owed most of its growth. Desiderius Erasmus (1466-1536), the greatest figure in the northern Renaissance, was a Catholic priest, born in Rotterdam. But in his aims and in his life he transcended nationalism, and hence cannot be considered a German humanist. Although he bitterly satirized the abuses flagrant in the Church, and directed much of his writings toward the reform of these, he was too intelligent to be caught by the mingled frenzy and chicanery of the Protestant Revolution. Erasmus, with the Frenchman Budé and the Spaniard Vives, formed the triumvirate of letters of the northern Renaissance. Of the three, Erasmus was the most forceful and effective writer, but Vives the most thorough-going educator.

Juan Luis Vives (1492-1540), after his early education at his birthplace, Valencia, in Spain, studied at the University of Paris for five years, whence he proceeded to Bruges, in the Spanish Low Countries, in 1514. Henceforth, although he travelled about much, he looked upon Bruges as his home. Erasmus welcomed him enthusiastically at Louvain, where he wrote, lectured in the University, and tutored. His treatise, *In Pseudo-dialecticos,* written when he was twenty-six years old, sharply criticized the debased Scholasticism of the period and advocated inductive methods of study. More, who admired him greatly, introduced him to the English Court, where Queen Catherine employed him as tutor to the Princess Mary. From 1523 to 1528, Vives divided his life between his tutorship to the Princess, a lectureship at Oxford, and his writings in Bruges. He published numerous educational works, the most important being his *De Tradendis Disciplinis* (1531), which Foster Watson reckons "probably the greatest educational work of the Renaissance." Vives was an excellent Catholic in his principles and in his life; a fact which Watson offers as one of the reasons why his name has been obscured in later ages.[1]

In France. France, through its naturally close relations with Italy, was early aware of the new educational development. Italian scholars visited various French centers of learning, and taught classes in Greek at Paris as early as 1458. But the Classic Renaissance did not take strong hold upon French minds until after the Italian campaigns of Charles VIII and Louis XII. In particular, the French Court at Milan, 1498 to 1512, became a channel for the spread throughout France of interest in the new learning. The foremost French leader in the new education was Guillaume Budé (1467-1540), the friend of Erasmus. Francis I welcomed him home from his studies in 1522, and made him royal librarian. Budé was a first-rate Greek scholar, and did much by his writings to promote that zeal for the study of Greek which became so notable in France. He was a sound Catholic, and in his many educational treatises manifests clear Catholic ideals of education. But because he was hostile to the dominance of Scholasticism at the University of Paris, and proposed that the new studies be put upon an academic equality with the chairs of philosophy and theology, the Scholastics accused him of Calvinist leanings: a charge from which he was completely exonerated only after his death. He was largely instrumental in persuading Francis I to found the *Collège de France*. During 1517 and 1518 Budé tried to secure the services of Erasmus as first rector of the College, but unsuccessfully. Hence the establishment of the College lagged for some time, but was finally accomplished in 1530. Budé's most important work on education was *De l'Institution du*

---

[1] *Cyclopedia of Education*, New York, 1913, Vol. 5, p. 739. See also estimate of wide influence of Vives in later pedagogy by K. A. Schmidt, *Encyklopadie des gesammten Erziehungs-und Unterrichtswesens*, Gotha, 1876-87, Vol. 9, pp. 843-51.

Prince, written in French in 1516, but not printed, through fear of comparison with a similar work by Erasmus, until 1547. seven years after the death of Budé.

II. Education in the Schools

Its limited connection with the Renaissance in general. Some histories of education naïvely assume that the large educational theories of a period, often the more or less original work of a few individual writers, are put into complete practice in the schools. It cannot be too often repeated that this assumption is not founded in fact. There are, and always will be, two great obstacles in the way of reducing educational theory to school practice; the very limited competence of most teachers, and the essential immaturity of their pupils. The result is that schools tend to drag everything they touch down to the low level established by these inevitable limitations. Renaissance treatises on education present splendid theories; Renaissance schools, with a few exceptions, show a drab practice which differs from that of mediaeval schools chiefly in the relatively unimportant point of mere curriculum. Almost all the Renaissance educational treatises follow the lead given by the best Italian writers, and whilst laying the intellectual and aesthetic foundations of education in the study of classic literature, insist strongly upon physical, moral, and even religious education, upon harmonious development of the whole individual. Yet even a cursory study of pedagogic writings makes it evident that this ideal of education was not new. It is to be found just as clearly expressed in scores of mediaeval treatises.[1] One can read

[1] See the excellent, and unheeded, criticism of Peter of Blois (who died in England about 1200) on the unbalancing of education by a craze for metaphysical subtleties. Epist. 101; Migne, *P. L.,* 107:311. For John of Salisbury, see the *Metalogicus,* lib. I, c. 24, and lib. II, c. 9, in Migne, *P. L.,* Vol. 199.

these theories admirably put by John of Salisbury, for instance, at the very time when the existing schools were already hardening into mere logic-chopping machines. In just the same way, the Renaissance schools, in spite of this renewed and excellent theorizing, promptly became grammar-chopping machines. The Renaissance ideals, like so many other 'revolutions' in education were largely another case of *parturiunt montes;* and the schoolboy mouse of which they were delivered was pitifully similar to other schoolboy mice of ages preceding and following. There is no lasting magic in a change of curriculum. Only a great teacher makes a great school; and even he demands, for more than mediocre success, conditions which are not always at his command.

The inspiring exceptions. However, there *were* great schools during the Renaissance, and they deserve study. It is true that a great many men whom history considers important in the Classic Renaissance confined their efforts to writing about education, and carefully shunned the schools. Erasmus, for instance, could never be tied down to a school. But some, especially of the early leaders in the movement, although attached to courts or universities, turned to actual teaching in schools, either to augment their scanty incomes, or from a generous desire to promote education in practice as well as in theory. Such men were great teachers, whose teaching work was of value, not merely to their pupils, but as an example to other less gifted teachers. Barzizza was such a teacher; so too were Vittorino da Feltre and the two Guarinos. The greatest of all seems to have been Vittorino, whose work cannot be passed by even in so condensed a book as this without some brief notice.

Vittorino da Feltre. Vittorino de' Rambaldoni, called generally da Feltre from the town in which he was born in 1378, studied under Barzizza at Padua, learned mathematics from Pelacani da Parma, and Greek from Guarino da Verona. In 1422, when he was forty-four years old, he succeeded his old master, Barzizza, in the chair of rhetoric at Padua; but resigned after a year, because he found the students wild and unmanageable. He then set about opening a school at Venice, but in that same year, 1423, was invited by the Marquis Gianfrancesco Gonzaga to come to Mantua and engage in the education of the Marquis' children. Vittorino accepted the invitation, with the stipulation that he be allowed to open a formal school and take other pupils besides the children of Gonzaga. He was given a villa for his school, the name of which he changed to *Casa Giocosa,* the Pleasant House. Here, in charming surroundings, without financial worries, he carried on a small, select school for twenty-three years, until his death in 1446. His pupils, in addition to the Gonzaga children, boys and girls, and the children of some of his friends, included a number of poor children. The basis of studies at Pleasant House was Latin and Greek literature, but genuine attention was paid also to history, mathematics, drawing, music, and such natural history as the times afforded. Everything reasonable was done to make study attractive. There was little punishment, plenty of recreation, excellent care of the health of the children. Games played an important part; though Vittorino aimed more at physical hardiness, health, and the moral control acquired in play, than at mere athletic skill. The children heard Mass every day, received the Sacraments every month.

Vittorino left no writings; but his pupils, who loved him as much as they admired him, spread his fame through the world as an excellent teacher, a model of the Christian gentleman and scholar. His school, which seems to have been even a finer piece of work than that of Guarino at Ferrara, is often hailed as the great pedagogical glory of the Classic Renaissance. Every discussion of the Renaissance brings it in as an instance of school work of the period, often with the implication that it was a 'typical' Renaissance school. Nothing can be farther from fact than to call the schools of Vittorino and Guarino 'typical.' They were, as Burckhardt is careful to point out,[1] quite simply "unique of their kind." They had advantages which no ordinary school can expect to have: in the unusual character of their teachers, in their physical and financial position, in the selection of their pupils. And it is to be noted that, with all its excellence, Vittorino's school turned out such a man as Lorenzo Valla, the mocking voluptuary.[2] This is not to belittle the school of Vittorino, but merely, for the sake of historical perspective, to indicate again the limited influence of even the best sort of school. A thousand schools like Vittorino's might have changed the whole character of the Renaissance; a single school merely lends to the Renaissance a fictitious glory.

The Brothers of the Common Life. Less excellent in individual quality than the schools of Vittorino and Guarino, but more influential because more numerous and more widespread, were the schools taught by the Brothers of the Common Life, a distinguished Catholic religious community founded about 1381 by Geert de Groote. De Groote was born at Deventer, in Gelderland of the Low Countries about 1340. He came of a wealthy burgher family, studied medicine, theology, and canon law at Paris, taught for a few years in the chapter school at Deventer. About 1364, still quite a young man, he was sent on a mission to Pope Urban V at Avignon. On his return he received two rich benefices, taught theology at Cologne,

[1] *Civilization of the Renaissance* (Middlemore's translation, 1898), p. 213.
[2] Cf. G. Voight, *Die Wiederbelebung des classischen Alterthums;* 2 Bde., Berlin, 1880-81, Vol. 1, p. 470.

lived a foppish life: until in 1374, through conversations
with a devout friend, he came to change his ways. He
gave up his house to a community of nuns, and spent some
years in religious meditation. About 1380, having been
ordained deacon, he got license to preach throughout the
diocese of Utrecht. His sermons, in the vernacular, produced great effect; young men in numbers flocked to him.
He encouraged them to study, set them at copying manuscripts, helped them to form sincerely Christian characters.
One of his disciples, Florentius Radewyn, suggested to him,
about 1381, that these young men should pool their earn-
ings from copying manuscripts and should live in common.
Gradually there was developed a permanent organization;
without vows, but pledged to practice poverty, chastity, and
obedience according to each one's conditions of life; forbidden to beg, obliged to maintain themselves by work.
De Groote's attacks on the vices of the clergy resulted
in the withdrawal of his license to preach. He appealed
his case to the Pope, but before any reply could be received
De Groote died of pestilence contracted whilst ministering
to those ill of the plague. He was only forty-four years
old at his death.

The educational work of the Brothers of the Common
Life began with their care for the moral and physical well-
being of poor scholars; whom they lodged in hostels, supplied with work as copyists, and tutored when they were
ill equipped for the established schools. Their tutoring
succeeded so well that many of them were asked to teach
in the schools. Here again their success led to their taking full charge of the schools or opening new schools. The
basis of that success was Christian character as well as
scholarly accomplishment. By 1470, Buschius, one of their
pupils, reckoned that they conducted more than fifty schools
in Flanders, France, and Germany. In 1500, the school
at Deventer had more than two thousand students. As

these schools were intensely Catholic, the Reformation broke up most of them. The best account of one of the schools is given by the Protestant Sturm, in his report to the magistrates at Strassburg in 1538.

The Brothers of the Common Life successfully adapted the new curriculum of the Renaissance to the Catholic ideal of education, their aim being expressed in the phrase *pietas literata*. They added to the study of Greek and Latin some mathematics, history, and geography. They divided their schools into two sections: elementary, for reading, writing, grammar, arithmetic; classical, for the languages, history, rhetoric, etc. They introduced a careful disciplinary organization, arranged classes into *decuries* under charge of monitors (a detail afterwards adopted by the Jesuits and others), offered prizes for good work. Their students gave performances of plays by Terence. Had the Brothers of the Common Life escaped the devastation caused by the Protestant Revolt, and continued their school work through the sixteenth and succeeding centuries, the history of the Jesuits might well have been quite different from the actuality. As it was, the influence of the Brothers was felt, not only in the eminent men they trained, such as the great Cardinal Nicholas of Cusa, Rudolph Agricola, Alexander Hegius, Sturm, and Pope Adrian VI, but even more in their wider spread of sound educational practice. The schools of following ages owe much to them.

Universities in the Renaissance. Almost without exception, the leaders of the Classic Renaissance were men trained in the universities; and their work was primarily a revolt against the universities. It was inevitable that the universities should be hostile to the Renaissance. The new learning was a terrifying threat to the established traditions which are always sacrosanct in an organized institution. It made its way, at first, outside of the universities: at courts, in writings. It had to batter at the university walls for entrance, or creep in with the sapper work of individual converts amongst the university lecturers.   But in the end the result was a gradual, slow surrender of the universities, scarcely completed before the seventeenth century.   However, the universities had their revenge.   A precious formula of the Scholastics was, *quidquid recipitur ad modum recipientis recipitur:* when the formalized universities admitted the new curriculum, they promptly set it in a mold.   The universities, together with the lower schools, succeeded in rendering futile the great educational dreams of the Renaissance leaders; they made of the new learning, in a short while, merely a change from Aristotelianism to Ciceronianism.   It is both amusing and tragic to observe the fiery zeal of Pierre de la Ramée[1] against the wooden Aristotelian dialectic of the University of Paris, and to note that the end of his campaign is an even more mechanical system based upon Cicero.   Both his friends and his foes called his system, Ramism; and fought about it fiercely for a hundred years.

Other Renaissance schools.   It is often shallow and dangerous to speak of a 'type' of schools; since there are such constant differences in schools even of the same period. Yet a summary account is forced to consider rather the things in which schools agree than those in which they differ; and it must be confessed that the agreements are more numerous than the differences.   The chief thing common to schools during the long time in which they were under the controlling influence of the Classic Renaissance was the general use of Latin and Greek literature as the

---

[1] More widely known as Petrus Ramus.   He was born at Cuth in Picardy, 1515; was a university lecturer and principal of several colleges; published fifty-two treatises.   The two most important were *Aristotelicae Animadversiones* and *Dialecticae Institutiones,* in 1543. He saw the evils of pedantry, but he could not get away from it.   He became a Calvinist in 1561, and was killed at Paris, in the St. Bartholomew massacre in 1572.

foundation of their studies. Most of these schools also borrowed a common stock of ideas about school organization from the schools of the Brothers of the Common Life. A third common quality they all soon acquired: the melancholy one of being dull, narrow, inflexible in academic routine. Some of the schools were already old when the Renaissance curriculum began to affect them; such as Winchester, which was founded in 1379, and Eton, established on the same model some sixty years later. Some were newly organized on the basis of humanism; such as Colet's foundation of St. Paul's in 1509, or Sturm's *gymnasium* at Strassburg in 1538. Some had masters, such as William Lilly and Johann Sturm, who were really eminent scholars and eager educators; some had to be content with bread-and-butter men who made no more mark in teaching than they would have made in any other profession. Sturm himself, for all his high qualifications, became a follower of the overelaborate Petrus Ramus, and developed in his Strassburg *gymnasium,* which he governed for nearly forty years, as narrow a sort of humanist school as can be found anywhere. A notable cause of the dull lifelessness of Sturm's school, as of most others, was the obvious fact that the approach to Latin and Greek *literature* was made upon an interminably long and winding road over the sands of *grammar*. The vast majority of the pupils never got out of the sands. In the course of time, the masters quite simply took this sand-trudging to be the essential school education. When they were reproached for this attitude, they fell back for defense upon some theory of 'formal discipline.'

Numbers and influence. On this most important point it is extremely hard to get compact and helpful information. The badly troubled times of the Protestant Revolution, coming so swiftly on the heels of the Renaissance influence in schools, naturally affected both the number of schools and their effective influence upon education.[1] But the Renaissance seems to have brought about some real increase in the number of schools. Further, it helped the organization of schools, since it led to a gradual sharper distinction between elementary and secondary schools by emphasizing the curriculum of the latter. When, however, we consider that the change in schools due to the Renaissance was chiefly a change in curriculum rather than in method,[2] we may reasonably doubt that the Renaissance schools in general were more efficient than those which preceded them. Schools continued, by economic law, to be the privilege mainly of the wealthier classes.

Conclusion. The Classic Renaissance was a challenge to existing ideals of education. It was stimulating, it prodded Europe out of a rut; and therefore it did a real service to education. It is a truism to say that routine is hostile to fine human development. The Renaissance broke an old routine; that is to its credit. But it ended in establishing a new routine; that marked its essential limitation.

Between the limits of the old and new routine, in the energetic ferment of the Renaissance, many great social and educational forces were set at work; the influence of which persists to our own day, and is likely to persist much longer. Some of these forces were beneficial, such as the wider tying together of the remote past and the present, the developing sense of human continuity. Even through the fog of grammar, that development has tended to widen

[1] Leach says that a moderate estimate of grammar schools for England in 1535 is three hundred; most of which were swept away under Henry VIII and Edward VI. *English Schools at the Reformation,* pp. 5, 6.

[2] The introduction of new grammars in place of the old *Doctrinale* of Alexander de Villa Dei, which disappeared with amazing rapidity after 1520, and the wide use of the *Dialogues* of Erasmus and Vives, do not indicate after all, any serious change in school method. The aim of schools continued to be chiefly the ability to read and write Latin, even though now they aimed more at Ciceronic Latin than before.

the vision of schools, and certainly has stretched the horizons of general thought. It could not bring classic beauty into the schools, if only because immature students can have little appreciation of beauty. Some of these forces were not beneficial, chiefly the reformulation of pagan ideals of life. Some hang in the balance, may be used for good or ill; and by that very fact would seem to indicate that they are of very great importance. Perhaps the most significant of these last is the new emphasis laid by the Classic Renaissance upon the individual.

The earlier semibarbaric ages, often called the Dark Ages, were strongly individualistic. Such organizations as existed during those ages, the Catholic Church, the religious orders, the various feudal societies, were comparatively loose in structure. Cluny gave the lead to organized stability, first in its own monasteries, then in the society which surrounded it. The great revival of learning in the twelfth century turned more and more to an *organization* of truths and opinions, to systematizing all human relations. Indirectly, it led to the development of national organizations, the various modern States. System became in time the fetish of the schools. In the fourteenth century, the schools sickened, and nearly died, of an overdose of system. The Renaissance was, in great part, a revolt against that oppression of too much system. Individualism, at times a wild and hysterical individualism, marked the Renaissance movement.

Now, every society recognizes instinctively that individualism is close kin to anarchy. Every society, so long as it has the physical power to do so, restrains the individual.[1] Theorists are forever contending, and rightly, for

[1] Clear historical records show beyond question that the Protestant States, which ranked their churches as governmental departments, were as severely repressive societies as any in history; in spite of the theoretical principle of 'private judgment.'

a balance between the two: between individual freedom
and social restraint. But the balance is hard to come by,
and is never stable. Ever since the recrudescence of striking individualism in the Renaissance, every society, Catholic or Protestant, ecclesiastical or civil, school or family,
has been wrestling, in varying degrees of poor success, with
the problem of asserting itself against the individual and
of granting to the individual such measures of freedom as
he must have for his true growth.

Hence, in political societies, we can trace the gradual
extension of the franchise, and the growth of political skill
by which governments render the franchise as nugatory as
possible; in the Protestant churches, we see a successive
surrender of authority, in the hope of placating individual
members, and of retaining them within the shadow of a
pulpit without doctrines; in the Catholic Church, with no
surrender of authority, we observe an increased consider-
ateness of discipline;[1] in the schools, we have attained the
amazing concession of 'elective curriculum,' the dominance
of paid athletics (half of the *panem* and *circences* of the
decadent Romans), and the charming insouciance of youth-
ful philanderings in coeducation.

To blame the Classic Renaissance for all the vagaries of
this struggle between the individual and society, would be
absurd. If we must strike a balance of praise and blame,
history seems to show that the Classic Renaissance, for all
its defects and limitations, gave a real impetus to vital
education, from which later ages profited. Many good results came from that loosening up of educational garments
which had grown too tight for the peoples of Europe. But
the Classic Renaissance did an irreparable harm to Western
civilization and education by enlisting men of force and

---

[1] See a stimulating and suggestive article by Archbishop Alban
Goodier, in the London *Month*, Vol. 152, No. 777, pp. 193-203, March,
1929.

influence in the service of pagan ideals, and by tending to establish those ideals in the minds of young and old at a time when the weakness of religious leaders had left the people without adequate guidance from Christian revelation. The pagan of today will see nothing to blame in that fact; the Christian, with an outlook beyond this present life, is forced to conclude that the Renaissance took away from its own and succeeding generations immeasurably more than it gave.

Finally, it must be remembered that the forces of the Renaissance were scarcely in full swing throughout Europe, when all European society was shocked and twisted by the cataclysm of the Protestant Revolution. We must consider the educational effect of that Revolution in the next chapter; but we must note here that it did not do more than momentarily halt the ultimate work of the Renaissance, for good and for evil.

TOPICS FOR DISCUSSION

1. The *Doctrinale* of Alexander de Villa Dei, and its influence through three centuries.
2. The educational work of Cardinal Nicholas de Cusa and Cardinal John Dominici.
3. The light thrown on schoolboy life by the Colloquies of Vives.
4. The position of women in Renaissance education.
5. An estimate of the educational writings of Erasmus.
6. A comparison of Erasmus and Vives on education.
7. Varying effects of the Renaissance in town and countryside.

BIBLIOGRAPHIC NOTE

In spite of a certain clumsiness in arrangement, the best general guide to sources for the Middle Ages and the Renaissance is U. Chevalier, *Repertoire des Sources Historiques du Moyen Age,* in two parts: the first, *Bio-Bibliographie,* 2 vols., Paris, 1877-86, 2d ed., Paris, 1905-07; the second, *Topo-Bibliographie,* 2 vols., Paris, 1894-1903. For Italy, of the many collections, these two may be mentioned: L. Muratori, *Rerum Italicarum Scriptores,* 28 vols., Milan, 1723-51 (new ed., Citta di Castello, 1900 sqq.); see Vol. 14 for Matteo Villani, *Historie Fiorentine,* and Vol. 19 for Leonardo Aretino, *Com-*

mentarius ab Anno 1378 usque ad Annum 1440; and the *Fonti per la Storia d'Italia,* Rome, 1887 sqq., especially the division, *Scrittori.* For France, see *Histoire Litteraire de la France,* Paris, 1862, Vol. 24; and the convenient L. Halphen (ed.), *Les Classiques de l'Histoire de France au Moyen Age,* Paris, 1923 sqq. There is a good collection of sources more directly referring to education in F. X. Kunz (ed.), *Bibliothek der katholischen Paedagogik,* Freiburg im Br., 1888 sqq.; see Vol. 7, 1894, for German translation by A. Roesler of Crd. Joannes Dominici, *Regola del Governo di Cura Familiare,* edited by G. Salvi, Florence, 1860. Brief extracts from the sources may be found in M. Whitcomb, *Literary Source-Book of the Renaissance,* 2d ed., Philadelphia, 1903. Adam of Usk, *Chronicon,* has been edited and translated by E. M. Thompson, 2d ed., London, 1904; it describes the Papal court at the beginning of the fifteenth century. Some of Petrarch's letters are translated in J. H. Robinson and H. W. Rolfe, *Petrarch, the First Modern Scholar and Man of Letters,* 2d ed. rev., New York, 1914; the *Epistulae de Rebus Familiaribus* have been edited by G. Fracasetti, 3 vols., Florence, 1859-63. R. Sabbadini has edited *Lettere di Guarino da Verona,* Venice, 1915; and R. Coulon, the *Lucula Noctis* of Cardinal John Dominici, Paris, 1908, his treatise on the use of pagan classics. R. H. H. Cust has translated *The Life of Benvenuto Cellini,* 2 vols., London, 1910. P. S. Allen's edition of *Opus Epistolarum Des. Erasmi Roterodami,* 7 vols., Oxford, 1906-28, is the best; the letters have been translated by F. M. Nichols, with a commentary, 3 vols., London, 1901-18. H. H. S. Croft edited Sir Thomas Elyot, *The Boke Named the Governour,* 2 vols., London, 1883.

A good introduction to the whole period is J. Burckhardt (English translation by S. G. C. Middlemore), *The Civilization of the Period of the Renaissance in Italy,* 2 vols., London, 1878; new ed., from 15th German ed., London, 1929. See also P. S. Allen, *The Age of Erasmus,* Oxford, 1914; F. A. Gasquet, *The Eve of the Reformation,* London, 1899; 3d ed., 1905; E. Gebhart, *Rabelais, la Renaissance, et la Reforme,* Paris, 1885; L. Geiger, *Renaissance und Humanismus in Italien und Deutschland,* Berlin, 1882; the three works of Eugene Muntz, *Les Precurseurs de la Renaissance,* Paris, 1882, *La Renaissance en Italie et en France a l'Epoque de Charles VIII,* Paris, 1885, *Histoire de l'Art pendant le Renaissance,* 3 vols., Paris, 1889-95; J. M. Stone, *Reformation and Renaissance, 1377-1610,* New York, 1904; J. A. Symonds, *Short History of the Renaissance,* New York, 1894; M. V. Clarke, *The Medieval City-State: an Essay on Tyranny and Federation in the Later Middle Ages,* London, 1926; J. E. Sandys, *The History of Classical Scholarship,* 3 vols., New York, 1903-08; J. Owen, *The Sceptics of the Italian Renaissance,* London, 1893.

Two valuable works on the *Doctrinale* are C. Thurot, *De Alexandri de Villa-Dei Doctrinali,* Paris, 1850, and D. Reichling, *Das Doctrinale des Alexander de Villa-Dei,* Berlin, 1893.

For Rome, see L. Pastor, *History of the Popes,* especially noting the Introduction to Vol. 1 and Vol. 5; J. B. Christophe, *Histoire de la Papauté pendant le XVe Siecle,* 2 vols., Paris and Lyons, 1863; and R. Lanciani, *The Golden Days of the Renaissance in Rome,* London, 1907.

For Italy, see P. de Nolhac, *Petrarque et l'Humanisme,* Paris, 1892; L. Barozzi and R. Sabbadini, *Studi sul Panormita e sul Valla,* Florence. 1891; S. Bellani, *Luigi Marsili degli Agostiniani, Apostolo ed Anima del Rinascimento Letterario in Firenze, 1342-1394,* Florence, 1911; L. Gabotto, *Lorenzo Valla e l'Epicureismo nel Quattrocento,* Milan, 1889; W. B. Skaife, *Florentine Life during the Renaissance,* Baltimore, 1893; C. de Rosmini, *Idea dell' Ottimo Precettore nella Vita e Disciplina di Vittorino da Feltre,* Bassano, 1801; R. Sabbadini, *La Scuola e gli Studi di Guarino Veronese,* Catania, 1896; and the two fine studies of W. H. Woodward, *Vittorino da Feltre and Other Humanist Educators,* Cambridge, 1905, *Studies in Education, 1400-1600,* Cambridge, 1906.

For the North, see P. Neve, *La Renaissance en Belgique,* Brussels, 1890; L. Einstein, *The Italian Renaissance in England,* New York, 1902, although this work is chiefly concerned with the sixteenth century; K. Grube, *Gerhard Groote und seine Stiftungen,* Cologne, 1883; J. Kettlewell, *Thomas a Kempis and the Brothers of the Common Life,* London, 1882; A. Hyma, *The Christian Renaissance,* New York, 1925; F. Paulsen, *German Education, Past and Present,* New York, 1908.

For Cusa, see C. Schmidt, *Kardinal Nikolaus Cusanus,* Coblenz, 1907; E. Vansteenberghe, *Le Cardinal Nicholas de Cues (1401-1464), l'Action, le Pensée,* Paris, 1920; and P. Rotta, *Il Cardinale Nicolo di Cusa: la Vita e il Pensiero,* Milan, 1928.

For Erasmus and Vives, see W. H. Woodward, *Desiderius Erasmus Concerning the Aim and Method of Education,* Cambridge, 1904; R. B. Drummond, *Erasmus, His Life and Character as Shown in His Correspondence and Works,* 2 vols., London, 1873; J. J. Mangan, *Life Character, and Influence of Erasmus of Rotterdam Derived from a Study of His Works,* 2 vols., New York, 1927; F. Watson, *Vives on Education* (his treatise *De Disciplinis*), London, 1906; *Tudor Schoolboy Life* (the *Linguae Latinae Exercitatio* of Vives), London, 1910; and *Vives and the Renaissance Education of Women,* London, 1910.

A good introductory study of the place of women in Renaissance education is M. A. Cannon, *The Education of Women during the Renaissance,* Washington, 1916. Alice A. Hentsch, *De la Litterature Didactique du Moyen Age s'Adressant Specialement aux Femmes,* Halle, 1903, briefly analyzes the writings of 114 authors, and covers the period to 1600.

CHAPTER XIII

THE REFORMATION AND EDUCATION

Reformation and revolution. In the year 1500, the situation of Christendom in the West was this: all the peoples of western Europe professed the Catholic religion, under the spiritual supremacy of the pope, whom they recognized as the vicar of Christ; they shared a fairly uniform culture, in which the differences were of degree rather than of kind; they still held some community in the Latin language, but it was diminishing steadily, and the vernaculars had become set in their permanent form and were truly national languages; they were divided into nations almost as sharply set apart from one another as those of today; they were more than a little confused in their relations with the pope, owing to the fact that he was a temporal as well as a spiritual sovereign; some of their national groups had long-standing political quarrels with the papal kingdom; they all had a good deal of distrust of the Catholic hierarchy, because it had become so worldly, and they envied it its enormous wealth and power; they had received a large leavening of pagan principles through one stream of Renaissance influence.[1] The situation was very compli-

[1] Perhaps to these should be added another item: they were infected with syphilis so extensively that the disease might be called pandemic. Apparently, the little handful of sailors who returned with Columbus from his first voyage in 1493 brought this new wave of syphilitic infection to Europe. It spread with a rapidity which is almost incredible. It was frightfully prevalent in Naples; and the soldiers of Charles VIII, who after a short siege entered Naples February 11, 1495, contracted the disease there. H. Haser says of these soldiers: "Those who had most to do with the further dissemination of the disease were the Albanian and Roumanian estradiots serving in the Venetian army, brutal and rapacious adventurers, and also the German and Swiss Landsknechte returning from Italy, who

cated. Social, political, and religious tension was high. Every man of developed intelligence realized that European civilization had reached an important crisis. The most intelligent appreciated that it was essentially a spiritual crisis, and that its proper solution depended more upon religion than upon political or economic changes. Practically, they saw that, if European civilization was to be saved and bettered, it must be through a reassumption of religious leadership, a reassertion of Christian principles in the conduct of life. That meant, in concrete terms, that the hierarchy of the Catholic Church must reform itself, and become once more capable of guiding and shaping the civilization over which it still claimed, by divine right, a control which it did not exercise.

Hundreds of really great men urged that reform, in word and in writing, with various degrees of patience or impatience, with varying realization of how huge a task the reform would be and how pitifully slow and dragging it must inevitably be. To many of these men the reform even seemed humanly impossible. It was, however, actually accomplished in the course of time; its great beginning

spread the disease over a large part of Europe." (*Lehrbuch der Geschichte der Medizin und der epidemischen Krankheiten,* 3d ed., Jena, 1882, Vol. 3, p. 256.)

How far the nervous irritability set up by syphilis influenced that impatience which largely caused the Protestant Revolution, it is beyond human power to determine. Certain it is that leaders of the Revolt, in common with many thousands of others, suffered from syphilis. Ulrich von Hutten died of it at the age of thirty-five. (D. F. Strauss, *Ulrich von Hutten,* Vol. 3, p. 165; in the abridged translation by G. Sturge, London, 1874, pp. 356-57. Von Hutten himself wrote a treatise, *De Guaiaci Medicina et Morbo Gallico,* published at Mayence, 1519.) There is good medical testimony that Luther and Henry VIII were syphilitic. (For Luther, see the letter of the physician Wolfgang Rychardus, dated June 11, 1523, and published by Theodore Kolde, a Protestant historian, in his *Analecta Lutherana,* Gotha, 1883, p. 50. Grisar discusses it in his *Luther,* Vol. 2, pp. 161-64. Charles MacLaurin, M. D., has gathered the evidence for Henry VIII in the third chapter of his book, *Mere Mortals,* Doran, New York, 1925.)

was made in the Council of Trent, 1545 to 1563. But before
that reform was begun, and perhaps as a necessary final
spur to the reform, an appalling spiritual catastrophe occurred; a number of ecclesiastical and civil leaders broke
definitely with historic Christianity and set up national
churches.[1] When the reform came, it was too late to save
these national churches to the Catholic Faith. Large sections of northern Europe split apart from the Church,
split into quarreling religious rivalries, took the negating
name of Protestant, and laid upon the centuries to come
the wasteful burden of emotional hostilities. This Protestant Revolution is generally, and most improperly, known
as the Reformation. The Reform itself is confusingly called
the Counter Reformation.

The causes of the Protestant Revolution. In a most
general way, it may be said that the causes of the Protestant Revolution were two: the gross and widespread corruption of the Catholic hierarchy and clergy; and the impatience of 'reformers' who were temperamentally incapable
of working for a real reform, and preferred instead the
suicidal action of revolt. The apparent justification of

---

[1] "Since the captivity of the Popes in Avignon and the great
Western schism, in every country in Europe, more or less, grave
abuses, galling inequalities, and a dangerous spirit of unrest had
heaped up, within the area of the Church, a mass of inflammable material which, if once unexpectedly kindled, was bound to break into a
terrible conflagration. Scandalous as the disorders in the Church
certainly were, damming up the well-springs of grace and truth,
there was, nevertheless, no ground for despair of recovery. Everywhere healthy forces still abounded by which gradually the elements of combustion might have been removed. That, instead of
such a process of regeneration, instead of the reform in head and
members longed for by all good men, the world-wide catastrophe
arrived which began by separating from the centre of Christian unity
a great part of Germany and, in the course of time, one-third of
Europe, seemed in the minds of contemporaries a judgment of God,
whose long-suffering was exhausted. The secularized clergy, epis-
copate, and Papacy needed chastisement; they must be cleansed and
purified through stern calamity." L. Pastor, *History of the Popes*
(English translation), London, 1923, Vol. 11, pp. 1, 2.

these latter must be that they had despaired of a reform; yet that, in reality, was not a genuine justification, but a new fault; since it was a flagrant distrust of the promise of Christ that He would not allow His Church to fail. In detail, there were other motives than this disordered zeal which urged on the leaders of revolt: envy of the wealth of the Church, unchristian and disgusting rivalries between religious orders, the conceit of theologians, the rude license of exaggerated individualism, the political ambitions of princes, the resentment of the masses against the privileges of the rich and powerful. In a word, for one part of high motive, the Revolt had nine parts of very low motives. Yet, granting all this, no amount of blame laid at the doors of the leaders of the Revolt can lessen the ultimate and terrible responsibility of Catholic churchmen for the conditions which gave occasion to the Revolt.

The character of the Protestant Revolution. The Protestant Revolution was not uniform in character. It was not a concerted movement; but a succession of mutually repellent explosions. In the Germanies, it was more characterized by moral indignation and emotional violence than elsewhere; in England, it was primarily concerned with pillaging the wealth of the Church; in Geneva, it was harshly and narrowly theological. Luther talked a frothy democracy in the beginning; but was quickly affrighted by seeing the peasants take him seriously, and became as violently authoritative and repressive as any. In no place, for more than a brief moment, did the Revolt keep a religious character; it immediately became political. Kings and princes seized upon it as a means of furthering their own schemes; indeed, without their backing it would soon have died out. Everywhere it was violent. The sixteenth century in Europe was noted more for heat than for light. Protestants persecuted Protestants as severely as they did Catholics, or as Catholics persecuted them.

It is hard to conceive of a competent historian who, at this distance of time, would take the stand that the Protestant Revolution was wholly disinterested or deserving of admiration. Because of the endless bitter feelings stirred up by it, the Revolution has been for centuries a subject, not for calm historical valuation, but for impassioned controversy. Perhaps the time has now come when men can view it with enough of cool and intelligent detachment to see that it was a blunder consequent upon a thousand other blunders, for which Catholic churchmen were chiefly to blame, and that the one emotion it should excite in us is a kindly and tolerant pity.

Its effect upon education in general. Excited dissensions, the bitterness of religious and political quarrelings, are always injurious to education, in schools or out of schools. To set peoples against each other in hatred is to thrust them backward in civilization, is to substitute prejudice for conviction, to make the acquisition of truth increasingly difficult, to do irreparable harm to character. As a simple historical fact, the Protestant Revolution had this bad effect upon education: a bad effect which still persists.[1] The immediate results of the Revolution, in cutting down attendance at the universities and other schools in the countries most affected by the Revolution, have been noted; but they were of little account in comparison with the huge educational disaster of the hatreds sown throughout Europe. Another important effect of the Revolution upon education was the entry of the State into the control and management of schools. This was a gradual consequence

---

[1] "It was prejudice and confusion of thought which allowed the very term, 'the new learning,' to be applied indifferently to humanists and Lutherans, and to make it connote anti-catholicism. In point of fact, Luther was as much opposed to the spirit of humanism as to that of catholicism." (J. W. Adamson, *A Short History of Education*, Cambridge, 1922, p. 134.) In this connection, see *infra*, p. 316, text and note 3.

upon the fact that the Protestant churches became departments of the States in which they were organized. In the long run, this State control unquestionably made for the material stability and wider spread of schools. Its influence, good and bad, upon the work done in the schools must be discussed later, when we come to consider the national systems of school education. In general, it can only be observed here that the education given in State-controlled schools tended to become exclusively secular in character. A final effect of the Revolution came from the introduction of the principle of 'private judgment' as to what constituted revealed truth in religion: religious anarchy, the gradual frittering away of Christian beliefs. This meant that the Protestant peoples little by little abandoned almost all of Christianity save its name and certain vaguely inherited elements of its moral code; so that today a man may be, not merely a Protestant in good standing in his church, but a minister of a Protestant religion, without believing even in the divinity of Christ. It meant also that a clear way was opened to the spread and development of that Renaissance paganism which had already done so much harm to the education of Europe, and which has since come to dominate so extensively in modern civilization. Sentimentally, Protestants regret that spread of pagan principles; logically, though unwittingly, they caused it.

Its effect upon school education. Erasmus, writing to Pirkheimer from Basle in 1528, uttered the statement so often quoted, "Wherever Lutheranism rules, learning dies."[1] After some four hundred years, a Protestant theologian substantiates the verdict of Erasmus in these words: "The immediate effect of the Wittenberg preaching was the collapse of the educational system which had flourished

---

[1] *Opera,* iii, col. 1139; Le Clerc (ed.), 10 vols., Ludg. Batavorum, 1702-06.

throughout Germany. . . . Nor was this merely the passing result of a misapprehension of Luther's preaching, since it endured for scores of years."[1] Erfurt, for instance, had 311 students enrolled in 1520; the number had fallen to 72 in 1522; and in 1527 the university was practically dead, with only 14 students. Eobanus Hessus, a friend of Luther, sent him in 1523 an elegiac poem entitled "Captiva," in which he bewails the sad decay of learning; and Luther answered it in tones of equal depression.[2] Eulenburg, in his study of university statistics, shows that conditions at Erfurt were paralleled at all the German universities, and follows his detailed figures with the general assertion: "The religious and social disturbances of the Reformation brought about a complete breakdown of studies. Some of the Universities were closed entirely, at others the students dwindled to a few."[3] The same state of affairs was brought about by the Protestant Revolution in England. At Oxford, there were 108 graduates in 1535, but only 44 the next year.[4] "In two years of Edward's reign, no student at all graduated at Oxford; in 1550, Latimer, a fierce advocate of the new movement (away from the Catholic religion), laments the fact that there seem 'ten thousand less students than within the last twenty years,' and remarks that 'it would pity a man's heart to hear that I hear

[1] *Preussische Jahrbucher* of Berlin, v. 132, 1908, pp. 381 sqq. Article by F. M. Schiele, "Luther und das Luthertum in ihrer Bedeutung fur die Geschichte der Schule und der Erziehung."

[2] *M. Luthers Briefe, Senschreiben und Bedenken,* edited by M. de Wette, Berlin, 1825-28, Vol. 4, p. 118.

[3] F. Eulenburg, "Uber die Frequenz der deutschen Universitäten in früherer Zeit," *Jahrbucher f. Nationalökonomie u. Statistik, 3,* 1897, Vol. 13, p. 525. Some of his figures for the decade 1521 to 1530 are: at Leipzig, a decrease in students from 340 to 100; at Rostock, from 123 to 33; at Frankfurt-on-Oder, from 73 to 32; at Wittenberg, from 245 to 174. See also Janssen, *History of the German People at the Close of the Middle Ages* (English translation, New York, 1900-10), Vol. 13, pp. 258, 266.

[4] R. H. Benson, in *Cambridge History of English Literature,* Vol. 3, p. 50.

of the state of Cambridge.'"[1]   Between 1542 and 1548, there was an average of only 32 graduates a year at Cambridge, and 28 a year at Oxford.[2]   In 1561, no doctor's degree was conferred at Oxford in any of the faculties.[3]   The spoliation of the monasteries closed some five hundred or more chantry schools.[4]

Of the grammar schools, Leach says: "Three hundred is a moderate estimate of (their) number in the year 1535, when the floods of the great revolution, which is called the Reformation, were let loose.   Most of them were swept away either under Henry or his son; or, if not swept away, plundered and damaged."[5]   In the Germanies, the grammar schools and elementary schools were not quite so hard hit as the universities, since they were not so directly involved in religious controversy.[6]   But indirectly, through the looting of their endowments, and through the growing materialistic temper of the people, which led them to despise any training not immediately needed for making money, these lower schools also suffered severely.   Indeed, it was the injury done to such schools which called forth Luther's two pamphlets on education.

Luther on school education.   The first of Luther's educational treatises was published in 1524, and was addressed

---

[1] Benson, *op. cit.*, p. 51.

[2] James Gairdner, *Cambridge Modern History*, Vol. 2, p. 468.

[3] W. H. Woodward, *Cambridge History of English Literature*, Vol. 3, p. 421.

[4] Professor Pollard reckons the 'chantry priests' as about two thousand in a population of two millions.   (*Cambridge Modern History*, Vol. 2, p. 502; *Political History of England, 1547-1605*, pp. 18-20.)   This estimate is conservative.   It is not known how many of these priests conducted chantry schools.   The number ventured in the text is a very moderate estimate.

[5] A. F. Leach, *English Schools at the Reformation*, Westminster, 1896, p. 5.

[6] A striking instance of the havoc wrought by religious controversy is found at Cologne.   This University, which began in 1389 with 737 matriculated students, and which a hundred years later regularly had about 2,000 students, was reduced by religious opposition to only 251 students in 1521, and to only 54 in 1534.

"to the Councillors of all the German towns," Catholic as well as Protestant.[1] It is a plea for the founding of schools, and a good plea; although it contains nothing new, it presents the age-old arguments for schools in a vigorous way. It deserves some attention here, because for a long time German Protestant writers made absurdly exaggerated estimates of its importance in the history of education, and on the basis of it hailed Luther as 'the father of the national schools.' Modern scholarship brushes aside such claims.[2] In reality, Luther's views on education were most narrowly limited, and his chief concern for schools sprang from a utilitarian desire to keep up the supply of preachers and rulers.[3] He scarcely had even a concept of the modern national school systems, with their insistence upon school education for all children. His compulsory education is limited to likely

[1] "An die Radherrn aller Stedte Deutsches Lands das sie Christlichen Schulen auffrichten und halten sollen." *Werke,* Weimar edition, Vol. 15, pp. 9 sqq.

[2] See the Introduction to the Weimar edition of "An die Radherrn," Vol. 15, p. 9. F. Paulsen says of Luther's educational writings that they are only "a cry for help, wrung from Luther by the sudden, general collapse of the educational system which followed on the ecclesiastical upheaval." *Geschichte des gelehrten Unterrichts auf den deutschen Schulen und Universitaten vom Ausgang des Mittelalters bis zur Gegenwart,* 2d ed., Leipzig, 1896-97, Vol. 1, p. 197. See also F. M. Schiele, in *Preussische Jahrbucher,* Vol. 5, p. 132 (1908), pp. 384, 386, who calls the supposed foundation of the national schools by Luther a fable.

[3] Kostlin-Kawerau, *Martin Luther, sein Leben und seine Schriften,* 5th ed., Berlin, 1903, Vol. 2, p. 37. Paulsen says: "Luther shared all the superstitions of the peasant in their most pronounced form; the methods of natural science were strange to him, and any scattering of the prevalent delusions he would have looked upon as an abomination." *Gesch. des gelehrten Unterrichts,* Vol. 1, p. 177. And again, according to Luther, "artistic education must be wholly rooted out as a work of the devil; the very most that can be tolerated is the use of those works which deal with form, but even these must not be commented on or explained." (*Ibid.,* p. 185.) "Neither Luther nor Knox had in mind a national system of elementary schools; their purpose was to secure control of all schools and universities, and to make the requirements of clerical education dominate the course of study." (J. W. Adamson, *op. cit.,* p. 135.) Grant records Knox's purpose in *History of the Burgh and Parish Schools of Scotland,* Edinburgh, 1876, pp. 76 sqq.

subjects for the Lutheran ministry; only "when the authorities see a clever lad," are they to force his parents to send him to school.[1] He had no enthusiasm for vernacular schools. Even for his grammar schools, in which Latin was to be begun early, his program is very modest; he wishes "the boys to attend such a school for an hour or two every day, and work the rest of the day at learning a trade, or doing whatever was required of them. . . . A little girl too might find time to go to school daily for an hour, and still thoroughly attend to her work in the house." Very sensibly, he wanted only the brighter children to devote "more time and longer hours to study."[2] Indeed, he wished the authorities to prevent any but 'clever boys' from going on to the universities, and had a forthright scorn for the ambition which made "every fellow want a doctorate."[3]

Luther's appeal had comparatively little effect. Melanchthon, who in general worked much more effectively than Luther for school education, founded a *gymnasium* at Nuremberg, on humanistic lines. The school, amply provided for by the city councillors, and intended as a model for other Lutheran schools, was opened May 6, 1526. Luther praised the school highly. Yet within four years the reluctance of the burghers to send their children to this grammar school led Luther to write, in July, 1530, his second lengthy treatise on the schools.[4] In it he combats the protest, "If my son knows how to read and reckon, he knows quite enough. We now have plenty of German books, we do not need Latin."[5] But his main plea is still for schools as 'seminaria' of preachers. He threatens with hell fire those

---

[1] This is taken from the second treatise, "das man Kinder zur Schulen halten solle"; *Werke,* Weimar edition, Vol. 30, 2, p. 587.

[2] *Werke,* Weimar edition, Vol. 15, p. 47.

[3] *Ibid.,* Vol. 6, p. 461.

[4] "Predigt, das man Kinder zur Schulen halten solle." *Werke,* Weimar edition, Vol. 30, 2, pp. 508 sqq.

[5] *Ibid.,* p. 519.

parents who refuse to send their clever boys to school or to let them become preachers. In general, no greater result came from these treatises than sporadic efforts to combine, here and there, a couple of decaying schools, and give them a new charter. Luther had no very definite or practical suggestions to offer the schools. The humanistic system which Melanchthon followed rather narrowly had lost popularity in Protestant Germany. Schiele says that "even towns like Nuremberg and Frankfurt, in spite of great sacrifices, could not introduce an orderly system into their schools. Camerarius and Micyllus, the two best and most practical schoolmasters of the time, were unable to keep their town-schools from decay."[1] Luther showed an intelligent good will toward school education; but he accomplished little or nothing practically to further it. A couple of treatises are weak weapons against a violent social upheaval. It was simply inevitable that school education should suffer in the catastrophe brought about by the Protestant Revolution. Only when the countries involved had settled down again to a routine existence, did the schools at all adequately revive.

The Catholic Reformation. Jesus Christ, in instituting His Church, had promised that "the gates of hell would not prevail against it."[2] That guarantee of indefectibility meant, not that its members, high and low, would always be faithful, but only that the faithless members would never be allowed to destroy the Church. It meant, therefore, that there would always be a body of Christians numerous enough, and strong enough in faith and practice, to keep the Church truly living even in the midst of widespread corruption; somewhat, to use a loose analogy, as in a human body its inherent vitality might combat and overcome the attacks of infection. History shows that even in

[1] *Preussische Jahrbucher*, Vol. 132, p. 391.
[2] Matt. 16:18.

the darkest hours of the Renaissance and the Revolt there were great numbers of men and women in the Catholic Church whose lives displayed Christian virtues even in heroic degree. The reform of the Church was largely brought about through the gradual extension of influence by these true Catholics over the corrupt members of the Church. As that Church had risen from beneath the weight of pagan persecution, as it had survived the more dangerous, because internal, assaults of Arianism, as it had emerged from the barbarism of the 'Dark Ages,' so now again it was to be rescued from the corroding selfishness, cupidity, and grossness of its own members and its hierarchy. The beginning of the reform, at first feeble and halting, was made in the Council of Trent; but it became sufficient to animate with new courage the little leaven of loyal and generous Catholics, and to give them the official backing they needed to carry out the slow, laborious work of re-educating the masses of their fellow religionists. It cannot be emphasized too strongly that their work was essentially a work of education, of intellectual and moral training.

The Council of Trent. Long before the outbreak of the Protestant Revolution, earnest Catholic men had been agitating for a general council of the Church, which should set on foot the needed reform. After the Revolt, there was still more urgent need of such a council; and it had now to take upon itself the further task of clearing Catholic doctrine from the misconceptions engendered through many years of unbridled theological speculation. But after the Revolt, the political and other difficulties in the way of convening the council became enormous. Many Catholic prelates were opposed to the council, because they dreaded the effects of a real reform upon their own lives. The two leading Catholic princes, the Emperor Charles V and Francis I of France, used the idea of the council as a politi-

cal makeweight in their own schemes. When the Farnese
Pope, Paul III, in 1537, nearly twenty years after the beginning of the Revolt, finally did issue the summons, the
Lutheran princes refused to send representatives to the
Council, Francis I forbade the French bishops to attend it,
and the Duke of Mantua, in whose capital the Council was
to meet, worked to impede the gathering. It was eight
years before the Council actually met, at Trent; and then
its members reckoned only four archbishops, twenty-one
bishops, and five general superiors of religious orders.[1]
Even in this little handful there was dangerous friction:
the partisans of the Emperor, Charles V, insisting that the
Council occupy itself primarily with a comprehensive
scheme of disciplinary reform, as against the Pope's wish
that the main business of the Council be with doctrinal
decrees, to oppose the new heresies. The Emperor viewed
the work of the Council chiefly as affecting his own political position in the German States; the Pope considered it
as benefiting the universal Church of Christ. The princes
who were profiting politically by the Revolt wished to have
nothing whatever to do with the Council. It would seem
almost incredible that, in the circumstances, the Council
should accomplish anything of real value.

It is a striking proof of the divine character of the Catholic Church that the Council of Trent, in the face of all
these difficulties, and in spite of the still greater difficulty
that even some of the bishops present at the Council had
no great stomach for a reform which would affect themselves, actually did function courageously and generously.
It met the opposition of Charles by a decision to discuss
discipline and doctrine simultaneously; and in each session
issued two decrees, one of doctrinal definition, one of reform. The number of bishops in attendance gradually in-

---

[1] St. Ehses, *Concilium Tridentinum,* Friburgi Br., 1904, iv, pp.
519 sqq.

creased. Their intelligent willingness to face real issues became more and more manifest. The Council struggled against ceaseless opposition for eighteen years, under five successive popes. In the end, it numbered as its members four cardinal legates of the pope, two cardinals, three patriarchs, twenty-five archbishops, one hundred and sixty-eight bishops, seven abbots, and seven general superiors of religious orders.[1] Its decrees, doctrinal and disciplinary, were more numerous than those of any other general council; and they met the needs of the times with a completeness and clarity which is nothing less than amazing. The hostile civil leaders who kept alive the religious controversy for political purposes spread detestation and contempt for the Council of Trent; but the Council made a new anchorage for the drifting faith and religious practice of the millions who still held allegiance to the Church established by Jesus Christ.

The spread of the reform. If the decrees of the Council of Trent had been promptly and thoroughly obeyed throughout the Church, the needed reform would have been secured within a few years. But, due to the massive inertia of human nature, there was, as always, a wide gap between reforms ordered and reforms carried out. Trent could only again point the way, the ancient way of the Church of Christ, to priests and people. It was the larger task of many generations of devoted men and women to get priests and people to walk in that way. That was a task of religious and moral education, a never-ending task, with the comparative success or failure of which all other educational efforts are bound up. It was not a new undertaking of the sixteenth century, but as old as Christianity itself. It was rendered, however, unusually difficult in the six-

---

[1] A. Theiner, *Acta genunia Conc. Trid.*, Agram, 1874, Vol. 2, pp. 509-13. In addition to those present, thirty-nine other members unavoidably absent were represented by proxies.

teenth and succeeding centuries, both by the long-standing abuses within the Church and by the embittered hostility of the peoples who had seceded in revolt from the Church. It is obvious that humanity, which always needs reform, is most difficult to reform when it needs it most.

Largely by means of new religious orders. The work of reform began, as Cluny had begun five hundred years before, in voluntary associations of men of high purposes. One of these, the Oratory of Divine Love, composed of both priests and laymen, was founded in Rome about the time that Luther began his revolt. Pastor does not hesitate to say that from this association "the Catholic reformation sprang."[1] Gian Matteo Giberti, one of its members, became Bishop of Verona, and with exquisite skill, patience, charity, and zeal, carried through a remarkable work of reform amongst his priests. "His masterly regulations were later taken as models by such devoted bishops as St. Charles Borromeo; indeed many of the enactments of the Council of Trent were borrowed from them almost word for word";[2] although Giberti died two years before the Council met. Two other members of the Oratory of Divine Love, Gaetano di Tiene and Gian Pietro Carafa, founded a new religious order, the Theatines, which became a training school for excellent bishops.[3] It is an undeniable fact that the older religious orders had become extremely corrupt. Hence, the Church, whilst still hoping to bring back the old orders to their former usefulness,[4] had to depend for the initial work of reform chiefly upon new voluntary associations of religious men and women. Paul III (1534-1549) and suc-

[1] *History of the Popes* (English translation), Vol. 11, p. 4.
[2] *Ibid.,* Vol. 11, pp. 504, 505.
[3] Good account in R. de Maulde-la-Clairere, *Saint Gaetan,* Paris, 1902.
[4] Note, for instance, the fine work of Girolamo Seripando in the Augustinian order, beginning in 1538. Cf. G. Calenzio, *Documenti inediti e nuovi lavori litterarii sul Concilio di Trento,* Roma, 1874, pp. 353 sqq. For the Dominicans and Franciscans, see B. Fontana,

ceeding popes did all in their power to foster and develop these new orders. In addition to the Theatines, the most important of these new religious associations were the Capuchins, the Jesuits, and the Ursulines. The Capuchins were a reformed branch of the Observant Franciscans (who had long ceased to be very 'observant'), begun in 1525 by Matteo di Bassi.[1] They stressed the rigorous poverty of St. Francis of Assisi, plain sermons for the uneducated masses, and work amongst the sick and poor. They were, in general, the most effective preachers of the sixteenth century, and were extremely well liked, especially by the poor. So many of the Observant Franciscans hastened to join them that the older order complained to the popes, and had various restrictions put upon the Capuchins.[2] The Ursulines were founded by St. Angela Merici in 1535.[3] They were the first teaching order of women established in the Church, to be followed by a very large number of others whose work in Catholic education has become so important in our times. Angela Merici, born in 1469 at Desenzano on Lake Garda, turned her home into a school for little girls when she was only twenty years old. But it was not until she was sixty-six that, with twelve companions, she founded the religious order of the Ursulines. In 1534, a year before the founding of the Ursulines, Ignatius Loyola and six companions formed a new group at Paris, which was to become the Society of Jesus. They were approved

Documenti Vaticani contro l'eresia Luterana in Italia (in Archivio della Societa Romana di storia patria, Vol. 15), Roma, 1892, pp. 390 sqq.; and L. Wadding, Annales Minorum, Romae, 1735 sqq., Vol. 18, pp. 410 sqq., 430 sqq.

[1] Pellegrino da Forli, Annali Capuccini, Milan, 1882. See also Vol. 13 of Franciscan Annals, Crawley, England.

[2] Cf. P. Tacchi Venturi, Vittoria Colonna, fautrice della riforma Cattolica, Roma, 1909, pp. 162, 173. Z. Boverius, Annales sive historiae ordinis minorum S. Francisci qui Capuccini nuncupantur, 2 vols., Lugduni, 1632, Vol. 1, pp. 197 sqq., 270 sqq. et passim.

[3] Postel, Histoire de la Sainte Angele Merici, 2 vols., Paris, 1878. An English life by O'Reilly, New York, 1880.

as a religious order by Paul III in 1540, the year of Angela Merici's death. It has often been noted that the Theatines were aristocrats in character and exerted influence chiefly amongst the wealthy and leisured, the Capuchins appealed to the masses of the poor, and the Jesuits found their sphere of activity principally in the growing middle classes.[1]

The manner of developing the reform. Christianity, from its first preaching by its Founder, was spread chiefly by *invitation* to accept its truths and its graces. The men who, in the sixteenth century, fanned to new flame the dulling embers of Christian life, relied upon that same sort of appeal to the human soul. They preached and taught and exhorted, they were insistent in presenting again and again the truths and principles of Jesus Christ, they strove by every skill they could develop to get people to avail themselves of the supernatural helps to living which were offered them in the sacraments and prayer. For adults, the most important approaches were necessarily sermons, books, conversations; for the young, the schools. There was nothing at all new in this, except the new earnestness and zeal which animated the Christian educators. The repressive measures, ecclesiastical censures and punishments, the various sorts of Inquisitions,[2] were not primarily educational, but were the unfortunately necessary instruments of moral surgery. They aimed at destroying out of the Christian body such members as were hopelessly corrupt, in order to safeguard the remainder against dangerous infection. Their part in the spread of Church reform was infinitesimal.

[1] Cf. Pastor, *History of the Popes* (Eng. trs.), Vol. 11, p. 540.
[2] These were more often social and civil agencies than ecclesiastical, even when they were staffed largely by ecclesiastics. Religious controversy has grossly distorted their true nature and function. Their grave defects we can readily acknowledge, without at the same time failing to see that they served a good and necessary purpose. Cf. *The Catholic Encyclopedia*, s. v.; also E. Vacandard, *L'Inquisition*, Paris, 1907; English translation, Longmans, New York, 1908.

The success of the reform. It would be absurd to claim that the reform of the Catholic Church was completely successful. In this world nothing of the sort ever is, or can be, completely successful. But the reform did meet with a great measure of success, a much greater measure than might humanly have been looked for. Many abuses were abolished, ecclesiastical greed was curbed, Church leaders were recalled to their true purpose and their zeal was stimulated, the masses of the people were increasingly better instructed in their religious beliefs and became increasingly more faithful in their religious practices, the general tone of Catholic life was elevated and purified. This successful progress of reform was decidedly gradual, and suffered occasional and local setbacks; but it was, on the whole, steady. Its results can be seen better in the long perspective of history than in a detailed study of the steps by which they were achieved. It is obvious that there are still defects in the Catholic body, as there always will be; but they are microscopic when compared with the gross faults of the fourteenth, fifteenth, and sixteenth centuries. The Catholic Church today is more vigorous than ever before. It has been helped much in this development by persistent opposition and even persecution.

The conclusion of the period: a dual educational system. By the close of the sixteenth century the splitting-up of Europe into Catholic and Protestant was completed, with an air of permanency. Henceforth, until such time as God's providence should heal the enormous wound, there were to be two cultures,[1] and therefore two educations, in Europe and in the Americas which Europe was beginning to colonize. The differences between these two systems of educa-

---

[1] One cannot add, 'two religions'; because, unhappily, there developed outside of the Catholic Church scores of religions, all calling themselves Christian, although holding quite contradictory opinions as to what were the doctrines taught, and the practices inculcated, by Jesus Christ.

tion were profound; yet, on the surface, the two had much in common. The differences, though very numerous, were chiefly these: the Catholic Church held to the truths revealed by Jesus Christ and taught unbrokenly since His time, whilst the Protestant churches variously lopped and modified these truths; the Catholic Church continued to administer the seven sacraments instituted by Jesus Christ, whilst the Protestant churches disavowed certain of the sacraments, often reducing them to only two; the Catholic Church maintained the essential principle of authority in deciding all points of uncertainty in religious doctrine and practice, whilst the Protestant churches abandoned this principle and left their peoples to the vague guidance of individual speculation. The result of these differences was, on the Catholic side, the ancient unity of faith and continuity with the Christian past; on the Protestant side, a progressive disintegration, which surrendered all security and definiteness of belief, and in time led to rationalism and agnosticism. It is significant that this break-up of Christian belief is praised as an exercise of 'liberty' by earnest and sincere Protestants, who would promptly see the absurdity of such 'liberty' if it were applied to the multiplication table. The points in common to the two educational systems were: their *emotional* acceptance of Jesus Christ as redeemer, teacher, and model; their common use of certain general means of education, preaching, writing, schools; and many elements of their ethical and social codes. The simple fact is that Catholic Christianity had so impressed itself upon the civilization of Europe that Protestant revolutionists could not possibly shake off all Catholic influences and ideals, except in the slow and gradual process by which they abandoned, one by one, the definite beliefs and principles of Christianity. As that process, fortunately, was never complete in the Protestant churches, they still retain a fragmentary resemblance to the Catholic

Church.   Of the working of the two systems in schools, we shall speak in the next chapter.

TOPICS FOR DISCUSSION

1. The position of Erasmus, Colet, More, in the Reformation.
2. The educational work of Melanchthon.
3. The influence of John Calvin on Protestant thought.
4. The educational methods of St. Philip Neri.
5. The Benedictines of St. Maur, and their effect on the study of history.
6. The educational influence of St. Teresa of Avila.
7. St. Peter Fourier and the 'simultaneous method.'

BIBLIOGRAPHIC NOTE

In addition to some sources indicated in the text, see the *Corpus Reformatorum,* edited by C. G. Bretschneider and H. E. Bindseil, 89 vols., Halle, 1834-1900, for the works of Melanchthon and Calvin. There are good bibliographies in *The Cambridge Modern History;* see especially Vol. 2, Cambridge, 1904.   For Huldreich Zwingli, see the *Latin Works,* edited by S. M. Jackson, New York, 1912.   U. von Hutten, *Opera,* edited by E. Boecking, 5 vols., Leipzig, 1859-62.   Calvin's *Opera quae Supersunt Omnia* in 59 vols., have been separately edited by Baum, Cunitz, and Reuss, Brunswick and Berlin, 1863-1900. For England, see Rawdon Brown, *Calendar of State Papers and Manuscripts Relating to English Affairs, etc.,* Vols. 5-7, London, 1873-90; and J. Gairdner, *Letters and Papers Foreign and Domestic of the Reign of Henry VIII,* Vols. 8-16, London, 1883-98.   Two source documents that throw light on the temper of the period are: S. Brant, *Das Narrenschiff,* 1494, edited and translated by T. H. Jamieson as *The Ship of Fools,* 2 vols., Edinburgh, 1874; and B. Sastrow, *Herkommen, Geburt, und Lauf seines ganzen Lebens,* edited by G. C. F. Mohnicke, 3 vols., Greifswald, 1823-24, and abridged translation by A. D. Vandam, *Social Germany in Luther's Time,* London, 1902. There are extracts from sources in B. J. Kidd, *Documents Illustrative of the Continental Reformation,* Oxford, 1911.   There are valuable documents scattered through J. Le Plat, *Monumentorum ad Historiam Concilii Tridentini Illustrandam Spectantium Amplissima Collectio,* 7 vols., Louvain, 1781-87; and in the *Liber Memorialis Ordinis Fratrum Minorum S. Francisci Capuccinorum,* Rome, 1928, as well as in the source collections for other religious orders previously mentioned.

Of the many works dealing with the period of the Reformation, the following may be suggested: J. Janssen, *History of the German People at the Close of the Middle Ages* (translated by A. M. Christie and M. A. Mitchell), 17 vols., London, 1896-1925; the compact work,

E. M. Hulme, *The Renaissance, the Protestant Revolution, and the Catholic Reformation,* New York, 1914, rev. ed., 1921; H. Belloc, *How the Reformation Happened,* London and New York, 1928; H. Stebbing, *The Reformation,* 2 vols., London, 1826-27; W. Busch (translated by A. Todd), *England under the Tudors,* London, 1895; J. Lingard, *History of England,* London, 1838 (especially Vols. 7 and 8); A. Baudrillart, *The Catholic Church, the Renaissance, and Protestantism,* New York, 1908; P. Imbart de la Tour, *Les Origines de la Reforme,* 3 vols., Paris, 1905-14; W. Cobbett, *A History of the Protestant Reformation in England and Ireland,* London, 1824-27, rev. ed. by F. A. Gasquet, New York, n. d.; A. O. Meyer (translated by J. R. McKee), *England and the Catholic Church under Queen Elizabeth,* London, 1916; C. Hollis, *The Monstrous Regiment,* New York, 1930; P. Guilday, *The English Catholic Refugees on the Continent,* New York, 1914; F. J. C. Hearnshaw (ed.), *Social and Political Ideas of Some Great Thinkers of the Renaissance and Reformation,* London, 1925; J. S. Schapiro, *Social Reform and the Reformation,* Columbia University, 1909; and G. O'Brien, *An Essay on the Economic Effects of the Reformation,* London, 1923.

For Luther, amongst the more impartial studies, these may be mentioned: J. Koestlin, *Martin Luther, sein Leben und seine Schriften,* 1875, as revised in the 5th edition by G. Kawerau, 2 vols., Berlin, 1903; H. S. Denifle, *Luther and Lutherdom* (English translation by R. Volz), Somerset, Ohio, 1917, an accurate but rather violent work; the careful, objective study of H. Grisar (English translation by E. M. Lamond), *Luther,* 6 vols., London, 1913-17; the brief analysis of J. Maritain, in *Three Reformers,* London, 1928; and R. H. Murray, *Erasmus and Luther,* London and New York, 1920.

For Calvin, see E. Doumergue, *Jean Calvin, les Hommes et les Choses de son Temps,* 7 vols., Lausanne, 1899-1927 (see especially Vol. 5); J. M. V. Audin, *Histoire de la Vie, des Ouvrages, et des Doctrines du Calvin,* Paris, 1841 (English translation by J. McGill, Louisville, Ky., n. d.); H. M. Baird, *The Rise of the Huguenots in France,* 2 vols., New York, 1879; and B. Warfield, *Calvin and Calvinism,* Oxford, 1931.

For the Catholic Reformation, see W. Maurenbrecher, *Geschichte der katholischen Reformation,* Noerdlingen, 1880; G. Kurth, *L'Eglise aux Tournants de l'Histoire,* Paris, 1905; A. W. Ward, *The Counter-Reformation,* London, 1889; A. von Reumont, *Vittoria Colonna,* Freiburg im Br., 1881. For the Benedictines of St. Maur, see J. U. Bergkamp, *Dom Jean Mabillon and the Benedictine Historical School of Saint-Maur,* Catholic University, Washington, 1928. For St. Teresa, see E. Lewis, *Life and Relations of St. Teresa of Avila,* 4th ed., edited by B. Zimmerman, London, 1911; and R. Hoornaert, *St. Teresa in her Writings,* London, 1931; for the Ursulines, P. M. Salvatori, *Vita della S. Madre Angela Merici,* Rome, 1807; M. O'Reilly, *Life of St. Angela,*

New York, 1880; J. Hubert, *Die heilige Angela Merici,* Mainz, 1891. For St. Peter Fourier, see J. Vuillimin, *La Vie de St. Pierre Fourier,* Paris, 1897; and for St. Philip Neri, L. Ponnelle and L. Bordet, *St. Philip Neri and the Roman Society of his Times,* London, 1933. There are some general data on the schools in E. Magevney, *The Reformation and Education,* New York, 1903; and A. F. Leach, *English Schools at the Reformation,* Westminster, 1896.

CHAPTER XIV

School Education from the Sixteenth to the Nineteenth Century

The schools religious and humanistic. For any proper understanding of school education in the period succeeding the Protestant Revolution and the Catholic Reformation, two facts must be kept clearly in mind. The first is that all school education in Europe for at least a thousand years had been religious and Christian in character. It is completely confusing to suppose, as many histories of education seem to suppose, that religious education in schools was a post-Reformation development. The testimony of history not merely disproves such a supposition, but indicates that it was the Protestant Revolution which led the way to the secularization of school education. In spite of this, it is also true that, for some considerable time, varying in different countries, there was, after the Reformation, added emphasis upon the religious content of school education. Quarrels over religion have a curious and sometimes unholy way of stimulating zeal. The second fact is that the influence of the Renaissance upon school education was, at most, only momentarily halted by the social, political, and religious upheaval of the sixteenth century. As soon as the first violence of that upheaval had passed, the Renaissance influence exerted itself quite vigorously in the schools. The result was that the schools of the sixteenth, seventeenth, and eighteenth centuries were, for the most part, both religious and humanistic in character. The religious side of the schools was shown in their being largely under the control of ecclesiastics, Protestant or Catholic, and in the avowed aims of the schools. Their humanistic

242

character consisted in the dominating concern of the schools with classical languages and literature, especially Latin.

The second cycle of school education. As humanistic, this long period of school education, extending from the middle of the fifteenth century to well into the nineteenth, marks the second of the cycles of school education outlined in pages 140-41 of this book. Humanistic school education had begun its course before the disturbances of the six-teenth century. It derived immediately from the Renais-sance. It could proudly claim such men as Vittorino da Feltre and Guarino da Verona as its great practical leaders. It never wholly and absolutely lost the ideals of those earlier humanist educators. But, as the humanistic schools grew in number, and spread more and more widely over Europe, after the Protestant Revolution, they inevitably solidified into a system; and the system would by no means have won the unqualified approval of Vittorino or Guarino.

The change in emphasis from content to form. The es-sential difference between the earlier, flexible, humanist schools, and the later rigid system, was a change in em-phasis. The earlier humanists looked to the antique for ideals: of beauty, of courage, of human achievement. They considered mere mastery of language as a necessary means, but only a means, to a larger educational end. Their schools were small, their pupils rather carefully selected; and they themselves were men of unusual ability, whose personal power gave life to their school work. When the schools multiplied in number, and became large, neither teachers nor pupils could measure up to the high standard of the earlier schools. Most of the teachers were necessarily and decidedly mediocre men; they had to lean upon the crutch of routine, they had to have cut-and-dried procedure to guide them. The result was that the later, numerous hu-manist schools became more and more literally 'grammar schools.' Erasmus saw the trend, and protested against it; so did Vives, even more intelligently. Both wrote *Colloquia,* meant as textbooks to help bring back the old emphasis upon content, in place of the new emphasis upon form. But they failed to make their protest effective; they were bound to fail. The post-Reformation schools settled gradually deeper into the linguistic and grammarian rut. There is no question of blame in saying all this. The deterioration came from the unavoidable limitations of school education.

Striking lack of originality. It can be said flatly that this humanistic school system was remarkably lacking in individual initiative or originality. The schools not merely turned for class material to the remote past, but did little to organize that material in any way newly adapted to the needs of their pupils. Much of the school method was as old as the texts studied. There was some development in school organization and management, brought about chiefly by the increasing size of the schools; but even that was for the most part an inheritance from the large fifteenth-century schools of the Brethren of the Common Life, who seem to have been the first schoolmasters to divide the pupils into graded classes.[1] Later writers have sometimes been eager to seize upon some point of method such as Ascham's 'double translation' as evidence of forward movement in educational detail. But such evidence is generally misleading. W. H. Woodward says of Ascham: "The method of Ascham, according to which a classical language is taught by the process of re-translation of construes, is at least as old as Cicero, and is of little importance in the history of instruction."[2] The whole period was one, not of discovery or innovation in school matters, but of stable organization and routine. What the Renaissance had begun

---

[1] Cf. A. Hyma, *The Christian Renaissance,* New York, 1924, pp. 288-98.
[2] *The Cambridge History of English Literature,* Vol. 3, p. 434.

in enthusiasm and under the guidance of brilliant men, was being reduced to a system to be conducted by very ordinary men. The schools were reaching more students, but reaching them in a more dull and lifeless manner; they were paying for quantity by quality. Sturm admitted in 1537 that he was copying at Strassburg the older schools of the Brethren of the Common Life. When, twenty-two years later, he visited the Jesuit school at Dillingen, he thought that the Jesuits were copying from him.[1] Comenius borrowed from the Irish Jesuit, William Bathe, both the title and the method of his *Janua;* and from Eilert Lueben, a Protestant theologian of Rostock, the plan for his *Orbis Sensualium Pictus,* published at Nurnberg in 1657.[2] The

---

[1] Cf. L. Kuckelhahn, *J. Sturm, Strassburgs erster Schulrektor,* pp. 9-13, 74-75; F. Meyer, *Der Ursprung des Jesuitischen Schulwesens,* p. 54; Ziegler, *Geschichte der Pädagogik,* p. 52; Schwickerath, *Jesuit Education,* pp. 32, 138. Of the Jesuits, Sturm writes in the *Epistolae Classicae,* "I note their method of teaching, which at present does not greatly differ from our rules and arrangements; so that it seems to be derived from us as a source." (R. Vormbaum, *Evangelische Schulordnungen,* Gutersloh, 1858, Vol. 1, p. 680). Charles Schmidt, *La vie et les travaux de Jean Sturm,* Strassburg, 1855, p. 221, suggests that it was this Jesuit competition which moved Sturm to write the *Epistolae Classicae* in 1565, and to make considerable changes in his Strassburg *gymnasium.*

[2] Bathe was born in Dublin, 1564, of wealthy Catholic parents. He entered the Society of Jesus at Tournay in Belgium, August 6, 1595. His *Janua Linguarum* was first published in Salamanca, in 1611. It was a collection of 1,200 sentences, in which no word was repeated. The student by studying and memorizing these, was expected to acquire in a short time a working vocabulary of Latin. Comenius acknowledged his borrowing from the Jesuit in the preface to his first edition of the *Janua Linguarum Reserata,* published just twenty years after Bathe's, 1631. Bathe intended his method to be used by missionaries, confessors, men of mature mind; Comenius designed his *Janua* for school children. *The Cyclopedia of Education,* Vol. 2, p. 136, makes the monstrous statement about Bathe's *Janua,* that "the sentences did not have a moral content." The author of that statement either could not read Latin, or had never seen Bathe's book. The moral sentences alone occupy twenty-three pages (283-306, in T. Corcoran, *Studies in the History of Classical Teaching,* Dublin, 1911). There is an excellent study of Bathe in *Distinguished Irishmen of the Sixteenth Century,* by Edmund Hogan, London, 1894, pp. 359-94. Corcoran, *op. cit.,* examines critically the work of Bathe and of Comenius, in what is beyond question the best study so far

only really important developments in schools during those long three hundred years were two, both of which we owe to St. John Baptist de la Salle, toward the close of the seventeenth century: the organization of normal schools, and the 'simultaneous method' of instructing a group of pupils at the same time.

Changes in the religious character of the schools. Catholic and Protestant schools were alike in being influenced by humanism in their curricula. For several generations after the Revolt, Protestant schools seemed even to carry on the age-old tradition of religious training, which, amongst other things, the various Protestant sects had taken with them when they split from the Church. It is true that, from the beginning of the separation, Protestant schools abandoned the Mass and most of the sacraments, and relied more upon a vague reading of the Bible and hortatory preaching. But as time went on, the differences between Catholic and Protestant schools in the matter of religious education became more and more pronounced: the Catholic schools continued in the unbroken traditions of Christianity; the Protestant schools increasingly abandoned them. There were three factors which made for these retrogressive changes in the Protestant schools: (a) the inevitable tendency of Protestantism to sporadic division, as the result of its lack of unifying authority; (b) the emotional hostility to all things Catholic which was so essential a part of Protestantism, and its consequent irrational impulse to differentiate itself from Catholic education, even in ways which endangered the avowed Protestant aim; and (c) the gradual subservience of Protestant churches to the several States in which they existed. In the course of little more than a lifetime, these causes brought about such a

published of the two men. Bathe has been ignored in most histories and encyclopedias of education, just as Comenius has been lauded most ridiculously beyond his deserts.

dilution of the Christian content of education in Protestant schools as to render it very ineffective. When, finally, the State in Protestant countries took over the major control of the schools, the step to complete secularization was so small as scarcely to be noticeable.[1] In sharp contrast to this, Catholic schools kept to the ancient Christian way, were clear and definite about the eternal purpose in education: even at the cost of conflict with the State, and of persecution. St. Augustine or St. Bernard would have found himself at home in any Catholic school of the sixteenth or succeeding centuries, as much as if it were of his own day.

With these preliminary observations to guide us, this chapter will consider school education from the sixteenth to the nineteenth centuries, in three divisions: the universities, the grammar schools, and elementary schools. The divisions were old and well organized when the period began; although their limits were more clearly marked in the later than in the earlier ages.

I. THE UNIVERSITIES

Loss of their international character. The universities had risen in Europe at about the same time as the beginnings of modern nationalism; yet, in spite of the increasingly sharp limits of political divisions, for three hundred

---

[1] The process of abandonment of Christianity by Protestants is, unfortunately, a slowly continuous one. Often, it is only in some startling incident that one realizes how complete it has become. Here is such an incident. In June, 1929, at Buck Hill Falls, Pennsylvania, U. S. A., there were assembled in a conference lasting some weeks, representative ecclesiastics and laymen of many Protestant churches. At one of the meetings of the conference, a layman, Jesse Herman Holmes, professor of philosophy at Swarthmore College, a Quaker school, made this statement: "I do not believe that the Church now, or its representatives, look upon its function as saving men from hell or getting them into heaven. The real values are human welfare, and the method of getting it is by human goodwill." (*Time,* June 24, 1929, p. 34.) Professor Holmes was merely clear-minded enough

years, from the thirteenth to the sixteenth century, the universities continued to be international in character. They were international for three great reasons: Europe had a common language, Latin, a single universal religion, the Catholic, and a common culture which derived from those two sources. Political separatism in Europe was feeble, compared with the binding force of those three unifying agencies: the universities were the symbol as well as the product of European unity. But the Renaissance destroyed Latin as a bond of unity, by making it the language of 'highbrows,' by contempt for the living Latin and glorification of the long-dead 'classic' forms; the Protestant Revolt broke the second, and strongest, of the bonds when it disrupted the unity of the Faith; and the unity of Europe in its culture went down with the other two. National divisions were of themselves becoming stronger. When to that strength was added the violence of religious hatred, the unity of Europe was irreparably shattered; and the international character of the universities disappeared in its ruins. "Cujus regio, ejus religio" was the final sentence for the destruction of both international culture and international schools. That is a very striking and significant fact in the history of education.

Their liberty of teaching curtailed. One of the most remarkable notes of the old Catholic culture in Europe was its ready tolerance of variety within its unity. When all the men of Europe were one in Faith, there was a freedom of discussion in the enormous field of thought beyond sharply revealed divine truth which was astounding. One might almost say that scholastic philosophy took its very origins in the twelfth-century controversy over 'univer-

to perceive the actual and practical stand of most Protestant churches today; and many millions in the United States and other countries who still call themselves Christians will agree in accepting his statement as the present position of the enormous majority of Protestants.

sals.'[1] Certainly the disputes between Peter Abaelard and the School of Chartres, which boasted such independent thinkers as Bernard of Chartres and William of Conches, gave a mighty impulse to the intellectual renaissance of the twelfth century. William of Conches (c. 1080-1154) taught a fairly clear 'atomic theory.'[2] After him, Roger Bacon (c. 1215-1292) and Ramón Lull (1235-1315) were remarkable, but by no means isolated, instances of freedom of thought within the Catholic unity.[3] When the writings of St. Thomas Aquinas were new, they seemed startlingly novel to the Franciscans, who promptly attacked them; for various reasons, the Dominicans rallied to the defense of Aquinas.[4] The fourteenth century, even in its debasement, was loud with the free contentions of Thomists, Scotists, Ockhamists. After the Protestant Revolt, the same spirit of frank discussion manifested itself amongst Catholics; for instance, in the controversies between Jesuits and Dominicans over the vexed points of 'essence and existence' and the mysteries of 'gratia efficax.' Comparatively few historians seem to realize how great that freedom was, or how much it was curtailed by what they often hail as the 'liberating' Protestant Revolt. When, in Protestant countries, religion became an appanage of the State, philosophical and theological argument could be, and was, forbidden by political authority. The universities could teach only

[1] Cf. M. de Wulf, *History of Medieval Philosophy,* London, 1926, Vol. 1, pp. 149-71, for a compact account of the controversy and the chief persons involved in it. On the active liberty of thought in the Middle Ages, see A. J. Macdonald, *Authority and Reason in the Early Middle Ages,* Oxford, 1933.

[2] See his *Elementa Philosophiae,* in Migne, *P. L.,* 90:1132.

[3] Roger Bacon's difficulties were not with the Church, but with his own Friars Minor. In 1257, five years after he entered the order, his superiors removed him from his chair at Oxford. The Pope, Clement IV, was his friend, and defended him against his superiors. But after the death of Clement, Jerome of Ascoli, the Franciscan General, confined Roger in prison for the last fifteen years of his life. (Cf. articles by Mondonnet in *Revue Neo-Scolastique,* 1910, 1913.)

[4] Cf. de Wulf, *History of Medieval Philosophy,* Vol. 2, pp. 37-55.

such doctrines as were acceptable to the civil powers. There is no need to illustrate in any detail the complete and rigorous dominance of the State over university teaching in England, Scotland, and the Protestant German principalities. Even in Catholic countries, rulers often caught the contagion spread by the spirit of revolt, and tried to use the universities for political purposes, thus hindering their liberty of teaching. To take a single instance, Louis XIV, March 23, 1682, ordered the University of Paris to adopt his views on the royal power in disposing of bishoprics; no degree in theology could be granted by the University except to candidates who maintained the royal doctrine in one of their theses.[1] We have become so used to this restraint upon teaching in our universities today that we take it for granted.[2]

Changes in curriculum. The enthusiasm for humanistic studies, which was an important part of the Renaissance, at first was met with resistance by the universities; but in the beginning of the sixteenth century, it had won a foothold in most of them. After the Protestant Revolt, for a time it seemed as if that enthusiasm might be thwarted, and philosophy and theology keep their old places at the head of the curriculum. Many of the Protestant leaders strongly distrusted the 'new learning,' and strove to keep alive an interest in the various theologies which the quarreling sects organized. That was more pronouncedly the case in such universities as were chiefly influenced by the teaching of Calvin. Thus, for instance, the Scottish universities were noted for their interest in metaphysics.[3]   But,

[1] For other instances, see Jourdain, *Histoire de l'Université de Paris au 17e et au 18e siècle,* Paris, 1866.

[2] See the excellent article on academic freedom in *Cyclopedia of Education,* Macmillan, 1911, Vol. 2, pp. 700-05.

[3] Mullinger points out the remarkable dominance of Scholasticism over the teaching of philosophy in Protestant universities, at least down to the middle of the seventeenth century. *History of the University of Cambridge,* Vol. 3, pp. 135, 373, 419, 435, 449-51.

gradually, in almost all the universities, language, rhetoric, and literature, principally Latin, took the place held for some three centuries by logic, metaphysics, and theology. Of the great universities, Paris was the only exception: there theology continued as a major study.[1] The Catholic universities were to some extent also influenced to this change in curriculum by the founding of seminaries, after the decree of the Council of Trent, July 15, 1563; these, as destined for the special training of priests, naturally emphasized the study of philosophy and theology. Although the seventeenth century was rich in genuine scientific discoveries, and although these discoveries were generally made by university men, they had little or no effect upon the curricula of universities.[2] Humanistic studies became the staple of teaching in the universities.

But not in method. There was singularly little change in method to correspond to this great change in curriculum. University teachers, with the conservatism characteristic of such men, instinctively adhered to the old lecture system, even though it was so poorly adapted to instruction in humanistic studies. Oxford had introduced the tutorial system, and Cambridge had adopted it from Oxford, early in the fifteenth century. But this excellent method, whereby a tutor, in private conversations, supervised the reading and study of a small number of students, was never much in use at Paris or other continental universities, and even in the English universities was rendered ineffective by the prevailing laziness there and the farcical system of exam-

---

[1] H. Rashdall, *History of Universities of Europe in Middle Ages,* Vol. 1, p. 556. Seminaries affected university teaching chiefly in southern France and in Italy.

[2] Cambridge, between 1702 and 1750, founded chairs in chemistry, astronomy, botany, geology. But the foundations were made at a time when both Cambridge and Oxford were decidedly in decay; and hence had no great influence on the character of university teaching. Cf. Christopher Wordsworth, *Scholae Academicae,* Cambridge, 1877.

inations.[1] An extreme formalism ruled everywhere, and most notably in the Germanies. Under the dull pounding of mechanical lecturers, classical culture ceased to have any real life in it. Paulsen says of the instruction given in the seventeenth-century German universities, that "toilsome compilation was the sole result of its activity."[2] The seventeenth and eighteenth centuries were a remarkably dull period in the history of universities. The temper of the age was alien to true university studies.

New universities. Oddly enough, that dullness and lack of real interest in the universities did not prevent a good deal of official interest in them, which led to the foundation of new universities. Melanchthon, who had declared that "philosophy was the worship of idols" and that the only knowledge a Christian needed should be drawn from the Bible, organized three new Protestant foundations: Marburg, in 1527, Koenigsburg, in 1544, Jena, in 1548; although Jena became a university only in 1577. Coulton reckons twenty-one new universities after the Revolt, in German-speaking lands alone: ten Protestant, eleven Catholic.[3] But the new foundations arose from no popular demand; they were founded by princes largely for political reasons; and they had no very vigorous life. About half of them failed to survive. Cromwell's attempt, in 1657, to found a new university at Durham, was based on the same principle of political expediency; but it was frustrated, in part by the opposition of Oxford and Cambridge, in part by the violent distrust of universities which was common

---

[1] "In 1675, candidates at Cambridge might put down caution-money as a guarantee that they would go through the statutory exercises; they could get the degree by forfeiting the money." J. W. Adamson, in *Cambridge History of English Literature,* Vol. 9, p. 410, n. 1. Conditions were worse in the eighteenth century. Wordsworth, *Scholae Academicae,* p. 23.

[2] *The German Universities,* New York, 1906, p. 42.

[3] *Cyclopedia of Education,* New York, 1913, Vol. 5, p. 661.

amongst the Puritans.[1]   There were three new French universities founded in the sixteenth century, at Douai, Lille, Pont-a-Mousson; two in Spain; one in Italy; but all these too were of feeble vitality.   The four Spanish-American universities, at Lima, Santo Domingo, Quito, and Cuzco,[2] had a more thriving existence, and considerably influenced the culture of Latin America.[3]   Of the later Protestant foundations, Halle, established in 1694, became one of the most important, since from it went forth the wave of rationalism which was to deluge the Protestant countries, and greatly destroy in them the lingering remains of Christianity carried over, in the Revolt, from the Catholic Church.

Waning influence.   Whatever their fortune in other respects, the European universities unquestionably failed in intellectual influence during the seventeenth and eighteenth centuries.   Even though an accurate estimate of the number of university students in those centuries is impossible, the general fact is evident enough that the students were fewer in relation to the total population than they were before the Protestant Revolt.[4]   Moreover, the life of the univer-

---

[1] The Barebones Parliament of 1653 debated "the propriety of supressing universities and all schools for learning, as unnecessary." Although the fanatics did not succeed in their purpose, they kept up a guerilla warfare of pamphlets against the universities.   Cf. *Cambridge History of English Literature*, Vol. 19, pp. 383-87.

[2] All founded between 1538 and 1598; the first of them, Santo Domingo, nearly a hundred years before Harvard, the first college in the English colonies.

[3] Cf. Menendez y Pelayo, introduction to *Antologia de Poetas Hispano-americanos*, Madrid, 1895.

[4] This statement might seem to be contradicted by Dr. Venn's estimate that the proportion of Oxford and Cambridge students to the total population of England was, in 1630, more than twice as great as it is today. (*Biographical History of Gonville and Caius College*, Vol. 1.)   But his estimate though it be correct for that year is misleading; since, as Mullinger points out (*History of the University of Cambridge*, Vol. 3, p. 9) 1630 was the high-water mark for attendance at Cambridge.   Immediately after, attendance fell off greatly, and remained low.   Undoubtedly, the political dominance of the Puritans

sities from the sixteenth to the nineteenth century was not vigorous enough to exert a strong influence over their students. The teaching offered in them had less character, less definiteness, less energy, than that offered in the mediaeval period. Paulsen says: "At the end of the seventeenth century, the German universities had sunk to the lowest level which they ever reached in the public esteem and in their influence upon the intellectual life of the German people."[1] English contemporary writers complain sharply of the academic and social conditions at Cambridge and Oxford.[2] Of the French universities in the seventeenth and eighteenth centuries, Compayré says: "Gradually these institutions declined and became nothing more than shadows of their former selves, without exercising any real influence. In fact, it may be said they no longer existed when they were abolished at the Revolution."[3] His biased statement has much fundamental truth, in spite of its exaggeration. As Mark Pattison points out, even the scholarship of the time was distorted and spoiled by the bitterness of polemics.[4] The true university spirit was scarcely possible in a Europe torn by religious dissensions, more actively engaged in hating than in studying.

badly hurt the universities. Milton, though himself a university man, rails at the universities in his pamphlet of 1659, "The Likeliest Means to Remove Hirelings out of the Church." He represents the Puritan attitude.

[1] *The German University,* New York, 1906, p. 42. See also H. Barnard's *German Educational Reformers,* pp. 284-85, in which he cites Melanchthon's bitter criticism of university students, as utterly lacking in interest or school discipline.

[2] For details, see Andrew Clark, *The Life and Times of Anthony Wood, Antiquary of Oxford, 1632-1695, described by Himself,* 5 vols., Oxford, 1891-1900; John Milton, *Of Education,* edited by O. Browning, Cambridge, 1895; A. D. Godley, *Oxford in the Eighteenth Century,* 1908.

[3] *Cyclopedia of Education,* New York, 1911, Vol. 2, p. 669.

[4] *Life of Isaac Casaubon,* 2d ed., Oxford, 1892, p. 466. Yet Casaubon was considered the foremost Protestant scholar of the seventeenth century.

II. The Grammar Schools

Their general character. From the sixteenth to well into the nineteenth century, the most important sort of school was the grammar school. Its influence had grown whilst that of the university was waning; and elementary school education had not yet been organized on the huge scale to which we are now accustomed. The grammar school, which thus dominated in those three centuries of school education, had a distinctive character in that it was concerned almost exclusively with humanistic studies, Latin above all;[1] but its range was rather vague and varied. It occupied a middle position between the university and the elementary schools, yet its limits were by no means sharply defined. Thus, Sturm's grammar school at Strassburg, and many others modeled on it, accepted boys at the age of six or seven, began their teaching with the alphabet, and had a

---

[1] An interesting exception is found in the Puritan 'academies' of England. After the restoration of the Stuart monarchy, a series of laws between 1662 and 1672 drove dissenting Protestant ministers from the churches, the schools, and the universities. There were some two thousand ministers thus thrown out of occupation. Although the Act of Uniformity, of 1662, forbade them to teach even in private schools, the law was not consistently enforced; and many of the ministers did conduct schools. Richard Frankland, for instance, promptly set up at Rathmill, his home in Yorkshire, a combination of grammar school and college, which he called an 'academy,' and which within a few years had three hundred pupils. The 'academies,' whilst keeping in mind the training of future ministers and the traditional grounding in the classics, added much to the ordinary grammar school curriculum, especially in emphasis upon English, mathematics, and history. After the Toleration Act of 1689 (which of course tolerated only Protestants), the 'academies' gradually merged into the general scheme of schools. (See Adamson, in *Cambridge History of English Literature,* Vol. 9, pp. 392 sqq.; Foster Watson's articles in the *Gentleman's Magazine:* "The Education of the Early Nonconformists," Vol. 291, September, 1901, and "Unlicensed Nonconformist Schoolmasters," Vol. 295, September, 1902.) By 1775, there were about thirty of these 'academies.' Brown, *The Making of our Middle Schools,* pp. 168 sqq., discusses briefly their program of studies.

ten-year course.[1]   Scholars entering at Eton, according to the statutes of Henry VI, were to have a knowledge of 'reading, Donatus,[2] and plain song,' and be not less than eight or more than twelve years old.   They were to be 'expelled' from the College when they were eighteen; except in the case of a scholar who was on the list for King's College, Cambridge, who might remain at school until he was nineteen.   In the earlier Jesuit schools, boys usually entered at ten or twelve years, and continued until sixteen or eighteen; yet the schools unquestionably included a year, or even as much as two years, of what in the United States is now considered college matter.   In general, therefore, the grammar schools covered variously the latter years of what we now call 'grade schools,' the whole of our present 'high schools,' and some part of the college course.   They were well named 'grammar schools,' since the study of Latin grammar loomed so large in them; but in the time of which we are treating, as for many centuries before, grammar really was the inclusive term for a study of literature.[3]

Their revival after the Protestant Revolution. The grammar schools, like all other schools, suffered disaster in the politico-religious turmoil caused by the Revolt.   In Eng-

[1] K. von Raumer, *Geschichte der Pädogogik,* in H. Barnard's *German Educational Reformers,* Hartford, 1878, p. 197.

[2] 'Donatus' was the very small primer of Latin grammar, some eight to ten pages in print, widely in use in elementary schools; in reality, the second of three parts of the *Ars Grammatica,* written by Aelius Donatus about the middle of the fourth century. St. Jerome had been one of the pupils of Donatus. The word 'donat' came to stand for the rudiments of any study, and is so used by Chaucer and Langland.

[3] Leach dates "the earliest use of the actual words 'grammar school' to a charter of the last half of the twelfth century," *Cyclopedia of Education,* Vol. 3, p. 139.   Yet he himself quotes, in his *History of Winchester* (p. 9), Ven. Bede's use of the words in recounting the establishment of a 'grammar school' by King Sigebert in 631 (*Historia Ecclesiastica,* edited by Chas. Plummer, Oxford, 1896, p. 162).

land, between twenty and thirty of them were revived under Edward VI, eight under Mary, about one hundred and twenty in the forty-three years of Elizabeth's reign.[1]   In spite of these revivals, the grammar schools of England, even after a whole lifetime, were only about forty per cent of those that had functioned just before the religious suppressions of Henry VIII.   In the Germanies, Bugenhagen in the north and Melanchthon in the south, together with such men as Neander, Sturm, Trotzendorf, and Valentin, lent their services to help princes reorganize the schools broken up in the Revolt.   But the greatest single impetus to the revival of secondary education came from the Catholic side, through the newly founded Society of Jesus.   The penal laws kept the Jesuit schools out of England, and in general the religious quarrels of the Revolution confined their work rather exclusively to the predominantly Catholic countries; yet even so, these schools exerted no little influence upon secondary education in the whole of Europe. At the close of the seventeenth century, the number of grammar schools was even greater in Europe than it had been before the Revolt; and some were already established in the colonies of America.   In Europe, by sheer weight of numbers, they had settled into a sleepy sort of dominance in school education.   Before attempting any conclusions regarding their effect upon education in general, it may be well to study briefly a few of the more representative schools: Eton, as the type of English public

---

[1] See article "Free Schools" by Leach, *Cyclopedia of Education,* Vol. 2, p. 697; also Vol. 5, p. 140; and Vol. 2, p. 455, under "Endowments." He emphasizes the fact that very few of these foundations were in any way new, that most of them were revivals of old suppressed schools. See also the vigorous statement of Hastings Rashdall, *Harrow School,* p. 12; Leach, *English Schools at the Reformation,* p. 6; and Thorold Rogers, *Six Centuries of Work and Wages,* Vol. 1, p. 165. For a detailed and sympathetic account of English grammar schools in the latter half of the sixteenth century, see J. Howard Brown, *Elizabethan Schooldays,* Oxford, 1933.

school; Sturm's *gymnasium* at Strassburg, as representing the German grammar schools; and the Jesuit schools.

"Our Lady of Eton." "The King's College of Our Lady of Eton beside Windsor" was founded in 1440, by Henry VI, on the model of William of Wykeham's "St. Mary of Winchester."[1] It was, and is, a 'free school,' in the sense that no charge is made for tuition.[2] Further, for seventy 'poor and needy' scholars, the foundation provided lodging and food.[3] But, about twenty years after the opening of the school, there began the system of taking other pupils, who paid large sums for boarding in the houses of the 'fellows' of the school and in the town of Eton. These were called 'oppidans.' By 1540, if not before, the oppidans outnumbered the scholars, as they have continued to do up to the present time, when the total number of students is well over a thousand. Eton has long been one of the most famous of the English public schools,[4] and is proud of its record as an aristocratic seminary of eminent politicians and military and civil officials. It was a Catholic school,

[1] Winchester had had a grammar school since 648, when the church was first founded. William of Wykeham, who as a poor boy had been educated in that school, became Bishop of Winchester July 4, 1367, founded 'New College' at Oxford in 1379, and endowed the "grammar school of the College of the Blessed Mary of Winchester" in 1382. See M. E. C. Walcott, *William of Wykeham and his Colleges,* Winchester, 1852. William of Wayneflete (Patten), who had been master of Winchester since 1429, became first master of Eton, and brought with him from Winchester five fellows and thirty-five scholars, half of the total foundation of the new school. Walcott, p. 135.

[2] Of course, *somebody* always pays for the tuition in 'free schools'; in the case of Eton, the paying is done by the royal founder's endowment, plus certain revenues from sequestrated religious houses; in the case of our modern governmental systems of 'free schools,' the people at large pay, through taxation.

[3] The 'poor and needy' scholars at Eton, as at Winchester, were, from the beginning, the sons of well-to-do people. See Sir H. C. Maxwell-Lyte, *History of Eton College,* London, 1875.

[4] Which means, in fact, intensely private and expensive schools for the sons of wealthy families. They are called 'public' merely because they are open to students from any part of the country. See Leach, *History of Winchester,* pp. 5-8.

of course, for more than a hundred years; the provost and the ten fellows were priests. Under Elizabeth, it became definitely a Protestant school; although traces of the old Catholic régime lingered in the arrangement of holidays and in some of the school customs.

Curriculum. A document of 1528 indicates six classes,[1] all concerned with Latin; beginning with Stanbridge's "Latin Grammar Rules" in English, and passing on to the reading of Erasmus' *Colloquia* and various Latin classic authors. There was much composition in Latin prose and verse. No mention is made of Greek, although there is evidence that it had been taught formerly,[2] and Greek grammar appears again in the two upper forms under Malim in 1561. The *Consuetudinarium*[3] of Malim, who became headmaster in 1560, indicates seven forms: first to third, the lower school; fourth, intermediate; fifth to seventh, the upper school. The matter studied was as follows:

I form, Cato's Moralia, Vives' Colloquia;

II form, Terence, Lucian's Dialogues (in Latin), Aesop's Fables (in Latin);

III form, Terence, Aesop (Latin), Sturm's Selections from the Letters of Cicero;

IV form, Terence, Ovid's Tristia, Epigrams of Martial, Catullus, Sir Thomas More's Utopia;

V form, Ovid's Metamorphoses, Horace, Cicero's Letters, Valerius Maximus, Lucius Florus, Justin;

VI and VII forms, Caesar's De Bello Gallico, Cicero's De Officiis, De Amicitia, Virgil, Lucan, and Greek Grammar.

There is no indication of any direct study of English, mathematics, or sciences. Latin was supreme. Every boy did daily exercises in composition: in the lower school,

---

[1] "The form order and usage taught in the Grammar School at Eton," attached to the charter of Cuckfield Grammar School, Sussex. *Cyclopedia of Education*, Vol. 2, p. 511.

[2] In the *Vulgaria* of William Horman, 1519. Horman had been headmaster of Eton in 1485-95.

[3] Printed in Creasy, *Eminent Etonians*, pp. 77-84.

translations of English sentences or passages into Latin; in the fifth form, a theme written in Latin on a subject set by the master; in the sixth and seventh forms, in Latin verse.

The school day.   The students rose at five in the morning, made their own beds, swept out the dormitories, then washed themselves.   There were no church services.[1]   At six o'clock, the usher read prayers.   The boys were occupied with various work until nine o'clock, and only then had breakfast, apparently a slender meal.   At ten, they went to class.   At eleven, they had dinner.   There were three hours of class from noon to three o'clock, then an hour for play, another hour of class; and at five, supper.   Supper-time ended the working day of the master and usher.   The boys studied from six to eight, under monitors chosen from the seventh form; but the study period was interrupted at seven for a collation of bread and beer.   At eight o'clock, night prayers were said in common, after which they went to bed.[2]   A private manuscript of the eighteenth century shows the studies and classes to have remained nearly the same; but the boys rose and retired later, and had more time for play during the school week.[3]

Discipline.   The master, usher, and their assistants, of course exercised authority over the students.   Incessant flogging marks the history of Eton until very recent times. But a distinctive disciplinary character of the English grammar schools is found in the prefects chosen from amongst the students.   The system seems to be almost as old as the grammar schools themselves.[4]   It is definitely pro-

---

[1] In this Eton was, from the beginning, unlike Winchester, where the day was begun with Mass.

[2] See analysis of the *Consuetudinarium* in Maxwell-Lyte, *History of Eton College,* Chap. 8.

[3] Maxwell-Lyte, pp. 311-22.   The MS was written between 1768 and 1775.

[4] See article by Leach, "Prefect and the Prefectural System," *Cyclopedia of Education,* Vol. 5, pp. 26-28.

vided for in the statutes of St. Alban's School in 1309, and in those of Winchester in 1382. At Eton, eighteen boys from the two upper forms were chosen as 'praepostors,' and given considerable disciplinary authority over the rest of the students. They enforced silence during studies, the speaking of Latin at certain times, and the observance of other school regulations. They could not inflict punishment; as Leach says, "they were not magistrates, but police constables."[1] But toward the close of the seventeenth century, and throughout the eighteenth century, the prefects assumed and exercised authority to cane offenders. By 1775, the 'fagging' system, whereby the younger boys were made servants to the older, was in full swing at Eton, and continued unabated for over a hundred years.[2] As might be expected, all this tended to abominable abuses. Within the past fifty years, the abuses have been done away with, and the prefectural system has been intelligently managed so as to secure its very real benefits of student self-government and training in leadership.

Games and holidays. Horman's *Vulgaria* in 1519 speaks of swimming, football, quoits, and tennis, as the games in vogue at Eton. Cust says that archery was practiced from very early times. But there seems to have been little encouragement of games before 1506, when the famous 'playing meads' began to occur in the accounts of the school. There were some restrictions on swimming, for a time, after the death by drowning of a scholar, Robert Sacheverell, in 1549. 'Fives,' a sort of handball game, was very popular. Football, played 'with a ball full of wind,' developed from a general hurly-burly into the highly technical 'Association' and 'Rugger' of later years. Tennis held sway

---

[1] *Cyclopedia of Education,* Vol. 2, p. 571.
[2] See Oscar Browning, *Reminiscences,* London, 1910. A good idea of some of the evils of fagging may be had from Hughes' novel, *Tom Brown's School Days.*

for a long time, but later gave way to rackets. The two most important forms of sport at Eton are comparatively late arrivals: cricket, appearing only after 1706; and rowing, after 1762.[1] No other public school in England keeps up such enthusiasm for rowing as does Eton.

In the sixteenth century, the holidays were numerous: a legacy from Catholic times. But, in the *Consuetudinarium* of Malim, the only vacation of schools was in the three weeks between Ascension Thursday and the Vigil of Corpus Christi. In addition, the daily order was much relaxed from the 6th of May, the feast of St. John before the Latin Gate, until September; work was much lessened, more time given to play. Two hundred years later, we find the vacation periods greatly increased: a month at Christmas, two weeks at Easter, a month at Bartlemetide, beginning the first Monday in August.[2] In the 'crow-baiting' of Shrove Tuesday, the sixteenth century retains traces of the old cruel sport of killing a cock with sticks: a custom which seems to have disappeared by the close of the eighteenth century. The curious ceremony of *Montem,* in which the students processionally marched out to a small nearby eminence called Salt Hill, was borrowed from the still more ancient Winchester institution of 'Hills.'[3] The Winchester 'Hills' was, at first, evidently a religious pilgrimage to the chapel on St. Katharine's Hill, about a mile from the College; later it became a mere recreational walk, overlaid with meaningless customs; and finally died out. *Montem* went through something of the same cycle. Its original and religious meaning was quite lost after the Protestant Revolution. The procession became an empty survival under Elizabeth, reduced to a rather absurd marching-out

[1] For a good account of games at Eton, see Lionel Cust, *History of Eton College,* New York, 1899, pp. 233-61.

[2] Maxwell-Lyte, *History of Eton College,* pp. 311-22.

[3] A. F. Leach, *History of Winchester College,* pp. 276-77. Maxwell-Lyte, pp. 452 sqq., gives Malim's account of *Montem* in 1561.

twice a year: about the feast of the Conversion of St. Paul, and in September to gather nuts. It later degenerated into a sort of initiation for new boys, and still later became a mere occasion for levying money toll on visitors to the school and hill.

Sturm's gymnasium. Johann Sturm, who was born near Cologne in 1507, was a pupil of the famous school at Liége, taught by the Brethren of the Common Life. At the age of seventeen, he went to study at Louvain for three years, then taught there for two more. At twenty-two he was in Paris, at that time still the capital of the intellectual world, where he studied medicine, married, and taught logic and the classics. In 1537, when he was thirty years old, he was called to Strassburg by the magistrates of the town, to conduct a school. At Strassburg, he was induced by Martin Bucer to become a Lutheran. He taught in the school of Strassburg for forty-five years, an amiable and dignified scholar, a devoted teacher, an industrious student of school education. His reward, after the forty-five years, was to be deposed from office because he ventured to write a pamphlet in which he took sides against the dominant party amongst the Lutherans, and to spend the remaining eight years of his life in poverty. He was thus punished despite the fact that, when the Emperor Maximilian II endowed the College of Strassburg in 1567, Sturm was appointed rector *in perpetuo*.[1] The College, a course of public lectures following the last years of the *gymnasium,* did not thrive well,[2] although Sturm took great interest in it. But the *gymnasium,* which within a very short time counted six hundred students, was successful from the be-

[1] K. von Raumer, in Barnard's *Teachers and Educators in Germany,* p. 194.

[2] It was empowered by Maximilian II to grant academic degrees in philosophy, but became a university only in 1621, thirty-two years after Sturm's death, under the Emperor Ferdinand II. (Barnard, *op. cit.,* p. 209.)

ginning, and became the model for many German schools. Sturm himself organized similar schools at Lauingen, Trasbach, and Hornbach. His pupils, Schenck and Crusius, planned the *gymnasia* at Augsburg and Meminger.

Sturm's system of instruction. In his plan of 1537, drawn up for the magistrates of Strassburg, Sturm proposed nine years of school education, ending at sixteen, and to be followed by five years of college lectures. Of the nine school years, seven were to go to the mastery of Latin, two to acquiring elegance of Latin style; the five years of college were to equip the student with eloquence. In the *gymnasium,* emulation was to be used as an incentive to study, prizes were to be awarded the two best scholars in each class. The religious atmosphere of the school was to be mildly Lutheran, with some study of the Bible and the German catechism each week. Twenty-eight years later, the number of classes had been increased to ten, as we learn from the 'Classic Letters' which Sturm wrote to his teachers in 1565. The elaborate records of a general examination in 1578 show no changes in the system. It was essentially a Latin school. Even the religious teaching was made to subserve Latin; for instance, in the seventh and sixth classes, on Sundays the German catechism was to be translated into classic Latin.[1]

The curriculum. Von Raumer gives an analysis of the ten-year course of studies in Sturm's Gymnasium, drawn from the 'Classic Letters' of 1565 and the examination of 1578.[2] The following is a brief summary of it:

10th class: the alphabet, reading of Latin declensions, memorizing of German catechism.

9th class: further work in declensions and conjugations, memorizing of selected word-lists.

---

[1] K. von Raumer, in Barnard, *op. cit.,* p. 199.
[2] Translated in Barnard, *op. cit.,* pp. 196-208.

8th class: more grammar, some letters of Cicero carefully parsed; in last months of year, written composition.

7th class: simple rules of syntax illustrated from Cicero's letters, brief written exercises in imitation of Cicero; on Sundays, written translation of German catechism.

6th class: some longer letters of Cicero to be translated into German, reading of short poetical selections; translation of German catechism on Saturdays and Sundays; Greek grammar begun.

5th class: Latin versification; mythology; Greek word-lists memorized; exercises in scansion, but not in verse writing; double translation, from Latin to German and back again; Saturdays and Sundays, interpretation of one of the shorter Pauline epistles.

4th class: the sixth oration against Verres; epistles and satires of Horace; Greek grammar, and reading in Greek "Book of Examples"; on Saturdays and Sundays, paraphrase of shorter Pauline epistles.

3d class: Herennius on rhetoric, together with the speech for Cluentius; in Greek, Demosthenes, and first book of Iliad or Odyssey; translation from Greek to Latin, or Latin to Greek; epistles of St. Paul memorized; comedies of Terence and Plautus to be acted, four upper classes taking part.

2d class: comparative study of classic orators and poets; elementary parts of rhetoric and logic; Demosthenes and Cicero, boys allowed to select the speeches to be read; Sundays, Epistle to Romans to be memorized; plays continued, boys encouraged to get up some on their own initiative.

1st class: rhetoric and logic continued, but with warning to keep to elements, and their laws applied in study of Demosthenes, Cicero, Virgil, Homer; Thucydides and Sallust to be divided amongst the boys for a written translation; plays to be acted more frequently, one a week; epistles of St. Paul to be expounded by students, passages amplified rhetorically.

Relations with other schools. Sturm's own schooling was closely bound up with the Brethren of the Common Life. He spent three years, from fourteen to seventeen, in their school at Liége, and the next three years at Louvain, where one of his teachers was Conrad Coclenius, who had been, a little later than Erasmus, a pupil of Alexander Hegius at Deventer. From the Brethren he took his practical ideas on school organization and management, and their great educational aim of *'pietas sapiens et eloquens.'* But his school was more narrowly grammatical and linguistic than Hegius' school at Deventer;[1] and being lukewarmly Protestant, it lost much of the practical religious purpose of the Brethren of the Common Life. From Valentine Trotzendorf, the Lutheran schoolmaster, who was a close friend of Melanchthon, and who, between 1523 and 1554, made the school of Gorlitz famous throughout the Germanies, Sturm borrowed some details of class management and school discipline;[2] although at least the germs of Trotzendorf's scheme would seem also to have come from the Brethren of the Common Life. But, in general, Sturm's system of school education was essentially the system evolved from the Renaissance, and already accepted for a long lifetime by practically all the existing schools of Europe. His successful work at Strassburg was, beyond question, one of the influences which helped to establish that school system for the next three hundred years; but it was relatively a minor influence.

[1] The "Dialogues" of Hegius pay much attention to mathematics and natural history, and insist strongly upon the ethical content of studies. See Barnard, *op. cit.,* pp. 65-67. Sturm's general indebtedness to the schools of the Brethren of the Common Life can be seen in G. Bonet Maury, *De Opera Scholastica Fratrum Vitae Communis.* In an appendix, he reprints Sturm's report to the Governors of the Schools of Strassburg, first written on his appointment to Strassburg. This report Sturm later developed into the treatise, *De litterarum ludis recte aperiendis,* which is given in R. Vormbaum, *Evangelische Schulordnungen,* Gutersloh, 1858, Vol. 1, pp. 653 sqq.

[2] For a succinct account of Trotzendorf's work, see von Raumer (in Barnard, *op. cit.,* pp. 185-91). Sturm seems to have taken from Trotzendorf the system of dividing each class into *decuriae,* with a student called *decurion* in charge, who was to collect themes, maintain minor points of discipline, and in various ways represent his group in the school. From whom the Jesuits adopted this practice is not clear; but it is obvious that they did not originate it.

Criticism of Sturm's system. The severe strictures laid upon Sturm's teaching by von Raumer[1] and many others, for its neglect of the vernacular, of arithmetic, geography, history, and all other sciences except logic, can be intelligently answered merely by pointing out two facts: (a) that the German tongue at that time scarcely had any literature;[2] and (b) that the exclusively Latin school was looked upon by most people with enthusiasm, as a great achievement of the Renaissance, and as the last word in school education. Sturm simply went with the educational world of his day, just as his critics go with the present educational fashions. It is singularly stupid to judge his work by our present-day requirements or preferences.

The Jesuit schools. Most textbooks succeed in being reasonably fair to all grammar schools during this long period, except in the case of the Jesuit schools. That hostility to all things Catholic, which seems to be quite an essential of the Protestant culture, tends to cause bias in the common accounts of the Jesuit schools, even when the writers of those accounts are honestly trying to be impartial. What is acclaimed, or at least defended, in other schools, becomes intolerably bad when done in a Jesuit school.[3]   Francis

---

[1] For von Raumer, see Barnard, *op. cit.*, pp. 213-23. Quick (*Essays on Educational Reformers,* edition of 1890, pp. 27 sqq.) is even more sweeping in his condemnation of "Sturmius"; and Charles Stuart Parker, whom he quotes, openly sneers at Sturm as a sort of political schoolmaster, more concerned with intrigue than with education.

[2] The only 'literature' in German that Sturm could refer to was Luther's sermons and translation of the Bible. Barnard, *op. cit.*, p. 222.

[3] A really amusing instance is quoted by Schwickerath, *Jesuit Education,* pp. 7-8. Dr. Conrad Rethwisch, in *Deutschlands höheres Schulwesen im neunzehnten Jahrhundert,* Berlin, 1893, defends the exclusive teaching of Latin in the school system of Saxony on excellent and convincing grounds; but blames the stress upon Latin in Jesuit schools to "the Romish-international tendencies of the Order." It is equally amusing to find that so intelligent a man as Professor S. S. Laurie of Edinburgh can write: "There is no record of any Jesuit school, so far as I know, which approached in its breadth of study or in the organization of school work the Protestant Gymna-

Bacon praised the Jesuit schools highly, in his *De Augmentis Scientiarum,* published in 1623;[1] an American professor of the history of education, nearly three hundred years later, concludes from the fact "that Bacon paid only casual attention to teachers and teaching"![2] It is simply taken for granted that the Jesuit schools *must have been* unworthy of praise, on the ancient and ever-living principle, "Can anything good come out of Nazareth?" Conceivably, if the world lasts long enough, men will deny that the Jesuits ever had any schools, just as they have denied Catholic schools in general before the Reformation. But, for the time being, it is still universally admitted that the Jesuits conducted a great system of secondary schools in Europe and America for nearly three hundred and fifty years, and that their system of schools still exists.

Their origin. About the time that Luther was touching a match to the tinder of religious revolt in the Germanies, a Spanish Basque of good birth named Iñigo de Oñez y Loyola, gave up his military career to devote himself singly to the service of God. At thirty-three years of age, he set about getting for himself a school education, which he completed at Paris, when, forty-four years old, on March 14, 1535, he received the degree of Master of Arts. Five years later, Pope Paul III, in the bull "Regimini Militantis Ecclesiae" gave legal existence to a new religious order founded by Iñigo, called "The Society of Jesus." Nearly twenty years before this, Iñigo had changed his name to Ignatius; and within four years of its origin his new order

sium of Sturm at Strassburg." (*Studies in the History of Educational Opinion from the Renaissance,* Cambridge, 1905, p. 87.) Apparently he cannot see that the remainder of his chapter on Jesuit schools, despite its obvious Protestant bias, completely refutes this amazing statement.

[1] "Consule scholas Jesuitarum: nihil enim quod in usum venit his melius," *De Augmentis Scientiarum,* lib. vi, cap. iv. (In Shaw's translation, edited by J. Devey, London, 1891, pp. 264-66.)

[2] Herman H. Horne, in *Cyclopedia of Education,* Vol. 1, p. 315.

became popularly known under the ironic title 'Jesuits,' a name which had been scornfully applied for more than a hundred years to those who in canting fashion used the name of Jesus freely in speech.[1]   After some ten years, the members of the Society accepted the new name in use, although Ignatius never used it.[2]   The work of school education was undertaken by the Jesuits almost from the beginning, and was definitely legislated for in their constitutions.[3]   Their school work was an essential part of their moral and religious program: a program almost universally misrepresented by non-Catholic writers.   The Jesuits were not founded to combat the newly arisen Protestantisms, as is so generally supposed, but to foster and develop Christian life in themselves and others.   Obviously, one of the ways of developing Christian character in others is through the medium of schools for the young.   The Jesuits could not possibly cover the whole field of school education (a fact which some of them are recently rediscovering): hence they centered their efforts chiefly upon grammar schools for boys and colleges for young men.[4]

Their system of education.   The Jesuit schools were not innovations.   They accepted the type of school education which was then prevailing: the religious-humanistic type. Their aims, Christian character and humanistic culture, were the same aims which had guided the schools of Europe for more than a hundred years before the Jesuits came into existence.   They accepted the curriculum then in vogue. They devised no startling new methods of instruction. There were three characteristics which distinguished their schools from other schools, and which were the true reasons

---

[1] J. H. Pollen, in *Catholic Encyclopedia,* Vol. 7, p. 641.
[2] J. H. Pollen, *The Month,* London, June, 1909.
[3] *Epitome Instituti Societatis Jesu,* Romae, 1924, pars 4a, sectio 2a, pp. 162-70.
[4] *Epitome Instituti Societatis Jesu,* pp. 162-63, outlines the sort of schools planned.

for their success. The first was their complete dedication to the work of teaching: they made it a life work, without salary, with sworn promises to seek no preferment in the Society or out of it; and this dedication was made in the spirit of unselfish love of God and of their neighbor.[1] The second was close organization, a common plan of work as well as a common purpose. The Society is military in its discipline, but the Plan of Studies was worked out democratically, from the actual experience of thousands of teachers and with their active co-operation. Fifty years of teaching experience went to furnish the data upon which the Plan was built. A committee of twelve men, skilled in school management, spent nine months of hard work in studying these data and devising a school program. Their recommendations, submitted in August, 1585, were again examined by two other committees. In 1586, the Plan of Studies was printed, but in only a few copies, and offered to the schools for trial. It was a whole treatise on education; it takes up one hundred and fifty pages in Pachtler.[2] It was revised three times between 1586 and 1593;[3] and it was tested in the schools for thirteen years, before it was issued in its final form, in 1599, as the *Ratio Studiorum* for Jesuit schools.[4] The whole procedure was a work of standardization of classes, methods, management, not imposed from the outside, but developed from the schools themselves: rather in contrast to the standardization with which schools in general are today so painfully struggling. The third characteristic was that the students did not pay

[1] This notion runs all through the constitutions. But see particularly *op. cit.,* pp. 233 sqq. for the vows which cut off all selfish ambition.

[2] *Monumenta Germaniae Paedagogica,* Vol. 5, pp. 67-217.

[3] Pachtler gives interesting details of the criticisms offered on the Plan in *Monumenta Germaniae Paedagogica,* Vol. 5, pp. 218 sqq.

[4] See *Monumenta Germaniae Paedagogica,* Vol. 5, p. 227, for Aquaviva's letter which ordered the adoption of the Ratio for general use.

for their tuition. That was paid for by an endowment, or, when the endowment was insufficient, by the begging and borrowing of the Jesuits themselves.[1] The 'free' school was not a new idea; all that the Jesuits added to it was the note of personal sacrifice which it often cost them. The purpose of endowment was to make the schools accessible, not to enrich the Jesuits; and it was an adequate endowment if it maintained the school buildings, and fed and clothed the teachers.

Jesuit contributions to school practice. The Jesuit *Ratio Studiorum* organized classes more carefully than had been done before. It presupposed elementary training in the students. It divided the school into five grades: three in 'grammar,' one called 'humanitas,' and one called 'rhetorica.' The first three aimed chiefly at mastery of Latin; the other two at a study of literature, chiefly with a view to developing the student's powers of expression. In all five attention was paid to history, geography, ethics, religion. The *Ratio Studiorum* set down definite subject matter and definite method for each class. But it avoided the unintelligent and mechanical rigor of our modern class systems, by making it clear that each grade meant, not a year, but a work to be done before the next division of work could be taken up.[2] The pace was set for the average boy; the dull boy might need four years or more for the three grammar classes; the clever boy might "pass through these forms in eighteen months, instead of three years."[3] The highest grade, 'rhetorica,' was expected to take two

---

[1] R. H. Quick, *Educational Reformers* (New York edition of 1909), p. 38. His statement that "want of money, however was not a difficulty which the Jesuits often experienced," is contradicted by the evidence offered in Pachtler, *Monumenta Germaniae Paedagogica*, Vol. 9, pp. 106, 110. A letter of the General, John Paul Oliva, says: "Thus far almost all the colleges, even such as have received endowment, suffer want regularly, and have frequently to borrow money."

[2] Hughes, *Loyola*, p. 89.

[3] Quick, *Educational Reformers*, p. 46. See Pachtler, in *Monumenta Germaniae Paedagogica*, Vol. 5, p. 360.

or three years,[1] and this longer term was urged upon 'the talented student.'[2] In other words, the Jesuit schools recognized the inevitable aristocracy of talent. Thus, the course might cover from five to eight years. This combination of definiteness with flexible adaptability should commend itself to every one who knows school work. Some educators today are trying to battle their way back to it.

The earlier grammar schools had long class hours. As early as 1567, even before the *Ratio Studiorum* was drawn up, the Jesuits saw the unwisdom of that, and cut the class hours to five daily, divided equally between morning and afternoon, with a long recess at midday.[3] John Dury, a Scotch Puritan minister, in his reported observation of a Jesuit school in 1645, says that classes took up only two hours in the morning and two in the afternoon: 9 to 11, and 3 to 5, in summer; 8 to 10, and 2 to 4, in winter.[4] But the amount of written work, reading, and memorizing, demanded of the students called for some four hours of work outside of class. The clever and industrious were urged to do more.[5] Work, and the conditions of work, were planned with an eye to the students' health.[6]

The abundant floggings of other schools were reduced to a minimum and were never inflicted by the Jesuit master

---

[1] Pachtler, *Monumenta Germaniae Paedagogica,* Vol. 5, p. 491.

[2] Hughes, *Loyola,* p. 89.

[3] Letter of Polanco ordering the change of hours for the German Province in *Monumenta Germaniae Paedagogica,* Vol. 2, p. 154.

[4] T. Corcoran, *Studies in the History of Classical Teaching,* pp. 236-37. Dury's report, printed by Corcoran (pp. 236-47) from the Sloane MSS., British Museum, Vol. 649, fol. 74-81, is extremely interesting, as it is one of the few early accounts of actual daily procedure in a Jesuit school. In its brief compass, it is quite complete.

[5] "For private study, besides written exercises and learning by heart, the pupils were recommended subjects to get up in their own time; and in this and also as to the length of some of the regular lessons, they were permitted to decide for themselves. Here, as everywhere, the Jesuits trusted to the sense of honour and emulation —those who did extra work were praised and rewarded." (Quick, *Educational Reformers,* p. 45.)

[6] Quick, *op. cit.,* p. 48.

himself.   Instead, the Jesuits sought rather to encourage industry by rewards than to discourage slackness by punishments.[1]   They made use of rivalry to stimulate interest in class work.   This is a point much emphasized by hostile critics.   They are shocked; they gravely reason, *a priori,* that such emulation must have a vicious moral effect on the students, lead to envy and bitterness, etc.   It is strange that such ardent disciples of 'induction' have not looked up the facts in the matter.   Students in the Jesuit schools could tell them that class rivalry is in actual practice quite wholesome, and has no such bad effects as the critics prognosticate.   Besides the Jesuit students, there have been thousands of observers of the Jesuit schools; none of whom has ever noted any vicious results from the Jesuit practice.   When the Jesuits were attacked in France on this score, Voltaire, who had come to hate the Catholic Church, defended them warmly, on the basis of his seven years' experience as a Jesuit student.[2]   Such emulation was used as a help chiefly to overcome the natural inertia of small boys, in the lower classes.   "In the higher classes a better kind of rivalry was cultivated by means of 'academies,' i. e., voluntary associations for study, which met together, under the superintendence of a master, to read themes, transla-

[1] The two methods were sometimes combined in an interesting way.   Thus, enforcement of the rule of speaking Latin at certain times was made a kind of game.   The last boy guilty of breaking the rule cried: "Do tibi signum!" when he heard another speaking the vernacular in time of Latin, thus passing on his liability to punishment.   Only the last boy guilty in the day was punished.   See Dury, in Corcoran, *op. cit.,* p. 237.   "If the Regent take notice of constant diligence in any Scholler, or if any make an extraordinary good exercise, he is honoured with a paper picture, sealed with the Colledge-Seal and signed by the Prefect and Regent to attest to the industry or will of the receiver.   The surrendering of this picture will free him or any of his friends, to whom he will give it, from the lash, whensoever they deserve it."   Dury, in Corcoran, *op. cit.,* p. 244.

[2] See his letter of February 7, 1746, in *Oeuvres* (edition of 1817), Vol. 8, p. 1128.   The letter was written to Father de la Tour, rector of the College Louis-le-Grand.

tions, etc., and to discuss passages from the classics."[1] Of course, plays, competitions for prizes, and other extra-class devices were also employed to lend interest to work.[2]

Extent of the system of schools. Since the suppression of the Jesuits by Pope Clement XIV in 1773, exact statistics about the older Jesuit schools are not available. There were about one hundred schools and houses of the Order in 1556, at the death of its founder; and 372 in 1615, at the death of Aquaviva. The high-water mark seems to have been reached about the close of the seventeenth and beginning of the eighteenth century, when there were 769 schools. A decline set in shortly after that. Fifty years later, there were only 728, with the papal suppression almost in sight. Some of the schools were large: the fourteen in the province of Paris reckoned, in 1627, 13,195 students, an average of nearly a thousand each. Many were small schools; although Hughes says he has found no record of any with less than 300 students.[3] It seems conservative to say that throughout the seventeenth century, the Jesuit schools had not less than 150,000 students, and in the eighteenth not less than 200,000. The Jesuits themselves were more than 22,000 in number at the time of the suppression. Even from such conservative estimates, the statement already made does not seem exaggerated: that for more than two centuries the Jesuit school system was the most important single factor in European school education.

---

[1] Quick, *Educational Reformers,* pp. 42-43.

[2] See Dury's account, in Corcoran, *op. cit.,* pp. 244-46. But these devices, as also the scheme of dividing each class into tens, under a sort of monitor, the decurion, who exacted from his group the work assigned them by the teacher, were borrowed from the practice of other schools: possibly from Sturm and Trotzendorf, very likely from the older, common source of the Brethren of the Common Life.

[3] Hughes, *Loyola,* p. 73. In pp. 68-74, he discusses the data at hand on the whole question. See also Pachtler, *Monumenta Germaniae Paedagogica,* Vol. 2, p. 20.

The general influence of grammar schools. Schools of
the sort briefly described in the preceding pages were dominant in European school education for some three hundred
years. What effect did they produce upon civilization?
That is always the most vital question in any historic
study; the most difficult to answer; and all too often any
answer can be only tentative and rather impressionistic.
One may venture to say that the widespread grammar
schools helped the development of a larger 'middle class'
in society, already established by economic conditions, and
that they increased considerably the number of those who
could lay some claim to the title of 'gentleman.' The
schools spread a thin layer of culture over a fairly large
number of people, and in so far 'humanized' them, by even
such superficial contact with great literature. Of a more
profound effect, in morals and religion, one may have serious doubts. The moral and religious tone of England and
the Germanies was obviously not improved during those
three centuries. In spite of the good work done by early
Wesleyanism, religion on the whole dwindled in England
up to the close of the eighteenth century. Formalism, and
later, rationalism, weakened religion in the German and
Scandinavian lands. Social and economic injustice grew
apace in every country. The millions of students who
passed through the Jesuit schools did not succeed in remedying the gross social and religious deficiencies of the
Catholic countries, did not prevent the spread of irreligion
fostered by the eighteenth-century 'encyclopedists,' did not
promote the political justice which would have warded off
the vicious extremes of the French Revolution, did not even
save the corporate existence of their Jesuit teachers. Some
day history may finally teach us that such achievements
are beyond the power of any school education, and make
us gauge aright how much more powerful than the schools
are the educational forces outside the schools. In the next

chapter, we may catch some glimpse of what those greater educational forces were, from the sixteenth to the nineteenth century.

III. ELEMENTARY SCHOOLS

Position of schools in sixteenth century. The notion of elementary schools as complete units of school education, self-contained and final, which is so widespread in educational theory and practice today, came into existence only in the nineteenth century. Up to that time, elementary schools were considered merely as first links in a chain of school education which continued through the grammar schools and the universities. Hence, in the sixteenth century, as for many centuries before that, the elementary school was chiefly concerned with teaching the rudiments of speaking, reading, and composing in Latin. During the later Middle Ages, it is true, schools of reckoning and writing were developed in the commercial cities, and by the sixteenth century many of these had become fairly complete elementary schools for training in use of the vernacular languages. But they were confined to the larger cities. The villages and small towns had only the schools of rudiments in Latin.

For a while it seemed likely that the Protestant Revolution, with its insistence upon Bible-reading in the vernaculars, would lead to a greater provision of elementary schools. The Duke of Wurtemberg, in 1559, and the Elector of Saxony, in 1580, issued school regulations which have been widely hailed as furthering elementary schools. They simply did nothing of the sort.[1] They were rather concerned with Latin secondary schools, which would prepare students for the Protestant ministry. The recommendations of Luther and Melanchthon may be classed with the

[1] F. Paulsen, *German Education,* New York, 1908, p. 77.

very numerous decrees of Catholic synods, as indicating some zeal for elementary schools on the part of churchmen; but both were quite ineffective. Popular apathy, as well as the Thirty Years' War (1618-1648), prevented any such counsels from being carried out. Elementary school development lagged far behind that of the grammar schools.

Religious character of elementary schools. Up to the nineteenth century, elementary schools were religious in character; which means that they were controlled by ecclesiastics and included in the subjects of study some religious instruction. Even in Protestant countries, where the State completely dominated the Church, elementary schools were still largely left in the hands of the Church.[1] It was only in the eighteenth century that Prussia took the lead in secularizing schools by a series of laws culminating in the code of 1794; yet Prussia at least kept a place for religious instruction in its State schools. But elementary schools were neither abundant enough nor vigorous enough to maintain religious belief and practice amongst the people, in the face of the inevitable rationalism and skepticism which gradually infected the Protestant groups. The Council of Trent, in the fifth session, May 10 to June 21, 1546, legislated for elementary schools, as well as for other schools.[2] Most of the provincial and diocesan synods of the sixteenth century tried to apply the laws of Trent to local conditions and needs.[3] But the Catholic Church had not the teaching facilities at hand to develop elementary

---

[1] This was obviously still more true where the Protestant church dominated the State, as it did in Massachusetts. The Massachusetts laws of 1638, 1640, 1642, and the penalizing law of 1647 (all of which were notably disobeyed) commanded the establishment of schools as a religious effort for a religious end. See E. Eggleston, *The Transit of Civilization*, New York, 1901, pp. 147, 230 sqq.

[2] Stephen Ehses, *Concilium Tridentinum,* Freiburg im Br., 1904, Vol. 5, pp. 238 sqq.

[3] See Mansi, *Collectio Conciliorum,* Vol. 33, for these decrees.

schools. These were to come in the seventeenth and succeeding centuries.

The Catholic teaching congregations. It is not difficult
to see that elementary school education in the sixteenth
century received much less practical attention from Catholic and Protestant alike than it now deservedly has. The
fundamental reason for that fact is quite simple: in the
earlier conditions of society, there was neither demand[1] nor
need for widespread elementary schools. Such a need developed only in a later, urban, capitalistic society. But
signs of the need began to appear even in the sixteenth
century. Now the Catholic Church had always been interested in schools; and when the time came for elementary
schools, she was interested in them too. But she lacked
teachers. For boys' schools, some attempt to supply the
need was made by such organizations as the Fathers of
Christian Doctrine, founded by a French priest, Caesar de
Bus, in 1593; the Piarists, founded by St. Joseph Calasan-
zio at Rome, in 1602;[2] and the more important organization

[1] It must puzzle many a modern mind to note how stubbornly the
people at large have opposed the development of elementary schools.
Luther's appeal for schools met with popular apathy, and drew from
him a second pronouncement on the subject (*Werke,* Weimar edition,
Vol. 30, 2, pp. 508 sqq.) which was equally ineffective. It was popular apathy which made the school regulations of the Council of Trent
so long inoperative. The Massachusetts law of 1647 was disobeyed
in many towns, "which found it cheaper to pay the fine imposed for
failure to establish a school than to pay for the services of a schoolmaster." (S. K. Wilson, *American History,* Chicago, 1929, p. 176.)
Even in the nineteenth century, the efforts of James Carter and
Horace Mann for the establishment of State schools in Massachusetts
required nearly sixty years, from 1824 to 1882, to overcome popular
opposition. (S. C. Parker, *History of Modern Elementary Education,*
Boston, 1912, pp. 257-59.) Instances might be multiplied almost
indefinitely.

[2] He had asked the Jesuits to open elementary schools; but the
rector of the Roman College (which had then more than 2,000 students) and the General Claude Aquaviva had to refuse him. He
then, in 1597, opened his first 'pious school,' which soon had 1,200
small boys in attendance. (Hughes, *Loyola,* pp. 260-61.) But after
1700, the Piarists transferred most of their attention to secondary
education. (*Catholic Encyclopedia,* Vol. 13, p. 588.) "The tenta-

of *laymen*, known as the Brothers of the Christian Schools, founded at Rheims nearly a hundred years later by St. John Baptist de la Salle. Women religious, devoted to the elementary education of girls, were not so abundant. What there were of them lived in cloistered seclusion. The Church at first looked askance at the very idea of uncloistered religious women.[1] But the women came, offering their services, and in time were accepted; and their work thrived wonderfully.[2] All this, of course, was a slow process; the real beginnings were made only in the seventeenth and eighteenth centuries. With characteristic conservatism, the schools lagged behind the social need, and the churchmen lagged behind the schools.

Curriculum. It is customary for modern writers to disparage the 'narrow' curriculum of the earlier elementary school, and to contrast it with the elaborate curriculum of

---

tives made in favor of boys by St. Peter Fourier (1565-1640) and Père Barré, in 1678, failed; the work of M. Demia at Lyons in 1672 was not to spread." (*Catholic Encyclopedia,* Vol. 8, p. 56.)

[1] St. Angela Merici labored for more than forty years before she gained papal approval for her congregation of Ursulines. Mary Ward who founded the "English Ladies" at St. Omer in 1609, could not get papal approval unless she consented to having the congregation cloistered. As she refused this, her foundation was suppressed by the Pope, Urban VIII, in 1630. (See articles by Mother Loyola, *Catholic Encyclopedia,* Vol. 8, p. 54, Vol. 15, pp. 551-52.) A second attempt, under the name of "Institute of Mary," succeeded in having its rule approved only in 1703; but even then the "Institute" as such was refused papal approval because it was not cloistered. It was 174 years later, 268 years after the first foundation by Mary Ward, before it was finally approved by Pius IX, in 1877.

[2] No adequate account of the rise and development of religious congregations of women devoted to teaching has been written. Information concerning them is scattered piecemeal in historical sketches of individual communities. P. J. Marique, *History of Education,* New York, 1926, Vol. 2, pp. 127, 128, 231, 232, gives names and dates of origin of a few congregations. See J. A. Burns, *Catholic School System in the United States,* New York, 1912, *passim,* for data on American sisterhoods; also, *The Catholic Church in the United States,* Vol. 1: *The Religious Communities,* New York, 1908. J. Prunel, *La Renaissance Catholique en France au Dix-septieme Siecle,* Paris, 1921, gives sketches of the religious teaching communities founded in France, chiefly from 1600 to 1650.

the present.   The earlier curriculum was limited to reading, writing, a little arithmetic, and some religious instruction, usually in the form of one or other of the catechisms. It simply took the place of the rudimentary instruction which might well be, and often was, received at home from the child's parents.   It was limited to a few years; after which the child either went on to a grammar school, or went to work.   But it must be remembered, as a cardinal principle in school education, that such a curriculum was quite well suited to the needs of the time.

Methods.   The methods used in elementary schools were not good.   Some effort was generally made to divide the children into groups, according to their progress in reading; but there was no group teaching before the last quarter of the seventeenth century.   The children studied alone as best they could, and recited individually at the teacher's desk.   St. Peter Fourier, who did good pioneering work for elementary schools, advocated that "the mistress take four or six children at a time, of about equal capacity, and whilst one is reading, the other five shall follow in their books, saying after her the same words in a low tone."[1] But even such an improvement had not penetrated into the New England schools so late as the beginning of the nineteenth century.   A pupil of a Connecticut school in 1800 writes: "The children were called up one by one . . . She [the teacher] then placed the spelling book before the pupil, and with a penknife pointed, one by one, to the letters of the alphabet, saying 'What's that?' "[2]   There was very

---

[1] From *Les Vraies Constitutions des Religieuses de la Congregation de Notre Dame*, 2d ed., Toul, 1694, sec. 4, p. 53; quoted by Brother Azarias, *Essays Educational*, p. 215.   The first edition of the Constitutions was printed in 1640, the year of Peter Fourier's death.

[2] Quoted from *Peter Parley* in C. Johnson's *Old time Schools and School-Books*, New York, 1904, p. 116.   See also the account of a Boston elementary school of about the same time, in H. Barnard's *American Journal of Education*, Vol. 26, pp. 209 sqq.

little in the way of school apparatus. The writing teachers spent hours in making and sharpening quill pens. Johnson says the first reference to a blackboard that he could find was a suggestion offered in the preface to a textbook on arithmetic, published in 1809 at Philadelphia.[1]

Two great advances. The two most obvious defects of elementary schools were poor teachers and poor methods. The procedure for remedying them was actively set afoot by a Catholic priest. John Baptist de la Salle, who was born at Rheims in 1651, founded the Brothers of the Christian Schools in 1682, died at Rouen in 1719, and was canonized as a saint by Pope Leo XIII in 1900. De la Salle had wealth, and a good ecclesiastical position as canon of the cathedral of Rheims. At thirty-two years of age he gave up his position to devote himself to the education of poor boys, and gave his money to the poor. He founded his organization of lay teachers, vowed to poverty, chastity, and obedience, and dedicated to teaching poor boys in elementary schools. He met with almost incredible difficulties: not merely with feeble co-operation, but with active ecclesiastical persecution.[2] But, with heroic virtue, he persevered in his purpose. At his death, his Institute reckoned 214 brothers, teaching more than 9,000 boys; but the Institute was not approved by the pope until six years after de la Salle's death, when Benedict XIII by a bull of January 26, 1725, made the community a religious congrega-

[1] Johnson, *op. cit.*, p. 107. It was suggested that the blackboard be "about three feet square, painted or stained with ink, and hung against the wall in a convenient place for a class to assemble around it."

[2] Ten years after he had founded the Institute, it "was so weakened by deaths and defections that de la Salle could hardly find two Brothers who were willing to bind themselves by vow to maintain the free schools. . . . In November, 1702, he was deposed by Cardinal de Noailles. . . . His name was attacked, and justice denied him before the civil tribunals. After thirty-five years of hard labour, his work seemed to be almost on the verge of ruin." (*Catholic Encyclopedia,* Vol. 8, p. 445; see also *idem,* Vol. 8, p. 56.)

tion.   The Christian Brothers' pupils now number more than 750,000.

Comenius, in 1657, had advocated the abandonment of the individual method of instruction in elementary school, and suggested that the teacher should instruct the children 'omnes simul et semel.'[1]   Charles Hoole used his suggestion successfully in an English school.[2]   De Nesmond, Bishop of Bayeux, worked out the same idea, independently of Comenius, in 1672.   About the same time, Charles Demia, a priest of Lyons, formed a plan for elementary teaching along much the same lines.   But these efforts were neither long lived nor greatly influential in affecting school practice.[3]   It remained for St. John Baptist de la Salle to give permanent form and lasting influence to the 'simultaneous method.'   "The pupils follow in the same lesson; they observe strict silence; the master, in correcting one, is correcting all: here is the essence of the Simultaneous Method."[4]   The method was not only employed in all Christian Brothers' schools, but was also widely copied in other schools.[5]

---

[1] *Didactica Magna,* Amsterdam, 1657, coll. 103.

[2] *Quarterly Journal of Education,* 1867, p. 262.   See *The American Journal of Education,* Vol. 17, pp. 191-207, 224-324 for the four treatises of Hoole's "A New Discovery of the Old Art of Teaching Schools," first published in 1660.   Hoole is more concerned with grammar schools than with elementary; though his "Petty Schoole" deals with elementary schools.

[3] See the excellent account of this whole matter in Brother Azarias, *Essays Educational,* pp. 207-40.   Another detail of method may be mentioned here, the use of question and answer forms for the catechetical instruction of children.   Some now doubt that it was much of an improvement in method.   The claim that the first to use the method was St. Jerome Emiliani (1481-1537) is made in *L'Ordine dei Chierici Regolari Somaschi,* Rome, 1928, a volume of essays by various hands, published to commemorate the fourth centenary of the congregation founded by St. Jerome Emiliani.

[4] *Idem,* p. 231.   De la Salle explained the method in detail in his *Conduite des Écoles Chretiennes,* Avignon, 1724.   An English version is *Management of Christian Schools,* New York, 1887.

[5] A. Ravelet, *Histoire du Venerable J. B. de la Salle,* 1874, pp. 369 sqq.

Many men had seen the obvious need of teacher training. Mulcaster touched on it in 1581.[1] Allain cites a petition presented to Louis XIV by de Chennevières, 'a priest serving the poor,' which urged seminaries for elementary teachers.[2] But, again, it was de la Salle who went forward from vague suggestions to actual practice. In 1684, he opened the first 'normal school.' The Duc de Mazarin offered money to help found other such schools. The Bishop of Rheims "refused to sanction the work";[3] but the Bishop of Laon gave it his approval; and the second normal school was established in his diocese. Thereafter the schools spread rapidly. August Hermann Francke took up the work at Halle in 1697; his disciple, Johann Hecker, opened his first normal school at Stettin in 1735. The Catholic priest, Johann Ignaz von Felbiger studied under Hecker, became his devoted friend, and carried his ideas back to Sagan, which became the normal school center for Silesia. In 1770, Felbiger founded a normal school at Vienna, reformed the whole system of Austria, and established or reorganized 3,933 primary schools.[4] But the idea reached the United States only well on in the nineteenth century.[5]

Position of schools at close of the period. In the nineteenth century, various forces combined to direct public attention more and more toward the elementary schools. They were shortly to become the most important of the agencies in school education. All the powers of the State were to be behind them. Their influence in shaping our

[1] *Positions,* edition by R. H. Quick, London, 1887, pp. 236-37.

[2] *L'Instruction Primaire en France avant la Revolution,* p. 128.

[3] Brother Azarias, *Essays Educational,* p. 252.

[4] Krieg, *Lehrbuch der Pädogogik,* Paderborn, 1905, p. 221; Barnard, *American Journal of Education,* Vol. 9, p. 600.

[5] "The first Catholic normal school in the United States antedated by at least twenty years the normal school established at Lexington by Horace Mann." J. A. Burns, *Catholic School System in the United States,* New York, 1912, p. 200. Mann's normal school was begun in 1839.

civilization, at least indirectly, was to become enormous. But when the nineteenth century opened, elementary schools scarcely gave any hint of this imminent huge development. In England, in the Germanies outside of Prussia, in the United States, in other Protestant countries, they were very feeble institutions. In Catholic lands, owing to the fine work of the Christian Brothers and the multiplying religious congregations of women, they had a somewhat stronger growth; yet even there they had not reached anything like the influence they were soon to exert. The new and astonishing spread of elementary schools depended upon conditions in society which were much more significant than the schools themselves. We shall consider those conditions in the next chapter.

TOPICS FOR DISCUSSION

1. The position of scholastic philosophy during the seventeenth and eighteenth centuries.

2. A comparative study of the school methods of (a) Vittorino da Feltre at Pleasant House; (b) the Brethren of the Common Schools at Zwolle or Deventer; (c) the Jesuit schools.

3. A comparison between (a) the *Colloquia* of Erasmus, Vives, and Cordier; and (b) the *Januae Linguarum* of Bathe and Comenius.

4. Points of resemblance and difference in the English prefectural system and Trotzendorf's student government.

5. The rise and development of 'academies' in England and America.

6. The development of 'primers' from Catholic religious manuals.

7. The story of arithmetic in the schools.

8. The school reforms of Johann Ignaz von Felbiger in Silesia and Austria.

BIBLIOGRAPHIC NOTE

Some of the more useful references, primary and secondary, have been already indicated. There is illustrative material for life at Eton in *The Paston Letters, 1424-1509*, edited by J. Gairdner, 4 vols., London, 1900-01; and the *Exercitatio* of Vives, Bruges, 1539 (translated by F. Watson as *Tudor School-boy Life*, London, 1908) and *Colloquiorum Scholasticorum Libri IV* of Maturin Cordier, Lyons, 1564 (English translation by C. Hoole, 1657; many reprints, especially in the abridged *Select Centuries*) give details of later school life. For the English universities, see Anthony à Wood, *Historia et Antiquitates Universitatis Oxoniensis,* 2 vols., Oxford, 1674 (English translation by J. Gutch, 2 vols., Oxford, 1791-96) and *Athenae Oxonienses,* 2 vols., London, 1691-92 (edited by P. Bliss, London, 1813-20) ; J. B. Mullinger, *History of the University of Cambridge,* 3 vols., Cambridge, 1873-1911; and C. Wordsworth, *Scholae Academicae: Some Account of the Studies at the English Universities in the Eighteenth Century,* Cambridge, 1877.

In the *Monumenta Germaniae Paedagogica,* begun in 1886 under the editorship of K. Kehrbach, there is some source material for the teaching of mathematics prior to 1525 in Vol. 3; documents for Melanchthon's educational work are given in Vol. 7, for Felbiger's work in Vol. 30, for the secondary schools of Bavaria in Vols. 41, 42, and G. M. Pachtler's edition of the *Ratio Studiorum et Institutiones Scholasticae Societatis Jesu* in Vols. 2, 5, 9, and 16 (1887-94). H. Barnard's *American Journal of Education,* 1855-87, contains translations or reprints of some sources (e. g., Charles Hoole's *Petty School* in Vol. 17). *The Ratio for Lower Schools* has been translated into English in W. McGucken, *The Jesuits and Education,* Milwaukee, 1932, pp. 271-315, and a full translation of the Ratio and Part IV of the Constitutions is given in E. A. Fitzpatrick, *St. Ignatius and the Ratio Studiorum,* New York, 1933. For a thoroughly intelligent and convincing defense of the Jesuit teaching methods, see Francis P. Donnelly, *Principles of Jesuit Education in Practice,* New York, 1934. For sixteenth-century arithmetic, see C. Clavius, *Epitome Arithmeticae Practicae,* Rome, 1583. For English colleges on the Continent, there is rich material in E. Petre (edited by Husenbeth), *Notices of the English Colleges and Convents Established on the Continent after the Dissolution of the Religious Houses in England,* Norwich, 1849; and T. F. Knox, *The First and Second Diaries of the English College at Douay,* London, 1878, and *Diaries III, IV, and V* (published by Catholic Record Society), London, 1911.

As a general introduction to schools of this period, see the fine chapters on education by J. W. Adamson, in *Cambridge History of English Literature,* Vol. 9, chap. 15, Vol. 14, chap. 14, with the bibliographies appended. For the Continent, see E. Allain, *L'Instruction Primaire en France avant la Revolution,* Paris, 1881; A. Sicard, *Les Etudes Classiques avant la Revolution,* Paris, 1887; E. Nohle, *History of German School System,* in *Report of the U. S. Commissioner of Education,* 1897-98, Vol. 1; H. Barnard, *Memoirs of Eminent Teachers and Educators, with Contributions to the History of Education in Germany,* Hartford, 1878; J. W. Adamson, *Pioneers of Modern Education, 1600-1700,* Cambridge, 1905. For English schools, see H. Staunton, *The Great Schools of England,* London, 1865; F. Watson, *The Old Grammar Schools,* Cambridge, 1906, and *The English Gram-*

mar Schools to 1660, Cambridge, 1908. For Scotland, J. Kerr, *Scottish Education, School and University, from Early Times to 1908,* Cambridge, 1914, carries on the incomplete work of J. Grant.

On Scholasticism, there are useful chapters in M. de Wulf, *Scholasticism Old and New,* New York, 1907; E. Boutroux, *Etudes d'Histoire de la Philosophie,* Paris, 1897, new ed., 1925 (translated by F. Rothwell, *Historical Studies in Philosophy,* London, 1912); and J. S. Zybura, *Present-Day Thinkers and the New Scholasticism* (especially pp. 371-532), St. Louis, 1926.

For the *Colloquia,* see L. Massebieau, *Les Colloques Scolaires du Seizième Siècle,* Paris, 1876; and the introductions to N. Bailey, *Erasmus' Whole Familiar Colloquies,* Glasgow, 1877, and Foster Watson's translation of Vives. On the development of the 'primers,' see W. Maskell, *Monumenta Ritualia Ecclesiae Anglicanae,* 3 vols., London, 1846, 2d ed., Oxford, 1882 (especially Vol. 3); G. Littlehales, *The Prymer or Prayer-Book of the Lay People,* London, 1891-92; H. Bannermann, *The Horn Book,* Fordham University, 1928; and H. Thurston, "The Mediaeval Primer," in *The Month,* February, 1911. For arithmetic in the schools, see L. L. Jackson, *The Educational Significance of Sixteenth Century Arithmetic,* Columbia University, 1906; F. Cajori, *A History of Elementary Mathematics,* New York, 1896, rev. ed., 1917; and D. E. Smith, *Rara Arithmetica,* Boston, 1908, and *Teaching of Elementary Mathematics,* New York, 1900.

For Sturm, see L. Kuckelhahn, *Johannes Sturm, Strassburgs ersten Schulrektor,* Leipzig, 1872; E. Laas, *Die Paedagogik des Johann Sturm, historisch und kritisch beleuchtet,* Berlin, 1872; and F. Collard, *La Pédagogie de Sturm* (in *Melanges d'Histoire Offerts a C. Moeller),* Louvain, 1914. For Trotzendorf's system of student government, see L. Sturm, *Valentin Trotzendorf und die lateinische Schule zu Goldberg,* Goldburg, 1888; and K. J. Loeschke, *Valentin Trotzendorf nach seinem Leben und Wirken,* Breslau, 1856. For the English prefectural system, see A. F. Leach, *History of Winchester College,* London and New York, 1899, and *Educational Charters and Documents,* Cambridge, 1911; T. F. Kirby, *Annals of Winchester College from 1382,* Oxford, 1892; H. C. Maxwell-Lyte, *History of Eton College,* London, 1875; L. Cust, *History of Eton College,* New York, 1899; and, for modern times, *The Public Schools from Within* (by various writers), London, 1906.

H. C. Barnard, *The Little Schools of Port-Royal,* Cambridge, 1913, is a sympathetic account. For the 'academies,' see I. Parker, *The Dissenting Academies in England,* Cambridge, 1911; and E. Eggleston, *The Transit of Civilization from England to America in the Seventeenth Century,* New York, 1901. For the schools of the Christian Brothers, see K. O'Meara's translation of Ravelet's *Life of St. John Baptist de la Salle,* New York, 1888, and R. Wilson, *The Christian Brothers, Their Origin and Their Work,* London, 1883; better still, J. Guibert, *Histoire de S. Jean Baptiste de la Salle,* Paris, 1901, with its excellent bibliography. For Felbiger, see J. Volkmer, *Johann Ignaz von Felbiger,* Habelschwerdt, 1890; and E. G. Walther, *Die Grundzuge du Pädagogik Ignaz von Felbiger,* Leipzig, 1903.

CHAPTER XV

A period of profound change. As has been seen in the last chapter, school education from the sixteenth to the nineteenth century underwent comparatively few changes. The universities lost influence; the grammar schools gained; elementary schools became better organized. But both decay and growth were rather quiet processes, which might scarcely impress the casual observer that there had been any change at all. Quite the contrary was the case with Western civilized society in general. That did change strikingly, profoundly. It changed in some of the most important activities which constitute and determine a civilization. The change was so vast, so forceful, so filled with presage for the future, as to have a remarkable effect upon education, upon the habits of thought, emotion, and conduct of the generations which lived through those three centuries and which were to follow. A history of education, no matter how condensed, cannot ignore the educational influence of such great changes in civilization. In this chapter, therefore, we attempt some brief outline of these important educational agencies which operated outside the schools.

The links with the past. It is quite necessary to any coherent view of the history of modern education to keep in mind that a great part of the Western world took a new direction in the Classic Renaissance, and has been moving in that direction ever since. The roots of that modern history are in two great occurrences: the spiritual decay of the fourteenth century, and the struggle between Chris-

tianity and a revived paganism begun in the Renaissance.
The Protestant Revolution complicated, but did not essentially change, the character of that conflict. All that it
really accomplished was to divide, and therefore weaken,
the forces of Christianity; and it did that at a most disastrous time, when Christianity had need of all its power for
the fight already begun. In that way, the Protestant Revolt contributed, unwittingly and unwillingly, to the important dechristianizing of society which has been going on
since the fourteenth century. A second complication,
though again no essential change, in the conflict between
Christianity and revived paganism, came from the amazing
surge of energy which swept through Europe in the fifteenth and sixteenth centuries. No man can hope adequately to explain either the enormous fatigue of the peoples of Europe in the fourteenth century, a fatigue which
had begun to be evident even before the devastation caused
by the Black Death, or the equally startling revival of
energy in the fifteenth century. But that there was such
a fatigue and such a revival is very clear. Unfortunately,
when the renewed energy came, the spiritual leaders of
Europe, the clergy and the schools, failed adequately to
guide and control it.

The enlarging world. First to strike the mind in a series
of great changes are the geographic discoveries of Vasco
da Gama (1460-1524), Columbus (1451-1506), and Magellan (1480-1521), and the astronomical discoveries of
Copernicus (1473-1543), and Kepler (1571-1630). Writers
of history are accustomed to labor the obvious point that
those discoveries were causes leading to great social effects;
but they not infrequently fail to consider the much more
impressive fact, that those discoveries were themselves effects of a most powerful and prophetic cause. That cause,
so seldom appreciated, was the sudden and astounding vigor
of action which surged through Europe in the fifteenth

century. Let the physiologists speculate on the reasons
why Europe, within two lifetimes after the Black Death,
manifested a vitality and enterprise which appear to have
been even greater than those shown in the twelfth century.
But whether or not they can explain it, the fact is there,
astounding and significant. New forces were unleashed,
which swept grandly clear of control by the old school education, which seethed through the peoples and urged them
to new achievements, which were quite literally to change
the face of the world. Men who had used the compass for
generations, now dared to trust its guidance beyond the
narrow seas of Europe. Men who had long read ancient
doubts about the Ptolemaic system of astronomy, a system
which made the earth the center of the universe, now bold-
ly tested the doubts, and proved the falsity of an astronomical theory which had been accepted for fourteen hundred years.[1] There is something mysterious and awe-inspir-
ing in this new energy. The first thing it did was to push
back the horizons of Europe. Men envisaged a new earth
and a new starry sky.[2]

The commercial revolution. The next thing that new

---

[1] Cardinal Nicholas of Cusa taught the motion of the earth round
the sun, nearly a hundred years before Copernicus. His statements
are to be found in his treatise *De Docta Ignorantia,* Vol. 2, p. 11.
(Cf. Max Jacobi, *Den Lahren des Nicolaus von Cusa,* Berlin, 1904.)
P. Duhem has discussed his influence on Leonardo da Vinci and
Keppler and on the Copernican theory, in *Bulletin Italien,* 1907, Vol.
7, pp. 87-134, 181-220, Vol. 8, pp. 18-55, 212 sqq., 312 sqq. In this
connection see also the excellent series of articles by Pierre Duhem
in *Annales de Philosophie Chretienne,* 1908, reprinted later as Σώζειν
τὰ Φαινόμενα, *Essai sur la Notion de Theorie Physique de Platon a
Galilee.*

[2] Curiously enough, the new spirit of geographic exploration, whilst
it opened up the great sea routes, did practically nothing to improve
communications between the various peoples of Europe itself. That
great Roman institution, the road, continued to be neglected. Indeed,
Ludwig Friedlaender estimates that the volume of travel in Europe
was greater in Roman imperial times than ever again until the nineteenth century. (*Roman Life and Manners under the Early Empire,*
4 vols., London, 1908-13, Vol. 1, p. 322.)

energy did was to set men digging earnestly into the new sources of wealth it had opened up. Pinched and parochial Europe thrust its arms up to the elbows in those riches of the sea-linked East, of which before it had had only a slow and laborious fingering. The Americas beckoned to a golden dream. The dreaded, unknown oceans were now the highways of the world. The trader and merchant became much more important in the eyes of Europe than the farmer and the craftsman. Portugal and Spain hilariously divided the world beyond Europe between them, and the Borgia pope, Alexander VI, drew a 'line of demarcation' for their claims. The English, the Dutch, and the French came in to wrest away great parts of the commercial spoils. The German and Italian city-states were out of it, and hence died on their feet. It was the new *nations,* Portugal, Spain, Holland, France, England, not the old city-states, which were to dominate the world for centuries to come. It was the *wealth* of those nations, not their culture or their chivalry, which was to determine their pre-eminence. The kings and rulers went into business; and the international bankers took the place of the popes in mediating between kings.

All this could not but color the thoughts and lives of the people at large. It sharpened their hopes and their interests in this present, material world. It brought new desires, and new possibilities, of material comfort in living. It created a new intellectual curiosity, a thirst for facts rather than for truths. It gave to education a new test of value, that of immediate, material utility: not how it might develop and fashion the individual, but how it might enrich him with new possessions. It built up a strong middle class; and taught the rich merchant to scorn the poor noble. It began to level society, in one sense; by making wealth the mark of distinction, and sneering at race and culture. It did not lift up the peasant, but it stirred him to new discontent and new envy. It made the cleric a decidedly unimportant figure in European society. For good or for evil, or for both, such changes are enormous in their influence.

Some social effects. The effects upon society of these great changes were manifold; but three of them especially may be noted.

(a) The separatist principle of nationalism, already strongly at work before the commercial revolution, was intensified in its action by rivalry for the control of colonies and colonial sources of wealth. Following upon that sharper limitation of nationalities, there came a vigorous development and fixation of the national languages. The peak of the national literatures comes in the late sixteenth century and the seventeenth century. This gave the final stroke to what the Classic Renaissance had begun: the destruction of Latin as the common living language of literate European men. The schools went on teaching Latin when it had small practical place in the world.

(b) Within each nation, as it grew in wealth, a plutocracy began to take the place of the old feudal aristocracy; and the new blood of the energetic bourgeoisie gradually forced the middle classes into leadership in the plutocracy. The economic system of capitalism was established. The old serfdom, which was dying out even before these great social changes, began to be replaced by the new serfdom of a proletariat, a people without land, who lived by hiring out their labor to merchants and industrial managers.

(c) Class hatred, now narrowed to the simple distinction between rich and poor, became more and more virulent.

If we add these forces to the religious hostility which had already begun to divide Europe, we may readily see how the social bonds were increasingly relaxed, the old controlling forces of society weakened almost to impotence. The European world was shaping itself, unconsciously, to a new culture. In comparison with the educative power of such social changes, all school education is a broken reed indeed.

The political changes. Changes in the political order were bound to follow upon such changes in society in general. The sixteenth century in Europe began with the established absolutism of the Tudors, and the developing absolutism of the Hapsburgs. The seventeenth century brought the even more rigorous absolutism of the Bourbons. But in England, Spain, Austria, and finally in France, the absolute power of the monarch was gradually broken by the rising force of the middle classes, and in each country various forms and measures of representative government were introduced. Toward the close of the eighteenth century, England's most important American colonies successfully revolted, to form, upon more or less democratic principles, the independent United States of America; in the early nineteenth century, most of Spain's colonies followed their example. The history of those political changes is impressive; but even more impressive is the attitude of mind in the various peoples which brought about those changes: a resolute insistence upon human *rights,* and the will to assert the power of the *masses.* In those three centuries, a new temper developed in the peoples of Europe and the Americas, new political principles showed active and compelling vitality.[1] It was all part of the huge change in the thoughts and emotions of Western civilization.

The growth of the positive sciences. The more strictly intellectual changes during those three centuries were as marked as the social and political changes. Metaphysical science had dominated the thought of Europe since the twelfth century. Now it was to be thrust aside by the

[1] "It was an inevitable, if unforeseen and undesired, consequence of the Protestant revolution, that where the individual had loosened the power of ecclesiastical authority, he should also shake that of secular political authority." G. N. Clark, *The Seventeenth Century,* Oxford, 1929, p. 225.

physical sciences. It has often been said that metaphysics was more concerned with truths than with facts. It is at least as true that the positive sciences are more concerned with facts than with truths. The distinction is, of course, relative in both cases. Each sort of science has suffered from its comparative lack; each needs the other as a correlative and corrective. But the efforts of men since the sixteenth century tended to turn more and more exclusively to the investigation of facts and laws of the material order. Physiology, physics, astronomy, chemistry, botany, geology, and kindred sciences have grown marvelously in both range and accuracy of observed facts. Real discoveries of great value have been made and continue to be made.

The mass of the people, obviously, never entered into any understanding of these discoveries, any more than they had ever possessed any grasp of metaphysical truth. But they became increasingly impressed by the succeeding discoveries, in the vague way of admiration and wonder; and they were soon to be more immediately awed by the remarkable development of practical inventions which came to apply scientific discoveries to the commodious uses of everyday life. 'Science,' ill-understood, or understood not at all, became a magic word amongst the populace. But it did not yet get strongly into the schools, which in this, as in other matters, always lagged behind the moving world.

The changes in religious thought. The Protestant Revolution had put Catholicism on the defensive, struggling hard, and not always successfully, to maintain its influence upon the peoples who still held to the ancient Faith. The newly discovered lands called forth fine efforts of missionaries, it is true; and the Catholic Church immeasurably outstripped the multiplying Protestant churches in the success of its missionary work. But the Catholic Church made practically no progress in winning back to the Faith the revolted peoples of Europe. Those peoples went their own way, and it was a way of almost constant change. The change was generally in the direction of latitudinarianism, rationalism, skepticism: in spite of such movements as those of the Pietists in the Germanies and of the Wesleyans in England.

An Englishman, Lord Herbert of Cherbury, seems to have given the first great impetus of this trend of Protestantism away from the fragmentary Christian beliefs carried over in the Revolt. Born in 1583, Lord Herbert published two books, *De Veritate,* in 1624, and *De Religione Gentilium,* in 1645, which urged the claims of natural religion rather than revealed religion. He found ready followers. Charles Blount (1654-1693) attacked the religious verity of the Bible, repudiated miracles as impossible, decried revealed religion. Scores of English writers, such as Thomas Woolston, Anthony Collins, Thomas Chubb, Thomas Morgan, between 1700 and 1750, carried on a violent warfare against all Christian beliefs, in books and pamphlets. In the Germanies, Christian Wolff (1679-1754), who became professor of mathematics and natural history at the University of Halle in 1706, quarreled with the Pietists and began to teach a rationalist opposition to Christianity. His opponents succeeded in having him exiled from Prussia in 1731; but Frederick the Great recalled him in 1740, and made him chancellor of Halle in 1743. His teachings gave a distinctive rationalist character to Halle; and the German universities largely followed the lead of Halle. Deism and rationalism crossed from England to France, and exercised even greater influence there than they did in England. Such men as Diderot (1713-1784), Rousseau (1712-1778), and above all, François Marie Arouet (1694-1778), who called himself Voltaire, took fiery leadership in spreading the new destructive ideas. Voltaire never explained what he meant by his 'natural religion'; his work, like that of most rationalists, was negative, devoted to tearing down Christianity, with little thought of substituting any positive beliefs in its place.

The educational significance of all this does not lie in the fact that some scores of men attacked supernatural, revealed religion, but in the more important fact that their writings were very widely accepted and grew in influence.

The spread of the printed word.　The part played by printing in spreading new ideas rapidly amongst the people is quite obvious.　Printing made possible cheap books and pamphlets, and in time produced the periodical and newspaper.　What should be particularly noted is the class of people who, from the sixteenth to the nineteenth century, bought and read most of the printed publications.　That class was, more and more, the developing middle class, the vague, intermediate world of merchants, shopkeepers, professional men, clerks, artisans: people of the towns and the cities for the most part.　The peasants were very little touched by the flood of print.　The well-educated brought some power of discrimination to their reading.　But the growing masses of men and women who had that little knowledge which is a dangerous thing, read eagerly, thought tumultuously, and were inclined to swallow whole whatever they saw in print.　Fanaticism, more especially in things affecting religion, has come to thrive most vigorously amongst members of the middle class.

The strange linking of 'science' and skepticism.　One of the curious phenomena in the history of human thought is the persistence with which, from the eighteenth century to the present time, overwhelming numbers of ill-informed men and women have maintained the superstition that scientific truth opposes the revealed truth of religion.　Among these ill-informed, or more plainly, ignorant and uneducated, people must be included by all means many teachers in schools, colleges, and universities.　Their private and public pronouncements make it clear that they have amazingly little knowledge of science, and still less knowledge of revealed religion. No first-class mind, of course, has ever entertained this superstition. But the masses are not impressed by that fact. They scarcely even know it. They have little to do with educated men; but spend most of their mental energy in trading opinions amongst themselves, and in establishing conventional attitudes of mind which they take for intellectual principles. One of their 'principles' is that increasing knowledge of the material world is hostile to divinely revealed knowledge concerning the origin and destiny of human beings! It is an accepted 'principle' amongst millions of literates today; it began to prevail in a small way in the eighteenth century, and has spread chiefly through the printed word and the schools. There should be no difficulty in perceiving that it is a decidedly educational 'principle.'

It may conceivably be traced to a merely ignorant *post hoc, ergo propter hoc.* Protestants in large numbers began to abandon Christianity shortly after a few geniuses (all Christians, by the way, and many of them Catholics) entered upon an astonishing series of scientific discoveries. The popular writers, and their gullible readers, ignoring the inevitable tendencies of Protestantism, and having but a superficial and inaccurate knowledge of the scientific truths discovered, violently concluded that it was those scientific discoveries which pushed Protestant Christianity over the cliff.[1] The men who babbled about 'science' without much knowledge of science, also shut their eyes to the

---

[1] This reference to the inherent tendencies of Protestantism is offered in no spirit of controversy, but as a statement of simple and much regretted historical fact. That Protestantism does tend to a vague Deism, has been admitted by many Protestants themselves. For instance, J. A. Gosselin quotes the genuine scientist, Jean Andre de Luc (1727-1817), a devout Protestant, who was reader to Queen Charlotte as saying: "I am convinced that Revelation can be guarded only by the Catholic Church, that all Protestant Churches lead to Deism." (*Vie de M. Emery,* Paris, 1861-62, Vol. 2, p. 32.)

steadfast Catholic faith of so many real scientists, from Regiomontanus to Pasteur.[1]

The decay of artistic taste. As a minor change occurring in the three centuries now under consideration, yet as having great educational significance, must be noted a pronounced decay in literature and the fine arts. It can be seen in every country, and therefore cannot be explained on grounds of some national condition alone. As illustration, one may point out that the Elizabethan age marked the last surge of the Christian Renaissance in England; after that came the cold pompositas of the Puritan age, the vapid coarseness of the Restoration, the dry intellectualism of the eighteenth century. The poets turned pamphleteers. The drama, in every country, became professional, lost the contact with the people which it had had in mediaeval times, grew stilted and unconvincing. Painting and sculpture became more mechanical, architecture more harshly utilitarian. The popular taste declined. This was almost as notable in Catholic lands as in Protestant lands. Spain, forgetting Burgos, produced the gingerbread facades of the 'Jesuit Style'; even Italy lauded the baroque. One explanation may be that amassing wealth had become much more important than studying how to create beauty. In any case, it must simply be said that the close of the eighteenth century marked the full ebb in literature and the fine arts, both in Europe and in its colonies.

Lack of Christian influence. Through all those great changes, distinctively Christian leadership played a very

[1] Many writers have undertaken to glorify the part taken by Catholics and other Christians in the development of the positive sciences. Some of their books will be listed in the bibliography. But it should be kept in mind that these writings have value only on the low plane of combating the vulgar superstition which insists that all scientists are anti-Christian. They are not properly works of apologetics. The Catholic faith neither stands nor falls with the conclusions of scientists. It has altogether another origin and another concern.

small part. The Catholic Church stood fast, of course, to its divinely revealed, and therefore unchanging, truths. But it claimed the allegiance of only a fraction of Europe, and of the less forceful and aggressive parts of the Americas. It was, as has just been said, very much on the defensive. Eighteenth-century democracy might borrow some of its ideas from St. Thomas and Bellarmine;[1] but it was scarcely conscious that it did so. The Catholic Church was not weakening during those three centuries; it was growing stronger, steadily engaged in the slow labor of reform within itself, building up spiritual power through the increasing use of the Sacraments. But before the nineteenth century, the reform had not progressed so far as to let the Church take a very active lead in inspiring the civilization of the period; it was full of promise, but still small in accomplishment.

On the other hand, the more vigorous elements in the various Protestant sects were inclined to be narrowly and repellently Puritan in character; they had no world vision; they were more concerned with detailed acts of individual conduct than with great, guiding principles; they were violent and repressive; and therefore, they too exerted practically no influence upon the large shaping of civilization. The formal 'establishments' of Protestant churches settled into the old human rut of easy living and smug self-satisfaction. The swift movements of those three hundred years went largely uncontrolled by thoughts or purposes which looked beyond the present life.

In this connection, one should not be misled by the

---

[1] M. Millar has shown the influence of the ideas of Bellarmine and Suarez upon the political principles of some of the founders of the American democracy, in *The State and the Church*, by J. A. Ryan and M. Millar, New York, 1922 (see especially Chapter 5, pp. 99-144), and in an article "Bellarmine and the Constitution," in *Studies*, September, 1930. The Fordham University Press has published an English translation of Bellarmine's *De Laicis*, by K. E. Murphy, Ph. D.

so-called 'religious wars' of the period. They were not religious wars, but strictly political wars, which used religion either as a political pretext, or to give popular color to political ventures. The religious tone of the world through those three centuries lowered as definitely as did the literary and artistic.

The relative positions of Catholic and Protestant countries. It was chiefly men of Catholic lands who took the lead in the discoveries which ushered in that period; but it was chiefly men of Protestant lands who won material advancement from the discoveries. By the time that the lines were quite fixed between Protestant and Catholic nationalities, roughly, 1600, Spain and Portugal were entering into decay; Holland was firmly established as a strong commercial power; France and England were in contest over commercial supremacy, out of which England was to come the victor. Poland was on the verge of breaking up, the Germanies and the Italian states had not yet become Germany and Italy, Russia was still outside the purview of Europe. In the matter of prestige, the pre-eminence gradually came into Protestant hands, and Catholics were relatively in the background of the world picture.

The educational trend. Even such a rough, condensed, and imperfect sketch as this may help one to evaluate what the gigantic forces of human activity were doing in those three centuries to fashion the character of the Western world. They began this shaping as unusually aggressive forces, in a period of history that brimmed with energy. There is plenty of excuse for those writers who label their chapters on the sixteenth century "The Great Awakening." It was even, if you will, a violent awakening. But, from the point of view of education, it is more important to consider the question: To what did Europe so awaken itself? The answer of fact is clear enough. The peoples of Europe began to focus their attention more exclusively than before upon the material concerns of life. The dreams of beauty in artistic creation, which once had stirred even the nameless craftsman working at a cathedral, the lure of metaphysical speculation, the search for those profounder truths which underlie the routine of living, the vision of eternal fulfillment held out by the Faith, all these lost much of their appeal to men; their place was taken by the attraction of wealth, and the power, prestige, and luxury which wealth could bring. Those centuries brought about a change in interests and in human values amongst large and dominant masses of mankind. There were enough men and women thus educated by the trend of events to make their aims, habits of thought, and conduct give a new character to Western civilization: the character of what is often ridiculously called 'realism,' as if the material things of life were the only realities.

Yet it would be utterly unfair to imply that money-making was the exclusive concern which occupied men's minds and efforts. As a secondary, but very real, activity, there went with that dominating aim a sharp intellectual curiosity, an enthusiastic interest in the knowledge of facts. It is true that the tendency constantly was to turn each new increase of that knowledge to material uses, to financial gain, to fighting diseases, to adding comfort to life in the way of better housing, speed in travelling, and facility of communication; but beneath those practical uses there remained a genuine interest in the positive sciences for themselves.

The people greatly abandoned religious beliefs and practices; partly because of their growing absorption in the present life, partly through a real and chafing irritation with religious truth. They were strengthened in this neglect, or even scorn, of religious truth by a widely fostered superstition that 'scientific' truth opposed and refuted religious truth.

The boastful, self-reliant spirit of individualism sponsored by the Renaissance and the Protestant Revolution developed in the masses a striking attitude of independence. It was often a petulant independence as is our human way. Because it was energetic, it was not always measured or balanced. It led to reckless experimentation, it was at times painfully cocksure. But it generally had in it great store of courage and a certain nobility. Men became highly critical of all authority, on the watch to demand an account of its stewardship; they were vigorously determined to keep the management of their affairs, so far as possible, in their own hands. But they had not now, any more than at other stages of the world's history, the power to carry out their determination. Political corruption did not diminish during those three centuries; skill in economic management did not increase; the crowding into the towns had already begun, and the way was preparing for the horrors of modern industrialism. But the ultimate characteristic of the world which was to face those and other intricate problems of life was that it looked to itself and its own forces alone for a solution. Although that blessed word, sociology, had not yet been invented, the turn of the nineteenth century found overwhelming masses of men ready to accept sociology in the place of theology.

TOPICS FOR DISCUSSION

1. How did the condemnation of Galileo link with the education of his times?

2. Was the eighteenth century notable for scientific discoveries? Why were many influential men of the eighteenth century so enamored of science?

3. The educational influence of the drama in the seventeenth and eighteenth centuries.

4. The educational foundations of modern notions of democracy.

5. What gave Voltaire his opportunity for educational leadership?

6. What educational causes have led Protestant countries to surpass Catholic countries in commercial and industrial wealth?

BIBLIOGRAPHIC NOTE

There are few books which discuss specifically the points raised in this chapter. The surge of energy which led to geographic and scientific discoveries must be sensed in many records. It appears between the lines in, for instance, most of the two hundred volumes of contemporary accounts of travel and exploration published at London since 1847 by the Hakluyt Society. It can be perceived in P. Jovius, *Historiae sui Temporis,* Florence, 1550-52; in C. B. Morisot, *Orbis Maritimi Historia,* Dijon, 1643; in Bartolomé de las Casas, *Historia de las Indias,* 5 vols., Madrid, 1878; in many of the writings of Galileo Galilei, particularly *Dialoghi delle Nuove Scienze,* Elzevir, Leyden, 1638.

A general introduction to the earlier stages of the great changes of this period may be found in L. Thorndike, *Science and Thought in the Fifteenth Century,* Columbia University, 1929; and H. O. Taylor, *Thought and Expression in the Sixteenth Century,* 2d ed., 2 vols., New York, 1930; which may be profitably supplemented by the wider view presented in C. S. Devas, *The Key to the World's Progress,* 2d ed., London, 1908, and by some of the earlier chapters in Arnold Lunn, *The Flight from Reason,* London, 1932. Some of the problems created by these changes are discussed in W. E. H. Lecky, *History of the Rise and Influence of the Spirit of Rationalism in Europe,* London, 1865, rev. ed., 2 vols., 1914; and W. N. Rice, *Christian Faith in an Age of Science,* 2d ed., New York, 1904.

On the economic changes which profoundly affected education, the following works are suggested: W. Cunningham, *An Essay on Western Civilization in its Economic Aspects,* 2 vols., Cambridge, 1898-1900; Max Weber (English translation by F. H. Knight), *General Economic History,* London, 1927; and for the eighteenth century and after, E. R. A. Seligman, *The Economic Interpretation of History,* rev. ed., New York, 1917.

For the influence of scientific developments on education, see D. Stimson, *The Gradual Acceptance of the Copernican Theory,* Columbia University, 1917; P. Duhem, *L'Evolution des Theories Physiques,* Louvain, 1896; A. Berry, *The History of Astronomy,* London, 1898; Sir A. Geikie, *The Founders of Geology,* London, 1905; W. Stirling, *Some Apostles of Physiology,* London, 1902; Brother Potamian, *Makers of Electricity,* New York, 1909; E. Wassmann, *The Problem of Evolution,* London, 1909; J. J. Walsh, *Catholic Churchmen in Science,* Philadelphia, 1909; Sir B. C. A. Windle, *The Church and Science,* 3d ed., London, 1924. A compact and impartial study is E. R. Hull, *Galileo and his Condemnation,* London, 1906. For an important development in law, see J. B. Scott, *The Spanish Origin of International Law,* Washington, 1928.

For illustrations of the educational influence of literature, especially of the drama, during this period, see Chapters 7-9 of G. W.

Shuster, *English Literature,* New York, 1926; Vol. 2 of E. Legouis and L. Cazamian, *History of English Literature,* 2 vols., New York, 1927; and the more inclusive summary in the earlier chapters of L. J. A. Mercier, *The Challenge of Humanism,* Oxford University Press, 1933. There are helpful discussions of the influence of seventeenth- and eighteenth-century drama in F. P. G. Guizot, *Le Temps Passé,* 2 vols., Paris, 1887; B. Matthews, *The Development of the Drama,* New York, 1903; B. H. Clark, *European Theories of the Drama,* rev. ed., London, 1929; and A. Eloesser, *Das Bürgerliche Drama: seine Geschichte im 18 und 19 Jahrhundert,* Berlin, 1898.

For the conditions which gave Voltaire his opportunity of leadership, see G. Desnoiresterres, *Voltaire et la Société Française au XVIIIe Siècle,* 8 vols., Paris, 1867-76; the less extensive work by E. Faguet, *La Politique Comparée de Montesquieu, Rousseau, et Voltaire,* Paris, 1902; and N. L. Torrey, *Voltaire and the English Deists,* Yale University, 1930.

An interesting thesis on the great social development of capitalism, with suggestive educational implications, is offered in R. H. Tawney, *Religion and the Rise of Capitalism: a Historical Study,* London and New York, 1926; with which may be read H. G. Graham, *Prosperity, Catholic and Protestant,* London, 1912; and M. Saint-Leon, *Histoire des Corporations des Métiers,* 3d ed., Paris, 1922.

CHAPTER XVI

SOME EDUCATIONAL THEORISTS AND THEORIES

I. THE UBIQUITOUS THEORIST

General character. Every man who spends ten consecutive minutes in thinking about the development of the young, or schools, or the advance of civilization, forms some sort of theory of education. As a rule, the theory is at least nine parts severely adverse criticism of the educational practices in actual use; and concludes with a fervent, but rather vague, statement: "Now what I'd like to see is . . ." Frequently enough, the adverse criticism is fairly well founded; since even a very limited intelligence and experience can catch the obvious fact that education, always and everywhere, falls short of the desirable. Occasionally, some theorist takes up a program of studies, or a method, of tried use by a skilled teacher, and urges its widespread adoption and development: as John of Salisbury, back in the twelfth century advocated the teaching methods used by Bernard of Chartres;[1] as Erasmus, Budé, and Vives tried to have the schools of their day follow the sound practice of the earlier humanists, such as Vittorino da Feltre and Guarino da Verona. But the positive suggestions for improvement in education are not always of great value: too often they have more froth than substance. What von Raumer says of Wolfgang Ratke is sadly true of a host of theorists: "He had sagacity enough to perceive the defects of the systems in vogue, but not enough to remedy them. . . . This conflict between his ideal and his lack of skill for the realization

---

[1] *Metalogicus*, Bk. I, c. 24; in Migne, *P. L.*, 199:854.

of it made him unsuccessful: and in this he is a characteristic forerunner of the later methodians, especially of Pestalozzi."[1]

The value of the theorist. Yet, in spite of his manifest shortcomings, the theorist does serve a valuable purpose in education. He is generally a fount of hope for the future; and hope is forever needed in the business of education. The facts of education, in schools and outside of schools, tend to breed discouragement in the minds of many. The theorist holds out the perennial hope that a new method, a new program, a new approach to the problems of education may do what humanity has failed to do in the past; and in the power of that hope he stimulates renewed efforts. Even though such efforts never attain the success that he looks for, they pull education out of its immediate rut, they do accomplish something; and men should be grateful for even the smallest advance in educational practice. The greatest weakness of the theorist is that he may ignore the sad facts of education too completely, that he may raise false hopes, that he may be disastrously one-sided in his view, that his enthusiasms may be misleading. That also happens, unfortunately, with painful frequency.

The power of the theorist. In what we may call modern times, and increasingly within the past hundred and fifty years, the power of the theorist has grown amazingly.[2] John of Salisbury and Roger Bacon were excellent theorists, but they had practically no influence upon education; Jean Jacques Rousseau was an almost incredibly stupid theorist, but he had an enormous influence, both upon his own and upon later ages. There are four factors which

---

[1] Translated in Barnard, *Teachers and Educators in Germany*, p. 344.
[2] Recall what has been pointed out, *supra,* pp. 191-92.

give the modern theorist his great power. The first is the printing press, which enables him to get his ideas and theories before large numbers of readers. This needs no emphasizing. The second is the development of normal schools, which are largely the seeding places of theories. The Jesuits adumbrated normal schools, in their junior houses of studies for their own members, in the exact provisions of the *Ratio Studiorum;* St. John Baptist de la Salle actually began them; they have since become a fixed part of every school system. Before the establishment of normal schools, individuals wrote out their precepts of teaching; but there was no machinery for translating those precepts into action, beyond the very slow process of general infiltration of ideas. With the wide spread of normal schools, the theorist came into his kingdom, with power to shape the future practice of his students preparing to teach. The third is the 'scientific' tendency of modern times, with its contempt of the past, and its restless seeking for novelty, and its huge conceit with its own accomplishments. The fourth is the *cacoethes scribendi* which urges many a little tenth-rate mind to rush into print with theories stolen from earlier theorists. These second-hand theorizers often seem to be the most powerful of all; they popularize, vulgarize, and often astonishingly distort, the more or less valuable theories of greater men; and because they speak in the accents of the mob, they are welcomed by the mob. When they get into normal schools and universities (and they very frequently do), they sometimes succeed in shaping school practice in a country for as much as five or ten years. Their powerful, but ephemeral, influence has contributed a great deal to the present-day jumble of schools in the United States. It is important to note in this connection that there has been, since the Renaissance, a steady tendency amongst theorists to ignore the Christian aim in education, and to center their theories increasingly upon that side of education which is concerned only with the present life. This essential weakness and unbalance in their theories has also, most unreasonably, added power to their immediate appeal.

Teaching and non-teaching theorists. Even for such brief treatment as this chapter can afford, it is difficult to make a selection amongst theories and theorists. The general practice in such selection has been to stress those which seem more significant from the immediate point of view of today; and that is often a practice made vicious by partisanship, by an unintelligent projection of the present into the past. Vives,[1] for instance, has been quite generally ignored; whilst other theorists have been magnified in importance because they appear to bolster up educational tendencies of the moment. Thus, Comenius, after lying in obscurity for two hundred years, has suddenly become a gigantic figure in the history of education;[2] Rabelais, who wrote a gross burlesque novel, is now solemnly weighed and analyzed as an educational reformer. In spite of all this, the present chapter will follow the accepted selection, for many reasons; one of which is simply the familiarity of that selection to students of education. But in discussing these educational theorists, this chapter will also observe the distinction which must be made between the theorists who are concerned with schools and draw much of their theories from actual school experience, and those who deal with education in a broader view than that of the schools. It is not easy to say which of the two sorts is more important;

---

[1] *Vide supra,* p. 204; *infra,* pp. 345-57.

[2] Some light may be thrown on this situation by the blunt statement of a Protestant writer: "Protestants in the time of Comenius were especially interested in the theory of education, because they were conscious that in the arts of teaching they were the inferiors of their great opponents, the Jesuits; but their theorists had in fact singularly little influence over the development of schools and universities." G. N. Clark, *The Seventeenth Century,* Oxford, 1929, p. 298.

but the second group evidently has a wider influence and a longer influence than the first, and in the end affects even the schools. Francis Bacon, for instance, did not write with a direct eye to school practice; yet he has influenced school practice in recent times much more perhaps than any other theorist. We shall consider first the non-teaching theorists.

II. NON-TEACHING THEORISTS

Erasmus (1466-1536). One may wonder at finding Erasmus listed here amongst non-teaching educational theorists, since he not merely served as tutor to Lord Mountjoy and others, but also taught at Cambridge between 1511 and 1514. The fact is that his teaching work was scarcely anything more than a distasteful necessity, part of his struggle to freedom for the literary career he ambitioned and achieved. By temperament and habit of mind Erasmus loathed school life, whether as pupil or as master. The wide world of letters was the only place in which he could breathe easily; that was his school, and in it he was an impressive, though not always a judicious, master. He constantly came near to being the most influential writer of his time.

Born at Gouda in the Lowlands, he was called at baptism Erasmus (the Desiderius was a Latin form of the same name later prefixed by himself) ; and he had no surname, because he was the illegitimate son of a Catholic priest. That bitter fact clouded all his life. Indeed, he cannot be understood at all without taking into account the effect upon his mind of the social disability which his birth laid upon him. His parents died when he was quite young, but had provided for the schooling of him and his elder brother Peter. In time, he became a canon regular of St. Augustine in the monastery at Steyn, not far from his birthplace.

He was ill fitted for the monastic life, neurasthenic,[1] hypersensitive, intensely ambitious. It is not improbable that his sensitiveness about his birth was a strong motive urging him to hide himself away in the monastic life. In any case, the life galled him intolerably, and after ten years of it,[2] when he was twenty-seven years old, he welcomed the chance to leave with permission to go as secretary to Henry of Bergen, the Bishop of Cambrai. This was in 1493. Erasmus had been ordained priest on April 25 of the preceding year.[3] On one pretext or another, he avoided returning to his monastery; but lived the life of a literary freelance, immensely industrious, irritable, discontented, suffering much in body and mind, and worrying about his means of livelihood until almost the close of his life.[4]

Erasmus was the most eminent figure in the literary renaissance in northern Europe. He was looked up to from all sides with a deference which is amazing. Kings,

[1] Dr. Mangan says he also suffered from chronic *pyelitis,* an inflammation of the kidney. *Life, Character and Influence of Desiderius Erasmus of Rotterdam,* 2 vols., New York, 1927, Vol. 1, p 39.

[2] There is disagreement about the year in which Erasmus became a canon regular. Mangan, *op. cit.,* Vol. 1, p. 39, says Erasmus was then twenty-one, which would set the year as 1487. Nichols and others give 1483.

[3] By Canon Law, illegitimate sons were barred from the priesthood and from holding ecclesiastical offices and benefices. The Bishop of Utrecht, who ordained Erasmus, must have secured for him some dispensation from the law. Thirteen years later, in 1505, Erasmus obtained a wider dispensation from Pope Julius II. But he was always rather scrupulous about his eligibility to benefices, and as late as 1517 asked for and was given a very complete dispensation by Leo X, by which the last disabilities of his bastardy were removed. Mangan, *op. cit.,* Vol. 1, pp. 278-80, Vol. 2, pp. 47-64.

[4] Mangan, *op. cit.,* and E. Emerton, *Desiderius Erasmus of Rotterdam,* London, 1899, accuse Erasmus of greediness in his constant anxiety to secure rich patrons, pensions, and gifts. But P. S. Allen, perhaps the foremost authority on Erasmus, points out that his begging aimed only at freedom for his work, and that "later on, in the time of his wealth, he was generosity itself with his money, and inexorable in refusing honours and places that would have hindered him from his work." *The Age of Erasmus,* Oxford, 1914, p. 133. Amongst such honors that he refused was the cardinalate offered him by Pope Paul III. Mangan, *op. cit.,* Vol. 2, p. 363.

popes, prelates, other literary men like himself, all heaped praises upon him. He was the intimate friend of Sir Thomas More, of the saintly Archbishop Warham, of Colet, of Cardinal Sadoleto (the secretary of Leo X), and of scores of others whose names ranked high in Church and State. The great ground of the esteem these men had for him was his literary scholarship; but there must have been in Erasmus admirable personal qualities to win him the warm regard of many of the fine men who valued his friendship.

His life work was writing; and he wrote exclusively in Latin, at his time still the common language of Europe. It is highly probable that he had no ease in any other language, except his native Dutch. His literary output was varied and large, the mere bulk of it all the more astonishing in view of his almost constant ill health. The *Bibliotheca Erasmiana*[1] lists two hundred and twenty-six works written by him. These works were of great variety in form; but Mangan properly notes that they are all serious in purpose, and most of them didactic in character.[2] Mangan ventures a classification of his writings, which, if not entirely accurate, is interesting and informing.[3] His first group is of fifteen, written directly for school use, a number of them definitely for Dean Colet's new school of St. Paul's in London. Two of the most popular of these were the *De duplici copia verborum et rerum,* a phrasebook, which had 139 editions, and the *Colloquia,* or dialogues, which went to 247 editions; both continued in active use for nearly two centuries after the death of Erasmus. Of this group of fifteen, a total of 1,106 editions have been published. Then there are twenty-five works, chiefly Latin and Greek classics, which he edited for more advanced scholars, and of which there have been published 854 edi-

---

[1] Published at Gand, 1893.
[2] Mangan, *op. cit.,* Vol. 2, p. 395.
[3] *Ibid.,* Vol. 2, pp. 396-98.

tions.   Linked with these are six other works for scholars, which went to a total of 337 editions; the most famous of these are the *Adagia,* or Proverbs, and the *Apophthegmata,* or Witty Sayings.   The fourth list is of six works on special subjects, the most important being two treatises against war.   He wrote thirty books of Catholic instruction and devotion, which went through 931 editions.   The most widely known of these, *Enchiridion militis christiani,* first published in 1503, and afterwards appearing in 120 other editions, is significant as showing his own solid Catholic orthodoxy and genuine piety. His *Novum Testamentum* had 293 editions, and his editions of various works of nine Fathers of the Church were published 169 times.   The *Moriae encomium,* an extremely sharp satire, has had about 210 editions, an English translation appearing in this country as late as 1929.   Mangan's figures of around 5,000 editions of all the writings of Erasmus, and a total publication of some 2,000,000 copies, are rather conservative.

The *Moriae encomium,* first published in 1509, and dedicated to Sir Thomas More, was, as Woodward calls it, "a sermon for the times, and a potent solvent of accepted stupidity and pretence."[1]   That, and the *Colloquia,* which was also filled with satire, castigated the follies of the clergy as well as the laity.   Both of these writings later dragged Erasmus into the Lutheran conflict: a position which was utterly distasteful to him.   He was berated by many Catholics as having weakened respect for ecclesiastical authority by his satires, and was hated by the Lutherans because he was intelligent enough to see that the faults of churchmen are no arguments against the Church. Men such as More and Colet were well aware that it was not Erasmus' satire on the clergy, but the gross defects

[1] W. H. Woodward, *Desiderius Erasmus concerning the Aim and Method of Education,* Cambridge, 1904, p. 20.

of the clergy themselves, that unfortunately broke down respect for the authority which the churchmen exercised and so often abused. But unthinking partisans, amongst both Catholics and Lutherans, were incapable of such discernment. The partisans are always the more numerous; and they have succeeded in clouding the name of Erasmus to this day.

Erasmus lived and died a sincere Catholic; a sincere Catholic, though by no means an heroic one.[1] He scornfully railed against the entrenched vices which did so much harm in the Church; but he had neither the patience nor the generosity to labor in the correction of those vices. Perhaps he was too self-centered in his literary ambition, perhaps his sensitiveness about his birth made a coward of him, perhaps he despaired of the possibility of reform in the Church; but whatever the reason, he fell short, for all his superb talents, of the spiritual measure of a great public man. Somehow his character failed to validate his writings. His 'sermons for the times' were only half-sermons.

His educational theories. The ideas of Erasmus on education are scattered through a very large number of his writings, yet he centered them considerably in five pieces, written at various times in a period of nearly thirty years. The first of these, *Enchiridion militis christiani,* published in 1503, is a simply written manual of Catholic belief and practice, in thirteen chapters. It contained the familiar Catholic principles, but presented, as Erasmus himself explained to Colet, "rather in the manner of a scientific textbook."[2] It wore a pretty sharp edge of criticism. It depre-

---

[1] In 1564, the Council of Trent placed on the *Index Librorum Prohibitorum* six or seven of Erasmus' works, including the *Colloquia* and *Moriae encomium.* In 1897, Pope Leo XIII removed the ban on all his writings. Mangan, who notes the condemnation (*op. cit.,* Vol. 2, p. 404) seems to ignore its revocation.

[2] *Erasmi Epistolae,* Ep. 181.

cated false piety,[1] the sentimental reverence for the Saints which is superstitious and not Christian,[2] mere externalism in religion,[3] the conceit of theologians.[4] Erasmus was all for reasonableness; but apparently had never grasped the fact that to demand any high degree of reasonableness from men in general is in itself unreasonable.

The second treatise, *De ratione studii et legendi,* published in 1511,[5] advocates the established humanistic procedure in education. The basis of it is Latin, as a means of literary expression; not grammar chopping, but wide reading, and much writing, with an ultimate view to forming a style. He sent this treatise at once to Colet; perhaps he wrote it with an eye to his school of St. Paul's.

It is certain that the third treatise, *Institutum hominis christiani,* (1516), was written for St. Paul's, and was used there. Three early editions, of the total of 45, were published in England. The little manual is a Latin metrical version of Colet's *Cathecyzon,* somewhat condensed. In character it is a good deal like the *Enchiridion.*

In the same year, 1516, Erasmus wrote for a boy of sixteen, just become Charles I of Spain, and three years later to become the Emperor Charles V, a fourth treatise, *Institutio principis christiani.* One catches echoes of Sir Thomas More all through this essay, for Erasmus and More were at one in their view of the nature of government and the duties of a king. It is a soundly Catholic view, emphasizing devotion to the interests of the people, and the promotion of peace.

Finally, in 1529, Erasmus wrote his lengthiest treatise on education, *De pueris statim ac liberaliter instituendis*

---

[1] Leyden edition, 1641, pp. 153-55.
[2] *Ibid.,* pp. 174-76.
[3] *Ibid.,* p. 327.
[4] *Ibid.,* p. 72.
[5] Translated into English for the first time in W. H. Woodward, *Erasmus concerning the Aim and Method of Education,* pp. 162-78.

libellus.[1]   It was addressed to William of Cleves, whose elder sister, Anne of Cleves, in 1539 became one of the later wives of Henry VIII.[2]   The ideas in it are familiar. Parents are charged with the education of their children as a duty to the State and to God.[3]   Education must begin in the very earliest years.[4]   Experience alone will not educate.[5]   Education, from the beginning, must be aimed at giving the child the power of expression.[6]   "A man ignorant of letters is no man at all."[7]   He discusses the psychology of the child,[8] the character of the teacher,[9] urges *public* schools, as against private or monastic schools,[10] is opposed to much punishment.[11]   There is nothing novel or startling in his theories.   They had been the stock commonplaces of humanists for a hundred and fifty years.   But in his hands, though they are written clearly, convincingly, in very readable Latin, they are somehow cold, dry, and brittle.   There is too much of the *book* in the education that he urges. Rather unconsciously, that education makes literature a complete end of life.   Woodward utters pretty nearly a final decision on Erasmus as an educational theorist, when he says that "the only region in which he had any thought-out system to offer for guidance of a practical world was the

[1] At that it is not very long.   It takes up folios 489-516 in Vol. 1 of the *Opera Omnia,* Leyden, 1703-06, edited by Jean Le Clerc.   Woodward has translated it into English, in *Erasmus concerning the Aim and Method of Education,* pp. 180-222.

[2] William of Cleves was elected Duke of Gelders in 1538.   The following year, he succeeded his father in the Duchies of Cleves, Berg, and Julich, the latter two of which he inherited through his mother.   In 1542, he joined the Protestant party in Germany.   *Cambridge Modern History,* Vol. 2, pp. 236, 243-45.

[3] *Opera Omnia,* Vol. 1, ff. 494-95, 511.

[4] *Ibid.,* ff. 486-90, 511-12.

[5] *Ibid.,* f. 497.

[6] *Ibid.,* ff. 501-02.

[7] *Ibid.,* f. 489.

[8] *Ibid.,* ff. 496, 499, 500.

[9] *Ibid.,* ff. 503-04.

[10] *Ibid.,* ff. 504, 514-16.

[11] *Ibid.,* ff. 504-07.

region of Latin scholarship and of education."[1]   In this
last treatise, Erasmus makes 'education' and 'Latin scholarship' practically synonymous.   That indeed was the central
weakness of Erasmus: that he was hard, unhuman, in his
preoccupation with an almost purely literary ideal.   With
the rest of life he was concerned chiefly as a field for his
excellent satire.   The satirist has a function in education,
it is true; but it is only a small function.   He may pull
down evil, for the moment, at least; but he is not a builder,
a developer.

Rabelais (1494-1553).   François Rabelais was a Catholic
priest, at first a member of the Franciscan Order.   In the
bad fashion common enough at the time, and in conscious
or unconscious imitation of Erasmus, who was some
twenty-five or thirty years his senior,[2] and whom he admired greatly, Rabelais got himself out of his Order
through the inadequate authority of a friendly bishop.   He
became a physician, was well received by Pope Paul III in
1536 under the patronage of Cardinal du Bellay, a few
years later was dispensed by the Pope from his conventual
obligations (including that of the Benedictine Order, which
Clement VII had permitted him to exchange for the Franciscan), and two or three years before he died got permission to hold the parish benefices of St. Martin-de-
Meudon and St. Christophe-du-Jambet.   Some Protestant
writers, displaying a not unusual ignorance of both the
man and his writings, try to make him out a rebel against
the Catholic Church;[3] just as one partisan writer amusingly

---

[1] Woodward, op. cit., p. 25.

[2] The dates of both birth and death of Rabelais are quite uncertain.
See the discussion of them in Abel Lefranc's critical introduction to
his edition of Oeuvres de François Rabelais, Paris, 1912.

[3] Thus, even the excellent Dr. Paul Monroe (History of Education,
p. 446, edition of 1921) describes Rabelais as "A monk, though expelled from one order and in constant hostility with the Dominicans
to whom he later belonged; a curé, though in open hostility to the
Church for most of his life . . . " Rabelais was never expelled from

refers to some school texts as "Protestant books, the most celebrated of which were those of Erasmus, Melanchthon, Sturm, and Lily,"[1] bracketing the two Catholics, Erasmus and William Lily (who died in 1522), with two Protestants.

Rabelais wrote in excellent French, a great, sprawling burlesque, in four parts or books (to which a fifth was later added by other hands), concerned chiefly with an incredible giant, Gargantua, and his son, Pantagruel. It is a mixture of sharp and shrewd satire with the grossest buffoonery. It reflects the curious blending of pagan and Christian ideas, upon which his own life, like that of so many of the Renaissance men, appears to have been ordered. La Bruyere confesses that the book is a puzzle to him;[2] it may well be a puzzle to any one who attempts to take it very seriously as more than an amusing piece of roistering, or who cannot understand a man writing with his tongue in his cheek. Its vitality and impetuous tumult of language has given it a deserved place in French literature.[3] Its interspersed satire on the institutions, educational, civil, and ecclesiastical, of its time, has been sourly accepted by 'reformers' incapable of grasping its genial humor, and has been used again and again to give support to theories of education which would in all likelihood have won the uproarious scorn of Rabelais. There is something very funny in seeing his novel dragged into solemn contro-

any order, was never a Dominican, and, far from being "in open hostility to the Church for most of his life," was the constant recipient of great favors from high ecclesiastics and from at least three popes.

[1] E. P. Cubberley, *The History of Education*, Boston, 1920, p. 343.

[2] Jean de la Bruyere, tutor to the Duke Louis de Bourbon, published in 1688 the collection of essays called *Caractères*. His criticism of Rabelais is to be found on page 19 of the Variorum edition by Charles Louandre, Paris, Charpentier (n. d.).

[3] Hilaire Belloc, in *The Path to Rome* and other writings, has often shown the marked influence of Rabelais' style at its best. The literary influence of Rabelais is thoroughly studied in L. Sainéan. *L'Influence et la Réputation de Rabelais*, Paris, 1930.

versies about schools and education in general, reverentially lauded by those who hail him as an apostle of materialistic education, frowningly damned by those whose stomachs are made queasy by his coarseness.[1]

All of Rabelais' significance for later times is in his writings; and the educational purport of his writings is practically nil. He burlesques the monks: at times in a delightful way, as when he solemnly warns his readers: "Never trust those men that always peep out through a little hole;"[2] this makes him a 'reformer' to the humorless Protestant, and is shocking to the humorless Catholic; and Protestant and Catholic alike often fail to see that his 'Abbey of Theleme,'[3] his religious house without rules, is as much a burlesque as anything in the four books. Out of some five hundred and fifty pages in Rabelais' novel, not more than a dozen pages can be considered as bearing in any way upon education; half of these pages are still a burlesque, as well of the new Humanism as of the old Scholasticism; the other half are vague generalities, absurdly exaggerated, which are nevertheless earnestly copied out today by some writers as if they were of great value.[4]

[1] See the adverse judgment in the final sentence of the article on Rabelais, *Catholic Encyclopedia,* Vol. 12, p. 620. The justification for such a judgment must be found chiefly in the mistaken evaluation which others have made of Rabelais as an educational theorist.

[2] Bk. II, c. 34; the last sentence in the chapter and book.

[3] Bk. I, cc. 52-58. In c. 57 is found a satiric praise of the Renaissance concept of 'honor': a satire which, again, escapes many modern readers.

[4] Particularly do the serious critics of Rabelais praise the letter which Gargantua wrote to his son, Pantagruel, when the latter was at Paris for his studies. (Bk. II, c. 8.) In it, Gargantua urges Pantagruel to "learn the languages perfectly": Greek, Latin, Hebrew, Chaldee, and Arabic; then History, "let there be no history which thou shalt not have ready in thy memory": then Cosmography, and "the liberal arts of geometry, arithmetic, and music"; then Astronomy, and "as for the civil law, of that I would have thee know the texts by heart, and then confer them with philosophy." After these trifles have been accomplished, Pantagruel is to set himself to acquiring an encyclopedic knowledge of the "works of nature . . . so that there be no sea, river, or fountain, of which thou dost not know

Cubberley speaks loosely of his "influence on later educational thinkers,"[1] without in any way indicating what that influence was. Rabelais' real contribution to 'later educational thinkers' (do modern writers ever wonder why he made no contribution to his contemporary educational thinkers?) was a roaring, ribald wealth of visceral and excremental humor; and it is quite impossible to see how the thinkers have made any educational use out of even that.

Michel Eyquem de Montaigne (1533-1592). Montaigne, a lawyer and petty politician, wrote in French, between 1570 and 1588, ninety-nine essays: most of them brief,[2] chatty, graceful, egotistical, slightly pedantic, witty, but without humor: of which only three essays are directly concerned with education.[3] His ideas in those three may be summed up as follows:

1. *Of Pedantry:* Mere knowledge is of little value, unless it be used as a means of developing intelligence and virtue.[4] This takes up fifteen pages.

the fishes; all the fowls of the air; all the several kinds of shrubs and trees, whether in forest or orchard; all the sorts of herbs and flowers that grow upon the ground; all the various metals that are hid within the bowels of the earth"; etc., etc. Next, he is to study medicine; and "at some hours of the day, apply thy mind to the study of the holy Scriptures; . . . In brief, let me see thee an abyss and bottomless pit of knowledge." Then, "thou must learn chivalry, warfare, and the exercise of the field." Furthermore, he is to test out all this "by maintaining publicly theses and conclusions in all arts, against all persons whatsoever." Only a Pansophist could keep from smiling at all this; and Rabelais tries to give even the Pansophist a hint by dating Gargantua's letter "From Utopia, the 17th day of the month of March."

[1] *History of Education,* p. 398.

[2] The most marked exception to this brevity is the last essay of all, seventy-six pages in Leclerc's edition. It is a cynical attack on the Christian notion of chastity.

[3] These three essays are in Bk. I, cc. 24, 25, in Bk. II, c. 8; in Leclerc's edition, Garnier, Paris, 1925, Vol. 1, pp. 135-90, Vol. 2, pp. 100-23.

[4] The following, on page 138, may be considered the topic sentences of the essay: "De vray, le soing et la depense de nos peres ne vise qu'a nous meubler la teste de science: du jugement et de la

2. *Of the Education of Children* (To Madame Diane de Foix, Countess of Curzon) : Get a tutor for your son, a stiff one, who will toughen him, body and soul. Let him keep the boy from being bookish, make him study life, even in books. Teach him to prefer judgment to mere knowledge. Let him make courage, moderation, justice matters of exercise rather than of views.[1] This takes up forty pages.

3. *Of the Love of Fathers for Their Children* (To Madame d'Estissac) : Compulsion has no place in education. Fathers should share their wealth with their children as soon as the latter grow up; should not compel reverence through fear. Educating a child is a more important part of fatherhood than begetting a child. Mothers should have only very limited authority over children; since women are more emotional than reasonable.[2] This takes up twenty-three pages.

vertu, peu de nouvelles . . . Il falloit s'enquerir qui est mieulx sçavant, non qui est plus sçavant."

[1] The following excerpts illustrate the above summary. "Qu'il luy face tout passer par l'estamine, et ne loge rien en sa teste par simple auctorite et a credit."   Vol. 1, p. 157.   "Le gaing de nostre estude, c'est en estre devenu meilleur et plus sage."   Vol. 1, p. 158.   "A cette cause, le commerce des hommes y est merveilleusement propre, et la visite des pais estrangiers."   Vol. 1, p. 159.   "Ce n'est pas assez de luy roidir l'ame; il luy fault aussi roidir les muscles . . . " Vol. 1, p. 160.   "Qu'on luy mette en fantasie une honneste curiosite de s'enquerir de toutes choses: tout de qu'il y aura de singulier autour de luy il le verra."   Vol. 1, p. 163.   "Il ne dira pas tant sa lecon, comme il la fera; il la repetera en ses actions: on verra s'il y a de la prudence en ses enterprinses, s'il y a de la bonte, de la justice en ses deportements; s'il y a du jugement et de la grace en son parler, de la vigeur en ses maladies, de la modestie en ses jeux, de la temperance en ses voluptez, de l'ordre en son economie; de l'indifference en son goust, soit chair, poisson, vin ou eau . . . " Vol. 1, p. 178.

[2] This wordy essay is really summed up in a single sentence: "J'accuse toute violence en l'education d'une ame tendre, qu'on dresse pour l'honneur et la liberte."   Vol. 2, p. 105.   His reason for denying much educational authority to women is a curious one to offer the woman to whom he dedicates this essay: "Car, n'ayant (les femmes) point assez de force de discourse pour choisir et embrasser ce qui le vault, elles se laissent plus volontiers aller ou les impressions de nature sont plus seules; comme les animaux qui n'ont cognoissance de leurs petits que pendant qu'ils tiennent a leurs mammelles."   Vol. 2, p. 118.

Montaigne writes charmingly, is at times shrewd, but never profound. He writes pedantically against pedantry; there are thirty-three 'classical' citations in his essay on pedantry. His point of view is that of the wealthy and leisured dilettante; a little aloof and reserved; elegantly, but slightly, tinctured with classical lore; having no lofty ideals; envisaging a pleasant and common-sense life, whose aim is the reasonable enjoyment of the present. He has dilettante doubts, he is cynically tolerant, he dodges most of the really searching interests of life, he is concerned chiefly with its superficial serenity. But he impressed his age, and still charms ours, by the easy, graceful, and sincere expression of his cultured personality, and by his *practical and moderate worldliness*. It is this last which has been seized upon, by those who emphasize its importance, as a splendid advance in educational theory. His influence has been very widespread.

Francis Bacon (1561-1626). Francis Bacon was the son of Sir Nicholas Bacon, who for twenty years held the great seal; he was connected through his mother's family with the Cecils, who were amongst the chief looters of England under Elizabeth; hence he was marked out from the beginning for a political career. He feathered his nest as best he could out of his political positions; but his interest was sincerely more in the field of scientific speculations than in that of politics. His talents were exceptional; so was his devotion to study; but his character did not match his intellectual equipment; he was largely ruled by expedience in his ethics. For a long time, his political advancement was slow; but toward the end, under James I, it speeded up. He moved swiftly to the high position of lord chancellor, and was made a peer, as Baron Verulam, and Viscount St. Albans. These honors came to him just when he was fifty-nine years old; with striking irony, they came just a few months before his fall. In 1620 he was accused of taking bribes in the exercise of his office.   As he saw the charges could be proved, he admitted his guilt.   The House of Lords made an empty gesture of punishment, sentencing him to pay an enormous fine, which was never collected, and to undergo imprisonment in the Tower for an indefinite term, which turned out to be, in reality, just two days. He spent the rest of his life in wealthy leisure, and died April 9, 1626.

During the past three hundred years, there is scarcely any name which has been invoked more often in the theory of education than that of Francis Bacon.   He was not a teacher, nor was he a discoverer of truth, scientific or of other sort; he was a theorist.   Of his many writings, those which chiefly carry his educational theories are two: *De Augmentis Scientiarum,* which appeared in 1623, and *Novum Organum,* published in 1620.   The first of these[1] is an enlargement of his English treatise *On the Dignity and Advancement of Learning,* which was first printed in 1605. The two books were meant to be parts one and two of a huge work in six parts, to have been called '*Magna Instauratio.*' He did write a rather inept third part, *Sylva Sylvarum,* in 1624, which was published a year after his death: " . . . . a foolish *omnium gatherum* drawn from all sorts of books, Pliny's *Natural History,* as well as works of Aristotle, Porta's *Natural Magic* and Cardan's *De Subtilitate* and *De Varietate.*"[2]   In his *Redargutio Philosophiarum,* he puts his purpose pithily: "Meditor instaurationem philos-

[1] Both are in Latin.   Bacon wrote much, and well, in English; but he said: "These modern languages will at one time or another play the bank-route (bankrupt) with books, and since I have lost much time with this age, I would be glad if God would give me leave to recover it with posterity."   (Church, *Bacon,* p. 210.)   For all his contempt of the past, he, like others of his age, still believed that literary immortality was to be had only in what was once the common language of civilized Europe.

[2] H. O. Taylor, *Thought and Expression in the Sixteenth Century,* rev. ed., 1930, Vol. 2, p. 371.

ophiae quae nihil inanis aut abstracti[1] habeat, quaeque vitae humanae conditiones in melius provehat." Macaulay, in a characteristic antithesis between Plato and Bacon, is not entirely fair to the latter, when he says: "The aim of the Baconian philosophy was to supply our vulgar wants"; although he makes the statement under the manifest impression that he is praising Bacon at the expense of Plato. Bacon did have some higher aim than that; but it was smothered beneath his interest in the immediately useful, and it was most thoroughly ignored by the 'Baconians.' The sixteenth and succeeding centuries were more and more exclusively concerned with improving this present world; and because that was Bacon's chief concern too, he has been welcomed as a leader.

No competent historian now credits Bacon with being the author of the 'inductive method' in reasoning, although he was widely hailed as such until rather recently. He did strongly emphasize the need of accurate and corrected observation in scientific research; but he could neither carry out such observation himself nor appreciate it when he saw it well done by others.[2] He did point out shrewdly some of the deficiences in the scientific work of the past, due to lack of observation and experiment; but that he gave any real stimulus to the scientific accomplishments which men have attained since his time, is frankly open

---

[1] 'Inane' and 'abstractum' were one for Bacon, who was immensely impatient of all abstract thinking. Note the inescapable fondness for duplicating synonymous adjectives and phrases, which constantly displays itself in his writings—except in the earlier Essays.

[2] He sneered at the very important work of Gilbert, *De Magnete* (cf. *Novum Organum,* lib. I, No. 70); he refused Galileo's demonstration of planetary motion; he rejected the Copernican theory—"which I am convinced is most false"; he ignored Harvey's discovery of the circulation of the blood. (Cf. *De Augmentis,* lib. III, cap. 4.) He called all the fine work being done in the sciences during his lifetime "vertigo quaedam et agitatio perpetua et circulus." (Prooemium, *De Augmentis Scientiarum.*)

to question; it most certainly has never been proved.[1] Bacon's true significance lies in his much wider and more far-reaching purpose, which was no less than that of re-educating the human race upon new lines and with a glamorous promise of success. In the Prooemium to *De Augmentis*, after a general indictment of past efforts, he says: " . . . . there is no other course left but to begin the work anew upon a better plan, and to commence a total reconstruction of sciences, arts, and all human knowledge, raised upon the proper foundations."[2]

In that vast aim of re-education, Bacon was rather a follower of his times than a leader. Already at the close of the sixteenth century, thinking men had become bitterly disillusioned about the earlier hopes of the Protestant Revolt: that it would achieve something finer in Western civilization than what had gone before. Fragmentary Christianity was having a rougher time of it with the minds and characters of men than entire Christianity had had. But hope dies hard. Large parts of the world were turning to still newer 'reforms,' in the eager, and often impatient, desire to improve mankind. They could not manage the supernatural aids given to men; they would try their hand at the natural. The newly developing sciences offered another field of spiritual hope; it must never be forgotten that all 'reforms' are at bottom spiritual in purpose. Bacon

---

[1] Huxley is outspoken on this point. He says: "No delusion is greater than the notion that method and industry can make up for lack of mother-wit, either in science or in practical life; . . . As a matter of fact, Bacon's 'via' has proved hopelessly impracticable; while the 'anticipation of nature' by invention of hypotheses based on incomplete inductions, which he especially condemns, has proved itself to be the most efficient, indeed an indispensable, instrument of scientific progress." T. H. Huxley, *Methods and Results,* New York, 1894, p. 46.

[2] The basic idea in Rousseau's *Emile* at once suggests itself in this connection. But in reality neither Bacon nor Rousseau had any monopoly in that tragic hope of new beginnings for humanity. Even Jesus Christ postulates a new beginning in "the Kingdom of His Father."

was one of the spokesmen, and a very clever one, of that new hope. "Knowledge is power!" he cried. If men but *knew* better, they would do better. In his plan he did not leave out the element of divine revelation (it needed several generations more for Protestants to become Deists); but he kept it only in an isolated corner. The domination of 'nature' by science was his vital theme; and it became practically the sole theme of his later followers. The whole race was to be improved by a *method* of scientific investigation. "The course I propose for the discovery of the sciences is such as leaves but little to the acuteness and strength of wits, but indeed rather levels wits and understandings."[1] And what he predicated for the sciences, he predicated for all living; since all living was to be based upon scientific knowledge. To a world more and more bound up in the tangible and concrete, that was an inspiring notion. Sectarian pulpits repeated it; educators and 'reformers' seized upon it; moral reform, reform of schools, reform by compulsory legislation, were built upon it. One wonders if those who acclaim Bacon as 'the Father of Modern Thought' recognize him also as the Father of Prohibition. His theory gave, and continues to give, a great impetus to schools. The testing of that theory by experience is often shirked; when such a test is made, the results are depressing.[2]

---

[1] *Novum Organum,* lib. I, No. 61.

[2] Nearly a century ago, Horace Mann indulged himself in the following prophecy: "*The common school is the greatest discovery ever made by man. . . .* Let the common school be expanded to its capabilities, let it be worked with the efficiency of which it is susceptible, and nine-tenths of the crimes in the penal code would become obsolete; the long catalogue of human ills would be abridged; man would walk more safely by day; every pillow would be more inviolate by night; property, life, and character held by a stronger tenure; all rational hopes regarding the future brightened." (From an Address delivered in 1840; quoted by T. Brosnahan in *American Catholic Quarterly Review,* Vol. 30, p. 514.) Dr. F. J. Kelly, then president of the State University of Idaho, might almost have been writing a commentary on Mann's rhapsody, when he said: "This sublime faith

René Descartes (1596-1650).   Descartes studied at first under the Jesuits in their college of La Flèche, until, when he was seventeen, he went to Paris.   For a few years he was a soldier, in the beginnings of the Thirty Years' War. Though not rich, he had some small independent means, which enabled him to travel about for several more years. In 1629, when he was thirty-three years old, he settled in Holland, in which country he did practically all his lasting work.   After twenty years in Holland, he went to Sweden at the request of Queen Christina; and died there the year following, of lung disease.

He was thirty-five years younger than Francis Bacon, but a contemporary; their lives ran parallel for thirty years. But there is a closer link between the two men than that of time.   Descartes, like Bacon, dreamed[1] of a new restoration of human knowledge, a new reform of humanity.   Like Bacon again, Descartes put his hope of this restoration in a *method*.   But his method ignored Bacon's observation

of the American people in education is of late years being subjected to severe tests.   People are looking about them and seeing that in this nation, which of all nations in the world is spending by far the most on education and in which more years of attendance are obtained by far larger proportions of her children, we have still the greatest disrespect for law; we have still amazing corruption amongst our politicians; we have still a larger proportion of the wealth of our country being concentrated in the hands of a smaller and smaller proportion of our people; we have still more crime and less efficient criminal procedure than in other countries; we have still an increasing proportion of our families breaking down in divorce.   These evidences of the failure in this country to bring about the essentials of successful democratic life are giving pause to people who have rested confidently in the assumption that if we but gave education a sufficient chance we could not fail to solve our social problems."   (From "The University in Prospect," in *School and Society,* November 24, 1928, p. 634.)

[1] Descartes literally dreamed of this.   He records, under date of November 10, 1619 (though some critics maintain that the date is only an old heading of a diary, and that the record is really much later), a dream which he interpreted as a divine impulse to devote his life to the reform of human knowledge; he was convinced that "it was the Spirit of Truth that willed to open for him all the treasures of knowlege."

and experiment; it worked from the inside outward; it was as contemptuous of induction as it was of deduction, subordinating both to that single act of the mind which we call 'intuition,' a mode of intelligence which is feeble and limited in men, but is characteristic of pure spirits, such as the angels. His method began with doubt even of the material world, and based all knowledge on the intuitive perception of one's self as the thinker: the famous 'Cogito, ergo sum.' From that point, he used the ontologic argument of St. Anselm[1] to establish human certainty of the existence of God. From God's excellence, he deduced our certainty that other realities correspond to our ideas of them.

This is not the place to go into the complicated, obscure, and often self-contradictory philosophy of Descartes. He is the forerunner of Spinoza, Hegel, and Kant, and therefore of the welter of modern non-Christian philosophers.[2] But it is his influence upon educational theory which is our present concern; and that influence comes, in part, from his leadership of modern philosophic systems, in part, directly from his method, embodied chiefly in two books, the French *Discours sur la Methode,* and the Latin *Meditationes.*[3] The essential points of his method are two. The first is the reduction of all human knowledge to something like a mathematical formula, which the intellect may take in at a single glance. It proclaimed a cold contempt for the 'humanities,' for history, for moral studies. It was, as

---

[1] *Vide supra,* p. 148, note 1.

[2] It is both amusing and pathetic to see how completely modern philosophy 'dates' from Descartes. Thomas, in his *Éloge de Descartes,* said: "From the age of Aristotle to the age of Descartes, I see a void of two thousand years." An Oxford Don writes: " . . . From this time (of Descartes) the history of philosophy can be understood with very little knowledge of what went before." (G. N. Clark, *The Seventeenth Century,* Oxford, 1929, p. 255.) Many of our so-called "Histories of Philosophy" solemnly build themselves upon that assumption.

[3] There have been many editions of Descartes' works. An excellent modern one is that by Adam et Tannery, Paris, 1896.

Maritain correctly says, "the principle and origin of the deep *inhumanity* of our modern science."[1] Boileau is reported to have said that "Descartes' philosophy had cut poetry's throat."[2] The second element of his method is his principle of accepting skepticism as the first step in philosophic investigation.[3] Within limits, and in competent hands, that principle *may* be reduced to mere balance and open-mindedness; but the limits are unknown and unobserved by most of those who have followed Descartes in his method; and the net result has unfortunately been to breed in many minds a thorough and devastating doubt as to whether or not any knowledge at all is valid. Such skepticism, in its extreme form, is very rare; and then, of course, it is intellectual suicide. But various illogical and incomplete measures of skepticism are now so common as to be considered almost a necessary part of sophistication. We poke fun at them under the title 'sophomoric'; yet they seriously color a great deal of what the world today likes to call 'thought'; they affect attitudes of mind both in the schools and in general society. To attribute this growth of skepticism to Descartes alone, would be absurd; yet he is decidedly important as one of the influences which has helped to establish and spread a skepticism derived from many other sources.

[1] Jacques Maritain, *Three Reformers,* London, 1928, p. 65.
[2] Idem, *op. cit.,* p. 89, quoting J. B. Rousseau.
[3] Descartes himself saw the dangers of that principle. In the *Discours (Oeuvres,* Adam et Tannery, Vol. 6, pp. 14-15), he wrote that "the distinctive effort to drop all one's formerly accepted opinions is not an example to be followed by every one"; and in a letter of March, 1637, to his great and constant friend, the Franciscan Father Mersenne (Adam et Tannery, Vol. 1, pp. 349-50), he admitted that "for weak minds" the metaphysical method of universal doubt might prove disastrous. Descartes always professed himself a Catholic. He was even very circumspect about any conflict with Catholic authorities; thus he deferred indefinitely the publication of his clever work, *Le Monde,* which he had completed as early as 1633, because he was alarmed at the condemnation of Galileo by a Roman Congregation.

John Locke (1632-1704). Locke was the son of an obscure Puritan clerk, who made his livelihood out of petty political appointments. Through the favor of a rich patron, the young Locke was educated at Westminster and Christ Church, Oxford. He took his degree B. A. in 1656, and M. A. in 1658.[1] He dabbled in medicine; he taught Greek, rhetoric, and philosophy at Oxford, from 1660 to 1664; he was superficially interested in chemistry and meteorology. He was an earnest, but vague, Christian; quite ready for religious compromise with any but Catholics; and therefore essentially Protestant; and therefore hostile to the Stuarts. He went into voluntary political exile in Holland with Lord Ashley, the first Earl of Shaftesbury, to whom he was a combination of physician, secretary, and tame philosopher; and stayed seven years in Holland, for his own safety, until the Prince of Orange became William III of England. He modestly enjoyed rich political preferments under King William. In 1690, the year after his return to England, he published the *Essay Concerning Human Understanding,* upon which he had worked for nearly twenty years, and three years later his *Some Thoughts Concerning Education.* To these must be added his *Conduct of the Understanding,* which appeared two years after his death. He died in 1704, in his seventy-third year.

Locke was a serene, humble, and gentle snob: who placidly believed that only 'gentlemen' (by which he clearly meant no more than men of wealth and social position) need be educated. If 'gentlemen' were educated, somehow the rest of the people would get along all right.[2] This atti-

---

[1] *Life,* prefixed to eighth edition of *Complete Works* (quarto, London, 1777), Vol. 1, p. 15.

[2] " . . . (The calling) most to be taken care of is the gentleman's calling. For if those of that rank are by their education once set right, they will quickly bring all the rest into order." From the Epistle Dedicatory to *Some Thoughts Concerning Education,* edition of 1801, Vol. 9, p. 5. See also par. 94 (p. 84) and par. 216 (last of Essay, pp. 204-05), and *passim.* In this connection, it is astonishing to find Pro-

tude is central to everything he wrote on education. Hence
he has no concern for schools; his scheme calls for a tutor.
Within the limits of that scheme, he is sensible and shrewd.
He prides himself on his logic; but he is not at all eminently logical.[1] He often contradicts himself.[2] But even
when he is not logical, he is always fairly reasonable. He
had read widely, and garnered ideas from his reading with
a cool common sense, of the superficial sort which is readily
grasped by readers in general, and which appeals to them.[3]
Although he is never very searching or profound, he rarely
offends or antagonizes his reader; he is plausible, and in
detail quite convincing, and not infrequently prosy and dull,
and infinitely repetitive. The English people of his day

fessor Parker acclaiming "Locke's preeminent achievement . . . as
formulator of the principles of Anglo-Saxon democracy . . . " (*The
History of Modern Elementary Education,* p. 150); and still more
astonishing to find him basing that claim upon Locke's defense of
the parliamentarians in the English Revolution of 1688. That revolution set up, not a democracy, but an oligarchy, of the sort known in
England as a 'squirearchy.' Nothing could be more remote from the
policy and practice of seventeenth- and eighteenth-century English
parliamentarians than that 'the people' should have any active voice
in government. The system of 'rotten boroughs' and close trading
of office amongst the very small ruling class is a curious thing for
any writer to label as 'democracy.'

[1] "He was not by any means a rigorous or even a lucid thinker,
and he loosely combined his empirical skepticism with a confidence in
the general conclusions which had been certainties to the rationalistic
method of Descartes." G. N. Clark, *The Seventeenth Century,* Oxford, 1929, p. 263.

[2] As a sample illustration, compare these two statements: " . . .
We are born to be, if we please, rational creatures, but it is use and
exercise only that makes us so, and we are, indeed, so no farther than
industry and application has carried us." *Conduct of the Understanding,* Vol. 3 (ed. 1801), p. 201. See also p. 195.
" . . . It is evident that strength of memory is owing to an happy
constitution, and not to any habitual improvement got by exercise."
Some Thoughts Concerning Education, Vol. 9 (ed. 1801), p. 169.
The Scholastic philosophy, in which he was educated, but which he
later despised, taught him the value of habits; educational theories
of his time began to sneer at the training of memory; Locke cheerfully embraces both.

[3] But perhaps Montaigne is his chief source of ideas. See Oscar
Browning, *Educational Theories,* pp. 84, 102 sqq.

and after were proud of him, and praised him; but were little influenced by him. It was the harder, more severely logical type of mind, on the Continent, which took him up with tremendous eagerness, exaggerated his amiable contradictions into rigorous logical conclusions (from which he himself instinctively shrank), and made him, in their rather distorted interpretation, a profoundly significant figure in the theory of education. Quite often, when writers of today refer to John Locke, they really mean Voltaire, Rousseau, Basedow, La Chalotais, or even John Stuart Mill or Professor Whewell. Locke's progeny would have startled him considerably.

Theories drawn from Locke. Locke rightly combatted the notion of 'innate ideas' maintained by Descartes and others. He wrote of the human mind as a *tabula rasa,* a blank paper.[1] "Let us then suppose the Mind to be, as we say, White-Paper, void of all Characters, without any *Ideas;* how comes it to be furnished? . . . To this I answer, in one word, from *Experience.*"[2] Although in his explanation of that answer, Locke sensibly follows scholastic philosophy, and makes reflection as well as sensation part of 'experience,' many of his followers centered their attention solely upon one source of ideas, sensation. From that error has come the long line of educational theory which magnifies out of all proportion the training of the senses, and which has been unfairly fathered upon Locke.[3]

Locke, unfortunately, did give real ground for having foisted upon him another theory, which he never formally sponsored: the radically destructive theory of religious

[1] These similes occur repeatedly in his writings. See, for instance, " . . . as white paper, or wax, to be moulded and fashioned as one pleases," offered as a description of his pupil, in the last paragraph of *Some Thoughts Concerning Education,* Vol. 60 (ed. 1801), p. 205.

[2] *Essay Concerning Human Understanding,* Bk. II, c. 1, par. 2.

[3] See the excellent brief discussion of this point in J. W. Adamson, *A Short History of Education,* Cambridge, 1922, pp. 204 sqq.

latitudinarianism, which results in rationalism. It is not merely that, as Davidson wrote, "in education Locke replaces the authority of God by the authority of society, the clergy by the landed gentry"; but, although he himself with characteristic illogicality holds to belief in a divine revelation, he minimizes its value, he leaves it open to the questioning of mere human reason. Thus, in Book IV, Chapter 18, of the *Essay Concerning Human Understanding,* he admits the supposition that revelation may be *opposed* to reason, and in such supposed dispute gives the prior right to human reason. In so judging (which is private judgment with a vengeance!), he was, it is obvious, only following the inevitable trend of Protestantism, which, whilst constrained to admit the need of authority for orderly human living and development, challenged the source of authority: at first admitting any authority save that of the Catholic Church, and later any authority save that of divine revelation. The effect of this upon education cannot be overestimated, since it meant the practical abandonment of everything in Christianity except the name, by men who still continued to cherish the name.

But it is in a theory which closely touches curriculum and method in schools, and therefore affects what modern writers almost exclusively consider education, that Locke's name and authority (though not his actual writings) are most often cited: the theory of 'formal discipline.' That theory, occasionally referred to previously in this book, now calls for specific consideration.

Formal discipline. The educational theory recently known under the technical or jargonized phrase of 'formal discipline' did not originate with Locke. One may say, without rashness, that it is as ancient as schools themselves. It is a protean theory, not always easily recognizable in its varying forms; but the idea underlying it seems to be that much of education is a mere discipline of human powers, which are developed and perfected by any orderly exercise. Put in that way, the notion appeals to common sense, and is verified by experience. But the theory seldom remains as simple as that basic idea. In the hands of schoolmasters, particularly, it next asserts that certain studies are especially adapted to develop and perfect the powers of the mind. A further form of the theory assigns a veritable hierarchy to these studies, systematizes the disciplinary concept of education, often beyond all reason.

It is significant to note that the extreme views of education as a discipline always recur in periods when some particular, dominating curriculum in the schools has fallen into a rut of staleness and dead routine. On the other hand, it must also be noted that the most fiery, and often quite unreasonable, opponents of the whole disciplinary notion of education are those who are enthusiasts for a new curriculum, or who at least are fighting for a place for their pet subjects of study in an old curriculum. Thus, the decadent scholastics maintained that logic-chopping was an adequate educational tool because it disciplined the mind to reasoning. The earlier humanists scouted that theory, and insisted that literature and the arts were necessary studies in any true education. Thus also, when humanism bogged down in grammar-drill and mechanical theme-writing, the schoolmasters declaimed on the training power of exact study of languages; and the 'scientists,' bent on ousting the 'classicists' from their pre-eminence in the schools, sneered at any training power of grammar, sometimes queerly denied that there were any faculties to be trained,[1]

---

[1] The violent quarrel in psychology about 'faculties' has simply no significance in the field of education. It is immediately evident as a matter of fact that the process of adding two and two differs from the process of recalling an historical event or the process of "giving to airy nothings a local habitation and a name." Whether we demand that these processes originate in distinct powers or faculties of the mind, or consider them diverse modes of functioning of a single central power, does not affect in the least the practical business of train-

and insisted that education was the acquiring of exact facts, not of grammar, but of the material world in which we live.

Locke expresses one form of the disciplinary concept of education in this often-quoted passage:

> The studies which he (the tutor) sets him (the pupil) upon are but, as it were, the exercise of his faculties, and employment of his time, to keep him from sauntering and idleness, to teach him application, and accustom him to take pains, and to give him some little taste of what his own industry must perfect.[1]

It may reasonably be objected that this view makes the work of tutor and pupil *only* a preparation for the education which somehow the pupil is later to acquire. In so far it is a narrow and defective view. But it is equally true that all education is preparatory to further education; that education is a process which should never end in this life; that every stage of it should link up with another stage. The value, therefore, of any of these theories of education reduces largely to a question of emphasis, of proportion. To claim that study, as a mental and moral discipline, has such educational value as to make of no moment what it is that one studies, is quite as silly as to claim that the student derives no benefit from any effort of study beyond the immediate acquisition of knowledge and skills. Both extremes are absurd; the truth lies between them. Every genuine education must combine the acquiring of knowledge, skills, habits, with the correlative increase in the power to assimilate further knowledge, to improve skills,

ing the mind in these processes. In this connection, it is amusing to note how many writers on education, who get quite worked up over what they consider the absurdity of classifying the activities of a single human being by 'faculties,' blandly venture to classify whole groups of men as 'realists,' 'humanists,' 'naturalists,' and the like. Logic and common sense are not always conspicuous in violent quarrels.

[1] *Some Thoughts Concerning Education,* par. 94 (10th ed., 1801, pp. 85, 86.)

to strengthen suitable habits. Far from there being any essential opposition between the two processes, they are necessarily interdependent and complementary.

How far the acquisitions in one line of study increase the students' capacity for more easily mastering another line of study, is, obviously, a question which cannot be answered in any general way. The answer to it must depend upon a variety of factors, such as the particular talents of the student, the more or less close relation between the studies involved, and the like. Darwin, for instance, confessed himself a badly educated man, in so far as excessive concentration on the study of material facts left him without any appreciation of poetry or the fine arts. But it is conceivable that, if he had spent all his time in trying to write poetry, he might have turned out an execrable poet. His talents may not have been in that order at all. Hence, most of the wordy quarrel about 'formal discipline' resolves itself into either a beating given to a straw man, made up of obviously absurd and extreme views, or a fruitless attempt to derive a general 'scientific' formula for infinitely variable situations. We can only conclude, in a common-sense way, that there is a disciplinary element necessary to education, and that it is neither as large as its extreme defenders claim nor as negligible as its irritated opponents claim.[1]

Jean Jacques Rousseau (1712-1778). It is an obvious truism to say that only God, the Omniscient, completely understands any human being; but there is a special reason for recalling this truism when one attempts to discuss Jean Jacques Rousseau. More than other men, Rousseau was a bundle of contradictions. More than any other man of his time, he divided those who studied him into violent par-

---

[1] For a balanced statement of the place of discipline in education, see A. Flexner, *Universities,* Oxford, 1930: the whole of Part I, especially the conclusions on pp. 30-31.

tisans, for and against him. He wrote his own autobiography, the *Confessions,* appallingly frank, ringing with sincerity, yet vitiated by false statements, needing frequent correction from other sources.[1] His life and character, even more than his work, is the subject of endless debate: there are those who call him a saint, as well as those who look upon him as one of the vilest of men: and both prove their opinions from his *Confessions.*[2] Manifestly, the cause of this obscurity of opposing judgments is to be found as much in the critics of Rousseau as in Rousseau himself; yet he remains a hard man to estimate.

He was born at Geneva, June 28, 1712, of a family that had removed from Paris to Geneva nearly two hundred years before, and had been Protestant all that time. His mother died at his birth; his early years were under the care of an affectionate aunt and a kind, but undisciplined, father. At the age of ten, he was put to school by his father, who thenceforth practically disappeared from his life. A sensuous dreamer, Rousseau never knew any real discipline. At sixteen, he was taken into the home of Madame de Warens, a divorcee of twenty-eight, a nominal convert to Catholicism, but in reality a sentimental Deist.

[1] An important source is G. Streckeisen-Moultou's two volumes of letters, published in 1865 as *Rousseau, ses Amis et ses Ennemis.* Another source is the *Memoires* of Mme. d'Épinay (3 vols., Paris, 1818); but these must be checked by Mrs. Frederika Macdonald's *J. J. Rousseau* (2 vols., London, 1906), an interesting, valuable, though not wholly convincing defense of Rousseau.

[2] The literature of discussion concerning Rousseau is of enormous extent. J. Grand-Carteret (*J. J. Rousseau jugé par les Français d'aujourd'hui,* Paris, 1890) collects a large number of French estimates, mostly laudatory. For some time, Rousseau's German and English admirers surpassed the French in enthusiasm. For the Germans, see Joseph Texte, *J. J. Rousseau et le cosmopolitisme litteraire,* Paris, 1895; English translation by J. W. Matthews, London, 1899; and L. Reynaud, *Histoire de l'influence française en Allemagne,* Paris, 1914. John Morley, *Rousseau* (2 vols., London, 1873; other editions as late as 1915), represents the more dispassionate and critical English view. There is a sound and sympathetic study of Rousseau in Jacques Maritain's *Three Reformers,* London, Sheed and Ward, 1928.

Under her urging, he too became a nominal Catholic. He also became her lover, sharing her favors with her gardener. He spent twelve years in her house, with intervals of wandering. When he was supplanted by another lover, he went to Paris, in his twenty-ninth year, filled with schemes for a new musical notation, although he had little knowledge of music. Penniless, he won friends, chiefly women, who secured him various secretaryships, none of which he held long. When he was thirty-three, he took as his mistress Theresa Levasseur, an illiterate laundress of twenty-two, by whom he had five children. He thrust each of these children, at its birth, into a foundling asylum. He loved a vagabond life, and hated cities. His rich friends humored him, gave him charming idyllic residences on their estates. He quarreled with all his friends, accepting favors from all, indignant if any neglected him, yet resenting to be under obligations to any one. In 1754, when he was forty-two years old, he again professed to be a Protestant, in order to secure his former rights as a citizen of Geneva. During the last twelve years of his life, his mind became increasingly unbalanced;[1] he suffered from a persecution-mania. He died July 2, 1778, on an estate of one of his friends, at Ermenonville, some twenty miles from Paris. A persistent rumor that he took his own life seems to have been untrue.

His writings. Although Rousseau dabbled at writing for many years, he was thirty-seven years old before he published anything. This first publication was written in the spirit which moved him throughout the remaining thirty years of his life: the spirit of a severe critic of all that

[1] Interesting studies of Rousseau's psychoses have been made by Victor Demole: "Analyse psychiatrique des Confessions" (*Archives Suisses de Neurologie et de Psychiatrie,* 1918, Vol. 2, n. 2); "Rôle du tempérament et des idées délirantes de Rousseau dans la genèse de ses principales théories," (*Annales Médico-psychologiques,* January, 1922).

men had done hitherto, the spirit of a reformer. His first published work was done as one of fourteen competing essays on this rather vague theme set by the Academy of Dijon: "Has the restoration of the arts and sciences contributed to purify or corrupt manners?" Rousseau answered with an impassioned attack upon the benefits of the arts and sciences and won the prize. His theory, which he was to cling to in general, although with many inconsistencies, postulated a primitive, happy 'state of nature,' a sort of distorted version of the earthly paradise referred to in divine revelation. Men had somehow fallen from that desirable state; and ever since had blundered more and more in their management of the affairs of life. He seems to have had no clear idea of the Christian doctrine of the Fall of Man: he certainly never grasped the supernatural element in that Fall, or the need of any supernatural help to restore men to their primal happiness. All that Rousseau could see was that men were blunderers; all he could urge was that they must cut loose from their bad past, and begin anew. Some ten years were to elapse before he attempted to set down his notions of how men were to make this new beginning.

The first of these attempts was *La Nouvelle Héloise,* published in 1761, when Rousseau was forty-nine years old. It is a novel, a story told in the form of letters. The characters and the language are stiff, the situations unreal and morbidly sentimental. It is coarse, yet pietistic; a mingling of seduction with rhapsodies on utopian family life; muddled in its thinking, yet rich in imaginative detail; utterly untrue to human nature in general, yet shrewd in individual observation. It is a duller work even than the novels of his contemporary, Richardson. Yet it was enormously popular, especially amongst women; and it affected much more than Richardson's novels did the beginnings of modern romantic literature. The great reason for its popularity may be set down as this: that it met the aspirations of countless men and women, who rebelled against the exact clarity of Christian teaching, yet shrank from the fierce rationalist assaults of the 'philosophers' upon that teaching; that it offered to such people a *via media* of sentimentality with which they could comfort their souls, inherently religious.

The next year, 1762, saw the publication of *Le Contrat Social,* and *Émile,* the two works upon which Rousseau's fame more generally rests. *The Social Contract* is an *a priori* study of the origins of society, quite illogical, often self-contradictory, but powerful in its sentimental defense of democracy and the rights of the 'common people.' It had much to do with shaping the ideas of the French Revolution;[1] and in a lesser way it influenced the political notions of the American Revolution. Of *Émile,* his treatise on education, we shall have to say more in a moment. His remaining works of importance are the *Confessions* (the greater part of which he wrote, in 1766-67, at Wootton, in England, where Hume had established him when he was exiled from both France and Geneva because of his subversive writings), and a sort of continuation of the *Confessions,* called *Rêveries du promeneur solitaire,* written mostly at Paris, from 1770 onward.[2]

---

[1] It is important to remember that Rousseau's political influence grew out of his writings in general at least as much as out of his more strictly political treatises. Moral and religious notions are inextricably bound up with the basic ideas of all government. When the Decree of the Committee, April 20, 1794, proclaimed: "One must entirely refashion a people whom one wishes to make free: destroy its prejudices, alter its habits, limit its necessities, root out its vices, purify its desires"; it echoed Rousseau's *Émile* as clearly as it echoed the *Contrat Social* or the *Considérations sur le Gouvernement de Pologne.*

[2] Rousseau's complete works were first published at Geneva, about five years after his death, in 47 small volumes. The most important edition is still that of Musset-Pathay, Paris, 1823, who, two years previously, had published *Histoire de la Vie et des Ouvrages de J. J. Rousseau.* Bosscha, 1858, and Streckeisen-Moultou, 1861, added some

Émile. *Émile* consists of five books, four devoted to an account of the boy Émile's education, in four sharply divided periods, from his birth to his twentieth year, the fifth to the education of Sophie, his future wife. The boy is to be brought up by a tutor, away from other human society: because all human society is vicious, and any true education must be cut off from the influence of the past. Rousseau does not, of course, tell his readers how the tutor is to be preserved from that influence; any more than he tells us how we are to secure enough tutors to go round. He borrows the ideas of Bacon and Locke on 'realist' instruction; Émile is to *discover,* for instance, "all the laws of statics and hydrostatics" (Book III). He invents most elaborate schemes to interest Émile in gardening, in the principles of commerce, absurdly complicated schemes, which are to cheat the boy into believing that he is making original discoveries. There is to be no use, or even expression, of authority in Émile's training; but only an involved process of getting him to make good choices on his own initiative. "Do not give your pupil any sort of verbal lesson, for he is to be taught only by experience" (Book II). All appeals are to be made to Émile's self-love: the only basis he will allow for education (Book IV). On this basis, Émile is taught a kind of stoic self-control, which Rousseau calls virtue; because it will make the boy's life interiorly comfortable, and therefore happy. Émile's social education consists of the inculcation of certain abstract ideals, of pity, of respect for the great mass of the people; but as a remote thing, not in actual daily contact with people. He is to hear nothing of religion: a matter to be left to his mature choice, when his education will have been completed. But in the fourth book there is introduced the

letters. Dufour and Plan (1924) edited the *Correspondance Generale.* The *Confessions* and *Émile* have been translated into English several times.

famous "Confession of Faith of the Savoyard Vicar," a vivid portrayal of Rousseau's religious ideal, at which he hopes to have Émile aim. This Confession of Faith is the precursor of what today we call 'Modernism' in religion: a vague grouping of pious sentiments, without doctrinal affirmation, without intellectual validity: a gentle and remote Deism, rich in emotional glow, incapable of intolerance or controversy, because incapable of definition. It brought upon Rousseau the scorn of Voltaire and the 'philosophers,' because it accepted the idea of God in a pious fashion; it brought him the repudiation of Protestants and Catholics alike, because it rejected the Christian teachings based on divine revelation. But it appealed immediately to millions, in his time and since, who, whatever their nominal religious adherences, had neither genuine faith nor the patience and humility to accept revealed truth.

Sophie's education is cavalierly dismissed in a brief account. She is to be the subject, rather than the companion, of Émile. Her training is that of the good housewife, without opinions or character of her own, guided by her husband in all things beyond the compass of her care for the children and her round of domestic duties. "The whole education of women ought to be relative to men: to please them, to be useful to them . . . "

Yet, in the midst of these unreasonable theories, there is a wealth of good notions in detail. Rousseau, for instance, urged mothers to suckle their own children;[1] urged study of children's temperaments and aptitudes as a foundation for all teaching; emphasized the advantage of leading over driving and of example over precept, the usefulness of curiosity as an intellectual stimulus, the value of manual training. Further, in attacking all educational traditions,

---

[1] Just as Vives had urged the same thing, some two hundred and thirty years earlier than Rousseau. Cf. *De Institutione Foeminae Christianae*, Antwerp, 1523; lib. I, cap. 1; translated in Watson, *Vives and the Renascence Education of Women*, London, 1912, pp. 39-41.

he naturally upset some bad traditions, such as the appeal to envy and vanity as motives for studying (Book II), the sheer memorizing of statements not understood (Book III).

Rousseau's popular appeal. Not in France alone, but in the Germanies, England, the Swiss Cantons, and the United States, Rousseau gained a wide influence which continued to grow strongly throughout the nineteenth century, and which has powerfully affected education down to the present time. In spite of that fact, it must be emphatically said that Rousseau was not really a leader of popular opinion. His talent lay rather in reflecting tendencies already clear and strong amongst the mass of the people, in making those tendencies articulate and expressing them with remarkable vigor and persuasiveness.[1]

He came upon the scene at a time when Western civilization was almost inevitably bound to undergo great changes: when Protestantism was largely breaking down into Rationalism and Deism, when absolution in government was piling up its last intolerable blunders, when Catholic prelates and clergy were again forgetting the sharp lessons of the Religious Revolt, when the minds of men were rebelling against the cold insufficiencies of the 'Age of Reason.' Rousseau, like Luther before him, did no more than throw a spark into a magazine already prepared for explosion.

He appealed to impulses in men which are as noble as they are often pathetically ill-guided: the love of liberty, so hard to distinguish from license; the resentment against formalism and bureaucracy, so likely to become resentment against all authority; the vague aspirations to goodness, provided there be no hardships in acquiring it; the undying and pitiful hope of perfect happiness on earth. Men in gen-

---

[1] As one of these tendencies Adamson reckons the developing hostility to the Jesuits, which, at the time when Rousseau was most energetic, resulted in the expulsion of the Jesuits from France and their later suppression. (J. W. Adamson, *A Short History of Education,* Cambridge, 1922, pp. 212-13.)

eral do not think; they feel: and Rousseau was the Hierophant of Sentiment. With greater passion and eloquence than Francis Bacon's, he held out a larger hope than Bacon's: that not the mere field of knowledge, but the whole field of living, could be transformed and perfected. The Christian hope in a perfection beyond this life, eternal, tries men's patience at times sorely. It is not hard for an eloquent man to embitter millions, who still call themselves Christians, against that far-off hope, and to arouse in them enthusiasm for a promise of more immediate results. The whole business concerns the emotions, with the vast majority of men, much more than it does the intelligence. Rousseau had a mastery of emotional appeal. It mattered nothing that he was illogical, that most of his writings were what he himself called a "collection of reflections and observations without order and almost without coherence."[1] The power of his writings was in their feeling, in their capacity to stimulate the imagination and emotions.

His influence upon education. In the narrower domain of school education, Rousseau's influence has been more good than bad. He did inspire men to the study of children as the foundation of school methods, even though that study later degenerated into pedantic absurdities. He did move men to fight for equality of educational opportunity, even though the movement culminated in Procrustean laws of compulsory schooling. Barring a few fanatics like Basedow, no one tried to carry out in schools Rousseau's ridiculous extremes.

But in the wider sense of education, Rousseau's influence has been almost wholly bad. He preached a sentimental softness to a world all too eager to avoid the divine responsibilities of life. He attacked the Christian concept of life much more effectively by his substitution of a vague-

---

[1] Opening sentence of his preface to *Émile*.

ly pious Deism than Voltaire did by his vehement and open negation. His teachings affect men today who have never even heard his name, much less read a line of his writings. He is the leader of the half-baked revolutionaries, who like himself chafe under the restraints of discipline and authority, and therefore repudiate divine revelation, and center their hopes and aspirations fruitlessly upon an impossible natural perfection. In that false hope lie the roots of much of the moral despair which overshadows the world today. To hope for too much from the present life is even a more saddening and enervating thing than to hope for too little. Although the more intelligent men of our time are in reaction against his influence, it is still very powerful. We shall consider some of the effects of that influence upon education in the succeeding pages; but for the moment we must turn now to some of the teaching theorists.

III. Teaching Theorists

Their common grounds. Histories of educational theory usually pay more attention to quarrels amongst theorists than to the larger field in which they agree. In this, as in so many other matters, we suffer from our human tendency to emphasize the unusual, the sensational, anything that has in it the dramatic element of conflict. As regards education particularly, it is an unfortunate fact that cool and steady sanity is seldom as impressive to the general run of men as is a startling eccentricity, or a pronouncement that raises revolutionary hopes. But this should not blind us to the fact that, in spite of all diversity, and even bitter opposition, amongst school theorists, they still have much in common. Certain basic problems of the school are the same even in changing conditions of society; and first-hand contact with those problems naturally produces a certain community of experience amongst school teachers. Hence, theorists who have faced the problem of group teaching agree upon the need of classification of pupils, of methods of instruction which can be applied to a group, of discipline to secure orderly procedure; they agree upon the necessity of some scheme for testing achievements in a class, even though they fight furiously about the merits of rival schemes; they unanimously see that there must be definite aims in teaching, no matter how bitterly they quarrel over the detailed value of certain aims.

The teaching theorist is more likely than the non-teaching theorist to avoid mere *a priori* speculations, and to keep his feet on the solid ground of experience. If Rousseau had ever taught in an actual school, it is scarcely conceivable that he would have denied the need of authority to enforce school discipline. One does not often find teaching theorists making that error of judgment. In fact, if teaching theorists were left to themselves, their points of agreement would be even more numerous than they are. It is the footloose theorist, who knows little or nothing of schools, and who would rather die than attempt to apply his theories in a real school, that most often flusters the schoolmaster, poor fellow, into extravagant experiments and dangerous fads.

There is another reason why teaching theorists have so much in common: the very obvious reason that they borrow theories so freely from one another. In that they show their good sense; although at times one wishes that they would display also the courtesy and justice involved in acknowledging the sources of their borrowings. These preliminary remarks may be found not inopportune when we consider the first of modern teaching theorists, the quarry from which so many other theorists have digged, Juan Luis Vives.

Juan Luis Vives (1492-1540). It may seem strange to many to call Vives the first of modern teaching theorists; but that is probably because the facts about him are not

so widely known as they deserve to be.[1] He was born in
March of the year in which Columbus discovered America;
he died in the year in which the Society of Jesus was approved by Paul III. A Spaniard of Valencia, his early
schooling was in the debased mediaeval type of routine
grammar and mechanical disputation; but at seventeen
years of age he went to spend five years in Paris, where he
broke with the bad traditions of decadent Scholasticism.[2]
His ripe manhood was passed during the first tumultuous
years of geographic exploration. He breathed the full air
of the Renaissance. He saw the breaking away of the
Germanies from the ancient unity of Christendom, and the
beginnings of the English separation under Henry VIII.[3]
He was living in Paris when Calvin's *Institute* was first

---

[1] W. H. Woodward first brought Vives to the notice of the present-
day English readers: in *Studies in Education during the Age of the
Renaissance,* Cambridge, 1906, chap. 10. Foster Watson followed,
with English translations of some of Vives' writings, to which he
prefixed excellent introductions. But the best studies of Vives have
been done on the Continent. Gregorio Majans y Siscar got out a fine
edition of Vives' collected works in eight volumes, Valencia, 1782.
A. J. Namêche published *Mémoire sur la Vie et les Ecrits de J. L.
Vives,* Brussels, 1841. Three studies of Vives in France are of some
value: Arnaud, *Quid de pueris instituendis senserit L. Vives,* Paris,
1887; Thibaut, *Quid de puellis instituendis senserit Vives,* Paris, 1888;
Lecigne, *Quid de rebus politicis senserit J. L. Vives,* Rennes, 1898.
Roman Pade, *Die Affektenlehre des J. L. Vives,* Munster, 1893, and
Gerhard Hoppe, *Die Psychologie des Juan Luis Vives,* Berlin, 1901,
have studied separate parts of his treatise *De Anima et Vita.* The
best book on Vives is in Spanish: Adolfo Bonilla y San Martin, *Luis
Vives y la Filosofia del Renacimiento,* Madrid, 1903.

[2] Five years later, whilst he was teaching at Louvain, he wrote
his book, *In Pseudo-Dialecticos,* attacking the still dominant logic-
choppers. He had already become the friend of Erasmus, who echoed
Sir Thomas More's praise of Vives in that same year 1519 (when
Vives was only twenty-seven) with the statement—very rare for the
jealous Erasmus—"He is one of those who will overshadow the name
of Erasmus." (*Erasmi Epistolae,* ed. 1642.) So far Erasmus has
not proven himself a valid prophet.

[3] Vives divided the six years, 1522-28, between England and the
Low Countries. He taught at Oxford, was tutor to the Princess
Mary, had a pension from the King; but took the part of Queen
Catharine in the divorce proceedings of 1528, and was for that exiled
and deprived of his pension.

published. Rabelais was his contemporary. Montaigne was a boy of seven, and Mulcaster a boy of nine, when he died. He saw, as Erasmus did, the break-down of the old mediaeval education; but he saw also, what Erasmus did not see,[1] the growing power of the vernaculars, consequent upon sharper national divisions, and he advocated their place in education.[2] A long lifetime before Francis Bacon, a century before Comenius, a dozen years even before there had begun, with Copernicus, the great era of scientific discoveries, Vives urged the importance of nature studies carried out by new methods of observation and experiment.[3] He was not merely the precursor of Francis Bacon in demanding a wider use of the inductive method, but vastly his superior in applying that method.[4] All the authors who have studied Vives show that he was the real founder of educational psychology.[5] No writer even of the present

[1] Nor did Bacon perceive it, though he was born some seventy years after Vives.

[2] For instances, see Foster Watson, *Vives on Education,* Cambridge, 1913 (a translation of the five books *De Disciplinis Tradendis*); p. 103, where Vives urges upon the teacher a thorough mastery of the vernacular in order to form his pupils in its correct use; p. 110, where he suggests precautions against corrupting the vernacular by mixing it with Latin; p. 265, "Laws should be written in the vernacular."

[3] *De Disciplinis Tradendis,* Bk. IV, c. 1 (in Watson's translation, pp. 166-71). Watson notes also how this new attitude of observation of nature is brought into Vives' Dialogues, *Linguae Latinae Exercitatio,* Bruges, 1539. Bomer, *Die Lateinischen Schulergesprache der Humanisten,* Berlin, 1899, reckons over a hundred editions of this work. Watson translated it as *Tudor School-Boy Life,* London, 1908. The dialogues referred to are VIII and IX, in Watson, pp. 39-64.

[4] See his studies of the origin of arts (Watson, *Vives on Education,* p. 20 sqq.); his applications of induction to the study of medicine (*ibid.,* pp. 221, 233); of law (*ibid.,* pp. 251, 262, 268); of positive sciences (*ibid.,* pp. 166-68). Note this particularly: "In teaching the arts, we shall collect many experiments and observe the experience of many teachers, so that from them general rules may be formed. Etc." (*ibid.,* pp. 87-88). The whole passage is noteworthy.

[5] His *De Anima et Vita,* written before the *De Disciplinis,* but published seven years after the latter, is an empirical treatise, which uses inductive methods in psychology for the first time. He always has in mind the application of psychology to educational practice.

time surpasses him in his clear view of the subordination of grammar to the acquisition of language, and of language itself to the purpose of expressing knowledge.[1] He revolutionized the old concept of history,[2] insisted upon critical standards, upon exact chronology, the value of contemporary sources. Finally, he taught the absolute necessity of religion as a part of education: a principle at once so old as to keep him a sincere Catholic in his life and thought, and so modern that many of our present-day theorists are only now, to their amazement, rediscovering it.

Sources from which Vives drew. It would be absurd to think that Vives invented all his ideas about education. He was a lifelong student of earlier writers, and he fully acknowledges his indebtedness to them. His originality lay in his power to appreciate the great changes that were taking place in the Western world, and in his foresight to adapt to the changed conditions of education old principles in a new application. Thus, for instance, Aristotle and the scholastic philosophers had taught that *"nihil est in intellectu quod non prius fuerit in sensu"*;[3] and Vives only says the same thing when he tells us that "the senses are our first teachers."[4] But Vives applies this principle in a way which most of the Scholastics never dreamed of. He links it up with Roger Bacon's great use of the principle back in

See Watson, *Vives on Education,* pp. 82, 169, 211, 225; W. A. Daly, *The Educational Psychology of J. L. Vives,* Washington, 1924.

[1] The idea recurs often; but see especially *De Disciplinis Tradendis,* Bk. III, c. 1 (in Watson's translation, pp. 90 sqq.); Bk. IV, c. 1 (Watson, p. 163).

[2] See Watson's translation of *De Disciplinis,* pp. 231, 232, and the whole of Bk. V, c. 2, pp. 237-49. In *De Causis Corruptarum Artium* (Majan's edition, *Opera,* Vol. 6), he wrote, "Herodotus may more truly be called the father of lies than the father of history." He praised modern historians (see Woodward, *Erasmus Concerning Education,* pp. 64-65), but with a critical eye (*De Causis Corruptarum Artium, Opera,* Vol. 6, p. 108).

[3] Cf. Mercier, *Manual of Scholastic Philosophy,* London, 1928, Vol. 1, pp. 240 sqq.

[4] *De Anima et Vita,* lib. II. cap. 8.

the thirteenth century, a use which took no general hold at the time.[1] So also, Vives' theories on the teaching of history had been formulated nearly a hundred years before him by Lorenzo Valla.[2] Vittorino da Feltre had given Vives the notion of the importance of choosing a proper site for a school;[3] which Mulcaster[4] and Milton[5] later borrowed from Vives. All the early Renaissance writers on education laid stress on the qualities needed for a good teacher; Vives merely applied their requirements to the actual conditions in which he lived.[6]

It is not belittling Vives to say that he leaned upon the past; it is, on the contrary, much to his credit. But it is a mark of his wisdom that he was not bound to past applications of principles which are independent of time. He not merely learned from his contemporaries, such as his admired Erasmus, Antonio de Lebrija, Sir Thomas More; but, since he was for years himself an active teacher, in public classes at Louvain and Oxford, and as a tutor,[7] he studied education in the field of reality, and tested the theories he read and meditated by the concrete experience of the classroom. His psychology draws constantly upon that experi-

[1] One of the most interesting facts to be observed in the history of education is the assumption that each theorist who stresses the importance of sense-training is the discoverer of that educational principle. Hence, each in his turn, Bacon, Locke, Rousseau, Pestalozzi have been hailed as pioneers in asserting a principle which, however badly it may have been applied or is still being applied, must have been fairly obvious to any intelligent man at any period in the history of mankind.

[2] Cf. *Cambridge Modern History*, Vol. 1, p. 602; and J. Vahlen, *Lorenzo Valla, ein Vortrag*, Berlin, 1864.

[3] Cf. Watson, *Vives on Education*, pp. 53 sqq.

[4] *Positions*, Quick's edition, p. 29.

[5] See "A Suggested Source of Milton's Tractate on Education," in *Nineteenth Century*, December, 1909.

[6] *De Disciplinis Tradendis*, lib. II, cap. 1; in Watson's translation, pp. 55-61.

[7] He was tutor both to personages, such as Cardinal de Croy and Princess Mary, and to humbler persons, such as Jerome Ruffault, who later became abbot of St. Peter at Ghent, and Margaret Valdaura, whom Vives married when she grew to womanhood.

ence for illustration and data of observation. It is this combination of grasp of established principles with accurate study of the conditions in which they are to be applied that makes his treatises so alive, so convincing, and so basically true. It seems likely that Foster Watson is pointing to this same combination in Vives, when he says, "He was the last of the Mediaevalists; and also, the first of the modern scientists."[1]

Vives' educational theories. Vives' theories are scattered through a number of treatises; but the most important of them may be found in *De Tradendis Disciplinis,* published at Bruges in 1531, and containing twelve books. The first seven books, *De Causis Corruptarum Artium,* discussed the reasons why education had lagged so far behind the social and political development of Europe. Vives found much fault with existing methods of study, especially in the natural sciences, in moral philosophy, in law, and in the languages; he found even more fault with the attitude of men toward learning, with their avarice, self-conceit, pretentiousness. The remaining five books are positive in character, and present his definite suggestions as to how the educational process may be improved. But with admirable modesty he insisted: "I do not wish to be the founder of a sect, or to persuade anyone to swear by my conclusions. . . . You who seek truth, make your stand wherever you think that she is."[2]

His basic idea is that education must be directed to the end for which man was made by God, which is the knowledge and love of God;[3] "so that every kind of learning may be valued to the extent that by its matter, its end taken as our end, its teachers, its methods, and its results, it agrees

---

[1] Introduction to *Vives on Education,* p. 118.
[2] Preface to *De Disciplinis Tradendis;* in Watson's translation, p. 9.
[3] See the whole of Bk. I, c. 4; in Watson's *Vives on Education,* pp. 28-36.

or does not agree with that standard."[1] He comes back to that idea constantly.[2] Education is based upon a divine obligation; since God gave men the power of thought and enquiry, men must use that power to further God's purpose in their regard.[3] Religious instruction is a necessary part of education;[4] but, beyond that, religious aims should control and guide all studies, both negatively[5] and positively.[6]

Perhaps next in importance is Vives' clear notion about the relation of all education to the various capacities of students. That, too, was no new idea. The ancients knew it; Vergerio and Barzizza had repeated it in the earlier days of the Renaissance, a century before Vives was born;[7] Erasmus emphasized it.[8] It is a fact obvious to any teacher that students differ in talents and disposition; and it should be an equally obvious conclusion that choice of studies, methods of instruction, and extent of instruction must reasonably be adapted to those variations.[9] Vives offers a practical suggestion as to how this principle may be applied in the circumstances of a school, where routine procedure

---

[1] Watson, *ibid.*, pp. 29-30.

[2] Cf. George Siske, *Willens- und Charakterbildung bei Johann Ludwig Vives,* Langensalza, 1911.

[3] See the opening sentence of *De Disciplinis Tradendis.*

[4] "First of all the fundamental truths of our religion should be taught." Watson, *ibid.*, p. 84. Vives wrote a textbook in religious instruction, *Introductio ad Sapientiam,* published in 1524.

[5] As, for instance, in his exclusion from the school of writings injurious to faith and morals. See Watson, *ibid.*, pp. 49-50.

[6] See especially Chapter 1 of the excellent Appendix to *De Disciplinis Tradendis;* Watson, *ibid.*, pp. 272-84.

[7] See *supra,* p. 197; also W. H. Woodward, *Studies in Education during the Age of the Renaissance,* p. 77.

[8] See Woodward, *Erasmus,* pp. 77 sqq.

[9] After long experience of compulsory schooling of a uniform sort for all children, some educators of today are coming to see the wisdom of this common-sense statement of Vives: "If a boy is not apt at his letters but trifles with the school tasks, and what is more serious, wastes his time, let him be early transferred to that work for which he seems fitted, in which he will occupy himself with more fruitfulness, and will be amongst the thoroughly trained, whom the Greeks used to call παιδομαθεῖς." (Watson's translation, p. 71.)

and mass-production methods are so likely to make discrimination difficult. He wants the masters in a school "every two or three months to deliberate and judge, with paternal affection and grave discretion, concerning the minds of their pupils, and appoint each boy to that work for which he seems most fit."[1]

In arranging his curriculum, Vives was guided by an educational theory of great moment. It is this: that a boy's school education should be of a general character, what we vaguely call 'liberal' or 'cultural.' He was opposed to plunging a youth into specialist studies before he had had the rounded training which would prepare him for life itself. His aim was the Christian aim, which, as has been seen, one section of the 'humanists' accepted and handed on from the early days of the Renaissance: "to order all our studies to the practical needs of life, to some definite gain for mind and body, and to the increase of personal piety."[2] It was the 'pietas literata' of the Brothers of the Common Life, and of Sturm. He believed, with Vittorino da Feltre, that such an education could and should be attained before the student entered a university; for the universities of his day, very much like our own, were centers of highly specialized studies.

He laid great stress on the importance of the early stages of education. In view of the unsatisfactory character of existing schools, he believed that this early education might be better conducted at home. He was particularly averse to boarding schools, which he thought were too often mercenary establishments and ill-disciplined.[3] But if the boy

[1] *De Disciplinis Tradendis,* lib. II, cap. 4; in Watson's translation, p. 82. See the same thought expressed, *ibid.,* p. 62.

[2] *De Disciplinis Tradendis,* lib. IV, cap. 1 (in Watson's translation, pp. 166-67). The idea is interwoven throughout the whole of the treatise; but note especially, in Watson's translation, pp. 62-71, 116-19, 133-34, 180, 184, 187. See also Woodward, *Education during the Renaissance,* pp. 203-04.

[3] *De Disciplinis Tradendis,* lib. II, cap. 2; in Watson's translation, pp. 64-66.

were to be tutored at home, he should have companions in his studies, to stimulate his progress.

Vives, however, contemplated the school as one of the normal instruments of education. He discussed rather fully the proper site of a school, and the selection of masters and pupils, before entering upon the plan of studies.[1] Then he considered the studies in this order: language, logic, nature study, elementary metaphysics, rhetoric, mathematics, the practical arts. Although it is impossible to examine his treatment of each, a few illustrations must be given to show his balance and breadth of view. For instance, he abandoned the old dialectic sort of grammar, with its endless investigation of details,[2] and advocated instead the simpler grammars of Antonio de Lebrija, Melanchthon, and Lily as revised by Erasmus.[3] He set the question of 'imitation' as a school method upon a new and sensible foundation, opposing the slavish imitation of the Ciceronians, and urging in all cases an imitation rather of the 'mind' of the model than of "the external form of his style."[4] He wished the student's reading to be wide, not limited to mere excerpts; and he was an early advocate of school libraries.[5] He realized the educational value of the vernaculars, as few men of his time seem to have done; and insisted upon competency in the use of the vernaculars, both at home and in school.[6]

Vives evaluated every study from the moral as well as from the intellectual side. Authors were to be chosen for reading with an eye to their effect upon the student's char-

---

[1] *De Disciplinis Tradendis,* the whole of lib. II; in Watson, pp. 53-89.
[2] *Idem,* lib. III, cap. 1; in Watson, pp. 96-98. More especially, in *De Causis Corruptarum Artium, Opera,* Vol. 6, pp. 50, 131.
[3] *De Disciplinis Tradendis,* lib. III, cap. 6; in Watson, p. 131.
[4] *Idem,* lib. IV, cap. 4; Watson, pp. 189-200.
[5] *Idem,* lib. III, cap. 5 (Watson, p. 124); lib. III, cap. 6 (Watson, p. 141); lib. III, cap. 7 (Watson, p. 149); lib. V, cap. 4 (Watson, p. 271).
[6] *Idem,* lib. III, cap. 1; Watson, pp. 90-91.

acter.[1] He would have the masters guard against developing contentiousness and conceit in the students: vices
easily fostered by the formal 'disputations' then in vogue in
the schools.[2] All intellectual effort must stimulate and
develop the love of truth.[3] Historical studies are not to
glorify war;[4] but should be the source of practical wisdom,
and the stay of piety.[5]

Finally, he took account of the place of play and games
in education; not merely to secure physical fitness, but as
an educational discipline.[6] With good sense, he recognizes
the necessary spontaneity of games; but he wants them
measured and ruled by reasonable purpose; and he even
thinks that games can be used for such a detailed aim as,
say, the practice of Latin speech.[7]

The education of women. As regards the education of
girls, Vives insisted that, whilst it must obviously be different from that of boys, it is of equal importance. He
wrote several treatises on the education of women;[8] a thing
he was qualified to do by his considerable experience as a
teacher of women. His general view, in which he was later

[1] *De Disciplinis Tradendis,* lib. III, cap. 5; Watson, pp. 124-25.
[2] *Idem,* lib. II, cap. 1 (Watson, pp. 57-58); lib. III, cap. 4 (Watson, p. 116).
[3] *Idem,* lib. IV, cap. 2; Watson, pp. 174-76.
[4] *Idem,* lib. V, cap. 1; Watson, p. 236.
[5] He regretted that men do not profit more by reading the lives of the saints; and noted as one reason for that lack the bad way in which so many lives had been written. "The writer has told us, not what the Saint actually did, but what the writer would have wished him to have done." *Idem,* lib. V, cap. 2 (Watson, pp. 248-49). Yet the two centuries following Vives continued to furnish 'edifying' lives of the saints, which ignored or distorted facts in favor of the pious fancies of the writers.
[6] *Idem,* lib. II, cap. 4; Watson, p. 82.
[7] *Idem,* lib. III, cap. 4; Watson, pp. 121-22.
[8] *De Institutione Foeminae Christianae,* Antwerp, 1523; dedicated to Catharine of England; *De Ratione Studii* and *Satellitium,* Louvain, 1524; written for Princess Mary; Chapter III of *De Officio Mariti,* Bruges, 1529. Foster Watson gives partial translations in *Vives and the Renascence Education of Women,* London, 1912.

followed by Erasmus,[1] was that the education of women should be chiefly moral, but that intellectual training and a certain erudition were admirable means to secure and enrich their moral development. He would prefer women teachers for women, if competent women teachers could be found;[2] but he did not think much of women teachers in general, "because a woman is a frail thing, and of weak discretion."[3] As Latin was the medium of learning in his time, he of course included it in the girl's studies; but it should be taught with and through the vernacular, and her prayers should be in the vernacular.[4] For the girl, as for the boy, Vives urged the use of paper notebooks, to make study a personal and active affair, not the mere passive absorbing into which reading may degenerate.[5] He set down a complete plan of studies for the English Princess Mary,[6] a plan which was carried out, and which resulted in giving her an excellent intellectual and moral education.[7]

Borrowers from Vives. Foster Watson, in his introduction to *Vives on Education*,[8] illustrates briefly the extent to which other educational writers have borrowed from Vives, quite often without any acknowledgment. He quotes verbatim passages from Ben Jonson's *Timber or Discoveries*,

---

[1] *De Matrimonio Christiano*, Basle, 1526.

[2] Watson, *Vives and the Renascence Education of Women*, p. 54.

[3] *Idem*, pp. 55-56. Yet Vives is not a misogynist, nor a mere railer at women. He repeatedly defends the intelligence of women, and their right to intellectual culture; but he wants that culture to conform to their natural place in human society. See *De Officio Mariti*, cap. 3 (Watson, *ibid.*, pp. 195-208). The same idea is expressed in *De Institutione Foeminae Christianae*, lib. I, cap. 4 (Watson, *ibid.*, p. 55), where Vives asserts that he sets no limit to the learning of women, any more than to that of men; but that a woman should be more concerned with such knowledge as she will later apply to improving the moral conditions of herself and others.

[4] *Idem*, p. 89.

[5] *Idem*, pp. 146, 243.

[6] *Idem*, pp. 137-49.

[7] Cf. Sir Frederick Madden, Introductory Memoir to the *Privy Purse Expenses of the Princess Mary*, London, Pickering, 1831.

[8] Pp. 30 sqq.

taken bodily from Vives. He traces Roger Ascham's notions on the use of notebooks, and his famous 'double
translation,' as well as a number of others, directly to
Vives.[1] Mulcaster once refers praisingly to Vives,[2] but
many times uses his writings without admitting that he is
borrowing ideas. The illustrations might be multiplied considerably. A. Lange, in 1887, made this definite statement:
"Whatever is really good in the Jesuit system can be traced
almost in detail to Luis Vives."[3] Jesuit writers have denied
that their founder borrowed from Vives, and have seemed
to prove their point conclusively. It is by no means clear,
however, that other Jesuits than St. Ignatius did not make
use of Vives' ideas without giving him credit as their
source.[4]

[1] For the double translation, see *De Disciplinis,* lib. III, cap. 3 (in
Watson's *Vives on Education,* pp. 113-14).

[2] *Positions,* Quick's edition, p. 259.

[3] In the *Encyklopadie des gesammten Erziehungs- und Unterrichtswesens,* Leipzig, Band ix, Abteilung III, pp. 843 sqq.

[4] For discussion of the relations between Ignatius Loyola and
Vives, see the following: In *Monumenta Historica Societatis Jesu,*
Juan Alfonso de Polanco, *Vita Ignatii Loyolae,* Vol. 1, p. 43, recounting the occasion (circa 1528-30) when Ignatius was a guest of Vives
at dinner. Ignatius took sharp exception to an academic remark of
Vives about the penitential value of Lenten diet. And though Vives
was favorably impressed by Ignatius, and afterward said he thought
him a saintly man, Ignatius seems to have kept a lasting distrust
of Vives. This may well have been added to by the fact that a book
of Vives', *Comentarii in XXII Libros de Civitate dei S. Augustini,*
dedicated in 1522 to Henry VIII, who had just been named "Defender of the Faith" for his book against Luther, was for a time on
the Index. At any rate, Ignatius repeatedly forbade the reading of
Vives in Jesuit colleges. (See *Monumenta Historica Societatis Jesu;
Monumenta Ignatiana,* Series I, Vol. 4, p. 106; Series I, Vol. 5, p. 56,
p. 421.) There were evident protests against this ruling; since we
find that on February 1, 1554, Ignatius whilst still forbidding Vives
to be read in the Roman College, tolerates him reluctantly in colleges
outside of Rome. (See *Ibid.,* Series I, Vol. 6, pp. 266-67; Vol. 8,
p. 35.) Although on October 27, 1554, an official letter to Father
J. B. Tavon at Padua significantly says: "The authors forbidden in
our college here, such as Terence, Erasmus, Vives, are not forbidden
outside of Rome. Yet, if the matter were in our Father's hands,
these authors would not be read at all; but for the time they are
allowed." (*Ibid.,* Series I, Vol. 7, p. 706.) Friederike Kayser, in

Influence of Vives. In attempting to estimate the influence of Vives on education one must remember that Vives was himself an inheritor of the great Christian tradition in education, as that tradition had been modified by the Renaissance. Something of his own personality and experience he added, it is true, to what he inherited; it did not flow through him entirely unchanged. Yet the tradition was not to stand or fall by anything that Vives added to it. Men took up details of his suggestions, who refused and broke with the whole Christian tradition in education. Men stood by the tradition, and therefore shoulder to shoulder with Vives, who had scarcely even heard of Vives. This much seems certain: that Vives was in spirit so thoroughly Catholic that his influence merged with the continuation of the Christian educational tradition, just as had merged with it the influence of the Brothers of the Common Life. Hence the Catholics soon came to ignore Vives as an individual source of educational theory; and the non-Catholics, although they borrowed from him in details of method, grew out of sympathy with his aims, and came under the sway of other influences. Until his memory was belatedly revived in Spain, Germany, England, in the twentieth century, Vives remained unknown for more than a century. He is still but little known, and therefore little honored or accepted as a leader in educational theory.

Roger Ascham (1515-1568). When Vives died, Roger Ascham was a young man of twenty-five. His is a great name amongst writers on English education; how much substance there is back of his reputation, is another ques-

the article "Johannes Ludwig Vives," *Historisches Jahrbuch,* Munich, 1894, Vol. 15, p. 350, offers the defense of the Jesuits that both their notions and those of Vives were already old, might come from common sources. See also Schwickerath, *Jesuit Education,* 2d ed., St. Louis, 1904, pp. 141-43; and J. B. Herman, *La Pedagogie des Jesuites,* Louvain, 1914, pp. 46-56. Both limit themselves to the Ignatian controversy; do not discuss the wider question of the relation between Vives and other Jesuits.

tion. Of middle-class family, he went up to Cambridge when he was fifteen, was graduated M. A. at twenty-two; was Greek reader at his college of St. John's the following year, and continued in the college for ten years, succeeding his old Greek master, Sir John Cheke, in 1546. Two years later, he was made tutor to the Princess Elizabeth. After another two years, he was a secretary in the embassy to Charles V. In 1553 he became Latin secretary to Queen Mary, and was later continued in his office under Queen Elizabeth. How he weathered the religious changes involved in the successions, we do not know. The Reverend J. A. Giles, who edited *The Whole Works of Roger Ascham* in 1865, says simply: "It is much to be feared that the real truth of Ascham's character has still to be discovered."[1]

Ascham's one great educational work is *The Scholemaster,* published in 1570, two years after his death. It has been highly praised as a piece of English writing, and quite as strongly condemned.[2] As a treatise on educational theory, it is narrow in scope. That is clearly indicated even in its full title: *"The Scholemaster, or plaine and perfite way of teachyng children, to understand, write, and speake, the Latin tong, but specially purposed for the private brynging up of youth in Jentlemen and Noble mens houses, and commodious also for all such as have forgot the Latin tonge, and would, by themselves, without a Scholemaster, in short tyme, and with small paines, recover a sufficient habilitie to understand, write, and speake Latin."*[3] The chief point of method is the 'double translation,' which he borrowed from Vives. He echoed the Christian Renais-

[1] *The Whole Works of Roger Ascham,* Vol. 1, part 1, p. 99.
[2] See E. H. Lewis, *The History of the English Paragraph,* London, 1894, p. 80. Edmund Gosse offers the blunt statement: "It is impossible to call Ascham an agreeable writer, and pure pedantry to insist upon his mastery of English." (*Short History of Modern English Literature,* 1897, p. 79.)
[3] Title page in Giles's edition.

sance aims of culture and virtue. He pleaded for milder discipline in schools, less whipping: in this also imitating Vives. From Thomas Fuller[1] on, writers praised him; but the English schools ignored him. In reality, he had comparatively little to offer.

Richard Mulcaster (c. 1531-1611). Mulcaster was graduated from Christ Church, Oxford, when he was about twenty-five years old. Five years later, when the Merchant Taylors Company of London founded their great day school, he was appointed the first headmaster of the school. He held that office for twenty-five years, and made a success of the school. Finally, in 1586, he quarreled with the governors of the school over the smallness of his salary, and resigned his position. Ten years later, he was made headmaster of St. Paul's, Colet's school, which the Merchant Taylors had imitated, and remained as head for twelve years. He died about three years after leaving St. Paul's, aged about eighty, and very poor.

He had had about twenty years' experience as headmaster of Merchant Taylors' School when he published his first book on education: *Positions wherein those Primitive Circumstances be examined, which are necessarie for the Training up of Children, either for skill in their Books or Health in their Bodie.* The following year, 1582, appeared *The First Part of the Elementarie.* The second part was not published, probably not written.

The *Positions* are fundamental principles, forty-five in number, offered as the basis for a system of education. The greater part of them are concerned with the training of the body and of the character by means of games. His ideas are for the most part eminently sensible: and every one of them might have been drawn from Vives. He was by no means, however, a mere copyist. He emphasized the

---

[1] Thomas Fuller, *Worthies of England,* 1662. See Nichols's edition, Vol. 2, p. 516.

importance of the vernacular more than Vives had done. He elaborated both the demand which Vives had made that school teachers be specially trained and his criticism of existing university education as a bad preparation for teaching; and he urged that "this trade requireth a particular college" in the university.[1]

The Elementarie chiefly stressed his views on the teaching of the vernacular. An important detail in that teaching which he discussed was that of the standards of excellence in a language, upon which the rules of grammar and rhetoric are built up. As the age of Demosthenes had furnished that standard for the Greek language, and the age of Cicero for the Latin, so for English he suggested that his own age was the Golden Age, and coolly proposed, not the writings of Gascoigne or North or Spenser, but his own writings as 'a general pattern.' In spite of that conceit, he wrote rather pedantically, and at times obscurely. It is strongly suspected that his place as a 'model' was only that of model for the schoolmaster whom Shakespeare ridicules in *Love's Labour Lost*. Neither of his two most important theories was accepted in English educational practice until nearly three hundred years after his death.

Wolfgang Ratke (1571-1635). Ratke was an embryonic Lutheran minister, who did not succeed in completing his theological course. When he was about forty, he blossomed forth as an educational reformer. He was a turbulent person, who several times got himself into prison by his contentiousness.[2] In 1612, he presented his famous 'Memorial' to the German princes and prelates assembled in the Imperial Diet for the election of the Emperor Matthias. It contained three great proposals: first, a method of teaching Hebrew, Greek, Latin, and other languages in a very short time; second, a new type of school, in which all the

---

[1] *Positions,* Quick's edition, London, 1888, pp. 248-49.
[2] G. Krause, *Wolfgang Ratichius,* Leipzig, 1872, pp. 7, 8, 39, 165.

branches of knowledge should be learned in German; third, a plan "to introduce conveniently and establish peacefully throughout the whole Empire a uniform speech, a uniform government and a uniform religion." Several of the German princes were attracted by his proposals. The Duchess Dorothea Maria of Saxe-Weimar made him her tutor and her pensioner. Her brother, Ludwig of Anhalt-Hoethen, gave him a school, complete with masters and scholars, as a means of putting his schemes into practice. Ratke mysteriously swore his masters to secrecy concerning his methods; and the experiment was begun, only to be brought to a disastrous close within three months by his violent eccentricities. Several other attempts to realize his grandiose schemes proved to be equally futile. When, in 1632, his patron Duchess got him introduced to Oxenstiern with a view to making another attempt in Sweden, the great Chancellor finally turned him away, with the conclusion that he was a sound cudgeller of existing bad practice in schools, but had nothing better to offer in its place. That judgment is supported by the opinions of those who have carefully studied Ratke's theories.[1] Ratke's one really important contribution to educational theory is contained in the statement which he made to the town council of Magdeburg in 1621: that the education of the young is exclusively the business of the State.[2] Ratke did not originate that

[1] Niemeyer of Halle and, after him, von Raumer and Quick have made grossly exaggerated claims for Ratke as an educational reformer, and have succeeded in building up a legendary importance for him. But Krause, by going properly to the sources, has corrected these errors of enthusiasm, and made clear how ill-founded are the claims set up by Ratke's admirers. J. W. Adamson, *Pioneers of Modern Education*, Cambridge, 1921, presents a balanced study of Ratke, based on G. Krause's *Wolfgang Ratichius*, Leipzig, 1872. In particular, Krause disposes of the claims that Ratke based his educational schemes on Bacon's theory of scientific education, or was consciously psychological in his methods. All he borrowed from Bacon was his hope of a millenium around the corner.

[2] See the article "Ratke," by Israel, in Rein's *Encyclopaedische Handbuch der Paedagogik*.

idea. It had been gradually forming itself in many minds as the result of the interlocking of Church and State in various countries. But he becomes a significant figure in the history of education because, a hundred years after the outbreak of the Protestant Revolt, he expressed publicly that notion of state monopoly in education which was later to exert so much influence upon school education.

John Amos Comenius (1592-1670). Jan Amos Komensky was a Czech, or Bohemian, who, in the usual fashion of his time, latinized his name. He was the son of a miller, and belonged to the small Protestant sect known variously as 'The Unity of Brethren,' or 'The Bohemian Brethren,' or 'The Moravian Brethren.'[1] After a rather belated and somewhat sketchy schooling, he was ordained a minister. He taught in a little school of his sect at Prerau for two years, during which time he began his career as an educational writer with a book for beginners in Latin.[2] He became pastor of the Moravian congregation at Fulneck when he was twenty-six years old. At about the same age, he married for the first time.[3] The Moravian Brethren were frequently in political troubles, with Protestants as well as with Catholics; as a result of which Comenius had to move from place to place, seeking the protection of powerful

[1] The oldest name is 'The Unity of Brethren.' It began in 1457, as a split-off from one branch of the quarreling Hussites. It later became vaguely Protestant, approaching Lutheranism, perhaps, most closely, but resolutely keeping its distinctive character. Its members emphasized Christian conduct of life rather than dogmatic tenets, and aimed at great simplicity and severity of life.

[2] *Facilioris Grammaticae Praecepta.* Cf. J. A. Comenius, *Opera Didactica Omnia,* Amsterdam, 1657, tom. i, col. 3. No copy of this grammar is now known to exist.

[3] His first wife, together with their two children, died of pestilence, apparently in 1622. Comenius married again in 1624, and had a son and four daughters by this wife. His third marriage seems to have taken place about 1649. (M. W. Keatinge, *The Great Didactic,* 1896, tom. i, col. 68.) The details of Comenius's life are but scantily known, and chiefly from scattered autobiographical notes in the *Opera Didactica Omnia.*

friends. Thus he spent the years from 1628 to 1640 at Lissa in Poland, where he taught in the small secondary school of the Moravians. It was during his stay at Lissa that he did most of his educational writings.[1] These writings promptly made him famous. Envy stirred against him. Fanatical attacks upon his orthodoxy by some of his own Moravian Brethren practically drove him out of Lissa in 1640. At the invitation of Hartlib, he went to London in September, 1641, and remained there until June, 1642, planning great schemes for an educational reform to be backed by Parliament. These schemes came to nothing, beyond the publication of some treatises outlining them. A new patron, Ludwig de Geer, a very wealthy Hollander, took up Comenius at that point, and settled him with his family and assistants at Elbing in Prussia, to give him facilities for writing his school books. The next five years he spent at that task, grudgingly, and with many quarrels between him and de Geer. In 1647, on the death of the aged Bishop Justinius, Comenius was elected as head of the Moravian Church,[2] and again took up his residence at Lissa. Three years later, at the invitation of Count Sigismund Rakoczy, he went to Saros-Patak in Hungary, where Rakoczy established him in a school, and gave him a printing press. There was much friction between him and his patron and his assistants. After four years at Saros-Patak, he returned to Lissa in 1654, and remained there three years, until his imprudence in espousing the cause of the Swedish king, Karl Gustav, who devastated large parts of

---

[1] He was a most indefatigable writer. Keatinge, *op. cit.*, tom. ii, col. 309-16, lists 127 separate works. Most of these are religious tracts; but the number of treatises on education is quite large.

[2] S. S. Laurie, *John Amos Comenius*, Edinburgh, 1884, p. 67, gives 1632 as the year of Comenius's election. According to Francis Vanous (in the *Catholic Encyclopedia*, Vol. 4, p. 599), Comenius was the last bishop of the sect; but it was revived about 1720 by Count Zinzendorf, and still exists. In the United States, it numbers at present some 25,000 adherents.

Poland, resulted in the burning of Lissa by the Poles. Laurence de Geer, the son of his old patron, brought Comenius to Amsterdam in 1657, liberally financed his publications there, and maintained him until his death in 1670. He died on November 15th of that year, and was buried at Naarden, near Amsterdam.

His qualities. Comenius was a great-souled man, devoted, unselfish, worthy of the highest regard. His aims were always noble. His interest in education sprang from motives of Christian zeal. He was a shrewd observer of teaching practice in his long years of school work, and a diligent reader of the observations and theories of others. But he was the victim of a curious emotional unbalance. From the age of thirty-three until his death in his seventy-ninth year, he was increasingly under the influence of visionaries and charlatans, who claimed to have revelations and to prophesy amazing political successes for Protestantism. His readiness to be duped by Christopher Kotter, whom he first met in 1625, by Christina Poniatowska, an hysterical girl of sixteen, and by Nicolas Drabik, a fellow-minister, from 1643 until his death,[1] brought him into disrepute toward the close of his life. With all the sympathy in the world for the sincerity of Comenius's ideals, it must be said that this gullibility sets him apart from the fine sanity of Vives, and that it was the unmistakable cause of his acceptance of the one thing he definitely borrowed from Francis Bacon, the belief that some educational *method* would bring about a millenium of widespread knowledge, virtue, and piety, and be the means of universal salvation. Comenius was but another instance, as pathetic as it is noble, of the sort of man who has not intelligence enough to disentangle his optimistic dreams from the bleak real-

[1] Keatinge, *op. cit.*, Vol. 1, p. 98, says that Drabik, eight months after the death of Comenius, formally retracted his prophecies, and became a Catholic.

ities of life; and in so far, he was not a sound Christian theorist. It is most important to appreciate that limitation of Comenius, because it enters constantly into his educational theories.

His theories. First and foremost, Comenius, with the limitation just noted, held to the Christian aim and ideal in education, and insisted constantly that education for this world alone is absurdly inadequate.[1] It is true that he was distressingly vague about how education for time and education for eternity were to be linked, and that he was positively wrong in his Baconian belief that "knowledge is power," in the sense that Christian conduct of life would follow upon an understanding of the Christian ideal of life. His own experience, so sensibly applied to the details of work in schools, should have proven to him the falsity of that belief; but his muddled optimism persisted against the facts of life. He thought that "a proper supply of comprehensive and methodical class-books"[2] could overcome the manifold difficulties in the way of his grandiose dream.[3]

It was with that end in view that Comenius wrote his school books. But his heart was not in that task; he complained of it often,[4] and wished by all means to devote himself entirely to his fabrication of large pansophic schemes. However, his patrons kept him to the task; and his reputation for all those two hundred years, until von Raumer, Laurie, and others gave it a new phase, was based upon the outstanding success of his school books. There

[1] See especially the first four chapters of *The Great Didactic;* in Keatinge's translation, pp. 25-39.

[2] *Didactica Magna*, xxxiii, 8; in Keatinge, Vol. 2, p. 296.

[3] See the whole of Chapter 33, *op. cit.*, in Keatinge, Vol. 2, pp. 295 sqq. Keatinge correctly says: "In his statement of the aims of education Comenius is weaker than in his exposition of method, and in this respect the modern educator resembles him. Comenius is weak in that he does not see the difficulties, the modern is weak in that he is overwhelmed by them." (*Op. cit.*, i, 159.)

[4] "Latinitatis studia mihi toties nauseata." (*Opera Didactica Omnia*, Amsterdam, 1657, tom. iv, col. 6.)

was nothing particularly original in any of those manuals. Erasmus, Vives, and above all, Cordier, had made 'Colloquies' a standard type of school book. Father William Bathe had published his *Janua Linguarum* in 1611, some twenty years before Comenius copied his idea. Bathe's book was devised, not for school boys, but for missionaries. Comenius adapted his idea to a book for children, and called the book *Janua Linguarum Reserata,* adding the pretentious subtitle *Seminarium Linguarum et Scientiarum Omnium.*[1] The method common to both Bathe and Comenius was to equip the beginner in a new language with a working vocabulary which he would master by reading graded sentences. No word, except the inevitable prepositions, copulatives, and the like would be repeated. Both books had many faults; but they were an improvement on the old grammar-chopping of the schools. Comenius later published a sort of introductory book, *Januae Linguarum Reseratae Vestibulum.*[2] He kept tinkering with the *Janua* for years;[3] he shortened it considerably, added illustrations, and turned out the *Orbis Sensualium Pictus: Hoc est, Omnium fundamentalium in Mundo rerum et in Vita actionum, Pictura et Nomenclatura,* which was published by Michael Endter at Nuremberg in 1658, and which had a deserved success as a first reading book. He also wrote a number of dictionaries, and several Latin grammars; but

[1] For Comenius's acknowledgment of his indebtedness to Bathe, and an accurate criticism of the work of both, see T. Corcoran, *Studies in the History of Classical Teaching,* New York, 1911, pp. 41-53. Comenius, by no means a first-rate Latin scholar, published in 1657 an *Apologia* for his Latin style in the *Janua:* of which defense Morhof (*Polyhistor Litterarius,* Lubeck, 1695, lib. II, c. 4) says that it also needed another *Apologia.*

[2] Written in 1633. Cf. *Opera Didactica Omnia,* tom. i, col. 303.

[3] One unhappy modification was the *Schola Ludus,* which Comenius subtitled *Januae Linguarum praxis comica,* and which the unfortunate boys were to use as an imitation of the plays staged by the students in Jesuit schools. It takes up a hundred folios in the *Opera Didactica Omnia.* Keatinge calls it "dismal stuff." (*Op. cit.,* Vol. 1, p. 80.)

the grammar written for the *Janua* was an intolerably complicated and bad piece of work.[1]

In 1637, he published at Lissa a treatise on school organization, the title of which amplifies still further the meta-
phorical names of his school books: *De Sermonis Latini
Studio, per Vestibulum, Januam, Palatium et Thesaurus
Latinitatis, quadripartito gradu plene absolvendo, Didactica
Dissertatio*. It proposed a six-year course for a secondary
school: the first half year to be spent on the *Vestibulum,*
the next year on the *Janua,* a year and a half on the
Palatium, and three years on the *Thesaurus*. The *Palatium*
and *Thesaurus* were yet to be written.[2] The *Palatium* was
to be divided into four parts: 'Palace of Letters,' a hundred
letters based on the *Janua;* 'Palace of History,' dialogues
containing facts mentioned in the *Janua;* 'Palace of Oratory' and 'Palace of Poetry,' repeating the same material
of the *Janua* in speeches and verses. The *Thesaurus* was to
be a collection of excerpts from the classic authors, which
would again cover the subjects discussed in the *Janua.*
The general scheme is clearly derived from the practice of
Jesuit schools, with the modification of a rather terrifying
insistence upon the *Janua* for the whole six years, based
upon the assumption (which some of his recent eulogists
have amusingly accepted without critical question) that
the *Janua* really introduces 'sense-realism' into the schools,
and entirely revolutionizes school procedure.

The Great Didactic. Unquestionably the most important
work of Comenius in the theory of education is a small
treatise[3] which he wrote in Czech between 1628 and 1632,

---

[1] See Keatinge, *op. cit.,* Vol. 1, p. 67.
[2] Apparently they never were written.
[3] In the curious hodge-podge, *Opera Didactica Omnia,* which
Comenius published at Amsterdam in 1657, the *Didactica Magna*
takes up only fifty-eight pages out of some 2,200 folio columns. In
Keatinge's translation, it forms a small octavo book of some 275
pages. At that, it is verbose and filled with repetitions.

and later translated into Latin, with the title: *Didactica Magna: Universale Omnes Omnia Docendi Artificium Exhibens*. Its aim recalls that of Bacon, Descartes, and so many other 'reformers'; it was to furnish "a *method, at once easy and sure . . .* by which the Youth of both Sexes, none being excepted, shall Quickly, Pleasantly, and Thoroughly become learned in the Sciences, pure in Morals, trained to Piety, and in this manner instructed in all things necessary for both the present and the future life."[1] Adamson reminds us that the belief that such a method was discoverable "proved to be a will o' the wisp for thinkers on education from Comenius's time onwards."[2] Comenius offers, as his contribution to this infallible method, some very sensible suggestions: as, that elementary schools should be open to all children,[3] that school premises should be pleasant places,[4] that the school should concern itself less with words than with things,[5] that pupils should understand before they commit to memory,[6] that later studies should be based upon earlier,[7] that the teacher should link each new subject with an old one,[8] that punishment should

[1] From the title page. See Keatinge, *op. cit.*, p. 3. An autobiographic note, in *Opera Didactica Omnia*, tom. i, col. 442, says that the reading of Ratke, Campanella, and Verulam, "glorious restorers of philosophy" showed him certain "defects and gaps" in their work, and urged him to perfect their beginnings. As a result, by bringing the whole matter in line with the fixed laws of nature, he produced *The Great Didactic*, "which sets forth a method for readily and thoroughly teaching everything to everybody."

[2] J. W. Adamson, *Pioneers of Modern Education*, Cambridge, 1921, p. 53.

[3] *Didactica Magna*, cap. 9; Keatinge, *op. cit.*, pp. 66-69.

[4] *Idem*, cap. 17, 17; Keatinge, p. 131.

[5] *Idem*, cap. 29, 5; Keatinge, p. 267: "What I have in view is an education in the objects that surround us." See also cap. 17, 41; Keatinge, p. 139: "As far as is possible, instruction should be given through the senses, that it may be retained in the memory with less effort."

[6] *Idem*, cap. 19, 45; Keatinge, pp. 177-78.

[7] *Idem*, cap. 18, 32; Keatinge, p. 151.

[8] *Idem*, cap. 19, 20; Keatinge, p. 167. This is suggested chiefly as a means by which the teacher may stimulate attention. It is not at all premature Herbartism.

be for moral offenses, not for intellectual defects.[1] All these are excellent, reminiscent of Vittorino da Feltre and his 'Pleasant House,' of Vives abundantly, of John Brinsley's *Ludus Literarius,*[2] even of the mysterious Ratke. Though he mingled with these suggestions a great deal of nonsense,[3] and suffused all the good things that he borrowed, or that he learned from his own experience, with his fantastic and unreasoned expectations,[4] Comenius assembled in this one treatise the most practical and most thorough details of schoolroom procedure which had up to that time been written. It is a pity, first, that his treatise should have been buried away in the ill-edited mass of the *Opera Didactica Omnia,* and second, that it should be so persistently vitiated by his pansophic dreams.

Pansophia. All his work on school books, on details of

---

[1] *Didactica Magna,* cap. 26, 4; Keatinge, p. 250.

[2] Published in 1612, the same year as Ratke's *Memorial.* For a summary account of it, see J. W. Adamson, *Pioneers of Modern Education,* pp. 20-31.

[3] Such, for instance, is his notion of teaching as a mechanical process. In *The Great Didactic,* cap. 19, 16 (Keatinge, p. 164), he says: "I maintain that it is not only possible for one teacher to teach several hundred scholars at once, but that it is also essential." And he proceeds to give some rather fantastic reasons for his statement, concluding thus: "In short, as a baker makes a large quantity of bread by a single kneading of the dough and a single heating of the oven, as a brick-maker burns many bricks at one time, as a printer prints hundreds of thousands of books from the same set of type, so should a teacher be able to teach a very large number of pupils at once and without the slightest inconvenience." Such also is his constant use of analogy as proof. Some instances of that may be found all through cap. 16, and in cap. 19, 41, 44, *op. cit.* Such are his patent self-contraditions; as for instance, in cap. 16, 18 and cap. 17, 23, *op. cit.;* in the first passage he insists upon giving "examples before rules," in the second he grows indignant over the mistake of "not starting with the fundamental principles . . . from which an unlimited number of results can be deduced."

[4] In six years, from 12 to 18, "the pupils should learn four languages and acquire an encyclopaedic knowledge of the arts" (*op. cit.,* cap. 30, 1; Keatinge, p. 274). But much more than any mere overburdening of the curriculum was his defect of expecting the impossible from the school. Thus, in cap. 9 (Keatinge, p. 69), he states baldly that great heresy, that the school can bring about a paradise on earth.

school organization, on method in teaching, which in reality
was his best work, was a minor affair to Comenius.   His
enthusiasm, which grew with his years, was for a vague,
vast scheme of co-ordination of all human knowledge.   It
was to be the realization of Bacon's dream of a 'Solomon's
House'; indeed, it was to be much more, since it was to
include the metaphysical nature of things as well as the
positive scientific knowledge of phenomena.[1]   The first
treatise in explanation and furtherance of the scheme seems
to be the *Conatuum Comenianorum Praeludia* which Hartlib, that likable but unbalanced enthusiast, caused to be
published at Oxford in 1637.   It was followed by an answer
to critics in 1639, *Conatuum Pansophicorum Dilucidatio,* by
the *Via Lucis: Hoc est, Rationabilis disquisitio, quomodo
Intellectualis animorum Lux, Sapientia, tandem sub Mundi
vesperam per omnes mentes et gentes feliciter spargi possit,*
which was written in 1641, though not published until 1688,
by the *Pansophiae Delineatio* in 1645, and by a number of
others.   In these treatises Comenius was very dogmatic.
He condemned the hypotheses of Copernicus, and Gilbert
de Magnete.[2]   Had he been a Roman cardinal, the modern
world would never cease to laugh at him.   He based his
demand for accuracy in scientific observations upon the
authority of Scripture.[3]   He laid down an exact procedure
for the mastery of universal knowledge, reduced to eighteen
aphorisms.   These are vaguely neo-Platonic: God, nature,
and art are the sources of all knowledge obtainable by men;
all things exist according to their 'ideas'; art gets its
'ideas' from nature, nature from God, God from Himself;

[1] That seems to be the sense of his claim to a wider scope than
Bacon's and his inclusion within his field of "rerum universitas," in
Opera Didactica Omnia, tom. i, col. 432.   But his scheme also included theology, as is evident from his adverse criticism of Peter
Laurenberg's *Pansophia,* in *ibid.,* col. 458.
[2] *Pansophiae Dogmaticae* . . . *Delineatio,* sec. 26.
[3] Cf. *Pansophiae Delineatio,* sec. 40, quoting Wisd. 2:20.

by induction we can abstract these 'ideas' of things from phenomena; if we know the fundamental 'ideas' and the modes of their differentiation, we shall know all things. On this foundation, *Pansophia* was to be built as a sort of encyclopedia inspired by piety and leading to union with God. All his writings were in one way or another linked up with this pansophic scheme. The school which he got Rakoczy to establish for him at Saros-Patak was to be a pansophic school. Even the early *Physicae ad lumen divinum reformatae synopsis,* written about 1633, was conceived in this spirit. Religious sentiment, deeply earnest Christian aspirations, struggled to link up 'science' with the vision of the world beyond this world which is hinted at by faith. His 'prophets' were seized upon by him as possibly divine aids to his pansophic projects. He tried, now from one angle, now from another, to envisage a working scheme by which he might make easily accessible to all men this transforming universal knowledge.

His influence. The Latin collection of Comenius's educational writings was the only likely means of spreading his theories, since his writings in Czech would be unknown outside of a very small corner of Europe. For various reasons, not least of which was the discredit brought upon Comenius by his 'prophets,' the great folio of 1657 seems to have made little impression upon the world of education. It was really quite forgotten, although Comenius's school books were in wide use, until von Raumer called attention to it in his *Geschichte der Paedagogik,* nearly two hundred years after it had been published. But within his lifetime Comenius wielded a very great influence throughout the Protestant countries of Europe, and beyond a doubt did much to perpetuate that tradition of sanguine reliance upon the school as an infallible instrument of social and religious reform which has always marked the Protestant culture. In that indirect way, his influence persists strongly to this day in all the lands where the Protestant culture is dominant. Unfortunately, those who passed on his optimistic hopes in the school failed for generations to carry out the excellent details of organization and method which he offered them as a means toward realizing his hopes.

The Gentlemen of Port-Royal (1637-1661). A group of men, high-principled, severe, some of them exceptionally gifted, withdrew in 1637 to the abandoned monastery of Port-Royal-des-Champs, near Versailles, for solitude and study, under the leadership of Jean Duvergier de Hauranne (1581-1643), better known as the Abbé of St. Cyran. They took no vows, but they formed a sort of religious community. They were ultra-rigorists, profoundly affected by the pessimistic teachings of Cornelis Jansen, Bishop of Ypres, and became the chief promoters of Jansenism throughout France. The Jesuits, as defenders of orthodoxy, vigorously opposed them, and caused the ecclesiastical and civil authorities to suppress them, when they had been in corporate existence only twenty-four years. The Port-Royalists, in turn, attacked the Jesuits, at times brilliantly, as in the famous *Provincial Letters* of Pascal. In this tense emotional atmosphere sprang up the 'little schools' of Port-Royal, to flourish for a scant fifteen years, to teach only a handful of children (amongst whom was Racine), yet to win for themselves a secure place in the history of education.

The aims of the Port-Royalists were in general Catholic, yet more than a little colored by the Jansenist notions they held of the total depravity of human nature. Although they wrote sincerely of their love for children, in actual fact they dealt with their pupils in an inhuman spirit of repression and mistrust. They did not punish; they restrained. They were moved by a theological pity; but they shrank fiercely from affection. St. Cyran extended the same mistrust to the general acquisition of knowledge, and feared that for many it might stand in the way of salvation. He is reported to have said: "Sometimes out of a hundred children not one should be allowed to study." That principle had much to do with his determination to keep his schools 'little,' although the schools were not really begun until three years after his death. They were usually limited to twenty or twenty-five boys in each, who entered at the age of nine and stayed six or seven years. There was one master for each five or six boys, who remained in constant watchfulness over them day and night. The pupils were brought up as little ascetics, drilled in formal *clichés* of behavior. Rewards for good work in the schools, or the spur of competition amongst their pupils, the Port-Royalists condemned as Jesuit trucklings to depraved impulses, and substituted instead the higher ethical motive of duty: with the result, as they themselves admitted, that their pupils were often indifferent and listless.

In further revolt against the teaching methods in Jesuit schools, the Port-Royalists laid their chief emphasis, not upon Latin, but upon French literature. In this they were following the French Oratorians (founded by Cardinal de Bérulle in 1611), who, especially in their excellent college of Juilly, which was established in 1638, offered a much wider curriculum than that of the Jesuits, and insisted upon a thorough grounding in French language and history, in mathematics and the natural sciences. As a minor point in this connection, the Port-Royalists invented a phonic method of spelling, as better suited to the French language than the alphabetical method based upon Greek and Latin.[1] But, although the 'little schools' were closed after fifteen years, and the Oratorians continued teaching for a hundred and thirty years longer, even taking over the Jesuit schools when the Jesuits were expelled from France in 1764, some

[1] Cf. the *Grammaire Générale et Raisonée* of Arnauld and Lancelot, chap. 6.

twenty-seven years before the Oratorians themselves were destroyed in the Revolution, it is a fact that the Port-Royalists effected more toward directing school education to the study of the French language and literature than did the Oratorians. There are two reasons for that fact: first, the Port-Royalists won prestige from their quarrel with the Jesuits; and second, they spread their influence, even after they were suppressed, through the clever writings of such men as Antoine Arnauld (1612-1694), Nicole (1625-1695), Lancelot (1615-1695), Coustel (1621-1704), Rollin (1661-1741), and the great Racine (1639-1699). The change in content from Latin to French was bound to come, once the French literature had developed as it had done; but the Port-Royalists gave the most vigorous impetus to the change.

Fénelon (1651-1715). François de Salignac de la Mothe-Fénelon was a younger son of a family that had more titles of nobility than money. Following a common practice in such cases, he was destined for the clerical life, and was ordained priest when he was twenty-four. He did some missionary work amongst the Huguenots. When he was thirty-six, he wrote for the Duchesse de Beauvilliers his *Traité de l'Éducation des Filles.* Two years later, her husband became governor of the grandchildren of Louis XIV, and had Fénelon appointed tutor to the eldest, the Duke of Burgundy. Fénelon had remarkable success in educating the rather vicious boy into an excellent character. He held his post as tutor for eight years (1689-1697), although in 1695, when he was forty-four years old, he was made Archbishop of Cambrai. During his years as tutor he wrote for his young charge his *Fables, Dialogues des Morts, Aventures de Télémaque,* delightful in their sprightliness, their irony, their charm of language, even though they are didactic in purpose and character.

Fénelon's *Treatise on the Education of Girls,* a compact

little book of thirteen short chapters, covers principles of elementary education in general, with special application to little girls. The first two chapters plead for greater attention to the education of girls. The third chapter is shrewd in its emphasis upon education during the period of infancy. The fourth faces the problem of protecting little children against their stupid elders.[1] Chapter V on the use of gradual and indirect instruction, is a study of child psychology not surpassed by any modern writer in so brief a compass.[2] Fénelon was far ahead of his time in urging the value of leading over driving, and in suggesting practical devices for applying the principle of interest as a motive in education.[3] The succeeding chapters (VI-XII) on the teaching of history and religion, on moral training, constantly embody that educational principle. The last chapter considers the needed qualities in the governess or tutor. Although all this is planned for the rich little girl who is to be educated at home, the principles he expounds are applicable to all children. Unfortunately, Fénelon's age was not at all ready to attempt the application on any large scale.

[1] This chapter alone, contained on a single octavo page, would justify Emile Faguet's comparison between Fénelon and Rousseau. (Cf. the edition Lutetia *De l'Éducation des Filles,* n. d., pp. viii, 32.) Rousseau would have children removed from the example furnished by a vicious society; Fénelon, more practical, suggests definite ways in which they may be armed against the inevitable.

[2] *Op. cit.,* pp. 33-54. It is not theorizing; it is concrete analysis, evidently based upon careful observation of children; most sound and convincing.

[3] It might come as a shock to many who think that our age has invented educational psychology to read this summary sentence written by a seventeenth-century French priest: "Souvent . . . pour exécuter ce projet d'education . . . il n'est question que de ne presser point les enfants, d'être assidu auprès d'eux, de les observer, de leur inspirer de la confiance, de répondre nettement et de bon sens a leurs petites questions, de laisser agir leur naturel pour le mieux connaître, et de les redresser avec patience, lorsqu'ils se trompent ou font quelque faute." (*De l'Éducation des Filles,* edition Lutetia, p. 121.)

Francke (1663-1727). August Hermann Francke, a Lutheran minister, was the most influential of the seventeenth-century theorists in the Germanies. He was a sincerely religious man, and of admirable gifts both as teacher and as organizer. Quite early in his career, he encountered much opposition from the conservative Lutheran theologians and ministers because of his unorthodox views on the Scriptures. In 1687, when he was twenty-four years old, he became a follower of Spener, the founder of Pietism.[1] Frederick Hohenzollern, the Elector of Brandenburg, who was to become in 1700 the first king of Prussia, invited Francke in 1691 to teach in the Ritterakademie[2] at Halle.

[1] Pietism, the real roots of which go much further back than to Philip Jacob Spener (1625-1705), was a development in Lutheranism not unlike that of Methodism in the Anglican Church. It emphasized works rather than doctrines. It was more than a little puritanical and Jansenist, accepting the latter's view of the total depravity of human nature. It developed other fanatical extremes. Under the leadership of Spener, Christian Thomasius (1655-1728; the first man to give theological lectures in German at a university), and Francke, it unintentionally broke down the weak intellectual coherence of Lutheran theology, and thus prepared the way for the later entry of rationalism. The first strong signs of the latter appeared in the teachings of Christian Wolff (1679-1754), who, as a professor of mathematics from 1706 to 1723, was driven out of Halle by the orthodox group. He was restored to a chair of philosophy at Halle in 1740 by Frederick the Great. When rationalism reached its full growth, in 1752, in the lectures of Johann Salomo Semler, the Pietists of Halle were as powerless as the other Lutherans to withstand it. It promptly spread through other German universities. See A. Ritschl, *Geschichte des Pietismus in der Lutheranischen Kirche des 17 and 18 Jahrhunderts,* Bonn, 1880-1886; A. Tholuck, *Geschichte de Rationalismus,* Berlin, 1865.

[2] Social distinction in types of schools, and particularly the notion of a distinctive education for the ruling classes, is probably as old as any idea in organized education. It is seen in the 'palace school' of Charlemagne. It is reflected in the *Polycraticus* of John of Salisbury, and the *De Regimine Principum* of St. Thomas Aquinas. The age of chivalry is marked by a special education for future knights and nobles. The Renaissance broadened somewhat the concept of that knightly education, although it gave it a pagan expression in Baldassare Castiglione's famous dialogues called *Il Cortegiano,* first published in 1528, and translated into English by Sir Thomas Hoby in 1561 (reprinted in the Tudor translations, London, 1900). The growing class of 'gentlemen' began to take up the tradition of a

Francke continued at Halle, in the university founded in 1694, until his death at the age of sixty-four. During those thirty-five years he was also pastor of the church of St. George at Glaucha, a suburb of Halle.

It was at Glaucha that he began his remarkable hierarchy of schools, which grew into the Francke Foundations, and have continued down to the present time. His first care and his first school were for the poor. In 1694, just after he had married, he began to teach poor children in his own house. Later he took in also children of burghers who could pay fees. He recruited part-time teachers from theological students in the university, and organized a normal school for them. He built an orphanage in 1695, which at his death housed 100 boys and 34 girls. He developed a Latin school in 1697. These rapidly multiplying ventures he financed in part by donations, but more largely by industrial and commercial enterprises which he managed very successfully. The story of his excellent administration is too long to be told here; but it deserves to be known and studied.[1]

special education in the seventeenth century, first in France, where the Oratorians established in 1638 the Academy of Juilly, and Richelieu, about the same time, the Academy of Tours. In less than ten years, there were twelve such academies in Paris alone. They taught young gentlemen, who had gotten their preliminary education from tutors at home, such things as riding, fencing, military arts, mathematics, some modern languages, courtly usages, and the like. The German courts, large and small, which at the time looked to France for social leadership, promptly imitated these French schools, called them *Ritterakademien*. They flourished in the Germanies until nearly the close of the eighteenth century. In spite of such writings as Sir Humphrey Gilbert's *Queen Elizabeth's Academy* (1572) and Milton's *Tractate of Education* (1644), and of many efforts to establish such types of schools in England, the courtly academy never thrived there. The Puritan academies, which did thrive in England, were of quite another sort.

[1] Much has been written in German about Francke; lives by Niemeyer (Halle, 1794), Guericke (Halle, 1827; English translation, 1837), G. Kramer (Halle, 1880-82), Hartmann (Stuttgart, 1897), and Otto (Halle, 1902). Karl Richter has collected Francke's pedagogical writings, *A. H. Francke, Schriften ueber Erziehung und Unterricht*,

In the field of educational theory, two ideas of Francke's greatly influenced German education. The first, an outgrowth of his Pietism, was the preponderance given to formal religious instruction, which each day occupied the four hours from 7 to 11 in the morning, only three hours, from 2 to 5 in the afternoon, being devoted to other subjects. When the lively enthusiasm of the early Pietists had died out and given way to a mechanical formalism, the many German schools modeled on Francke's Foundation became merely rather dull catechism classes, and continued as such throughout the eighteenth century.

Francke's second idea was an extreme utilitarianism. He aimed at pointing all school studies, beyond the strictly religious, almost exclusively to the business of gaining a livelihood. This too was in part a result of his Pietism, with its severely puritanical outlook, its scorn for the graces of life. But in part it was due to his generously assumed task of helping poor children, upon whom the necessity of immediate toil for a livelihood pressed so hard. Christopher Semler tried, in 1707, to carry out Francke's lead and organize a complete *Realschule;* but he failed. The first successful foundation was made in Berlin, in 1747, by Johann Julius Hecker (1707-1768), who had been under Francke's influence at Halle in 1726.[1]

Both of these tendencies were widely spread through Francke's normal school, which furnished many teachers to Prussia and other German states. But of the two the second was the more enduring.

Basedow (1723-1790). Johann Bernard Basedow was a

Leipzig, 1872; other collections by Kramer (Langensalza, 1885), and A. Stein, 1894. Knuth has a good history of the Foundations, *Die Francke'schen Stiftungen* (2d ed., Halle, 1903). A brief English account is given in Adamson, *Pioneers of Modern Education,* Cambridge, 1921, pp. 237-57.

[1] See F. Ranke, *J. J. Hecker, Gruender der Koenigliche Realschule,* Berlin, 1861; F. Paulsen, *Geschichte des Gelehrten Unterrichts,* Vol. 2, pp. 63 sqq.

hard-drinking, bad-tempered, lecherous boor, and more than a little a charlatan and impostor; but he had talents out of the ordinary. He was born in Hamburg, son of a wig-maker, and of a mother who died insane. Although he never made many friends, he did so impress some people by his ability and forcefulness that they secured for him opportunities of schooling and sent him to the University of Leipzig. All his life he was first to impress people, and then to disgust them. After an incomplete theological course at Leipzig, ending when he was twenty-four years old, he became tutor to the children of a nobleman in Holstein, named von Quaalen. His five years in that occupation seem to have been the most successful years of his life. In 1753, von Quaalen got him a place as teacher of ethics and literature in the academy at Soroe, Denmark. There he spent a troublous eight years, quarreling, drinking, writing attacks on Christian doctrines, preaching educational reforms based upon Comenius and Locke. After reading Rousseau's *Émile,* he centered his efforts chiefly upon education, as a means of spreading the gospel of rationalism and naturalism. That is his great distinction, that he was the first to attempt to translate Rousseau's fundamental theories into school practice.[1]

In 1768, when he was forty-five years old, Basedow published *An Address to Friends of Humanity and Men of Means, on Schools, Studies, and their Influence upon the Public Weal,* which proposed a school system separated from the Church, under control of the State, and asked for aid to the publication of a projected work which should

[1] Basedow followed chiefly the theories expressed in *Émile,* although he was not averse to the theories urged by Rousseau in Chapter 4 of the *Considérations sur le gouvernement de Pologne et sur sa reformation projetée,* which Rousseau published some ten years later than *Émile.* The fact that these later theories most amazingly contradict those of *Émile* caused no concern either to Rousseau or to his disciple.

reform elementary schools. In response, money poured in from all sides, including generous donations from the rulers of Austria, Russia, and a number of the German states. With this money he published, in 1774, and again in 1785, his *Elementarwerk,* in four volumes, with ninety-six illustrations by Chodowiecki. The work, a sort of children's encyclopedia, supposed to contain all needed instruction for children up to fifteen years of age, was an admitted imitation of the *Orbis Pictus* of Comenius, but discarded Comenius' Christian views and his foundations of instruction in language. It was very diffuse and wordy, enthusiastic, preachy, and imprudent. Book II contained frank sexual instruction for children. Book IV was a treatise in popular style, on 'natural religion.' The illustrations were no improvement upon those of the *Orbis Pictus*. But the book suited the temper of the times in the Germanies, and not merely was widely distributed and used, but inspired many imitators, so that, as Schlosser says, "Germany was soon deluged with a silly literature for children by men whose extreme views sought to turn grown up people into children."[1]

In 1774, Prince Leopold of Dessau founded a school in which Basedow might carry out his theories. This was the famous *Philanthropinum,* upon which so many schools were modeled in the Germanies, in France, and Switzerland. It was a boarding school for children of the well-to-do. All teaching was to have in it the spirit of play. The principle of interest was to be stressed. Appeal was constantly to be made to the senses. Latin and French were to be taught by conversation. Only 'natural religion' was to be inculcated. At the close of two years the school numbered thirteen pupils, two of whom were Basedow's own children. After two years more, Basedow's impossible character

[1] *History of the Eighteenth Century,* 8 vols., London, 1843-52, Vol. 2, p. 203.

forced his removal from the school. Joachim Heinrich Campe (1749-1818) conducted it for a time; within a few years it ceased to exist. Christian Gotthelf Salzmann (1744-1811), who had been a teacher in Basedow's *Philanthropinum*, began one of his own in 1784, at Schnepfenthal in Saxe-Gotha. His first pupil was Karl Ritter, who led the great reform in geography. Salzmann, a well-balanced man where Basedow was a violent fanatic, kept the improvements in method suggested by Basedow, and long antedated the reforms later urged by Pestalozzi, but avoided many of Basedow's extreme views. His school continued for more than a hundred years. Campe and Salzmann wrote voluminously in support of the reform idea in schools, and tried, not very successfully, to add an evangelical flavor to Basedow's naturalism. But the hundreds of petty writers who took up the reform imitated Basedow's pretentiousness and charlatanism rather than the improved class methods which he, in turn, had borrowed from Comenius. For the most part, the educational writings echoing the *Philanthropinum* are a sorry mess. It was a sentimental movement from which only two sharp, clear tendencies were to emerge: the first, toward a dominating utilitarianism in school education; the second, toward State control of schools.

Conclusion. This chapter and the two preceding chapters cover the same period in time: the sixteenth, seventeenth, and eighteenth centuries. The first of the three chapters discussed school education in those three centuries; the second roughly outlined the larger educational agencies outside the schools; and the third offered a brief account of the more outstanding educational theories developed during the same three centuries. The theories sprang from the past experience of the society in which they were developed, and pointed the way to future educational efforts. They are, therefore, links binding together the past and the future. They reveal historical changes, and they prophesy.

Even in so summary an account as is offered in the present chapter, one must see how the development of educational theories illustrates the great separation between Christian and pagan education, begun in the Renaissance, and only momentarily halted by the Religious Revolution. The Catholic theorists, and some of the Protestant theorists, kept to the ancient Christian aims. The pagan theorists fixed their aims more exclusively upon this earth, and prepared the way for a State system of education which was to ignore Christian ideals pretty thoroughly. There was throughout those same centuries a gradual development and improvement in school methods, to which both Christian and pagan theorists contributed. Vives, Comenius, Fénelon, and de la Salle helped at least as much toward that improvement as did Bacon, Montaigne, Rousseau, and Basedow. Changing conditions in society compelled both types of theorists to make new adaptations of school efforts, to experiment with new schemes of organization and curriculum, to work out new techniques in the classroom. But the underlying differences in aims affected even those details of method, tending to make the Christian theorists careful and conservative, and the pagan theorists irritable, vacillating, and somewhat reckless. That contrast in temper is profoundly significant, just because it came from a difference in educational aims; for aims always give life and meaning to methods.

As for the prophetic element inherent in those educational theories, the surest prophecy was that of continued war between the two diverging aims in education. For various reasons, with which educational theories often had very little to do, the State came to assert more and more control over schools; and as the forces of the State became increasingly pagan in character, the influence of pagan theorists upon actual schools was inevitably to grow. The State, under that influence, was also to lend itself more and more to the fevered search for the complete and perfect *method* in schools; but the value of even improved methods was often to be lost through vague, uncertain, and sometimes quite wrong, *aims* in the schools. The nineteenth and twentieth centuries were to see the followers of Montaigne, Bacon, and Rousseau armed with great official power in school education, and flaunting that power as a proof of educational superiority in the face of Christian schools shorn of political encouragement and often even forced to struggle heroically for existence. The story of that contrast is matter for succeeding chapters.

TOPICS FOR DISCUSSION

1. The educational writings of Cardinal Jacopo Sadoleto.
2. The *Ludus Literarius* of John Brinsley.
3. Jesuit borrowings from Vives.
4. Comparison between Rousseau's theories of education as outlined in *Émile* and in *Considérations sur le Gouvernement de Pologne*, Chapter 4.
5. How far educational theories influenced the suppression of Jesuit schools.
6. The influence of eighteenth-century 'enlightenment' on educational theories.
7. The development of some of the popular forms used in spreading educational theories; e. g., novels, plays, pamphlets, periodical articles.
8. The effects of nationalism on educational theories.
9. Educational theories in relation to the growing 'middle classes' in society.

BIBLIOGRAPHIC NOTE

It need scarcely be necessary to remind the reader that the published material dealing with even the limited range of theories touched upon in this chapter is very large. For the works of Erasmus, the references given in the text and notes may suffice. Perhaps the best edition of *Oeuvres de François Rabelais* is that by P. d'Espezel, 4 vols., Paris, 1930; there are many editions of the standard Urquhart-Le Motteux translation of *Gargantua* and *Pantagruel*, of which one of the best is that by A. J. Nock and C. R. Wilson, 2 vols.,

New York, 1930. For the man himself, a scholarly work, inclined to deal severely with its subject, is J. Plattard (English translation by L. P. Roche), *The Life of François Rabelais,* New York, 1931. There is a great wealth of material published by the Société Rabelaisienne, including E. Gilson's *Rabelais Franciscain.* Montaigne's *Essais* have been well edited by J. V. Leclerc, Paris, 1837, of which edition Garnier, Paris, published a cheap issue in 1925. The English translation by Charles Cotton, has been edited by W. C. Hazlitt several times; e. g., 5 vols., New York, 1923.

The standard edition of Francis Bacon's *Works* is that of Spedding, Ellis, and Heath, London, 1857, of which the best American reprint is Houghton, Mifflin's in 15 volumes. The Oxford Press between 1876 and 1915 issued several partial editions and translations. The *Novum Organum* and *Advance of Learning* have been conveniently published in English versions in Everyman's Library. Descartes' *Oeuvres* have also been frequently edited; recent popular editions are those of the Lutetia Classics, Paris, and Nelson, London. Everyman's Library contains an English translation of the *Discourse on Method* and *Meditations,* New York, 1912. For a compact view of his underlying philosophy, see M. J. Mahoney, *Cartesianism,* Fordham University, 1925.

The *Works* of John Locke are easily available, in many editions. One of the basic editions is the quarto, 4 vols., by Bishop Law, London, 1777. J. W. Adamson has edited *John Locke's Educational Writings,* London, 1912. A standard life is H. R. F. Browne, *Life of John Locke,* 2 vols., London and New York, 1876. There are good editions of Rousseau in the Lutetia Classics; *Émile* in 2 vols.; an English translation by B. Foxley, New York, 1911. In addition to the references given in the notes, see also W. Boyd, *The Educational Theory of J. J. Rousseau,* London, 1911, and the laudatory *Rousseau* by H. Davidson, New York, 1898.

J. Morley, *Voltaire,* London, 1886, is a sound work; it and E. J. Lowell, *The Eve of the French Revolution,* Boston, 1892, discuss the 'naturalist' movement; but better than either is D. Mornet, *La Pensée Française au XVIIIe Siècle,* Paris, 1926 (English translation by L. M. Levin, New York, 1929). G. Hibben, *The Philosophy of the Enlightenment,* New York, 1910, gives an outline of the chief theories; but his Chapter 10, "Practical Influences" is still theoretical, confined to the spread of theories through writers, not through educational practice.

E. T. Campagnac has ably edited *Mulcaster's Elementarie,* Oxford, 1926, and *Brinsley's Ludus Literarius,* Liverpool, 1917. Mulcaster's *Positions* edited by R. H. Quick, has been published by Bardeen, Syracuse, New York, n. d. In addition, see F. Watson, *Mulcaster and Ascham,* London, 1893, and *Richard Mulcaster and his Elementarie,* New York, 1899; H. Barnard, *English Pedagogy,* Hartford, 1876; and H. Mark, *Educational Theories in England,* London, 1899.

For Comenius, in addition to the references given in the notes, see J. Kvačsala, *J. A. Comenius, sein Leben und seine Schriften,* Vienna, 1892; W. S. Monroe, *Comenius and the Beginnings of Educational Reform,* New York, 1900; and the reprint of the 1728 English Latin edition of *Orbis Pictus,* by Bardeen, Syracuse, 1887.

On the Port-Royal schools, see G. Carré, *Les Pédagogues de Port-Royal,* Paris, 1887; H. C. Barnard, *The Little Schools of Port-Royal,* Cambridge, 1922. F. Cadet, *L'Éducation a Port-Royal,* Paris, 1887 (English translation by A. H. Jones, London, 1898), gives extracts from Port-Royal writers (pp. 69-248) and castigates the Jesuits. Another work by G. Carré, *L'Enseignement Secondaire a Troyes du Moyen Age a la Révolution,* Paris, 1888, includes a discussion of the general educational scheme of the French Oratorians. This should be supplemented by C. Hamel, *Histoire de l'Abbaye et du Collège de Juilly,* Paris, 1901. There is a good summary account of earlier educational theories in J. Guibert, *Histoire de S. Jean-Baptiste de la Salle,* Paris, 1901. K. Lupton has translated *Fenelon's Education of Girls,* Boston, 1891.

The best study of Ratke is Krause's; but see also I. C. G. Schumann, *Die aechte Methode W. Ratke's,* Hanover, 1876. For Francke, see K. Richter, *A. H. Francke, Schriften ueber Erziehung und Unterricht,* Leipzig, 1872; for Basedow, Th. Fritzsch and H. Gilow, *Elementarwerk: kritische Ausgabe,* 2 vols., Berlin, 1909, and O. H. Lang, *Basedow, His Life and Work,* New York, 1891. A. Pinloche, *La Réforme de l'Education en Allemagne au 18eme Siecle,* Paris, 1889, offers a brief account of a number of theorists. W. L. Gage, *The Life of Karl Ritter,* New York, 1867, sketches the general educational background of the period.

Sadoleto's *Opera Omnia* were published in a good edition, 4 vols., Verona, 1737-38. The *De Pueris Recte Instituendis* was translated into English, with an introduction by E. T. Campagnac and K. Forbes, as *Sadoleto on Education,* Oxford, 1916. See also A. Joly, *Étude sur J. Sadolet,* Caen, 1856, and L. Gerini, *Scrittori Pedagogici del Secolo XVI,* Turin, 1891.

As regards the effect of nationalism on educational theories, J. W. Adamson, *English Education, 1789-1902,* Cambridge, 1930, is excellent; E. H. Reisner, *Nationalism and Education since 1789,* New York, 1922, and *Historical Foundations of Modern Education,* New York, 1927, offers a compact summary of facts, but no authorities, and shows some Protestant bias.

CHAPTER XVII

Administrative Evolution in Education

Education as right and duty. As soon as we begin to think of the administrative side of education, the question of authority comes up: who has the right and the duty to direct education? It is a thorny question. Unless we answer it clearly, we shall be in hopeless confusion in dealing with the historical facts of the development of education. Yet the important truths upon which that answer must be based are so obvious that they need only plain expression in order to be recognized as truths. In the first rank of these truths is this: each normal human being has both the right and the duty to educate himself; he has that right and duty just because he is a rational being, capable of self-development, needing education to become what he can become; he has that right and duty, therefore, from God, the author of man's nature. But it is the mark of each man's imperfection that he must share that right and duty of education with three other moral persons: his family; the civil society of which he is a member; and the religious society which, in the providence of God, claims his allegiance. He must share that right and duty with his family, and specifically with his parents, first of all, on the ground of his sheer physical necessity; because of his long infancy, and because of the assistance he must have during his physical and mental immaturity. Then the State, because of its essential purpose, which is to secure the temporal well-being of its citizens, has authority from God to see to it that individual and family carry out their duties in the important affair of education. Finally, the Church, because it is divinely commissioned to pass on to individuals the revealed truths committed to its charge, to administer the means of grace, and to shepherd its members in the conduct of life leading to eternal happiness, has a two fold right and duty in the education of each member of the Church: the first, which it has in common with the State, is to urge the individual and his family to fulfill the duty of education; the second, which is exclusively its own, is to direct and guide the religious education of the individual.

The authority of parents in education diminishes with the increasing maturity of the child; but so long as it lasts, it is prior to the authority of the State. The authority of the State and the Church endure as long as the individual is a member of civil and religious society. How all these rights and duties are to be given effect, how the shifting borderlines of authority in education are to be adjusted, constitute one of the major problems of humanity, a problem that in the whole history of mankind has never been solved adequately and to the satisfaction of all concerned. The reason for this is not far to seek; it lies in the very limited intelligence and virtue of all the human beings who try to exercise those rights and perform those duties. If education is left too much to the control of the individual and his family, it is most often neglected, through laziness, short-sighted selfishness, mere incompetence. If State and Church interfere too far with the individual and his family, there is enervating paternalism, bad coercion, even tyranny. There is also the endless difficulty of proper co-ordination between the two complete and autonomous societies, Church and State, having different aims, yet a considerable common field of activity.

In the earlier civilizations. In the earlier civilizations, State and Church interfered very little, as a general rule, with the business of education. Those Greek city-states, of which Sparta in a leading fashion stamps the type, were an exception to the rule; since in them the State dominated education pretty thoroughly, and determined the aim, manner, and even the details of the education to be given to each individual. But the rule held good amongst the Hebrews. Although the Hebrew State was a theocracy, it contented itself with a moral insistence upon the duty of parents to educate their children. Only when the theocracy had ceased to exist, and within a few years of the final destroyal of the nation itself, was compulsion in education attempted. The type of city-state represented by Athens also insisted that parents must care for the education of their children, but left the extent and manner of that education largely to the parents' choice. Roman education was more completely a family concern than was education amongst the Greeks. In both Greek and Roman societies, religion, even when it entered strongly into the national life, was too vague a thing to be conceived of as a church. Hence there was for the Greeks and Romans no practical problem of adjustment of educational authority between Church and State.

In the early centuries of Christianity. The concept of a church is a Christian concept: a visible society functioning in this world for ends beyond this world, and using means toward its end which also originated beyond this world. Such a society instantly asserted its supreme authority over the education of its members. As those members, during the early age of the Christian Church, were largely recruited through the conversion of mature persons, the concern of the Church was more narrowly limited to the religious education of adults. That sort of education is, obviously, a distinctive right and duty of a religious society, belonging to it by its very nature and not affected by changes in time, in social organization, or in social conditions. In that particular field of education the Christian Church ignored the Roman Empire, as it has since ignored all succeeding States. It is a field in which the State, as such, has no business at all. Attempts on the part of any State to restrict or restrain the Christian Church in its work of religious education must be considered by the Church as persecutions, whether they occur under Nero, or a Bourbon king, or a modern republic.

After Christianity was politically recognized. From the time of Constantine, the Christian Church took its place in the Western world as a society marching abreast of the civil society, with its existence recognized, and at least tolerated, by the State. That fact brought two consequences: the enlargement of the field of education in which the Church was bound to exercise guidance, and inevitable relations with the State in the same field of education. The Church realized that religion affects the entire life of the individual, and therefore was concerned with his education at every stage of his life. Its ministries began with the baptism of the newly born infant, and ceased only with his final anointing in death. Its teachings were to shape belief and conduct from the very first moment at which belief and conduct came under the voluntary control of the individual member of the Church. That meant that schools had to be a part of the Christian program, almost as necessarily as churches were. But the State also was rightly interested in schools, since its concern in the education of the individual for temporal ends, as a citizen, extended just as surely and properly to the entire length of life of the individual as did the concern of the Church. The situation called for reasonable co-operation between Church and State. In theory, that co-operation is quite simple, since Church and State have ends which, although diverse, are not conflicting; each has merely to recognize where the essential purpose of the other begins and ends, and to respect those limits. In practice, that co-operation is enormously difficult: both because it is by no means always easy to see in detail where the borderlines of civil and religious activities actually are, and because Church and State are administered by men subject to tragic weaknesses, to ambition, to impatience and irritability, to blinding self-conceit, to all the various forms of stupidity which characterize fallen human nature.

And into the Dark Ages. Yet there were two facts which, for some five or six hundred years, kept the difficulties of co-operation between Church and State in the matter of education from obtruding themselves very seriously. The first fact was the extremely old tradition of noninterference, of leaving the details of education to the family. Both Church and State accepted that tradition; their acceptance kept them from clashing. The second fact was that, except for the great Arian heresy, which died out in the seventh century, there was no serious religious split amongst those who called themselves Christians. That meant that, from an administrative standpoint, the Church presented a stronger front to the possible aggressions of the State; there were no traitors in the camp to join forces with any hostile agency which might develop without. But unquestionably the Dark Ages became dark not merely because of civil insecurity resultant upon the break-up of the Roman Empire, but also because the tradition of leaving education almost solely to the initiative of the individual and his family had come to mean a great practical neglect of education by both.

Church and State in the Middle Ages. Even the bitterest enemies of the Catholic Church cannot deny that she kept alive the tiny sparks of knowledge which survived through the Dark Ages, and that she took the lead in the revival of learning, of civilization, and of religion which marked the change into the Middle Ages. As a result, education came into her hands in the Middle Ages almost without any challenge from the civil governments; and what co-operation there was between Church and State in education was effected decidedly under the leadership of the Church. But, as the Middle Ages progressed, two developments tended to make co-operation between Church and State increasingly difficult. One was the temporal sovereignty, not of the Church, but of the popes. The other was the sharpening of national divisions throughout Europe. The first brought on political quarrels between the pope, as temporal ruler, and other sovereigns, in which quarrels it was not at all easy for the papal opponents to distinguish between the pope and the Church. The growth of nationalism also occasioned certain modifications of educational procedure within the different States; and in guiding these modifications the State felt that it had a particular interest at stake and a special claim to exercise its authority in education. One side of the Renaissance movement, its paganizing side, tended to strengthen the State in its assertion of authority in education, not on the wholesome ground of the State's undoubted right in the matter, but simply out of hostility to Christian principles of conduct.

After the Religious Revolt. The Protestant Revolt of the sixteenth century found a situation at hand already filled with quarrels between Church and State. It intensified the quarrels, as between the Catholic Church and various States of Europe, by setting up the destructive thesis, *Cujus regio, ejus religio;* so that the many forms of Protestantism accepted subservience to the States in which they existed, in order to use the civil power as a weapon against the Catholic Church. In Protestant States, thenceforth, the tendency was for Church and State to work together in education, with the State as the master and the Church as the servant. In Catholic States the Church was to have a checkered career, at times of struggle with the State, at times of attempts at co-operation more or less successful. In the end, Catholic and Protestant States alike came to establish systems of schools, from the elementary to the university, which the State directly controlled, financed, and administered. The Church, Protestant or Catholic, could take its choice between coming into the State school system, as an auxiliary force, and paralleling the State schools with a system of its own.

Gradual entry of the State into education. The tendency of the civil authority to control schools is inherent, as has just been said, in the nature and purpose of the State. That tendency showed itself even in the Middle Ages, when the Catholic Church had for several centuries been almost the sole source of education in Europe. The manifestation began in a small way in the towns. The growing number of lay teachers made it increasingly possible for the burgher schools to function outside the direct control of the Church. Churchmen, but not the Church, opposed that extension of civil authority.[1] It was a good and proper extension, naturally bound to come when the civil authority was strong enough. In the larger, national way, the State also waited only until the differentiated nations were sufficiently organized to assert its authority in school education. It turned first to the universities, because of the strategic position of these in each nation. University charters, which first derived from ecclesiastical authority, soon came to get their chief force from civil authority.[2] The

---

[1] The distinction, always important, is particularly clear here, where the supreme authority of the Church repeatedly overruled the jealous actions of individual bishops and chapters. See *supra,* pp. 178-79.

[2] Up to the Protestant Revolt, the primary chartering authority was always the pope, as alone having the power to confer the *jus ubique docendi.* The State, except in the cases of Palencia, founded by Alfonso VIII in 1212, and Naples, founded by Frederick II in 1224, contented itself with issuing to the universities a secondary or confirming charter. Thus the charter granted to the University of Paris in 1200 by Philip Augustus actually released the students to ecclesiastical authority. Papal Bulls, on the other hand, legislate as if by direct right; even regulate details of economic administration, as in the Bull *Parens Scientiarum* of Gregory IX, in 1231. (Du Boulay,

fourteenth and fifteenth centuries saw civil governments interfering with grammar schools.[1] But not until the sixteenth century did the State begin to thrust itself into the management of elementary education: the field which was ultimately to become the most important of all in State systems of schools.[2] Even then, the development of State

Historia Universitatis Parisiensis, Paris, 1665-73, tom. iii, p. 106.) When the Emperor Charles IV founded the University of Prague, he asked a papal charter, which was granted by Clement VI on April 7, 1347. Only on September 14, 1349, did the emperor issue his own charter. But as time went on, kings and emperors were impelled to take measures regarding student discipline, as Queen Blanche did with disastrous results at Paris in 1228-29, or to regulate medical practitioners by examinations and licenses, as Roger II did at Salerno as early as 1137, or to tie the important teaching bodies to the crown, as Henry III did at Oxford in 1258, or to drag the universities into their disputes with the popes, as in the famous case of the English Statute of Provisors, wherein Edward II, in 1350, rejected the papal claim to appoint to benefices in England. These assertions of State authority were, of course, only gradually successful. Thus, when the English Parliament in 1421 revoked the old papal privileges of Oxford, and ordered that the university be subject to the common law of the land (9 Henry V, St. i, c. 8), its decree was quite simply ignored. (J. E. G. de Montmorency, *State Intervention in English Education,* Cambridge, 1902, pp. 73-74.) But the natural result of thousands of such acts of intervention in the conduct of the universities, by a State authority which was close at hand and growing in strength, was to bring the universities into closer dependence on the civil power.

[1]By way of illustration these instances may serve. In 1312, Richard Hall, a student at Canterbury, was excommunicated by the Archbishop for an offense to school authority, but was freed by a crown writ. (A. F. Leach, *Schools of Medieval England,* pp. 189-90.) Richard II, in 1392, used funds from suppressed alien priories to endow Charterhouse School. (Leach, *op. cit.,* p. 222.) Henry IV, in 1400, appointed the headmaster of Higham Ferrers School. (Leach, *op. cit.,* p. 254.) From that time onward, at least, a royal license was required for the founding of any grammar school. In 1496, the Scottish Parliament under James IV ordered "all barons and freeholders that are of substance" to put their eldest sons at school until they had mastered Latin. (de Montmorency, *op. cit.,* p. 112.) This is one of the earliest instances of compulsory education.

[2] As an English instance, the Chantry Act of 1546, under Edward VI, urged the chantry priests to conduct elementary schools, almost with the air of its being a new duty, instead of one which the chantry priests had carried out for centuries. The Act of 1548, which abolished the chantries, also abolished the chantry schools. The first distinctive elementary school which Foster Watson notes as begin-

control of schools was a slow affair. Between the opening of the Protestant Revolt in the Germanies and the first establishment of a definite State system of schools there was a period of about two hundred and fifty years. The first State school system came into existence in Austria, a country that was overwhelmingly Catholic in population; it dates only from the legislation of the Empress Maria Theresa in 1774. Prussia came second with its code of 1794, although its school system did not begin to be effectively organized until after 1807.[1] In reality, the development of State school systems had to wait upon the development of elementary schools by private agencies.

Some conditions affecting the spread of elementary schools. As has already been noted, the social turmoil in Europe following upon the Protestant Revolt for a time halted the development of all schools. But in that same sixteenth century certain profound social changes set in, which in time were to have a great, though indirect, effect upon furthering the spread of elementary schools. It would

ning to take the place of the chantry schools came into being only eighty years later. (*English Grammar Schools to 1660,* p. 154.)

[1] There were earlier attempts, but most of them never got beyond official decrees. Such were the attempts made in Württemberg in 1559, in Brunswick in 1570, in Saxony in 1580. The Duchy of Weimar decreed compulsory school education in 1619, to affect all children between the ages of six and twelve. The decree was a dead letter. (*Cyclopedia of Education,* Vol. 1, pp. 285-86.) It is true that Duke Ernst of Saxe-Gotha, the son of Ratke's old patroness, established, between 1642 and his death in 1675, an elementary school system, under the direction of Andreas Reyher, with Lutheran pastors as supervisors of the schools. School attendance was compulsory, between the ages of five and thirteen; parents were fined when their children did not attend school. The curriculum was fixed, the textbooks prescribed; it was all quite 'modern.' But the system embraced only twenty schools in a small duchy, some five hundred square miles in extent; and it promptly passed out of existence under Duke Ernst's sons and successors. (K. A. Schmid, *Geschichte der Erziehung,* Stuttgart, 1884-1902, Vol. 4, Pt. I, pp. 1-74.) Much has been made of the Massachusetts law of 1642, ordering selectmen to compel parents to instruct their children themselves or to send them to school; but not even two hundred and thirty years later was any such law enforced in Massachusetts. (*Cyclopedia of Education,* Vol. 1, pp. 287-88.)

be out of place here to attempt anything like a full discussion of those changes. Yet four of them stand out so prominently, as influencing the growth of elementary schools and leading to the establishment of State school systems, that they must be at least briefly considered.

The first was the multiplication of books. The exact relation between opportunity to read and desire to read is obscure. But, whichever comes first, their interrelation is undoubted. With printing, ready access to books became more and more common. After a while, even a poor man might buy a book.[1]

Yet more than the mere abundance of books was needed to stimulate large numbers of people to read. That stimulation came from various sources. Some of it, no doubt, came from the Protestant insistence upon the Bible as the sole depository of revealed truth. Some of it came from religious controversy, which promptly broke into print. But perhaps most of it came from the great increase in town life, in commerce, in manufacturing industries connected with commerce. These made written records more and more important as part of daily life, of the process of making a living. Wealth began to take a more fluid form, banking grew, commercial accounts multiplied; in a word, the apparatus for accumulating and guarding wealth called

---

[1] But the day of the poor man's book was many years removed from that of the *Biblia Pauperum*. Early printed books might cost from one-fourth to one-tenth as much as manuscript books; yet even that left their prices relatively high. Fust, in 1462, got fifty crowns a copy in Paris for his folio Bible. Trade restrictions and governmental licensing tended to keep the price of books high. In England, it was only as late as 1738 that the book trade was set free sufficiently to allow it to develop vigorously. The Germanies had always more liberty in publishing, and better facilities for distribution; hence books were cheaper there. But in every country, lowered cost of books had to wait upon increased demand for them. Cf. Mumby, *Romance of Bookselling. A History from the Earliest Times to the Twentieth Century*, London, 1910; and H. B. Wheatley, *Prices of Books; An enquiry into the changes in the price of books which has occurred in England at different periods*, London, 1898.

for a wider spread of literacy. All this constituted the second great social change, as a result of which the demand for elementary education grew.

A third change was the increasing complexity of life, especially in the growing urban centers. The range of knowledge was widening on one side, the physical. Curiosity was more widely aroused. The phenomenon of the newspapers was, it is true, still distant; but there was lively news in the sixteenth and seventeenth centuries, and plenty of popular eagerness to be in touch with it. Oral literature gave way to written literature, and that in the vernaculars: no longer simple and naïve, but elaborate, provocative, prodding ambitions, stirring passions, and raising questions.

And finally, social and political discontent grew enormously during those centuries. The middle classes were asserting themselves against the old feudal nobility; and later, as large numbers of the peasants came into the commercial and manufacturing centers and became an urban proletariat, they too grew restive under the oppressive condition of their lives. Political absolutism, in whatever form, was menaced by this widespread discontent. The masses of the people, in the uneasy view of governments, needed shepherding; and one way of shepherding them was through a State system of schools. It is not without significance that the first modern State schools were projected contemporaneously with the French Revolution, and that the amazingly rapid development of State school systems should come when the Western world was seething with social and political unrest.

The sort of private agencies which developed elementary schools. The slow work of development of elementary schools which preceded the establishment of State school systems was carried out in a curiously haphazard fashion, all the more strikingly casual when one considers how widespread and persistent was the social, religious, and economic pressure which stood back of those private efforts. Sometimes a single individual began the work of promoting an elementary school, as did von Rochow, and Robert Owen. Sometimes organized groups undertook the work, generally groups with a more or less clearly defined religious character. The motives urging those varied individuals and groups were also varied; but we may reasonably sum them up as, in the main, these three: (a) a genuinely altruistic desire, often based upon Christian teachings, to improve the physical, mental, and moral equipment of their individual fellow men; (b) a forward-looking concern for the social good, which was to be secured, they hoped, by the wider spread of school education; (c) a selfish need on the part of commercial and industrial magnates for employees who could read, write, figure accounts, and the like. In particular instances these motives often blended in such a way as to obscure our view of them at this distance of time.

The philanthropic agencies. The most unselfish and the most efficient agencies for the development of elementary schools were, beyond question, the Catholic teaching congregations: groups of men and women dedicated to the work of Christian education in a communal and celibate life. There were more than thirty of these religious congregations founded between the years 1525 and 1700, the total about equally divided between congregations of men and congregations of women.[1] Most of their teaching was done in elementary schools. They covered pretty widely all the European countries from which they were not excluded by sectarian State laws. They were very numerous. For instance, one congregation, that of the Sisters of Char-

---

[1] A partial list of these, with approximate dates of foundation, will be found in P. J. Marique, *History of Christian Education,* New York, 1926, Vol. 2, p. 128.

ity of St. Vincent de Paul, counted six thousand members in 1789.[1] The Visitation Order of nuns had 167 convents in 1792, most of which conducted schools.[2] The Christian Brothers had 920 members, and were teaching 36,000 pupils in their elementary schools, in 1790. They, like all the other Catholic congregations in France, were destroyed in the French Revolution. Yet by 1821 they had so well revived that their pupils again numbered 50,000.[3]

Next to the Catholic teaching orders, though reaching a much smaller number of children, came the various continental Protestant churches which conducted elementary schools. Of this sort were the schools of Comenius at Prerau and at Saros-Patak, of Francke, Hecker, Campe, Salzmann. Such were the Lutheran parish schools conducted, often in rather haphazard fashion, throughout northern continental Europe. One of the most efficient of the Protestant parish school organizations was that set up by the Dutch Reformed Church at the synod of Dort in 1618. But the Protestant parish schools had not the great help toward a supply of teachers, who were at least devoted, which the Catholic schools had in the religious congregations.

Both Catholic and Protestant elementary schools faced two great obstacles to their development: the dull, passive resistance of the people in general to school education, and the slow but steady decay of religious belief and practice throughout Europe in the eighteenth century.[4]

[1] *Catholic Encyclopedia,* 1st ed., Vol. 3, p. 605.
[2] *Ibid.,* Vol. 15, p. 481.
[3] *Catholic Encyclopedia,* 1st ed., Vol. 8, p. 57. For a good account of much Catholic effort toward elementary schools in the seventeenth and eighteenth centuries, see J. Guibert, *Histoire de S. Jean Baptiste de la Salle,* Paris, 1901.
[4] James Grant, *History of the Burgh and Parish Schools of Scotland,* Glasgow, 1876, pp. 27, 307-11, 314, indicates the rather remarkable contrast in Scotland between the eagerness of its people for schooling before the Religious Revolt and the long-persisting hostility they showed toward compulsory school laws after the Revolt.

In England.   Conditions were particularly bad in England, where the wretched industrial system degraded vast masses of the people to a level nearly approaching the bestial.   Here and there, an individual, touched by their great need, set up a 'charity school,' which might teach a score or two of children.[1]   Thomas Gouge, an Anglican clergyman in difficulties with his ecclesiastical superiors, got leave to attempt an evangelization of Wales in 1672, and formed with others in 1674 a Trust to set up schools and to distribute bibles and tracts.   A year later, he had 1,850 children in his schools.[2]   But the venture came to an end with the death of Gouge in 1681.   Another Anglican clergyman, Dr. Thomas Bray, founded in 1698 a more successful and more lasting organization, the Society for the Promotion of Christian Knowledge.   This made rapid growth.   By 1704, its schools contained about 2,000 chil-

This is a point sometimes missed by those who, justly, praise the excellent later influence of school education upon the Scottish people. In 1567, Calvinism, as introduced by John Knox, was established as the State religion.   In 1592, the State church was given by law complete control of education.   It must be said that the Church officials were eager to promote schools.   They got the Scottish Parliament in 1633 to impose a school tax "on every plough of land"; in 1639, and again in 1641, they petitioned Parliament to have the act enforced. But 'the nobility' objected (de Montmorency, *op. cit.*, pp. 118-19), just as they had objected to Knox's scheme for financing schools from the confiscated properties of the monasteries, and the people at large were apathetic about the whole business.   The real growth of popular interest in schools came in the eighteenth century, and was due to the religious devotedness of the parish schoolmasters, often men of university training themselves, who stirred the ambition of clever poor children, and even prepared such pupils for the universities. (John Strong, in *Cyclopedia of Education,* Vol. 5, p. 301.)   Those Scotch schoolmasters were admirable exceptions to the general run of lay teachers.   Their zeal and industry brought about a thin but wide diffusion of learning, for which some moderns praise the Scottish people, but of which Dr. Johnson said in 1775, "Their learning is like bread in a besieged town: every man gets a little, but no man gets a full meal."   (Boswell's *Life,* ed. of 1824, London, Vol. 2, p. 339.)

[1] See some instances in Adamson, *Pioneers of Modern Education,* pp. 202-03.

[2] See article in *Dictionary of National Biography,* Vol. 8, pp. 269-71.

dren,[1] and in 1729 it reported 1,658 schools with 34,000 children.[2] After 1740, interest in the work fell off greatly. In the meantime, when the National Society for Promoting the Education of the Poor was founded in 1811, the S. P. C. K. turned its schools over to the new educational body. The National Society had 52 schools in 1812, with 8,620 pupils. The following year it had 230 schools, with 40,484 pupils.[3]

Back of these attempts in elementary education by large organizations lay the efforts of many private individuals. Griffith Jones (1683-1761), an Anglican clergyman, in 1730 started a system of 'circulating schools' in Wales. At his death, thirty years later, 10,000 children were getting at least a few weeks each year in school. His work was largely supported by a Welsh woman, Mrs. Bevan, who died in 1779, and left her estate to the schools. But the will was held up in chancery for twenty-five years, and the schools

[1] John Strype's edition of John Stow's *Survey of the Cities of London and Westminster,* London, 1720, Bk. V, pp. 43-48.

The same year, 1704, marks a curious development. The tiny Isle of Man, in the Irish Sea, having a quasi-independent existence as a British crown colony, with an area of 220 square miles and a probable population of 4,000 or 5,000, passed a law making school attendance compulsory for children until they were able to "read English distinctly." The school fees were sixpence a quarter for those who learned reading only, ninepence for those who learned also to write. Parents were to be fined if children were not sent to school. De Montmorency (*op. cit.,* p. 104) thinks this law may have been inspired by the Puritan Act of 1649 (Commonwealth, act 31) which allotted £18,000 of the king's tithe rent to pay salaries of "preaching ministers and schoolmasters," and £2,000 for salaries of masters at both universities. The Isle of Man law continued in force, how effectively is not clear, until the general English system was followed in 1872, and was made compulsory in 1878. (*Cyclopedia of Education,* article by de Montmorency, Vol. 4, pp. 114-15.)

[2] De Montmorency, *op. cit.,* p. 202, note 3, questions the accuracy of these figures, and judges that they include a number of school foundations much older than the S. P. C. K. See also Adamson, *Short History of Education,* pp. 254-55.

[3] *Cyclopedia of Education,* Vol. 5, p. 206, says that the National Society schools in 1813 had only 12,000 children. Perhaps the larger figure includes the number of children in the S. P. C. K. schools.

died out.[1]   Andrew Bell (1753-1832), another Anglican clergyman, who had been a superintendent of an orphanage in Madras, India, developed a mechanical system of conducting classes in which he used some of the older children as 'monitors' to instruct the rest.   He published a pamphlet about it in 1797.[2]   His scheme seemed to offer a cheap solution to the problem of finding teachers for the schools. Joseph Lancaster (1778-1838) borrowed Bell's method, and opened a school in 1801.   Bell and Lancaster had rival followings which quarreled.   In 1808, Lancaster secured the royal patronage of George III, and the Royal Lancasterian Institution was founded.[3]   This, in turn, promptly fell into conflict with the National Society, and in 1814 changed its name to the British and Foreign School Society.   It was just vaguely Protestant in character, not closely linked with the Anglican Church, since Lancaster had a strong secularist leaning.   Thomas Stock, curate of the Anglican church of St. John the Baptist, Gloucester, with the aid of Robert Raikes, owner of the *Gloucester Journal,* opened in 1780 four schools in his city to give poor children some instruction on Sundays.   Raikes succeeded in spreading the idea, until in 1785 the 'Sunday Schools Union' was established.[4]   Robert Owen (1771-1858), a Welshman, became

---

[1] De Montmorency, *op. cit.,* pp. 203-04.

[2] *An Experiment in Education made at the Male Asylum of Madras, suggesting a System by which a School or Family may teach itself under the superintendence of the Master or Parent.*

[3] De Montmorency, *op. cit.,* pp. 206-07.   Adamson, *Short History of Education,* pp. 244-57.

[4] In Manchester, the Sunday schools engaged the children who attended them for five and a half hours on Sunday, and about two hours besides on two evenings of the week.   (De Montmorency, *op. cit.,* p. 205.)   Fifty years after the beginning of Sunday schools, Frederic Hill said of Birmingham, then a city of 120,000 population, "Sunday Schools have to this day been the principal means of diffusing education."   (*National Education, its present state and prospects,* 1836, p. 113.)   See A. Gregory, *Robert Raikes, Journalist and Philanthropist: a History of the Origin of Sunday Schools,* London, 1877.

in 1799 head of a company owning cotton mills at New Lanark, near Glasgow. He had about two thousand factory hands, including some five hundred children between four and eleven years of age, who went from the parish poorhouses as apprentices. Owen raised the entrance age for working children to ten years, and set up a free school for the children from five to ten years old, conducted on the Lancasterian system. He attracted much attention, became a national figure of reform, and was so extremely modern as to combine advocacy of legal prohibition of all liquor with public attacks upon Christianity. Between 1824 and 1828, he sank much of his fortune in a communist venture at New Harmony, Indiana, U. S. A. For the next thirty years he devoted himself to spreading socialist theories. A few years before his death he became a Spiritist. His school venture fell through when he went to develop communism in the United States.[1] But in reality none of these various schools was well conducted. Francis Place, testifying before the Select Committee on Education in 1835, said of the charity schools that "they taught children next to nothing, and nothing likely to be useful to them."[2] The plain fact is that the teachers in those schools were mostly untrained and incompetent, and that the monitorial method which made for cheapness made also for a terrible inefficiency.

In Prussia. Over in Prussia, another individual, Friedrich Eberhard Baron von Rochow (1734-1805), avoided the

---

[1] Frank Podmore, *Robert Owen, a Biography,* London, 1906. Owen wrote much. The most notable of his many works are: *A New View of Society,* 1816; *The Revolution in the Mind and Practice of the Human Race, or the Coming Change from Irrationality to Rationality,* 1849; *Address to Teachers of the Human Race in all Countries,* 1851; and the *Life of Robert Owen, Written by Himself,* 1857. Owen was a generous-souled man, caught in the long tradition of human perfectibility from Francis Bacon through Rousseau, a man who never realized the terrible truth involved in the Fall of Man.

[2] Quoted in de Montmorency, *op. cit.,* p. 203.

English mistake of cheap teaching in his efforts to help in the education of poor children living on his estates. He wrote pamphlets on the subject in 1772, 1773, and 1776. He opened schools with good teachers in 1773 and following years. His schools, containing in all several hundred children, were very practical. They taught morality, but not religion, the 'three R's,' 'useful knowledge,' all in German. Rochow's book, *The Improvement of the National Character by Means of Popular Schools,* published in 1779, created opposition from the Lutheran clergy, but made wide appeal to the growing spirit of nationalism.[1] His work linked up with that of Basedow, Campe, and Salzmann.

In France and Spain. There were two lines of endeavor affecting elementary education in France and Spain: one, practical, working through actual schools, carried on by the Catholic teaching congregations; the other, strong in political theory, secularist, concerned first to destroy the character of the existing schools, later to build up State systems. The first was destined to a long eclipse, in the social and political upheaval of the French Revolution. The second was to shape the educational policy of Europe and the United States throughout the nineteenth century. The principles guiding the latter were those of 'The Enlightenment,' the deistic, rationalistic, and vaguely humanitarian, culture fostered by the French *philosophes* and spread by them throughout Europe. When the violence of the French Revolution and the Napoleonic Wars had exhausted itself, there were to be various compromises between the Catholic and anti-Catholic forces in education, unhappy compromises, unstable, shot through with distrust from both parties, breaking down from time to time into open conflict.

---

[1] K. A. Schmid, *Geschichte der Erziehung,* Stuttgart, 1898, Vol. 4, Pt. 2, pp. 446-76. See also M. Reiniger, *Friederich Eberhard von Rochow, der Reformator des preussischen Landschulwesens,* Langensalza, 1905.

It was, and is, essentially a conflict between education for this world alone and education which envisaged this world as only an antechamber of eternity, between pagan and Christian education.

The final moves toward State control in education. The idea of complete control of education by the State was in the air all through the eighteenth century. It was already put into practice to some extent, in an indirect fashion, through the acknowledged supremacy of State over Church in most Protestant countries, and through the increasing interference in Church affairs by the autocratic Bourbon and Hapsburg dynasties in Catholic countries. Frederick William I (ruled 1713-1740) made school attendance compulsory in 1717. His son, Frederick the Great (ruled 1740-1786), by the code of 1763 made further detailed regulations for schools. But both left the immediate supervision of schools in the hands of the Lutheran clergy.

The great impetus to establishing direct and complete State control over schools came from France. Louis René de Caradeuc de la Chalotais, Attorney-General of the King in the Parliament of Rennes, published in 1763, the year before the Jesuits were expelled from France, his *Essai d'éducation nationale, ou plan d'étude pour la jeunesse.* He claimed to be only writing a commentary on the principles expressed by Locke, Fleury, and Nicole.[1] But he was bitter against existing education, as monkish, and lacking in national feeling.[2] He was concerned, it is true, chiefly with secondary education, and railed at the Christian Brothers for teaching the children of the poor to read and write instead of to use the plane and file. But he offered two sweeping notions that were to affect all education. The first was that the schools should have nothing to do with teaching

---

[1] *Essai*, p. 147. The *Essai* was published at Geneva, and was almost immediately translated into Dutch, Russian, and German.

[2] *Essai*, p. 20.

religion, which should be the concern of the home and the parish church.[1] The second was that "education should be dependent on the State alone, because education belongs essentially to the State."[2] The State schools should teach morality, based on the natural law.[3]

In 1768, Rolland, President of the Parliament of Paris, and, more importantly, Turgot, the Minister of Finance, in 1775, proposed plans for a national system of schools founded upon the theory of la Chalotais.[4] In the Constituent Assembly (1789-1791) Mirabeau and Talleyrand, the apostate Bishop of Autun, offered similar plans, that of Talleyrand being the more radical and religiously intolerant of the two. Other plans were drawn up, by Condorcet,[5] and by Pelletier.[6] For the time being, nothing came of all those plans; but they pointed the way to future efforts. Poland and Russia accepted the French lead enthusiastically in this matter, since French intellectual in-

---

[1] *Essai*, p. 16. It must be remembered that la Chalotais was a Catholic, but of the sort known as 'Gallican,' those who claimed exaggerated rights for the king in the disposition of Church affairs. He had been very active against the Jesuits. His *comptes rendus* to the Parliament of Brittany in December, 1761, and May, 1762, led Grimm to say that he was the destroyer of the Jesuits in France. (*Catholic Encyclopedia*, Vol. 12, p. 773. See also J. Delvaille, *La Chalotais, Educateur*, Paris, 1910.)

[2] *Essai*, p. 17.

[3] *Essai*, p. 132.

[4] V. Duruy, *History of France*, p. 523.

[5] Submitted April 20, 1792, to the Legislative Assembly, which had succeeded the Constituent Assembly. Condorcet's plan called for a primary school for every four hundred inhabitants, secondary schools in each department, one hundred and ten institutes, nine university colleges, all to be under the control of 'The National Society of Arts and Sciences,' a not unlikely forerunner of Napoleon's 'University of France.' The plan was not, of course, carried out; but, after the religious teachers were suppressed, a futile law of June 8, 1793, established, on paper, a system of primary schools throughout France. (De Montmorency, *op. cit.*, p. 104.)

[6] July 13, 1793. It was "a national compulsory system, modelled on the system of Sparta. Of this plan Robespierre said that it was inspired by the genius of humanity." O. Willmann, *The Science of Education*, 2d ed., Latrobe, Pa., 1930, Vol. 1, p. 304.

fluence dominated those two countries at the time. Rousseau, Diderot, and others wrote out educational schemes for the Eastern lands. Charles Emmanuel of Sardinia, Filangieri in Naples,[1] Pombal in Portugal, Aranda and Campomanes in Spain, welcomed the French ideas in their educational reforms.

In Austria. Maria Theresa, who in 1740 at the age of twenty-three had succeeded to the throne of Hungary, Bohemia, and Austria, began about 1760 to take an active interest in the schools of her wide domains. But up to 1770 she contented herself with trying, not very successfully, to stimulate Catholic prelates in promoting schools. In 1765 her son, Joseph II, became emperor, and co-regent of Austria with his mother. Joseph espoused the intensely national and secular theories in education emanating from France, and was able to get his mother to adopt them in a limited measure. In 1773, when the Jesuits were suppressed by Pope Clement XIV, their confiscated property was used to further elementary schools. The plans outlined in a new education law, of 1774, were committed to the charge of Johan Ignaz von Felbiger, the Abbot of Sagan in Silesia, who was called to Vienna in that year and appointed General Commissioner of Education.[2] Von Felbiger

[1] Filangieri, *Scienza della legislazione,* Naples, 1780-85, Bk. IV.

[2] Von Felbiger was born on January 6, 1724, at Gross-Glogau, Silesia. He was a tutor in a wealthy family from 1744 to 1746, then joined the Canons Regular of St. Augustine at Sagan. He was ordained priest in 1748, and ten years later became abbot of his monastry. The schools under his jurisdiction as abbot were in very bad shape. In 1761 he drew up a plan for their reform. The next year he went to Berlin, where he was much impressed by Hecker's *Realschule* and by the teaching methods of J. F. Hahn. In 1763 he established a normal school at Sagan. Frederick the Great commissioned him in 1765, with von Schlabrendorff, to draw up a program of schools for Silesia. He was working at the regulation of higher schools in Silesia, in 1774, when Maria Theresa invited him to Vienna. In 1775 he published his *Methodenbuch fur Lehrer der deutschen Schulen.* (Panholzer has made a study of this in Volume 5 of *Bibliothek der katolische Paedagogik,* Freiburg, 1892.) He published

worked earnestly and autocratically at his task, opened new schools, imposed rigorously exact methods of administration and teaching. Besides the usual passive resistance of the people, he created plenty of opposition on the part even of those who might have been expected to help him. At the death of his patroness, he was deposed from office by Joseph II, who thereupon cut the national school system further away from clerical control.

In Prussia. A similar development of State intervention in schools took place in Prussia. As early as 1717, King Frederick William decreed compulsory attendance 'whereever schools existed,' daily attendance in winter, two days a week in summer. The law had little effect. Forty-six years later Frederick the Great (1712-1786) issued an elaborate code of school laws, fixing the age of compulsory attendance at from five to thirteen or fourteen, and imposing on the Church the obligation of paying tuition for children whose parents were too poor to pay. This set of laws was also pretty widely ignored. Zedlitz, from 1771 to 1788 Minister for Lutheran Church and School Affairs, seized upon von Rochow, whose educational work and writings had won him a good deal of popularity, as a helper in his scheme to take education out of the hands of the Lutheran clergy and secularize it. He succeeded in his purpose in 1787, the year after Frederick the Great had died. Zedlitz was a warm champion of Basedow's ideas. But the new king, Frederick William II, removed Zedlitz from office and modified his secularizing policy. It is true that in Chapter XII of the great code of Prussian laws completed in 1794, and known as the *Allgemeine Landrecht,* the principle of State control was very definitely asserted, but with a recognition of the religious rights in education of both Lutheran

seventy-eight treatises on education, displaying high ideals, but a very mechanical concept of school methods. He died at Pressburg in Hungary, May 17, 1788.

and Catholic children. Frederick William III, who succeeded his father in 1797, did little to carry out the educational provisions of the code of 1794. But after Napoleon's great defeat of the Prussians at Jena in 1806, a succession of strong prime ministers, Stein, Hardenburg, Scharnhorst, with the aid of Fichte the philosopher, roused a spirit of fiery nationalism which, from 1808 onward, when the Ministry of Public Instruction was established, made the Prussian system of State schools the most closely organized and the most complete in Europe. Between 1815 and 1825 the Lutheran clergy were finally ousted from any control of the school system. By 1840, Prussia had thirty-eight normal schools, nearly thirty thousand elementary schools, and about one-sixth of the total population was in school. Frederick William IV (ruled 1840-1861) blamed the irreligious schools for the revolution of 1848,[1] and lent considerable influence to the religious elements in the nation which strove to recapture control of the schools. But both religious and irreligious contenders admitted the State supremacy.

In England. The idea of State control of education made slower progress in England than on the continent. Adam Smith, in 1776, urged the right of the State over elementary education "for the common people . . . the labouring poor."[2] Tom Paine, who publicized many of the French Revolutionary theories in his *Rights of Man* (1792), wanted

---

[1] F. Paulsen, *German Education, Past and Present,* p. 246.

[2] *An Inquiry into the Nature and Causes of the Wealth of Nations,* London ed. of 1893, p. 613. Smith had great scorn for schools, "public institutions for education," because they taught useless things, and had a high regard for the home education of women. "There are no public institutions for the education of women, and there is accordingly nothing useless, absurd, or fantastical in the course of their education." (p. 612) But he would have compulsory schools for "the labouring poor," for one reason, because "the more they are instructed, the less liable they are to the delusions of enthusiasm and superstition which, among ignorant nations, frequently occasion the most dreadful disorders." (p. 618.)

the State to allot £4 a year for the schooling of every child under fourteen, and to compel parents to send their children to school until they had learned reading, writing, and arithmetic. But most of the advocacy of State intervention in education which began in the later eighteenth century was based upon the need of reforming the horrible and dangerous system of apprenticeship then in vogue in English manufacturing industries: a system which placed children as young as four years old at work in factories, under conditions ruinous to health and morals. The 'Health and Morals of Apprentices' Act of 1802 cut down the working hours of children to twelve a day, and ordered daily instruction in reading, writing, and arithmetic.[1] The Act was

---

[1] There was an odd vagueness about this. Apprentices were to be instructed "in some Part of every working Day . . . in Reading, Writing, and Arithmetick, or either of them, according to the Age and Abilities of such Apprentice." (42 George III, c. 73, sec. 6.) They were also to be taught, one hour on Sunday, "the principles of the Christian Religion." (sec. 8.) The full title of this Act of 1802 is worth recalling: "Health and Morals Act to Regulate the Labour of Bound Children in Cotton Factories." Its provisions were strictly limited to child laborers in one industry, that of cotton spinning, and in that one industry to those children who were *formally indentured,* only about one per cent of the children employed in the cotton factories. Not until the Act of 1819 was any protection offered to the other child laborers, and that was still limited to the cotton factories. This Act of 1802 has often been hailed as the first education law in England. It was obviously nothing of the sort. Besides the instances already mentioned in connection with the universities, State intervention under Henry VIII, Edward VI, Mary and Elizabeth even decreed that the grammar of Colet and Lily "and none other" must be used by "all you schoolmasters . . . within this our realm, and other our dominions." This decree was issued by Henry in 1542, and repeated variously as late as 1604. (J. W. Adamson, *Short History of Education,* pp. 124-25.) Moreover, this may be a proper place to notice a State intervention in schools all too seldom commented on. That was the notorious system in Ireland known as the charter schools. These were set up in 1733 by Hugh Boulter, the prime minister, under a royal charter, for the express work of proselytizing amongst the poor children of Ireland. Between 1745 and 1831 the Colonial Parliament granted aid to these schools amounting to more than a million pounds sterling. In 1781 and again in 1787 John Howard, the prison visitor, examined these schools and found conditions in them absolutely horrible. His reports, ordered printed by

resented and poorly enforced. Samuel Whitbread, five years later, proposed a national system of parish schools, financially assisted from the taxes, to provide two years of schooling for children somewhere between the ages of seven and fourteen. Parliament rejected the bill. In 1816 Henry Brougham, who had taken up Whitbread's work after the death of the latter in 1815, got Parliament to appoint a Select Committee to enquire into the 'education of the lower orders,' a Committee which functioned for many years in gathering information, not all of it very reliable. Brougham introduced a bill in 1820 substantially repeating Whitbread's proposal of 1807, and the proposal was again rejected. In the meantime the various school societies were succeeding in increasing the voluntary attendance of children at school. There were more than a million in the schools by 1833, representing about one-third of the children in England between the ages of three and twelve. Brougham, who had become Lord Brougham, looked upon this increase as "rendering resort to compulsion needless."[1] Parliament was asked, and in August 1833 reluctantly granted, £20,000 to aid in "erecting school-houses for the education of the poorer classes in Great Britain," the money to be used only where at least an equal amount was raised by subscription for the same purpose. In 1846 the par-

the Colonial Parliament in 1799, were successfully repressed until 1856. (*Studies,* Vol. 16, p. 140.) No industrial exploitation of children in England surpassed this carried on in Ireland under State approval. (See *Reports on Education, Ireland; Commissions,* 1791, 1810, 1856; Winifrede M. Wyse, *Notes on Education Reform in Ireland,* Waterford, 1901; *Catholic Encyclopedia,* Vol. 13, p. 576.) For the whole subject see O. J. Dunlop and R. D. Denman, *English Apprenticeship and Child Labor,* London, 1912.

[1] Adamson, *Short History of Education,* p. 265. Mr. J. A. Roebuck in July 1833 asked the House of Commons to "oblige by law every child in Great Britain and Ireland from perhaps six years of age to twelve years of age to be a regular attendant at school." (*Ibid.,* p. 292.) This proposal was rejected, but its rejection prepared the way for the successful request, a month later, for the first grant in aid since the days of the Puritan Commonwealth.

liamentary grants were extended to maintenance as well as to construction of schools. In 1847 Catholic and Wesleyan schools were admitted to share in the grants. The Committee of the Privy Council on Education was created in 1839 "to superintend the application of any sums voted by Parliament for the purpose of promoting public education." On April 13th, three days after it was appointed, the Committee advanced a scheme for a national normal school, which aroused such fierce opposition that it was abandoned forever. The annual grants by the government were increased from the £20,000 of 1833 to £663,000 in 1858. During the years 1853 to 1868 a long series of compulsory education bills were proposed in Parliament and though they were not approved, the discussion about them got the minds of legislators ready to accept W. E. Forster's education bill of 1870. The period after 1832 was also a time of much social unrest, of the Chartist movement of 1838-1848. The franchise had been more widely extended by the Act of 1867. Government felt strongly the need of controlling by education the vast number of restless, discontented, and ill-instructed voters. Forster's bill did not go so far as compulsory attendance, but concerned itself rather with the national provision of schools; yet even so it was passed only with some difficulty. Compulsory school attendance became law only with the passing of Mundella's act in 1880.

In France. The Revolution brought, as has been seen, a number of projects for nationalizing education, but also made it impossible to carry out any such project. All it did for schools was to drive the Catholic teachers out of France. The Christian Brothers were suppressed in 1792, all other teaching congregations in 1793. When Napoleon had restored order, he outlined a vast system of education, in 1802, the year in which he entered into the concordat with Pope Pius VII, and a year before he recalled the Christian Brothers to France. His plan called for no direct support of schools by the national government, nor did it make attendance compulsory upon the children. The compulsion was upon the *communes,* of which there were then about 37,000 in France, and which were ordered to furnish each a school building and a house for the teacher. The commune might demand tuition, but was to grant free schooling to one-fifth of its children. In secondary education the State interfered more directly, turning over to various municipalities former Catholic school buildings to be used as *lycées.* The municipality was to equip the school building, and to collect tuition fees from the students; but the State allotted scholarship grants to 6,400 students in secondary schools each year. In 1806 Napoleon founded the 'University of France,' not a teaching institution, but an executive body, composed of a grand master and council of twenty-six members, appointed by the government, and set over the entire nation geographically divided into twenty-seven 'academies' or districts, each 'academy' governed by a rector and council of ten. It was a huge bureaucracy with a great force of inspectors, all centrally appointed by the grand master to superintend all the schools of the nation. In 1815 the grand master became commissioner of public instruction, and in 1850 the whole apparatus became the State Department of Education. The system endured many changes without entirely losing its national character. It was put practically under the control of the Catholic clergy by Charles X on his accession in 1824. It was secularized again in 1830 when Louis Philippe became king.[1] After the revolution of 1848, for which, just as in Prussia, the secular schools were

---

[1] Under Louis Philippe, the education law of 1833 reiterated the provisions of 1802 obliging each commune to maintain schools. There was no State financial aid for these schools, nor any pressure of true compulsory attendance.

blamed, Catholic schools were again encouraged. The number of Catholic schools grew from 6,464 in 1850 to 11,391 in 1864. But the Third Republic, after 1870, was increasingly hostile to religious schools. In 1881 all teaching of religion was forbidden in the communal elementary schools. On March 28, 1882, elementary education was made compulsory. In 1886 members of religious congregations were replaced in the elementary schools by lay teachers, and in 1904 all religious congregations were by law suppressed.

Opposition to State control. The above sketchy summary of the events leading, in the course of a little more than a hundred years, from the first strong assertion of the principle of State control to its practical application in the national school systems would be inadequate and misleading without some mention of the severe opposition which met both principle and practice of State control during that hundred years: roughly, from 1780 to 1880. That opposition was naturally varied in character, but it may be said that it came everywhere from two main sources: first, the inherent Christian tradition that religious training is an essential part of education; and second, the equally inherent reluctance of the mass of the people to surrender to governments the enormous social power implied in State-controlled schools.

Religious opposition. The religious opposition to State schools expressed itself, as a matter of course, through the organized Church, Protestant and Catholic.[1] Yet it found

[1] Some of the earliest religious opposition to national schools in England came from a woman, Mrs. Sarah Trimmer (1741-1810). The mother of twelve children whom she largely educated herself, she was one of the founders of the Sunday School Union and active in its work. From 1802 to 1806 she published a periodical, *Guardian of Education,* at first monthly, later quarterly, to promote religious education and oppose secular education, which she believed to be inspired by the Deism of Voltaire and the French *philosophes.* She attacked the secular character of Lancaster's schemes in 1805 in a

support, a gradually dwindling support, it is true, in the long traditional attitude of peoples whose Church affiliations were becoming of the slenderest, and whose Christian belief had considerably succumbed to the rationalism and indifferentism which characterized that period in Western history. It can simply be said that it was the decay of religious belief and practice throughout the Western world which made it possible for State governments to control and secularize education. Possibly that decay was in turn due to the neglect or inability of the churches to build up adequate school systems. But it seems historically sound to say that religious principles alone would have been a bond capable of holding together in any effective way the loose popular opposition to State control, an opposition which in the main was based upon reasons other than religious.

General popular opposition. A vague hostility to educational schemes is a phenomenon often observed amongst the masses of the people. It was a fact with which every

pamphlet entitled *A Comparative View of the New Plan of Education promulgated by Mr. Joseph Lancaster . . . and of the system of Christian education founded by our Pious Forefathers, etc.* A sort of biography of her appeared in 1814, 1816, 1825: *Some Account of the Life and Writings of Mrs. Trimmer, with Original Letters and Meditations and Prayers Selected from her Journal.* See *Dictionary of National Biography,* and Adamson, *Short History of Education,* pp. 231, 233, 249 sqq., 256-57. At the death of Mrs. Trimmer in 1810 Dr. Herbert Marsh, Lady Margaret professor at Cambridge University, with the aid of Anglican bishops, carried on her work, to result in 1811 in the founding of the "National Society for Promoting the Education of the Poor," with the definite idea of heading off a national system of secular schools. The religious opposition to State control was so strong in England that Forster's Bill of 1870 was really a compromise measure. (Adamson, *op. cit.,* p. 310.) In Prussia and other German States it led to arrangements for denominational schools. In France it was the cause of a series of shifts in management of schools from 1824 to 1904, in which latter year religious education was given a practical death blow. In Spain the Church went into a wavering partnership with the State, dissolved in 1931.

government had to contend in its efforts to establish a national system of schools. It is a fact which still makes the truant officer a common necessity. Some of that hostility comes from mere inertia, some from ignorance and a sullen unwillingness to forego the profits accruing from child labor; but perhaps most of it comes from the individualism which sets citizens 'agin the government,' from a mistrust of the civil authority, and of those who interfere in what people consider their private rights and duties. Along about 1790 Miss Hannah More, a zealous promoter of Sunday school work amongst the poor children of Somerset, wrote of the children's parents: "A great many refused to send their children unless we would pay them for it; and not a few refused, because they were not sure of my intentions, being apprehensive that at the end of seven years, if they attended so long, I should acquire a power over them, and send them beyond sea."[1] In every country the early laws making school attendance compulsory became inoperative through dogged popular opposition.[2] It was the general opposition aroused throughout England which killed Brougham's bill in 1820,[3] and which did much to win Brougham himself to its side in 1833, when that same opposition defeated Roebuck's bill.[4] O'Connell expressed a view very widely held, not in England only, but in every nation, when he said in the debate of 1833, "Facility of education should be encouraged, but all domination ought

[1] William Roberts, *Memoirs of the Life and Correspondence of Mrs. Hannah More*, London, 1834, Vol. 1, p. 390. There was also a religious element in the quarrels arising from Miss More's Sunday schools. See *Dictionary of National Biography*, Vol. 13, p. 864.

[2] As instances may be mentioned: the Weimar decree of 1619 (*Cyclopedia of Education*, Vol. 1, pp. 285-86), the Scotch laws of 1646, 1696 (de Montmorency, *op. cit.*, p. 119), the Prussian law of Frederick William in 1717, and of Frederick the Great in 1763, the French law of June, 1793 (de Montmorency, *op. cit.*, p. 104), the English apprentice law of 1802 (de Montmorency, *op. cit.*, pp. 210-15).

[3] De Montmorency, *op. cit.*, pp. 229-33.

[4] *Ibid.*, p. 236.

to be abolished."[1]   Before that popular opposition could be effectively broken down great changes were to occur in political theory, changes even more important socially than they were politically, changes which involved a new concept of society, a new concept of the place of the individual in society, or at least the revival of a concept so old as to be capable of becoming new again, and a new philosophy of education.   The following chapter will try to give some notion of what those changes were and how they affected education.

Conclusion.   The struggle begun in the Renaissance between the Christian and the pagan ideal in education, and modified by the bitter dissensions amongst Christians caused by the Protestant Revolt, reached one of its most decisive phases when it aligned the national States on the side of universal and compulsory attendance of children at schools which increasingly abandoned the religious element in education.   The distinctive character of that development was not the mere entry of the State into the business of education, but the fact that the great financial and coercive powers of the State should back the pagan ideal in its compulsory schools.   Yet, since the State took up the work of schools in a world disrupted by the Protestant

---

[1] The whole debate brings out the principles back of the widespread opposition.   See *Hansard,* Vol. 20, cols. 139-74.   The most biting statement of that opposition was given expression a hundred and ten years before this time in the *Essay on Charity and Charity-Schools,* which Bernard Mandeville in 1723 added to his first edition of his *Fable of the Bees.*   His attack was directed against those private attempts at furnishing free schooling to the poor which so long preceded the entry of the State into education.   His arguments were drawn from economic, moral, social, and psychological reasons to support the general thesis that "nothing should be taught for nothing but at Church." (F. B. Kaye's edition of *The Fable of the Bees,* 2 vols., Oxford, 1924, Vol. 1, p. 297.)   Similarly, Mirabeau, in his *Travail sur l'Education publique,* published after his death in 1791 by his friend Cabanis, speaks in terms almost exactly the same as those of O'Connell, denying the right of the State to impose compulsory schooling upon its people.

Revolt, it not unnaturally thought to save itself further friction by shelving the whole content of religion in its scheme of education. On the other hand, those who positively held to the pagan ideal in education were every whit as sincere in their convictions as were the Christians, and not unfrequently were more devoted in promoting their concept than the Christians were in upholding the Christian ideal. Moreover, the struggle between the two was complicated and confused by the fact that Christianity, even where it had been rejected, had so influenced the whole of Western civilization that the pagan ideal had come to contain many inheritances from the Christian moral code. That partial content of the pagan concept of education often bewildered its Christian opponents and rendered them only half-hearted in their opposition. The Christians were further bewildered by the ugly rivalries and dissensions existing amongst their own sects, and serving not merely to destroy unity, but also to obscure the truths of Christian revelation. Yet with all this, it is important to remember that State-controlled systems of secular schools are only a phase in that struggle between Christianity and paganism which began long before the Renaissance, and which in all likelihood will continue to the end of the world.

TOPICS FOR DISCUSSION

1. The growth of burgher schools in the Middle Ages, and the increase of lay teachers.

2. The attitude of the Church and of churchmen toward lay teachers, from the twelfth to the sixteenth century.

3. State interference in the administration of the Universities of Paris and Oxford.

4. The influence of the *Illuminati* on the administration of education.

5. Gallicanism and Josephism as affecting State control of education.

6. The development of French educational administration from the 'University of France.'

7. State-controlled schools as a means of furthering governmental policies.

BIBLIOGRAPHIC NOTE

Data on lay schools in the Middle Ages must be exhumed here and there from local chronicles, and from occasional references in such works as the earlier histories of universities, or the 13 volumes of D'Achery and Mabillon's *Spicilegium Veterum Scriptorum,* or their supplement, J. Mabillon's *Vetera Analecta,* 4 vols., Paris, 1675-85, or Mabillon's *Acta Sanctorum Ordinis Sti. Benedicti Seculo Sexto,* 2 vols., Paris, 1701; or from such more recent works as A. T. Drane, *Christian Schools and Scholars,* rev. ed. by W. Gumbley, London, 1924, G. Manacorda, *Storia della Scuola in Italia,* 2 vols., Palermo, 1913, and L. Maitre, *Les Ecoles Episcopales et Monastiques en Occident avant les Universités, 768-1180,* 2d ed., Paris, 1924. J. Launoy, *De Scholis Celebribus a Carolo M. et post Carolum M. in Occidente Instauratis Liber,* Hamburg, 1717, has a few scattered references to the growth of lay schools.

For the question of lay teachers, as well as for State interference in the universities, see the works of Rashdall, Denifle, and Chatelain, already mentioned, as also H. K. Mann, *The Lives of the Popes in the Middle Ages,* Vols. 9-15, London, 1925-29. For the official decrees, one must ransack the later volumes of J. Mansi's huge *Concilia,* 31 vols., Florence and Venice, 1758-98.

For the influence of the *Illuminati,* besides such contemporary works as A. Barruel, *Memoirs of Jacobinism,* 4 vols., London, 1797, and the famous J. Robison, *Proofs of a Conspiracy against all the Religions and Governments of Europe, carried on in the Secret Meetings of the Free Masons, Illuminati, and Reading Societies,* 3d ed., London, 1798, see L. Engel, *Geschichte des Illuminaten-Ordens,* Berlin, 1906; R. L. Forestier, *Les Illumines de Bavière et la Franc-Maçonneries Allemande,* Paris, 1915; and V. Stauffer, *New England and the Bavarian Illuminati,* New York, 1918.

The effects on school administration of Gallicanism and Josephism may be summarily viewed in R. Parsons, *Studies in Church History,* 2d ed., New York, 1897, Vol. 4. For a somewhat wider view, see B. J. Kidd, *The Counter-Reformation,* London, 1933; D. Ogg, *Europe in the Seventeenth Century,* London, 1925; H. E. Bourne, *The Revolutionary Period in Europe (1763-1815),* New York, 1922; W. H. Jervis, *The Gallican Church from 1516 to the Revolution,* 2 vols., London, 1872; G. Holzknecht, *Ursprung und Herkunft der Reformideen Kaiser Josefs II,* Innsbruck, 1914; G. Strakosch-Grassmann, *Geschichte des osterreichischen Unterrichtswesens,* Vienna, 1905; F. Paulsen, *German Education, Past and Present* (translated by T. Lorenz), New York, 1908.

For the administrative development in France, out of a vast amount of material the following books are suggested: E. Allain,

La Question d'Enseignement en 1789 d'après les Cahiers, Paris, 1886, and *L'Oeuvre Scolaire de la Revolution, 1789-1802,* Paris, 1891; C. Hippeau, *L'Instruction Publique en France pendant la Revolution,* Caen, 1871; A. Delfau, *Napoleon Ier et l'Instruction Publique,* Paris, 1902; A. Aulard, *Napoleon et le Monopole Universitaire: Origines et Fonctionnement de l'Université Imperiale,* Paris, 1911; O. Greard, *Législation de l'Instruction Primaire en France depuis 1789 jusq' a nos Jours,* Paris, 1890; A. Beauchamps, *Recueil de Lois et Réglements sur l'Enseigement Superieur, 1789-1909,* Paris, 1880-1909; E. Brouard, *Essai d'Histoire Critique de l'Instruction Primaire en France de 1789 jusq'a nos Jours,* Paris, 1901.

For other countries in general, there is an excellent summary of legislative development in J. Monti, *La Libertad de Enseñanza,* Madrid, 1930. For Italy, see G. Carenzi, *Manuale di Legislazione Scolastica,* Milan, 1919; for Belgium, P. Verhaegen, *La Lutte Scolaire en Belgique,* Ghent, 1905; for Holland, C. Heutzen, *De Politicke Geschiedenis van het Lager Onderwijs in Nederland,* Gravenhage, 1927; for early State intervention in Irish schools, see Chapters 10 and 11 of A. S. Green, *The Making of Ireland and its Undoing,* London, 1908.

For the development of school administration in England, one of the best general introductions is J. W. Adamson, *English Education, 1789-1902,* Cambridge, 1930. A useful book for early background is W. Bowden, *Industrial Society in England toward the End of the Eighteenth Century,* New York, 1925. The two larger societies are dealt with in W. O. B. Allen and E. McClure, *Two Hundred Years: The History of the Society for Promoting Christian Knowledge,* London, 1898, and C. G. Pascoe, *Two Hundred Years of the S. P. G.: An Historical Account, 1701-1900,* Milwaukee, n. d. There are valuable data in A. W. Tuer, *The History of the Horn Book,* 2 vols., London and New York, 1896, 1 vol., 1897. Some details of the development in England are given in W. Chance, *Children under the Poor Law,* London, 1897; D. Salmon, *Education of the Poor in the Eighteenth Century,* London, 1908; F. Adams, *History of the Elementary School Contest in England,* London, 1882; J. C. Greenough, *The Evolution of the Elementary Schools of Great Britain,* New York, 1903; Sir James Kay-Shuttleworth, *Four Periods of Public Education,* London, 1862; and a summary of laws in Sir Hugh Owen, *Elementary Education Acts Manual,* 23d ed., London, 1906, and G. N. Morrison, *Education Authorities Handbook,* Edinburgh, 1919.

A few useful books on the development in the United States are: M. Alma, *Standard Bearers,* New York, 1928; B. Confrey, *Secularism in American Education: Its History,* Washington, 1931; and the following on educational laws: H. C. Voorhees, *The Law of the Public School System of the United States,* Boston, 1916; *A Manual of Educational Legislation,* United States Bureau of Education, Bulletin 22, 1926; H. R. Trusler, *Essentials of School Law,* Milwaukee, 1927.

On the contribution of Catholic teaching congregations, besides the references already given, see M. Monica, *Angela Merici and her Teaching Idea,* New York, 1927; M. M. Drummond, *The Life and Times of Margaret Bourgeoys,* Boston, 1907; and the condensed account of teaching congregations in M. Heimbucher, *Die Orden und Kongregationen der katholischen Kirche,* Paderborn, 1908.

CHAPTER XVIII

'DEMOCRACY' IN EDUCATION

General outline. In the course of two long lifetimes, or four generations, the jumble of ideas loosely and elusively expressed in the word 'democracy' have come to dominate educational efforts in the Western world. Our fathers' grandfathers saw the beginnings of this new enthusiasm for democracy. Our own grandfathers began to be severely, even cynically, disillusioned about the possibilities of political democracy on any scale larger than, say, that of a dozen families; and the present generation has no illusions whatever on the subject. But the influence of the democratic ideal on school education survived in spite of this disillusionment. Of the hundred and fifty years or so which cover the history of modern democracy up to the present, roughly the first half was taken up with the struggle to get the confused ideas involved in democracy so widely accepted as to establish control of the schools by them; the second half was filled with the amazing development of schools under that control. For the sake of perspective, it must be added that the past dozen years have seen the disillusioning process gradually extend from the political aspect of democracy to the educational, in a way to make one suspect that another great change in school education may be approaching. But that last is prophecy, not history.

The coming of 'democracy.' When the notion of State control of schools was first strongly advocated, the various nations of the Western world were governed by political systems which were traditionally monarchic and more or less absolute in character, yet which were all beginning to change profoundly under the influence of social and eco-

421

nomic developments, and of still more important religious and philosophic developments. Long before universal and compulsory schooling was to become a commonplace of our Western civilization, all the governments were to have changed their character, even though some (England and Prussia, for example) were to keep their old external form. The essential change was that of endowing a larger number of individuals in each nation with at least an apparent voice in the management of the affairs of the nation. The structure of government was to become 'representative.' The actual conduct of government was to be controlled, remotely and indirectly, by the power of the citizens to select and approve by suffrage the officials who governed the people in the name and place of the people themselves. No one individual could again utter the legendary 'L'État c'est moi!' But the millions empowered to cast a vote in each State could say (in varying degrees of accuracy, it is true), 'WE are the State.' The process of imposing compulsory schools then became that of persuading the masses of the citizens that they themselves were doing the imposing. That process marked the beginning of a technique of propaganda which reached its climax in the Western world during the years 1914 to 1918, and perhaps found its most tragi-comic expression in the phrase, 'Making the world safe for Democracy.'

The roots of 'democracy.' The beginning of this great political, social, and educational change came from France, which had been for many centuries the center of cultural influences in Europe. Its roots may be traced to four important facts: (a) the growth of a bourgeois 'middle class,' of a numerically large section of the people, financially independent, jealous of aristocratic prestige and power, increasingly articulate and capable of effective organization; (b) the development, not merely of manufacturing industries and commerce, but even more strikingly of remarkable mastery of the means of communication, in the steamship, railroad, telegraph and telephone, with the consequent spread of bourgeois discontent and ambition, the growing consciousness of the political power of the manufacturer and trader; (c) the decay of the influence of supernatural religion, the weakening amongst the masses of the people of that outlook upon eternity which had been a reassuring hope in adversity and a restraint upon too gross a resentment against the inequities of this present life; and (d) the revival, or rather the renewed vigor in survival, of a materialist philosophy; the *carpe diem* of a paganism at once antique and undying.

The growth of 'democracy.' The process of the growth of democracy is confused, because it is human. It was nourished by both the highest aspirations of man, and his most corroding selfishness. Underlying the movement, vitalizing it, was the truly spiritual concept of the dignity of the individual man, of his human claim to have that dignity recognized, of a bond of brotherhood which should shape the group activities of man. That meant hostility to the idea of privilege as such. But inevitably the spiritual concept was phrased in very material terms; and selfishness made each man stress his rights and slur over his duties. Privilege became a hateful thing only when others had it, not when it was within the reach of one's own grasp. *Fraternité,* which might have meant Christian charity, could very practically mean only a humanitarian sentimentalism which one could shout vociferously even whilst one's hands were plundering his 'brother's' pockets in sharp business practices or gripping his 'brother's' throat in political chicanery. If the whole jumbled notion of democracy can be crowded at all intelligently into one small group of ideas, it may be in some such fashion as this: men tried once more to translate their eternal destiny out of terms of a remote and uncomprehended heaven into terms of this immediate earth. Each man was the image of God, each man was capable of endless happiness, each man was given equal rights to that happiness by his Creator; he was to set himself, therefore, to assert those rights before his fellow men, and to grasp that happiness here before death closed his eyes.

The place of education in 'democracy.' Bacon and Locke, still holding feebly to a diminished Christian concept of life, had ventured only a vague hope of an unlimited perfectibility of human nature, to be accomplished by education. Rousseau and Voltaire resolutely cut away from all Christian limitations and pictured the vague hope as a prophetic certainty. Man could make of himself whatever he chose to be; and he needed no God to help him in the process. Every man, in the later classic American expression of the idea 'was as good as the next man, and maybe a damn sight better.' *Liberté, egalité, fraternité!* was the cry introducing a new heaven upon earth; new political governments, purged of privilege and selfishness, purely ordered 'of the people, by the people, for the people'; new social alignments, in which the State, which was now to be the people themselves, would absorb the individual; a new morality, discarding divine authority, self-contained, having its rules and its sanctions in the individual human being and in the mass of humanity. To bring this to pass, all that was needed was enough schools, of the right sort, the common property of all, freed of the superstitious churches, 'democratic' as the State itself was to be. Man was to be redeemed anew, not by Jesus Christ, but by himself through the schools. Education was to make him the perfect social being, altruistic, lost in devotion to the common good, yet somehow acquisitive enough to secure for himself a full share of wealth and pleasure and fame and power without preventing his neighbor from attaining the same success.

The excellences in 'democracy.' There is something stirring to every human being in the history of the late eighteenth and early nineteenth centuries. That history is filled with an air of liberation. The rubbish of 'divine right' of kings, the concept so vigorously refuted by Bellarmine and Suarez, was being swept away. A great experiment was begun, of entrusting to the rank and file of men the power of decision regarding their political destiny. There was a specious appearance of religious tolerance, even though it was at bottom mostly religious indifference. There was an emphasis, at least in talk, upon the dignity of man as man, independently of the accidental circumstances of his political and social position. There was an emphasis on each man's right to *equality of opportunity,* to a chance to make use of his capacities, unhindered by tyrannical privileges. New energies were set free in the individual, a new stimulus was given to his development, new hopes were aroused in him.

The fallacies in 'democracy.' The most pathetic weakness of the whole movement was that it aroused exaggerated hopes, hopes inevitably doomed to disappointment. It made men confuse a remote political control, through the vote, with an immediate and practical control. It led men to believe the absurdity, so bitterly proven such since then, that 'representative' government could not become as corrupt as 'absolute' government. It fostered the translation of 'equality of opportunity' into a vicious equality of persons, mischievous in every field of human endeavor, but most mischievous of all in the field of education. It made men's hopes too self-centered, too reliant upon their own inadequate powers, and in so doing destroyed the essential and necessary balance between the human and divine which Christianity struggles to achieve. It made the goal of individual effort material success, wealth, comfort, display. And in all this it tended to create an enormous impatience which has embittered the lives of countless millions, and perhaps has added as much unhappiness to the world as all the bad actions of tyrants put together.

The attitude of Christianity toward the new 'democracy.' The Christian Church, keeping inviolate the divine truths committed to it, intelligently recognizes the changes in human circumstances which time brings. Its never-ending task is to apply unchanging truths to changing conditions of human life. It has a divine assurance that its truths will never be destroyed by human stupidity and viciousness. It has a confident hope of divine aid and guidance in applying those truths to human needs. But it has not the same absolute assurance in the latter as in the former. It must depend upon human skill very largely in meeting new human conditions. Hence the Church moves cautiously, slowly. Some of its members are swept away by new enthusiasms, without sufficient discrimination; some of them are temperamentally hostile to any innovation, no matter how excellent it be. But the Christian Church itself goes its deliberate way, in balance. It welcomed all that was admirable in the new 'democracy'; it showed that welcome in its own changes of administration and discipline.[1] But it stood resolute against the suicidal pagan content of the new ideas, against the basic self-sufficiency of the philosophy behind them, against the false hopes which would most certainly create disaster for men. Where Christian principles still had any influence over nations, those nations were kept from the extremes of irreligion and materialism in the character of their schools. Instances of this will be seen later, in both Protestant and Catholic lands. But where Christian principles had little or no influence, the leaders of

---

[1] As illustrations, may be mentioned the increase in Church schools, the adaptation of religious congregations to new social needs, the moderation of authority in religious congregations and the limiting of tenure of office in such congregations, sympathy with labor organizations, the increasing use of the laymen in Church activities.

the new movement in education were unhesitatingly hostile toward Christianity, and forced war upon the Christian Church which could make no compromise in its principles.

Some of the early difficulties of 'democracy' in education. The violent excesses of the French Revolution, its political, social, and religious destructiveness, halted in all the Western peoples their enthusiasm for 'democracy' in education; but only for a surprisingly short time. Human nature, bereft of divine hope, was too hungry for a substitute to go long without it. It must have something to animate it in its efforts; and the human hope in education was better than none at all. Napoleon re-established the leadership of France, released again the halted enthusiasm. When his troublous domination was stilled in St. Helena, that enthusiasm for a human perfection independent of God, fed by new human achievements in science, in exploration of the riches of this earth, in mastery of communication, in comfort of living, was checked only by the search for a perfected *method* of securing to man the glamorous utopia created by his own magnificent desires and his unbounded imagination. The search was taken up by individuals, in diverse lands, with glowing devotedness, with heroic persistence. Every discovery of theirs was heralded with joy, and urged upon the people who were told that now they had in their own hands the media needed for carrying into effect their hungry hopes.[1]

Conquered by individuals. The significance of individuals as leaders, begun centuries before this in the Classic Ren-

---

[1] Just in passing, it may be mentioned that the nineteenth century's remarkable fertility in 'inventions' flattered still further this hope based upon man's self-sufficiency. The age which applied steam power to ships and railways, which produced the telegraph and telephone, which gave men the convenience of electric light, was quite ready to believe that men could remake themselves by means of schools. The cleverness of a few gifted men was vaguely attributed to "the people," as if *Demos* himself had become an inventor, a genius in applied mechanics.

aissance, was magnified. Pestalozzi, Herbart, Froebel, Darwin, Spencer, Dewey became magic figures. Their pronouncements ranked as high in growing popular esteem as once had ranked the inspired scriptures of Christianity. There was all the old fanaticism, once so pitifully inflamed by religion, in the new devotees of the new salvation by schools. No State could stand against that developing enthusiasm; to do so was to court revolution. The men who fostered the enthusiasm were relatively few; but they had the power of propaganda over the masses. 'Naturalism,' the fundamental philosophy of man's self-sufficiency, was in the saddle. A new crusade swept the Western world, to the cry, not of 'God wills it!' but of 'The Citizens will it!' But the painful difficulty remained, even after getting the citizens to shout the battle cry, of getting them actually to will anything of the sort. It took a long time to surmount that difficulty, even with moderate success. *Demos* had his own crude ideas of what his *cracy* should be; and he was slow to envisage schools for his children as essential to those ideas. The rest of this chapter is concerned with the more important of the individuals whose work helped to the early growth of the idea of 'democracy' in education.

Pestalozzi. In the forefront of those promoters of 'democracy' in education stands Johann Heinrich Pestalozzi. Every student of education is familiar with his name. There is a whole library of books about him. Yet as an educator he was ridiculously inefficient; as a writer, he was cumbersome, confused, inept; he was not a scholar, not a clear thinker, not eloquent. In spite of all that, it is proper to give him a most important place in any study of modern education. He was a promoter. His position in the nineteenth century is not unlike that of Martin Luther in the sixteenth.[1] Pestalozzi, like Luther, found a powder maga-

---

[1] Indeed, Fichte made the comparison, in 1808. See Rede IX of *Reden an die deutsche Nation.*

zine at hand, into which he threw a lighted match. The resultant explosion in each case was out of all proportion to the talents and qualities of the match-thrower; but, in our human way, we attribute the importance of the explosion to the human agent who set it off.

His life. Johann Heinrich Pestalozzi was born at Zurich, January 12, 1746, of a middle-class family, for two centuries Swiss and Calvinist, in spite of the Italian surname. His father died when he was five years old; and although his mother was devoted to him, and sent him through the successive schools of Zurich, he had an ill-disciplined childhood and youth, from which he emerged emotionally unbalanced, very superficially instructed, and quite unprepared for the practical conduct of life. He began to study for the Calvinist ministry, abandoned that for the study of law, abandoned law for agriculture. Rousseau and the 'naturalists' enthralled him; he became an enthusiast for 'reform.' He gave up his Christian profession for the vague Deism then popular.[1] Yet he never developed any religious intolerance, and he spoke respectfully, if vaguely, of Christianity.[2] When he was twenty-three years old, he married Anna Schulthess, an excellent woman, some seven years older than he, who bore him one son. He bought land near Zurich for a farm, which he called Neuhof. He failed signally as a farmer. In 1774, he established on his farm a cotton-spinning industry, in which he employed seventeen boys and twenty girls, deported to him by the government

---

[1] Cf. his *Meine Nachforschungen uber den Gang der Natur in der Entwickelungen des Menschengeschlectes,* published in 1797. Much earlier, he had joined the revolutionary and deistic society known as the *Illuminati,* founded in May, 1776, by Adam Weishaupt. It was suppressed in Bavaria in 1784; and the suppression drove it afield, into Prussia and France. Its members claimed credit for having brought about the French Revolution. See Nesta Webster, *World Revolution,* Boston, 1921; *Catholic Encyclopedia,* Vol. 7, p. 661.

[2] This last is especially notable in his *Uber die Idee der Elementarbildung,* § 47-50, 56, 57, 85.

of the Canton of Berne as 'poor and outcast children.' This farming out of poor children was a pitifully common practice throughout Europe in the eighteenth century. Pestalozzi's scheme was frankly intended as a means to make his unsuccessful farm pay; but he sentimentally, yet sincerely, linked with this financial hope a dream of making his workhouse farm an educational experiment inspired by Rousseau's *Émile*. He raised a public subscription, and borrowed money to carry on the project. But his utter incapacity for management doomed it to failure. It collapsed in 1780. The children were turned back on the Canton, and the loans subscribed were repaid to the extent of about 30 per cent by Mrs. Pestalozzi's family.

But there was no lack of men who were willing to back anyone with Pestalozzi's enthusiasm for educational reform. Encouraged by a few of these, Pestalozzi began to express his views on education in the journal of his friend Iselin, *Die Ephemeriden der Menscheit*. He wrote a number of essays and a social novel, *Lienhard und Gertrud: ein Buch fur das Volk,* which appeared in four widely separated parts between 1781 and 1787. His other writings fell dead from the press; but *Leonard and Gertrude* had an instant and widespread success. He leaped into fame. He conducted a weekly journal of his own; which promptly failed. He corresponded with such men as Count von Zinzendorf, the Austrian Chancellor of the Exchequer,[1] von Hohenwart, Prime Minister of the Grand Duke of Tuscany, who half promised him a chance to put some of his educational ideas into practice, and the philosopher Fichte, who was himself interested in State educational projects.

In the meantime, Neuhof, Pestalozzi's farm, continued to be a failure; and he and his family owed most of even a wretched livelihood to a heroic servant, Elizabeth Näf, the

---

[1] Son of the man who revived and reorganized the Moravian Brethren, the sect of which Comenius had been bishop.

model for 'Gertrude' in Pestalozzi's books. He had a reputation as a writer on reform in education, but he had no
money, and was incapable of earning any money. He sought
a government appointment, which would maintain himself
and his wife (his son, Jacob, was already apprenticed to
Felix Battier, a merchant of Basle), and at the same time
let him try out his educational theories. The new government of Switzerland gave him such a post, at the close of
1798, as manager of an orphanage at Stanz, in the Catholic
Canton of Nidwalden. In his own chaotic way, Pestalozzi
seems to have made a vivid impression on the sixty-two
children put in his care.[1] But the project lasted only five
months. That same year he was given a place as a teacher
in a school at Burgdorf. But his experiments were resented, and he was transferred to an infants' school conducted by Fräulein Stähli. Stapfer, the Swiss Minister of
Arts and Sciences, was his devoted patron, secured for him
government subsidies, had him promoted to the larger
school in the castle at Burgdorf. Hermann Krüsi, the elder,
joined him there, tried to put order and method into his
work, secured two more teachers to help in his scheme, and
helped to raise a public subscription of money. Pupils
flocked in. Pestalozzi was delighted. He wrote a series of
fourteen letters on education, the first two largely autobiographical, which he called *Wie Gertrud ihre Kinder lehrt*.
It was published in 1801, and was a popular success, serving to spread his reputation still more widely. His political
friends secured increased government support for him. But
for various reasons, one of which was suspicion of his radi-

---

[1] There were two supervisors over the orphanage, Truttmann and
Businger, the latter being the Catholic priest of the parish. Their
reports on Pestalozzi's work begin by enthusiastic praise of him in
the first month or so of the work, then become puzzled and doubtful,
and finally wind up by admiring his manifest good will but lamenting
his equally manifest incompetence. (See A. Pinloche, *Pestalozzi*,
New York, 1901, pp. 35-36.)

cal political ideas, the Canton of Berne moved him out of the castle at Burgdorf in 1804, withdrew its grants in aid, even asked repayment of loans made to him; but turned over to him for his school an old monastery at München-buchsee. That made him a neighbor of Philipp von Fellen-berg, a Swiss noble, who five years before had bought in that place a six-hundred-acre estate, Hofwyl, which he devoted to a project for the education of poor children. Krüsi and the other assistants induced Pestalozzi to turn over the management of his school to von Fellenberg, in order to leave himself free, with an annual pension, to inspire the work and spread its influence by his writings. The arrangement wound up in a violent quarrel three months later.

Pestalozzi had had an invitation to bring his Institute to Yverdon, a little town at the south end of Lake Neufchatel, a few miles from the French border. He went there in July, 1805, and remained for twenty years, the most glorious, but the most troubled, of his turbulent life. He made Yverdon a sort of educational sounding board for Switzerland and the German-speaking countries. His Institute was essentially, though not always professedly, a normal school, and became famous throughout the Western world. Pestalozzi did not teach;[1] he directed, and propagandized. His disciples, especially Krüsi, Niederer, and Schmid, quarreled with him and with one another. Pestalozzi was as incapable as ever of any competent management, or even of self-control. The work of the Institute was confused and disorderly. Yet visitors came daily to the place, drawn by the renown which popular acclaim had built up for Pestalozzi. A few clever boys were put up to dazzle the visitors; the quarrels of the staff were momentarily hushed; the visitors went home to sing Pestalozzi's praises. Yet,

[1] H. Morf. *Zur Biographie Pestalozzis,* 4 vols., Winterthur, 1868-89, Vol. 3, p. 105.

curiously enough, even the students accepted the notion that the school was accomplishing pioneering wonders.[1] Finally, the quarrels reached such a scandalous stage that the government had to intervene; and Pestalozzi was forced to leave. On March 2, 1825, he returned to Neuhof. His son, Jacob, had died in 1801, his wife, Anna, in 1816. Pestalozzi fell into new three-handed quarrels at Neuhof with his grandson, Gottlieb, the ancient servant, Elizabeth Näf, and his faithful disciple Schmid. He got into new controversies with von Fellenberg. All this exhausted the old man, and on February 17, 1827, in his eighty-second year, he died at Brugg, and was buried, with no display, in the cemetery at Birr. In 1846, on the centenary of his birth, the Canton of Argovie put up a belated monument to him in front of the school at Birr.

His character. Writers in Pestalozzi's own time and since have glorified his qualities out of all proportion. The simple fact is that his gifts were more of the heart than of the head. His enthusiasm for elementary education was a veritable passion, but it was matched by no corresponding power to think out adequate ways and means in education,

---

[1] See Vulliemin's interesting account of his experiences as a pupil at Yverdon, in J. Guillaume, *Pestalozzi, Étude Biographique*, Paris, 1890, pp. 225-29. "We were told constantly that we were sharers in a great piece of work, that the world was watching us, and we readily believed what we were told. . . . What was so enthusiastically called Pestalozzi's 'method' was a complete mystery to us, and to our teachers." In 1809, the Helvetian Diet sent a commission to investigate the Institute. The head of the commission was the remarkably able educator, Père Girard, director of the Catholic schools at Freiburg. His *Rapport sur l'Institut de M. Pestalozzi* is quoted in Guillaume, *op. cit.*, pp. 271-77, and is an excellently fair and balanced criticism of the school and of Pestalozzi. He admires Pestalozzi's modesty in admitting that "we but try to put into practice what *common sense* taught men thousands of years ago." But he intimates that that modesty is not reflected in the staff. He cannot find any distinctive *method*, except in the teaching of drawing and singing. He praises Pestalozzi's zeal and perseverance, but asks pity for a man "who has never been able to do exactly what his soul desires." But Pestalozzi was angry with the report.

or to carry into practical effect the inchoate and rudimentary methods he was capable of devising. His pupils, Louis Vulliemin (1797-1879), who was with him as a child of eight to ten years, and Johann Ramsauer,[1] who was both pupil and teacher under him, have left descriptions of Pestalozzi that have become famous: his extraordinary ugliness, his pockmarks, his dirtiness and untidiness, his disordered clothing, his nervous tics, his irascibility and violence, his hobby of picking up stones and carrying them about with him, his utter disregard of time and of the conveniences of others, his fits of melancholy, his touchy vanity alternating with intense self-depreciation, his theatrical posturings,[2] his suspiciousness, all the vivid details of the impression that he was an unbalanced freak; yet shining through that, something that made the pupils love him, and call him *Father* Pestalozzi, that could win enthusiasm and make a confused and almost meaningless lecture somehow interesting, that could get his teachers to work without salary, that created a confidence which no eccentricities, no incompetencies, could entirely destroy. The basic thing in him was essentially noble, an unselfish devotion to an ideal. No wonder men forgave him all his defects, or even tried to turn them into good qualities! His staggering limitations, which might make absurd the claims set up for him as an educator, did not stand in his way as a promoter. Indeed, there are always plenty of persons who almost demand oddities as the hallmark of genius, and are quite willing to believe that muddy water must be deep.

[1] Johann Ramsauer, *Kurze Skizze meines pädagogischen Lebens, mit beonderer Berückstigung auf Pestalozzi und seine Anstalten,* Oldenburg, 1838, pp. 7-10.

[2] From 1806 onward he kept in his room, usually under his bed, a coffin marked with a death's head. When he wanted to harangue his staff with special effectiveness, he made his speech with the coffin beside him, picturing himself as dead, appealing to their remorse for thwarting him, etc.

His theories. In one sense, it is misleading to speak of Pestalozzi's educational theories. He himself, with as much truth as modesty, wrote, a year before his death, "My life has brought forth nothing whole, nothing complete; my writing therefore cannot produce anything whole or complete."[1] What he contributed to education was an impetus, rather than a theory. He *felt* his way along the path of development which he ardently and generously desired for every human being. Ways and means were matters which he had neither the patience nor the skill to handle. His writings are filled with age-old commonplaces on the value and necessity of education. He had what A. C. Benson once called, in another connection, "a distressing grip on the obvious." The moment he lets go of the obvious, he flounders. Thus he tells us, over and over again,[2] that education must aim at the complete and harmonious development of all human powers. He saw that the educational procedure of his time did not accomplish that,[3] and could point out particular deficiencies well enough.[4] But he became vague when he had to venture positive suggestions for improving the procedure. He fell back upon the generality of 'following nature';[5] he even despaired of the usefulness of any theory, and roundly plumped for the practical sense of mothers as superior to all the learned the-

---

[1] "Mein Leben hat nichts Ganzes, nichts Vollendetes hervorgebrancht; meine Schrift kann auch nichts Ganzes und nichts Vollendetes leisten." (Foreword to *Schwanengesang* (Swan Song), 1826.)

[2] For instance, in *Wie Gertrud ihre Kinder lehrt*, X, § 22; *Über die Idee der Elementarbildung*, §§ 13, 194, 198, 247; *Von der Erziehung* (in his short-lived weekly, *Schweitzerblatt*, 1782), §§ 1-11.

[3] See *Über die Idee der Elementarbildung*, §§ 67-82, 112-19; *Wie Gertrud ihre Kinder lehrt*, II, §§ 8-13; IV, § 3; X, § 18; *Schwanengesang*, §§ 88, 91.

[4] As when he rails at the Philanthropinists for trying to coax children into studying by pretending that study is a game. (*Von der Erziehung*, §§ 18-20.)

[5] See, for instance, *Wie Gertrud ihre Kinder lehrt*, X, § 22; *Über die Idee der Elementarbildung*, §§ 92-111, 247; *Schwanengesang*, §§ 1-10.

orists.[1] He thought that faith in God and love of God 'naturally followed' from the child's love of parents, brothers, and sisters.[2] He did take up again, it is true, the extremely old and entirely correct notion, so frequently rediscovered in education, that sense perception precedes thought. He did try to work out a psychological method of teaching, based upon sense perception, through a curiously forced analysis of all perceptions into *number, form,* and *language.*[3] But even his admirers were compelled to admit that he got hopelessly lost in trying to formulate some actual *method* involving this distinction, which seemed to be vividly convincing to himself, yet which he could neither put into practice with children nor make clear to other teachers. In fact Pestalozzi recognized this incapacity in himself.[4] It is not without significance that the enthusiastic followers of what they called Pestalozzianism should have quarreled so often over the very nature of the theories and method each professed to follow.[5] He had not

[1] *Von der Erziehung,* §§ 3-8. One of his thoroughly excellent ideas was that of equipping women to educate their own children at home. With this purpose in view he published in 1803 the *Buch der Mütter, oder Anleitung für Mütter, ihre Kinder bemerken und reden zu lassen.* It contains many sensible suggestions, but forces the idea of sense-perception into mechanical generalizations which must certainly have been a queer puzzle to most mothers attempting to guide themselves by the book.

[2] *Schwanengesang,* § 18.

[3] See Letter VI in *Wie Gertrud ihre Kinder lehrt,* especially §§ 8-13, and Letter VIII, §§ 1-10; he works out the details for language in Letter VII, §§ 20-44. For his psychology of language see *Über die Idee der Elementarbildung,* §§ 34-35.

[4] See the frank statement in *Wie Gertrud ihre Kinder lehrt,* VII, § 56, in which he confesses that "all this is just a speculation about the mysterious processes of education, concerning which he is not at all clear," and that his projected *Book of Methods* had not been written because "he had not thought his way through to it."

[5] This instance may illustrate. Charles Mayo, a young English clergyman of twenty-seven, became a chaplain at Pestalozzi's Institute in 1819 (two years after Hermann Krüsi's son was born at Yverdon), and remained three years with Pestalozzi. He then returned to England, lectured and wrote about Pestalozzi, and set up a Pestalozzian school, first at Epsom, later at Cheam. The school

the distinctive gifts, and at heart he had not the desire, to work out a coherent theory of education. The flattering hubbub of Yverdon, whilst it may have pleased his innocent vanity, confused him. He wrote, some time after he had moved to Yverdon, "At Burgdorf I began my work, and at Burgdorf I finished it."[1] That work aided the promotional development of education in two ways: by giving a vigorous sentimental impulse to the idea, already formed and growing that 'democracy' demanded school education for every child; and by further inspiring the search for a more perfect educational method based upon a study of the child's psychology. But at the end of his long life, Pestalozzi knew that what he strove for was an ideal, most worthy of pursuit, yet never to be attained in this life. "Human nature itself fights against this ideal. Our knowledge and our capacities are only a makeshift, patchwork, and will never be anything more."[2] In those late years, too, he returned to the simple ideas he had begun with at Neuhof. The final pages of the *Schwanengesang* repudiate his work, not merely at Yverdon, but at Burgdorf, and claim as his real own the emotional generalities of Neuhof and of *Leonard and Gertrude*. Whilst he thanks the Swiss government for having given him the castle at Burgdorf, he says bluntly, "It was a grave mistake on my part to have accepted it." Now, the compelling idea of the Neuhof days was simply industrial education, the training of poor children to manual labor. In his report of 1777 (the second

---

acquired a great name, had a long waiting list of applicants. In the year in which Mayo died, 1846, the young Hermann Krüsi, then twenty-nine years old, became a teacher in Mayo's school. He left at the end of the year, in open disgust, protesting that the methods of the school were not at all the methods of Pestalozzi. (H. Krüsi, Jr., *Recollections of My Life, etc.*, edited by Elizabeth Alling, New York, 1907.)

[1] H. Morf, *Zur Biographie Pestalozzis,* Winterthur, 1868-89, Vol. 3, p. 105.

[2] See the whole passage in *Schwanengesang,* §§ 36-39.

of three issued for the cotton-spinning venture at Neuhof),
he emphasizes his opinion that children of seven "should
be devoted to their true destiny, learning to do manual
work. Reading, writing, reckoning should not be begun
until they are several years older." In this he was following Rousseau's guidance, probably the one persistent inspiration of his life.[1]   A recent writer insists that this
industrial education was the central aim of Pestalozzi, and
complains that Pestalozzian schools have neither grasped it
nor applied it.[2]   Apparently he does not see that such an
aim would not have served the purpose of 'democratic'
propaganda into which poor Pestalozzi had to fit.

His influence. It was very definitely in that line of school
development, the propaganda of the 'democratic' idea, that
Pestalozzi's influence was powerful. He was, of course,
only one of many promoters; but it was his fortune to be
the outstanding one so as to catch the imaginations of the
historians. Von Fellenberg was doing his industrial education much better than Pestalozzi could ever do it;[3] Père

[1] See *Émile*, Bk. II.   T. Corcoran (*Studies*, Vol. 16, pp. 138-39) tells
of Pestalozzi's boasting that his son, Jacob, at twelve years of age
could not read or write; but quotes Pestalozzi's friend, Emmanuel
Frohlich (in his *Souvenirs*), as authority for the statement that Mrs.
Pestalozzi had taught the boy to read, write, and figure, without
Pestalozzi's being aware of the fact.

[2] L. F. Anderson, *History of Manual and Industrial School Education*, Appleton, New York, 1926.

[3] Philipp Emmanuel von Fellenberg was born at Berne in 1771, and
educated at Tübingen. After the formation of the Swiss Republic
he was ambassador at Paris. Wealthy, and of noble family, he had
been taught by his father to take a generous interest in social and
political problems and in the education of the poor. He conceived
an early admiration for Pestalozzi's ideas. When he was twenty-
eight years old he bought the estate of Hofwyl with the purpose of
dedicating it to educational experiments. In 1804 he tried to get
Pestalozzi, who had become his neighbor, to work with him; and
made another like attempt in 1817. But collaboration between him
and Pestalozzi was simply impossible. His Institutions at Hofwyl
began to attract notice from 1808 onward, when that excellent
teacher, Jacob Wehrli, joined him. They included schools for poor
boys (and after 1823 a school for poor girls, founded by his wife),
an academy for children who would pay their way, a normal school,

Grégoire Girard[1] was organizing elementary schools at Freiburg with a skill utterly beyond Pestalozzi's powers; Bernard Overberg, a full contemporary of Pestalozzi, was conducting at Münster a much better normal school than

various technical schools. All were linked with his two central ideas: that education should be built upon manual labor, and that religion was an essential part of education. In its day, Hofwyl was at least as world famous as Yverdon, and undoubtedly of much greater practical influence on Swiss education. But it lacked the glamor of Pestalozzi's large dreams. Von Fellenberg died in 1844. His son William undertook to carry on his Institutions but they died off within four years. His notion of manual labor in education was carried over to England and the United States, and for a time affected schools. There was even a Manual Labor Society organized in New York in 1831, to spread von Fellenberg's ideas in schools; but it died the same year. Somehow, the new 'democracy' had no great taste for manual labor. (See W. King, *The Institutions of de Fellenberg*, London, 1842; and H. Barnard, *American Journal of Education,* Vol. 3, pp. 591-96; Vol. 13, pp. 323-30; Vol. 26, pp. 359-68.)

[1] Jean-Baptiste Girard was born at Freiburg in Switzerland, December 17, 1765. He became a Franciscan at Lucerne in 1781, taking the name 'Grégoire.' He was ordained priest at Freiburg in 1789. At once, he was set to teaching philosophy to his fellow Franciscans at Freiburg. Ten years later, Stapfer, who was also Pestalozzi's patron, put him on his official staff, as consultant and archivist. Girard's own tolerance and charity did much to break down the common hostility toward Catholics. He visited Pestalozzi at Burgdorf in 1802, and always showed a friendly interest in his work, although he was too intelligent not to see how grossly imperfect that work was. From 1804 to 1823 he was superintendent of the Catholic schools for French children at Freiburg. He introduced lay teachers (one of them from Pestalozzi's school at Burgdorf), he improved teaching methods, and of course he made the Christian aim a central part of his teaching. He made skillful use of a modified 'monitorial' system, based rather on the old Jesuit scheme than on those of Bell and Lancaster, which he called 'mutual instruction.' He had great success, attracted visitors from all parts of the world. His admirers called themselves Girardists, even founded a Girardine review in Italy to spread his ideas. When the Jesuits sought to return to Freiburg in 1814, Girard at first opposed the move. The Jesuits finally succeeded in 1818. From that time onward, Girard met much official opposition. He was accused of 'Gallicanism,' of being a disciple of Kant. The Bishop of Freiburg at first defended him, and in 1819 commended his educational system; yet four years later, on May 25, 1823, he condemned it as "unmoral and irreligious." Girard resigned from his position in charge of schools. He was offered a Canonry at the cathedral of Lyons, France, with the prospect of carrying on his work there on a large scale; but he refused it, because it would involve his leaving the Franciscan order. He went

the Institute at Yverdon,[1] and had published in 1793 an admirable manual of pedagogy, of which a new edition was issued as late as 1908.   But von Fellenberg was a noble, keeping to the aristocratic tradition even in his work for the poor, and Girard and Overberg, although thoroughly in sympathy with the 'democratic' movement, were Catholic priests.   *Non tali auxilio* did the men who dreamed of a new approach to the earthly paradise plan the spread of schools which were to realize the great 'democracy.'   Most

instead to Lucerne, and there for twelve years took care of the schools for poor children.   During this time, Froebel submitted his theories to Girard for criticism.   The last fifteen years of his life he spent at Freiburg, much honored, engaged in writing.   He died there, March 6, 1850, at the age of eighty-five.   He wrote a good deal.   His most important educational works are: *L'Enseignement régulier de la langue maternelle,* Paris, 1844, which won the Montyon prize of the French Academy; and *Cours éducatif de la langue maternelle,* 7 vols., Paris, 1845-48.   There is an excellent monograph on Girard by Andrew Maas (Wagner, New York, 1931), which contains a summary of his report on Pestalozzi's Institute.

[1] Bernhard Heinrich Overberg was born at Höckel, a village of Westphalia, May 1, 1754, of a poor family.   His father was a peddler, and he himself had to take up the same occupation whilst still a boy. Even had he had opportunity for school education, the local schools were wretched affairs, conducted by ignorant and incompetent teachers.   A Catholic priest took interest in the boy, taught him privately, and prepared him to enter the seminary.   Overberg was ordained priest in 1779.   Immediately afterward, he joined teaching to his work as a curate.   The vicar-general of Münster was eager to start some normal school work, and commissioned Overberg to undertake it in 1783.   The work was done in the summer and autumn, the courses lasting about four months.   Overberg continued in the work for forty-three years, until his death in 1826, although he was given the added task of rector of the diocesan seminary after 1809.   He was the first man in Germany to make provision for women in his normal school, and may be said to have opened up teaching as a profession for lay women.   He wrote a great deal about education, including a number of textbooks.   His chief work was *Anweisung zum zweckmässigen Schulunterricht,* Münster, 1793, which was translated into French, from the 7th German edition, in 1838, as *Manuel de Pédagogie,* and has since then been re-edited a number of times. The *School Regulations for the District of Münster,* 1801, was almost entirely drawn up by Overberg.   In spite of his humility and modesty, high honors were given him toward the close of his life.   He died November 9, 1826, at the age of seventy-two.   (H. Krabbe, *Leben Overbergs,* Münster, 1831; there is an English translation.)

histories of education scarcely deem such Catholic educators worthy even of a footnote. It was not quality of work
which would make any man an effective leader in the new
educational trend, but adaptability to the uses of emotional
appeal. For all his incompetence, Pestalozzi was highly
acceptable to the emotional aspirations of his time and of
later times, and that in the two hopes which fired the new
enthusiasm: the general hope that schools would renew
mankind, and the more definite hope that a method would
be found to make all schools efficient for that high purpose.

On education in general. Speaking of the time when
Pestalozzi was moved from Burgdorf to Münchenbuchsee,
one of his biographers says, "On all sides people declared
that his institute ought to be kept up, if it were only on
account of the enthusiasm excited by it throughout Europe."[1] There is the real nub of his influence. Fichte said
the same thing. He urged that the State system of schools
in Prussia should be based on Pestalozzi's 'method of instruction,' not because it was the best in itself, but because
"Pestalozzi's aim is to raise the lower classes to an equality
with the most highly educated . . . and because his theory
can enable the nation and the whole human race to rise
above our present miserable conditions."[2] Stein, the Prime
Minister of Prussia, sent some student-teachers to Pestalozzi, with definite instructions not to be cajoled into
thinking Pestalozzi's 'method' of any great value, but to
catch Pestalozzi's flame of enthusiasm.[3] The visitors who
came in such numbers to Burgdorf and Yverdon, even if
they were able to see through the little trick of putting up
the bright boys to dazzle them, were tremendously impressed by Pestalozzi's talk. As early as 1803, Ström and
Torlitz, sent to Pestalozzi by the Danish government,

[1] A. Pinloche, *Pestalozzi*, New York, 1901, p. 61.
[2] *Reden an die deutsche Nation,* 1808, Rede IX.
[3] Bruno Gebhardt, *Die Einführung der Pestalozzischen Methode in
Preussen,* Berlin, 1896, pp. 33 sqq.

opened a Pestalozzian school at Copenhagen. It lasted only three years. In 1805 another visitor, Gruner, went back to Frankfort and began a school modeled on Pestalozzi's; and although the school survived for only five years, it was an important center of influence, because in it Froebel did his first teaching. But no number of failures, no amount of evidence that Pestalozzi's 'method' was hopelessly mechanical, could affect the influence which he had in promoting the schools that raised such great hopes. Prussia showed the result of that influence more quickly, and in some ways more strongly, than any other country. But Maine de Biran, in the second stage of his journey from rationalism back to Catholicism,[1] founded a Pestalozzian school at Bergerac in 1808. The Swiss Voitel carried Pestalozzi's influence into Spain, in the days when French rationalism swayed the *politicos,* and from 1806 to 1808 was head of the short-lived State-endowed *Real Instituto Pestalozziano Militar* at Madrid. William Maclure,[2] the rich Scotchman who became a United States Commissioner to Paris under Jefferson, visited Yverdon in 1806, and brought back to the United States, not merely a Pestalozzian enthusiasm, but a Pestalozzian pupil, Joseph Neef, an Alsatian, who had been a Catholic seminarist before he went to Yverdon. Maclure wrote the first American account of Pestalozzi's work. Later he associated himself with Robert Owen in his communistic venture at New Harmony, Indiana, and contributed $150,000 toward promoting it. Neef organized Pestalozzian schools at Philadelphia, Village Green, Pennsylvania, and Louisville, Kentucky, and was to have made New Harmony another Yverdon. He taught in the last named place from 1825 to 1828, then conducted schools

[1] Cf. Couailhac, *Maine de Biran,* Paris, 1905; W. Turner, *History of Philosophy,* Boston, 1903, pp. 606 sqq.

[2] Maclure published at New Harmony in 1831 *Opinions on Various Subjects,* which contain twenty essays on education.

at Cincinnati and Steubenville for six years, and finally returned to New Harmony, to spend the last twenty years of his life there in writing propaganda. In England, James Pierrepont Greaves, who had gone to Yverdon at the age of forty, and spent eight years associated with Pestalozzi, became secretary of the Infant School Society for seven years, then conducted several Pestalozzian schools. In 1827 he translated and published *Letters on the Early Education of the Child,* which Pestalozzi had written to him. He named one of his schools after Amos Bronson Alcott, the American teacher and writer, who in 1830 had founded the famous Temple School at Philadelphia. These scanty illustrations[1] of the spread of Pestalozzi's influence are offered to bring out the essential fact that the men who welcomed Pestalozzi's ideas were already filled with great dreams of a new social order, of economic and moral reforms, basically rationalistic, ignoring, though not always actively opposing, Christian principles. Their energy was admirable and more than admirable was their generous devotedness to the cause of the reform which they hoped to effect through schools. Their most pronounced results were obtained in Prussia and in the United States, in the very remarkable growth of State-endowed and State-controlled school systems.

[1] They might be multiplied considerably. See, for instance, A. P. Hollis, *The Oswego Movement,* Boston, 1898, for an account of the work begun at Oswego, New York, by Dr. Edward Austin Sheldon, in which he was aided by Margaret Jones of the London Home and Colonial Training School in 1861, and, after 1862, by Hermann Krüsi Jr. Another center of Pestalozzian influence was William Torrey Harris (1835-1908), who was superintendent of the public schools in St. Louis, Missouri, from 1867 to 1880, and introduced into the schools a sort of Pestalozzian method. In 1881 he was one of the founders of the Concord School of Philosophy and Literature. He was a leading exponent of Hegelian philosophy. For seventeen years, from 1889 to 1906, he wielded great influence on schools as United States Commissioner of Education. He wrote enormously. The bibliography published in the *Report of the Commissioner of Education* for 1907 (Vol. 1, pp. 37-72) includes no less than 479 of his articles on education. Cf. G. Karr, *Dr. W. T. Harris' Lehre von den Grundlagen des Lehrplans dargestellt und beurteilt,* Jena, 1900.

On methods in schools. Pestalozzi's own methods, so far as they may be said to have ever had any definite existence, failed to make any great impression on schools. His influence rather lay in the fact that he stimulated the efforts of others to discover the perfect method for schools. The absurd claim that Pestalozzi originated the 'psychological movement' in schools has only this much foundation, that under his inspiration a host of teachers and writers became increasingly conscious of the need to study the mental processes of the child at school. The success of those efforts has naturally been varied. He himself contributed little or nothing of any value to that study. He repeated the age-old formulas of 'following nature,' 'concrete before abstract,' and the like, the common stock of educational writers from Vives onward; but he was incapable of applying the formulas in any practical way. In reality, however, what Pestalozzi fostered was an educational movement, dating back to Francis Bacon and Comenius, much wider and more significant than a mere study of pupil psychology. It was a movement to discover and formulate a 'science of education'; and as such it is still continuing, undeterred by a long succession of failures.

From Vittorino da Feltre and Vives down to 'Mark Hopkins on one end of a log,' all the great teachers have known that teaching is an art, that the success or failure of almost any method in schools depends upon the personal gifts and acquirements of the teacher himself. That fact demonstrates the essential aristocracy of education, the class distinctions in teacher as well as in pupil set by the Creator. The new temper of 'democracy' chafed under that limitation. Men harked back to Bacon's grandiose promise of a 'method' which would 'level all wits.' The business of education must be reduced to unchanging 'laws,' to a positive 'science,' a set of rules of procedure which anyone may master. Pestalozzi believed that all that could be done;

even now and then believed that he himself had actually accomplished the task.[1] His great significance lies in the fact that he exerted his influence in an age which was ready and waiting for it, in an age which had largely abandoned the guidance of revealed truth to trust in its own self-sufficiency, which had built up an imaginary 'conflict' between science and religion and had declared for science as the victor over religion, which had replaced theology by sociology. Such an attitude of mind has, of course, no essential connection with 'democracy.' It just so happened that the new social and political enthusiasms came into being in a world which had developed that rationalistic and irreligious temper. But that temper was precisely what caused men to raise such exaggerated hopes of what the efforts of multiplied secular schools could accomplish toward the reconstruction of mankind. The immediate result of Pestalozzi's influence on school methods was to usher in a period of new theorizing and experimentation: in which the dominating individual names are those of Herbart, Froebel, and Spencer. We must briefly consider the work of each of these.

Herbart. Pestalozzi had given a tremendous emotional shove to the movement for 'democracy' in education. But even his most ardent admirers had to admit that he left unsolved the great problem of 'method.' Herbart came to attack that problem. His significance for the new development in schools comes in part from the actual and valuable aid he offered in improving the technique of instruction in schools, but in greater part from wide conclusions to which he at least pointed the way, and which, after his

---

[1] See, for instance, Fischer's letter of December 20, 1799, to Steinmuller, outlining Pestalozzi's plans and hopes, which Pestalozzi reprinted in part in *Wie Gertrud ihre Kinder lehrt* (1st letter; in Holland's translation, pp. 34-42), with his own running commentary on the letter. See also his acceptance of Glayre's summary: "Vous voulez mécaniser l'éducation." (*Ibid.*, Holland's translation, p. 25.)

death, were to form the basis for the universal education imposed upon the new generation by 'democratic' national governments.

His life. Johann Friedrich Herbart was born at Oldenburg, capital of the little country of the same name, up near the North Sea, on May 4, 1776. His father was a lawyer. Of his mother the most notable fact recorded is that she studied Greek with her son. His parents were divorced when he was a young man. He was given the orthodox education of his social class, the *gymnasium* from his thirteenth to his eighteenth year, and then the university: in his case, Jena. He studied philosophy under Fichte (1762-1814), and though much influenced by him, was opposed to his philosophic idealism, and at the age of twenty began a philosophic system of his own.[1] In 1797 he became tutor to the three sons, eight, ten, and fourteen years of age, of von Steiger, a Swiss official at Interlaken. As tutor, he was to render a report on his work each two months. The five reports which have been preserved contain much of his educational theories. After two years he gave up this work to complete his doctorate at Göttingen in 1802, where he then taught and wrote until 1809, in which year he was appointed to the chair of philosophy, formerly held by Kant, at Königsberg. In that same year, 1809, he married an eighteen-year-old English girl named Mary Drake. He continued at Königsberg until 1833, when he fell into political disfavor with the Prussian government, and in consequence removed to Göttingen, where he taught until his death, August 11, 1841.

His philosophy. We are not here concerned with Herbart's philosophy except in so far as it affects his work in

---

[1] Although of a genial and cheerful temper, Herbart was so much discouraged by the doubts raised through Fichte's teaching that he was strongly tempted to drown himself. Cf. his *Ein Augenblick meines Lebens*, 1796, in Vol. 1 of the *Sämmtliche Werke*, edited by Kehrbach and Flugel, Langensalza.

education. In opposition to Fichte's idealism, he conceived a rather narrow realistic explanation of the universe, which in the department of psychology led him to assert that the soul, like other substances, is a monad, endowed with no faculties or activities, and simply postulated as the subject of the presentations which combine and interact to form the only knowable reality of our mental life. He tried to devise mathematical formulas for the interactions of these presentations. His teaching had little influence during his own lifetime. But later it became the foundation both of the 'psycho-physics' developed by Fechner, Weber, Wundt,[1] and others, and of a general mechanical view of the mind, which Herbart himself would scarcely have accepted. In these two ways he affected the foundations of education with a powerful indirect influence, which seems quite to overweigh the many excellent contributions he made to methods of instruction.

Herbart as educator. During the second of his two years of tutorship, when he was a young man of twenty-three, Herbart visited Pestalozzi at Burgdorf. His work as tutor had already created in him an intense interest in educational theory. Pestalozzi's enthusiasm fired that interest still further. He began writing about Pestalozzi's ideas.[2] He set himself to organize his own experience as tutor into principles of method. Although he went on to prepare himself for a professorship in philosophy, that interest in education never waned. He lectured on education at Göttingen. At Königsberg he founded a pedagogic seminar, in which he lectured every week, and for which he secured a practice

---

[1] Wundt's *Outlines of Physiological Psychology*, which appeared in 1874, became a sort of standard textbook in the United States after G. Stanley Hall brought German psychology to Johns Hopkins University in 1883.

[2] In 1802 an appreciation of *Wie Gertrud ihre Kinder lehrt*, and a criticism of *Idee eines A B C der Anschauung*; in 1804, *Standpunkt der Bertheilung der Pestalozzischen Unterrichtsmethode*.

school to serve to demonstrate his principles. He wrote a great deal on education.[1] The students in his seminar became heads of schools and school systems throughout the Germanies, and in that way spread his theories. But his greatest influence upon education came after his death, and was perhaps most noted in the United States. That influence affected both the general character of education and the methods used in school instruction. We must consider his theories in each of these ways.

Herbart's theories. Herbart thought of education as fundamentally a training for virtue.[2] But the virtue to be aimed at had little or no connection with either revealed divine law or the social nature of man.[3] It was determined by a morality based upon *aesthetic necessity,* and was to be secured by (a) government, which essentially consists in

[1] The most important of his many educational works are these: *Die aesthetische Darstellung der Welt als das Hauptgeschaft der Erziehung,* 1804; *Allgemeine Pädagogik,* 1806; *Briefe über Anwendung der Psychologie auf die Pädagogik,* 1831; *Umriss pädagogischer Vollesungen,* 1835; *Umriss der allgemeinen Pädagogik,* 1841. Of English translations may be noted here the following: H. M. and E. Felkin, *The Science of Education,* London, 1892; M. K. Smith, *Textbook of Psychology,* New York, 1894; W. J. Eckoff, *A. B. C. of Sense-Perception and Introductory Works,* New York, 1896; B. C. Mulliner, *Application of Psychology to the Science of Education,* New York, 1898; A. F. Lange, *Outlines of Educational Doctrine,* London and New York, 1901.

[2] See Lange's translation, *Outlines of Educational Doctrine,* pp. 7, 44: "the term *virtue* expresses the whole purpose of education."

[3] This view is elaborated in *Die aesthetische Darstellung der Welt, u. s. w.* Herbart was not irreligious nor asocial. In §§ 18, 19 of the *Outlines of Educational Doctrine* (Lange, p. 14), he admits the need of religious training; he discusses religious instruction in §§ 232-38, *ibid.,* but he concludes that all this is the work of the church and the home, not of the school. In the same way, he recognizes that the school itself is a little world, that the pupils have social relations even as pupils (§§ 14, 15, 182, 318, *op. cit.*); but these are only circumstances in which the individual is to work out his 'inner freedom,' or harmony with his own nature, as the prime constituent of virtue; they do not constitute any basis of law. Even the religious training is valued chiefly, if not singly, because it makes for a humility which is a proper part of the individual 'inner freedom.' That is the only reason given in §§ 18, 19, *op. cit.* for the need of religious training. His morality is entirely self-centered.

keeping children occupied, (b) instruction, the immediate purpose of which was to set up a 'many-sided interest,' and (c) training, through the sympathetic personal relations between teacher and pupil. Of these three means, Herbart devotes most of his study to instruction, not merely because he denies the existence of a faculty of will,[1] but because the presentations which come through instruction, as also those got through experience,[2] actually constitute the mind of the pupil. Hence his detailed study of method is so largely concerned with the method of presenting ideas in instruction. He did not lose sight of his other two elements of education, namely, government and training, but he made it altogether too easy for those who followed him to lose sight of those elements.

In the matter of method, Herbart based his theories upon what he called 'apperception.' The word itself seems to have been first used by Leibnitz.[3] The idea it expresses can be traced at least as far back as Aristotle, and was familiar to scholastic philosophers in the ancient maxim, *Quidquid recipitur ad modum recipientis recipitur:* What you are colors what happens to you. Herbart's psychology gave this a new twist. His theory was that the first presentation made to a human being was not recognized as such, but became part of the unconscious mind. A second presentation evoked this former one, interacted with it; and the two then formed the beginning of an 'apperceiving mass,' which practically *is* the human mind.[4] Interest is self-activity,

---

[1] *Op. cit.,* § 58; Lange, p. 40.

[2] *Ibid.,* §§ 36, 78, 83; Lange, pp. 24, 69, 76.

[3] Leibnitz designates by 'apperception' nothing more than reflection, or a consciousness of an idea. Cf. G. W. Leibnitz, *Principes de la nature et de la grace,* § 4; *Monadologie,* § 14; in H. Schmalenbach's edition, *Ausgewahlte philosophische Schriften,* Leipzig, 1914, Vol. 2, pp. 124, 135.

[4] This basic notion of apperception can easily be made out in his *Textbook of Psychology.* It runs so thoroughly through his educational writings that specific instances of it would be entirely inade-

which is most powerfully exercised in education when the mass of ideas the pupil already has are reproduced and united with new presentations.[1]

Upon this foundation Herbart established a procedure for instruction, calculated to arouse the 'many-sided interest' of the pupils. He divided it into four parts: (a) clear presentation of ideas, analyzing them so as to be readily grasped; (b) association of these new ideas with what the pupil already knows; (c) system, or the ordering of the ideas through classification, reduction to principles, and the like; and (d) method, the application of this procedure by the pupil to assigned tasks, or to problems of his own devising. It is quite unlikely that Herbart had much acquaintance with the class method indicated in the Jesuit *Ratio Studiorum;* yet anyone familiar with it must see at a glance that Herbart's method is strikingly akin to the old Jesuit method; but with the important addition of a psychological analysis.[2] Herbart did not limit his view of method to the mere technique of presentation, but took in the wider question of material to be presented, and based his choice of material on both the psychological development of the pupil and the educational aim to be secured.[3]

quate. See Lange, *Über Apperception,* translated by the Herbart Club in America, Boston, 1892, pp. 200-45.

[1] *Outlines of Educational Doctrine,* § 71; Lange's translation, p. 60.

[2] The distinctive element in the Jesuit method was the *praelectio,* which, whilst it naturally varied for the different sorts of classes, grading all the way from university lectures to elementary instruction in grammar, nevertheless had a common structure throughout. Its essential purpose was to facilitate the student's grasp of new ideas, by a clear analysis of these and a linking up with his former knowledge. Cf. the *Ratio Studiorum, ann 1586, 1599, 1832,* tom. II, of G. M. Pachtler's edition (in *Monumenta Germaniae Paedagogica,* Band V), Berlin, 1887; pp. 165 sqq. for the *Ratio* of 1586; pp. 398-442 for the *Ratio* of 1599 and 1832. See also T. A. Hughes, *Loyola and the Educational System of the Jesuits,* New York, 1892, pp. 232 sqq.

[3] As illustration may be noted his emphasis upon the Odyssey as a beginners' book for boys, presenting ideals which make for his aim of virtue as the end of education, and presenting them in a way especially suited to appeal to younger minds. See *Outlines of Edu-*

His influence. Herbart deserved to have a considerable influence upon education. He contributed to the theory of education a remarkable wealth of shrewd, first-hand observations on the psychology of pupils. He analyzed with much clearness the problem of attention. He stressed the essentially moral purpose of education. His practical suggestions throughout his many writings are generally sound, convincing, and helpful. Unquestionably, educators like Stoy, Rein, Paulsen, and Willmann have profited much from those practical suggestions. But equally beyond question, the best things in Herbart's writings have not had the widest or deepest influence. There was in Herbart a general temper of sane realism which did not quite match the democratic enthusiasms; even though he praised generously the school system of the United States, on the very point of its 'democracy.'[1] Paul Natorp (1854-1925) began in 1897 an attack upon Herbart, contrasting him with Pestalozzi, whom he insistently hailed again as the founder of modern education.[2] Herbart was too individualistic. He

cational Doctrine, § 283 (Lange, pp. 282-85). Tuiskon Ziller (1817-83), whose *Grundlegung zur Lehre vom erziehenden Unterricht,* published in 1865, really first brought Herbart into wide public notice, developed Herbart's use of the Odyssey into the 'culture-epoch' theory, according to which each child parallels in his individual development the rise of mankind in general from savagery to civilization. The course of studies for the child should, therefore, be built up out of past epochs in the racial and national culture which correspond to each stage of the child's own psychological development. Wilhelm Rein (1847-1929), professor of pedagogy at Jena from 1885 onward, worked out, with the aid of two other teachers in the normal school, Pickel and Scheller, an elaborate scheme, in eight volumes, for reducing Ziller's theory to practice in elementary schools: *Theorie und Praxis des Volksschulunterrichts,* Leipzig. A fairly good idea of this may be gathered from C. de Garmo, *Herbart and the Herbartians,* New York, 1895, pp. 141-66.

[1] *Outlines of Educational Doctrine,* § 340; Lange, p. 322.

[2] See his *Herbart, Pestalozzi, und die heutigen Aufgaben der Erziehungslehre,* Leipzig, 1908. Others have gone further than Natorp. Such men as Paul Bergemann, director of State schools in Silesia, John Dewey, the present foremost influence in public education in the United States, Professor Findlay of Manchester, England, and Georg Kerschensteiner, for twenty-five years head of State

refused to consider the State the central agency in education, and he said plainly that State schools could scarcely affect the inner lives of their students.[1]

Yet in spite of these facts, Herbart has influenced the modern theory and practice of education profoundly, and, unfortunately, in rather a mischievous manner. In the first place, his theories concerning the human soul and mind have been made use of to bolster a mechanistic psychology which goes beyond Herbart in denying the substantial and spiritual nature of the soul. The 'stream of thought' definition of the mind is the practical basis of, perhaps, most of the educational psychology of the moment. In the second place, Herbart has helped to center educational efforts almost exclusively upon instruction. Even though he made clear the importance of what he called 'government' and 'training' in education, most of his work was concerned with instruction. In the minds of those who used Herbart, that preoccupation fitted well with the Baconian principle that 'knowledge is power,' which has been so thoroughly adopted in modern educational theory. Those two notions, of a mind that functioned rather like a material machine, and of an education largely centered upon the acquisition of knowledge, in turn helped to establish what has become the strongest belief affecting modern schools, the belief that education is a science, and that its exact laws can be laid down for the guidance of schools as sharply as the physical laws of, say, light or gravitation. What 'democracy' had been led to hope for, in Bacon's promise of a method universally applicable by all teachers to all pupils, seemed to

schools at Munich, have developed Natorp's theory of State supremacy in education to include almost the complete subjugation of the individual to society, and certainly to exclude religion most completely from the schools. For an excellent brief discussion of these and other radicals amongst modern educators, see E. B. Jordan's English translation of Franz de Hovre's *Philosophy and Education,* New York, 1931, pp. 85-203.

[1] *Outlines of Educational Doctrine,* §§ 331-32; Lange, pp. 317-18.

be brought much nearer by the labors of Herbart and by the curious conclusions drawn from his writings by the men who came after him.

Froebel. Pestalozzi had furnished the vague, humanitarian, emotional impetus to the new 'democracy' in education. Herbart offered it a sort of intellectual assurance, a psychology of instruction, and a new stirring of the hope that school procedure could be reduced to a science. There were still some gaps to be filled before the scheme would be complete. Two of the desiderata were these: an organization of the very early stages of child life; and something to be done about that troublous problem of religion in education, which refused to be ignored completely, despite the heroic efforts of the most enlightened educators. Froebel came to supply these deficiencies. A brief sketch of his life will throw some light on how he carried out his task.

His life. Friedrich Wilhelm August Froebel was born April 21, 1782, at Oberweissbach, a village of the Thuringian Forest. His father was a Lutheran minister. His mother died before he was a year old, leaving five sons. His father married again three years later, and the stepmother paid little attention to Friedrich. When he was ten years old his mother's brother, also a Lutheran minister, took him to his home a few miles away, at Stadt-Ilm, and sent him to school. But the boy was not a good school subject, being dreamy, introspective, shy. He was of the emotional and imaginative type, so very common, which finds routine oppressive and therefore avoids it as much as possible. At fifteen he was apprenticed to a forester, but he spent his two years with the forester chiefly in metaphysical speculations about the 'unity of nature.' At seventeen he joined his elder brother at the University of Jena for a year, restless, wandering from one lecturer to another. Then he was set to study farming; but he took no hold of that. He tried successively surveying, accounting, a private secretaryship. He studied architecture for a while at Frankfort, abandoned that to teach for some time between 1805 and 1807 in Gruner's Pestalozzian school. In the work of a teacher he found a field in which to sow his vague metaphysico-religious ideas. He went to Pestalozzi at Yverdon, stayed there two years, 1807 to 1809. Then he wandered again for two years, finally going to Göttingen in 1811, and on to Berlin, studying natural sciences, chiefly mineralogy, seeking some connection between crystallization and God. In 1813 he enlisted as a volunteer in the Prussian army, and served a little over a year, although he was never in battle.[1] In 1814 he became an assistant curator in the Berlin Museum of Mineralogy. Whilst in the army, he had acquired two devoted friends, Langenthal and Middendorf, with whose aid, and five of his nephews as pupils, he opened a school at Griesheim in 1816. Froebel was then thirty-four years old. The school did not thrive. He removed to Keilhau, another village of Thuringia, in 1818, married an educated woman, Henrietta Wilhelmina Hoffmeister, set up an educational community with his friends, and conducted a struggling school[2] until 1830. In that year his friend Schnyder invited him to establish a branch school in his castle at Wartensee, in the Canton of Lucerne, Switzerland. The district, largely Catholic, resented what the people looked upon as a Protestant invasion. After three years there, Froebel moved to Willisau, nearby, in 1833, but with no better results. The Swiss government helped to set him up as an instructor of a diluted normal school at Burgdorf, Pestalozzi's former

[1] *Cyclopedia of Education,* New York, 1919, Vol. 2, p. 719.
[2] Yet Johann Arnold Barop, a disciple who had married one of Froebel's nieces (Middendorf and Schaffner married two other nieces and Langenthal married an adopted daughter of Frau Froebel), took over the school at Keilhau in 1832 and made such a financial success of it that he was able to give aid to the rest of the community of teachers. (H. C. Bowen, *Froebel,* New York, 1892, p. 35.)

place.[1] There the idea came to him that schools failed of their purpose because the children were already spoiled by bad education in their infancy. This was in 1836, when Froebel was fifty-four years old; and it marked his entry into a new career which was to lead to fame. He thought for a while of taking his new schemes to the United States, but finally went back to the Thuringian Forest, and, in 1837, at Blankenburg, near Keilhau, opened the first *kindergarten,* 'Garden of Children.' His wife died there two years later. His kindergarten suffered the same financial difficulties as all the other schools he conducted, and had to be closed in 1844. But in the meantime he had been writing about his system of infant education in the weekly *Sonntagsblatt* for nearly three years.[2] His writings began to win wide attention. After the failure of the kindergarten he travelled through the Germanies for five years, lecturing before groups of women. Toward the close of his lecture career he won the friendship of a clever woman, the Baroness von Marenholtz-Bulow,[3] who did more than any other one person to spread his theories, and by whose aid

[1] The elementary teachers of the Canton of Berne were to spend "three months every alternate year" at Burgdorf, and receive instruction in school methods from Froebel and Bitzius. (R. H. Quick, *Educational Reformers,* New York, 1902, p. 393.)

[2] This was not his first publication. At Keilhau, back in 1826, he had written his most important educational work, *Die Menschenerziehung, die Erziehungs—Unterrichts—und Lehrkunst, angestrebt in der allgemeinen deutschen Erziehungsanstalt zu Keilhau, dargestellt von dem Vorsteher derselben, F. W. A. Froebel.* He definitely subtitled it, *I Band bis zum begonnenen Knabenalter* (Volume 1, to the Beginning of Boyhood), but he never wrote any succeeding volumes. W. N. Hailmann, who had opened a German *kindergarten* in Milwaukee, Wisconsin, U. S. A., in 1873, published a rather free translation of this book as *The Education of Man,* New York, 1887.

[3] Bertha von Marenholtz-Bulow-Wendhausen was thirty-nine years old when she first met Froebel in 1849, and spent the remaining forty-four years of her long life in propagating his ideas by lectures, writings, practical demonstrations in London, Paris, Berlin, and several cities of Italy. Amongst her many writings are the *Reminiscences of Friedrich Froebel,* translated by Mrs. Horace Mann, Boston, 1887.

he founded a training school for kindergarten teachers at Liebenstein in 1849. The next year, in his sixty-ninth year, he married Miss Louisa Levin. But on August 7, 1851, von Raumer,[1] the Minister of Education, ordered the closing of all kindergartens in Prussia. Froebel felt this keenly, of course. On June 21, 1852, he died, and was buried at Schweina, a village near Marienthal.

His character. Froebel was a man of good intelligence, of high moral purpose, and of earnest religious sentiments. But he was temperamentally averse to disciplined effort under any guidance save his own. In spite of his gentle and modest willingness to co-operate with others externally, he was an extreme individualist, obsessed by a quite fanatical religious belief. He had sensed, early in life, as many another before and since his time has sensed, the gross imperfections in our management of life. He was intelligently aware that the final solution of life's problems lies in religion. Yet such religion as was offered to him in the Lutheranism of his age was anything but satisfactory to him. His life therefore became a quest for religious truth and for the means of making such truth active in human conduct through education. But in that quest he worked almost alone (or at least he thought he did), because he felt that the leaders with whom he was thrown were as much in the dark as he was. His search for truth in religion and education was a groping search, bewildered in

---

[1] Karl Otto von Raumer (1805-59), a Pomeranian, not to be confused with Karl Georg von Raumer (1783-1865) who was the first modern writer on the history of education (*Geschichte der Paedagogik, u. s. w.*, 4 vols., 1843-55). Karl Otto became Prussian Minister of Education in 1850. The revolution of 1846 had been largely fomented by schoolmasters; and von Raumer, as a conservative, distrusted the whole tribe. Moreover, one of Froebel's nephews, Karl Froebel, had published socialistic writings attacking the government. Von Raumer may have linked uncle and nephew, not realizing that they were opposed in their ideas. But it seems more likely that he thought Friedrich Froebel's theories were actually subversive.

the presence of problems which man alone has never solved. We must respect and admire his earnestness and devotedness. But our admiration must not blind us to the fact that he was also pitiful in his attempts to do what was beyond unaided human powers, and in his lack of that authoritative guidance which Divine Truth has given to men.

His theories. What Froebel offered to the developing schools of 'democracy' falls into two divisions: his technique of education in infancy, and his religious basis for all education. The latter is by all means the more important of the two, and pervades all his work. His kindergarten theories are a late development, begun when he was fifty-four years old, and are colored throughout by his ideas of religion. Those ideas are elusive and vague in his writings; partly because he was not a competent writer, partly because the ideas were nebulous even to himself; but the essential and fundamental concept he makes clear enough.

When he began to think about religion at all, the Protestant world had already become pretty largely rationalistic. For a great many Protestants, faith in the divinity of Jesus Christ had become an acute problem, because of the strain set up in their minds between an inherited emotional attachment to the Founder of what they still professed as Christianity and the intellectual uncertainties which two hundred and fifty years of 'private judgment' had inevitably bred. Froebel solved this problem handsomely by believing in the divinity of everything. That allowed him to include the divinity of Jesus Christ, without becoming involved with the authoritative limitations of Christianity.[1] His pantheism then gave him his definition and

[1] "The divine effluence that lives in each thing is the essence of each thing." (*Die Menschenerziehung, u. s. w.*, opening paragraph. Hailmann's translation, *The Education of Man*, p. 2.) That idea recurs constantly throughout his writings. See particularly *op. cit.*, §§ 15, 18, 24, 60, 61, 63, 66, 76, 88. The very ancient doctrine of pantheism had been revived by a number of German thinkers around

formula for education, which is "the unfolding of the divine essence of man."[1]   He foggily refused some of the implications of this basic principle.   Whether with the conscious purpose of avoiding too sharp controversy, or because of the dreamy vagueness of his own mind, he at times obscured his pantheistic notions by references to 'the teaching of Jesus'[2] and by speaking of man and of external nature as 'creatures.'[3]   But he is resolute and explicit in applying a religion of pantheism to education.   He more than accepted Rousseau's theory of the 'natural' goodness of each human being; he made it the 'divine' goodness of each human being, and the foundation of his significant principle that education should be 'passive' as regards all interference with free 'self-activity.'[4]   A god, even if one confusedly thinks of him as a god in the making, should not be curbed. Any "categorical, mandatory, and prescriptive education of man" is justifiable only "when the original wholeness of the human being has been marred."[5]   His kindergarten aimed at preventing such marring, by simply presenting to infants various means of 'self-expression' and by withdrawing examples and influences which might set up any strains in their 'original wholeness.'   In his view, the play of children became a sacred thing;[6] his devices, the 'gifts' and

Froebel's time.   He does not admit borrowing it from any of those, Fichte, Hegel, Schelling, or Krause, who filled the German universities and learned journals with pantheistic idealism; but the air was full of it.

[1] *Die Menschenerziehung*, § 5 (Hailmann, pp. 4-5).

[2] Whom he never calls 'Christ.'   For some references cf. *op. cit.*, § 11 (Hailmann, pp. 12-13); § 61 (Hailmann, pp. 144-51).

[3] E. g., "Are not man and nature creatures of the same one God?" *Op. cit.*, § 76 (Hailmann, p. 205).

[4] "Education, from its fundamental principles, must be passive, following, not prescriptive, categorical, interfering."   *Op. cit.*, § 7 (Hailmann, pp. 7-11).   See also § 9.

[5] *Op. cit.*, § 8 (Hailmann, p. 10).

[6] *Die Menschenerziehung*, § 30.   "Play is the purest, most spiritual activity of man at this stage (childhood), and, at the same time, typical of human life as a whole, of the inner, hidden, natural life in

'occupations'[1] with which they are to pass their time, were discussed, not merely with great pedagogic nicety, but with a constant interweaving of religious symbolism, such as a strange modern distortion of thought likes to call 'mysticism.' Moreover, he made it quite clear that this divine wholeness had not to wait for a future life to find its fulfillment. Indeed he was rather severe and bitter in his condemnation of any appeal to a future reward.[2] The right education was to make 'men as gods,' not in heaven, but right here on this 'democratic' earth. One is not astonished to find that he opposed all dogmatic teaching of religion, although, as a matter of course, he himself constantly dogmatized: as, for instance, in his extraordinary definition of Christianity.[3]

His influence. To an educational world which had rather completely lost sight of the clear concept of Christianity, such theories came as most welcome, soothing, inspiring, satisfying. They were better than Rousseau's, because they were more vague, more tender, more sincere, more appealing to sensibilities not yet entirely dissociated from the long traditions of Christian culture. They appeared to be simply soaked in religiousness, and of a sort to seem orthodox enough to men and women who had reduced Christianity to a collection of reverent sentiments. In addition, they flattered that optimism which is an essential part of modern 'democracy,' the hope of immediate approaches to human perfection. Moreover, Froebel's life, simple, decent, kindly, created no such difficulties for his theories as had Rousseau's life. In particular, his theories appealed to the

---

man and all things." (Hailmann, pp. 54-55.) The whole paragraph is highly significant, as one of his braver conclusions from pantheism.

[1] Sphere, cube, etc., with which children are set to play, and thus arouse their 'self-activity.' See Froebel's essays, translated by Josephine Jarvis as *Pedagogics of the Kindergarten*, New York, 1895.

[2] *Die Menschenerziehung*, § 88 (Hailmann, pp. 244-45).

[3] *Ibid.*, § 61 (Hailmann, pp. 144-51).

hopeful tendencies of women; and the women, with von Marenholtz-Bulow-Wendhausen at their head, carried the kindergarten throughout Europe, and over the seas to the fallow lands of the United States.[1] Von Raumer's opposition was considered neither more nor less than a rather unusually stupid persecution. Study clubs were organized widely to bring the new gospel of our innate divinity to the homes and the school. 'Democracy' in education had its religious sanction.

Spencer. The nebulous, obscure, vaguely tender pantheism of Froebel, as a solution of the religious problem in education, appealed strongly, not merely to many women, and to those men who were already indoctrinated with the philosophic 'idealism' then prevalent in German universities, but also to the general type of sentimentalist of

---

[1] Froebel himself sharply pointed his *Kindergarten* theory to the United States. In an essay written in 1836, he indicated his hope that his chief field of influence would be in America. (Cf. Richard Lange's edition, *Friedrich Froebels gesammelte paedagogische Schriften,* 3 vols., Berlin, 1861-62, Vol. 2, appendix.) Kindergartens were established in the United States within a few years of Froebel's death. From the time that W. T. Harris, in 1873, introduced Froebel's theories into the public schools of the United States, the enthusiasm for Froebel grew rapidly. Within twenty-five years there were more than 3,000 kindergartens in the public schools (*Report* of the United States Commissioner of Education, 1903-04), and about 1,500 private kindergartens. Translations of all of Froebel's writings have been published in the United States, and the books concerning him are numerous. For a partial bibliography, see H. C. Bowen, *Froebel and Education through Self-Activity,* New York, 1892. But one of his most successful and most widely known followers is the Italian Maria Montessori. Born at Rome, 1872, she was the first woman physician graduated from the University of Rome. Her work amongst feeble-minded children led her into educational theory. Although her methods immediately derived from Edouard Seguin (1812-80), a French physician who resided in New York after 1848, she had read Froebel and caught his ideas. Later she developed her method for the training of feeble-minded children into a general scheme for all children between the ages of three and seven. The two essentials of her method are sense training and self-discipline through liberty. The method is outlined fully in her book, translated by A. E. George as *The Montessori Method,* New York, 1912; in which is also an historical sketch of its development.

either sex and of any nation. It left untouched, of course, all Catholic thinkers and the considerable number of Protestants who still held to the broad framework of Christian belief. It also left untouched a large class of men and women at the other extremes, Deists and Rationalists, the harder-headed opponents of Christianity in any form or any dilution. To these, Froebel's delicately veiled pantheism was an offensive sentimentality, an insult to their rationalism only slightly less gross than Christianity itself. That large class of persons found their champion and major prophet in Herbert Spencer and his cold, hard, 'scientific' theories. As in the case of some other theorists, a brief sketch of Spencer's life will do much to illuminate his theories.

His life. Herbert Spencer, born at Derby, England, April 27, 1820, came of a family closely connected with the origins of Wesleyanism. His grandfather, father, and uncles were school teachers. Young Herbert attended a local school, where he developed a vigorous dislike for Latin, Greek, and language studies in general, and an equally vigorous enthusiasm for the natural sciences. From his thirteenth to his sixteenth years, he lived with his uncle, Thomas Spencer, an Anglican curate at Hinton Charterhouse, near Bath. This uncle was rather noted as a social reformer and advocate of teetotalism. When he was seventeen, Herbert was set to work as a minor clerk in the construction department of a railway. He continued there for a little over three years, and in 1841 was dismissed on account of his cockiness. He puttered about at home and in London for a few years, incidentally publishing a political essay on 'The Proper Sphere of Government' in 1843. In 1844, he was employed as a subeditor on 'The Pilot,' a Birmingham journal, but got into trouble by his radical, anti-religious temper, and was dismissed the same year. He went back to railway work for two years. Then he spent a year or more, 1846-1847, in attempts at mechanical inventing. For the five years, 1848-1853, he was subeditor of 'The Economist.' During that period he published his first book, *Social Statics,* in 1851, and wrote some essays for reviews. By 1853, when he was thirty-three years old, he set himself free from other occupations to begin a series of philosophical works. The first of these, *Principles of Psychology,* afterwards incorporated into his *magnum opus, Synthetic Philosophy,* appeared in 1855. Because of his intense application to the writing of that book, he suffered a nervous breakdown, from which, although he lived forty-eight years more, he never fully recovered. In 1857, he began the huge *Synthetic Philosophy,* upon which he spent nearly forty years, and which mounted up to eighteen large volumes. The last years of his life he occupied in writing a voluminous autobiography. He died at Brighton, December 8, 1903, and his body was cremated at Golder's Green.

His qualities. Spencer unquestionably was a man of great talents; but his talents never equalled the audacity of his self-conceit; and most certainly did not include a sense of humor. He was by temperament self-centered, irritable, and had built up a morbid fear of misrepresentation. An extreme individualist, in practice as well as in theory, he resented praise almost as scornfully as he resented blame.[1] His emotional equipment seems to have been chiefly neg-

---

[1] He refused all civic honors offered to him when his work had brought him fame. But he engaged in many controversies to maintain his right to priority in promulgating his ideas. Curiously, he does seem to have antedated Charles Darwin in asserting the theory of evolution, although he borrowed much from Darwin in his later expansion of the theory. It is possible that he got his notions of the evolutionary theory from the writings of Buffon (1707-88), or Erasmus Darwin (1731-1802), the grandfather of Charles, or Lamarck (1744-1829). In any case, there was much speculation about theories of descent throughout the late eighteenth and early nineteenth centuries. Spencer seems to have coined the phrase "survival of the fittest." (See *Principles of Biology,* London, 1898, Vol. 1, p. 530.)

ative, his hostilities more pronounced than his loyalties. All his writings, no matter how pretentiously 'scientific' in tone, were colored by a hostility to Christian dogmas, which may quite possibly have been derived from an early disgust with the narrow Wesleyanism which surrounded his boyhood. In other respects also he manifested a disposition strangely alien to the calm balance, objectivity and care for accuracy that one looks for in even a *soi-disant* philosopher. He read little or nothing of previous writers when he was preparing for his own work on psychology.[1] He wrote *Principles of Biology* without having bothered to acquire any wealth of knowledge concerning biology, and trusted to Huxley, who read the proofs for him, to catch any notable errors of fact.[2] All his work displays an overbearing cocksureness.[3]

His educational theories. Between 1856 and 1859, Spencer contributed to three different English reviews four articles on the subject of education; and later published them as four chapters of a book, first printed in New York in 1860. The American edition was due to the refusal of 'The North British Review' to surrender the second article of the four for publication in book form.[4] Possibly an

---

[1] *Dictionary of National Biography,* 2d Suppl., Vol. 3, p. 362. He does not refer in his book even to Herbart and those German psychologists who followed Herbart's lead in developing a mechanics of psychology, with the exception of E. Weber, whose work he cites briefly in *Principles of Psychology,* 3d ed., New York, 1880, Vol. 2, pp. 228, 269.

[2] *D. N. B., Ibid.,* p. 363.

[3] "Huxley . . . laughingly said that Spencer's definition of a tragedy was the spectacle of a deduction killed by a fact." (*D. N. B., Ibid.,* p. 366.) But it was a tragedy only if the deduction were Spencer's own. Professor Sidgwick stated a similar criticism more bluntly: "Spencer suffered from the fault of fatuous self-confidence." (E. T. Raymond, *Portraits of the Nineties,* p. 121.) Criticism infuriated him almost as much as it does that perfect disciple of his, Mr. H. G. Wells.

[4] *Education, Intellectual, Moral and Physical,* Appleton, New York, 1860, Preface, p. v.

American 'pirating' was prophetic of the fact that Spencer's influence was to be much greater in the United States than in England. The general thesis of the book may truthfully be said to be that the best education for all men is the education which produced Herbert Spencer.

The first chapter establishes, lengthily, and with a ponderous dotting of 'i's' and crossing of 't's,' this basic principle: "To prepare us for complete living is the function which education has to discharge; and the only rational mode of judging of any educational course is to judge in what degree it discharges such function."[1] The rest of the book makes plain the fact that Spencer's 'complete living' is limited most severely to life on this earth. For that sort of 'complete living' he undertakes to prove that 'science,' by which he means only the physical sciences, is the necessary and sufficient educational instrument. His hostility to the cultural subjects, especially to language as a tool in education, recalls his own boyhood's dislike of languages. But he uses one argument which shows a deeper basis for his dislike even than his habitual approval of all that he himself had done. He says, "The learning of languages tends, if anything, further to increase the already undue respect for authority. . . . (The pupil's) constant attitude of mind is that of submission to dogmatic teaching. And a necessary result is a tendency to accept without inquiry whatever is established. Quite opposite is the attitude of mind generated by the cultivation of science."[2] It is true that he devotes the following four pages to proving that science is religious, and "that not science, but the neglect of science, is irreligious."[3] But that is by way of paradox, and as a defense against criticism.[4] He makes his defense hinge

---

[1] *Op. cit.*, p. 12.
[2] *Ibid.*, p. 79.
[3] *Ibid.*, p. 82.
[4] When his *Principles of Psychology* had appeared in 1855, R. H. Hutton criticized it adversely in an article in *The National Review*,

upon a loose *apologia* for 'natural' religion as opposed to the Christian religion.

But it is in the second chapter that his animus against Christian teachings appears most unveiledly. He repeats the already stale accusations of the Rationalists that the Catholic Church stifled intelligence, and "considered that the best education which most thwarted the wishes of children."[1] As a contrast to that, 'science' is now to revolutionize education and to find 'the true method' in education. The test of this true method is to be "the constant exhibition of its results." He falls back upon the comforting assumption of all the 'democratic' theorists, that children instinctively know what is best for them in education, and that we need only the right method to make education pleasant.[2] He praises Pestalozzi's 'principles,' although he admits that "the Pestalozzian system seems scarcely to have fulfilled the promise of its theory."[3]

In the third chapter he makes a great to-do about the punishment of children being 'natural,' so that they may see it as the logical consequences of their wrong conduct, not the interference of hated authority. The fourth chapter considers bodily health as an aim of education, and discusses the subject in a sensible way, albeit with much

entitled "Modern Atheism." Spencer, however, was not an atheist; he was an agnostic—and a good deal of an anarchist.

[1] *Op. cit.,* p. 89. He emphasizes that it is the Catholic Church he means, by glorying that "Protestantism has gained for adults a right of private judgment and established the practice of appealing to reason." (*Ibid.,* p. 88.) In reality, as his life showed, he cared nothing for any of the many Protestant forms of religion. The praise here is merely a stick with which to beat the Catholic Church.

[2] *Ibid.,* pp. 101 sqq. Yet he stumbles upon the need of authority in education when he writes of the teacher's task "in providing from day to day the right kind of facts, prepared in the right manner, and giving them in due abundance at appropriate intervals" (*Ibid.,* p. 108); and yet does not dare indicate that the child himself is to decide *which* are the right facts, and the right manner, and the due abundance, and the appropriate intervals.

[3] *Ibid.,* p. 109.

elaboration of the obvious and the usual heavy dogmatism which characterized all the utterances of this foe of dogma.

His psychology. Back of his immediate pronouncements on education lay the views which he expressed later in his two volumes on *The Principles of Psychology*.[1] Although Spencer did not formally deny the spiritual character of the human mind, he insisted that we cannot *know* any such character,[2] and he reduced all the functions of the mind to material activities in the order of physical and chemical changes.[3] He quite definitely denied the freedom of the will, or for that matter any distinctive power of willing at all.[4] He carefully avoided using even the word 'soul' in the entire 1,300 octavo pages of his work on psychology— no mean specimen of a Hamlet-without-the-Prince. He stood for the complete application of the theory of evolution to human beings and to all human functions.[5] The whole trend of his psychology is materialistic. That psychology reflected itself constantly in his educational theories, and gave to his insistence upon 'science' as the one means of education a meaning which his disciples have never failed to catch.

His influence. Spencer's treatise on education has been translated "into all the chief languages."[6] It was received with enthusiasm by many educators, but most enthusiastically of all in the United States and in Japan. When Spencer visited New York in 1882, he was astonished by

---

[1] 3d edition, Appleton, New York, 1880.

[2] "Impressions and ideas are the only things known to exist, and Mind is merely a name for the sum of them." (*Op. cit.*, Vol. 1, p. 146. See the whole passage, pp. 145-62.)

[3] This notion recurs constantly, in various ways. As an instance: "All that we call Reflex Action, Instinct, Memory, Reason, Feeling, and Will are a cumulative result of physical actions that conform to known physical principles." (*Ibid.*, Vol. 1, p. 614.)

[4] "Will is nothing but the general name given to the special feeling that gains supremacy and determines action." (*Ibid.*, Vol. 1, p. 503.)

[5] *Ibid.*, Vol. 1, pp. 291 sqq. See especially pp. 325 sqq.

[6] *Dictionary of National Biography, loc. cit.*, p. 363.

the ebullient welcome he received from American educators. Here was an eminent English philosopher more than confirming the educational principles which the American Herbartians had dug out of Herbart. He is still hailed widely as the foremost philosopher of the nineteenth century. But he rather shocked the English people, who, if they are not religious, have at least a tradition of respect for religion. Even in England, his glorification of scientific studies as the supreme means of education may possibly have influenced the larger place given to such studies in modern schools, although the tendency to enlarge the scientific content of education was in operation long before Spencer wrote. It was the Japanese, who, with their astonishing mimetic tendency and their delight in hard, exact outlines, undertook to follow Spencer to the letter. That remarkable man, Yukichi Fukuzawa (1834-1901), imported Spencer's theories into Japan, after a visit to England in 1862. His three-volume work, *Sei Yo Jijo* (Western Ways), which appeared in 1866, had enormous effect toward basing the new Japanese civilization on the materialistic philosophy of Spencer.[1] In the United States, Spencer's influence has been rather through his principles than through his suggestions of method in education. The secularist view in education, already highly developed in the United States, found Spencer an impressive ally. He made articulate what millions of men had gropingly felt: their emotional revolt from the teachings of the Christian religion, and from a philosophy inspired and guided by Christianity; their impatient despair over the apparent failure of education as hitherto conducted; and their eager hope that, by concentrating its efforts on the immediate, tangible affairs of life, mankind with the magic aid of 'science' might be able to make our life on earth more comfortable—or, as they would

[1] Cf. B. H. Chamberlain, *Things Japanese*, London, 1891; and S. Okuma, *Fifty Years of New Japan*, New York, 1909.

say, happier. Spencer's work fitted in very well with the grandiose dreams of 'democracy' in education.

Summary and conclusion. The movement toward 'democracy' in education, which came to mean primarily a wide spread of compulsory school attendance, was in part a true social evolution, corresponding to the political evolution which was taking place in governments. It was also in part an engineered movement, pushed forward by a comparatively small number of private individuals, who had material aid and moral support from various governments, and who were in a position to exert a powerful and effective propaganda upon the masses of the people. These individuals were of many sorts, Catholics, Protestants, Deists, Pantheists, Rationalists, Agnostics; some eager to keep the influence of Christian teachings in the 'democratic' education, at least in some vague way; others equally eager to get rid of the last remnants of Christian dogma, and to found the new 'democracy' on naturalism. The two camps tended to become confused on their fringes, chiefly because many secularists still had a lingering sentimental association with Christianity, and many Protestants were so vague in their beliefs that the admixture of a little pantheism or rationalism scarcely caught their attention; but the main opposition stood out clearly enough. Of the two camps, Christian and naturalist, the latter became in the early nineteenth century numerically much the larger, and politically much the more powerful.

The four men briefly discussed in this chapter, Pestalozzi, Herbart, Froebel, and Spencer, were spokesmen for the Naturalists and Rationalists. Their writings, and those of the hundreds of their followers who were articulate enough to write, controlled educational theory in all the public normal schools, and through practically all the professional journals. The Catholic and Protestant theorists who worked parallel with these men in promoting the spread of school education, and in developing improved methods in schools had little or no influence in forming the educational principles which guide the huge modern machinery of State school education.[1] For one thing, the means of propaganda

[1] This point is well worth illustrating. One instance may be taken from France, where the Catholic body, under the exceptionally able leadership of an active educator, Felix Antoine Philibert Dupanloup, began in 1844 a concerted effort to put Christian principles into school education. They were aided by political circumstances, through the fear of revolution fostered by irreligion which was then imminent throughout western Europe. The Second Republic of 1848, which in 1852 became the Second Empire, was conservative in its policies. Falloux, the prime minister, was friendly to religion. In this favorable atmosphere, Dupanloup, for whom Falloux had secured the bishopric of Orleans in 1849, wrote several excellent treatises on education; notably, *L'education en general* (1850) and *La haute education intellectuelle* (1850). These treatises embodied the best thoughts of the modern theorists on widening school opportunities, on enriching the curriculum, on improved methods in teaching. But they insisted that physical, mental, moral, and religious education is a unity, and that to neglect any element of it is to unbalance education and to destroy its effectiveness. The *loi Falloux* of 1850 responded to Dupanloup's principles, encouraged private schools, gave a freer hand to the Catholic communal schools. These latter grew in number from 6,464 in 1850 to 11,391 in 1864; and even hostile critics had to admit that in administration, curriculum, and methods they were an improvement upon the lay schools which had preceded them. Many of the anti-religious propagandists in education fled into exile. The prospects for complete education seemed rosy. Yet this success was astonishingly short-lived. The Second Empire fell in 1870, and was succeeded by the Third Republic. Before Dupanloup died, in 1878, he saw the old forces opposed to religion in education once more assuming power. The history of education in France since 1890 has been a history of mounting anti-religious persecution, and of the triumph of secularism. Most histories of education gloat over that last fact, and call the period from 1850 to 1879 one of "reaction" against "true progress." Another instance may be found in the United States. John England, an Irishman born in 1786, became bishop of Charleston, South Carolina, in 1820. As able a man as Dupanloup, he set himself to the promotion of education. Within two years he founded a journal, *The United States Catholic Miscellany,* in which for twenty years he wrote admirably upon Christian principles in education. In 1830 he established a school "to educate females of the middling class of society," and in 1832 founded a college for boys, Catholic and non-Catholic. Chancellor Kent said of him that "he revived classical learning in South Carolina." He was admired and loved by all classes of people. Yet he had simply no effect on the secularist propaganda conducted by Horace Mann and his followers, nor upon educational policies in general throughout the developing school systems in the

for 'democracy' in education were not to any great extent in their hands. Moreover, for several generations before the project of 'democratic' schools approached its fulfillment, a very large number, perhaps a majority, of men and women in our Western civilization had ceased to be practical Christians of any denomination, or to be willing to accept religious leadership in education. The dominating theories in education were, therefore, secularist, and for the most part positively rejected any religious influence in the schools.

Those theories, which began to control State schools and many private schools, although they varied in some details, had the following points in common. They all effectively denied the doctrine of original sin, and assumed a human perfectibility to be made actual in this life, and by means of school education. They envisaged as the immediate aim of school education a raising of the physical, mental, and moral level of mankind, such as would make a true democracy possible. They offered, or hoped for in the very near future, some perfected 'method' which would enable schools to attain that aim. If they admitted religion into their view at all, as an element in education and in life, it was a vague 'natural' religion, certainly not Christianity.

United States. His own college, after a brilliant short career, was forced to close its doors. The Catholic population of South Carolina, in the century from his coming to Charleston, grew only about 40 per cent in numbers, whilst the population of the State grew more than 400 per cent. In the field of pure theory, a greater man than Dupanloup or England did work which was more thoroughly lost sight of than even that of Overberg. Antonio Rosmini-Serbati, the founder of the Institute of Charity and author of a remarkable system of philosophy, worked out an astonishingly shrewd application of psychology to classroom methods. His book on the subject, begun in 1839, was published in 1857, two years after his death, and has been translated into English as *The Ruling Principle of Method Applied to Education*. Davidson wrote an English discussion of his philosophy in 1882. But only research students know anything about him. The world of education has passed him by completely. Instances of this sort can easily be multiplied.

They stressed 'science' as both the content and the guide of education, in the form of 'natural studies,' or 'direct observation methods,' or 'induction,' or even the materialistic philosophy which they so often, and so mistakenly, offered in the guise of 'evolution.' They leaned strongly toward a mechanistic psychology, as the foundation on which to build an exact 'science' of education.

When those theories were reduced to popular form for that appeal to the masses which political 'democracy' made necessary, they pointed to wealth, comfort, social prestige, political or economic power as the goal of the new education, and the chief inducements for universal school attendance. They sought to stimulate in every individual his natural ambition for success in this world. They sought to make school procedure pleasant and alluring. They combined persuasion for the masses with pressure upon the governments to bring about a universal schooling of children. To a rather remarkable extent, that propaganda was successful, and by the close of the nineteenth century had approximately attained its aim so far as the spread of schools and compulsory attendance were concerned, in the western lands of Europe, in Canada and the United States, in several of the South American and South African countries, in Japan, and in Australia. What sort of school systems resulted from this great movement, it will be the business of the next chapter to consider.

TOPICS FOR DISCUSSION

1. Hegel and the doctrine of State supremacy in education.
2. The governmental support afforded to Pestalozzi, Herbart, and Froebel.
3. The influence of Fichte in German education.
4. The relation between the Industrial Revolution and schools.
5. The work of James Pierrepont Greaves in English education.
6. The theories of Bell and Lancaster as regards religion in education.

7. The work of Overberg in establishing teaching as a profession for lay women.

8. A comparison between the theories of Froebel and Rosmini-Serbati.

9. The 'method' of Joseph Jacotot.

10. The influence of Darwinian 'evolution' upon educational theories.

11. The place of William Torrey Harris in the history of school education in the United States.

BIBLIOGRAPHIC NOTE

So much has been written on the principles underlying the modern 'democratic' developments in education that only a few of the more important works can be indicated here. Many books on the subject display an uncritical enthusiasm which is unscientific and misleading. J. K. Hart, *Democracy in Education,* New York, 1918, is an instance of that sort of book. European Continental writers have studied those principles more dispassionately and objectively. Amongst the best of such studies are: O. Willmann (translated by F. Kirsch), *The Science of Education,* 2d ed., 2 vols., Latrobe, Pa., 1930; F. De Hovre (translated from French edition of G. Simeons by E. B. Jordan), *Philosophy and Education,* New York, 1931; R. Eucken (translated by W. S. Hough and W. R. Boyce Gibson), *The Problem of Human Life as Viewed by the Great Thinkers from Plato to the Present Time,* New York, 1910; A. Eymieu, *Le Naturalisme devant la Science,* Paris, 1911; E. Boutroux (translated by J. Nield), *Science and Religion in Contemporary Philosophy,* London, 1909; Cardinal Mercier, *Les Origines de la Psychologie Contemporaine,* 3d ed., Louvain, 1925; F. Brunetière, *Sur les Chemins de la Croyance,* Paris, 1905; and the searching work of F. W. Foerster, *Politische Ethik und politische Paedagogik,* 4th ed., Munchen, 1920, and *Christentum und Paedagogik,* Munchen, 1920. In England, A. F. Leach, J. E. G. de Montmorency, and J. W. Adamson have written with detachment and good sense. Cardinal Newman, in "The Tamworth Reading Room" (reprinted in *Discussions and Arguments*), written five years before he became a Catholic, and in *The Idea of a University,* offers an excellent consideration of principles. In the United States, together with a vast amount of nonsense, there are such sane writings as N. M. Butler, *The Meaning of Education,* New York, 1915; and R. R. Rusk, *The Philosophical Bases of Education,* Boston, 1928; but perhaps the clearest American writer is J. L. Spalding, *Means and Ends of Education,* Chicago, 1895; *Thoughts and Theories of Life and Education,* 3d ed., Chicago, 1901; *Education and the Higher Life,* 14th ed., Chicago, 1922. Some convenient selections of earlier writings can be found in W. H. Kilpatrick, *Source Book in the Philosophy of Education,* New York, 1923. F. De Hovre, *La Catholicisme, ses Pédagogues, sa Pédagogie,* Bruxelles, 1930, presents a good analysis of Catholic principles, as maintained by Newman, Spalding, Dupanloup, Mercier, and Willmann.

A thorough bibliographic study for Pestalozzi has been made by A. Israel, in *Monumenta Germaniae Paedagogica,* Vols. 25, 29, and 31, Berlin, 1903-05. Pestalozzi's collected works have been published several times; in 15 vols., Stuttgart und Tübingen, 1819-26; in the 18 vol. edition by Seyffarth, Brandenburg, 1869-73, and in the enlarged edition by Seyffarth, Liegnitz, 1899-1901. H. Barnard, *Life, Educational Principles, and Methods of John Henry Pestalozzi,* New York, 1859, translated some fragments of his works. J. P. Greaves translated his *Letters on the Early Education of the Child,* London, 1827; Eva Channing, an abridgment of *Leonard and Gertrude,* Boston; Lucy Holland and F. Turner, *How Gertrude Teaches her Children,* 1844, 5th ed., Syracuse, N. Y., 1915. For his life, there are K. von Raumer, *Geschichte der Paedagogik,* Stuttgart, 1843-47, Vol. 2 (translated by Barnard, *op. cit.*); the huge work of H. Morf, *Zur Biographie Pestalozzis,* 4 vols., Winterthur, 1868-89; and perhaps the best study of all, J. Guillaume, *Pestalozzi, Étude biographique,* Paris, 1890. For his intellectual background, see H. Higgs, *The Physiocrats,* New York, 1897. For his theories and influence, one may select out of the hundreds of studies the following: H. Barnard, *Pestalozzi and Pestalozzianism,* New York, 1862; E. Biber, *Henry Pestalozzi and his Plan of Education,* London, 1831; H. Krüsi, Jr., *Pestalozzi, His Life, Work, and Influence,* New York, 1875; M-A Jullien, *Exposé de la méthode d'éducation de Pestalozzi,* Paris, 1842; F. Herisson, *Pestalozzi élève de J. J. Rousseau,* Paris, 1886; B. Gebhardt, *Die Einfuhrung der Pestalozzischen Methode in Preussen,* Berlin, 1896; A. Pinloche, *Pestalozzi,* Paris, 1901 (English translation, New York, 1901); R. de Guimps, *Pestalozzi, his Life and Works,* New York, 1889; W. S. Monroe, *History of the Pestalozzian Movement in the United States,* Syracuse, N. Y., 1907. Most of these, although colored by enthusiasm, give material for a fair estimate.

O. Willmann, who esteemed the many excellent things in Herbart, and who edited his *Paedagogische Schriften,* 2 vols., Leipzig, gives a balanced criticism of his theories in his *Didaktik,* 2 vols., Braunschweig, 1882-89. (In Kirsch's translation, see Vol. 1, pp. 28 sqq., 42 sqq., 54, 57, 328 sqq., 335.) See also Stoy's article in *Encyklopaedie der Paedagogik,* 2d ed., Leipzig, 1878. Besides the references in the text, fair evaluations of Herbart will be found in C. de Garmo, *Herbart and the Herbartians,* New York, 1895, and L. Gockler, *La Pédagogie de Herbart, Exposé et discussion,* Paris, 1905. For some of the developments based on Herbart, see W. Rein, *Paedagogische Studien; alte Folge,* 2 vols., Vienna; and T. Ziller, *Einleitung in die allgemeine Paedagogik,* Leipzig, 1856. These are also touched upon in C. C. Van Liew, *Life of Herbart and Development of his Pedagogical Doctrines,* London, 1893. A summary of Herbart's psychology is given in T. Ribot, *German Psychology of To-day*, New York, 1880. C. A. McMurry, *The Elements of General Method Based on the Principles of Herbart*, Bloomington, Ill., 1892, is an illustration of the American adaptation of Herbart. J. Adams, *Herbartian Psychology Applied to Education*, Boston, 1906, is a good presentation of some of the best in Herbart. J. Darroch, *Herbart, a Criticism*, New York, 1903, is a rather angry attack.

W. Lange edited a fairly complete *Friedrich Froebel's gesammelte paedagogische Schriften*, 3 vols., Berlin, 1861-62. Many of Froebel's writings have been translated into English. The following are the most important: *Autobiography* (translated by Michaelis and Moore), Syracuse, N. Y., 1889; *Education of Man* (translated by W. N. Hailmann), New York, 1887; *Letters* (translated by A. H. Heinemann), Boston, 1893; *Mothers' Songs, Games and Stories* (translated by F. and E. Lord), London, 1885-86; Josephine Jarvis's translations of *Pedagogics of the Kindergarten*, New York, 1895, and *Education by Development*, New York, 1899. H. Barnard groups together a great deal of translated material about Froebel in *Kindergarten and Child-culture*, Hartford. Most of the books written on Froebel take the kindergarten work for their immediate subject and bring in his pantheistic idealism incidentally. A bibliography of detailed studies in Froebel's methods is given in H. C. Bowen, *Froebel and Education by Self-Activity*, New York, 1893, pp. 203-04. A contrast to the rather sugary adulation of Froebel may be found in J. Guillaume's article on him in *Dictionnaire de Pédagogie*, Hachette, Paris. P. R. Cole, *Herbart and Froebel, an Attempt at Synthesis*, New York, 1907, is interesting but superficial.

Herbert Spencer's *Autobiography*, 2 vols., was published in New York, 1904. A laudatory *Life* is by H. Elliot, London, 1917. H. F. Collins wrote an *Epitome of the Synthetic Philosophy of Herbert Spencer*, London, 1901, to which Spencer himself contributed a preface which was an epitome of the epitome. W. Waite, *Spencer and his Critics*, Chicago, 1900, quotes large passages from Spencer, refutes his agnosticism. W. Ward, *Naturalism and Agnosticism*, London, 1903, traces the genesis of Spencer's theories and opposes them. An interesting study of principles is M. F. Shepperson, *Comparative Study of St. Thomas Aquinas and Herbert Spencer*, University of Pennsylvania, 1925. H. Macpherson, *Spencer and Spencerism*, New York, 1900, discusses his influence. G. Compayré (translated by Maria E. Findlay) deals favorably with Spencer in *Herbert Spencer and Scientific Education*, New York, 1907. Lucas, *Agnosticism and Religion*, Baltimore, 1895, confines himself to Spencer's general principles, although implying criticism of their effects upon education.

Of those whom the bulk of historians consider minor figures in this period, von Fellenberg reveals himself in *Blätter von Hofwyl*, Berne, 1843, and is given some notice by H. Barnard in *American Journal of Education*, Vols. 3, 13, 26. For Père Girard, besides Father Maas' monograph there are A. Daguet, *Le Père Girard et son Temps,* 2 vols., Paris, 1896; E. Naville, *Notice biographique sur le Père Girard de Fribourg,* Geneva, 1850; G. Compayré, *Le Père Girard et l'éducation maternelle,* in *Les Grands Éducateurs,* Paris, n. d.; E. Lüthli, *Pater Gregor Girard,* Berne, 1905; J. Schneuwly, *École du Père Girard,* Freiburg, 1905. Barnard has a brief notice of Father Overberg, *American Journal of Education,* Vol. 13, pp. 365 sqq. Lagrange has a good account of Dupanloup's educational work in *La Vie de Msgr. Dupanloup,* Paris, 1883. For Rosmini, there are his own works: *Del Supremo Principio della Metodica, e di alcune sue Applicazioni in Servigio dell' Educazione,* Turin, 1857 (translated into English by Mrs. M. Grey, *The Ruling Principle of Method Applied to Education,* Boston, 1887); *Saggio sull' Unita dell' Educazione,* Florence, 1826; *Psychology* (English translation), 3 vols., London, 1884-88. See also W. Lockhart, *Life of Antonio Rosmini-Serbati,* 2 vols., London, 1886, and Thomas Davidson, *The Philosophical System of Antonio Rosmini-Serbati,* London, 1882 (which gives also a biographical sketch and bibliography). For Bishop England, see Peter Guilday, *Life and Times of John England,* 2 vols., New York, 1927, especially Vol. 2. pp. 133-72, 404-79.

CHAPTER XIX

Modern School Systems

Diversity of character. The whole tradition of schools, for at least a thousand years, had been linked with religion, when State governments began to enter upon the direct organization and management of schools. That tradition was to persist, even though a different type of school, the secularist, was to oppose it in overwhelming numbers, with vast financial support, and with the sanction of large masses of the people in all the Western nations, who had abandoned all definite belief and religious practice.

The improvements in school administration and school methods, which came in great part as the result of the new enthusiasm for schools, were common to both religious and secularist schools; but secularist educators claimed the larger credit for those improvements, and, because of their stronger financial position, were often able to anticipate religious educators in taking advantage of the improved school technique.

As a result of these conditions, the religious schools naturally found themselves on the defensive, and tended more and more to lose influence over the masses of the people. But there is an inherent vitality in the Christian religion which enables it to withstand even such conditions as these. The history of modern school systems is, therefore, primarily a history of State schools, but by no means exclusively so; it is shot through with the struggle of religious education to maintain itself in a world grown hostile to Christianity. The present chapter will attempt a brief sketch of the school systems in a few of the leading nations; keeping in mind the two great agencies, governmental and private, and the two opposed characters of schools, secular and religious. The school systems of the United States will be considered in another chapter.

But it is important to note that the division of schools as governmental and private does not necessarily and always coincide with the division of schools as secular and religious. Some governmental schools are religious; some private schools are secular. Moreover, the interweaving of social elements in modern times is so complex that not infrequently an avowedly secular school is staffed by teachers who have a religious purpose in education and give a religious character to their instruction; whilst at the same time there are private schools, conducted under the apparent control of religious bodies, in which the teaching is openly irreligious, even atheistic. It is especially necessary to remember these facts when, as in the present chapter, consideration is limited to only the broad outlines of school systems.

General organization of schools. From the time of the early Roman Empire, schools had been divided into three classes, roughly corresponding to the periods of childhood, adolescence, and young manhood. In modern times we have come to think of those classes under the generic names of elementary, secondary, and higher schools. That classification is accepted in all modern school systems to such an extent that even the considerable differences of organization in the various modern systems are still confined within that general framework. As those differences of organization mainly affect the manner in which elementary schools are articulated with secondary, and secondary with higher schools, they may properly be said to concern the lower and upper limits of secondary schools, as determined by the age of students, by the aim of the schools, and by the curriculum devised to attain that aim. To illustrate this, it may be pointed out that the type of school now familiar in the United States as the 'high school' has no exact equivalent in any European system. In the age of its students, the American high school corresponds to the last four years of a German *gymnasium;* but in curriculum, it is more on a level with a *gymnasium* student-age at least three years younger; and its aim is rather like that of the Prussian *mittelschule* and continuation school.

Two types of school systems. But amongst European school systems there is this point of organization in common, that for all students beyond the age of 8-10 years, the schools branch into schools for the leaders and schools for the masses: the former serving the education of 10 per cent or less of the children, the latter of 90 per cent or more. The type of secondary school for future social leaders, represented with some approximation by the American senior high school and college, is called *gymnasium* in Germany and Austria, *lycée* and *collège* in France, *ginnasio* and *liceo* in Italy, grammar school or college in England, *collège* in Switzerland, *athénée* in Belgium, *lärowerk* in Sweden, *colegio* in Spain and Latin America. All these have minor differences; but they all stress a cultural or liberal training and most of them envisage a linking up with higher schools of the university type. The schools for the masses, equivalent to a compact combination of the American elementary and high schools, are variously known as *volksschule,* board school, *école primaire,* etc., carry their pupils to the age of 14-16 years, and are designed as the final school education of those who attend them. In the last two or three school years, these schools for the masses often divide, to give industrial or commercial training, or normal school work, or the like. European higher schools, like those of the United States, fall into two great groups: schools of culture and research, of the traditional university type, and professional schools.

State control of school systems. In the matter of State

control of schools there is naturally much diversity in the various countries. But in general that control is exerted in two ways, one direct, and the other indirect. Directly, in each modern State, the government controls its own school system, through its financial appropriations, through its determining the qualifications of teachers and its appointment of executives and teachers, through its limitation of the character and aim of its schools, and the curriculum to be followed in the schools. Indirectly, the government exercises considerable control over private school systems, sometimes by means of monetary grants, sometimes by setting up qualifications for teachers, or issuing licenses to teachers, or by enforcing standard requirements for degrees, or compelling students in private schools to pass a governmental examination based on the curriculum in State schools; and always by the prestige which mere bulk, numbers, and the backing of State authority give to its own system of schools, and which is a powerful psychological force affecting private schools. The result is usually a general uniformity in each nation between the State school system and the private school systems, as regards school organization and curriculum, however much the private schools may try to direct that organization and curriculum to an aim different from the aim of the State schools.

Limitations of school education. All the greater leaders who formed the principles on which modern school systems are built envisage education as physical, mental, and moral; some of the leaders, as also religious. The schools do attempt, in varying measures, some physical training, in the way of organized games, athletic exercises, and the like; and most of them give instruction in elementary hygiene. But moral education is inefficiently handled. Scarcely any effort is made to teach morality in practical ways; and in the secular schools, even moral instruction is weakened by its lack of adequate sanctions. The school systems which include religious education in their aim all too often are content with doctrinal instruction, as a rule crowded into a small corner of the curriculum, and seldom give their pupils much exercise in religious practice. These short-comings are the result of the natural tendency of all schools to concentrate upon instruction, upon an approach to education through the mind alone. They are defects to be noted in ancient and mediaeval, as well as in modern schools. But the close and rigorous organization of modern schools, with their almost mechanical alignment of class schedules and assigned material for instruction, tends to make the defects unusually pronounced.

With these few broad considerations as guides, even a cursory view of some modern school systems may show how they fit into the history of education. Such a cursory view is all that this chapter will try to offer; nor will it attempt even to touch upon the most recent developments in the various countries discussed. For one reason, some of those very recent developments, such as the movement toward the *einheitsschule* in Germany and the *école unique* in France, are so fluctuatingly still in the present that an historical view of them is scarcely possible.[1]

I. GERMANY

Prussia the model for German school systems. Germany as a state is one of the youngest. Until 1870, the name 'Germany' stood, not for a nation, but for a rather shifting geographical area in Europe and a medley of peoples of diverse race and culture who happened to speak approximately the same language. Before the downfall of Napo-

---

[1] The reader who desires a detailed and immediate view of education in England, France, Germany, Italy, Russia, and the United States, will find it in I. L. Kandel, *Comparative Education,* Boston, 1933, a compact treatise in some 900 pages, with good bibliographies.

leon, there were some four hundred 'German' States. The
Congress of Vienna, in 1815, amalgamated those into thirty-
eight. Under Bismarck's management, in 1870, twenty-two
of those States and three free cities united in a federation
to form the German *Reich*. In that group Prussia stood
out, largest in area and in population, and assumed an
aggressive leadership. Particularly did Prussia take the
lead in establishing a State system of schools; and the
school systems set up in the other German States showed
the influence of Prussian leadership. Thus, in spite of the
considerable divergences in the various German school systems, the schools of Prussia are fairly representative in
general structure and character of all the German schools,
as well in Austria and other German-speaking countries as
in the States which made up the former German Empire
and now constitute the present republican *Reich*.

Prussian State schools. Prussia had accepted the principle of State control of schools in legislation begun as
early as 1713, under Frederick William I, and culminating
in the great Code of 1794. The theory was established;
but it took some time to put it into practice. Prussia's
position in Europe was insecure. Napoleon defeated the
Prussians badly at Jena, in 1806, and humiliated them in
the severe terms of the Treaty of Tilsit, in 1807. When the
Prussian State set about plans for its recovery from those
disasters, Fichte, during the winter of 1807-1808, delivered in Berlin nine 'Addresses to the German Nation,'
in which he urged a national school system as the chief
instrument in building up a national spirit. His ideas were
received with great enthusiasm; and prompt action followed.[1] In 1808, a Department of Public Instruction was
added as a branch to the Interior Department of State. In

---

[1] F. Paulsen, *German Education, Past and Present* (translated by
Lorenz), New York, 1908, pp. 183, 240.

1809, Karl August Zeller (1774-1847) was empowered to set up a State normal school, inspired by what the Prussians thought to be the theories of Pestalozzi; for the State shrewdly realized that to control principles of education is even more important than to control the mere material organization of schools. By 1840, there were thirty-eight normal schools for elementary teachers, and nearly 30,000 elementary schools. It was a remarkably rapid, enthusiastic growth; but like many a first rush it soon spent itself. About 1840, a reaction set in against the whole program.

The grounds for that reaction were fundamentally religious. Although Lutheranism was the official State religion of Prussia, the ministers of that religion were in a servile position under the State, and had long been deprived of influence in the management of schools.[1] The State school systems were developed under influences definitely irreligious and anti-Christian. Yet the Lutheran ministers had not lost all influence amongst the Prussian people, especially of the powerful middle class. The long traditions of Christianity were not to be destroyed even by the aggressive dominance of anti-Christian philosophy in the early nineteenth century. Moreover, the Prussian king, Frederick William IV (ruled 1840-1861), took alarm at the powerful propaganda of irreligion in the schools, and even blamed that sort of teaching for the political revolution of 1848.[2] The result was a new set of school regulations in 1854, by which the exaggerated claims of naturalism in the school aims and plans were restricted, and religious instruction was again made a part of the school curriculum. The need of religious instruction has ever

[1] As regards elementary schools, the Lutheran clergy were ousted by the State regulations of 1763 and 1765. They lost all voice in the affairs of secondary and higher schools in 1787. See F. Kretzschmar, *Handbuch der preussischen Schulrechts*, Leipzig, 1899; L. Clausnitzer, *Geschichte des preussischen Unterrichtsgesetzes, u. s. w.*, Berlin, 1892.

[2] F. Paulsen, *German Education, Past and Present*, p. 246.

since been given consideration in the Prussian State school system,[1] even though Bismarck's *Kulturkampf* of 1872 for a time threatened to banish again from the schools all religious influence.[2]

Denominational schools. In the elementary schools, Prussia[3] makes provision to have Protestant, Catholic, and Jewish children taught by persons of their own faith. The State higher schools are undenominational; but arrangements are made for certain periods, usually two, of religious instruction each week. Practically all secondary education is given in the State schools. In 1908, for instance, out of a total of 922 secondary schools in Prussia only 21 were not State schools.[4] Bavaria, in which the Catholics are about 70 per cent of the population, followed a similar arrangement; and only nine out of 158 secondary schools were private schools. In Austria, another predominantly Catholic country, State schools are the rule, the school system dating from the *Studienhofkommission* established by Maria Theresa in 1774. The regulations provided for instruction in the Catholic religion even in schools for the crown lands, and the State system included parish schools

[1] Taking the period just before the World War for illustration, one finds that the Prussian 'middle schools' gave exactly the same amount of time to classes in religion as to classes in needlework for girls, but only two-thirds as much time to religion as to gymnastics for boys. In the *Gymnasien,* religion and 'nature study' were each accorded the same number of class periods, which was just about one-half as many as were given, respectively, to German, Latin, French, and mathematics. (Cf. *Cyclopedia of Education,* Vol. 3, p. 78, for detailed statistics in tabular form.)

[2] E. Nohle, *History of German School System* (in *Report of the United States Commissioner of Education,* 1897-98, Vol. 1, p. 179), admits that Bismarck's attack was specifically directed against the Catholics. But it naturally tended to weaken all Christian influence, including that of the Lutherans.

[3] With a few exceptions, such as Baden and Hesse, the other German States follow Prussia in providing for denominational elementary schools. In 1906, about 90 per cent of Protestant and Catholic children were in denominational schools in Prussia; but only about 25 per cent of Jewish.

[4] *Cyclopedia of Education,* Vol. 3, p. 91.

under the immediate direction of the parish priests. By a decree of Joseph II in 1781, freedom was granted to Protestants to have their own schools within the State-controlled system.[1] In all the schools, about the same amount of time is given to religious instruction as in the Prussian and other German schools.

German universities. Fichte, in 1807, had urged the King of Prussia to found a new university at Berlin. It actually was founded in 1810, under the wise direction of von Humboldt, and upon a generous plan of work for research, rather than upon the older notion of a training place for teachers. The introduction of the seminar, small groups of students working out problems under the direction of a teacher, and the concentration of study upon rather narrowly specialized fields, marked the new university. Since Prussia had lost most of her universities by the Treaty of Tilsit, other new universities were founded on the model of Berlin.[2] The older universities throughout the German States, as well as those newly established at Breslau (1811), Bonn (1818), and Munich (1826) were also much affected by the type of work done at Berlin: the exact, searching, and sometimes pedantic work of scholarship conceived in the modern scientific spirit. The old scheme of the four faculties, still including that of theology, was maintained in most of the German universities; although the theology not infrequently was a strange blend of rationalism. German philosophy wandered vaguely between a sort of Kantian agnosticism and the pantheistic idealism of Fichte and Hegel. The State allowed no universities save its own; but it did grant a wide academic freedom to its own. The Austrian universities, more Catholic in doctrine, were more subservient to the State in character and purpose than were the Prussian. Joseph II

---

[1] *Cyclopedia of Education,* Vol. 1, p. 305.

[2] There were six by 1840, and eleven at the close of the century.

had stamped the universities as essentially intended "for the training of State officials,"[1] and they never quite lost that mark.

General summary of German school systems. The school systems of the German-speaking lands have these fundamental characteristics in common:

(a) There is political diversity in the controlling organization, together with a good deal of uniformity in actual school systems; the latter due to the influential leadership of Prussia;

(b) Attendance is compulsory in all up to the age of 13 or 14, and in most of them for an additional two or three years of continuation school;

(c) Religious instruction is provided for in the elementary schools, with due regard to denominational differences;

(d) Different types of schools are carefully arranged to meet the needs of different classes of students: a broader cultural formation for those who have the talent and the leisure to profit by it; and a more immediate practical training for those whom lack of educational capacity or stringency of circumstances compels to leave school at the age of 15 or 16;

(e) There is freedom for private school systems, below the universities; but with an indirect control over these by the various 'leaving examinations' and the grant of privileges based upon examinations set by the regional and central governments.

II. FRANCE

Napoleonic origins. The eighteenth-century Revolution had destroyed religion in France, and with religion the

---

[1] O. Willmann (Kirsch's translation), *The Science of Education,* Vol. 1, p. 313.

schools.   Napoleon, in 1806, set up a system of national schools which, in its essential structure, still is the school system of France, and has been copied largely in Holland, Belgium, Italy, and other countries.   It is a highly centralized system, corresponding in that to the political organization of France.   It was built up to its present status through a whole century of development, strongly marked by the conflict over religion in the schools.   Napoleon himself undertook to legislate only for secondary and higher schools, and established the University of France, not as a teaching body, but as the national corporation in control of all schools.   In his plan, France was divided into twenty-seven administrative districts called 'academies,' under officers appointed by the central government: for each, a rector, a council of ten, and a corps of inspectors.   All schools, communal or private, were under the jurisdiction of the academies.   The basis of instruction set down by the central government was the Catholic religion and patriotism.   The general scheme was kept by the restoration governments of Louis XVIII (1815-1824) and Charles X (1824-1830) ; but little was done to develop it.   Elementary schools in those years were largely in the hands of enthusiasts for 'mutual instruction,' the makeshift theories of Bell and Lancaster, imported from England.   Under the King, Louis-Philippe (1830-1848), the *Loi Guizot* was passed in 1833, by which each commune was obliged to maintain elementary schools.   With the establishment of State elementary schools, there began the inevitable conflict concerning religious instruction which has continued to the present day.

The religious question in French schools. Protestantism had never made great headway in modern France; the people were for the most part either Catholics or infidels; and all through the nineteenth century infidelity had increased markedly amongst all classes. There was a temporary reaction in favor of religion after the fall of Louis-Philippe in the revolution of 1848. The Catholics of France, numbering then perhaps a majority of the population, succeeded, under the leadership chiefly of Dupanloup, in securing recognition for the religious character of elementary instruction. The *Loi Falloux* of 1850 encouraged denominational schools as the best means for promoting religious education, and gave such schools a standing equal to the communal and secular schools. The Catholic schools grew both in numbers and in quality. But the growth of infidelity was only halted, and the anti-religious factors were only embittered by the momentary ascendancy of the French Catholics. By the time of France's humiliation at the hands of Prussia in 1870, the forces working against religion had quite dominated the French government, and have held supremacy ever since. They realized that a complete destruction of religion in France depended primarily upon its destruction in the schools. Jules Ferry, Minister of Public Instruction for the most of the years between 1879 and 1885, began the attack by making the elementary schools secular in 1881, and carried it on by the law of compulsory school attendance in 1882. A law of October 30, 1886, forbade clerics to teach in any State school. The dwindling Catholics of France turned to private schools.[1] But the State, between July 17, 1902, and July 7, 1904, suppressed 6,159 private schools, 1,288 schools for boys, conducted by the Christian Brothers, and 4,869 schools for girls,[2] conducted by teaching sisterhoods, and ended in 1904 by driving all teaching congregations out of France. How-

[1] In the decade 1887-97, Catholic schools grew from 11,754, with 907,346 pupils, to 16,129, with 1,447,310 pupils: a growth of about 38 per cent in schools, and of about 63 per cent in pupils attending.
[2] These figures are given by Gabriel Compayré (*Cyclopedia of Education,* Vol. 2, p. 670). The *Catholic Encyclopedia* (Vol. 13, p. 559a) more than doubles his figures; says that 14,404 "congregational schools" out of a total of 16,904 were closed by July, 1904.

ever, members of the teaching congregations, in lay garb,
succeeded by 1909 in reopening 3,069 schools, 922 for boys,
2,077 for girls.[1] The superb example of patriotism shown
by Catholic priests and religious during the World War
shamed the hostile government into a temporary mildness
in enforcing the laws against Catholic schools; but the laws
remained unchanged. Those laws are also made to apply
to the older French colonies; but in the newer colonies,
where the government is still eager to profit by the influence
of the missionaries, certain measures of toleration are
granted.[2] The laws proclaim religious 'neutrality' in the
schools; but as a matter of demonstrable fact, much of the
teaching is actually hostile to religion, and the bishops
have constant ground for protesting against the use of
anti-religious textbooks.[3]

School organization. The compulsory laws for elementary
schools demand attendance in the *écoles primaires* from six
to thirteen years of age; but children who by examination
secure a *certificat d'étude primaire* may leave school at as
early age as eleven, and many do so leave. There is a
non-compulsory 'higher primary' school, usually of two
years, for those who wish to get some vocational training.[4]
The schools are maintained by the communes, but under a
rigid system of inspection by the central authority of the
minister of public instruction.

Secondary schools receive pupils at the age of ten, and
offer seven-year courses. The first four years present a

---

[1] Charles L. Souvay, "The Catholic Church in Contemporary
France" (in *The Catholic Historical Review,* Vol. 18, pp. 205-28, July,
1932), gives as the total number of Catholic schools for 1910-11 the
impressive figure of 14,428, with 960,712 pupils (p. 207). This, however, contrasts not so impressively with the State schools, which in
that same school year numbered 71,491, with 4,135,886 pupils.

[2] *Cyclopedia of Education,* Vol. 2, pp. 675-79.

[3] *Ibid.,* Vol. 2, p. 657; article by Gabriel Compayré.

[4] In 1910 there were 229 of these 'higher primary' schools for boys,
with 26,649 pupils; and 135 similar schools for girls, with 18,259
pupils. *Cyclopedia of Education,* Vol. 2, p. 658.

choice of two lines of curriculum, the humanistic and the scientific; the latter three years subdivide the curriculum again into four lines by distinguishing between 'classic' and 'modern' in the cultural subjects. At the end of the seven years there is an examination for the baccalaureate, which covers the entire range of secondary studies. Students must be at least sixteen years of age to qualify for this examination; most of the entrants are seventeen. In 1910, out of 26,761 who entered for the examinations, only 10,370, or less than 40 per cent, passed successfully. Secondary schools in the State system are two: *lycées,* which are national; and *collèges,* which are communal. In 1908 the *lycées* for boys had 60,548 students, the *collèges* 36,282; girls' *lycées* and *collèges* had about 33,000; at the same time, private colleges, almost all Catholic, enrolled about 60,000 students.[1] Fees are demanded in the State secondary schools, as in the private.

The universities were destroyed in the eighteenth-century Revolution, and were not revived by law until July 10, 1896. There are fifteen State universities, all coeducational, and no private universities are allowed to exist. However, private 'faculties,' or departments of universities, are tolerated, although they may not grant degrees, but must submit their candidates for degrees to the State university examinations. The Catholics now have seventeen such 'faculties' in France. In 1909 the universities numbered about 41,000 students, of whom 17,512 were enrolled in the University of Paris.[2]

[1] That is less than one half of the number in State secondary schools; but in 1900, before the State suppression of Catholic schools, the Catholic secondary schools had 91,140 pupils, which was 6,668 more than those in the State schools. (Souvay, *op. cit.,* p. 209.)

[2] Most of the statistics given in these paragraphs have been taken from the article by Gabriel Compayré, "Education in France" in *Cyclopedia of Education,* Vol. 2, pp. 656-75. Souvay's figures claim that by 1914 the attendance at Catholic *collèges* was about equal to that at the State secondary schools. (*Op. cit.,* p. 209.)

Taking 1910 again as illustration, there were, all told, about 240,000 students in all French schools above the primary grades; a proportion of about 1 in 25 to the total school population; for comparison, in the United States, for the same year, the proportion was about 1 to 16.

French influence on other school systems. Three countries in particular, Holland, Belgium, and Italy, have shown strongly the influence of France upon their State organization of schools. The Kingdom of the Netherlands, set up in 1815, and including what are now Holland and Belgium, adopted the scheme of nationalization and secularization of schools proposed in 1806 by Van den Ende. It was Catholic opposition to secular schools that chiefly caused the revolution of 1830, which terminated in the separation of Holland and Belgium. After the separation, the Protestant population of Holland outnumbered the Catholic in the proportion of about 3 to 2; the population of Belgium was nominally almost entirely Catholic. But the progress of infidelity in Belgium has been nearly as marked as in France; it has been estimated that in the twentieth century the Catholics scarcely number one half of the people of Belgium;[1] the remaining half disclaim all religion.

In Holland, by a law of January 3, 1842, whilst religious instruction was still forbidden in State schools, a concession was made to have Protestant and Catholic teachers assigned in the State schools, so far as practicable, in accordance with the religious beliefs of the children attending the schools; and ministers of religion were permitted to give religious instruction before or after the regular school classes. These concessions were repeated in the law of 1857; and in 1889 were enlarged to include the granting of State subsidies to religious schools. In July, 1900, attendance in elementary schools between the ages of seven

---

[1] *Catholic Encyclopedia,* New York, 1907, Vol. 2, p. 405.

and thirteen was made compulsory. Taking the year 1910 as illustration, Holland had 5,229 State elementary schools, with 562,284 pupils, and 1,889 subsidized religious elementary schools (1,003 Protestant, 880 Catholic) with 341,318 pupils; relatively, 62 per cent in State schools, 38 per cent in religious schools.

Belgium, besides the religious problem,[1] had also the difficulty of two main languages: the French, spoken by about 44 per cent of the people; and the Flemish, by about 51 per cent. Flemish was finally given equality with French as official language, in 1873, and primary schools were directed to conduct classes in the language used in each locality. Elementary schooling is compulsory between the ages of six and fourteen; and no fees are charged. The national government bears about three-fourths of the cost of the schools, the communes about one-fourth. The control of education was centralized, May 2, 1907, in the Ministry of Sciences and Arts. As in Holland, ministers of various religions are permitted to arrange for religious instruction before or after the usual class hours, in elementary, secondary, and normal schools; but, generally speaking, this provision is a dead letter. The secondary schools have six-year courses, divided pretty much as in France; and charge fees ranging from 100 to 350 francs. In 1910, there were twenty national *athénées,* with about 6,000 pupils, and seven communal *collèges,* with about 1,000 pupils. Private schools are permitted, but the teachers in them must acquire by examination a State certificate. Private schools may also receive State subsidies, if they submit to supervision by State inspectors. In 1910, there were about 90 Catholic *collèges,* with some 18,000 pupils; nearly three times as many as in the State secondary schools. There are four universities: two, at Ghent and at Liege, being national;

[1] Cf. Verhaegen, *La lutte scolaire en Belgique,* Ghent, 1905.

one, at Brussels, conducted by a private corporation; and the Catholic University of Louvain.[1]

Italy derived its school law from the Sardinian Act of Casati, passed on November 13, 1859, which based the organization of schools on the French plan of centralized control. The Casati law kept the original Napoleonic feature of including religious instruction in elementary schools and did not make school attendance compulsory. The first compulsory law was that of Coppino, July 15, 1877, which also abolished religious instruction from the schools. The compulsory school age was set at 6 to 9 years. The Orlando Act of 1904 added stringency to the old compulsory law, which had been badly enforced, and raised the school age, at least for some *communi,* to 6-12. It was estimated that in 1908 there were about 4,500,000 children in Italy between the ages of six and twelve, of whom about 3,000,000 attended State schools, and about 150,000 were in 3,504 private religious schools. There are two divisions of secondary schools: the *ginnasio,* with a five-year course, and above that the *liceo,* with a three-year course. The usual age of students in these secondary schools is from ten to eighteen. Under Mussolini's government, an able man, Giovanni Gentile, Minister of Education from 1922 to 1925, reformed the entire national school system, and amongst other changes restored the teaching of religion to the elementary schools.[2]

Switzerland also borrowed from the French system in its article 27 of the Federal Constitution, adopted May 29,

[1] Cf. J. F. Abel, *Education in Belgium,* United States Office of Education, Bulletin No. 5, 1932.

[2] For an account of Gentile's purpose and plans, see his *Il fascismo al governo della scuola,* Palermo, 1924. E. A. Miller, ("Il Fascismo, Italian Education, and the Church," in *School Review,* September, 1930, Vol. 38, pp. 510-24) discusses the religious aspect of Gentile's work. In 1929, the population of Italy was 42,115,606, of which total 40,009,826 were Catholics, 351,617 Protestants, and 1,717,622 disclaimed any religion. (*La Documentation Catholique,* XXVI, col. 311; August 29, 1931.)

1874, whereby it orders the Cantons to provide elementary schools. By the article 27 bis, adopted November 23, 1902, it makes elementary schooling compulsory and secular, and arranges for the Federation to subsidize the Cantons for the maintenance of schools. But Switzerland has also borrowed from the German scheme, by allowing the twenty-two Cantons and three half-Cantons liberty in managing the details of the schools. There are only seven Catholic Cantons; but the general population of Switzerland is about 60 per cent Protestant and 40 per cent Catholic. The Swiss Federation is very old, but its present character has been determined largely by the revolt of the Catholic Cantons in 1847, in which the school question was a most important issue. The Catholics were defeated, and a new Constitution strengthening the Federal authority was adopted September 12, 1848. Later developments allowed the Catholics to organize the University of Fribourg, one of the seven Cantonal universities. But zeal for elementary schools was vigorous in many of the Cantons long before the Federation stressed it, and the Swiss were proud of having been one of the first countries that practically banished illiteracy.[1]

General summary of French school systems. There is a certain hard, clear quality, characteristically French, about the State school system. The central idea of State dominance and supremacy determines both the rigid organization of schools and the steady hostility to Christian teachings. The State suffers no compromise with its principle of absolute supremacy; and bases that claim to supremacy upon a theory of 'democracy' which has been more thoroughly refuted by political facts in France than in any other country professing to accept the theory. France has

[1] In this connection it is interesting to read Stephen Gwynn's comment upon his observations during a six-months' stay in the Canton of Vaud, in 1887: "Everybody could read and write, and nobody did either, except to make out a bill." (*Experiences of a Literary Man,* New York, 1926, p. 89.)

long been a political oligarchy, in which even the apparent differences of party have been no bar to the interchange
of governmental office amongst the small group of politicians. The Catholic population, long a minority as contrasted with those scouting all religion, maintains with
great difficulty schools equalling in number less than one-
tenth of the State schools, but conforming in general organization of courses to the types established in the State
systems. All schools are very practically conducted, with
a clear, matter-of-fact recognition of the relatively small
number of children capable of any school education beyond
the elementary.

III. SPAIN

Its confused history. Another country which has shown
the influence of French principles on its school system is
Spain. Amongst Western nations, Spain has perhaps the
most confused, and least understood, recent history. Its
peoples had long been traditionally Catholic in religion and
monarchist in politics. But they have never been a real
unit. Castilians, Basques, Catalans, Andalusians, and Gal-
legos differ in language, character, customs, occupations,
and even in the climate of the regions they inhabit. Based
upon those fundamental differences, others have been built
up, of grave political import, and of bewildering intricacy.
There are dynastic quarrels amongst the monarchists,
through which each group plays into the hands of anti-
royalists, republicans, communists, and anarchists. The
Catholics, sapped from without by the growing infidelity
largely inspired from France, are internally divided over
racial, cultural, economic, and political questions. Out of
this political confusion, a small well-organized minority,
markedly hostile to all religion, has recently succeeded in
overturning the enfeebled and inept monarchy, and setting

up a republic, which is avowedly anti-Catholic in its aims and plans. If that now dominant minority can bring material order and harmony to Spain it will have achieved something that Spain has lacked since the death of Philip II.

Effects upon schools. Non-Catholic writers have little sympathy with the Spaniards, often incline to gloat over their national decay, and ascribe that decay to the vicious influence of the Jesuits and the Spanish Inquisition. The explanation of their attitude is simple; it is the explanation offered by Dr. Johnson for a gross error in his dictionary: "Ignorance, Madame, pure ignorance." They might as well blame the Jesuits for the Spanish climate. But non-Catholic writers are correct in pointing out Spain's deficiencies in schools. For the past hundred years or more, schools in Spain have been a political football in the hurly-burly of internal dissensions.

Article 14 of the 'Liberal Constitution' adopted by the Cortes of Cadiz in 1812, after the defeat of Napoleon, provided for the establishment of schools as a national project. But the Constitution itself was the subject of internal wars for sixty-four years, until the Restoration of the Bourbons in 1876; and in the meantime no less than six Constitutions were set up and overthrown. Antonio Gil de Zarate, Director of Public Instruction from 1845 to 1849, introduced the secularizing element as regards schools in 1845, when he had a law passed banishing religious instruction from secondary schools.[1] The law was rather generally ignored. The Constitution adopted September 9, 1857, ordered the provincial and municipal *juntas* to establish elementary schools, made the compulsory school age 6 to 12, exempted the poor from school fees, made obligatory a government certificate for teachers, and kept religious instruction in the elementary schools. After the revolution

---

[1] His ideas are also embodied in his book, *De la Instrucción Pública en España,* Madrid, 1855.

of 1868, another Constitution exempted all pupils in elementary schools from paying fees, and released the certification of teachers to the local boards, or *juntas*. The local board was made up of the chief executive officers of the city or province, with one priest, and at least two heads of families, as additional members. The clergy used their position to strengthen the assurance of religious teaching in the schools. Thereupon, the anti-clericals founded, in 1876, a compact, well-financed organization to campaign against clerical influence in the schools.[1] In 1887, the State declared a monopoly in normal schools, and placed restrictions upon the religious teaching congregations. These restrictions were renewed and increased in 1902. On June 9, 1909, the State established the *Escuela Superior del Magisterio,* or higher normal school, in which all teachers in other normal schools and all inspectors of schools were to be trained. In the following month, anti-Catholic riots broke out in Barcelona, under the leadership of Francisco Ferrer, a violent advocate of lay schools. When, three months later, Ferrer was tried and executed for the wholesale arson, rape, and murder he had instigated, 'liberals' all the world over execrated the Spanish government.[2] Even anarchy is applauded if it be directed against Catholics. In 1911, the government took over from the local *juntas* complete control of elementary schools, and placed them under a special director. On April 14, 1931, the King was driven out, and a republic proclaimed. A republican Constitution dissolved religious orders and confiscated their property, granted that marriages be divorced by mutual consent, assumed entire jurisdiction over educa-

[1] Their chief organ of agitation was a bulletin, *Institución Libre de Enseñanza,* published monthly from 1877 to 1894, semi-monthly from 1894 to 1908.

[2] See, for example, William Archer, *The Life, Trial and Death of Francisco Ferrer,* London, 1911, in which Ferrer is glorified as a martyr.

tion and private property, and in general pointed the way to a Russian type of communism.

Organization of schools. As might readily be expected, the organization of schools in Spain was a shifting and fluctuating affair. The State early assumed the French principle of central control; but was never able to put the principle into effect. There was a ministerial director of public instruction from at least 1834; but the real jurisdiction over schools was local, nominally through the school boards, more often actually by the *caciques,* regional political bosses, who were the real masters of Spain and very nearly throttled the central government. The State system of schools at times expanded by the adoption of parish schools and private schools, at times contracted its sphere, as political circumstances changed. Real vigor of organization it could not have, under the strain of a central claim to control which could not be exercised. The insistent attacks of anti-clericals upon religious instruction in schools further added to the kaleidoscopic character of the schools, which in different localities varied all the way between Catholic and atheistic. The Spanish people, largely peasants, were generally apathetic about schools anyway. Under the circumstances, it is rather remarkable that in 1910 there were 34,954 elementary schools in the State system (nearly a third of the number being parish schools) and 8,100 private schools, with a total school enrollment of more than 2,000,000 in a population of less than 20,000,000.

Spain was divided into ten university districts, corresponding in many ways to the seventeen academies of France. The rector and advisory council in each district had jurisdiction over secondary schools as well as over the university. All executives and teachers in universities and secondary schools were appointed by the king, and were required to have a degree of doctor, or at least licentiate, in philosophy or arts, from a State university. Only State universities could grant degrees.

The State secondary schools were generally called *institutos,* private secondary schools generally *colegios.* Both offered two types of courses: a six-year cultural course, with some subdivision after the first two years, leading to the university; and a four-year vocational course, again dividing after the first two years, with the latter two years usually given to industrial training. The private secondary schools were, as a rule, much hampered and handicapped by official regulations.

General summary. Spain, a Catholic agricultural country for the most part, cut off by the barrier of the Pyrenees from France, and, after Napoleon's invasion, entertaining an almost violent popular antipathy to France, was nevertheless infected by the spirit of religious infidelity which spread from France. Latterly, enthusiasm for a republican form of government had also developed, and had linked itself with the hostility to religion. Against those two forces, and weakened by dynastic quarrels and local caciquism from within, a Catholic monarchial government struggled with the problem of schools. It asserted a central control which it could not exercise; and thereby lost much of its possible influence over the actual local control. It wavered between Catholic support and infidel support, until it lost the respect of both. Its schools became the pawns of politicians, in the face of a populace neither greatly caring nor greatly daring to express its convictions about them. Ultimately, the anti-religious and anti-monarchial elements, a definite minority, seized control of government and schools. What they will do with both remains to be seen.

IV. ENGLAND

The tradition of religious schools. The Religious Revolt of the sixteenth century had most profound social results in England. The hostility between Catholics and Protestants went into the last details of living, and resulted in almost the total destruction of the Catholic tradition as an influence upon English life. The Anglican Church, which succeeded the Catholic, became grossly subservient to the civil government, and steadily diminished in spiritual vitality. But in spite of those facts, the schools of England continued to be controlled by religious bodies, with no government intervention beyond the varying amount of persecution which the government indulged in with regard to Catholics and dissenting Protestant sects. The great private societies which, throughout the eighteenth century, worked for the development of elementary schools were religious in character. Even most of the individual agencies fostering schools were religious. Hence the English people were thoroughly habituated to the association of religion with their schools. This tradition persisted into the nineteenth century, even after a very considerable decay of religious belief and practice amongst the mass of the English people.

Respected by the State. The English government kept that long tradition in mind when it made its gradual entry into the direct control of schools. The first modern parliamentary grant in aid of schools, made on August 30, 1833, four years after the Catholic Emancipation Act, consisted of £20,000 to be expended for school buildings only, and to be apportioned as a supplement to private subscriptions for the erection of schoolhouses. The government did not even reserve the right to supervise the distribution of this grant, but turned it over to the National Society and the Foreign School Society. Those two societies controlled the grant in aid until 1856. In 1847, the government sanctioned the admission of Catholic and Wesleyan schools to share in the grant. Even when government aid was extended to meeting part of the cost of teachers' wages,[1] the chief restriction put upon the distribution of the money was academic, the apportioning of the grant 'by results,' greater or less payments depending upon the success with which pupils passed examinations.

Attacked by private bodies. The demand for secular schools came, not from the government, but from private agencies. Joseph Lancaster (1778-1838) had urged that a national system of schools should be established, in which 'undenominational religion' based upon 'general Christian principles' should be taught.[2] Dr. Walter Farquhar Hook (1798-1875), the Anglican Vicar of Leeds, proposed in 1846 that no grant-aided schools should furnish religious instruction.[3] His proposal was rejected by the government; but it was welcomed by a considerable group in Manchester, who demanded a system of secular schools for the County of Lancaster (one of the strongholds of Catholicism), and who soon formed the National Public School Association, devoted to promoting secular schools for the whole of England. Birmingham followed suit with its League. The movement spread rapidly to all the larger towns, and was carried on vigorously by the organizations until 1887, and after that date by sporadic efforts up to as late as 1908. To oppose these activities, the Manchester and Salford Committee on Education was formed, which proposed municipal school systems, with Bible reading as a prescribed subject, but exempting from denominational instruction children whose parents objected to it. These

---

[1] This was the result of recommendations made by the Duke of Newcastle's Commission, appointed in 1858.

[2] J. Lancaster, *Improvements in Education as it Respects the Industrious Classes,* London, 1803.

[3] Hook had outlined this idea in a letter as early as 1838. His formal proposal of the scheme was made in a letter to Bishop Thirlwall. Hook was not a secularist, but a man of great heart, zealous for the growth of the Anglican Church, yet eager to avoid any offensive proselytizing. He wanted religious instruction to be given out of school hours by ministers of the various denominations. See his *Life and Letters,* by W. R. W. Stephens, 2 vols., London, 1878.

divergent schemes were each so warmly championed that every attempt at national school legislation from 1853 to 1868 was defeated. But the discussion stimulated interest in schools; the government grant was steadily increased, until it amounted to £663,000 in 1858; and in the same year private subscriptions for schools reached the annual total of £1,250,000. After 1858 the government grant was for a time reduced.

Forster's Bill, 1870. In one way and another, and from a great variety of motives, pressure was being brought to bear upon the government to do something about a national school system. The essential difficulty lay in the contentions about religious instruction in the schools. Forster's Bill was a compromise, moderately acceptable to the religious bodies, but bitterly assailed by Joseph Chamberlain, who represented the secularists. It provided for the creation of elective local school boards, and empowered such boards to organize schools *wherever needed to supplement the voluntary religious schools.* Both board schools and voluntary schools were to share in the parliamentary grants of money; but only the board schools were to receive support from local taxes. The principle of 'payment by results' was kept, although furiously denounced by the more radical 'democrats.' Religious instruction was to be given before or after school hours, and only to those children whose parents wished them to receive such instruction. The school boards were empowered to compel attendance between the ages of five and thirteen. Both board and voluntary schools were subject to government inspection. The religious bodies hastened to do their part in this plan for promoting elementary schools. In 1870 they built 1,500 new schoolhouses. The government grant was again increased, amounting in 1871 to £562,000. A general compulsory school law was passed in 1876, and again in 1880. The tendency throughout the years following 1870 was to increase the central control over schools, quietly and tact-fully, in part through the influence of parliamentary grant in aid, in part by closer organization of school manage-ment. Thus, for instance, in 1891 an extra grant of ten shil-lings a pupil was made to schools which ceased to charge tuition fees; in 1893, 1899, children of eleven or twelve years were exempt from school attendance upon passing an examination; special schools were established about the same time for the blind, deaf, and other defective children; and in 1899 a central board of education was set up.

The continuing conflict between secular and religious school systems. Forster's Bill by no means settled the con-flict between the secularists and the religious schools. The latter won a small victory in 1897, when they received a special grant of five shillings per pupil to help them com-pete with the wealthy board schools, were allowed to fed-erate in such a way as to deal with the government as unit groups, and were empowered to dispose of the parliamen-tary grant in aid turned over in a lump sum to each re-ligious group. On the other hand, the pensions bill of 1898, whereby the government contributed with the teachers to a pension fund, tended to bind the teachers to the State rather than to the religious groups. The Balfour Education Act of 1902 abolished the local school boards, and gave con-trol of the State schools to the county and borough coun-cils.[1] It further extended State control over the voluntary schools by offering them a share in the local taxes, in ex-change for the right to appoint two of the six managers of the voluntary schools. The latter eagerly grasped at the offer of increased revenue, of which they stood in real need. In 1903, they got 56 per cent of the £8,000,000

---

[1] The schools of Scotland, as a result of the Duke of Argyll's Com-mission (1864-67), had been consolidated by the Education Act for Scotland, 1872, which instituted school boards with jurisdiction over all grades of school education. In its effects on religious schools this Act of 1872 was the equivalent of the Act of 1902 for England.

granted by the government. In that same year all but 7 per cent of all elementary schools had ceased to exact any fees for tuition.[1] The net result of the various moves in the educational battle was this: between 1896 and 1923, the Anglican schools suffered a loss of 600,000 in enrolled pupils, the other Protestant schools lost 400,000. Only the Catholic schools held their own; the number of their pupils increased 36,000, to a total in 1931 of 425,000.[2] In 1906, the Liberal majority in the House of Commons enthusiastically passed Birrell's Bill, which refused to recognize any longer the religious schools; but the Lords killed the Bill. A similar bill by McKenna in 1908 was withdrawn because its promoters foresaw that it too would be defeated in the upper house.

Secondary schools. The English grammar schools had a long history before the Protestant Revolt. Leach has told the painful story of their destruction under Henry VIII and Edward VI, and their slow rebuilding. In the nineteenth century the number and the quality of secondary schools was still entirely inadequate to the needs of the country.[3] In 1867 the British Schools Inquiry Commission (Taunton) made a rough grading of secondary schools into three classes: the first grade, which included the famous public schools, carried their pupils to the age of eighteen, and prepared them for the universities; the second grade had courses shorter by two years, and the third grade shorter by four years, carrying their pupils, respectively, to sixteen and to fourteen years of age. Balfour's Act of 1902 (part 2, sec. 2, no. 1) ordered the county and borough

[1] *Cyclopedia of Education*, Vol. 2, pp. 465-67.

[2] Daniel Sargent, "The Catholic Church in Contemporary England," in *Catholic Historical Review*, Vol. 18, p. 70. *Catholic Encyclopedia*, Vol. 13, p. 559, reckons the Catholic schools in 1870 as 354, with 101,933 pupils; and for 1906 as 1,062 schools, with 284,746 pupils.

[3] See the *Report* of the Taunton Commission, 1867, Vol. 1, p. 102. The *Report* in 23 vols., was published 1868-69.

councils to provide secondary schools, and particularly envisaged a popular type of 'higher elementary schools' with
a three-year course, for which special parliamentary grants
were given, but on condition that the pupils were at least
twelve years of age on entering, and had attended a public
elementary school for at least two years. In 1910 there
were 841 secondary schools receiving government grants
in aid, of which 325 were council schools, and the remaining 516 were voluntary schools having some of their officials appointed by the councils.[1]

Universities. The Anglican Church had virtually complete
control of the older universities until 1871. But as early
as 1826 the University of London was founded as a protest
against Anglican control. It opened in October, 1828, with
some three hundred students. It had, however, no charter,
no official recognition. From the beginning it definitely
excluded any sort of religious instruction. It got its charter in 1836, under Peel's ministry; but after 1858, when
it broke its affiliation with University College and King's
College, the teaching institutions, it was for forty years
only an examining body. Between 1854 and 1857, Oxford
and Cambridge relaxed some of the Anglican tests; and in
1871 the Universities Tests Act abolished all doctrinal tests.
The University of Durham, chartered in 1837, modeled itself upon Oxford; but after 1850 the colleges and universities sponsored by the government all followed the lead
of the University of London in excluding religion from the
higher schools. Commissions were appointed in 1850 to
reorganize Oxford and Cambridge. By various statutes enacted between 1854 and 1858, the monopoly of the colleges
in each university was broken, private halls were again
authorized, the revenues of the colleges were applied more
liberally to teachers' salaries, and a new form of governing

[1] *Cyclopedia of Education,* Vol. 2, p. 476.

body set up similar to that which had functioned before the Protestant Revolt.

Entry of science into secondary and higher schools. The tradition by which instruction in all English schools above the elementary was based upon the humanistic studies was as old as the Renaissance, and was even more firmly established than the religious tradition. But for a hundred years efforts have been made to break that humanist tradition; and there is evidence that the efforts are succeeding. The inspiration for the attack on the exclusive 'classic' tradition came from Germany. Thomas Campbell, the poet, visited the University of Bonn in 1820, two years after it was founded. It was his enthusiasm for the German scientific type of higher school which led him, in 1825, to urge the foundation of a similar university in London; although it was another motive which kept the new University of London from imitating Bonn in its Catholic and Protestant departments of theology. The matriculation examinations of the University of London demanded, in addition to the traditional 'classic' subjects, one modern foreign language, mathematics, and natural science. For many secondary schools those examinations came to be pretty much what the German 'leaving examinations' were, and thus exercised much influence on the curriculum of secondary schools. The Taunton Commission recommended the German *realschulen* as models for the English second and third grade secondary schools.[1] Spencer's *Education,* in 1861, made science the staple of all school education; but perhaps angered more than it converted. J. S. Mill more successfully pleaded for a mixture of classical and scientific studies; and Thomas Huxley wanted the proportions of the mixture preponderant on the side of science.[2] Darwin's work became the foundation for a 'scientific' interpretation of all human life;

---

[1] *Report,* 1867, Vol. 1, pp. 284-87.
[2] Huxley, *A Liberal Education and Where to Find It,* London, 1868.

and the interpreters beat manfully on the doors of the schools.

It will be remembered that all this went apace with the wide dissemination of the idea that 'science' and religion are hostile to each other, mutually exclusive; and that England in general, during those decades, was undoubtedly falling off badly in Christian belief and practice. Yet there was a stubborn core of resistance to the new dominance of science in the schools. The new universities, it is true, took up science eagerly; the proprietary secondary schools emphasized elementary science courses; but Oxford and Cambridge, and the old established public schools admitted it grudgingly, with the air of its being a concession. Gradually, however, the 'modern side' grew in secondary schools, and 'stinks' became an accepted part even of Eton vocabulary. But the Cross Commission of 1886 still found it necessary to urge the teaching of science in secondary schools,[1] and the Bryce Commission in 1894 was emphatic in pointing out how badly science was taught. Even as late as 1918 a commission testifies to the reluctance with which the larger secondary schools of the first grade still handled scientific studies.[2] One gets the impression that back of that attitude lie the fragmentary remains of an aristocratic tradition which held that 'science' is part of a technical training, not of a human education. In any case, the new universities are now teaching brewing, dyeing, metallurgy, and other applied sciences; and Oxford and Cambridge have courses in engineering, agriculture, and forestry.

General summary of English school systems. The English school systems exemplify two pronouncedly British characteristics: an ingrained, conservative respect for traditions, and a genius for compromise. Even when religion

---

[1] *Report,* 1888, p. 183.
[2] *Report of the Committee on the Position of Natural Science in the Educational System of Great Britain,* 1918.

had lost its hold upon a majority of the English people, their respect for religion somehow survived. "The English-man is rather sorry if he is told that there is no God; it seems to him that another of the old landmarks is dis-appearing, and he doesn't want it to disappear."[1] That national attitude acts as a balancing force in the large mass of people standing between the minority of earnest Chris-tians who maintain that religious instruction is an essential part of school education and the smaller minority of earnest agnostics and secularists who want religious instruction banished from all schools. It has made possible the careful compromises in legislation which permit nearly 40 per cent of English school children still to be in religious schools. It has enabled the schools to temper the rather unbalanced modern enthusiasm for scientific studies, and as a result to secure for the English schools as flexible and well-balanced a curriculum as is to be found in any modern system. There is an equilibrium about the English systems which much commends itself, but which naturally demands constant vigilance to keep it from being upset by the fanat-ical enthusiasts for a completely secularized 'democracy.'

V. JAPAN

The modernizing of Japan. One of the startling phe-nomena of history has been the rapid development of Japan within the past sixty years. Young compared with China, but an old nation compared with many European states, Japan had been slightly in contact with Europeans ever since the Portuguese first began trading with the Japanese in 1542. There was even a period of some forty years, from the coming of St. Francis Xavier in 1549 to the first edict against the Christians in 1590, when it seemed possible, if

[1] Ronald Knox, "The Future of Religion in England," in *Studies,* 1926, Vol. 15, p. 21.

not probable, that the Japanese people might become Catholic. But the Japanese toleration of missionaries, and even the early facilitating of their work, were due to rivalries between native princes and the desire of some of these to secure muskets from the Portuguese. The fact was significant and prophetic. In no great time, the instinctive native hostility to Christian teachings, supported by the influence of Dutch traders who hated the Portuguese, led to repressive measures and savage persecution of the Catholics, and ended in the massacre of 45,000 Catholic Japanese in the siege of Hara, April 12, 1638, and the final expulsion of the missionaries.[1] Japan thereafter remained thoroughly closed to European influence until Commodore Perry, in 1853, secured the opening of some ports to foreign commerce. Between 1854 and 1858 Japan entered into treaty relations with the United States, England, Russia, Holland, and France. In 1867 the military government of the Shogunate, which had dominated the country for centuries, restored the civil power to the emperor, under a modern Constitution, elaborated in 1889. From that time onward, Japan set itself to take its place as a great political power in the world. Within twenty-five years it humiliated China, a nation ten times its size, and took from it Korea. Within ten years more, it defeated Russia. It made itself felt in world commerce. It blustered and threatened other nations that stood in the way of its policies, in quite the approved Western fashion.

The coming of Western schools. The Japanese, mentally

[1] The amazing survival of the Christian religion in Japan through more than two centuries was made manifest on March 17, 1865, when some fifteen Japanese Catholics presented themselves to Père Petitjean, of the Paris *Missions Étrangères,* in the new church built at Nagasaki. It was then found that many thousands of Japanese had inherited the teachings of the early missionaries. (*Catholic Encyclopedia,* Vol. 8, p. 307.) Persecution soon broke out again, in 1867, one of the last acts of the Shogunate. In 1873 the laws against Christians were abrogated.

alert and energetic, have a remarkable talent for super-ficially imitating others. Their government set that talent to work, with the vigor possible to a closely organized State, having a central and nearly absolute power over its people. The government saw how much the Western world had outstripped the East in manufacturing, especially in mass production of goods, in commerce and communication, in military and naval equipment. It wanted the apparent benefits of Western methods for its own people. It had no concern for the artistic, social, or religious ideals of the West, save in so far as these might possibly be of help in attaining material advantages. It sent thousands of the Japanese people to study in the United States and Europe. It hired more than 5,000 *Yatoi,* foreign specialists in industrial, commercial, military, and naval affairs, to bring their knowledge and skill to Japan. It realized promptly that to compete with Western peoples its own people needed a wholesale training in Western ways, and that a new school system was the obvious means of giving them that training. For the hard, narrow purpose in view, the writings of Herbert Spencer instantly appealed to them; and Spencer became their guide in the organization of schools. With a certain naïve cynicism, the Japanese caught from the strange Western civilization the tenets of what Raymond Thompson has somewhere called 'Christian atheism,' a selective borrowing of Christian moral maxims, quite dissociated from the Christian religion, and a very liberal borrowing of unchristian practices. Most industriously they copied the details of Western school procedure, almost with the same exactness with which they copied even the flaws and accidental defects of Western manufactured products. That school procedure they superimposed upon their own cumbersome language[1] and entirely alien culture. The re-

---

[1] The Japanese language, whatever its original basis, has borrowed from China for some fourteen centuries. It is agglutinative, with a

sult is a system of schools mechanically like the European and American schools, but fundamentally hostile to the tradition which shaped all Western schools.

The organization of schools. In 1872 *Gakusei,* the State educational code, was promulgated. Under a central government control, the whole country was divided into eight university districts, each university district to contain thirty-two middle school districts, each middle school district having 210 elementary school districts. This organization, borrowed evidently from the Napoleonic scheme, was too ambitious to be carried out completely. It called for 53,680 elementary school districts, a number not yet attained. It was replaced by another code, *Kyoikurei,* in 1879, and by the *Shogakkurei* code for elementary schools in 1886. The present system of schools was inaugurated in 1900, and has since been several times revised. But it follows three broad principles which were laid down in 1890: compulsory elementary schooling;[1] moral instruction, based upon an imperial rescript of October 30, 1890, and definitely non-religious;[2] and a close control of all schools, public and private, by the State ministry of education. In the first quarter of the twentieth century the number of pupils in elementary schools tripled itself, amounting in 1925 to 9,020,619 children out of a total population of 61,081,954, and representing 98.6 per cent of all

small range of sounds, but an enormously complicated script, involving six thousand or more ideographs. It has been constantly changing. See J. H. Gubbins, *The Making of Modern Japan,* Philadelphia, 1922; and G. Bourgois, *Dictionary and Glossary for the Practical Study of the Japanese Ideographs,* New York, 1918.

[1] In 1890, only four years of elementary school attendance was made compulsory. In 1907 this was raised to six years, 6-12.

[2] The imperial rescript consists of a brief paragraph, a score of printed lines in the English translation, which urges family affection, modesty and temperance, benevolence toward all, zeal for learning and the arts, devotion to the common good, and loyalty to the State. See the article by Nobuaki Makino, former Minister of Education, in *Encyclopedia Americana,* 1932, Vol. 15, p. 666.

Japanese children of compulsory school age.[1]   No tuition is charged in these compulsory elementary schools.   But there are 'higher elementary schools,' generally with a two-year course, in which tuition is charged, and which are scantily attended.   Secondary schools for boys cover the ages twelve to seventeen, and for girls twelve to sixteen.   Both are insufficient in number to accommodate all who wish to enter them,[2] and are inadequately staffed.   In general, Japanese teachers do not measure up to the standards set by State regulations; chiefly because of the meager salaries paid them, which range as low as 15 yen (at par, $7.50) a month.[3]   Private secondary schools are allowed if they conform to government regulations; but, with the exception of the peers' school in Tokio, no private elementary schools are allowed.   There are four official State universities, and twenty-two other institutions permitted to call themselves universities.   In 1925 these twenty-six universities had a total enrollment of 35,163.

VI. RUSSIA

Schools in the Empire.   Russia began to be a Western nation, so far as it ever was or is such, under two sovereigns: Peter the Great, who ruled from 1689 to 1725; and the German princess who became the remarkable Catherine II, and ruled Russia from 1762 to 1796.   Both of these looted Courland and Poland of great libraries,[4] and other-

[1] Figures from the *Report* of the Department of Education, Tokio, 1926.

[2] *Cyclopedia of Education,* Vol. 3, pp. 523-24.   In 1925, the boys in secondary schools numbered 219,102 in 422 schools; the girls, 206,864 in 618 schools.   The eagerness of the Japanese for school education is shown by the large figure of 1,007,561 enrolled in technical continuation schools for the year 1925.

[3] *Cyclopedia of Education,* Vol. 3, p. 523.

[4] The Russian government, at the third and last partition of Poland, October 24, 1795, carried away from Warsaw to St. Petersburg the famous Zaluski Library, a collection of more than 300,000 volumes.   *Encyclopedia Americana,* 1932, Vol. 17, p. 339.

wise showed considerable zeal for the spread of learning amongst their peoples. But the mass of the Russian peasants had little desire for school education; and the Russian government disdained the Western device of flattering the masses into imposing schools upon themselves. As a result, it was not until 1864, three years after Alexander II had freed 20,000,000 serfs, that the first primary school law was passed, by which a State system of schools was set up, open to all children without distinction, but also without compulsion. The system was governed by a central ministry of public instruction, under which the huge country was divided into fifteen administrative districts: another echo of the Napoleonic plan for France. The schools developed rather slowly. By 1912, there were about 126,000 primary schools, with an enrollment of 8,264,000 pupils, or about one-fourth of the children of school age.[1]

Soviet schools. After the Bolshevist revolution of 1917, the new communist government, immeasurably more autocratic than the old Empire, took hold of the schools with great definiteness and vigor of purpose. It retained central control of the system, under a commissariat of education, but with elaborate organization of both management and finances,[2] due to the federation of seven soviet republics in the Union of Socialist Soviet Republics, the new name of Russia. The Commissariat reports that about $500,000,000 was spent on schools in 1927-1928, and more than double that sum in 1929-1930. Yet, strangely, the number of primary schools reported is only 114,111, or some 12,000 less than functioned under the Empire, just before the World War. However, the total number of children in schools has

[1] The average percentage of persons able to read and write was estimated as about 21 per cent for the Empire. *Encyclopedia Americana,* 1932, Vol. 24, p. 36.

[2] About two-thirds of the appropriations for schools are local, and one-third charged against the constituent republics. *World Almanac,* 1932, p. 704.

increased about 45 per cent and represents about one-third of the children of school age.[1] The school system comprises three groups: (a) Institutions for infants, including infant schools, which are comparatively few; creches, which may number as many as 2,000; and 8,223 playgrounds; (b) 'institutions of social education,' chiefly primary schools, but including also 10,534 varied technical, agricultural, and continuation schools, some of them of the secondary type; (c) vocational schools, amongst which are 1,054 technical high schools, 1,368 trade schools, and a great variety of 'workmen's faculties,' apprenticeship schools, workmen's lecture courses, etc.[2] The status of the universities is difficult to evaluate. There has been a great deal of reorganization since 1917, with a tendency to destroy all academic freedom, and to make the universities seminaries for training communist propagandists. In 1929 four new universities were planned expressly as centers of propaganda.[3] In general, the curriculum throughout the various grades and kinds of schools is carefully planned to secure three immediate aims: (a) a great increase in the number of those who can read, as an important condition for propaganda; (b) the technical training of industrial workers; and (c) the destruction of all religious belief and practice.[4]

[1] *Encyclopedia Americana,* 1932 edition, Vol. 24, p. 36, gives the figure for schools quoted in the text. *World Almanac,* 1932, p. 705, sets the number of elementary schools for 1928-29 as 120,012, with 11,101,372 pupils. It estimates that from 1927 to 1931 an average of over 50,000 schools for adult illiterates had been conducted, with an enrollment in 1928-29 of about 2,700,000 pupils. The Commissar for Education claims that the census of 1926-27 shows that the average of literacy has been raised to 51 per cent.

[2] *Encyclopedia Americana,* 1932, *loc. cit. World Almanac, loc. cit.,* reckons for 1928-29 the number of 'Workmen's Faculties' as 105, with 60,200 students.

[3] *Encyclopedia Americana,* 1932, Vol. 24, p. 37.

[4] See the *Encyclopedia of State and Right,* published in 1925 by the Communist Academy of Moscow. See also Article 37 of the Soviet Code of 1926. The whole question is discussed, with citations from soviet authorities, in B. Mirkine-Guetzevich, *La Théorie générale*

The ultimate aim is, of course, the established security of the Marxian communist regime. There is great earnestness shown in the conduct of soviet schools. Zealous inspectors particularly see to the carrying out of the third aim. The greatest lack of success seems to be in attaining the second aim.

The use of libraries. Soviet Russia has some remarkable libraries, such as the National Public Library of Leningrad, which contains more than 4,500,000 volumes and 231,000 manuscripts, and the Lenin Public Library at Moscow, with 3,500,000 volumes. In Leningrad alone, other public libraries total some 2,000,000 additional volumes; and the Library of the Communist Academy at Moscow, founded in 1918, has about 1,000,000 volumes. Under the soviet regime the old Russian libraries were ruthlessly purged of books opposing communist teachings, and hundreds of thousands of religious books were destroyed. The reorganized libraries, and many others newly founded, have been made a part of the State system of education. This is a logical step following upon State control of schools, and is a matter of technique in which the soviet government has surpassed all other States. The people are taught to read, urged to read, supplied with great facilities for reading, and their reading rigorously controlled by the State to further its own purposes.[1]

General summary of the chapter. This rapid survey of

du Droit Soviétique, Paris, 1928; and in Waldemar Gurian (English translation by E. I. Watkin), *Bolshevism: Theory and Practice,* London, 1932.

[1] *Encyclopedia Americana,* 1932, Vol. 17, p. 339. See also H. G. Eddy, "Beginnings of United Library Service in U. S. S. R.," *Library Journal,* 1932, Vol. 57, p. 61; and "Library Progress in Russia," *Libraries,* 1930, Vol. 35, pp. 454-55. Most of the American writers on the Soviet use of libraries are enthusiastic in their approval. See especially the articles of Mme. L. Haffkin-Hamburger, "The Moscow Institute for Library Sciences," in *Library Journal,* 1925, Vol. 50, pp. 991-93; "Libraries in the Soviet Union," in *Libraries,* 1926, Vol. 31, pp. 502-06.

the school systems of some modern countries has for its purpose to give the reader a compact view of the systems, and to enable him to form some reasonable estimate of the effect of modern schools upon the unending process of education. It is almost a truism to say that schools at any time are only one of the means of education. In this book an effort has already been made and in the last chapter will be made again to consider some of the educational agencies which function outside and beyond the school. The schools are part of a large pattern, and get their value from their place in the pattern.

But in the past twenty-five years of history the startling fact emerges that schools have been actually dealt with as if they were the sole means of education.[1] The attention of statesmen, educators, parents, children has been focussed more and more during those years upon the schools. Church and State have found their central point of contention in the schools. The schools themselves have been multiplied as never before. The physical power of the State has been seriously used to compel the attendance of children at schools. The school population, managers, teachers, and pupils, have become a larger part of the total population than ever before in history. Upon no other means of education does the State lay any significant stress. The common thought of mankind has everywhere come to accept schooling as the complete synonym for education. The idea of education now evokes no other connotation than that of the school. That astounding fact is of fundamental importance.

The second fact to be noted in the general view of modern

---

[1] This is not, however, the case in Soviet Russia. In its anti-God education, the government cleverly makes use of periodicals, museums, mocking processions, the theatre, libraries, posters, games; has set up a six-day week, to break up even the memory of Sunday; etc., etc. Cf. J. Busteed, "Soviet Russia," in *Studies,* 1932, Vol. 31, pp. 531-48.

schools is the widening split between religion and the concept of education. The steady tendency has been toward strengthening the position of the secular schools and weakening that of the religious schools. Everywhere the religious schools are on the defensive; and what religious influences have been tolerated in the secular schools have their existence constantly threatened by energetic and zealous bodies of secularists. One can see a link between this fact and the fact noted just above: emphasis on the schools became a kind of negation of the Church; and the popular mind joined the official political mind in concluding that, since education was the work of the schools and religion the work of the Church, religion had no place in education.

The third fact is the almost unchallenged assumption by the State of the primary right in education.[1] One must say 'almost' unchallenged; because some Catholics and Protestants still publicly protest against such an assumption as a usurpation. But the vast masses of the people in all countries have, however grudgingly, acquiesced in the complete and primary authority of the State in education, as a *de facto* jurisdiction. It is noted that in most countries even when other systems than the State system of schools exist, they exist on sufferance. No fact in modern history is more manifest than that the wide development of schools, which began as part of a program of 'democracy,' has become one of the most important fields for the exercise of State autocratic authority. The ultimate sole defense that can be made for that autocracy, even by its devoted admirers, is that it is a benevolent form of despotism.

Finally, as a matter of fact, not of theory, the practical aims of the wide-flung school systems appear in the records of history. By a natural process of interrelation, made easy through the remarkable modern development of means

[1] Recall what has been said on the authority of the State in education, *supra,* pp. 386-87.

of communication, the practical aims of schools have become pretty much the same everywhere. The most important of those aims appear evidently as these two: for the elementary schools, literacy, in the narrow sense of a facility in reading and writing; for the upper schools, the acquisition of factual knowledge and technical skill. The Soviet schools have defined these aims more sharply than some others; but the aims are historically evident in all the large modern school systems. The most common reckoning used to measure the results of a State system of schools is the percentage of illiterates in the State 'before and after taking.' The growing exclusion of religion from the schools, and the consequent decay of moral training in the schools, have quite naturally centered the interest and efforts of teachers and pupils upon intellectual instruction; and the dominance of the natural sciences over content and method in the schools has made that intellectual instruction factual and technical, instead of, as it had once been, disciplinary and cultural.

TOPICS FOR DISCUSSION

1. The curriculum in schools for classes and schools for masses.
2. The effect of religious rivalries on denominational school systems.
3. The influence of partisan politics in the management of State school systems.
4. The effects of the 'scientific-religious' conflict as carried into the schools.
5. The content and method of religious instruction in Catholic, Protestant, and Jewish schools.
6. The content and method of moral instruction in non-religious schools.

BIBLIOGRAPHIC NOTE

One of the most convenient sources of statistical information about modern school systems is the annual series of *Bulletins* issued by the United States Bureau of Education. In addition to school statistics covering most of the countries of the world, these *Bulletins* also contain detailed studies of the historical development and the actual functioning of many school systems; studies which naturally vary a great deal in value. As illustrating their wide range of topics, the following titles, out of more than a thousand, may be mentioned: *German Views of American Education, with Particular Reference to Industrial Development* (1906, No. 2); *Education in Formosa* (1908, No. 5); *Daily Meals of School Children* (1909, No. 3); *The Movement for Reform in the Teaching of Religion in the Public Schools of Saxony* (1910, No. 1); *Teaching Language through Agriculture and Domestic Science* (1912, No. 18); *Present Status of the Honor System in Colleges and Universities* (1915, No. 8); *Training in Courtesy* (1917, No. 54); *Motion-Pictures* (1919, No. 82); *The School Janitor* (1922, No. 24); *Federal Aid to Public Schools* (1922, No. 47); *Negro Education* (1916, Nos. 38, 39, about 1,150 pages, with many charts). Unfortunately, many of the writers or compilers of these Bulletins display a narrow tendency to evaluate all other school systems in terms of the public schools of the United States, and are inclined to depend too much upon mere literacy as a test of education. *A Cyclopedia of Education,* edited by Paul Monroe, 5 vols., New York, 1911-13, and the general encyclopedias, such as *Americana, Brittanica, Herder, Larousse,* have good summary outlines of modern school systems.

Most present-day histories of education devote a great deal of space to accounts of the modern school systems, often with more enthusiasm than judgment. Some, such as S. C. Parker, *A Textbook in the History of Modern Elementary Education,* Boston, 1912, and E. P. Cubberley, *The History of Education,* Boston, 1920, rejoice in the banishment of religious instruction from State school systems, and generally view State control of schools as an unmixed blessing. J. W. Adamson, *A Short History of Education,* Cambridge University Press, 1922, is much more objective and better balanced. P. J. Marique, *History of Christian Education,* 3 vols., Fordham University Press, New York, 1924-32, is sound in view, but rather ill-ordered and inadequate in presentation. The works of O. Willmann, F. W. Foerster, and F. De Hovre, mentioned in the note to Chapter 18, are valuable studies of the principles underlying modern school systems. De Hovre and Foerster offer good bibliographies. F. W. Roman, *The New Education in Europe; an Account of Recent Fundamental Changes in the Educational Philosophy of Great Britain, France, and Germany,* London, 1923, is the result of a four years' personal investigation of reforming groups. F. De Hovre, *German and English Education, a Comparative Study,* New York, 1917, is broad and enlightened.

Based generally on the many statistical reports issued by various governments, the following works may be noted as discussing both historical developments and modern trends in some of the more important school systems: J. F. Abel and N. J. Bond, *Illiteracy in the Several Countries of the World,* United States Bureau of Education,

Bulletin No. 4, 1929; J. F. Abel, *National Ministries of Education*, United States Bureau of Education, Bulletin No. 12, 1930 (a summary account of State organization of school systems, with bibliography); A. P. Newton, *The Universities and Educational Systems of the British Empire*, London, 1924; B. Darwin, *The English Public School* (English Heritage Series; an account of the large secondary schools of England), London, 1929; I. L. Kandel, *The Reform of Secondary Education in France*, Columbia University Press, New York, 1924; T. Alexander and B. Parker, *The New Education in the German Republic*, New York, 1929; for the development of the Prussian school systems during the later nineteenth century the best account is the semi-official one of Wilhelm Lexis, *Das Unterrichtswesen im Deutschen Reich*, 4 vols., Berlin, 1904, of which an extract was published in English, translated by G. J. Tamson, as *A General View of the History and Organization of Public Education in the German Empire;* A. S. Jensen, *The Rural Schools of Norway* (historic and present; good bibliography), Boston, 1928; A. Gabelli, *L'Istruzione in Italia,* Bologna, 1903; V. de Lafuente, *Historia de las Universidades, Colegios, y demás Establecimientos de Enseñanza de España,* 4 vols., Madrid, 1884; Hijos de J. Espasa, editores, *España* (Sexta Parte), Barcelona, 1925; for general understanding, Ward, *The Truth about Spain,* London, 1911; E. Baelz, *Awakening Japan,* New York, 1932 (diary of a German doctor in Japan, 1876-1905; valuable for understanding national temper back of modern school system); for Japan there are many recent studies, such as *Present Day Japan,* by Yusuke Tsurumi, Columbia University Press, 1926; beginning with its *Outlines of the Modern Education in Japan,* Tokyo, 1893, the Japanese Department of Education has translated into English and published many reports on its school system; T. Y. Feng and T. T. Lew, editors, *Education in China,* Peking, 1923 (papers by Committees of Society for the Study of International Education); W. Gurian, *Bolshevism: Theory and Practice,* London, 1932.

CHAPTER XX

The Western inheritors. Up to the present, this sketch of educational history has been deliberately kept away from the American scene. There were two main reasons for reserving consideration of American education. The first reason, a minor one, was to make it easier to offer a compact view of school education in the Western hemisphere. The large reason was that the most important elements in American education were an inheritance from Europe. European civilization had already reached the great climaxes of the Renaissance and the Protestant Revolt before the Americas were discovered and colonized by Europeans. In what we think of as the modern age, say, roughly from 1500 to 1800, the educational development of the Americas was shaped by European ideas; the educational dependence of the Americas upon Europe was nearly as complete as their political dependence. This is true in spite of the fact that some of the native Americans, notably the Zapotecs, Mayas, and Quechuas, had had a high culture and civilization for centuries before the Europeans came.[1] But the

---

[1] Accounts of this American civilization are generally inadequate, as might be expected. Garcilaso de la Vega, a *mestizo* of Inca stock, wrote the best we have about the Quechuas. It has been translated by C. R. Markham as *The First Part of the Royal Commentaries of the Yncas,* Hakluyt Society, London, 1869. For the Mayas see T. Gann and J. E. Thompson, *The History of the Maya,* New York, 1931. Diego de Landa, Bishop of Mérida in Yucatan from 1573 to 1579, destroyed in 1562 hundreds of hieroglyph manuscripts, containing the ancient Mayan literature. He afterwards wrote a *Relación de Las Cosas de Yucatán,* which Diego Lopez de Cogolludo used a good deal in his *Historia de Yucatán,* Madrid, 1688. De Landa and Cogolludo are valuable, but suspect. Later studies have been forever handicapped by de Landa's intolerance and vandalism. One of the best

high native culture had already begun to decay when the white men came from Europe; and those adventuring white men came with an amazing energy of body and mind, with superior weapons, and with the military advantage of having horses, which made it possible to subjugate the Americans, and either to impose the European civilization upon them, or to drive them away and gradually kill them off. The result has been the fairly complete dominance of European principles and practices of education in the Americas. It seemed sensible then to defer the study of American education until we had reviewed the developments in Europe.

The modification of the inheritance.   The native culture had comparatively very little influence upon the education developed in the Americas by the colonizing Europeans. But the European colonists in time gradually wrought changes themselves in the educational procedure they had inherited from the long traditions, Roman and Christian, of Europe. Their way of life in a new land, vast, richer than Europe, relatively unsettled, could not be completely the European way. The new circumstances affected the pioneers physically, mentally, morally. Certain graces of manner and of language were lost, to be compensated for by a hardihood of body and a new mental aggressiveness in all who survived the harsh conditions of exploration, conquest, and colonization. A certain resolute, vigorous temper was necessary for the successful colonist: a temper which was to lead, ultimately, to political independence, and which was certainly to give a distinctive stamp to educational practices borrowed from Europe. The tradition which the first colonists had brought from Europe learned in the New World to cock its hat and swagger a bit; it took on, for all its age, some qualities of youth. That modifica-

bibliographies on such researches as have been made is given in H. Beuchat, *Manuel d'Archéologie Américaine,* Paris, 1912.

tion of the European inheritance was gradual, and quite varied. It differed in Latin America, in British America, in the United States; but it became in time unmistakably a group of characteristics which made American education obviously different from European education.

The division of the inheritance. The colonization of the Americas was undertaken chiefly by the peoples of the Atlantic seaboard of Europe. The Spaniards came first, quickly followed by the Portuguese. The Spaniards settled in that part of North America lying south of the Carolinas, in Central America, and in South America. The Portuguese began their colonial empire in Brazil in 1531. In the years in which Luther was beginning to rend Christendom, Magalhaes went through the Straits of Magellan into the Pacific, and definitely made clear that the Americas were not a part of Asia. After the Spanish and Portuguese came the French, under the Florentine Verrazano in 1524, directing their course northward from the Carolinas to Newfoundland. Their colonization of the northern part of North America began with the settlement of Cartier and Roberval in 1534-1541. England had sent another Italian, John Cabot, over as early as 1497-1498, but began colonizing only in 1585, with the unfortunate venture of Raleigh at Roanoke. The English field of settlements ranged from the Floridas to Newfoundland. The Dutch, with an Englishman, Hudson, to lead them, came to found New Amsterdam in 1609. The Swedes planted a colony in what is now New Jersey in 1637; but were conquered by the Dutch, who in turn were conquered by the English in 1664. French Canada became British in 1763. French Louisiana became part of the United States shortly after the latter came into existence. By the time the great modern era of school education was about to begin, the cultural traditions of the Americas had been split into two major divisions and one minor division: the major divisions of Iberian and British, which also meant Catholic and Protestant; and the minor division of French, in Quebec and Louisiana. The United States developed, culturally, out of the British, Protestant tradition. Canada developed out of an unfused mixture of British Protestant and French Catholic.

The place of the native Americans. But there was another point of major division, and a supremely important one, which came from the attitude of the colonists toward the native Americans. All the colonists exploited the natives, but with a difference. The earlier colonists, Spanish, Portuguese, and French, because they were Catholics, retained in their dealings with the natives some shadowy remnants of the Catholic tradition of the spiritual equality of men. They robbed the natives as ruthlessly as the later Protestant colonists did; but they also seriously and persistently tried to Christianize the natives, and they intermarried with them. Their policy was one of peaceful robbery wherever possible, and it led to much miscegenation, lawful and unlawful. Now, if one remembers that the mingling of the white and native races was almost always of a white man with a native woman,[1] and keeps in mind the elementary fact that early education, in the most formative years, is in the hands of mothers, not fathers, it is easy to see how the descendants of whites and natives got a very diluted share in the inheritance of European cultural tradition. The Catholic priests did set up churches and schools, did instruct the growing *mestizo* population in the rudiments of religious belief and practice and in some of the elements of European school education. But such in-

[1] The Spanish Crown rigorously controlled emigration to the American colonies. Unmarried women were never allowed to go to the colonies. Cf. C. de Lannay et H. van der Linden, *Histoire de l'Expansion Coloniale des Peuples Européens*, 3 vols., Brussels, 1907-21, Vol. 1, p. 362. As late as 1803, Humboldt reckoned that only one-tenth of the Spaniards in Mexico were women. For other figures on this point, see W. W. Sweet, *A History of Latin America*, New York, 1919, pp. 122-24.

struction came to them after their early foundation upon the decayed native traditions, and never succeeded in lifting the mass of the intelligent, docile Indian and *mestizo* peoples to the general educational level of European peoples. The British, Protestant colonists, on the other hand, made very feeble and short-lived attempts to Christianize or educate the native Americans. It must be admitted that the Indians with whom they dealt were not as readily susceptible to European education as the Indians of the South; but they were the same sort of Indians as those with whom the Catholic missionaries in Canada and in the West labored so hard and so successfully. The British Protestant policy with the natives soon settled down to relentless warfare.[1] The prime result of that policy was the more complete transfer of European culture and education to the British Protestant colonies and the predominant peopling of their lands by white men. From a material point of view, their policy was more efficient than that of the Catholics. But even from that point of view their efficiency rather overreached itself when it led them to bring negro slaves into their colonies, and to produce by miscegenation with those slaves a very considerable body of mulattoes who still remain below the educational level of Europeans.

The educational provinces of the Americas. When, therefore, the modern period of school education opened in the Americas, the Western hemisphere presented three great educational provinces:

[1] There is a core of truth in the rhetorical statement of Francis Parkman: "Spanish civilisation crushed the Indian; English civilisation scorned and neglected him; French civilisation embraced and cherished him." (*France and England in North America*, Boston, 1865, p. 44.) In the same tenor are the testimonies of J. Douglas, *New England and New France*, New York, 1913, p. 513, and of travellers such as Isaac Weld (*Travels through the States of North America and the Provinces of Upper and Lower Canada during the Years 1795, 1796, and 1797*, 2 vols., London, 1800, Vol. 2, p. 25) and Alexander Henry (*Travels and Adventures in Canada and the Indian Territories, 1760-1776*, New York, 1909, p. 34).

(a) Latin America, from Mexico southward; characterized by a population in which native blood predominated, which was generally Catholic in religion, and relatively slow in industrial development;

(b) British America, including Canada, some West Indies islands, and the tropical coastal colonies of British Honduras and Guiana; characterized by a population having some admixture of native and negro blood, but predominantly white,[1] largely Protestant, but with a few strong centers of French Catholic tradition, and moderately advanced in industrial development; and

(c) The United States, characterized by a population about nine-tenths white, with admixtures of all European peoples, but predominantly British and Protestant in its traditions, and most energetic and swift in industrial development.

The school education built up in each of these great divisions of America is so diverse in character that any intelligent treatment of it must be a separate treatment by divisions. The rest of this chapter, therefore, will contain three parts.

I. SCHOOL EDUCATION IN LATIN AMERICA

Some conditions in common. Latin America is made up at present of seventeen countries of Spanish speech and culture, and one large country, Brazil, of Portuguese speech and culture. The one great difference between them is found in the larger part played by negro slavery in Brazil.[2]

---

[1] People of unmixed white race form a little less than five-sixths of the total population of British America. In Canada, the admixture is of white and Indian; in the rest of British America, largely of white and negro.

[2] The Portuguese, who had first introduced negro slaves into Europe in 1441, brought some negro slaves to Brazil in the early years of the colony. But after 1663, when the Jesuit Antonio Vieira secured a royal order forbidding further enslavement of the Indians,

Otherwise the Latin American countries are all pretty much alike. So far as education is concerned, the most important fact common to them all is this: the Catholic religion was, from the earliest colonial days, the official State religion, but in such a way that the Catholic Church was reduced to what was practically a department of the State.[1] That put the schools in the hands of the Church, and, since the Church was governed by the State, created a school situation unsatisfactory to both Church and State. No Christian church has ever really done its work well when it was closely linked with a political State. The officials of the church become involved in political intrigue, lose something of their religious character both in actual fact and in the esteem of their people, and find their influence for good greatly diminished between the jealous hostility of the civil officials and that mistrust on the part of the people in general which so often develops into anti-clericalism. Church-

negroes were imported from Africa in enormous numbers, and were sent chiefly to work the sugar plantations in the northern captaincies. At the close of the colonial period, the slaves outnumbered the white population in the proportion of two to one. There was so much miscegenation that it became almost impossible to determine what proportion of the population was mulatto. A rough estimate of the population about 1800 would give half a million or less of white race, a million negro slaves, and a million and a half made up of free negroes, mulattoes, and a comparatively small number of Indians and *mestizos*. Slavery was abolished only in 1888. (See Roy Nash, *The Conquest of Brazil*, New York, 1926.) The Spaniards also brought negro slaves to America, but not in such great numbers as the Portuguese did. In New Spain the number of negroes did not exceed six thousand. The Spaniards rigorously opposed miscegenation between negroes and Indians; and *zambos*, offspring of the two races, were relatively few. But in Cuba and Porto Rico there were more than half a million negroes at the close of the colonial period. No serious attempts were made anywhere to educate the negroes. The heroic labors of St. Peter Claver and others on their behalf were necessarily limited to relieving their extreme spiritual and material needs. (See C. O. Bunge, *Nuestra America: Ensayo de Psicologia Social*, 4th ed., Buenos Aires, 1912.)

[1] Perhaps the clearest view of the relations between Church and State to be had in English is in the well-documented work of C. H. Cunningham, *The Audiencia in the Spanish Colonies*, University of California Press, 1919 (Vol. 9 of Publications in History).

men in Latin America, trying to promote school education, were faced by those two difficulties: a half-hearted co-operation from the State and from the people; and a lack of freedom in their efforts which hampered their initiative. In addition, one must note the fact that many of the priests were low-grade specimens, cast-offs from their own European countries, of a sort to add new difficulties in the way of the good and competent priests who seriously strove to educate the people.

Another important condition common to all Latin America is that all the countries are predominantly agricultural. The short-sighted economic policy of Spain repressed colonial industries and commerce. One consequence of that was that the commercial and industrial activities of the colonies did not call for many employees who could read and write. Literacy, therefore, was not judged so much by its financial value as by its value as a possible means of culture.

A third important condition is that in all Latin American countries the ancient distinction of classes was taken for granted; a distinction emphasized by the additional barrier of race. The modern enthusiasm for 'democracy' as a social creed was slow in making its way into Latin America. In those few countries where the notion has recently made itself felt politically, it has been imposed by an organized minority, and often in the most brutally autocratic fashion. 'Democracy' is still rather an alien concept in Latin America, where it appears all too often as a mere pretext for political intrigue. As a result, there has been less forcing of schools upon the people than in Europe and the United States; and the conviction that higher school education is a luxury has not been entirely destroyed.

Elementary schools in colonial times. In the Spanish viceroyalty of New Spain, which included the settlements in North and Central America and what is now Venezuela, elementary schools were fairly abundant. They were less abundant in the viceroyalty of Peru, established in 1556; and were very scantily supplied in colonial Brazil. The earliest schools were the work of Franciscan missionaries; the very first of all being connected with the convent of San Francisco in Santo Domingo, which was begun in 1496. On the mainland, too, the Franciscans were the first school-masters. Fray Pedro de Gante came to Mexico in 1523, and within a short time had a school caring for from eight hundred to a thousand Indian boys, in which they were taught, besides the three R's and the catechism, drawing, music, and certain handicrafts.[1] In general, the religious orders were more concerned with the establishment of schools than were the secular clergy. Much of the actual teaching was done by laymen; but the schools were almost exclusively conducted by priests. Yet there was no attempt to stop others from opening schools, and in later colonial times there were a considerable number of schools conducted by laymen. In the cities, the school facilities were generally sufficient for only the children of the whites and wealthier *mestizos*,[2] but in the missions the Indians had

[1] Mariano Cuevas, *Historia de la Iglesia de Mexico,* 3d ed., 5 vols., El Paso, 1928, Vol. 1, p. 385.

[2] Cuevas, *op. cit.,* Vol. 2, p. 151, reckons that there were 470 parishes in Mexico by the year 1600. It is by no means certain that there was a school in every parish, although the claim is made that there was one in every town where there were friars. (Cf. *Códice Franciscano,* pp. 64-66, ed. by Joaquín García Icazbalceta, in Vol. 2, *Colección Nueva de Documentos para la Historia de México,* 5 vols., Mexico, 1886-89, Vol. 2.) Juan Lopez de Velasco estimated for 1574 that there were in Spanish America 200 cities, 160,000 Spaniards, and 5,000,000 civilized Indians. (*Geografía y Descripción Universal de las Indias, Recopilada desde el año de 1571 al de 1574,* first published, as edited by D. Justo Zaragoza, Madrid, 1894.) Alexander Humboldt, at the close of the colonial period, estimated the population as comprising 3,276,000 whites, 5,328,000 *mestizos,* and 7,530,000 Indians. (*Voyage aux Regions Équinoxiales du Nouveau Continent fait en 1794-1804,* 3 vols., Paris, 1814-25.) The estimate of whites seems rather high, even though they obviously included both Europeans and *Criollos,* white descendants of Europeans. One may sus-

good schools, some of them of higher grade than elementary.[1] Religious instruction was, of course, given in all schools. In the cities, the medium of all instruction was Spanish or Portuguese; but in the missions the native languages were kept up;[2] and in the ecclesiastical seminaries care was taken to cultivate a good use of the native languages.[3] The natives often showed considerable talent for the fine arts, and their teachers succeeded in developing it with such effect that Spanish-American artists compared favorably with those of Europe in the seventeenth and eighteenth centuries.[4] Murillo's son taught painting in

pect that many numbered amongst these latter were *mestizos,* descended from whites and Indians.

[1] In the earliest years these schools were compulsory (J. Icazbalceta, *La Instrucción Pública durante et Siglo XVI,* Mexico, 1893, p. 6). But after 1540, the Spanish Crown did little to promote schools for the Indians. That was left to the initiative of the missionaries (Cuevas, *op. cit.,* Vol. 2, p. 286). All honest historians praise the zeal of the missionaries to educate the native Americans. The most famous missions were those of the Jesuits in Paraguay, begun in 1587 at the request of the Franciscan Bishop of Asunción, Alonso Guerra. To protect the Indians against enslavement, the Jesuits organized them as a nation, with about a hundred towns and a population in 1767 of about one million. As a work of education, those missions merit study. Portuguese greed began to destroy them in 1750; the Jesuits were expelled in 1767. A good study of the missions is R. B. Cunninghame Graham's *A Vanished Arcadia,* London, 1901. But the missions of Paraguay were only a small part of the missionary and educational work done amongst the Indians. J. García Icazbalceta notes the interesting fact that in Mexico City, although the friars would not admit Indians into their orders, Indians taught in the monastery schools and had amongst their pupils young Spanish or Creole friars. (*Op. cit.,* p. 12.)

[2] A printing press was set up in Mexico City as early as 1536 or 1537, and in Lima about 1587. In 1546, Bishop Zumárraga had catechisms printed in Nahuatl, one of the commoner languages of Mexico. (Cuevas, *op. cit.,* Vol. 2, p. 198.) Primitive newspapers began to appear in Lima as early as 1594, but were very sporadic affairs in all the viceroyalties until after the establishment of the *Gazeta de México* in 1722, and the *Diario de Lima* in 1790. Of course, newspapers were in Spanish.

[3] Cuevas, *op. cit.,* Vol. 2, p. 313.

[4] See M. G. Revilla, *El Arte en México,* 2d ed., Mexico, 1923; F. H. G. Kreeble, "The Colonial Art of Quito," in *International Studio,* December, 1922; J. G. Navarro, "Art in Ecuador," in *Bulletin of Pan-American Union,* August, 1925.

Lima and Quito. Miguel de Santiago, a *mestizo,* and Caspuara, an Indian of Quito, won international renown. In woven stuffs, household furnishings, and architectural ornament, there was developed a distinctive American style.

Girls had almost everywhere less school opportunities than boys had. One of many reasons for that fact was the lack of teachers. Juan de Zumárraga, first Bishop of Mexico, brought back from Spain in 1534 a few women to conduct a school for girls. They were unsuited to the undertaking and failed at it.[1] The first nuns came from Spain to Mexico in 1540;[2] very timid and uncertain; and were thirty years in the city before they organized a single new convent.[3] It was not until 1754 that a congregation was formed for the definite work of teaching.[4] The religious policy was weak with regard to women. For more than two hundred and fifty years no congregation of nuns in New Spain would admit native girls as members.[5] The number of convents in colonial Mexico was never more than fifty-six, and the highest total number of nuns was less than 1,700, of whom only a minority were engaged in teaching.[6]

Higher schools in colonial times. Although the Franciscans were the first religious priests in America and opened the first elementary schools, it was the Dominicans, coming some fifteen years later than the Franciscans, who first conducted higher schools. Their traditions linked them closely with the European universities, and hence it was the university type of school they envisaged when they began their work in America. By 1538, they had secured

[1] Cuevas, *op. cit.,* Vol. 1, p. 400.
[2] *Ibid.,* Vol. 4, p. 178.
[3] *Ibid.,* Vol. 4, p. 180. Cuevas (*op. cit.,* Vol. 1, p. 402) speaks of a "Colegio de niñas" opened in 1555 at Mexico City for *mestizo* girls, not for white girls; but this seems to have been rather a protectorate than a school.
[4] Cuevas, *op. cit.,* Vol. 4, p. 195.
[5] *Ibid.,* Vol. 4, p. 198.
[6] *Ibid.,* Vol. 4, p. 199.

from Pope Paul III a bull empowering them to establish a university in Santo Domingo. But because the subordination of Church to State rendered papal decrees valueless until approved by the king, the University of Santo Tomas had to wait twenty years for a decree of Philip II in 1558. In the meantime, the same order of Dominicans had proceeded more cannily in South America; and got permission from Charles V to found the University of Saint Mark, at Lima, in 1551. With that they could go ahead, although this time it was the pope who made them wait twenty years for his sanction; and when it came, in 1571, they were ordered to turn the university over to seculars; but the Dominicans continued to teach philosophy and theology in it. In the same year 1551, the University of Mexico was founded by royal decree; but classes were not begun until 1553; and the papal bull recognizing it was not issued until 1596.[1] The University of San Antonio Abad, founded at Cuzco in 1598, was second in importance only to San Marcos at Lima. The Augustinians founded the University of San Fulgencio at Quito in 1586; but it was soon overshadowed by the University of Saint Gregory the Great, founded in the same city by the Jesuits in 1620. At Bogotá, the Jesuits had the College of San Luis from 1592; and it became the Xaverian University shortly after the Dominicans, in 1627, opened there the University of Santo Tomas. Further south, the Jesuits had a college in Chile as early as 1593; but the first university in Santiago, Santo Tomas, was established by the Dominicans in 1619. There was always rivalry between the religious orders, never less than keen and sometimes less than wise. The Jesuits in Santiago promptly got a papal bull from Gregory XV in 1621, raising their school to university rank. A third university at

---

[1] Cuevas, *op. cit.*, Vol. 2, p. 287. See also José Adame y Arriaga, *Constituciónes de la Real y Pontifical Universidad de México*, Mexico, 1775.

Santiago, San Felipe, was founded in 1738, by decree of
Philip IV of Spain. Although it had a very feeble existence
until 1759, when the vigorous Valeriano Ahumada became
rector, it was this third university which managed to persist to the present as the National University. In what is
now the Argentine, the Jesuits had a college at Córdoba del
Tucumán from about 1618. Gregory XV and Philip III
raised it to a university in 1622. When the Jesuits were
expelled by the Spanish Crown in 1767, the Franciscans
took over the university.[1] The Jesuits had another university, called Saint Francis Xavier, at Chuquisaca, now
Sucre, the capital of Bolivia, founded in 1624. Venezuela
saw its old seminary of Santa Rosa, at Caracas, become a
university by decrees of Innocent XIII and Philip V in 1722.
The Dominicans got a papal bull in 1721 for the founding
of a university in Havana, but the Bishop of Havana succeeded in preventing its foundation until 1728, and it
secured the royal sanction only in 1734.

In addition to these universities, there were many
colegios, roughly equivalent to a combination of our modern
high schools and junior colleges. The Jesuits, sixteen of
whom came to Mexico in 1572, had twenty-seven *colegios* in
Mexico within a hundred years.[2] The other religious orders
and some of the bishops also conducted secondary schools;
but, just as in Europe at the time, the Jesuits had most of
the *colegios.* It need scarcely be said that these higher
schools were planned for the whites and the upper-class
mestizos, and that the Indians rarely found their way into
them.

The number and spread of higher schools in colonial
Latin America is impressive. Attention has often been
called to the fact that there were twelve universities and

---

[1] J. V. Gonzalez, *La Universidad de Córdoba en la Cultura Argen-
tina,* Madrid, 1872.
[2] Cuevas, *op. cit.,* Vol. 2, pp. 328, 332; Vol. 3, pp. 27, 437.

nearly forty colleges established in Latin America before the founding of Harvard College in 1636. The Latin American universities were also impressive in the number of students enrolled,[1] in the wide range of their studies,[2] in the quality of their teachers,[3] and in their influence upon colonial culture.[4] Just as in Europe, Latin was the ordinary language used in lectures and disputations in the higher schools. Although religious teaching in the universities tended to be relegated to the official courses in the department of theology, there was some practical religious instruction in the secondary schools. Moreover, there was at least a negative safeguard for all the schools. The Inquisition, which was extended from Spain to Peru in 1570 and to

---

[1] For instance, San Marcos, at Lima, by the year 1700, had more than 1,800 students. Between 1558 and 1775, the University of Mexico had conferred the degrees of doctor or master upon 1,162 graduate students. (Cuevas, *op. cit.,* Vol. 4, p. 260.)

[2] The undergraduate college of arts, with a curriculum patterned generally on that of Salamanca, was the core of each university. Some universities had several such colleges, as the University of Mexico had, not only in Mexico City, but in five other dioceses. Practically all the universities had the standard four faculties, of arts, philosophy, and law, civil and canon law; some had more; Santa Rosa, at Caracas, had nine departments in all, including schools of medicine and music. The most noted law school was that of the University of San Francisco Javier, at Chuquisaca, which drew students from all over South America.

[3] One thing that tended to keep up the high standard of teachers was the rivalry between religious orders, which spurred them to draw well-equipped professors from Europe, and to be eager in recruiting the cleverest and ablest scholars from the creoles of the colonies.

[4] See Quesada, Menendez y Pelayo, Cuevas, Oliveira Lima, for lists of eminent scholars and literateurs who wrote during colonial times. Their number and quality is in striking contrast to the intellectual poverty of the North American colonies. An interesting survey of the general culture of the sixteenth century in Mexico is offered in the English translation of Garcia Icazbalceta's "Education in the City of Mexico during the Sixteenth Century," in *Historical Records and Studies,* United States Catholic Historical Society, Vol. 20, New York, 1931. See also A. L. Coester, *Literary History of Spanish America,* New York, 1916; and I. Goldberg, *Brazilian Literature,* New York, 1922. Icazbalceta (*op. cit.,* p. 137) points out that many of the earlier manuscripts and printed books have been destroyed. That they once existed is known only from references in other works.

Mexico in 1571, had for its chief concern the censorship of books, in the effort to keep false doctrines out of Latin America.   That was an educational service, which, naturally, irritates non-Catholic historians, but for which much can be said in the way of rational defense.[1]

The transition.   Between 1803 and 1823, the Spanish and Portuguese colonies in America, with the exception of Cuba, won their independence and began to break up into nations. Back of the complicated political and economic conditions which led to the wars of independence were important social causes which touch the schools of Latin America.   One of the most important was the resentment of the creoles and the wealthier *mestizos* against the social and political dominance of the Spaniards.   In the matter of school education, they had been on an equality with the *cachupines,* those born in Spain; but socially they were looked down upon by the Spaniards, and they were excluded from all the higher offices in the State and in the Church controlled by the State.[2]   In time they came to outnumber the Spaniards, perhaps by as much as ten to one;[3] they were an unacknowledged 'middle class,' as contemptuous toward the

[1] See H. C. Lea, *The Inquisition in the Spanish Dependencies,* New York, 1908; E. Vacandard, *The Inquisition* (English translation from 2d ed., by B. L. Conway), New York, 1908.   The least that can be said of the Inquisition in Spanish America is what Mr. Hoover said of prohibition, that it was "noble in purpose."   But, unlike prohibition, it was effective in its main business of censorship, for the excellent reason that it had large popular support.   The Spanish Americans, whatever else they were, were generally averse to heretical teachings.

[2] Forty-nine of the fifty viceroys of New Spain had been *cachupines, chapetones, peninsulares* (born in Spain); of 602 local governors in New Spain, all but fourteen were Spanish born.   (M. Williams, *People and Politics of Latin America,* p. 231.)   In like fashion, the bishops and religious superiors were exclusively Spanish born.   (E. Ryan, *The Church in the South American Republics,* p. 43.)   Archbishop Pascal Diaz (consecrated 1925, Bishop of Tabasco) is the first Mexican prelate of Indian blood.

[3] Cuevas (*op. cit.,* Vol. 5, pp. 43 sqq.) quoting the famous summary of Abad y Queypo on the social classes in Mexico.

Indians and lower-class *mestizos* as the *cachupines* had
been toward them.   All writers, earlier and later, agree in
describing them in general as quick in intelligence, but
inclined to be superficial and unstable in character.

At the revolt from Spain, power came into the hands of
these men, men with a grievance, suffering from what our
present-day psychology likes to call an 'inferiority complex.'   Ambition in such men tended to become violent,
vindictive, unmeasured.   Masonic lodges attracted them
powerfully, because they appeared to offer strong and secret
help toward political advancement.   Masonry grew rapidly amongst them, of the type that was hostile to Catholicism and often to all religion.[1]   In the first few decades
of independent national life, almost everywhere the schools,
even when taken over by the States, continued to be administered by the Catholic clergy.   But friction between Church
and State inevitably developed in the new regime, due to
faults on both sides, and was added to by these three vital
facts: (a) although the lower ranks of the clergy, secular
and regular, were staunch adherents of the new governments, many of them were dissolute and undisciplined, and
alienated the people by their lives;[2] (b) the higher ranks

[1] Cuevas, *op. cit.*, Vol. 5, chap. 2, pp. 130 sqq.
[2] For Mexico, Cuevas estimates that 6,000 of the 8,000 priests
actively favored the revolution.   (*Op. cit.*, Vol. 5, p. 92.)   Hidalgo,
Morelos, in Mexico, and Cortes Madariaga in Venezuela, with many
other revolutionary leaders, were priests.   Cuevas tries to qualify
the hostility of the bishops and religious superiors (mostly Spaniards)
toward independence; but that hostility is well known and generally
acknowledged.   (See E. Ryan, *The Church in the South American
Republics,* pp. 43 sqq.)   There are many accounts of the irregular lives
of friars and secular priests.   See, for instance, that of the viceroy
Francisco Moreno y Escandón, *Estado del Virreinato de Santa Fé de
Granada,* 1782; Vol. 85 in *Colección de Documentos Inéditos para la
Historia de España,* 112 vols., Madrid, 1842-95; also A. F. Frézier,
Voyage à la Mer de Sud, Paris, 1717, Vol. 2, pp. 430-50.   In the early
years of the new Latin American nations, this condition grew worse
because the quarrel between the Spanish crown and the Church over
the 'patronage' prevented the consecration of bishops for the new
republics.   (See E. Ryan, *op. cit.,* pp. 48 sqq.)

of the clergy had not been in sympathy with the revolution, and were disgusted by the new type of politicians with whom they had to deal; (c) the wealth of the Church, much exaggerated in popular esteem,[1] stirred up envy in a people all too prone to envy.

These revolutionary elements churned and fermented for some thirty or forty years, with much political and social disturbance. Out of the ferment emerged small, compact political organizations, drawn for the most part from two professional classes, the military and the legal, bitterly contending with one another for political power, but all accepting a common attitude toward school education. That attitude, which was to shape State policy as regards schools in almost all Latin America, was one of regret and shamed apology for their past, and a naïve eagerness to be 'modern.' It led the various nations to enact compulsory school laws, which they could not enforce, and have not enforced. It led them to reorganize university education on the narrowest basis of professional studies. The old humanistic curriculum was discarded, both because it was old, and because Latin literature was somehow associated with the Catholic Church. It was in this temper that the modern school systems of Latin America were begun and developed.

Modern elementary schools. All the Latin American countries, except Colombia,[2] have laws that make attendance at elementary schools compulsory. The compulsory school age is usually six or seven years to twelve or thirteen years; averaging about six years, or until completion of the school course. But not all elementary schools offer six years of work. The periods vary, from as low as two

---

[1] Cuevas (*op. cit.*, Vol. 5, pp. 289 sqq.) notes the significant fact that Callcott and others have confusedly given the capital wealth of Mexican dioceses as their income.

[2] G. W. A. Luckey, *Outline of Education Systems and School Conditions in Latin America* (United States Bureau of Education, Bulletin No. 44), Washington, 1923, p. 33.

years in Brazil[1] to six years in the Argentine,[2] Chile,[3] Panama,[4] and a theoretical eight years in Cuba;[5] but the average is about three years in Brazil and not more than four in most of the Spanish-speaking nations. Except in the cities and larger towns, scarcely any effort is made to enforce the compulsory law; and often only a feeble effort in the towns and cities. Boys and girls are usually taught in separate schools.[6] In their intense desire to be 'modern,' the men who control schools in Latin America swallowed whole the 'modern' pronouncements against memory work; and quite logically banished all textbooks from their schools.[7] Recently, the textbooks have begun to return; and one country, Uruguay, has even swung to another 'modern' extreme, and now furnishes the textbooks free to the school children.[8] The general result of the experiment is simply that Latin American schools have very poor textbooks. To make matters worse, the schools have adopted another 'modern' enthusiasm, for an 'enriched curriculum.' For instance, in the elementary schools of the Argentine, Luckey lists fifteen subjects taught: including physiology, physics, chemistry, domestic science, music, and nature study, as well as history, geography, manual training, geometry, the three R's, drawing, and physical education.[9] This overloading operates to bring back the worst features

[1] Luckey, *op. cit.,* p. 11.
[2] *Ibid.,* p. 4.
[3] *Ibid.,* p. 20.
[4] *Ibid.,* p. 108.
[5] *Ibid.,* p. 76.
[6] Except in the Argentine, Chile, and Mexico, in each of which the majority of elementary schools are coeducational. (E. E. Brandon, *Latin American Universities and Special Schools,* United States Bureau of Education, Bulletin No. 30, Washington, 1912, p. 127; gives table of figures.)
[7] Brandon, *op. cit.,* pp. 141-43.
[8] Luckey, *op. cit.,* p. 57.
[9] Luckey, *op. cit.,* p. 4. Cuban elementary schools offer about as many subjects (*Ibid.,* p. 77); Uruguay, in a three-year elementary school course, presents fourteen obligatory subjects (*Ibid.,* p. 57).

of mechanical memorizing; since the children can do no more with such a variety of subjects than cram a few facts for examination.

The Catholic religion is still the professed religion of the peoples of Latin America. In some States provision is made for religious instruction in the schools, generally before or after the regular school hours.[1] In Mexico and Panama no religious instruction is allowed.[2] Similarly, all the governments except Mexico, which for the past twenty years has carried on violent anti-Catholic persecutions, permit the establishment of private religious schools, but under State supervision and with the curriculum imposed by the State. In the Argentine, for the year 1919, private schools cared for about one-fifth of the children at school;[3] the largest proportion in Latin America. In general, throughout Latin America the Church has not attempted to compete seriously with the State in the field of elementary schools.

Modern secondary schools. Although there are many types of secondary schools at present in Latin America, the most important of them fall into two classes: the *colegio* or *liceo,* more numerously attended by boys; and the normal school, in which most of the students are girls. There is practically no coeducation in secondary schools. The *colegio* or *liceo* in every Latin American school system leads to a bachelor's degree, and qualifies its graduates for the university; although graduates must also pass an entrance examination. The course is generally of five years' dura-

---

[1] Some States put further conditions to this permission. Venezuela, for instance, insists that parents of at least ten children must request that religious instruction be given. (Luckey, *op. cit.,* p. 64.)

[2] *Ibid.,* pp. 67, 108.

[3] *Ibid.,* p. 4; he cites the figures: 7,801 public elementary schools, 1,467 private schools. (*Ibid.,* p. 2.) More characteristic of general conditions is the situation in Costa Rica, for the year 1921: State elementary schools, 398; private schools, 25; a proportion of about sixteen to one. (*Ibid.,* p. 103.)

tion,[1] based on a six-year elementary school.[2]   The normal school varies from two to four years in courses offered. Both types of secondary schools are alike in (a) the large number of subjects taught;[3] (b) fixed curriculum; no electives; (c) the fact that no Latin or Greek is taught.[4] Latin, above all, had been a staple of the older curriculum; it is, therefore, part of 'modernity' to exclude it absolutely.   Its place is taken by modern languages, amongst which French is in the first rank.[5]

Most governments permit of private secondary schools; but control their studies by making their students pass an examination in the courses set up for the State schools. The Catholic clergy center most of their educational efforts in secondary schools.[6] But classes in religion or philosophy in Catholic schools must be added to the already heavy schedule.[7]

Attempts to compare Latin American secondary schools

[1] Some schools, as in Chile and Colombia, have a six-year course. See Luckey, *op. cit.*, pp. 21, 34.

[2] The maximum elementary period in Brazil is five years.   (*Ibid.*, p. 12.)

[3] For instance, in the Argentine, students of the *colegio* must study twenty-three subjects; normal-school students have seventeen subjects. (*Ibid.*, p. 5.)   In Brazil the normal schools demand twenty-one subjects. (*Ibid.*, pp. 12, 16, 17.)

[4] The *colegios* of Venezuela are an exception.   The four-year general courses there offered are divided into three sections, one of philosophy and letters, two of physical sciences.   In the section of philosophy and letters, Latin is taught for two years, and Greek for one year.   The first four years of the six-year course offered in the *liceos* follow the same arrangement. (*Ibid.*, p. 65.)

[5] See E. E. Brandon, *op. cit.*, pp. 132-40, for a sound discussion of this question of languages.

[6] In the Argentine, about one-third of the secondary schools are private, and almost all Catholic. (Luckey, *op. cit.*, p. 4.)   The proportion runs to one-half in Chile. (*Ibid.*, p. 21.)   In Bolivia, in 1922, there were fourteen State secondary schools, and ten private. (*Ibid.*, p. 29.)   The Protestant missionary societies also devote themselves chiefly to secondary schools. (Brandon, *op. cit.*, p. 66.)

[7] See the detailed schedules of subjects and hours per week in Luckey, *op. cit.*, p. 25, in which the Catholic student is shown to have thirty-three fifty-minute periods a week in each year.

quantitatively with high schools in the United States are often misleading. Luckey affirms that graduates of the better *colegios* and *liceos* are usually ranked in the United States as on a level with graduates of the four-year high school.[1] Such an 'accrediting,' however, is hardly fair. The better *colegios* and *liceos* are at least the equivalent of junior colleges in the United States.

There are in the Latin American countries a large number of commercial schools and schools for training in industry and agriculture; in most of which the latter years may be reckoned as giving secondary education. The commercial schools are the most important of these, and attract large numbers of students.[2] The character of all these schools is strictly utilitarian.

Modern universities. It may be said that none of the Latin American universities of today has had an educational life continuous with that of the old universities; not even when they continue in the name and place of the old universities. When the independent States took over the old universities, they soon changed their character. The old universities were primarily cultural; the present universities are almost exclusively utilitarian and professional. The faculty of philosophy and literature, which had been usually the most important, has now been abandoned in almost all universities.[3] Brazil had no colonial university. The one federal university at present, the University of Rio de Janeiro, was founded only in 1920, by consolidating schools of medicine, law, and engineering already function-

[1] *Op. cit.*, p. 22.

[2] Brandon, *op. cit.*, pp. 94-125, studies these various sorts of special schools in some detail.

[3] There are a few exceptions, as in San Marcos at Lima, and the University of Havana; but the number of students in the faculty of philosophy and letters is quite small. At Buenos Aires, the faculty has become a normal school, attended chiefly by women. San Marcos has even kept the faculty of theology, although the teaching is done in the seminary. (Luckey, *op. cit.*, pp. 6, 23, 54.)

ing.[1] Those three faculties, with sometimes a fourth of agriculture, constitute the whole of most universities. The courses are organized to lead to a doctorate, and vary from four to six years in length.[2]

Within the past twenty-five years women have been attending the universities in increasing numbers. The old faculty of philosophy and letters has been metamorphosed, in many of the universities, into a higher normal school. Latin American women, as Brandon observes,[3] go to the universities, not for general or cultural education, but for vocational training as teachers, physicians, pharmacists, or dentists. Although the law schools are open to women, very few women study law; nor do women attend commercial schools, except in Brazil.[4]

There are very few universities in Latin America not directly controlled by the State. At present there are only three Catholic universities; and one private university, that of Concepción, Chile.[5] The Catholic universities are: Santiago de Chile, founded by Archbishop Casanova in 1888, with four faculties, law, mathematics, engineering, and agriculture; Valparaiso, Chile; and Buenos Aires, which has only two faculties, law and social sciences.[6] The Colegio de Nuestra Señora del Rosario, at Bogotá, and Mackenzie College, at São Paulo, Brazil (affiliated with the University of the State of New York), although not universities, are recognized by the State as of university rank.[7]

Attendance at all universities and higher schools has grown enormously in the past thirty years. The University

---

[1] Luckey, *op. cit.*, p. 13.
[2] For example, at Buenos Aires, four years for philosophy and letters (normal school), four years for dentistry, five for pharmacy, six for medicine, five for law, five and six for engineering. (*Ibid.*, p. 6.)
[3] *Op. cit.*, p. 129.
[4] *Ibid.*, p. 130.
[5] Luckey, *op. cit.*, p. 23.
[6] E. Ryan, *op. cit.*, p. 59.
[7] Brandon, *op. cit.*, pp. 66-69.

of Buenos Aires now numbers more than 11,000 students; Santiago de Chile about 4,500. The medical faculty almost everywhere vastly outranks all others in number of students; although not more than one-half its graduates ever enter professional practice. In the absence of liberal arts colleges, most of those students who go to the universities for a general education study law or medicine. Perhaps not a third of the law graduates ever practice law.[1]

Summary and conclusion. School education in Latin America has been conditioned by three factors: (a) social distinctions based on race; except for the earlier missionary work, the vast Indian population has not had much schooling, and of course has not desired schools; (b) the agricultural character of the countries, which until recently stood in the way of any great demand for widespread school education; and (c) the action and reaction concerning religion, which linked the schools with the Catholic Church for three centuries, and in the past century committed them to politicians varying from suspicious to hostile in their attitude toward Catholicism. The result has come to be systems of schools completely controlled by the State (directly or indirectly), rather inadequate in extent and method, narrowly utilitarian in purpose, and weak in both cultural and religious influence.

II. School Education in British America

The field and its divisions. British America at present falls into two natural divisions. The first, and more important, is the Dominion of Canada, a federation of States within the British Empire. The second comprises the coastal crown colonies of British Honduras and British Guiana, and the British West Indies, broken groups of

---

[1] E. E. Brandon, "Education in Latin America," in *Encyclopedia Americana,* New York, 1932, Vol. 17, pp. 11 sqq.

islands from the Bermudas to Trinidad. The population of Canada, in 1929, was estimated as 9,796,000; the population of the rest of British America is about 2,250,000, of whom at least nine-tenths are negroes or mulattoes.[1] Most of these possessions were gained by England in the eighteenth century, Canada only some twenty years before the revolt which issued in the formation of the United States. There were traces of the educational influence of Spain or France, varying in degree and force, in these countries when the English took possession; but, with the exception of the Province of Quebec, English ideas in educational development promptly prevailed in all the colonies.

The general temper of school administration. Throughout British America there has been evident the attitude toward school education which developed in England during the nineteenth century. That attitude may be summed up somewhat in this fashion: it is conservative and conscientious; aware of the inevitable changes in school methods and school administration, yet not unmindful of educational traditions; much affected by the lingering hostility toward the Catholic minority, yet honestly striving to make allowance for that bias, and to be fair to the minority; vaguely respectful toward religion in education, even when the State officials are no longer influenced by religious belief. The few details possible to offer in this condensed sketch may serve to illustrate that temper of school administration in British America.

In the smaller colonies. A fairly uniform procedure with regard to schools, the natural result of the central policy in England, exists throughout the British colonies and de-

[1] The white population ranges from as high as 18,000 out of a total 170,000 in Barbados to less than 15,000 out of about 1,000,000 in Jamaica, and less than 200 out of 12,000 in Montserrat. For details, see *The British Empire, a Survey,* edited by H. Gunn, 12 vols., London, 1924, Vol. 5; *Dominions and Dependencies; New International Year Book,* 1932; and *Encyclopedia Americana,* 1932, *sub vv.*

pendencies. Generally there are two parallel systems of schools: the government schools, directly managed by the State officials; and voluntary schools, under the immediate management of religious bodies, but strongly helped financially by a State grant in aid, and subject to indirect control through government inspection and examinations. In most of the colonies the old English system of 'payment by results,' a graduation of grants according to the success of the pupils in passing the governmental examinations, is still in force, and apparently works satisfactorily. For illustration, the largest colony, Jamaica, and one of the smallest, British Honduras, may be considered a little in detail.

Jamaica became a British possession by capture in 1655. Cromwell populated it by sending 2,000 young Irish men and women into exile there, and another 2,000 Scotch criminals.[1] In 1660 there were 4,500 whites and 1,500 negroes on the island. In 1807, when England prohibited the slave trade, there were 320,000 negro slaves in Jamaica. Slavery was abolished in 1834; and in 1844 as the freed negroes were unsettled about working, Hindu coolies began to be brought in. After 1820, the English parliament had granted annual sums of money for schools; and forty schools for slaves and seven for free children were established before the abolition of slavery in 1834. About 1840 a considerable private bequest was added to the government grant, and some fifty schools were built.[2] But in the first year in which coolies were imported, the parliamentary grant was withdrawn; and until 1865 only the colonial legislature's grant of £3,000 a year was available. The legislature then bestirred itself in a reform of the school system. In 1867 it adopted the English plan of granting aid to schools under

[1] See C. B. Davenport and M. Stegerda, *Race Crossing in Jamaica,* Washington, 1929; and J. J. Williams, *Whence the Black Irish of Jamaica?* (bibliography), New York, 1932.
[2] *Cyclopedia of Education,* Vol. 3, p. 515.

these heads: (a) partial payment of costs of building new schools, where local contributions made up the major part of the cost; (b) payment of teachers' salaries, based upon both the grade in which the teacher qualified in an examination for his certificate from the government, and the success of his pupils in passing the annual school examinations. Denominational schools shared in this grant in aid. In 1870 the Anglican Church was disestablished and disendowed in Jamaica, and some of its former endowment went to the aid of schools, enabling the government that same year to establish its first normal school. From 1885 to 1892 a government commission studied the school question anew. As a result of the study, the legislature, in 1892, created a Central Advisory Board in Education, in which the various denominational bodies also had representatives, and levied a house tax to do away with the need of collecting fees in elementary schools. This latter, of course, is what is called making the schools 'free.' There was a revised code of regulations issued by the Education Department in 1900; but it left the general scheme unchanged.

In 1929, there were 656 elementary schools in Jamaica, with 133,495 pupils enrolled.[1] There are four government normal schools. The Catholics and Anglicans each have a secondary school. The Catholic school, St. George's College, was begun by Spanish Jesuits in 1850, and after a checkered career of forty-five years, was moved from Kingston to a suburb, Winchester Park. Until 1927, it included elementary classes. At present it has about 160 pupils. Franciscan teaching Sisters came from Scotland to Jamaica in 1857, and English Sisters of Mercy in 1890. Both conduct a number of elementary schools, and the latter several industrial schools, aided by the government.[2]

---

[1] *Encyclopedia Americana*, 1932, Vol. 15, p. 600.
[2] *Catholic Encyclopedia*, Vol. 8, p. 273. See also F. C. Delany, *A History of the Catholic Church in Jamaica, B. W. I.*, New York, 1930.

British Honduras, or Belize, lying just south of Mexico on the Caribbean coast, is about the size of New Jersey, with a population of some 50,000, of whom only 650 are whites. About half of the population is negroid, the other half of various types and admixtures of Indian stocks. Originally a rendezvous of buccaneers, Belize just drifted into being a British colony. Its largest single influx of people came in 1848, when some 7,000 Yucatecans, driven out of Mexico by Indian uprisings, came south into the colony.[1] These new settlers were Catholics, and succeeded in getting two Jesuit priests from Jamaica in 1851.[2] About the same time, Baptists from the United States settled in the colony; and in 1868 some Methodists came from the Southern States, self-exiled during the bitter period of 'reconstruction' following the Civil War.[3] In 1883, Sisters of Mercy from New Orleans opened in Belize a school for girls; and in 1887, English Jesuits began a school for boys. In time, these, as well as the Anglican, Wesleyan, and Baptist schools in Belize, developed into secondary schools. Practically all the elementary schools in the colony are denominational, and all share in the government grant in aid, in the same way as indicated for Jamaica. In 1894, a central board of education was set up, in which the denominational bodies are represented.[4]

In 1930, there were in the colony 77 elementary schools, with 7,619 pupils enrolled, and an average attendance of 5,812. The government grant was about $70,000, or rough-

[1] The population of the colony before the coming of the *mestizos* from Mexico was probably not more than 6,000. See A. R. Gibbs, *British Honduras,* London, 1883, p. 85 (where population for 1829 is given as 3,833), and p. 153 (where population for 1871 is given as 24,710).

[2] The Anglican Church was established in 1810 (Gibbs, *op. cit.,* p. 77); the first church begun in 1812, consecrated in 1826 (*Ibid.,* pp. 77, 83); only one clergyman until after 1850 (*Ibid.,* p. 99). First school begun in 1816 (*Ibid.,* p. 78).

[3] *Ibid.,* p. 151.

[4] *Encyclopedia Britannica,* 14th ed., 1929, Vol. 4, p. 201.

ly about $12.50 per child.[1]   Most of the schools also demand some fees from the parents.   The five secondary schools have about 530 pupils; and no secondary school receives financial aid from the government.   The secondary curriculum, as in many British colonies, is largely shaped by the Cambridge Local Examination.   These, held annually all over the Empire, are set by Cambridge University, and made attractive both by the educational standing they create and by money prizes awarded to the schools presenting successful candidates.

The foundations of education in Canada.   In all the vicissitudes of its three centuries of history, Canada has borne the imprint of a French and Catholic character; and nowhere has this character shown itself more strikingly than in the development of its school education. French colonization was slow in starting,[2] and slow in developing.[3] But from the very beginning the interest in education was evident.   Missionary zeal at once took the form of instruction,[4]

---

[1] *Encyclopedia Americana,* 1932, Vol. 14, p. 352.

[2] There was no permanent settlement until that of Port Royal in 1605.   This became the capital of the region known as Acadia, comprising what is now Nova Scotia, New Brunswick, and part of Maine. Destroyed by the English in 1613, it repeatedly changed hands between French and English, until finally taken for the English by Nicholson in 1810, and called Annapolis.   In 1749, England landed 3,000 Protestant colonists in what was thenceforth known as Nova Scotia, and founded Halifax.   In 1753, the Acadians, to the number of about 8,000, were transported into exile, and their place taken by people from Scotland and Ulster.   For a fair discussion of Acadian history, see A. G. Doughty, *Acadian Exiles,* Toronto, 1914 (Vol. 9 of Chronicles of Canada).

[3] There were only about 6,000 colonists in Canada in 1700.   (*Encyclopedia Americana,* 1932, Vol. 5, p. 297.)   At that time, the population of the English colonies was 262,000.   (*Encyclopedia Americana,* Vol. 27, p. 340.)   In 1775, when the rebelling American colonies had a population of 2,500,000, including 500,000 negro slaves, Canada had only about 60,000 in all.   (*Encyclopedia Americana,* Vol. 27, p. 341; C. W. Colby, *Canadian Types of the Old Regime,* New York, 1908, p. 41.)

[4] See J. Douglas, *New England and New France,* New York, 1913, p. 513; and H. J. Boam, *Twentieth Century Impressions of Canada,* Montreal, 1914, p. 37. For the educational work of the missionaries

and schools followed close everywhere upon the entry of the missionaries. As early as 1616, the Franciscan Recollect, Brother Duplessis, opened a school at Three Rivers.[1] Quebec was founded by Samuel de Champlain in 1608; and the Jesuits, who came in 1625, opened there the first permanent school in 1635.[2] Montreal was not founded until 1642, by the heroic Maisonneuve; and although for thirty years the settlement lived under constant dread of the Iroquois, Marguerite Bourgeoys came to Montreal in 1653, and in six years was able to found the first American congregation of nuns. In 1657, ecclesiastical control of Canada was taken out of the hands of Louis XIV, so that henceforth the educational work of the colony was carried on independently of the French crown.[3] Indeed, practically the only aid given the missionaries in Canada was the royal grant of lands;[4] their help from France came from private contributions of money, but most of all from the devoted men and women who gave their lives to the colony. In

amongst the Indians, the great historical source is *The Jesuit Relations and Allied Documents,* edited by R. G. Thwaites, 73 vols., Cleveland, 1896-1901. A single volume of selections from these was edited by E. Kenton, New York, 1925. See also F. Parkman, *The Jesuits in North America in the Seventeenth Century,* Boston, 1895, especially pp. 63 sqq., 133 sqq. The French treatment of the Indians was generally most humane; yet strangely there were in 1930 only 110,596 Indians in Canada. (*Encyclopedia Americana,* 1932, Vol. 5, p. 409.)

[1] J. G. Bourinot, *The Intellectual Development of the Canadian People,* Toronto, 1881, p. 24.

[2] *Encyclopedia Americana,* 1932, Vol. 5, p. 379.

[3] C. W. Colby, *op. cit.,* pp. 272, 286.

[4] These lands were later taken over by the English administration, and were long a subject of litigation. In 1839, the lands of the Sulpicians were restored to them. But the lands of the Recollects and Jesuits were not so readily disposed of. In 1831, the Jesuit lands were definitely confiscated by the government, to be used for education of both Catholics and Protestants. Protests were made, until finally, in 1889, the Jesuits were paid a sum equal to about one-fifth of the value of their lands, as a compromise; although as a further compromise, 15 per cent of that sum was taken for Protestant schools in Quebec. (F. B. Tracy, *The Tercentenary History of Canada,* 3 vols., New York, 1908, Vol. 3, pp. 996-98.)

1659, the year in which Marguerite Bourgeoys founded the Congregation of Notre Dame,[1] François de Montmorency Laval came to Quebec as the first bishop in Canada. Quebec at the time had only 500 inhabitants, and all the colonists in Canada numbered less than 2,200; yet Laval, within four years of his coming, opened the Seminary of Quebec, and five years later, in 1668, a secondary school for boys.[2] One important result of this early foundation of schools was that a considerable supply of teachers and priests could be furnished within the colony itself, and that the culture of Canada could develop a character of its own.[3] In 1727, elementary schools were everywhere turned over to the care of the parish priests; and by 1750 there were schools in nearly every parish, even in the country districts.[4]

[1] Twenty years before that, French Ursuline nuns had opened a school for girls in Quebec. J. Douglas, *op. cit.*, p. 361, points out the vastly better education given to girls in Canada than in New England. The obvious reason for that was the existence of the teaching congregations, whose members devoted themselves heroically to the work. The standard life of the Venerable Marguerite Bourgeoys is that of M. Faillon, 2 vols., Montreal, 1853. Many others have since been published; the latest, anonymously, by Kenedy, New York, 1932.

[2] Auguste Gosselin, *Vie de Mgr. de Laval, Premier Évêque de Québec*, Quebec, 1890; F. X. Garneau, *Histoire du Canada depuis sa Decouverte jusqu'a nos Jours*, 3 vols., Quebec, 1859, Vol. 1, pp. 170 sqq. J. Douglas, *op. cit.*, p. 385, calls Laval's industrial school at St. Joachim "the first technical school on the continent."

[3] Between 1665 and 1765, there labored in Canada 572 French priests and 179 Canadian priests. (C. W. Colby, *op. cit.*, p. 283.) By 1773, the Congregation of Notre Dame alone had fourteen houses. (*Catholic Encyclopedia,* Vol. 3, p. 234.) In striking contrast, note this testimony of the Reverend Jonathan Boucher, an Anglican clergyman and schoolmaster in Maryland and Virginia from 1759 to 1775: "At least two-thirds of the little education we receive are derived from instructors who are either indented servants or transported felons. Not a ship arrives with redemptioners or convicts, in which schoolmasters are not as regularly advertised for sale as weavers, tailors or any other trade; with little other difference that I can hear of, excepting perhaps that the former do not usually fetch so good a price as the latter." (*A View of the Causes and Consequences of the American Revolution,* dedicated to George Washington, London, 1797, Discourse IV, "On American Education," p. 184.)

[4] Some of these country schools had Latin classes. (*Encyclopedia Americana,* Vol. 5, p. 379.)

The coming of the English. When the English aggression against Canada began to be effective, it did much injury to school education.   After 1710, there were no schools in Nova Scotia for more than forty years.[1] The school of the Notre Dame nuns at Louisbourg, Cape Breton, was closed by the English in 1758.   The persistent attempts of the English to wrest Canada from the French finally succeeded.[2] By the Treaty of Paris, 1763, the entire country became an English possession.   Unquestionably, religious intolerance, as well as racial hostility to the French colonists, marked the early years of English rule.[3] Even though Sir Guy Carleton, in 1774, succeeded in getting the English Parliament to pass the Quebec Act, which gave legal freedom to Catholics,[4] the clash between the conquering English and the conquered French continued to disturb education for many years.   In 1801, the government tried to give a monopoly in school education to the Royal Institution for the Advancement of Learning, an Anglican body; but popular resentment was strong enough to withstand the at-

[1] There had been boys' and girls' schools at Port Royal as early as 1640, and again after the temporary English conquest of 1654. (*Encyclopedia Americana,* Vol. 5, p. 380.)

[2] The English had held Quebec from 1629 to 1632; and from 1621 onward had held and lost the maritime Provinces until their final possession in 1710.

[3] J. C. Bracq, *The Evolution of French Canada,* New York, 1926, pp. 55-73, gives a brief, but substantial account of those early years; valuable as from a fair-minded Protestant.   As a source, see Sir H. Cavendish, *Debates in the House of Commons in the Year 1774,* London, 1839.

[4] It infuriated the New Englanders and many of the other American colonists, and was actually made one of the grievances against England which led to the American Revolution.   For a summary account of anti-Catholic bigotry in this connection, see P. Guilday, *Life and Times of John Carroll,* New York, 1922, Vol. 1, pp. 73-82. See also R. Coupland, *Quebec Act,* Oxford, 1925, and C. M. Andrews, *Colonial Background of the American Revolution,* Yale University, 1924.   As to the effects upon education of the supremacy of the British, the facts may be simply summarized thus: "The British Conquest was followed by a decline in education."   (*Encyclopedia Americana,* Vol. 5, p. 380.)

tempt.[1] In the endeavor to revive their schools, the French Canadians organized in 1821 La Société d'Éducation du District de Québec.[2] Their efforts were so successful that in 1824 the government recognized the separate Catholic and Protestant schools; and after 1829, for a few years offered grants in aid. Indeed, for a time there was a greater abundance of money than of competent teachers, either English or French.[3] The armed rebellion of 1837, very complicated in its motives, and shared in by both English and French, did not lack the dispute over education as one of the motives. When the revolt was quelled, the English Parliament granted most of what the rebels had demanded. Upper and Lower Canada, separated since 1791, were reunited in 1840; and in 1841 an act of Parliament sanctioned separate religious schools throughout the colony. In Upper Canada, now Ontario, men hostile to the old tradition, French and Catholic, fought against this act until 1863, when the Canadian Assembly passed the Scott Act.[4] These years were a period of revival and reorganization for the Catholic schools in Quebec; new religious congregations of men and women came into the work of teaching;[5] it was the great period for the establishment of Cath-

[1] See A. Buies, Le Saguenay et le Bassin du Lac St. Jean, Quebec, 1896, p. 160; and N. Burwash, Edgerton Ryerson, Toronto, 1903, p. 142.

[2] Les Ursulines de Québec, 4 vols., Quebec, 1864-66, Vol. 4, p. 668.

[3] See The Report of the Earl of Durham, British North America, London, 1905, pp. 67, 94. The Catholics met this difficulty by the aid of the religious congregations in France, which sent many members during the following years, and by the establishment of new Canadian teaching congregations. But the improvement took time for both Protestants and Catholics.

[4] Named after Richard William Scott (1825-1913), knighted in 1909, who as member of the Canadian Assembly, 1857-63, was author of the act putting into effect the parliamentary sanction of 1841, and carried it despite the bitter opposition of Ontario Orangemen. (See F. B. Tracy, The Tercentenary History of Canada, 3 vols., New York, 1908, Vol. 3, p. 918.)

[5] Between 1837 and 1918, there came from France or were founded in Canada, 27 congregations of men and 51 of nuns. (Le Canada Ecclésiastique, Montreal, 1918, pp. 399 sqq.)

olic secondary and higher schools.[1] When confederation of
the Provinces into the Dominion of Canada was brought
about in 1867, the Canadian people were ready to solve
their school problems intelligently and, on the whole,
amicably.

Modern elementary schools. As it affected education, the
situation in 1867 was somewhat like this: (a) the population was made up of three elements; the French Canadians;
the English, Scotch, and Irish immigrants; and a considerable influx of people from the United States; the French
Canadians were Catholics, the rest mostly Protestants,
many of them, like the Orangemen of the West, virulently
hostile to Catholics; (b) all elements were loyal to the
British sovereignty, and loyally suspicious of the neighboring United States; and the English government, appreciating that loyalty, was eager to deal fairly with the Canadian people; (c) the principle of admitting separate religious
schools was accepted both in England and in the Dominion,
although with persistent reluctance by a large body of
Protestants, who preferred rather to have no recognition
of religion in schools than to allow the Catholics the right
of religious education.

Each Province in the Dominion was to have control of its
schools, with a limited general revising authority exercised
by the Dominion government. As the school systems were
actually worked out, they divided into three types. The
first is that of Quebec, in which there are two complete
systems of schools, Catholic and Protestant,[2] with separate

---

[1] Most important was the founding of Laval University in 1852.
The College of Montreal had been established in 1767; but in 1876 a
branch of Laval University was opened at Montreal, which became
an independent university in 1889. Of the impressive list of colleges,
these may be mentioned: Nicolet, 1803; St. Hyacinthe, 1809; St.
Theresa, Montreal, 1825; Assumption, Montreal, 1832; Levis, Quebec,
1853; St. Francis Xavier, Antigonish, 1854; Regiopolis, Kingston,
1866; Ottawa, 1866.

[2] The division is also linguistic and racial, French and English:

school committees for each, functioning under the Province's Council of Public Instruction, and coming together from time to time to consider questions of common interest. In both systems, schools are neither compulsory nor 'free.'[1] The second type is that of Ontario, Saskatchewan, and Alberta, in which five or more heads of families in a locality may set up a separate school, may be exempt from taxes levied for the common schools, and may elect trustees empowered to tax their property and administer the school. These separate schools also receive a proportionate share of the grant in aid. All schools, common and separate, are under the same regulations as regards qualifications of teachers, curriculum, compulsory attendance, and inspection.[2] The third type of school is the rigidly secularist,

although most of the French schools also teach English. The Catholic system enrolls about nine-tenths of the children of the Province. (*Cyclopedia of Education,* Vol. 1, p. 521.)

[1] Financial support of elementary schools in Quebec comes from three sources: (a) a grant from the general funds of the Province, amounting to about one-eighth of the total school expenditure; (b) local taxes, which each tax-payer at his own choice assigns to the Catholic or the Protestant schools, and which furnish more than half of the school funds; (c) school fees, which amount to about one-third of the total. School fees do not exceed 50 cents a month, and are remitted in many cases. (*Cyclopedia of Education,* Vol. 1, p. 519.) It is particularly interesting to note that in Quebec, the only Province without compulsory school laws, the average of school attendance has always been much higher than in the provinces which compel school attendance. For instance, for the first quarter of the twentieth century, 1901-25, the average enrollment of pupils in the Province of Quebec was 425,602, or one in four of the total population, with an average attendance of 77.5 per cent of those enrolled. The average attendance in Ontario, with the same proportionate enrollment, one in four of the population, was only 63.3 per cent, and in the whole of Canada only 67 per cent. (Based on figures in the official *Canada Year Book,* Dominion Bureau of Statistics, Ottawa.) Newfoundland, which is not in the Dominion of Canada, but is a separate crown colony, has a system of separate religious schools very like that noted in British Honduras. The Catholics, Anglicans, and Methodists each form roughly about one-third of the population. The schools charge fees, and also receive government grants. *The Year-Book of Newfoundland* for 1928 shows a total school attendance of 59,088, or nearly one in four of the total population.

[2] Most of the separate schools in these Provinces are Catholic, since

which is found in Nova Scotia, New Brunswick, Prince Edward Island, British Columbia, and Manitoba.[1]   In practice, however, the systems are influenced by the temper of religious tolerance which marks the Canadian people as a whole; and in some districts in these Provinces the schools are often conducted as religious schools.[2]

Throughout Canada the organization of elementary schools is fairly uniform. The compulsory school period is generally five years.[3]   The schools are, as a rule, divided into five 'forms' or 'grades'; the first three of which are concerned rather closely with the three R's. The choice of subjects for study is usually sensible; the curriculum is not overloaded, yet is not left too meager to meet the practical needs of the children.[4]   Except in Quebec and a few other

Protestants generally do not show as much zeal as Catholics for religious schools. The rather burdensome procedure for establishing and maintaining separate schools appears also to be wearing down the Catholic zeal. In Ontario, for instance, there were 537 Catholic elementary schools in 1915, but only 415 in 1928. (*Encyclopedia Americana,* Vol. 5, p. 381.)

[1] Manitoba had followed the arrangement permitted in Ontario until 1890, when it refused to recognize separate schools. In 1916, it made school attendance compulsory (yet raised the average attendance only about 2 per cent: see *Canada Year Book,* 1918) and forbade the use of French as the language of instruction in schools. Both the 1890 and 1916 acts were bitterly, but unsuccessfully, opposed.

[2] An exception must be made for British Columbia, in which no sort of conniving at religious schools is allowed. (*Encyclopedia Americana,* Vol. 5, p. 383.)

[3] In 1919, Ontario increased the period of compulsory attendance to the ages 8 to 16, with the alternative that those who left school at 14 should attend continuation schools for 400 hours each year (an average of 2 hours a day, 5 days a week) until the age of 18. The new regulation added about 10 per cent to the number of enrolled pupils, but increased the average attendance only about 5 per cent. (*Canada Year Book,* Ottawa, 1924, p. 852.)

[4] Taking Ontario as illustration, the elementary schools teach these subjects, in addition to the standard three R's: hygiene (including instruction on temperance in drink), music, calisthenics, morals and religion. In the fourth form, some elementary notions of agriculture are added; and in the fifth form some commercial subjects, leading into the new vocational courses of the continuation schools. (*Cyclopedia of Education,* Vol. 1, p. 515.) Quebec schools have an admirable

large cities, elementary schools are usually coeducational. Teacher training is amply provided for, both in model schools and in normal schools. The number of pupils assigned to each teacher is controlled by regulations.[1] The material equipment of schools is good, and school libraries are provided almost everywhere.

Modern secondary schools. In the organization, as in the nomenclature, of secondary schools there is wide diversity. But this diversity is due primarily to the effort to adapt the secondary schools to the needs and circumstances of their pupils. Some secondary schools are only a year or two added to elementary schools, and administered as one with the elementary school. Some, especially amongst the private schools, include a year or two of elementary schooling, a full secondary course, and a year or more of university work. In Ontario, there is a distinction between 'high schools' and 'collegiate institutes,' both conducted by the State, both giving secondary education: but the latter have a more highly qualified staff and a more liberal financial

flexibility of curriculum. Formal provision is made for adapting the subjects studied to the needs of children according to locality and circumstances: rural, urban, industrial, commercial, etc. Each 'grade' in Quebec schools means a definite work done, and advance made; not necessarily a year's time, but longer or shorter. For detailed studies of the system, see *L'Enseignement Primaire.*

[1] Generally, fifty pupils to each teacher is the maximum number allowed; but actual practices greatly vary. Thus, for instance, the official figures in the *Canada Year Book* show Quebec as maintaining for the years 1901-25 a steady ratio of one teacher to each 30 pupils, whilst Ontario varied from a ratio of 1 teacher to 50 pupils in 1901, to 1 to 43 in 1911, and 1 to 40 in 1922. It may be of interest also to compare the expenditures for schools in Quebec and Ontario for the same years:

	1901	1911	1922	
Quebec	$2.09	$3.34	$10.15	per capita of population
Ontario	2.49	4.79	14.12	per capita of population

The differences are due chiefly to the fact that in Quebec the ratio of teachers to pupils is about 25 per cent higher in Catholic schools than in Protestant schools, and that of the Catholic teachers some 48 per cent are religious brothers and nuns, who are content to teach for a smaller salary than that paid to lay teachers. (*Cyclopedia of Education,* Vol. 1, p. 520.)

allowance.[1]　In Quebec, there are three types of school, covering eleven grades: (a) the strictly elementary schools, teaching the first seven grades; (b) the model schools, including nine grades; and (c) the academies, covering all eleven grades.　The Catholic classical colleges are not in the Province system; but nineteen of them receive an annual Province grant of $10,000 each.　There are, however, under the Province management, nineteen normal schools, eighteen Catholic and one Protestant, which give secondary education.[2]　Except in the classical colleges, there is a considerable amount of vocational training in secondary schools throughout the whole of Canada: courses in manual training, in household sciences, in agriculture, in mechanical drawing, are given in most high schools and normal schools; and there are besides, especially in the larger cities, a good many definite technical and commercial high schools.[3]

---

[1] See *Encyclopedia Americana,* 1932, Vol. 5, p. 366.　In Ontario, no separate secondary schools are recognized.　There are at present 32 Catholic secondary schools, privately maintained by religious congregations.

[2] The statistics given for 1916 for the Province of Quebec are as follows:

Catholic:　　680 model schools,　　with 108,475 pupils
　　　　　　　308 academies,　　　　　"　83,227　"
　　　　　　　21 classical colleges,　"　7,696　"

Of the total of 7,407 teachers in these schools, an average of about 1 to each 27 pupils, the religious teachers outnumbered the lay teachers nearly five to one.

Protestant:　58 model schools,　　with　5,416 pupils
　　　　　　　41 academies,　　　　　"　12,038　"

The total number of teachers was 602, or about 1 to each 29 pupils.

[3] For illustrative statistics, see the article on secondary schools in *Encyclopedia Americana,* 1932, Vol. 5, pp. 365-71. The arrangement of subjects in the Ontario secondary schools is worth noting.　The schools have four 'forms,' or years, of which the first two offer instruction which has a commercial outlook: in languages, a choice amongst Latin, French, or German; an obligatory course in bookkeeping.　The latter two years point more toward the university: Latin is obligatory, the choice in studies being between Greek and a

Higher schools.   Canada is well supplied with higher schools, since it reckons twenty-three universities and eighty-eight colleges.[1]   Of the twenty-three universities, six are State-controlled, and the remaining seventeen are divided amongst four undenominational, six Catholic, three Anglican, two Baptist, and two Methodist.   Moreover, the two largest and best-organized of the State universities, Toronto and Manitoba, have affiliated colleges under the guidance of Anglicans, Catholics, Methodists, and Presbyterians.   Hence it is obvious that religious influence is not wanting in the higher schools of Canada.   The oldest university, McGill, at Montreal, is undenominational; and in 1929 had a total of 3,191 students in four faculties, arts, law, medicine, and applied science.[2]   The four strongest universities are McGill, Toronto, Laval, and Montreal.[3]   The universities that are not State-controlled receive some financial aid from the government.[4]   Most of the universities

combination of French or German with physics or chemistry.   (See *Cyclopedia of Education*, Vol. 1, p. 517.)

[1] Of the colleges, 50 are in Quebec, chiefly 'classical colleges' and seminaries.   Of the 10,894 students enrolled in these 50 colleges in the year 1929 (*International Year Book*, 1931, p. 138), it is impossible to say how many are preparatory students.   There is some similar blurring of figures for higher schools all through Canada.   Thus, the 10,069 students enrolled in the Catholic Laval University for 1928, and the 11,029 in the Catholic University of Montreal, undoubtedly include some who are taking secondary courses.   The total of university students proper for 1929 was reckoned as 28,870.   (*Ibid.*)

[2] The other three undenominational universities all began as denominational: Dalhousie at Halifax in 1838 and Queen's at Kingston in 1841, both as Presbyterian; Western University at London, Ontario, as the Anglican Huron College.   (*Encyclopedia Americana*, 1932, Vol. 5, p. 373.)   The four affiliated colleges of McGill University are all Protestant.

[3] Montreal had been a branch of Laval from 1876 to 1920, when, after a fire which destroyed most of its buildings, it became a separate university, with faculties of law, medicine, arts, philosophy, theology, dentistry, political science, and a polytechnic school for engineering and architecture.   In 1931, it began a $10,000,000 building program.   It has twelve affiliated colleges.

[4] Thus, Laval and Montreal each receives an annual grant of $25,000; and the Polytechnic School of Montreal a grant of $80,000.

have excellent laboratories and libraries,[1] and some of them well-equipped museums. The interlinking and affiliation of colleges and universities in Canada has been of real benefit in maintaining high standards of scholastic work.[2]

Summary and conclusion. School education has been generously cared for by people and by government in Canada, and has been at least adequately provided for in the rest of British America. The organization of schools has been, for the most part, practical and well-balanced, intelligently and realistically adapted to circumstances. In spite of the inevitable and unfortunate friction between Catholics and Protestants,[3] the place of religion in the schools has not been ignored; and, except in the west of Canada, reasonable efforts have been made by governments to adjust the school opportunities and school burdens equitably to the

[1] McGill has 285,000 volumes, Toronto, 252,486 volumes, Laval, 140,000 volumes. (*Encyclopedia Americana*, 1932, Vol. 5, p. 373; Vol. 17, p. 81; Vol. 19, p. 417; Vol. 26, p. 704.)

[2] Thus, for instance, the following are affiliated with the Universities of Oxford and Cambridge: the Universities of King's College, Dalhousie, and Acadia, of Nova Scotia; the Universities of New Brunswick, Mount Allison, and St. Joseph, of New Brunswick; Toronto and McMaster Universities, of Ontario; and the State Universities of Alberta and Saskatchewan. Almost every college in Canada is affiliated to some Canadian university. (See *Canada Year Book*, Statistics on Education.) The linking varies in significance. Thus, the Colleges of St. Michael's, Trinity, and Victoria really form a part of the University of Toronto; just as Manitoba, St. Boniface, St. John's, and Wesley Colleges are constituents of the University of Manitoba; the Jesuit College of Edmonton, Alberta, has its courses and degrees controlled by Laval University, Quebec; and some of the affiliated colleges of the University of Montreal merely have their degrees sanctioned by Montreal.

[3] British America is predominantly Protestant. The Catholics are not more than 5 per cent in Jamaica, 7 per cent in British Guiana. In the small colony of British Honduras, the Catholics are a majority: some 30,000 out of a total population of about 50,000. In Canada, during the past quarter of a century, the Catholics have averaged about 40 per cent of the population; Anglicans, Methodists, and Presbyterians each about 15 per cent. In 1925, the Methodist, Presbyterian, and Congregational churches joined to form the United Church of Canada. It has now about 3,000,000 members, or some 30 per cent of the total population. (*Encyclopedia Americana*, 1932, Vol. 5, p. 392.)

rights and duties of denominational adherents. Of Canadian school education in general, it can be said that it is the best in the Americas.

III. School Education in the United States

A general view of the people. The population of the Americas is at present about 235 millions. Of these a little more than one-half, about 123 millions, are in the United States, 100 millions in Latin America, and some 12 millions in British America. The people of the United States have long assumed to their country the whole name of 'America,' and have called themselves 'Americans'; as a people they are not much conscious of the other 112 millions in the Americas. It will be convenient to accept this bumptiousness, and use the name 'Americans' in that sense for the rest of this chapter.

The growth of the Americans in numbers and wealth is one of the striking phenomena of modern history. In 150 years, their numbers had multiplied the original 2½ millions about fifty times; and the national wealth had grown from 750 millions to 360,000 millions of dollars, that is, had multiplied about 480 times.[1] The growth in population came very largely by immigration, chiefly from the various nations of Europe.[2] The population is therefore hetero-

---

[1] For the sake of comparison we may note that the national wealth of the United Kingdom of Great Britain and Ireland had multiplied, in the same period, only about 15 times; in other words, at a rate less than one-thirtieth as rapid as that in the United States. (*Encyclopedia Americana*, 1932, Vol. 29, pp. 125-26.)

[2] It is hard to estimate the numbers of the aboriginal population when the colonists first came; perhaps it was not much more than 200,000. The United States census of 1930 gives a total of 340,541 Indians. (*Encyclopedia Americana,* Vol. 15, p. 57.) As to involuntary immigrants from Africa, there were 500,000 negro slaves in the colonies in 1775, about 700,000 in 1790, about 2,000,000 in 1830. An act of Congress, March 7, 1807, forbade further importation of slaves; and additional enforcing acts were passed in 1818 and 1820. But some importation continued up to the Civil War. Slavery was

geneous, in language, racial origins, social traditions. The one thing the Americans have had in common is nervous energy, restless aggressiveness, eagerness to exploit the great natural wealth of a new and rich country. It is not unnatural that this polyglot people, uprooted from their native customs, scattered throughout a huge, rich, raw land, and inflamed by the material ambitions which the opportunities of the country aroused, should have made slow progress in cultural development, and should have ceased to be much affected by religious beliefs and practices.[1]

On the other hand, there have always been in the United States two elements which made strongly for a lavish expenditure in the development of schools. The first, and more basic, is the popular enthusiasm for 'democracy,' which has meant in America the unlimited desire and hope that each man might attain to great wealth, prestige, and power. Schools were readily envisaged as a means toward realizing such an ambition. The second element has been the existence, especially in the latter two-thirds of the history of the United States, of a body of men and women devoted almost fanatically to the idea of school education, eager and aggressive to spread schools, to improve school methods, to secure financial and political backing for the development of schools. Most of these advocates of school

finally abolished by the Thirteenth Amendment to the Constitution, December 18, 1865, which set free about 4,500,000 negroes. In 1930, there were 11,891,143 negroes in the United States. The earlier immigration of whites came chiefly from northern Europe, the later immigration chiefly from southern and eastern Europe.

[1] In 1931, the estimated number of persons in the United States who made any profession of religion was 49,752,443. (*Daily News Almanac*, Chicago, 1933, p. 427.) That left over 72,000,000, or about 60 per cent of the population, quite indifferent to religion. There is good reason to estimate that the percentage of persons without religious affiliation was much higher in the past. *The Yearbook of American Churches*, 1932, sets that percentage as high as 93 per cent in 1800, 82 per cent in 1870, 65 per cent in 1900.

education have been sincere and unselfish in their purpose, fired by the conviction that school education is the most important means for the improvement of social and political conditions, radiantly expecting a utopian perfection of national life as the result of widespread schools.   They have succeeded in so imposing their view upon the mass of the American people that belief in the school has come to hold the place which religious belief holds in other civilizations, and is now the first article in the American *credo*.

The colonial background.   The American colonists, although of mixed origins, were mainly British and Protestant in traditions.   The thirteen colonies in the East may be roughly divided into three groups: New England; the central group of New York and Pennsylvania; and the southern group.[1]   All three were at one in their policy of driving off the native Americans.[2]   In all three the influence

---

[1] The New England group comprised Massachusetts, New Hampshire, Connecticut, and Rhode Island; but it had been a shifting group, owing to the claims of Massachusetts on other colonies.   The middle group was New York, New Jersey, Pennsylvania, and Delaware, which had split off from Pennsylvania in 1692.   The southern group was Virginia, Maryland, North and South Carolina, and Georgia, the youngest of all, founded only in 1733.

[2] It would be unfair to deny to the English colonists any concern for the civilization and education of the Indians.   There are several indications of official interest in that education.   In 1618, Virginia set aside 1,000 acres of land as endowment for an Indian school. (E. D. Neill, *History of the Virginia Company of London,* 1885, p. 137.)   In 1624, the General Assembly of Virginia ordered that each borough should educate some Indian children.   (J. Fiske, *Old Virginia and her Neighbors,* 2 vols., Boston, 1902, Vol. 1, p. 246.)   In 1650, Connecticut ordered that "one of the teaching elders of the church . . . be desired, twice at least in every year to go amongst the neighboring Indians and andeavor to make known to them the counsels of the Lord . . . "   (B. A. Hinsdale, *Documents Illustrative of American Educational History,* Report of Commissioner of Education, Washington, 1892-93, Vol. 2, p. 1252.)   There is no evidence that these schemes ever got off paper, or that any practical missionary or educational work resulted from them.   Lord Baltimore's grant of 10,000 acres in 1651, set apart at Calverton Manor as a reserve for the Indians, was more effective, because it followed upon active missionary efforts by the Jesuits, who went amongst the Indians almost immediately upon coming to the colony.   (J. G. Shea, *The*

of the Protestant religions in school education was acknowledged.   But there were striking differences in the attitude of each toward schools.   In the Southern group of colonies, education was generally looked upon as the concern of the family, and the question of schools was left to parental initiative.   In the central group, the organization

Catholic Church in Colonial Days, New York, 1886, p. 73.)   There were Catholic mission schools for the Indians in Maryland from at least as early as 1677 (B. C. Steiner, *History of Education in Maryland,* Baltimore, 1894, p. 16); but later religious persecutions broke up those schools.   (For the almost incredible official hostility to Catholics in Maryland, see the acts of the Assembly in 1704, 1715, 1718, in J. T. Scharf, *History of Maryland,* 3 vols., Baltimore, 1879, Vol. 1, pp. 367-71.)   Individual Protestants made some generous efforts to aid the Indians.   The most renowned of these was John Eliot, a Puritan clergyman, who began preaching amongst the Indians of Massachusetts in 1646, translated the Bible into Algonquin in 1661-63, and is said to have had as many as 3,600 Indians receiving his instructions.   (See W. G. Polack, *John Eliot, the Apostle to the Indians,* St. Louis, 1925.)   But the war with King Philip, chief of the Narragansetts, utterly destroyed his work.   A more lasting success attended the missionary work of the Anglicans, about 1750, and later of the Congregationalists and Methodists, amongst some of the Iroquois tribes in New York.   (See W. L. Stone, *Life and Times of Sir William Johnson, Bart.,* 2 vols., Albany, 1865; and E. H. Brush, *Iroquois Past and Present,* Buffalo, 1901.)   At present, the Indians of the New York reservations, some 5,000 in number, are mostly Protestants.   As regards actual schools for Indians, Dartmouth College grew out of a Protestant venture, Moor's Indian Charity School, which was begun with two Indian boys by Eleazar Wheelock, a Congregational minister at Lebanon, Connecticut, in 1754.   When the school was removed to Hanover, New Hampshire, in 1770, its students were eighteen whites and six Indians.   As Dartmouth College, it promptly ceased entirely to be an Indian school. (See B. P. Smith, *History of Dartmouth College,* Boston, 1878.) There was little body or persistence to Protestant colonial work for the Indians.   It becomes almost negligible beside the heroic work of the Jesuits amongst the Hurons, in which thirty priests and more than forty assistants labored between 1626 and 1649, or the work of Menard amongst the Ojibwa of Michigan, begun in 1660, and Allouez in Wisconsin, of Rasle in Maine, of Kino and Salvatierra in the Southwest after 1683, or the really superb work of the Franciscans in California after 1768, when the Jesuits had been driven out by Spain.   Scharf, *op. cit.,* Vol. 1, p. 190, points out that the first printing press in British America was set up by the Jesuits about 1642, and that Father White had printed catechisms, a grammar and dictionary in Indian languages before the press was destroyed in the persecutions of 1655.

of schools was a parish work, in which the government had no direct part beyond lending a moral, and at times financial, support to the schools.[1]   But in New England school education early became a State affair, for the curious reason that the Puritan church completely controlled the State, and used the power of the State to promote and enforce school education.   The early legislative acts of 1642, 1647, 1671, 1677, 1683 aimed at establishing elementary schools in every town of fifty families, and secondary schools in every town of a hundred families.[2]   It was from Massachusetts, and from the New England tradition of State-controlled schools, that the modern American school system was to stem.   The huge West was but sparsely settled by Spanish and French Catholics, who were to contribute little or nothing to the educational policies developed in the United States.[3]   When the men of the East took possession of the Western lands, they brought the ideas of New Eng-

[1] When the English took New Netherlands in 1674 and made it New York, they discontinued the aid to the parish schools; but soon the Society for the Propagation of the Gospel and similar bodies began to advance that aid.   (E. B. O'Callaghan, *New York Colonial Documents,* Albany, 1849, Vol. 1, pp. 112, 317; Vol. 3, pp. 233, 407.) Colonel Thomas Dongan, the Catholic governor of New York, was patron of a Jesuit school conducted there from 1684 to 1688.   (J. A. Burns, *The Catholic School System in the United States,* New York, 1908, p. 104.)   Most of the Catholics in the Eastern colonies were in Pennsylvania and Maryland; by 1783, about 7,000 in Pennsylvania, and 16,000 in Maryland.   (Burns, *op. cit.,* p. 148.   See also J. P. Wickersham, *History of Education in Pennsylvania,* Lancaster, 1886.)

[2] The texts of the acts may be conveniently found in E. G. Dexter, *History of Education in the United States,* New York, 1919, pp. 584-89.

[3] Although English Catholics established one colony, Maryland, in 1634, they not merely were without much influence in the East, but were generally persecuted even, after a short time, in Maryland itself.   The first school in Maryland was the Jesuit school at Newtown, 1639-59.   (M. P. Andrews, *History of Maryland,* New York, 1929, p. 265; J. A. Burns, *op. cit.,* pp. 92-93.)   The Puritans gained control of Maryland, and in 1654 proscribed Catholics.   (*Archives of Maryland,* Baltimore, 1883, Vol. 1, p. 341; Andrews, *op. cit.,* pp. 123-25.)   For other Catholic schools in Maryland, Indian as well as white, see Steiner, *op. cit.,* p. 16; Burns, *op cit.,* pp. 89-118.

land with them.   But long before that time, the religion of
New England had ceased to be an active influence in Amer-
ican life.   The State-controlled school to be developed from
Massachusetts was to be a secular school.

Early trend of school policies in the United States.   The
government of the United States developed gradually from
the raw Congress of 1774 into a system of difficult balances
between a limited central authority and a limited sovereign
authority in each State.   It took fifteen years to effect that
development; and it was seventy-five years more before the
development reached one stage of its stability at the close
of the Civil War.   Those seventy-five years were years of
eager material expansion, of building roads, canals, railways, of opening up the great western country.   The time
was marked by all the uncouthness of a pioneering age.   In
comparison with other activities, schools were decidedly a
minor interest, especially in the newer parts of the country.
Yet during those years American school policies were also
being gradually developed; and at the close of the period
the essential structure of the American school system was
already erected.

Two characteristics marked the early schools of the
United States: they were religious in temper and purpose,
usually linked with some church organization;[1] and they
were local in their control and administration.[2]   The early

---

[1] The early textbooks offer one evidence of the religious temper of
the schools: e. g., *The New England Primer,* largely scriptural and
catechetical in content, and in widespread use for a hundred and fifty
years, until supplanted by Noah Webster's school books.   See P. L.
Ford, *The New England Primer: a Study of its Origin and Development,* New York, 1897.   See also Clifton Johnson, *Old-Time Schools
and School-Books,* New York, 1904.   It may also be pointed out that
one of the chief aims of the schools above elementary was to maintain a supply of clergymen.

[2] Even in Massachusetts, the first State to establish legal unity in
its school system, the actual unit of administration was the 'school
district,' the very small organization built up in the immediate locality of each school.   Long recognized as the *de facto* administrative

attitude toward schools is well illustrated in the famous Ordinance of 1787, by which Congress organized the lands west of the Alleghanies and north of the Ohio into the Northwest Territory, and in which occurs this much-quoted statement: "Religion, morality, and education being necessary to good government and the happiness of mankind, schools and the means of education shall forever be encouraged." Schools, in that view, are agencies, in a rather vague way, for the promotion of virtue; they are linked somehow with 'religion and morality' as well as with 'education.' The vagueness of the relation tended to increase in American minds throughout the early nineteenth century; and ultimately the relation itself was to be completely ignored.[1] The vast majority of the people were indifferent to religion. In fact, the religious tolerance of which the American people so often and so amusingly boast is perhaps nine-tenths sheer indifference. Moreover, those Americans who professed any religious belief, small minority as they were, looked upon each other with profound mistrust and jealousy, and were inclined to resent any arrangement by which public moneys should be expended upon schools controlled by a religious body other than their own. Each religious group, just because it acknowledged that school education should be religious in character, dreaded that any

unit, the 'school district' was legalized in 1789, and was not abolished until 1882. See W. Burton, *The District School as it Was,* Boston, 1833.

[1] Many of the intellectual leaders of America had accepted the Deistic teachings so rapidly spread throughout Europe during the eighteenth century. The two most influential men in early educational policies, Benjamin Franklin and Thomas Jefferson, were Deists, and showed decided hostility toward any association of schools with Christian church organizations. For Franklin, see *Autobiography* (edition in Harvard Classics, Vol. 1, New York, 1909), pp. 57-58, 80-81. For Jefferson see Letter to Peter Carr, August 10, 1787 (*Writings of Thomas Jefferson,* edited by H. A. Washington, 9 vols., New York, 1853-54, Vol. 2, pp. 237-41); Letter to Dr. Priestley, April 9, 1803 (*Ibid.,* Vol. 4, pp. 475-76); also Vol. 4, pp. 422, 525; Vol. 5, pp. 416, 471, 492; Vol. 6, pp. 217, 412.

governmental support of schools should become an entering wedge for the establishment of a State religion. Yet, in the very nature of modern political development, the State inevitably would take up the maintenance of schools, and would merge the local autonomy of schools into some general scheme of control. The people at large might be content with isolated schools, hovering vaguely under the shadow of some Christian church, but their political leaders could not long tolerate such a state of affairs.

French and German influences. The ferment of ideas affecting European education worked also in America. Up to 1830, the political leaders drew their educational ideas and ideals chiefly from France. Jefferson spoke much of a *national* scheme of schools. The State of New York created in 1784 a controlling but non-teaching university, inspired by the same French ideas that led Napoleon in 1808 to establish the University of France.[1] But the American spirit was chary of too much centralization. The power of controlling schools was never surrendered by the several States to the United States.[2] When government

[1] Dupont de Nemours' *Sur l'Éducation Nationale dans les États-Unis*, published in 1800, was well known in the United States; but the plan brought to New York by John Jay and embodied by Alexander Hamilton in the University of the State of New York really goes back to Chalotais' *Essai* of 1763, and to the schemes of Rolland, in 1768, and of Turgot, in 1775. Jefferson wished to carry out the same notion in Virginia; and Judge Woodward, in frontier Detroit, in 1817, outlined a like plan for the "Catholepistemiad, or University of Michigania." See S. Sherwood, *The University of the State of New York,* United States Bureau of Education, Circular No. 3, 1900; B. A. Hinsdale and I. N. Demmon, *History of the University of Michigan,* Ann Arbor, 1906.

[2] The Federal government has, from its earliest years, done much to aid schools. Its total land grants for schools are 149,299,775 acres. (*Cyclopedia of Education,* Vol. 4, p. 382; see also F. W. Blackmar, *History of Federal and State Aid to Higher Education in the United States,* Washington, 1890.) Frequent, and of late persistent, attempts have been made to bring the schools of the entire country under Federal control. The National Education Association, founded at Philadelphia in 1857, as the last and strongest of a series of like associations, has made one of its chief aims the establishment of

schools came, it was in the American tradition that they should be controlled by the individual States. Moreover, another educational influence began to oust that of the French. About 1815, American students began to go to Göttingen and other German universities, and to catch the German enthusiasm for Pestalozzi and the 'reformers'; the Prussian school system delighted them. These men became influential when they returned to America, and brought with them an admiration for the Prussian schools which has never died out in the United States.[1] It did not, however, suit their plans to adopt the German arrangements for religious instruction in schools. It seemed an easier and simpler way out of sectarian jealousies to make the schools entirely secular.

The significance of Horace Mann. Horace Mann, a Massachusetts lawyer and politician, was born in 1796. A member of the State legislature at thirty-one, and of the State senate at thirty-seven, he became much interested in the political side of philanthropy and education. In 1837, a fellow member of the legislature, James G. Carter, secured the passage of a bill establishing the first State board of education; and Mann, who had backed the bill, was appointed secretary of the board. A writer who admires Mann says of him: "He hated with an equal hatred ignorance, slavery, drink, tobacco, war, and Calvinism. He be-

a Federal Department of Education, with financial control over State schools. Since 1917, the National Education Association has centered its activities on Washington.

[1] See B. A. Hinsdale, *Notes on the History of Foreign Influences upon Education in the United States*, in *Report* of the Commissioner of Education, Washington, 1898. Ticknor, Everett, Cogswell, Motley, Tappan, Mann, W. T. Harris, the men who shaped school policies in the United States, were all Prussian enthusiasts. Victor Cousin's *Report on the State of Public Instruction in Prussia*, published in 1833, and translated into English by Sarah Austin (Wiley & Long, New York, 1835), made a tremendous impression on the American proponents of school reforms, and added to the Germanic influence already in existence.

lieved firmly in phrenology."[1]   Mann was not a practical
schoolman; he was that much more powerful figure, the
school theorizer working through political agencies.   At the
bottom of his theories were two sincere convictions, one
positive, the other negative: the positive conviction of the
perfectionist, rampant since the days of Francis Bacon,
that properly organized schools could bring about an ideal
human society; the negative conviction that Christianity,
as Mann saw it in Calvinism, the only form of religion with
which he had close acquaintance, had nothing to contribute
to that happy idea.

For twelve years, by writings, lectures, public assemblies,
he agitated for an organization of schools modeled on the
Prussian system; he edited a monthly periodical, *The Massachusetts Common-School Journal;* he secured the aid of
enthusiasts in a yearly 'campaign' of meetings and addresses to advocate secular schools directly controlled by
the State.   He met strong opposition to his schemes, especially from school teachers.   He carried some of his proposals; lost some others, at least temporarily.   He got the
State to double its appropriation for schools, to found three
normal schools, to increase the pay of teachers, to add a
month to the school year.[2]   His proposal to refuse State
aid to denominational schools was for the time defeated;[3]
he lost his fight against the local control of schools.[4]   But it

[1] E. E. Slosson, *The American Spirit in Education* (Vol. 33 in
Chronicles of America), Yale University Press, 1921, p. 136.   There
is subject for interesting study in the number of Americans who
have fiercely resented Puritan theology, yet have advocated Puritan
moral and conventional attitudes.   They are frequently sociological
crusaders.

[2] G. H. Martin, *Evolution of the Massachusetts Public School System,* New York, 1894, p. 174.

[3] From 1830 to 1853, Lowell, Massachusetts, had given financial
aid to Catholic parish schools.   In 1855, after several previous attempts, and seven years after Mann had given up his post in education, a constitutional amendment was passed, which permanently
excluded religious bodies from sharing in public funds for schools.

[4] The 'school districts' were not legally abolished until 1882; but

is true to say that his proposals were not so much defeated as delayed in acceptance; and their ultimate acceptance was much wider than in Massachusetts alone. His annual Reports were read in all parts of the country. He was recognized as the devoted and effective spokesman for that group, growing in numbers and in power throughout the northern and western States, who substituted 'democracy' for Christianity in their high and unselfish dreams for mankind; who looked to 'free' schools, maintained by State taxes, and dissociated from any religious teachings, as the most important means for turning their dreams into actuality; and who insisted that the State should supply those schools and make school attendance universally compulsory. As such, Mann is properly acclaimed 'the father of the American public schools.' He gave up his secretaryship in 1848, to become a member of Congress for the next four years; then became president of the newly founded Antioch College in Ohio, where he remained until his death in 1859.[1]

The dual systems of schools. Against considerable opposition, from large numbers who resented new taxes, from local school authorities, from those who believed in religious education, from those who mistrusted the wisdom of enforced schools, and from many others, the States one by one followed the lead given by Massachusetts, and established a system of tax-supported secular schools.[2] The process often began with State aid to existing schools, even

before that date many, if not most, of them had voluntarily given up their authority.

[1] For his work at Antioch, see G. A. Hubbell, *Horace Mann in Ohio,* New York, 1900.

[2] The early school funds, before regular taxes were levied for schools, came from many sources; sometimes from local rates; sometimes from the sale of lands set aside by the State or Federal government; sometimes from public lotteries, a much-used source. New Hampshire, in 1821, exacted a levy of ½ of 1 per cent on the capital of all banks in the State. In 1837, the Federal government turned back to the twenty-seven States then constituted, a treasury surplus of more than $42,000,000; sixteen of the States gave at least part,

when of a religious character, over which aid there was so much quarreling.[1] The second step, in a number of the eastern States, was the formation of a private group opposed to religious schools, or aiming at setting up 'free' schools and turning the State aid to them, or openly campaigning for a State system of schools.[2] The legislature would next enact laws which determined a general plan of schools.[3] Gradually the machinery would be built up to

and eight gave all, of their share of this money to the school fund. (See A. D. Mayo, *Original Establishment of Public School Funds*, in *Report* of Commissioner of Education, 1894-95, Pt. II, pp. 1513 sqq.)

[1] In practice, most of the early schools were Protestant, even when they claimed to be nonsectarian. The various Protestant denominations watched each other jealously in their demands upon the school funds, and all united to watch the Catholics, who, though a minority everywhere, were growing in numbers. The classic field for illustration of these quarrels over school funds is New York City up to 1842, when an act of the State legislature created the New York City Board of Education, and forbade any financial aid to schools which taught religion. (A. E. Palmer, *History of the Public Schools of New York City*, New York, 1905, p. 84.) Even two Catholic parish schools, St. Peter's from 1806, and St. Patrick's from its opening in 1816, shared in the State funds until the Free School Society succeeded in having this grant cut off in 1824. (T. Boese, *Public Education in the City of New York*, New York, 1869, pp. 98 sqq.; H. J. Brann, *The Life of John Hughes*, New York, 1892.) An interesting instance of the conflict over establishing State schools is found in Indiana. The State constitution of 1816 called for 'free' schools; but it was thirty-one years before the public school party succeeded in getting taxes levied. (R. G. Boone, *History of Education in Indiana*, New York, 1892.)

[2] De Witt Clinton, in 1805, founded the Society for Establishing a Free School in the City of New York, which opened a Lancasterian school in 1806, and began getting State aid in 1807. In 1826, the Society got a new charter from the State, changed its name to the Public School Society of New York, and entered upon its long fight to keep other schools from getting a share of the State funds. In 1827, there was organized in Philadelphia the Pennsylvania Society for the Promotion of Public Schools. The Society got the State legislature to pass a school law in 1834, constituting school districts, setting up a system of school officers and inspectors, and offering a State grant of money to those districts which would levy a local tax to maintain schools. Of the 987 school districts in the State, 485, or nearly half, refused the bait. (J. P. Wickersham, *History of Education in Pennsylvania*, Lancaster, 1886, pp. 101 sqq.)

[3] In most States ultimately the plan included compulsory school attendance, beginning with the modest requirement of the Massa-

enforce the general plan.   In most States, because of the representative form of government, some of the delay in setting up the State system of schools came from a desire to reconcile, so far as possible, conflicting views about schools.[1]   But inevitably the system in each State became a system of secular schools.   The minority, Catholic, Protestant, Jewish, who valued the religious element in education, could not accept secular schools, and therefore had to maintain schools of their own.   The States did not forbid the existence of such schools; but those who supported them had also to pay taxes for support of the State schools. Thus there gradually came to be a number of systems of private and parochial schools outside the State school systems.   Of the religious schools the most tenacious were the Catholic and the Lutheran schools, and the most important in numbers the Catholic.[2]

Catholic schools.   The Catholic parish schools are organ-

chusetts law of 1852 that children between the ages of eight and fourteen should attend school for *twelve weeks* each year, of which six weeks were to be consecutive, and mounting up to a required full term attendance.   (See E. G. Dexter, *A History of Education in the United States,* New York, 1919, pp. 623-27, for a compact table of compulsory school laws up to the year 1902.)   In 1889, R. G. Boone, *Education in the United States,* p. 330, declared that the compulsory school law was inefficient and poorly enforced.

[1] There have been a number of experiments in including parish schools in the State or city public school system.   St. Peter's School, Poughkeepsie, New York, in 1873 was rented to the city for one dollar a year; and thereafter the city, by written contract, engaged to pay the salaries of the nuns who taught in the school.   The school had about one-third of all school children in the city.   The arrangement lasted until 1899.   In Minnesota, Archbishop Ireland, of St. Paul, got the State to try a similar experiment at Stillwater and Faribault in 1891.   Catholics as well as Protestants attacked the plan, which fell through after a few years of successful working. In Nebraska, there were Catholic and Lutheran schools in the State system as late as 1917.   (See J. A. Burns, *Catholic School System in the United States,* New York, 1908, especially pp. 356-77.)

[2] "The elementary and secondary education of Protestant children is now almost wholly carried on by public schools or by private institutions having no sectarian affiliations."   E. E. Slosson, *The American Spirit in Education,* p. 181.   See also A. A. Brown, *A History of Religious Education in Recent Times,* New York, 1923: a study of

ized by dioceses, under general legislation of the ecclesiastical councils held at Baltimore. The first Provincial Council, in 1829, urged the establishment of schools "in which the young may be taught the principles of faith and morality, while being instructed in letters," but made no specific rules in the matter.[1] The second Provincial Council, in 1833, appointed a committee to discuss uniformity in textbooks.[2] The five following Provincial Councils, held every three years until 1849, *made no pronouncement whatever about education*. In the meantime, the Catholic population had grown a great deal; the trend of State school systems was pretty well settled; and there was no likelihood of any general inclusion of religious schools in the State systems. Hence, the First Plenary Council of 1852 strongly *advised* building parish schools.[3] The Second Plenary Council repeated the advice.[4] But in 1884, the Third Plenary Council took up the question of schools very earnestly; nearly one-fourth of its decrees concern education.[5] It ordered a school to be built in each parish within two years; an order which the parishes have not yet completely carried out.[6] But the Catholics of the United States

religious education in the Protestant churches of the United States from colonial days to the present.

[1] P. Guilday, *History of the Councils of Baltimore,* New York, 1932, p. 94.

[2] *Ibid.,* p. 106.

[3] *Ibid.,* pp. 179-80.

[4] *Ibid.,* p. 211.

[5] *Acta et Decreta,* Tit. VI, Baltimore, 1886. Cf. Guilday, *op. cit.,* pp. 237-39; T. Jenkins, *Christian Schools,* Baltimore, 1889, pp. 128 sqq.

[6] At no time have Catholic schools been able to accommodate all Catholic school children. Some of the reasons for the large attendance of Catholic children in non-Catholic schools are given in J. A. Burns, *Growth and Development of the Catholic School System in the United States,* New York, 1912, pp. 357-59. Father Burns (*ibid.,* p. 353) sets down the enrollment in parish schools for 1909-10 as 1,237,251 children out of an estimated school population of about 2,875,000; and says that the proportion had been about the same for the sixteen years preceding. *The Catholic Directory* for 1930 gives a total of 2,248,571 children in parish schools, out of a school population which, from other sources, may be reckoned as above 4,000,000.

have made generous efforts to build and maintain their parish schools, under the handicap of having also to pay taxes for the support of the public schools; and they have succeeded in establishing an impressive system of secondary and higher schools. The success of the Catholic school system is due in part to the zeal of the Catholic people for religious education, but in greater part to the heroic devotedness of the Catholic teaching orders, without whose self-sacrifice the Catholic schools could not exist.[1]

In 1920, of 10,608 parishes in the entire United States, 5,852 had schools; in 1930, of 12,413 parishes, 7,225 had schools.

[1] The Catholic parish schools are chiefly indebted to the teaching communities of Sisters. Many of these have their origins in Europe; but the larger number are native to the United States. A complete bibliography of these congregations is not called for here; but the following brief notes may be useful. The best single work giving a conspectus of the teaching orders of women is E. T. Dehey, *Religious Orders of Women in the United States,* Hammond, Indiana, rev. ed., 1930. Two other books dealing with the subject in a general way are: J. B. Code, *Great American Foundresses,* New York, 1929; D. A. Lord, *Our Nuns,* New York, 1924. Many of the detailed studies of individual congregations are anonymous, written by some member of the congregation. Here are a few of the more outstanding: J. B. Code, *Mother Seton and her Sisters of Charity,* New York, 1930; M. A. McCann, *The History of Mother Seton's Daughters,* 3 vols., New York, 1917; M. J. Brunowe, *The College of Mt. St. Vincent,* New York, 1917; M. B. Downing, *Chronicles of Loretto,* New York, 1897; A. C. Minogue, *Loretto: Annals of the Century,* New York, 1912; A. McGill, *Sisters of Charity of Nazareth, Kentucky,* Chicago, 1917; *In the Early Days* (Sisters of Charity of the Blessed Virgin Mary), St. Louis, 1912; H. C. Semple, *Ursulines in New Orleans,* Kenedy, New York, n. d.; *Fifty Years in Brown County Convent* (Ursulines), Cincinnati, 1895; *The Springfield Ursulines,* Springfield, Ill., 1909; M. E. Mannix, *Memoirs of Sister Louise, Superior of the Sisters of Notre Dame,* Boston, 1907; M. L. Savage, *The Congregation of St. Joseph of Carondelet,* St. Louis, 1927; *Mother M. Xavier Warde, Foundress of the Order of Mercy in the United States,* Boston, 1902; *Story of Fifty Years* (Sisters of Holy Cross), Notre Dame, Ind., 1905; J. E. Stuart, *Society of the Sacred Heart,* London, 1914; *Mother Theodore Guerin* (Sisters of Providence), New York, 1904; *History of the Sisters of Charity of Leavenworth, Kansas,* Kansas City, 1898; *Gleanings of Fifty Years* (Sisters of the Holy Name), Portland, Ore., 1909; J. M. Ory, *Origin of the Order of Our Lady of Charity,* Buffalo, 1918; *Our Community* (Sisters of 3d Order of St. Francis), La Crosse, Wis., 1920; *A Retrospect, Three Score Years and Ten* (Sisters Servants of the Immaculate Heart of Mary), New York,

General character of American schools. Despite the fact that each of the forty-eight States is quite independent of the others in its control of schools, and that there are a number of systems of schools outside the State-controlled systems, there is throughout the United States a fairly close uniformity in school organization and in the general character of schools. Some of that uniformity is due to pressure exerted upon schools by standardizing agencies,[1] some of it to the practice (roughly equivalent to the German 'leaving-examinations') of admitting pupils from one level of schools to another on certification of having complied with the requirements of the lower school, some of it to the curious mob-thinking about schools which prevails in the United States and is fostered by newspapers and periodicals. As a result of all these, it is possible, and may be instructive, to consider the common characteristics of American schools as a whole.

In Europe, from which Americans have drawn their basic ideas about schools, education was aristocratic in concept,

---

1916. *The Catholic Encyclopedia* has brief articles on most of the Sisterhoods. In 1930, there were in the United States 216 distinct congregations of religious women, with a total membership of approximately 122,500, of whom 67,715 were engaged in teaching. (*Directory of Catholic Colleges and Schools,* National Catholic Welfare Conference, Washington, 1933.) Their diversity has been compared with that of Protestant sects, which they slightly surpass in number of varieties in the United States. This diversity is a possible source of weakness, in overlapping of work, in multiplied overhead, above all in rivalries which stand in the way of unified action. There are, also engaged in parish schools, fifteen congregations of Lay Brothers. A characteristic sketch of their life and work may be found in J. J. Trahey, *The Brothers of Holy Cross,* Notre Dame, Ind., 1907.

[1] These are mostly volunteer associations, without official authority, but exercising great power through a kind of blackballing. To become a member of such an association, a school must carry out the association's detailed and often arbitrary requirements; not to be a member involves a sort of scholastic ostracism, a penalizing of the school through refusal of 'recognition.' These standardizing agencies are regional, specialized by subjects, often overlapping, but mutually supporting. For some summary data see *Encyclopedia Americana,* 1932, Vol. 9, pp. 696-99.

recognizing the hierarchy of talents and the limitations of individual possibilities of culture, until the spirit of the age which produced Pestalozzi, Girard, Owen, Froebel, and their followers, introduced the notion of democracy into education, and stressed the importance of wider schooling for the masses of the people.   Thereafter, schools in Europe developed on *parallel* lines, very clearly in Germany and in England, less clearly in France: of one system of schools meant to carry children to the age of 13 to 16 before they should leave school finally for their work in industries or commerce; and of another system of schools, pointing to the universities, the professions, the military and civil services.   The distinction in school opportunities was not founded solely upon the different capabilities of children, but largely upon class distinctions of wealth and social position; yet it did keep in mind the limitations of individual capacity.   It was not very hard for the leaders of educational thought in America to persuade Americans that any distinction in school opportunities was 'undemocratic,' and therefore hateful and to be rejected.   During the years, say, 1850 to 1880, in which the structure of American school systems was being solidified, the men who controlled schools labored to change the European scheme of *parallel* schools into a system of *cumulative* schools.

Elementary schools in America were planned for eight years; above them, the high schools of four years; and above the high schools, four years of college, leading to the bachelor's degree.   Then persistent and widespread efforts were made to raise the age limit of compulsory school attendance, and where compulsion failed, to use every inducement to secure a further continued attendance at school.[1]   By the year 1900 it took uniformly sixteen years

---

[1] The growth of school attendance above the age of 14 years has been remarkable.   *The Biennial Survey, 1926-1928,* United States Bureau of Education, shows that attendance of children 15 to 18

to attain a bachelor's degree, from two to four years longer than in European countries. To meet the condition of an inflated school attendance, the work in schools was diluted, spread out. With compulsory school laws driving in the children from below, administrators of schools had perforce to advance children from one grade to another, irrespective of their fitness, simply to keep the procession moving.[1]

Another characteristic of American schools has been the zeal displayed for experimentation in methods, curriculum, and administration. Every theory fathered in Europe found a home in America. Back of this readiness to experiment was the noble hope of finding the perfect method and curriculum: the ancient hope of Francis Bacon. It led to a wild multiplicity of subjects of study.[2] It embarrassed capable teachers by the vagaries of methods introduced. Its defense was sometimes the plea for 'enrichment' of the curriculum, sometimes the honest admission that the schools were trying to do something for the vast number of pupils who were uneducable by the ordinary procedure.

years of age in secondary schools has grown from about 11 per cent of the total children of that age in 1900 to about 55 per cent in 1928 (p. 433); and that the percentage of persons 19 to 22 years of age taking some form of college work has grown from 2.8 per cent in 1900 to 17.9 per cent in 1928 (p. 431). In other words, where in 1900 one boy or girl of each ten of high-school age attended high school, more than five of each ten attended in 1928; one person in each thirty-five of college age attended college in 1900, but one in each six in 1928.

[1] See "Forced Promotion" in *Elementary School Journal*, February, 1930, Vol. 30, p. 409. In a paper read at the annual meeting of the National Education Association, July, 1929, Fannie W. Dunn, Associate Professor of Education, Columbia University, could offer only this solution of the jumble of bright and dull children in a forced-motion system of schools: " . . . All the facts point to a necessity, for the average children of our schools, of a *longer period of elementary education* . . . Let us set up our curriculum at a slope such that the average child can go up it in high." (*Proceedings,* National Education Association, 1929, pp. 529-30.)

[2] It has been noted previously how the Latin American schools imitated this feature, under the belief that it was an educational improvement.

Observers are inclined to attribute to the forcing process of putting pupils indiscriminately through long years of schooling, and to the chaos of subjects studied, many of them at the pupil's own choice, a resultant superficiality in the product of American schools.[1]

Finally, owing to the distinctive organization and traditions of American politics, there has been much political jobbery in the American schools, and an occasional airing of scandals in the management of school funds.[2]

Elementary schools. The story of the American elementary school is really a sort of epitome of the spiritual history of the American nation: the story of a young, vigorous people, pretty well abandoning religion, and with very little of cultural traditions, setting forth on the high quest of a remedy for their social and spiritual ills. It cannot be told adequately here; one can only hint at its glory and its pathos. Andrew Jackson, the headstrong, romantic swash-

[1] Educated Europeans, as a rule, are shocked at the American schools. But a kindly Englishman, R. E. Hughes, in an article on "The Public School System" in 1905, offered this plea in extenuation: "It is true that the pupils from the high schools often have but a poor knowledge of the subjects of instruction; nevertheless, they have preserved the natural curiosity and acquisitiveness which children always take to school but rarely bring away with them, their physical stamina has not been lowered by excessive mental toil, the school games have developed their muscular powers and nourished their self resource, and they leave school, not indeed cultured citizens, but with a certain mental alertness. . . . " (*The Making of America*, 10 vols., edited by R. M. La Follette, Chicago, 1905, Vol. 1, p. 123.) There is no indication that this was written ironically.

[2] It is not without significance that while school attendance between 1900 and 1926 showed a growth of 59 per cent, and the number of teachers a growth of 90 per cent, the increase in salary expenditures was 700 per cent, of cost of buildings 1,050 per cent, and of other expenses 1,130 per cent. (Based on figures given in *Biennial Survey, 1926-28*, United States Bureau of Education.) The general cost of living in the United States increased 66.6 per cent between 1913 and June, 1930; in the same period the average cost per child in the public schools mounted from $38.35 a year to $108.90 a year, an increase of 284 per cent, or about fourfold the increase in cost of living. (*World Almanac*, 1933, pp. 247, 308.) In the year 1927-28, the total school enrollment was 29,276,068; and the total expenditure for schools was $3,033,706,590. (*Biennial Survey, 1926-28*, p. 425.)

buckler of the frontier, the self-sufficient, uncouth, but not irreverent man of the masses, symbolizes it better than the urbane Thomas Jefferson, the balanced intellectual aristocrat; but Jefferson also is in it, with his despairing hope that 'democracy' might be a way to the aristocracy of mind which he essentially cherished. The form of the American elementary school was given it by legalistic, Puritan Massachusetts; but its spirit came from the woods and plains of the West. It glorifies its origin, 'the little red schoolhouse,' the rural center of rudimentary beginnings in letters, self-limited to a thin but wide dispersion of knowledge, and committed to an enormous hope of great things to come from that little knowledge. No other school system has had a more continuous and earnest purpose in view: the conscious elevation of a whole people. No other school has had more devoted propagandists. No other school system glories in such popular pride. You may criticize the American government with impunity; but if you dare belittle the American public school, you rouse the anger of most Americans.

The first task in building the elementary school system was the task of legislators: to secure its basic organization, its schoolrooms and equipment, its financial support.[1] This was done in all the northern states within fifteen years after the close of the Civil War. The South had never taken to the project with as much enthusiasm as the North; and the effects of the Civil War delayed the legal establishment of schools in the South still more.[2] The next

[1] "Most school money comes from local taxation." (*Encyclopedia Americana,* 1932, Vol. 9, p. 685.) In all States, the financial provision for schools has constantly increased, not merely in total yearly amounts, but in per capita proportions. (United States Bureau of Education, *Biennial Survey, 1926-28,* pp. 452 sqq.)

[2] New York State passed the first compulsory school law in 1874; Mississippi, the last State to fall into line, enacted its school law in 1918. (*Encyclopedia Americana,* 1932, Vol. 9, p. 601.) School terms also are generally shorter in the South than in the North; the

step was provision for the training of teachers. This was begun by the first State normal school, set up in 1839, at Lexington, Massachusetts.[1] The training work was carried on with such zeal that by 1928 the increase in number of persons in training to be teachers exceeded the growth of teaching positions more than elevenfold.[2] In the earlier elementary schools, men teachers were more numerous; later, the number of women teachers increased so greatly that by 1928 the women teachers outnumbered the men more than eight to one.[3] The third step was the elaboration of schools, in organization, in enrichment of curriculum, in hygienic supervision, in vocational training, in such additional facilities as 'free' school lunches, textbooks, transportation to and from schools. 'Movements' flared up, and died down. For instance, the first kindergarten was opened in St. Louis, Missouri, in 1873; by 1898 there were 4,363 kindergartens, with 8,937 teachers, and 389,604 children enrolled. Thereafter, the enthusiasm waned. The Montessori method began to displace Froebel. The rapid growth of kindergartens stopped. In the next thirty years the number of children in kindergartens did not even keep pace with the increase of total numbers in schools.[4] The Pestalozzian enthusiasm deserves a separate study: there is no room for it here.[5] But some of the other 'movements,'

terms ranging in 1928 from as short as 138.9 days a year in Arkansas to as long as 188 days in New Jersey. (*Biennial Survey, 1926-28*, p. 461.) In many of the Northern cities, the term of school is 200 days.

[1] By the year 1930, there were 382 State-controlled normal schools, and 67 private normal schools. (*Encyclopedia Americana*, 1932, Vol. 9, p. 608.)

[2] *Biennial Survey, 1926-28*, p. 315.

[3] The increase of women teachers began notably in the 1880's. In 1890, there were 232,925 women teachers in elementary schools, and 121,877 men teachers; a ratio of nearly two to one. (*Biennial Survey, 1926-28*, p. 426.)

[4] *Encyclopedia Americana*, 1932, Vol. 9, p. 610.

[5] See W. S. Monroe, *The History of the Pestalozzian Movement in the United States*, Syracuse, N. Y., 1907.

especially those that involved wider expenditures of public moneys, have thriven steadily.[1]

Elementary schools in the United States, public and private, are most often coeducational;[2] although in the larger Catholic parish schools boys and girls have separate classrooms or even separate buildings. Within the past thirty years, all schools have been uniformly graded on an eight-year basis; but there is a vague opinion in the air that this grading needs revision. Some approach to the problem has been made in recent years by the organization of junior high schools, which include the two latter years of the elementary grades and the first year of the high school.[3]

The total enrollment in elementary schools for 1928 was 21,268,417 in the public schools, and 2,289,455 in private schools.[4] Of the latter number, 2,195,569, or about 96 per cent, were enrolled in 7,680 Catholic schools.[5] The United States Bureau of Census estimates that illiterates, ten years of age and over, have been reduced from 6 per cent of the total population in 1920 to 4.3 per cent in 1930.[6] That is an achievement of which the Americans are justly proud. How far it has set them on the road to the high purpose aimed

[1] The increased distribution of 'free' textbooks may be mentioned as one illustration. As another, Massachusetts, back in 1869, passed a law to consolidate small country schools into larger district schools, and to provide transportation for the school children because of the longer journeys involved in attending the consolidated schools. In 1890, the sum spent on transportation was less than $23,000; in 1915, it was more than $500,000. (*Encyclopedia Americana*, 1932, Vol. 9, p. 645.) For instances of recent developments, see *Biennial Survey, 1926-28*, pp. 412-13.

[2] "Today 96 per cent of the pupils of American elementary schools are in coeducational institutions." (*American Universities and Colleges*, New York, 1928, p. 10.)

[3] This experiment is taking place chiefly in larger cities. For a group of city school systems, the *Biennial Survey, 1926-28*, p. 501, estimates that the number of junior high school pupils increased 83.5 per cent from 1922 to 1924, 49.2 per cent from 1924 to 1926, and 29.4 per cent from 1926 to 1928.

[4] *Biennial Survey, 1926-28*, p. 425.

[5] *Directory of Catholic Colleges and Schools, 1932-33*, p. 194.

[6] Quoted in *World Almanac*, 1932, p. 252.

at in widespread school education is another question, the answer to which must be deferred for the moment.

Secondary schools. The early American secondary schools were simply transplanted English grammar schools, of the type that had persisted with relatively little change since the Renaissance.[1] They were, as a rule, organized with a view to preparing their students for college; they made no pretense to being articulated with the elementary schools. Only a few of the colonies and early States attempted to combine secondary schools into systems; for the most part, each school was an isolated unit.[2] The first great change in the character of secondary schools began with the founding of 'academies.' These borrowed their idea and their name from the Puritan secondary schools in England, of which about thirty were established between 1672 and 1775.[3] Benjamin Franklin's academy, opened in Philadelphia in 1751, seems to have been the first to use the name.[4] These academies boasted of being more 'practical' than the grammar schools. They still kept the study of Latin and Greek as the core of their curriculum, but gradually edged out to include a larger share of English, history, geography, mathematics, and the physical sciences. They multiplied in numbers rapidly. In Mas-

---

[1] One such school, the Boston Latin School, founded in 1635, has had a continuous existence. A study of its history would furnish a sort of microcosmic view of secondary education throughout the United States. See H. F. Jenks, *Catalogue (and History) of the Boston Public Latin School,* Boston, 1886.

[2] After the middle of the seventeenth century, Massachusetts, Connecticut, New Hampshire, and Maryland had something like systems of secondary schools. Instances of isolated colonial schools were William Penn Charter School, in Philadelphia, University Grammar School in Warren, Rhode Island, and the Free School, in New York.

[3] Referred to *supra,* p. 255, note 1. See also *Cambridge History of English Literature,* Vol. 9, chap. 14; Vol. 10, chap. 16; Vol. 14, chap. 14.

[4] It was chartered in 1753, and not long after became the University of Pennsylvania. See T. H. Montgomery, *History of the University of Pennsylvania from its Founding to 1770,* Philadelphia, 1900.

sachusetts alone, 150 academies were incorporated between 1778 and 1865. Dexter reckons that in 1850 there were in the United States 6,085 academies, with 12,260 teachers and 263,096 pupils.[1] The figures indicate that the academies were mostly small schools, since they had on an average only about two teachers and forty-four pupils each. The two Phillips Academies, that set up at Andover, Massachusetts, in 1778, and that at Exeter, New Hampshire, in 1781, seem to have been the most important models for the later academies in the West.[2] All the early academies had some religious affiliation; but most of the Protestant academies soon abandoned any distinctive religious character.[3] The Catholic academies grew slowly in numbers, compared with the growth of other schools; yet oddly enough, the Catholic girls' academies outnumbered those for boys. The latter were generally connected with a college, and formed a continuous lower division of the college.[4]

The American high school. The American high school

[1] E. G. Dexter, *History of Education in the United States,* New York, 1919, p. 96.

[2] The founders of these academies, John Phillips and Samuel Phillips, were uncle and nephew. See J. L. Taylor, *A Memoir of His Honor Samuel Phillips, LL. D.,* Boston, 1856; C. H. Bell, *Phillips Academy, Exeter,* Exeter, 1883; H. Adams, *Some Famous American Schools,* 1903.

[3] *Encyclopedia Americana,* 1932, Vol. 9, p. 648.

[4] In 1835, when there were eleven Catholic dioceses and 341 priests in the United States (*Catholic Almanac,* Baltimore, 1835, pp. 65-70), there were nine Catholic colleges for boys, with academies attached, and twenty-eight 'female academies.' Although no data are given for numbers of students, most of those academies seem to have been small. In one congregation, the Sisters of Charity, the number of nuns assigned to each academy ranged from three to seven (*Ibid.,* pp. 140-41), which would indicate small schools. But 'St. Joseph's Academy for Young Ladies,' Emmitsburg, Maryland, announced that it had recently added another building, "calculated to accommodate 200 boarders." (*Ibid.,* p. 107.) By 1850, when the number of dioceses had increased to 34, and the number of priests to 1,303, there were thirty-six 'literary institutions for young men,' and eighty-seven 'female academies'; a creditable showing for a Catholic population of 1,334,500, most of whom were quite poor. (*Catholic Almanac,* 1850, p. 224.) Yet the Catholic academies, if Dexter's reckoning is correct,

was a development from the academies. In 1821 there was founded in Boston the English Classical School, apparently modeled on the high school of Edinburgh, Scotland, with a three-year course covering English, mathematics, navigation and surveying, geography, natural philosophy and astronomy, history, logic, moral and political philosophy. It definitely did not aim at preparing its students for college. But that fact was found to be a handicap to the school; hence, after a few years, the school added Latin, Greek, and modern languages to the course, which became thereafter of four years instead of three.[1] This school marked a beginning. In 1838, Philadelphia organized its Central High School, by a special act of the legislature. High schools in Providence, Rhode Island, and in Hartford, Connecticut, were opened in 1843 and 1847, respectively. On the eve of the Civil War, in 1860, there were high schools of the new type in 69 cities.[2] The distinctive marks of the new high school were two: it was linked with the elementary school below more closely than with the college above; and it considered the immediate utility of its subjects of instruction more than their general cultural value.

were in 1850 only about one-fiftieth of the total number of academies, although the Catholics numbered one-seventeenth of the total population of 23,191,876.

[1] See A. J. Inglis, *The Rise of the High School in Massachusetts,* New York, 1911.

[2] E. T. Cubberley, *History of Education,* Boston, 1920, p. 701; based on statistics given in *Report* of United States Commissioner of Education, 1904, Vol. 2, pp. 1782-1989. Of the 321 public high schools in the United States in 1860, more than one-half were in three States, Massachusetts (78 high schools), Ohio (48), and New York (41); and nearly nine-tenths were in northern States. Although the United States Bureau of Education was established in 1866, with the eminent Henry Barnard as first Commissioner (1867-70), statistics for secondary schools are rather jumbled until 1890. But the figures since then are quite significant. The 2,526 public high schools of 1890 nearly doubled their number in five years (4,712 in 1895); by 1910 were 10,213, and by 1924 were 22,500. In those thirty-four years, 1890 to 1924, private high schools increased in number only from 1,632 to 2,500. (*Encyclopedia Americana,* 1932, Vol. 9, p. 650.)

It was, in effect, an extension of the public elementary school system. It was indiscriminate in its inclusion of pupils: which is what is most often meant by calling any type of school 'democratic.' It thus lent itself more readily to the campaign for enlarging the scope and length of compulsory schooling, with the result that by 1928 the American public high schools had enrolled 4,217,313 pupils, or more than 50 per cent of the population between 14 and 18 years of age.[1]

The courses of study in the high schools have steadily increased in multiplicity.[2] The 'elective system' permits pupils a wide range of choice in subjects of instruction. Yet, even with these developments, the larger cities at first, then the smaller, have thought it necessary to establish special high schools: such as 'manual training high schools,'[3] 'commercial high schools,'[4] 'agricultural high

[1] These figures include the last year students in junior high schools. (*Biennial Survey, 1926-28,* p. 960.) Some of the public high schools are very large; the Carl Schurz High School in Chicago had 9,897 pupils in March, 1933. Coeducation is general in the public high schools, but is exceptional in the private high schools. Of the private high schools, the Catholic schools number more than five-sixths. In 1928, there were 2,129 Catholic secondary schools, with 13,489 teachers (belonging to 139 religious orders of men and women, and including 1,943 lay teachers), and 225,845 students. (*Directory of Catholic Colleges and Schools, 1932-33,* pp. 109 sqq.) The Council of Church Boards of Education, in its *Handbook* for 1928, reports a total of 227 Protestant secondary schools, with 2,863 teachers, and 36,629 pupils (pp. 593 sqq.). By far the greater part of these Protestant schools are in the South and East.

[2] The United States Bureau of Education in 1928 reported enrollments of high-school students in *250 different subjects.* (*Biennial Survey, 1926-28,* p. 963.) For the incapacity of teachers to instruct in this appalling range of subjects, see E. A. Fitzpatrick and P. W. Hutson, *The Scholarship of Teachers in Secondary Schools,* New York, 1927.

[3] The first of these was begun in 1880, at St. Louis, Missouri, in connection with Washington University. By 1890 there were such special schools in thirty-eight cities, and by 1905 in sixty-three cities. (*Encyclopedia Americana,* 1932, Vol. 9, p. 653.)

[4] Pittsburgh opened the first commercial high school, in 1872. The United States Bureau of Education in 1914 reported 2,914 such schools, with 178,707 pupils.

schools.'[1] and recently 'technical high schools' giving a rudimentary engineering course.[2]

Control of secondary schools. The direct control of public high schools is generally by a local board of education. But there is a tendency to assert and increase a more remote and centralized control by the State, through certification of teachers and inspection of schools and methods, in return for an offer of financial aids from the State taxes. Indirect control is largely exercised by the various 'standardizing agencies' through the machinery of 'accrediting': which results in admitting pupils of one school into another without examination. The 'accrediting' is variously done: by the State university, or by the State department of education, within each State; and by the powerful private 'associations' within a region. Some of these associations are: the New England Association of Colleges and Preparatory Schools,[3] founded at Boston in 1885; the North Central Association of Colleges and Secondary Schools, founded at Evanston, Illinois, in 1895; and the Association of Colleges and Preparatory Schools of the Southern States, founded at Atlanta, Georgia, also in 1895. The requirements of these 'standardizing agencies' vary somewhat; but, in the name of efficiency, they all tend toward greater complexity in school organization and greater expenditures of money upon schools. They control private schools even more effectively than public schools.

[1] This movement began in Alabama about 1910, in Wisconsin about 1915. In 1928, 4,750 public high schools had courses in agriculture. (*Biennial Survey, 1926-28*, p. 967.) But the enthusiasm for the subject seems to be dying out.

[2] Technical high schools are still rather scarce. The first seems to have been Lane Technical High School in Chicago, and the Technical High School in Cleveland; both opened in 1908. (*Encyclopedia Americana*, 1932, Vol. 9, p. 653.)

[3] Out of this Association in 1902, there grew the establishment of the New England College Entrance Certificate Board, which now has more than 400 schools 'accredited.' (*Encyclopedia Americana, ibid.*, p. 651.)

Higher schools. There had been twelve colleges founded in the American colonies, of which nine survived. Seventeen more were added to these between 1776 and 1800; so that a population of 5,308,483 in 1800 had twenty-six institutions of higher instruction. Practically all of these higher schools had some religious affiliation. They were all rather poor in wealth of buildings, libraries, and endowments.[1] Most of them had begun to function with an eye to providing ministers of religion.[2] They inspired no enthusiasm in the country at large; many of the more ambitious students went abroad for university education. Criticism of the schools began to be voiced, and early plans were afoot for their improvement and development. Washington wanted a 'National University'; but nothing came of his plans. Jefferson's scheme of keeping all schools within the jurisdiction of the separate States was more consonant with the American political temper. The plan of Jefferson for his own State, Virginia, envisaged one university, to be fed by a rigorous selection of excellent students from the lower schools.[3] A distrust of private schools

[1] The total value of the twenty-six colleges was about $1,000,000, or an average of about $40,000 each. (*Encyclopedia Americana*, 1932, Vol. 9, p. 619.) Their total libraries amounted to approximately 30,000 volumes; and of those one-third were at Harvard alone. (*Public Libraries in the United States*, Bureau of Education, 1876, pp. 775-77.) As a contrast, the total property value of American colleges and universities in 1928 was the huge sum of $2,413,748,981; and their libraries counted 40,498,291 volumes. (*Biennial Survey, 1926-28*, p. 697.)

[2] See, for instance, the much-quoted *New England's First Fruits*, a tract printed in 1643, in which are given the reasons for founding Harvard College; it is reprinted in *Massachusetts Historical Collection*, Vol. 1. See also A. F. West, *Princeton University*, Princeton, 1893; R. H. Guild, *Brown University*, Providence, 1867; F. B. Dexter, *Documentary History of Yale University*, Yale University Press, 1916. The Universities of Pennsylvania and Virginia seem to be exceptions amongst the early higher schools.

[3] In American history, Jefferson is almost a symbol of 'democracy.' Yet his plan of a school system is aristocratic. He wished that there should be elementary schools for all the people; but under local control, even to the extent that should the local company of voters "de-

grew up. The State was urged to take over higher schools. In the older States, this tendency was resisted.[1] But in the new States carved out of the West, the idea of State universities was dominant from the beginning. The Federal government encouraged the States by repeated grants of land and of annual subsidies.[2] Thus there grew up a State system of higher schools alongside the older and strongly entrenched private colleges and universities. By 1928, there were 1,076 schools above secondary level, of which 226 were controlled by State or city, and 850 were private. Of the 919,381 students enrolled in all these schools, about 40 per cent were in State schools and 60 per cent in private schools.[3]

cide that it would have no school, let them remain without one." (*Complete Works,* edited by H. A. Washington, 9 vols., New York, 1853; February 2, 1816, letter to Joseph C. Cabell, Vol. 6, p. 542). There were to be secondary schools for those "in easy circumstances" (*ibid.,* Autobiography, Vol. 1, p. 48) and for *one* clever boy from each elementary school. Of these clever boys, at the end of the first year of secondary schooling, twenty were to be chosen for a six-year course, at the close of which half of the twenty were to be sent out as teachers, and the other half to be sent on to William and Mary College for three years' study of "such sciences as they shall choose." (*Ibid.,* "Notes on Virginia," in Vol. 8, pp. 386-91.) The plan was embodied in a bill for the Virginia legislature, which was passed in part.

[1] The famous 'Dartmouth College Case' sprang from an attempt by the legislature of New Hampshire in 1816 to take over the College as a State school. The trustees of the College brought suit, but lost in all the State courts; took the case to the United States Supreme Court in 1819, were defended by Daniel Webster, and won a favorable decision. But the decision suggested that States might in future reserve power to break the contract implied in a school charter. See W. S. Shirley, *The Dartmouth College Causes and the Supreme Court,* St. Louis, 1879.

[2] Federal land grants for schools began in 1787; but the most important grants for higher schools were conceded by the Morrill Act of 1862, which allotted school lands in the measure of 30,000 acres for every representative in Congress. By acts of 1890 and 1907, the Federal Congress gave $50,000 annually to each State for agricultural and engineering schools; and in 1887 and 1906, gave $30,000 annually for agricultural experiment stations. See *Survey of Land-Grant Colleges and Universities,* 2 vols., United States Office of Education, 1930, Bulletin No. 9, especially Vol. 1, pp. 1-33.

[3] *Biennial Survey, 1926-28,* pp. 691 sqq.

Following German models. The early American colleges followed the methods of instruction used in the English universities, in which were combined elements of the old scholastic practice, such as disputations, with methods developed in the Renaissance.[1]   But by the second quarter of the nineteenth century the increasing number of American students who flocked to the new type of university at Göttingen, Berlin, and Leipzig, imported an enthusiasm for the German lecture system.   This method of instruction has prevailed for the past seventy or eighty years in most of the American higher schools.   The essential aim of the German university was the pursuit of absolute knowledge, *Wissenschaft*.   The crown of its work was 'research,' the cold, accurate, often pedantic, and generally inhuman, labor of dissociated erudition.   This aim and character of the German university was first taken over with thoroughness by Johns Hopkins University, founded in 1876 at Baltimore; and was caught in varying degrees by other American universities.   Yale University, it is true, had had a graduate school since 1847; but the true growth of 'research' began with Johns Hopkins and with the graduate school at Harvard in 1877.[2]   There has been some excellent work done in American universities.   But gradually, because of the mechanical inclusion in those universities of an ill-assorted student body, the work tended to become narrow and superficial, and in the end both the process and

[1] For some interesting details of teaching procedure in England, see J. Timbs, *School-Days of Eminent Men,* London, 1858.   For the early course of studies and some hints of method, at Harvard, see *New England's First Fruits,* in *Massachusetts Historical Collections,* Vol. 1, pp. 242-46.   One of the earliest of the western State universities, Michigan, was chartered in 1837, opened in 1841.   Two years later, when it had 53 students under three professors and one tutor, its course of studies and its methods were still those of the colonial colleges.   (See *Joint Documents of the Legislature of Michigan,* 1852, p. 388.)   In 1852, the German influence reached Michigan.

[2] S. E. Morison, *The Development of Harvard University,* Harvard University Press, 1930, pp. 454 sqq.

the results of American 'research' all too often have been ridiculous.[1] Of late years, the value of current university methods has been questioned even by American educators, and there are hopeful signs of a return to the serious and scholarly point of view which should mark university education.[2] The great and insuperable difficulty in the way of such a return is the concept of 'democracy' prevalent in America, which makes it almost impossible to exclude from higher schools the incompetent and the trifling student.

The supremacy of the German influence was one of the causes of the remarkable development of American school

[1] For some of the absurd recent developments in 'research' see the devastating instances given in A. Flexner, *Universities, American, English, German,* New York, 1930, pp. 102 sqq. The Ph. D. degree was first conferred in the United States in 1861. (*Cyclopedia of Education,* Vol. 2, p. 286.) By 1908, American colleges and universities were conferring 47 différent degrees. (*Report,* United States Commissioner of Education, 1908, p. 615.) In 1928, the 1,076 colleges and universities conferred, besides the 83,065 bachelor's degrees, 13,834 graduate degrees, of which 1,447 were the Ph. D. degree. (*Biennial Survey, 1928-30,* p. 462.) For 1931, the United States Bureau of Education estimates the total number of bachelor's degrees granted as 123,853: men, 75,353; women, 48,500; and the total of higher degrees as 17,000: men, 10,812; women, 6,188. (*World Almanac,* 1932, p. 260.)

[2] Some of the larger eastern universities are introducing parts of the English tutorial system, looking toward a closer relation of teacher and student. Some are getting away from the 'cafeteria' method of extreme electivism in studies, through a comprehensive examination at the close of school periods. For a summary of some recent tendencies, see *Biennial Survey, 1926-28,* pp. 26-32, and *1928-30,* pp. 481 sqq. The summarizer admits that "the further evolution of our higher educational system is not entirely clear." (*1928-30,* p. 499.) One development that may have important implications for the future is the growth of 'junior colleges,' which are schools offering the first two years' work of the standard four-year course leading to a bachelor's degree. They do not purposely link with major colleges; but are in reality a further extension of secondary schools. They aim either at being the final stage in the pupil's schooling or at preparing the pupil to take up study for one of the professions. In 1922, there were 207 junior colleges, enrolling somewhat over 16,000 pupils. In 1931 the number of junior colleges had grown to 436, and the number of pupils enrolled to nearly 75,000: of whom 45,021 were in 178 public schools, and about 30,000 were in 258 private schools. (*Biennial Survey of Education, 1928-30,* Vol. 1, p. 128.)

libraries. Both the lecture method of instruction and the growth of 'research,' which most often has meant only laborious compilation, have driven the students to rely more upon books than upon teachers.[1]

Control and maintenance of higher schools. Slightly more than one-fifth of the higher schools, 21 per cent, are directly controlled by State or city;[2] but that 21 per cent of the schools in 1928 received more than 41 per cent of the operating income of all higher schools, and had 35 per cent of the school property, exclusive of productive endowments. There was justification for that situation in the fact that the public higher schools in the same year enrolled 38.5 per cent of the total number of students in higher schools. The actual number of students enrolled in public colleges and universities was 335,009;[3] and the total income was $205,-

[1] A history of the place of the library in American higher schools would illustrate interesting changes in methods of instruction, especially during the crucial years, 1850 to 1890. But after 1876, when the library movement developed a momentum and a character of its own, the growth of libraries is not so intimately related to classroom methods as to the important social phenomenon that reading was becoming a recreational necessity. That fact must be considered later. For the earlier development, there is the detailed study issued by the Bureau of Education in 1876, *Public Libraries in the United States;* and E. Edwards, *Free Town Libraries,* London, 1869 (of which Bk. III, pp. 269-344, is taken up with non-school libraries in the United States). For the recent period, see *Statistics of Public, Society, and School Libraries, 1929,* United States Office of Education, Bulletin No. 37, 1930; and "Library Service" in *Biennial Survey, 1928-30,* pp. 643-94.

[2] Seven cities conduct complete higher schools, in addition to the junior colleges. All these schools are maintained in whole or in part by taxation: e. g., in New York, wholly by taxes; in Detroit, half by taxes, half by student fees; in Cincinnati, about one-third by student fees. (See *American Universities and Colleges,* issued by the American Council on Education, New York, 1928.)

[3] Some of the State and municipal universities have huge enrollments of students. Of the State 'land-grant' universities, California in 1931 had 19,235 students, Illinois had 14,896. The University of Michigan had 12,531 students. The Municipal College of the City of New York had 18,300 students. (*World Almanac,* New York, 1932, pp. 264-67; based on statistics of United States Bureau of Education.)

753,979, or about $612 for each student.   Most of the money was derived from taxes; but the public higher schools in 1928 had productive endowments totalling $110,505,241.[1]

The private higher schools are generally under direct control of a private corporation, and indirectly are subject only to the same sort of control by 'standardizing agencies' as has been noted in the case of secondary schools.   Some of the private schools are so strong in wealth of property, in prestige, and in number of students, that they are quite free even of that indirect control, and may and do carry out such experiments in higher education as they choose.[2] Most of the private schools have some productive endowment funds;[3] some of them have very large endowments; the total of all in 1928 was $1,039,607,010, which was an increase of 67 per cent since 1922.[4] This is unequally distributed; ranging from the large endowments, such as Harvard's $86,702,843, Columbia's $63,597,416, Yale's $58,- 024,459, and Chicago's $43,408,468, down to the microscopic $1,960 of Wingate College.[5] Practically all exact student fees.   The total operating income of the 850 private higher schools for the year 1928 was $290,775,330.   This sum, against 533,784 students, means an average income of $545 for each student.[6]

---

[1] *Biennial Survey of Education, 1928-30,* Vol. 1, pp. 460-63.

[2] But it should be noted that professional schools, private as well as public, have been closely controlled in recent years.   The most rigorous control has been over medical schools, of which more than one-half have been forced to close since 1900.   Yet the growth in numbers of students for the professions has mounted until it reached over 350,000 in 1928.   For detailed statistics, see *Biennial Survey, 1928-30,* pp. 461 sqq.   The increase in those preparing for teaching (274,348 in 1928, more than double the number in 1920) has created a problem of over-supply. (*Ibid.,* pp. 501 sqq.)

[3] This does not hold for the Catholic schools, very few of which have any endowment of money.   What they most often have is an 'endowment of service' in the fact that religious teachers get no salary, but only a meager sustenance.

[4] *Biennial Survey of Education, 1928-30,* Vol. 1, p. 463.

[5] *Ibid., 1926-28,* pp. 837 sqq.

[6] *Ibid., 1928-30,* Vol. 1, pp. 460-62.

Social life in higher schools. American colleges and universities, like all others, have always had their own social atmosphere. Fashions in dress, in carriage and manner, in smoking and drinking, in *clichés* of slang, in mental attitudes, spread like measles from campus to campus, until the whole collegiate world became one uniform rash. But the two institutions which have chiefly given a distinctive character to social life in American higher schools are Greek-letter societies and coeducation.

Greek-letter societies, or 'fraternities' and 'sororities,' are for the most part student social organizations in which the members are pledged to secrecy.[1] The oldest, Phi Beta Kappa, was founded in 1776, and has made high academic standing one of its requisites for membership. It was the only society of its kind until 1825. The huge growth of college fraternities came in the Middle West after 1839, when Beta Theta Pi was founded at Miami University in Ohio.[2] Each society is national, with one branch, called a chapter, permitted to each school in which it is organized. In 1928, there were 3,429 such chapters in nearly 700 schools.[3] In 1930, the 275 societies had a total membership of 1,040,003,[4] and owned 3,125 fraternity houses valued at $90,678,434. Princeton University and some others prohibit fraternities. Most fraternity houses are residence clubs, en-

[1] The secrecy is generally of a trifling character. Delta Upsilon, founded at Williams College in 1834, and having 54 chapters and 21,253 members in 1930, is not a secret society.

[2] The largest in membership, Phi Delta Theta, was also founded at Miami University, in 1848. In 1930 it had 97 chapters and 36,876 members. The 'sororities' are of later date, the first having been established in 1872. The largest is Pi Beta Phi, founded in 1888, which in 1930 had 20,100 members. (*Encyclopedia Americana*, 1932, Vol. 13, p. 402.) Most of the private colleges for women do not permit the organization of Greek-letter societies.

[3] *Biennial Survey, 1926-28,* p. 25.

[4] This number includes many alumni. Indeed the alumni are generally important both for the financial help they give the fraternities and for their power, political and financial, to maintain the existence of the societies in schools which might wish to abolish them.

tirely under the control of their members; except for the matter of discipline, they are not altogether unlike the 'colleges' at mediaeval universities.[1] Their rivalry over recruits, and their other activities, often lend color, and sometimes rowdiness, to the social life of American higher schools.[2]

The first college to introduce coeducation was Oberlin, in Ohio, when it was founded in 1833. Now, although there are still a large number of separate higher schools for men and for women,[3] the majority of colleges and universities are coeducational. The State universities, beginning with Michigan, Illinois, Missouri, and California, in 1870, have all become coeducational, but with some restrictions upon the enrollment of women in the southern States. In 1928, of the total enrollment of 919,381 in all higher schools, 356,137, or nearly 39 per cent, were women;[4] and of these more than three-fourths were in coeducational schools.[5] One result of this extensive mixing of young men and women in colleges has naturally been philandering and distraction in work; another has been the curious feminizing of the higher schools, due to the social leadership of women students.[6]

[1] "Almost one-tenth of the entire college student body of the country is housed and fed in fraternity houses." (*Biennial Survey, 1926-28*, p. 25.)

[2] For the whole subject, see W. R. Baird, *Manual of College Fraternities*, edited by F. W. Shepardson, 12th ed., Menasha, Wis., 1930.

[3] The separate colleges for women are mostly in the East. Some few of them (for instance, Radcliffe at Harvard, Barnard at Columbia) are associated with men's colleges, somewhat as at Oxford and Cambridge, and share to some extent the staff and facilities of the men's colleges, especially the libraries. Students in women's colleges, after sophomore year, flit in considerable numbers to coeducational colleges. (*Biennial Survey, 1926-28*, p. 13.)

[4] *Biennial Survey, 1926-28*, p. 692.

[5] Catholic secondary schools are scarcely ever coeducational. But in 1930, out of a total enrollment of 105,926 students in Catholic colleges and universities, 50,898, or a little over 48 per cent, were women; and of that number, 25,960, or more than half, were in coeducational colleges. (*Directory of Catholic Colleges and Schools, 1932-33*, p. 29.)

[6] See J. A. Hawes, *Twenty Years amongst the Twenty Year Olds*,

Religious influences in higher schools. Almost every American college and university has a chapel, in which are conducted, with greater or less regularity, chapel services. In the earlier years, attendance at chapel was generally compulsory, often with the not unnatural result of arousing repugnance and hostility. In the past thirty years, not merely have chapel services become increasingly optional, but they have quite lost definite religious character in all public higher schools; and in most private higher schools, outside the Catholic group and a few of the smaller Protestant colleges, they have become little more than occasions for vague moral exhortations without any implications of religious belief or sanctions.[1] The Catholic group of higher schools has steadily grown, from the foundation of Georgetown College in 1789, to 162 colleges and universities,[2] with 7,768 teachers (of whom 3,114 were members of religious orders), and 105,926 students.[3] Yet, in spite of the fact

New York, 1929, p. 244; see also *ibid.*, pp. 94, 101 sqq., 243 sqq.; and C. F. Gauss, *Life in College*, New York, 1930.

[1] "In State universities required chapel is usually an assembly of all students. The program consists of administrative announcements and an address of general inspiration to good citizenship." (*American Universities and Colleges*, New York, 1928, p. 41.) For a brief account of the gradual decay of religious influences in American higher schools up to about 1875, see C. F. Thwing, *American Colleges, Their Students and Work*, New York, 1878, pp. 55-68. There have been all along, it is true, professional theological schools. But their history too reflects the waning interest in religion. For instance, 165 theological schools in 1898 conferred 1,693 degrees; there were exactly the same number of schools in 1924 (although 38 had been closed and others had taken their places), and those graduated only 1,319 persons. Catholic theological seminaries alone seem to have shown a steady increase in numbers both of schools and of students. In 1930, there were 99 Catholic seminaries of collegiate rank, with 886 teachers, and 7,632 students. (*Directory of Catholic Colleges and Schools, 1932-33*, p. 13.) Of the non-Catholic theological schools, in 1926, somewhat less than a hundred schools represented twenty-six denominations; seven were 'non-sectarian,' four interdenominational, three had no denominational name, forty-one admitted women students. (*Encyclopedia Americana*, 1932, Vol. 9, p. 665.)

[2] The 99 major seminaries and 88 minor seminaries are not included in this total.

[3] *Directory of Catholic Colleges and Schools, 1932-33*, p. 29.

that the student body in Catholic higher schools had grown more than threefold in numbers between 1920 and 1930, it is estimated that in the latter year there were still twice as many Catholic students in non-Catholic higher schools as in Catholic schools. In 1926-27 there were 349 universities and colleges, having 14,464 teachers and 229,533 students, listed as affiliated with Protestant churches.[1] It must also be noted that, since the attitude toward religion in the schools can scarcely ever maintain itself as merely neutral, there is found, outside the explicitly religious schools, a positive tendency in much of the teaching in American higher schools to undermine religious belief and practice.[2]

Summary and conclusion. In school education, as in geographical position, the United States is above Latin America, but below Canada. The glory and the boast of the United States is that from a standing start its people have outdistanced others in material completeness of school systems and in lavish wealth of school opportunities for every youngster in the land. Yet, in spite of their many excellences, one cannot help thinking that a single word describes American schools: they sprawl. They have been based upon a sentimental hope rather than upon a realistic philosophy: the hope that schools, dissociated from re-

[1] Council of Church Boards of Education, *Handbook for 1928,* pp. 566 sqq. It should be noted, however, that sixty-two of these schools are junior colleges; and that many of the larger schools, especially sixteen universities with an enrollment of 84,418 students, are to all intents and effects, outside of their theological departments, secular schools of the same character as the State universities. The influence of the various Protestant religions on higher schools is felt chiefly in the smaller Protestant schools.

[2] Particularly since the World War, there has been a good deal of discussion in periodicals about the religious influences in American higher schools. As random samples of such discussion, these may serve: "Agnosticism in the Colleges," *Literary Digest,* July 7, 1928, p. 30; "Why Doubt Thrives on the Campus," *ibid.,* June 29,1929, pp. 25-26; "The Religion of College Men," *Outlook,* March 21, 1928, p. 455.

ligious teachings and sanctions, may accomplish adequately all that former schools, even with the aid of religion, were able to accomplish only very inadequately. It is that hope, at once alluring and distracting, which has maintained enthusiasm for every sort of experiment in schools, whilst it has blurred the aim of schools. Because of the weakness and insecurity of philosophic principles back of the school procedure, American schools, for all the generous support given them, have failed to equip their pupils in sufficient measure with that discipline of mind and character which gives direction to thought and life.

TOPICS FOR DISCUSSION

1. Humanistic education in Latin American higher schools.
2. The effects of anti-Catholicism in Latin American State schools.
3. The influx of communistic principles into Latin American schools.
4. Comparison between courses of study of elementary and secondary schools in Canada and in the United States.
5. Points of resemblance between the early college in the United States and the modern classical colleges of Canada.
6. The growth of secularism in schools of the United States.
7. The history of coeducation in schools of the United States.
8. The education of negroes in the United States and in British America.
9. Points of contrast between higher schools in the East and in the West of the United States.
10. The development of teachers' colleges in the United States.
11. How the land-grant colleges became universities.

BIBLIOGRAPHIC NOTE

The native American civilizations are significant in this history of education only as background for some of the influences which continued to affect large sections of the people. Some of the sources may be found in Lord Kingsborough's huge collection of inscriptions, monuments, texts, etc. (pseudonym, Augustine Aglio), *Antiquities of Mexico*, 9 vols., London, 1830-48; and in C. E. Brasseur de Bourbourg, *Histoire des Nations Civilisées du Méxique et de l'Amérique Centrale durant les Siècles Anterieurs à Colomb*, 4 vols., Paris, 1857-59. C. R. Markham has translated Garcilaso de la Vega, London, 1869, and Cristobal de Molina's *Rites and Laws of the Incas*, London, 1872. Of modern discussions of the subject, these may be recommended: H. J. Spinden, *Ancient Civilizations of Mexico and Central America*, 3d ed., New York, 1928; and T. A. Joyce, *South American Archaeology*, New York, 1912.

The most important single work on education in Latin America during colonial times is V. G. Quesada, *La Vida Intellectual en la América Española durante los Siglos XVI, XVII, y XVIII*, Buenos Aires, 1917. For the beginnings of education in Mexico, there is a translation of J. Garcia Icazbalceta's little book, "Education in the City of Mexico during the Sixteenth Century," in *Historical Records and Studies*, United States Catholic Historical Society, Vol. 20, New York, 1931. Icazbalceta's larger works are scholarly, extremely valuable. An honest and well-informed little book, useful as background study, is E. Ryan, *The Church in the South American Republics*, Milwaukee, 1932. Most studies in educational history of Latin America are detailed, and concern particular institutions. But M. de Oliveira Lima, *Aspectos de Literatura Colonial Brasileira*, Leipzig, 1896, and M. Menendez y Pelayo, *Historia de la Poesia Hispaño-Americana*, 2 vols., Madrid, 1911, give a broad view of colonial education and its results. There are good chapters on education in these: E. G. Bourne, *Spain in America, 1450-1580*, New York, 1904 (Vol. 3 of the American Nation Series); M. W. Williams, *The People and the Politics of Latin America*, Boston, 1930; H. G. James and P. A. Martin, *The Republics of Latin America*, New York, 1923; and W. R. Shepherd, *Latin America*, New York, 1914. The literary histories of A. L. Coester, New York, 1916, and B. Moses, London, 1922, are also of value for broad surveys of education in colonial times. For recent statistics, see references in text. Brandon's work is highly intelligent; Luckey's is useful for its statistics, but is otherwise rather stupid.

For a brief general introduction to education in British America, there are good chapters in W. H. Woodward, *Short History of the Expansion of the British Empire*, 2d ed., Cambridge, 1902. Sir Charles Bruce, *The Broad Stone of Empire*, 2 vols., London, 1910, is fairly thorough in outlining school systems for the crown colonies in America. The administrative side of education is well handled in H. Wrong, *Government of the West Indies*, Oxford, 1923; and the book also covers British Honduras and British Guiana, and contains a bibliography. A. P. Newton, *Universities and Educational Systems* (Vol. 10 of *The British Empire, a Survey*, edited by H. Gunn in 12 vols., London, 1924), gives an excellent comprehensive view.

There is great abundance of material on education in Canada. Some of the earlier works are unscientific, and are spoiled by partisanship. Thus, for instance, J. G. Hodgins, *History and System of Popular Education in Upper Canada*, Boston, 1855, is unfair to Catholics; H. R. Casgrain, *Oeuvres Complètes*, Montreal, 1885, is unfair to Protestants. (It is only just to add that the latter work, a one-volume collection of sketches which was reprinted in 1897 as *Biographies Canadiennes,* is not characteristic of the mature, scholarly writings afterward published by the Abbé Casgrain.) More recent works are generally written with improved accuracy and impartiality. Thus Vols. 11 and 12 of *Canada and its Provinces, a History of the Canadian People and their Institutions,* by One Hundred Associates, edited by A. Shortt and A. G. Doughty, deals with education quite satisfactorily. For education in Lower Canada, there are two admirable works: Amedie Gosselin, *L'Instruction au Canada sous le Régime Français,* Quebec, 1911 (published also in condensed form as Vol. 16 of *Canada and its Provinces*); and G. W. Parmelee, *Education in the Province of Quebec,* Quebec, 1914. Education in Ontario is surveyed competently and impartially in W. H. Moore, *The Clash, a Study in Nationalities,* Toronto, 1918. For detailed studies of the school systems, the periodical *L'Enseignement Primaire,* published in Quebec since 1879, is a rich source. The Canadian government has also been publishing a bilingual *Statistical Report on Education in Canada,* the first of the present series being for the year 1921. The compact articles on education in the *Encyclopedia Americana,* 1932, are by men who know their subjects and deal with them intelligently.

An obvious source of information on schools in the United States is the long series of *Reports, Surveys, Bulletins,* and *Circulars of Information* issued by the United States Bureau of Education. Another is Henry Barnard's *American Journal of Education,* 32 vols., 1855-82. For general background, an excellent, compact work is S. K. Wilson, *American History,* Chicago, 1929; unusually rich and clear in its cultural details. Besides the various books mentioned in the text, W. H. Small, *Early New England Schools,* Boston, 1914, and E. W. C. Parsons, *Educational Legislation and Administration of the Colonial Governments,* New York, 1899, are recommended for contemporary accounts and records. An interesting book is R. B. Culver, *Horace Mann and Religion in the Massachusetts Public Schools,* Yale University Press, 1924. B. Confrey, *Secularism in American Education,* Washington, 1931, gives a summary history and view of State laws affecting religion in the schools. A more comprehensive view is had in S. W. Brown, *The Secularization of American Education,* Columbia University Press, 1912. The twenty monographs on *Education in the United States,* edited by N. M. Butler, New York, 1900, cover the entire field up to that date. C. H. Brewer, *A History of Religious Education in the Episcopal Church to 1835,* Yale University Press, 1924, stops at about the period when religious influence began to disappear from the common schools. For the early Catholic schools, see J. A. Burns, *Catholic School System in the United States,* New York, 1908; and for the later period, after the great increase in immigration that began in 1840, his *Growth and Development of the Catholic School System in the United States,* New York, 1912; both volumes have bibliographies. E. H. Reisner sums up the various tendencies in *The Evolution of the Common School,* New York, 1930. W. A. Squires, *Educational Movements of Today,* Philadelphia, 1930, evaluates current school theories for their influence on religious education. For secondary schools, a standard work is E. E. Brown, *The Making of our Middle Schools,* New York, 1903. On the trend toward reorganizing secondary schools, see L. V. Koos, *The Junior-College Movement,* Boston, 1925; W. M. Proctor and N. Ricciari (ed.), *Junior High School,* Stanford University Press, 1930; and W. C. Eells, *Junior College,* Boston, 1931. A useful work on the land-grant colleges is F. W. Blackmar, *History of Federal and State Aid to Education in the United States,* United States Bureau of Education Circular of Information, No. 1, 1890. For some of the earlier developments in higher schools, see C. F. Thwing, *History of Higher Education in America,* New York, 1906; and G. P. Schmidt, *The Old-Time College President,* Columbia University Press, 1930. For the later developments, out of the many books on the subject, these are suggested as well-informed and honest: E. Deller, *Universities in the United States,* London, 1927; A. Flexner, *Universities, American, English, German,* New York, 1930. Two books valuable for current opinions on university problems are: W. M. Kotschnig and E. Prys (ed.), *The University in a Changing World, a Symposium,* Oxford, 1932; and *The Obligations of Universities to the Social Order,* New York University Press, 1933.

CHAPTER XXI

Educational Agencies Other Than Schools: Nineteenth and Twentieth Centuries

Their importance. A recent writer entitled one of his chapters in a book about college students, "The Social Life—90 Per Cent of Their Time."[1] Even during the period of school attendance, the work of the school takes up only a small fraction of the student's time, energy, and interest. The fraction becomes much smaller when one considers the average lifetime of an individual. Moreover, in all ages of the world, the larger activities of life have constantly shaped the character of the schools themselves. The period of modern development of schools was contemporary with swift and impressive changes in the industrial, commercial, political, social, artistic, and religious activities of the world. Many of those activities were inevitably educational in their influence upon each rising generation; hence it would be unintelligent entirely to neglect consideration of them in a history of education. In this chapter a few of the more important educational agencies other than schools will be briefly discussed. But first should be noted some striking general phenomena affecting human living in the nineteenth and twentieth centuries.

The century of expansion. The late fifteenth and the sixteenth centuries stand out in history as the centuries of discovery and exploration; the seventeenth and eighteenth, as the centuries of colonization; but the hundred years from the close of the Napoleonic Wars to the opening of the World War was decidedly the century of expansion. That

[1] J. A. Hawes, *Twenty Years among the Twenty Year Olds,* New York, 1929, chap. 6.

expansion included a great increase in the population of the world, a corresponding spread of human energies over new lands and an increase in the total wealth of the world (though not in its equal distribution), a remarkable improvement in means of transport and communication, and, perhaps as a result of all those, a growing complexity in the affairs of life. The expansion did not bring spaciousness of living, but a new crowding. The population of Europe and the Americas rather more than trebled in that century, from about 220 millions to nearly 700 millions.[1] There was a notable exodus from Europe to the Americas; thus, between 1825 and 1925, the United States received 37 millions of immigrants, and the rest of the Americas perhaps 15 to 18 millions. The population of the Americas in general multiplied eleven times, from about 20 millions in 1820 to 225 millions in 1925; but if one takes into account the fifty millions or more who came to America from Europe, the American growth is just about the same as the European. During that century, the population of Australasia and of Africa each increased by only about one-half, and the population of Asia about twofold. Any accurate estimate of the increased wealth of the world is impossible. It can only be noted here that that wealth was added to, not merely through the labor of an increased population, but by the quite unusual amount of discoveries of coal, petroleum, precious metals, and the like.[2]

[1] Exact figures are out of the question. For a summary of some approximations, see *Encyclopedia Britannica*, 1929, Vol. 18, pp. 229 sqq. (based on estimates of International Statistical Institute); *Encyclopedia Americana*, 1932, Vol. 22, pp. 365 sqq.; *Proceedings of the World Population Congress*, 1927; W. S. Thompson, *Population*, Columbia University Press, 1915; J. S. Sweeney, *Natural Increase of Mankind*, New York, 1926; E. B. Reuter, *Population Problems*, Philadelphia, 1923.

[2] An illustration may be taken from the production of gold, of which a fairly accurate account has been kept. The Director of the United States Mint estimated (*Report*, 1930) the total amount of gold produced in the world from 1492 to 1929 as 1,041,232,774 fine

Causes of population growth. Apparently men have not yet discovered the adequate explanation of the sudden and rapid increase of population during the nineteenth century. Various reasons are suggested, not all equally convincing. The opening up of rich lands in the Americas to an influx of European immigrants resulted in an abundance of food-stuffs; from the Americas, from Africa and Asia, improved means of transportation facilitated increased exports of raw materials to Europe. These facts have been offered as at least partial explanation for the growth in population.[1] Some of the developments in medical science, greater attention to hygienic laws, help to account for a lessening of infant mortality, and perhaps for the slight general increase in average span of life. Against those advantages must be set such facts as these: that there was what might be called the normal amount of war in Europe and the Americas during the nineteenth century, and a quite abnormal amount in the twentieth century; and that there were wide-ranging epidemics of cholera, yellow-fever, typhus, typhoid, malaria, and influenza, during those hundred years. Moreover, there was a definite, and in some countries a sharp, decline in the birthrate during the latter half of the nineteenth century.[2] One rather unusual explanation of increase in population is that poverty, crowding, malnutrition, bring about an increased fertility; that

ounces, reckoned as equal to $21,525,005,673. Of this total amount only one-ninth was produced between 1492 and 1800; slightly more than one-third between 1801 and 1900; and rather more than one-half between 1901 and 1929. The exact figures given are: (1492-1800) $2,476,988,829; (1801-1900) $7,695,570,400; (1901-1929) $11,-352,447,444. In the nineteenth century, most of the gold came from the California placers (discovered in 1848), Australia (in 1851), the Transvaal (in 1886), and Alaska (in 1897).

[1] See, for instance, R. Pearl, *The Biology of Population Growth*, New York, 1925.

[2] See the graph illustrating that decline, in *Encyclopedia Britannica*, 1929, Vol. 18, p. 237. See also R. de Guchteneere, *Judgment on Birth Control*, London, 1931.

increase in population is the attempt of nature to meet bad conditions of living.[1] There is at least some substantiation for that view in the spread of large-scale industrialism, with its attendant poverty due to destruction of ownership amongst the masses of the people, and the enormous movement of peoples from the countryside to the cities, both of which were outstanding phenomena of the nineteenth century. The twentieth century saw a gradual halting of population growth in the Western world, an approach to a stable or a declining population. But more important than this increase in the number of men were the conditions in which those men lived.

The modern scene. Men are always trying to reduce the history of large periods to a phrase. One such phrase calls the past hundred years, 'the machine age.' In the material order, it is evident that the machine dominated that hundred years. The energies of falling water, electricity, heat (in the form of expanding steam or exploding gasses), were harnessed to ingenious devices for manufacturing articles of necessity and of luxury; for carrying men swiftly on land and water, and through the air; for communicating over long distances by telegraph, telephone, and radio; for furnishing amusement and instruction, through books, newspapers, motion pictures; for adding to the comfort of housing, in electric lighting, central heating, sanitary systems, and the like. In many fields of industry, the workman ceased to be akin to the artist, and became instead the custodian of a mechanical apparatus. The first apparent result of the dominance of the machine was economic. It required large capital to own and operate machines in the competition set up by increased manufacturing. Wealth

---

[1] This explanatory theory seems first to have been advanced by Thomas Doubleday in *The True Law of Population*, London, 1841. It is discussed fully by C. E. Pell, *The Law of Births and Deaths*, London, 1921. See also R. R. Kuczynski, *Balance of Births and Deaths*, New York, 1928.

tended to concentrate more and more in the hands of the relatively few who did succeed in owning the machines. The masses of men gradually ceased to be true owners at all, and became a proletariat, dependent upon a wage. Thus, in the large-scale industrial countries, there came about an inequality in the distribution of wealth which can be matched only in the civilizations built upon slavery, or in the non-slave proletariat of decadent Rome.

The supremacy of the machine brought indirect social consequences: the leveling down of the middle classes, the political dominance of plutocracy, the growth of the city slums,[1] the menace of unemployment for millions, the further spawning of discontent and class hatreds. Religious beliefs and practices had already been much undermined before 'the machine age' began. Men lacked spiritual supports with which to meet the hurrying social changes. The philosophy of life of hundreds of millions of human beings had been shattered; a large part of humanity drifted leaderless. It was in this age that the leaderless were called to be their own leaders, through 'democracy'; when men without a program undertook to shape control of their affairs according to the immediate demands of the moment. There

---

[1] In the twentieth century, the exodus from the countryside to the cities, already begun two generations before, when large-scale industries were made possible by the introduction of steam-driven machinery, became so great, especially in England, Germany, and the United States, as to change the entire social structure of whole nations. A condition of industrial slavery developed in the manufacturing centers. Men lacked freedom of choice because they lacked ownership of the means of livelihood. Their work and wages and living conditions were determined for them, in such a way that they had no choice but to accept those conditions or starve. To illustrate the growth of urban population, it may be noted that in England it had grown from about one-fourth of the total population in 1800 to more than three-fourths in 1921; in Prussia, from about one-tenth in 1800 to one-half in 1914; in the United States, the population of towns and cities of more than 2,500 inhabitants had increased more than threefold between 1890 and 1930, from 22,298,359 to 68,954,283. (*World Almanac*, 1933, p. 335.) See A. F. Weber, *Growth of Cities in the Nineteenth Century*, Columbia University Press, 1899.

began in that age the startling phenomenon of what has been called 'the Revolt of the Masses'[1]: the mob-rush toward a thoughtless enjoyment of the present, without recognition of the past, or provision for the future.

Speeding things up. In very modern thought, one of the most overworked ideas is that of 'progress.' It has had all sorts of meanings; but through all the vagueness, it has always kept one quality attached to itself, the quality of speed. Perhaps this connotation came as a result of improved means of travel and of communications, or as a result of the pressure of increased competition in industries and commerce; but whatever the cause, it is evident enough that life for most people in the past two or three generations has been sharper-paced. The greedy pursuit of wealth, which men had always known, became more fevered. Men tired themselves more swiftly in the effort to compass and enjoy bodily pleasures. There was a restlessness even in achievement, which dulled the edge of delight. Only the peasant peoples escaped this hag-ridden urge of 'progress'; a fact which earned them the scorn of the rest of the world. The note of the very modern world came to be impatience. The ultimate cause of that is not new; it is as old as the sin of Adam; it is the hunger for our lost Paradise. But the impatience became more bitter as men narrowed their search to the limits of the present time and place. They were not merely contemptuous of the past; they became intensely contemptuous of the present. Will-o-the-wisp proved to be a hard pacemaker. Although 'progress' brought increased speed of living, it was very largely a driven speed.

Regimented life. This, indeed, from the educational point of view, is one of the most important things to be noted about the modern peoples: that, crowded so much as they

---

[1] J. Ortega y Gasset, *La Rebelión de las Masas,* Madrid, 1930; translated as *The Revolt of the Masses,* New York, 1932.

were into cities, politically vociferous, yet shackled to a wage for maintenance, their life had become a mass-life, with their lines of thought, of amusement, of artistic or spiritual interests, even of fashions in dress and colloquial speech, pretty well determined for them by a comparatively small number of persons. Something of this mass-life has always existed in highly organized societies; it is part of the social implications of human nature. But in modern times it became exaggerated to the point where individual preferences were all but smothered. Consider, for instance, the complete mental dependence of most modern adults upon the newspapers, not for news alone, but for political, economic, sociologic, scientific, and ethical opinions. Consider the compelling universality of public amusements, in theatrical performances, moving pictures, public dances, and the like, which created a passive instead of an active attitude in even the recreations of the individual. Just as the machine had destroyed much of the creative spirit in industry, so the regimentation of opinions, tastes, amusements, and leisure pursuits in general, reduced the vast majority of modern people to a deadly routine even in their pleasures. The tempo of modern life was swift, but it was appallingly monotonous; it had the terribly even beat of slaves in a treadmill. It may be worth while to look at some of that regimentation a little in detail.

The uses of literacy. As has been seen, the immediate purpose of the widespread elementary schooling, of which modern times boasted, was to equip every individual with the power to read and write. That is in itself a valuable power, since it extends human communications from the spoken word to the written word; from the manifestation of another's thought, passing with the sound that utters it, to the whole conserved world of literature. It is the written word now that makes Homer and Dante and Shakespeare live again. No wonder the purpose of widening human experience through the sharing of great literature inspired and moved thousands of men and women to promote schools! The schools came. Practically all the Western world was able to read, and a rather terrifying number of men and women had learned the mechanics of writing for publication. The publishing business advanced by leaps and bounds. Of the utmost educational importance is the answer to these questions: What was printed for men to read, and what did men read? There was an enormous amount printed and it did find readers. The technique of selling books became as highly developed as the technique of selling bonds. To pass any summary judgment on the massed 'literature' of the nineteenth and twentieth centuries would be absurd. It contained much that was really literature, much that was mediocre but not unworthy, and very much that was trash. But the unquestionable fact, and educationally much more important fact, is that the circulation of that printed matter was in inverse ratio to its worth. Men did read a great deal in the nineteenth and twentieth centuries; they spent more average time per person in reading than men of any age before them. They read newspapers, magazines, and books; and quantitatively in that order.[1] The newspapers, with very rare exceptions,

[1] The development of newspapers in the nineteenth and twentieth centuries was most remarkable. There had been newspapers of a sort since the first quarter of the seventeenth century. By 1702 there was even a daily newspaper in English, the London *Daily Courant;* and in 1784, just after the Revolution, an American daily newspaper, *The Pennsylvania Packet and Daily Advertiser.* (W. G. Bleyer, *Main Currents in the History of American Journalism,* Boston, 1927, pp. 16, 101.) But the real spread and power of the press came only in the latter half of the nineteenth century. The advent of the steam printing press and cheap wood-pulp paper were some of the causes that brought about the great growth of newspapers. The great *London Times,* founded in 1785, had a circulation of only 5,000 copies in 1815, the year of Waterloo, and had grown to only 50,000 circulation in 1854. (*Encyclopedia Britannica,* 1929, Vol. 16, p. 337.) Now there are several English and French newspapers with a daily circulation of 2,000,000 copies. In 1900, there were, by estimate, 50,000 newspapers in the world. By 1914, this number had grown to 60,000;

were deliberately written down to a quite childish level of intelligence.[1] They deliberately catered to the more ignoble forms of curiosity, to the almost pathological craving for sensational stimulation. This character of the newspapers was more emphasized in the United States than in Europe. One reason for that low level of newspapers was that they were primarily commercial ventures, and had as their first aim a large circulation as an advertising medium, procured by almost any means that would serve. The magazines, again with some exceptions, followed the same line of endeavor as the newspapers, and played up sensational and often salacious appeals. The novel, the most widely read of modern books outside of school texts, has been called "a species of higher journalism . . . at once ephemeral and momentous."[2]

All the forms of reading material presented to the masses of the people readily lent themselves to a centralized control, governmental or private. Some of that control was of

of which 23,167 were in the United States, 9,500 in Great Britain, 8,500 in Germany, some 3,000 each in France, Italy, Austria-Hungary, 2,000 in India, 1,800 in Japan. Scarcely any European country had less than 1,000. (*New International Encyclopedia,* 1930, Vol. 17, p. 55.) As to circulation, one may illustrate from the United States, in which the total circulation grew from 426,409,978 in 1850 to 11,898,-353,613 in 1909; a growth of nearly 2,800 per cent. (*Ibid.*) After the World War, there was, in several countries, a tendency to merge newspapers into fewer but larger units. In 1932, the newspapers of the United States circulated about 15,000 millions of copies. (Ayer, *Directory of Newspapers and Periodicals,* 1932.) A good compact account of the development of newspapers is in *Encyclopedia Britannica,* 1929, Vol. 16, pp. 334-60. See also G. H. Dibblee, *The Newspaper,* New York, 1913; J. D. Symons, *The Press and Its Story,* London, 1914; J. M. Lee, *History of American Journalism,* Boston, 1923; S. Morrison, *The English Newspaper,* Cambridge, 1932.

[1] See F. R. Leavis and D. Thompson, *Culture and Environment,* London, 1933, p. 3; M. Eastman, *Journalism versus Art,* New York, 1916.

[2] W. Follett, *The Modern Novel,* revised edition, New York, 1923, p. xxvi. See also Q. D. Leavis, *Fiction and the Reading Public,* London, 1930. In 1929, there were published in the United States alone 45,880,162 volumes of fiction. (*Publishers' Weekly,* 1932, Vol. 121, p. 368.)

an economic or commercial sort;[1] some of it was political.[2] The World War stressed the use of the press to manufacture public opinion; but the press has been so employed both before and after the war.[3] Even when the newspaper is considered merely as a purveyor of news, its intellectual and moral deficiencies were pronounced.[4] Most significant of all is the fact that newspaper reading was the *only* use of literacy made in every modern country by a considerable majority of those who read.

The growth of libraries. Collections of books open for public use have been a familiar part of the intellectual history of the past two thousand years or more. But never in previous history had libraries been so abundant and so urgently thrust upon popular use as were the libraries of the late nineteenth and the twentieth centuries. The growth of public libraries, and the insistent campaigns to popularize their use, were consciously aimed at the continued education of adults by means of books; they were a logical extension of the purpose and hopes back of the modern school movement. There had been a slow, steady increase in public libraries throughout continental Europe during the first half of the nineteenth century.[5] But the crusade

[1] See H. Belloc, *The Free Press*, London, 1918. A more extreme indictment, limited to the American press, is U. Sinclair, *The Brass Check*, Pasadena, Calif., 1919. After the World War, a number of commercial organizations sprang up, whose purpose was to push the sales of particular books. Under such names as Book-of-the-Month Club, Book Society, Book Guild, they selected for their subscribers a new volume each month. It was a striking illustration of modern mental dependence that many thousands of readers willingly submitted to having their book reading thus regimented for them.

[2] N. Angell, *The Press and the Organization of Society*, rev. ed., Cambridge, 1933; E. T. Cook, *The Press in Wartime*, New York, 1920; Sir Philip Gibbs, *Now It Can Be Told*, New York, 1920; R. E. Park, *The Immigrant Press and Its Control*, New York, 1922.

[3] R. G. Scott-James, *The Influence of the Press*, London, 1914; W. Lippmann, *Public Opinion*, New York, 1922.

[4] L. M. Salmon, *The Newspaper and the Historian*, Oxford, 1923; G. Seldes, *You Can't Print That*, New York, 1929.

[5] When Edwards began his efforts, France had 107 free public

for public libraries begun in England, in 1848, by Edward Edwards, gave an impetus to their development which spread to all the Western countries. Five years later, Charles C. Jewett set on foot a similar movement in the United States. After some twenty-five years more, organizations of libraries were founded,[1] which in time secured larger grants of public moneys, and considerable private benefactions, to further the development and influence of public libraries.[2] Modern libraries grew to vast proportions, not merely in the very large collections of books housed for public use in the great cities,[3] but in the wide distribution of branch public libraries and other smaller libraries scattered throughout even the lesser towns.[4] In

libraries of more than 10,000 volumes each, some of them quite large; Austria had 41 such libraries; whilst England had only 29. (*Encyclopedia Americana*, 1932, Vol. 17, p. 331.)

[1] The American Library Association was organized in 1876; the Library Association of the United Kingdom, in 1887; l'Association des Bibliothécaires Français, not until 1906.

[2] In America there were such library gifts as those of John Jacob Astor in 1849, James Lenox to New York City in 1870, Walter Loomis Newberry to Chicago in 1876. But topping them all were the donations of Andrew Carnegie (1835-1919), a Scotchman who came to the United States and amassed a fortune of $500,000,000 in the steel industry, and who, after his retirement in 1901, gave $64,000,000 to the building of some 3,000 municipal public libraries. (*Encyclopedia Americana*, 1932, Vol. 17, p. 324.)

[3] Some statistics for 1932 were: The Public Library of Leningrad, 4,832,948 volumes; The Lenin Library, Moscow, 3,900,000 volumes; The Library of Congress, Washington, 4,477,431 volumes; Bibliothèque Nationale, Paris, 4,000,000 volumes; Library of the British Museum, London, 3,200,000 volumes. (*World Almanac*, 1933, p. 279.)

[4] For instance, in the United States in 1929, there were 10,397 libraries having more than 1,000 volumes each, with a total of 161,-975,385 volumes in all. (United States Bureau of Education, 1930, *Bulletin* No. 37.) Of those libraries, 4,508 had between 1,000 and 3,000 volumes each; 3,901 had from 3,000 to 10,000 volumes each; 270 had more than 100,000 volumes each, and 34 had each more than 500,000 volumes. (*World Almanac*, 1933, p. 279.) In other words, nearly nine-tenths of American libraries were small libraries. But the greater use of the libraries was made in the large cities, partly because there the students are sent to the libraries for supplementary reading. In 1932, for instance, the Chicago Public Library, having 1,687,288 volumes, circulated 15,588,622 books: an average of 22.37

general, the major part of the reading done through these
public libraries was in fiction, which formed as high as 70
per cent and 80 per cent of the circulation of many libraries;[1] but they supplied opportunities for more serious reading to hundreds of thousands of adults. In more recent
years, public libraries aimed to have their librarians guide
and direct the reading of those who frequented the libraries.[2] Soviet Russia made the most complete and thorough
organization of that guidance of reading.

Modern wars. The nineteenth century was as thoroughly
filled with wars as any century in history. Even a partial
list of the major conflicts is impressive: the Napoleonic
Wars, the Crimean War, the Prussian-Austrian War, the
Franco-Prussian War, the American Civil War, the Spanish-
American War, all leading up to the World War of the twentieth century. Into all those wars there entered strongly
the cocky nationalism which had disrupted the Western
world after the religious break-up of Europe. That was a
cause of wars for the three hundred years before the nineteenth century. But back of the later wars were found new
causes, closely linked with the larger education of the nine-

---

books per borrower. The highest average circulation per borrower,
38.05, was in Milwaukee Public Library, which had 937,114 volumes,
and a total annual circulation of 6,320,933. Readers in the Milwaukee
Public Library were less than one-fourth as many as those in the
Chicago Public Library; but they had about twice as many books per
borrower in the library, and they read nearly twice as many books
each. (Figures from *A. L. A. Bulletin,* May, 1933, Vol. 27, p. 226.)

[1] Satisfactory figures are not available. For an estimate for 1929,
see "Fiction in Libraries," *Publishers' Weekly,* January 11, 1930, Vol.
117, pp. 216-17. After the World War, there was a popular turn to
works of biography of a novelized type, and a considerable enthusiasm for pseudo-scientific works, such as Wells' *Outline of History,*
which belittled Christianity and glorified the present age.

[2] Besides the direct expression of that purpose in the American
Library Association publications, there is such indirect evidence as
this: that in the six years previous to 1929, the number of librarians
in the United States grew 67 per cent, or nearly three times as
rapidly as the growth of libraries and numbers of books in those
same years. (See statistics in United States Bureau of Education,
Bulletin No. 37, 1930.)

teenth and twentieth centuries. The 'machine age' made
its influence apparent, not merely in the increased range
and destructiveness of weapons, and in the large-scale
movements of soldiers, but in the conditions which led to
wars. The clamor of industrial States for new sources of
raw materials and new markets for manufactured goods
brought about most of the European wars;[1] the rivalry between the agricultural South and the industrial North was
the deepest lying cause of the American Civil War; and the
Spanish-American War can pretty nearly be explained by
one word, Sugar.[2] Moreover, the masses of people in the
nineteenth and twentieth centuries, through the spread of
literacy and the universal habit of reading newspapers,
could be and were, more readily than earlier peoples, stirred
to that popular indignation and mutual hostility which is a
necessary prerequisite to war. Then, the nervous tension
and irritability which was so marked a result of modern
urban life and of the competitive character of modern industries, rendered rulers and subjects alike more susceptible
than ever to internecine rages. If one lumps all those conditions together, it is not hard to see how the strong central
governments of modern times, under the economic pressure
of an industrialized world, could through the press rapidly
create in their regimented peoples the mind and will to
wage war.[3] Finally, the one power which might have stood
as mediator between angry governments, the papacy, was
discredited and rejected on either political or religious

[1] A. J. Grant and H. Temperley, *Europe in the Nineteenth Century,*
London, 1927, especially Parts 3 and 4, pp. 209 sqq.; P. W. Slosson,
Twentieth Century Europe, Boston, 1927, especially chapters 6, 7,
and 8, pp. 133-268.

[2] S. K. Wilson, *American History,* Chicago, 1929, pp. 477 sqq., 644.

[3] J. B. Scott, *Diplomatic Documents Relating to the Outbreak of
the European War,* 2 vols., Oxford, 1916; G. A. Schreiner, *The Craft
Sinister,* New York, 1920; G. P. Gooch, *Recent Revelations of European Diplomacy,* London, 1927; H. D. Lasswell, *Propaganda Technique
in the World War,* New York, 1927; N. Angell, *Public Mind,* New
York, 1927; C. H. Grattan, *Why We Fought,* New York, 1929.

grounds, or on both.   Indeed, the papacy itself was engaged, from 1860 to 1870, in a war to preserve the temporal kingdom of the pope.

The arts in modern life.   One may cynically observe that governments always play upon the gullibility as well as upon the passions of their peoples when there is question of war, and that the nineteenth and twentieth centuries witnessed only an amplification of the ancient ways of propaganda.   But it has always been considered that the fine arts were essentially spontaneous creations, and as such were true indices of the culture from which they sprang.   In the earlier and poorer half of the nineteenth century public efforts were begun to stimulate popular appreciation of the arts by means of public art galleries.   The popular response was not so great as some had expected it to be; but it was considerable.   Schools of art multiplied; at first rather mechanical in their following of older ideas, in a fashion which, if it did no great good, also apparently did no great harm.   The whole atmosphere and temper of the 'machine age' was not favorable to the development of any high spontaneous art.   Nevertheless, in the latter half of the nineteenth century and in the twentieth century, distinctive tendencies in the various arts began to emerge, and to assume the challenging title of 'modern.'   This is not the place for even a cursory review of the modern artistic denominations, from impressionism to dadaism.   But it may be pointed out that the characteristics which modern art movements had in common were their irritation with the past and their evident purpose to force a new esthetic, rather sharply limited in general by the materialistic point of view.   That the results produced by that tendency were often bizarre, is irrelevant; that they lacked warmth, kindliness, spiritual reach and insight, is extremely important.

The pictorial and plastic arts in recent times tended to become distressingly 'high-brow,' remote from common humanity, scornful of much that men in all times intuitively loved. As a result, they lost influence upon the people in general; they bewildered the observer who was not trained in the esoteric tenets of the particular 'schools' represented: and modern artists were, for the most part, rather bad-temperedly willing that this should be so. Architecture, after running the gamut from gingerbread Gothic to a resolute bareness of line, frankly cast away all spiritual significance, and aimed at impressing, not through beauty, but through sheer massiveness and structural engineering.

The art of the theatre, when it had struck a moral depth below that of the Restoration theatre, was nearly destroyed by the 'art' of the moving pictures, which attained a popularity far surpassing that of the theatre.[1] Of the moving pictures as means of recreation and instruction this must be said: that, in addition to their being on a low moral and intellectual level, they also atrophied mental activity, since they called for only a passive acceptance by those who witnessed them. In all the modern arts there tended to be this note of passivity. The multitudes absorbed, but did not create; they were played upon by the relatively small group who supplied them with a fixed medium of visual stimulation. The contrast with, say, the Greek arts, or with the mediaeval arts in architecture, sculpture, parish and village plays, folk-songs and folk-dances, balladry and pageantry, is both obvious and striking.

[1] Exact figures for attendance at moving-picture shows are not available. But the *Motion Picture Almanac of 1932* offers the estimate of 65,000,000 to 90,000,000 attendance weekly in the United States; and an approximate 185,000,000 for the weekly attendance throughout the world (p. xx). The production of motion pictures in California, one of the greatest centers of the industry, just about doubled between 1925 and 1927. (*World Almanac*, 1933, p. 542.) The number of motion picture theatres in the world in 1931, as estimated by the United States Department of Commerce, was as follows: Europe, 29,316; United States, 20,000; Latin America, 5,435; Far East, 4,925; a total of 58,676. (*Daily News Almanac*, 1933, p. 419.)

One reason for the modern purveyed recreation was that there was less leisure for the working people in modern times than in mediaeval times. From the thirteenth to the sixteenth century, throughout most of Europe, the ordinary workingman had from twice as many to three times as many holidays a year as the workingman of the nineteenth and twentieth centuries.[1] The modern workingman's leisure was limited to about fifty-five days a year; except when the affliction of unemployment gave him enforced leisure without sustenance.[2] The modern workingman found that his amusements, like his toil, were regimented by the conditions of modern industry; and when leisure did come, he had lost the skill of former ages to shape it to his own purposes.

Outdoor amusements. The modern city-dweller naturally needed and sought some recreation out of doors. The best, and most spontaneous, of those recreations was walking, which the urban man and woman did, for the most part, in crowded city streets. The modern man also took much

---

[1] Lynn Thorndike reckons for France in the fifteenth century fifty holidays a year, besides Sundays. (*History of Mediaeval Europe,* Boston, 1917, p. 333.) For the Rhine country, Gina Lombroso sets the annual holidays as high as 160 to 180. (*The Tragedies of Progress,* New York, 1931.)

[2] Unemployment was the spectre which forever stalked the modern industrial world. The wage-earner went in constant dread of it. The intricate industrial, commercial, and financial structure in which he found his means of livelihood was beyond his control; at times it used him, at times it cast him forth. In very recent times, there were as many as 30,000,000 workers unemployed. (Estimate for November 1, 1932, in principal countries of Europe and America; *Daily News Almanac,* 1933, p. 640.) Lest one think that phenomenon due only to conditions after the World War, Gina Lombroso lists a succession of industrial crises and periods of unemployment in England, continental Europe, and the United States from the beginning of modern industrialism to the year 1907. (*The Tragedies of Progress,* p. 207.) Two facts are worth noting about those periods of unemployment: that the half dozen of them since 1857 occurred nearly simultaneously in all the countries given to large-scale industries; and that they affected very little the countries in which large-scale industries had not been developed, and scarcely touched at all the agricultural countries.

interest in athletic games and sports; but again in a curious mob-fashion. For one man who actually engaged in cricket, tennis, baseball, football, boxing, polo, or the like, there were hundreds, perhaps thousands, who were content to take their sports vicariously, to watch professionals play, or to read long newspaper accounts of games played by professionals. A distinctively modern recreation was travel, very often of a rather aimless sort. The popularizing of the automobile brought the strange spectacle of suburban roads crowded, on Sundays and holidays, with a slow-moving procession of motor cars meandering in an atmosphere of gasoline fumes and carbon dioxide, or of the excellent modern roads traversed at high speed by automobiles, in which modern men dashed from one place to another under the restless urge of change. The human quality most common to all those forms of outdoor recreation was a nervous tension and irritability. Modern recreations appear to have been often more exhausting than enjoyable.

Modern home life. In all previous ages, family life had been a large element in education.[1] Social training not merely began, but reached its finest development, in the close contacts between parents and children. The educational influence of the family still persisted in modern times; but in a much lessened measure. The first reason for the decay of that educational influence was the fact that both labor and leisure became less of a family concern than ever before in history. The factory, warehouse, office, commercial exchange, and school, separated the members of the family during the working hours of the day; public amusements, and the growing custom of eating in hotels and restaurants, tended to break up the family during leisure hours. Home was frequently only a lodging for the night.

---

[1] C. S. Devas, *Studies of Family Life*, London, 1886; W. Goodsell, *A History of the Family as a Social and Educational Institution*, New York, 1930.

The second reason was that the employment of married women in factories and offices, and the prevalence of divorce, had in many cases destroyed the stability and security necessary for a vigorous family life. Especially in the cities, the family gradually ceased to be the decisive unit in modern social life. The Soviet aim to abolish the family completely seemed to be but a logical extension of the process long ago begun by modern industrial civilization.[1]

The educational influence of Christianity. Nothing is more clearly evident than that the dominant working principles of the nineteenth and twentieth centuries were materialistic, quite simply opposed to Christianity, acknowledging no aim beyond the immediate present, and having as their highest range of virtues those social compromises necessary as minimum requisites for peace and security during man's life on earth. Most men, it is true, in all ages since the promulgation of the teachings of Christ, have never guided their conduct consistently by those teachings, even when they accepted the teachings in theory. But so long as Christian principles were at least accepted, they had some influence upon private and public policy; they were, if nothing more, a corrective norm, by which conduct at a lower level could be intelligently judged. During the nineteenth and twentieth centuries, the larger numbers of men in the Western civilization became what Devas called 'After Christians';[2] they repudiated Christian principles in theory as well as in practice. There was, of course, a strong minority who still held to the ideals, truths, and ministrations of the Christian religion: in very recent years, some part of the 300,000,000 Catholics, and of the 260,000,000 Orthodox and Protestant Christians who shared with the Cath-

---

[1] R. P. Coulet, *L'Église et la Problème de la Famille*, Paris, 1924; S. Schmiedeler, *An Introductory Study of the Family*, New York, 1930.

[2] C. S. Devas, *The Key to the World's Progress*, London, 1906, Part I, sec. 12.

olics a considerable amount of Christian beliefs and practices.[1] There was even an intensification of religious life in some countries, such as was brought about by the Wesleyan movement and the Oxford movement in England and the strong development of Catholic parishes in some of the *cities* of the United States. In addition, one should reckon with a large number of persons, impossible to estimate with even approximate accuracy, but perhaps in very recent times as many as 75,000,000 or 100,000,000, who, although they had lost or abandoned the Christian faith, still clung to many moral principles which they held as an unconscious heritage from Christian teachings. Christianity, therefore, remained as a strong, though minor, educational influence in the modern world. Its enemies had succeeded fairly well in driving it from the schools of many countries, and from any practical guidance in politics, industrial management, and commercial relations. Nevertheless, except latterly in a few countries such as Russia, Mexico, and Spain, the adherents of Christianity were allowed to express their convictions, at least in a limited way, through the press and books. There was even some small evidence, perhaps more a hope than an evidence, that the very modern world, chastened by the material disasters consequent upon savage industrial competition and the resultant World War, might be inclined to accept some measure of guidance from Christian principles.

The growth of religious cults. Mankind is incorrigibly religious. The decay of Christian influences in the nineteenth and twentieth centuries did not necessarily mean the entire disappearance of religious tendencies amongst modern men and women; it often meant only the rise and development of sporadic religious cults. Most of those cults were a more or less legitimate offspring of Protestantism, al-

[1] Statistics based on those in *Lutheran World Almanac,* 1933; see *Daily News Almanac,* 1933, p. 428.

though some, such as Theosophy and Bahaiism, linked with the pagan East. The official census of 1926 lists, for the United States, 212 religious denominations, exclusive of oriental religions. Most of these are small; more than half of them have less than 7,000 members; there are fifty or so with less than 1,000 members, such as the 'Two Seeds in the Spirit Baptists,' numbering 304, the 'Bullockites' (Baptists) with thirty-six members, and the 'Primitive Friends' with twenty-five members.[1] The larger Protestant denominations were in existence by the middle of the eighteenth century; but the great shoal of present-day cults sprang to life in the nineteenth century, and chiefly in the United States.[2] For the most part those nineteenth-century cults displayed two characteristics: the intense earnestness to be looked for in new religions, and a determined purpose to achieve happiness in this life so far as that can be done. Their origins were in the modern impatience with human limitations and imperfections, and in a sort of despairing faith in the perfectibility of mankind. It is curious and significant to note that even amongst those who scoffed most loudly at all religion, there persisted that embittered and irritated hope that some means might still be discovered of making this earth a Paradise again. One of the latest forms of that hope, inspired by what its adherents thought was 'evolution,' fixed itself upon eugenics as the desired means.[3]

Moral education of adults.   The breakdown of religious influences in any age naturally affects the moral principles

[1] For a brief survey of the United States census returns as regards religions, see C. L. Fry, *The United States Looks At Its Churches,* New York, 1930.

[2] See the lively account of some American cults given in G. Seldes, *The Stammering Century,* New York, 1928. For a compact sketch of some of the major denominations, see V. H. Krull, *Christian Denominations,* 13th ed., Cleveland, 1925.

[3] George Bernard Shaw was one of the major prophets in popularizing that hope. See, for instance, the Prefaces to *Getting Married* and *Man and Superman.* In spite of his advocacy, the hope became rather extraordinarily widespread.

of the age. The nineteenth century merely endured a continuation of the process begun in the sixteenth century: the rejection of religious authority, of religious certitude, the unrestrained growth of 'private judgment' and the resultant *laissez faire* in economics. The nineteenth century did not originate the moral principle of unlimited competition; but it applied that principle savagely. The result was a degrading economic morality, in complete contradiction to the Christian principles of justice and charity. Men grumbled and rebelled against the social consequences of that bad morality; but they still accepted it. They accepted it, because it was thrust upon them at every turn, in their newspapers and magazines, the chief sources of their ideas. Even when, in very recent times, it brought to the world the new and paradoxic spectacle of men starving because there was too much wheat, meat, coffee, and sugar, men still hoped to reconstruct the economic edifice on the old foundation of unlimited competition. It had become part of the moral attitude, in which the modern world was educated, to hate restraints even when actual conditions demonstrated the absolute need of restraints. That same attitude impressed and educated adults in domestic life, and was responsible for the growing prevalence of divorce and the immoral use of contraceptives. Not that moral anarchy was anything new in the world; human nature, ever since the Fall of Man, had always known anti-moral impulses. The distinctive point in modern moral education was that the spirit of the age justified itself in its materialistic morality. The major part of such printed material as the people in general actually read was committed to a glorification of modern standards and principles, to a scorn of the past which precluded even learning much from the mistakes of the immediate past. The ideas which dominated in the press, in fiction, in plays, taught modern men and women to be self-satisfied in the midst of moral blunders which brought poverty out of the too greedy pursuit of wealth, and pain out of the petulant search for pleasure.

In one particular, the nineteenth and twentieth centuries apparently achieved a moral advance over previous centuries. That was in the general softening or humanizing of manners; or, if not in so positive a quality as that, at least in the diminution of crimes of violence and turbulence. Whilst thankfully appreciating whatever measure of voluntary practice of civic virtues may be implied in that improvement, one must also in honesty admit that much of the improvement was due to the exercise of a closer police surveillance than was known in previous centuries. What has been called "the more refined tyranny of an industrial age,"[1] through its sharper regimentation of life, must be credited with enforcing restraints upon conduct, which made for peace and security and certain habits of civic orderliness, yet were not real virtues. One may doubt, for instance, if theft was really lessened because highwaymen became fewer; it is conceivable that the robbers might have changed their pistols for pens, and gone from the roads to the stock exchanges and the managers' offices.

Again, the World War had the moral result of intensifying hatred of war in general. A vigorous campaign was carried on, through the press, pamphlets, and books, and from many pulpits, with the aim of educating people to 'peace-mindedness.' Such agencies as the Carnegie Endowment for International Peace devoted much money and effort to the work. The weakness of the results obtained lay in the fact that what was actually promoted was rather a mere negative shrinking from the hardships and horrors of war than a positive and practical desire on the part of peoples and governments to make the self-sacrifices necessary for peace.

---

[1] W. T. Walsh, *Isabella of Spain*, New York, 1930, p. 131.

A minority press, and still more decidedly minor presentation in pamphlets and books, advocated Christian ethical principles in the conduct of industry, commerce, and finance, in the activities of governments toward their own peoples and toward other nations, in relations between the sexes, and in the integrity of family life. This educational work of Christian writers was much strengthened, except where positive anti-Catholic hostility prevailed, by the encyclical letters of the popes, notably those of Leo XIII and his successors. Although that assertion of Christian principles was of immense value in orienting individuals, it was not able to affect very strongly the dominant moral tone of the modern world.

Summary and conclusion. Education outside of schools was a more self-conscious process in the past hundred years than it had been before that time. Many of the activities which influence the spread of knowledge, and the development of ideals and principles of conduct, were deliberately controlled by governmental and private agencies. The control exercised by those agencies was often inspired by high purpose, by a genuine desire to promote the welfare of the people; but it was also often inspired by political expediency, commercial greed, and the instinctive human ambition to dominate others. In effect, because that control was rarely based upon sound ethical principles, its general good result was chiefly an improved superficial orderliness in social life; its bad result was in the destruction of economic and civic freedom, and in the establishment of a routine of life upon rather low pagan levels. Thus, whilst men were cajoling themselves with self-satisfaction over their 'democracy' and 'rugged individualism,' they were losing true ownership of property and becoming slaves of an industrial system. Thus, also, whilst they flattered themselves that they were living in an age of 'progress,' they were losing the very capacity for spontaneous self-development, and were surrendering what leisure they had to the exploitation of commercial entertainers. There was, therefore, much self-deception in the larger education of the nineteenth and twentieth centuries. The complexity of living made it increasingly difficult for men to pit themselves against untoward circumstances, material or spiritual, even made it difficult for men to realize what new handicaps to decent living had been brought them by large-scale industrialism and a materialistic civilization.

TOPICS FOR DISCUSSION

1. Modern city environment as an educational influence.
2. The diverse uses of leisure by men and by women.
3. Comparison between the 'Little Theatre movement' and the conditions which produced the mediaeval miracle play.
4. Reading as a mental and moral opiate.
5. The conditions fostering development of artistic taste.
6. Physical education in rural life and in urban life.
7. The moral influence upon the individual and upon society exercised by class hatreds.
8. The educational influences of the feminist movement.

BIBLIOGRAPHIC NOTE

The field covered in this chapter is so wide that anything like an adequate bibliography is out of the question. At most, there are offered here a few suggestions for further reading. For the general background, one of the best summary accounts of the modern expansion of Europe is C. H. J. Hayes, *A Political and Social History of Modern Europe*, 2 vols., New York, 1928, Vol. 2, Part 5, pp. 547-726. J. A. Hobson, *Imperialism: A Study*, London, 1902, points out some of the unhappy consequences of that expansion. For full treatment of the subject, perhaps the best book is P. T. Moon, *Imperialism and World Politics*, New York, 1926. A very well written summary of American developments is S. K. Wilson, *American History*, Chicago, 1929; particularly valuable for its balanced view of the cultural elements in that development.

For detailed studies of some of the principal European countries, the following will be found useful: A. W. Benn, *Modern England: A Record of Opinion and Action from the Time of the French Revolution to the Present Day*, 2 vols., London, 1908; A. L. Guerard, *French Civilization in the Nineteenth Century*, New York, 1914; and W. H. Dawson, *The German Empire: 1867-1914 and the Unity Movement*,

2 vols., London, 1919. For social and cultural conditions in the United States, the following are recommended: S. Chase, *Men and Machines,* New York, 1929; R. S. and H. M. Lynd, *Middletown, A Study in Contemporary American Culture,* New York, 1929, an extremely valuable work; and E. C. Hill, *The American Scene,* New York, 1933, graphic, but limited to the most recent developments.

A general work of great importance is J. A. Hobson, *The Evolution of Modern Capitalism: A Study of Machine Production,* 4th ed., London, 1926; with which should be read H. Belloc, *The Servile State,* London, 1912, one of the most searching social analyses written in modern times. Some other general works of value are: G. Lombroso (Ferrero), *The Tragedies of Progress* (English translation by C. Taylor), New York, 1931; M. de la Bedoyere, *The Drift of Democracy,* London, 1932; and J. Drinkwater, *This Troubled World,* Columbia University Press, 1933.

An admirable, but all too brief, survey of "Twentieth Century Life and Culture" is Chapter 21 of P. W. Slosson, *Twentieth Century Europe,* Boston, 1927. H. Jackson, *The Eighteen Nineties, A Review of Art and Ideas at the Close of the Nineteenth Century,* New York, 1923, chiefly discusses individual writers and artists, but interweaves a good general impression of the period. Books about the press are sufficiently indicated in the footnotes to this chapter. Books about the theatre are multitudinous, and often too partisan. A fairly well balanced view is had in W. L. Phelps, *The Twentieth Century Theatre,* New York, n. d. On the moving pictures, two books are suggested: E. Schneiderhahn, *Motion Pictures,* St. Louis University, 1917; and W. M. Seabury, *The Public and the Motion Picture Industry,* New York, 1926. E. K. S. Key, *The Woman Movement,* New York, 1912, is by the Swedish pioneer in the movement; G. Lombroso (Ferrero), *The Soul of Woman,* New York, 1923, is a conservative and critical discussion of modern feminism.

Of the first importance, as presenting a comprehensive and sound view of the larger education of modern times, is the series entitled *Essays in Order,* edited by C. Dawson and T. F. Burns, London, 1931—; particularly in the first three of the series: J. Maritain, *Religion and Culture;* P. Wust, *Crisis in the West;* and C. Dawson, *Christianity and the New Age.* These stress principles. Concrete illustrations of the conditions and forces shaping that larger education may be had in many biographical sketches, such, for instance, as the following: G. D. H. Cole, *The Life of William Cobbett,* which gives a wide view of English conditions up to 1835; W. H. Mallock, *Memoirs of Life and Literature,* the record of an English conservative during the latter half of the nineteenth century; and, for America, J. T. Adams, *The Adams Family,* Boston and Oxford, 1930, an illuminating commentary on four generations of American education. For the laboring classes in England, there are singularly accurate and vivid studies by J. L. and B. Hammond: *The Town Labourer, 1760-*

1832, the New Civilization, London, 1917; *The Village Labourer, 1760-1832,* new ed., New York, 1920; and *The Rise of Modern Industry,* New York, 1926.

INDEX